The Gypsum Construction
Handbook

Centennial Edition

Published for the Construction Industry by
USG Corporation

Important Notes to This Edition

This fifth edition of the Gypsum Construction Handbook is a guide to construction procedures for gypsum drywall, cement board, veneer plaster and conventional plaster construction in effect in 2000.

Information, standards, products, product names, properties, application methods, procedures, etc., contained herein are subject to change. For the latest available information concerning USG products, systems or recommended application procedures, contact your local USG sales office or representative toll-free at 877-874-6655, call the USG product information and literature line at 800-874-4968 or see the USG website (http://www.usg.com).

All information, details, specifications, data, applications, procedures, etc., contained in this handbook are intended as a general guide when using USG-manufactured or supplied products. USG assumes no liability for failure resulting from the use of this handbook or for failure from improper application or installation of its products.

USG products must not be used in the design or construction of any structure without a complete and detailed evaluation by qualified engineers, architects and/or acoustical consultants to verify the suitability of these products for use in any given structure. Competent supervision of component installation is recommended to achieve desired results.

Information from this publication should be used only in conjunction with USG-manufactured products or products supplied by USG, as physical properties among competitive products may vary.

Information about USG products that contain recycled materials, as well as a discussion on environmental acceptability of USG products and what steps USG is taking to protect the environment in the future may be found on page vii.

Trademarks

The following trademarks used herein are owned by United States Gypsum Company or affiliated companies: ACOUSTONE; ACOUSTIBOND; ACRYGLO; AIRTROL; AP LITE; AQUA TOUGH, AURATONE; AX; BEN FRANKLIN; BRIDJOINT; CADRE; CELEBRATION; CENTRICITEE; CHAMPION; CLEAN ROOM; *CLIMAPLUS*; COMPÄSSO; COVER COAT; CURVATURA; DIAMOND; DIAMONDFLEX; DONN; DURACAL; DUR-A-BEAD; DURABOND; DUROCK; DUROSCREEN; DX; DXL; DXLA; DXW; EASY SAND; ECLIPSE; "F" FISSURED; FACTS-ON-DEMAND; FIBEROCK; FIRECODE; FROST; GLACIER; GRIDWARE; GYP-LAP; HIGHLINE; HYDROCAL; IMPACTION; IMPERIAL; INSULSCREEN; LEVELROCK; LIGHTFRAME; LINEA; MARS; MERIDIAN; METAL FACE; MILLENNIA; ORIENTAL; ORION; PANZ; PARALINE; PARALOCK; PLUS 3; PREMIER HI-LITE; PREMIER NUBBY; QUADRA; QUADRADOME; QUIK & EASY; QUICK-RELEASE; RC-1; RADAR; RED TOP; RENDITIONS; RIGID-X; ROCK FACE; ROCKLATH; ROTUNDA; SANDRIFT; SHEETROCK; SILENT BAFFLES; SILENT EXPRESSIONS; SILENT SQUARES; SKYFRAME; SKYLITE; SMOKE SEAL; SNOW WHITE; SPEED BEAD; STAR; STRUCTO-BASE; STRUCTOCORE; STRUCTO-GAUGE; STRUCTO-LITE; TEXOLITE; TRANSPARENCIES; TUF TEX; ULTRACODE; ULTRASCREEN; ULTRAWALL; USG; USG ACTION; USG EXTERIOR; WIREWORKS, ZXA; and ZXLA.

BONDCRETE; GRAND PRIZE; IVORY; MORTASEAL; and SNOWDRIFT are trademarks of GenLime Group L.P. THERMAFIBER is a trademark of Thermafiber LLC. BUILDEX, CLIMASEAL; CONDRIVE; TAPCON; TYPE S; and TYPE S-12 are trademarks of ITW Buildex. TYVEK and HOMEWRAP are trademarks of DuPont. MASTERSPEC is a trademark of American Institute of Architects. MASTERFORMAT is a trademark of Construction Specifiers Institute. SWEET'S is a trademark of McGraw-Hill Sweet's Group. COLORTREND and AMBIANCE are trademarks of Creanova, Inc.

Editorial Committee

The Editorial Committee for the fifth edition of the Gypsum Construction Handbook was headed by William Leavitt and Bob Grupe, and included Jeff Johnston, John Lieske, Phil Shaeffer, Mike McGovern, Tom Sheppard, Rich Kaczkowski, Fred Tolson and Jim Thayer. Julia Archer was Creative Director, Steven Kalter was Technical Artist and Diane Cosentino was Print Production Manager.

Published by USG Corporation
Copyright 2000, USG Corporation
Printed in U.S.A.

ISBN:
0-9636862-2-4 (Paper Cover, H17)
0-9636862-3-2 (Cloth Cover, H18)
0-9636862-4-0 (Spanish, H20S)

A Century of Building

This "Centennial Edition" of the *Gypsum Construction Handbook* recognizes not only the dawning of a new century, but also the fact that United States Gypsum Company is about to celebrate its 100th anniversary in supplying building materials to build America and the world. We intend that this new edition will be a valued companion for you for many years into the twenty-first century.

Since its earliest version in 1905, the *Gypsum Construction Handbook* has been the best reference for gypsum products and systems in the building industry. Throughout the years it has evolved and changed as the building industry itself has evolved and changed. This edition has been reorganized to make it easier than ever to use and to find the specific information you are looking for.

— It has been printed in a larger size to make it easier to read and more pleasing to look at.

— We've divided the "Finishing" chapter into separate chapters on drywall finishing and veneer plaster finishing to help you find the specific information you are seeking.

— We've added improved photos and illustrative details to make information clearer for you.

— We've provided more information on subjects that readers of our previous editions have asked for, including entire chapters on acoustical ceilings and safety.

— We've added many new products and construction techniques concerning not only gypsum products, but cement board products as well.

— The most popular feature of previous editions has been the comprehensive key word index; we've further expanded and improved it to make it even more valuable.

Founded in 1902, United States Gypsum Company's concentration on quality has ensured its success in the development of gypsum plasters and cements for the construction industry. Continued research and innovation enabled the Corporation to revolutionize the industry in the early 1930s with the introduction of Rocklath Gypsum Lath, a paper-bound gypsum board that replaced conventional wood and metal lath as a base material for conventional plaster. Later in the same decade, advancements in production technology and research in gypsum-based compounds resulted in the development of larger gypsum panels. As the Corporation perfected systems to join the panels together, it introduced the Sheetrock Brand Drywall Systems that have become the standard of the construction industry throughout the world.

The innovations continue to this day. In this last twenty years alone, the Corporation has pioneered major advances in Durock Brand Cement Board construction, lightweight Sheetrock Brand Joint Compounds, high performance sound-control assemblies, fire-rated systems, high-strength veneer plasters and drywall surface preparations. The most-recent innovations have been in the area of abuse-resistant construction, where a variety of drywall and plaster products, including Fiberock Brand Abuse-Resistant Panels, have been developed.

For nearly 100 years USG has been the name to be trusted for quality and fire/sound performance. The Corporation's spirit of innovation will help us retain our reputation as construction moves into the twenty-first century and USG's second century.

Introduction and Contents

The Purpose of the Handbook

This fourth edition of the *Gypsum Construction Handbook* is a guide to good construction procedures for gypsum drywall, veneer plaster, cement board and conventional plaster construction. It contains the newest developments in products and systems including time-saving, lower-cost methods of installation to simplify and speed construction.

The book, which has become a standard handbook in other countries as well as the United States, serves as a valuable reference for those with broad experience and those who wish to learn about gypsum con-struction. The *Gypsum Construction Handbook* will soon be available in a Spanish version. Also, there is a version of the *Gypsum Construction Handbook* specifically written for the Canadian building industry. Information on obtaining copies of either the Canadian version, or the Spanish-language version, is inside the back cover.

Architects and Engineers Technical information on gypsum product construction standards, including available system descriptions, fire- and sound-rated construction, limitations and installation procedures.

Contractors, Builders and Dealers Full data on all aspects of gypsum products and accessories, tools and equipment, and application including information for estimating and planning.

Apprenticeship Training Schools Well organized, easy-to-understand, illustrated directions for applying gypsum products from framing to finish.

Journeymen A comprehensive index to contents and clear, concise illustrated directions and techniques for applying gypsum products from framing to finish.

Building Inspectors and Code Officials Fire, sound and physical test data; proper construction procedures for gypsum products to ensure compliance with performance criteria.

How to Use the Handbook

To find the information you want, use the table of contents or the fully cross-referenced index in the back to find the applicable reference on drywall, veneer or conventional plaster, or cement board construction. The handbook is organized as follows:

Environmental Responsibility

USG Corporation and its subsidiaries work hard to be as friendly to the environment as possible. The following general statement provides an overview of USG's commitment to the environment. Specific information about percentage of recycled material in specific products or answers to other questions may be obtained by writing to Dept. 147-3, USG Corporation, 125 South Franklin Street, Chicago, IL 60606-4678 or by calling (800) USG 4YOU (874-4968).

Assurance We recognize the importance of safeguarding the environment. We offer our customers products that are environmentally acceptable, safe and effective when used as intended. We are committed to our employees, our customers and our communities and believe that health, safety and environmental well-being can and should be compatible with economic health. We will continue to conduct our operations worldwide in compliance with applicable laws and regulations, continuously reviewing all procedures, practices and products.

Dedication We are a leading manufacturer of drywall, plaster, cement board, joint treatment, ceiling tile and suspension systems, relocatable wall systems and commercial life-safety systems. With plants throughout North America, we remain dedicated to environmental issues while maintaining our high standard of product quality and service. We use recycled and sustainable raw materials in product formulation and development. Using recycled goods as raw material provides numerous environmental benefits such as reducing demands on municipal landfills, mitigating mining and logging operations, and preserving depletable natural resources.

Leadership USG has a long history of utilizing recycled materials in manufacturing building products. We use synthetic gypsum, a byproduct of various industrial processes, to manufacture ceiling products and wallboard, in addition to natural gypsum. In 1993, USG (as a founding member) help established the U.S. Green Building Council, a coalition of principal building industry groups whose mission is to promote energy, health, productivity and environmental improvement for "whole" buildings. USG is also involved in construction of recycling demonstration projects with the National Association of Home Builders (NAHB).

USG Corporation Metric Policy

USG Corporation supports the intent of the metric conversion program. USG has manufactured metric sized products for export for many years on a special order basis. USG will make every reasonable effort to make metric products available to the federal market on a special order basis.

USG is prepared to offer metric sizes in most of its acoustical panel and suspension systems.

Metric width and length Sheetrock Brand Gypsum Panel products will be available from designated manufacturing plants throughout the

United States. Metric length and width Durock Brand Cement Board products will also be available from designated manufacturing plants. Certain minimum order quantities and up-charges may apply, as determined by local market conditions.

Bag and pail products, including Sheetrock Brand Joint Treatment Products, spray textures, gypsum plasters and other products carry soft metric designations for size and/or weight.

Important: The basic USG product line remains unchanged. Standard foot/inch/pound products previously available from USG will still be readily available. The addition of metric length/width products will allow us to supply all job requirements, whether standard or metric.

USG Corporation will offer assistance to construction professionals with regard to design, specification and installation issues involving our metric products, just as we always have with our standard products.

In metric construction, many building materials, systems and documents are affected.

Dimensions Units have changed from feet and inches to millimeters, scales from inch fractions to feet (for example, 1/4″ = 1′ 0″) to true ratios (such as 1:20). Drawings are not to be dual dimensioned, in order to avoid dimensional conflicts and errors.

Specifications Specs call for metric linear dimensions, areas, and volumes.

Construction Products A majority of construction products do not change in size since they are not modular or panelized. They are simply "soft converted" or re-labeled in metric dimensions.

Framing Stud spacing has changed from 16″ to 400 mm and 24″ to 600 mm. Wood studs keep their nominal name, or may be relabeled a nominal 50 mm x 100 mm or a more exact size.

Batt Insulation Width has changed from 16″ and 24″ nominal to 400 mm and 600 mm nominal.

Ceiling Systems Grids and lay-in ceiling tile, air diffusers and lighting fixtures, from 2′ x 2′ to 600 mm x 600 mm and from 2′ x 4′ to 600 mm x 1200 mm. Grid profiles, tile thicknesses, air diffuser capacities and fluorescent tubes have not changed.

For more information and assistance on metric projects, see the current USG literature on product sizing and availability. Information on specific metric product availability in your market area may be obtained from USG sales or customer service representatives. They can be reached at your local sales office. See inside the back cover of this book for information on reaching your nearest USG sales office. Also, there is more information on metric terms and a table of metric equivalents on pages 470-471 of the Appendix.

USG Products and Systems

USG offers a wide variety of quality products and performance-engineered systems. These systems are designed to consider all major factors: cost, sound control, fire resistance, structural capacity, esthetics and overall utility and function.

Thin, lightweight gypsum panel drywall and cement board assemblies are noted for their fast installation and low cost. They are used in the majority of new residential buildings and have gained similar acceptance in commercial buildings.

This handbook contains the latest information about proper gypsum drywall, plaster and cement board construction available at the time of its writing. The text covers framing installation, drywall and veneer plaster construction, joint treatment and plaster finishing, interior cement board construction, and conventional plaster application, as well as the tools required for each job. It also covers special engineered systems, product application factors, problems and remedies, and various repair and remodeling techniques.

The Manufacture of Gypsum Products

The development of all gypsum products begins with a mined mineral rock, gray to white in color, called gypsum. The basic mineral is composed of calcium sulfate chemically combined with water of crystallization — $CaSO_4 \cdot 2H_2O$. The combined water makes up approximately 20% of the weight of gypsum rock. This is the feature that gives gypsum its fire-resistive qualities and makes it so adaptable for construction purposes.

After gypsum rock is mined or quarried, it is crushed, dried, and ground to flour fineness, then calcined to drive off the greater part of the chemically combined water as steam. This calcined gypsum, commonly called plaster of paris, is then mixed with water and other ingredients and sandwiched between two sheets of specially manufactured paper to form various types of gypsum board or specially formulated and bagged for shipment as gypsum plaster or cement.

While mined gypsum has been the traditional raw material for drywall and plaster products, more and more "synthetic" gypsum is used in the manufacturing process. Synthetic gypsum is a material that is a byproduct of an industrial process. For example, in most power plants, the burning of coal produces undesirable emissions of sulfur, a leading cause of acid rain. A wet lime-limestone scrubber is a common method for removing this pollution from the air. It works via a device installed on the exhaust (smoke stack) of the coal-burning furnace; as the exhaust smoke rises through the scrubber, the pollutants are chemically removed. The calcium and water in the wet limestone combine with the sulfate in the exhaust to create calcium sulfate (gypsum) and water. This material is called either "synthetic" or "chemical" gypsum and can be readily used to manufacture gypsum products.

Gypsum manufacturers are increasingly using this material as a substitute for mined gypsum. The U. S. Bureau of Mines estimates that roughly 20 million tons of synthetic gypsum were generated in 1993 by electric utilities equipped with wet lime-limestone scrubbers. USG and other gypsum manufactures have worked with the utilities on sourcing synthetic gypsum for wallboard production.

Gypsum boards are formed in a highly automated continuous process. After the gypsum core has set, the boards are cut to length, dried, pre-finished if required, and packaged for shipment. All processing is in strict accordance with specifications to meet quality standards.

Cement board products have some of the same characteristics as gypsum boards, but without the disadvantage of being sensitive to water. Cement boards are manufactured from strong, water-durable portland cement, formed in a continuous process of aggregated portland cement slurry with polymer-coated, glass-fiber mesh completely encompassing edges, back and front surfaces, in a patented process. The ends are square cut. The most-popular use for cement board is as a substrate for ceramic tile on walls and floors, because of its durability. A wide variety of sizes are available for floors, walls, ceilings, countertops and as a wall shield for solid-fuel room heaters and fireplace stoves.

The continued advancement of gypsum construction depends on maintaining quality while reducing construction time and costs. USG has consistently been at the forefront of this effort. New products for broader uses and new cost-saving systems with improved fire and sound resistance are continually being developed and tested at the USG Research Center. Once quality is ensured, strategically located operating plants produce and/or stock the building materials described here.

Advantages of Gypsum Product Construction

Life Safety Protection Fire resistance is inherent in gypsum or cement board construction. Systems provide permanent fire resistance not subject to loss of water pressure or other malfunctions and problems that may occur in sprinkler systems.

Fire Resistance Neither gypsum nor portland cement panels will support combustion. When attacked by fire, the chemically combined water in the gypsum crystal is released and turns to steam to help retard the spread of flame and protect adjacent constructions. Cement board, too, is an effective fire barrier. Both constructions meet fire resistance and flame spread requirements of all model building codes. Fire resistance ratings up to four hours are available with specific gypsum partition, wall, floor-ceiling, beam and column fireproofing assemblies.

Sound Control Gypsum and cement board constructions offer excellent resistance to airborne and impact sound transmission without excessive bulk or weight. Resilient attachment of gypsum panels or bases and sound insulating blankets further improve sound ratings, making partitions ideally suited for party walls. Walls and floor-ceiling assemblies are available which meet STC (Sound Transmission Class) and IIC (Impact Insulation Class) requirements of applicable building codes, and tenant/owner needs.

Durability Veneer plaster combines the best features of drywall and conventional plaster. The high-strength and abrasion-resistant features of veneer finishes offer the durability needed in high-traffic areas. Conventional plaster surfaces are highly resistant to impact and abuse. Finished with a USG joint system, gypsum panels form walls and ceilings that are better able to resist cracking resulting from minor movement and variations in temperature and humidity than other, more rigid materials. Cement board is an exceptionally durable substrate that does not deteriorate in water.

Light Weight Gypsum and cement board constructions weigh much less than masonry assemblies of the same thickness. They reduce material-handling expense and may permit the use of lighter structural members, floors and footings. Veneer plaster construction compares with the weight of gypsum drywall and is considerably lighter than conventional plaster.

Low Installed Cost Gypsum and cement board systems offer lower installed costs than more massive constructions. The lighter weight systems reduce material-handling costs. The hollow-type constructions provide an ample cavity for thermal and sound insulation, simplify fixture attachment and permit routing of utilities in walls. Low material cost and large, quickly erected panels combine to provide a lower cost for gypsum drywall, cement board and veneer plaster systems than for conventional plaster or masonry. Fast veneer plaster finish application plus savings in decorating time make veneer systems competitive to gypsum drywall in many instances.

Fast Installation Gypsum and cement board construction eliminates costly winter construction delays, permits earlier completion and occupancy of buildings. Cement board and gypsum panels and bases are job-stocked ready for use; they are easily cut and quickly applied. For high-volume applications, conventional plasters are readily pumped and spray-applied. Veneer plasters, which set in approximately one hour, eliminate drying delays and are usually ready for next-day decorating or painting with breather-type paints.

Easily Decorated Gypsum construction offers smooth surfaces that readily accept decoration with paint, wallpaper, vinyl coverings or wall tile and permit repeated decoration throughout the life of the building. Plain or aggregated textures are easily applied to gypsum panels or produced during finish coat plastering. The smooth, hard surfaces obtained with veneer finishes and conventional plasters are more sanitary and easier to maintain than exposed concrete block. Cement board can be finished with ceramic tile, thin brick or synthetic stucco finish.

Versatility Gypsum and cement board constructions are suitable as divider, corridor and party walls; pipe chase and shaft enclosures; exterior walls and wall furring; and membrane fire-resistant constructions. Adaptable for use in every type of new construction—commercial, institutional, industrial and residential—and in remodeling. They produce attractive joint-free walls and ceilings; and they easily adapt to most contours, modules and dimensions.

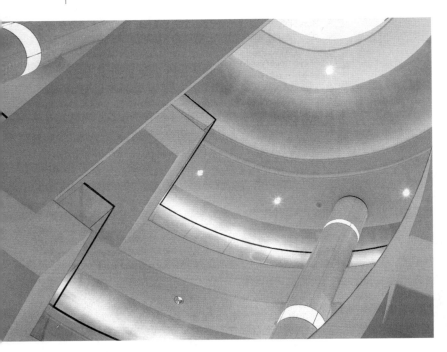

Commercial ceiling of drywall attractively houses the building's structural systems, mechanical and electrical services.

Abuse Resistance The variety of USG products available allows for wall construction to be done with high abuse resistance relative to weight and cost. Specially manufactured gypsum and gypsum-fiber panels, combinations of gypsum panels and veneer plaster, and combinations of cement board and veneer plasters have added an entire new series of solutions to low-cost abuse-resistant systems.

The Manufacture of Ceiling Products

USG is also a leading manufacturer of ceiling tile and suspension systems, relocatable wall systems, and commercial life-safety systems. As the nation's largest producer of ceiling suspension systems and second in manufacturing ceiling tile in the United States, USG operates 11 ceiling product plants in North America.

One of USG's principal raw materials for ceiling tile is slag, a byproduct of iron-ore reduction. Nearly 150,000 tons of slag per year are used in manufacturing mineral wool for ceiling panels. In certain processes, USG uses corn starch as a binder in manufacturing ceiling tile and drywall products. Since this material comes from renewable agricultural resources, it is less demanding on the environment than many chemicals typically used for binding that are derived from non-renewable petroleum reserves.

In addition, USG recycles large amounts of pre-consumer and post consumer waste paper (newspaper, phone books, old corrugated containers, cartons and cuttings from cardboard manufacturing) into ceiling panels and various other products. This reduces manufacturing costs while utilizing materials that would otherwise be a landfill burden.

As the largest U.S. user of synthetic gypsum, USG uses more than 2.75 million tons annually in the production of acoustical ceiling panels, wallboard, and other gypsum products. Synthetic gypsum is a byproduct of the flue gas desulfurization (FGD) process, which removes sulfur dioxide from the emissions of coal-burning electrical power plants.

As for USG suspension systems, light gauge carbon steel is roll-formed into grid components. These products can be 100 percent recycled by melting and salvaging the metal. Currently, two-thirds of all scrap metal is recycled into new steel products. The metal coil stock that USG purchases from vendors for its grid operations contains about 25 percent re-melted scrap steel.

Overall, USG offers ceiling and gypsum products that are manufactured to be environmentally acceptable, safe, and effective when used as intended. For more information regarding the recycled content of USG ceiling products, call 800-950-3839.

Other USG Products and Systems

Related USG companies manufacture a wide range of products and systems beyond the scope of this book. Unless otherwise noted, information about any of the following quality products can be easily obtained by calling 800-USG-4YOU (874-4968) or looking us up on our website (http://www.usg.com).

Exterior Construction Products

USG Exterior™ Products and Systems USG markets a wide range of "water-managed" exterior wall systems. These are available as Exterior Insulation and Finish Systems (EIFS) that use insulation panels and a flexible textured finish on the outside surface; these are known as InsulScreen™ Systems. Direct-applied exterior wall systems use conventional insulation in the stud cavities rather than on the outside wall surface and have a direct-applied exterior finish. These are known as DuroScreen™ Systems. Both exterior wall types incorporate water-management details to assure long-term, reliable performance. These systems feature a wide range of performance benefits from hurricane/high-wind-resistant systems to exciting textured and colored finishes. Substrates available include high-strength Durock Brand Exterior Cement Board and Fiberock Brand Sheathing with Aqua Tough, as well as more conventional Sheetrock Brand Gypsum Sheathing. USG also has many related accessory products for these systems.

Highway Sight & Sound Walls The UltraScreen Sight and Sound Barrier is a wall system developed specifically to act as a sight and sound barrier along highways in areas where visual privacy is needed for residents close to the roadway and/or where it is desirable to minimize noise distractions. UltraScreen Barriers may also be used as a privacy fencing system around residential or commercial properties. Built from a combination of a lightweight core sandwiched between Durock Brand Exterior Cement Board panels, the system has good acoustical performance and excellent strength-to-weight ratio in heights of up to 20 ft. Texture finishes in various colors provide esthetic options.

Security Walls

STRUCTOCORE **Security Walls** This wall system consists of specially formed steel sheets that provide continuous reinforcement for monolithic, high-strength, fire-resistant plaster finish applications. STRUCTOCORE Security Walls are ideal for use in lieu of reinforced concrete or concrete block. Applications include jails, prisons, correctional centers, vaults and storage rooms for valuable items. Tests show these walls are capable of ultimate load for fixture support of 4850 lbs. Partitions are 3″, 4″ and 4-1/2″ thick and can weigh as little as 35 psf.

Industrialized Construction

Manufactured Housing and Industrialized Construction Products USG has a whole assortment of products specifically designed for use in manufactured housing and industrialized construction environments, including gypsum board products, joint treatment products, metal beads and trims, special sealants, primers, cement board and texture products. All are under the SHEETROCK MH Brand.

Industrial Products

LEVELROCK **Brand Floor Underlayment** Poured gypsum floor underlayment systems provide an economical way to achieve lightweight, fire-resistant, sound-rated, self-leveling floors in residential and light-commercial construction. Gypsum floor underlayment can be applied to a variety of substrates. This product is excellent for new construction as well as providing solutions for rehab flooring. Typical applications are less labor intensive than many other types of construction and provide the high fire ratings and sound isolation, for which gypsum systems are well known. Gypsum floor underlayments currently offer a range of benefits unmatched by other commonly specified underlayment. Some of these benefits include:

— LEVELROCK Brand Floor Underlayments provide compressive strengths up to 5,000 pounds per square inch. They can be applied at thicknesses of only 0.75 inches over plywood.

— Gypsum floor underlayments provide crack-free surfaces. In addition, the slight expansive nature of gypsum underlayments seals openings around pipes and other penetrations to enhance sound control.

— Gypsum underlayments install quickly allowing for up to 30,000-sq. ft. to be installed in a day. Fast setting allows for the return of light construction trade traffic within hours.

To learn how gypsum floor underlayments can save you money and provide solutions for your next project, call our toll free hot-line at 800-487-4431.

Plaster Casting and Glass-Fiber Reinforced Gypsum Products USG Moulding Plaster and HYDROCAL Brand White Gypsum Cement are ornamental plasters for specialized cast work, such as ornamental trim, running cornices and castings. HYDROCAL Brand FGR-95 Gypsum Cement is designed to be used with chopped glass fibers or glass fiber mat for fabricating lightweight fire-resistant decorated shapes, architectural elements, column covers, cornices and trims.

Agricultural and Landscaping Products USG Industrial Gypsum Division has many other specialty products for agricultural and landscaping use, as fillers in the manufacture of products as diverse as brake linings and plastics and for food and pharmaceutical uses. A small sampling includes BEN FRANKLIN Agricultural Gypsum, AIRTROL Plaster (erosion control), USG Terra Alba and SNOW WHITE Filler (both calcium sulfate fillers for food and pharmaceutical applications), FIRECODE CT Gypsum Cement for fire stop applications and DURACAL Cement for patching roads and highways.

Retail Products

Many of USG's products are sold in retail outlets. They are the same high quality products used by construction professionals. Examples are SHEETROCK Brand Gypsum Panels, DUROCK Brand Cement Board, FIBEROCK Brand Abuse Resistant Panels and SHEETROCK Brand Joint Compounds. Many of the joint treatment products are packaged in smaller packages that are more appropriate for retail sales. Certain products, including many ceiling products and remodel/repair products, are produced especially for retail sales.

Contents

2 | Framing

Framing practices and procedures for wood and steel framing. Includes details for resilient channel installation, chase walls, furred ceilings and walls, and door and window openings.

3 | Drywall and Veneer Plaster Cladding

Detailed instructions for installing drywall and veneer bases in single and multiple layer configurations. Also covers predecorated panels, water resistant panels, sheathing, insulation, fixtures and specialty materials. Provides information on fastener requirements and special constructions such as curved surfaces, arches, soffits, etc.

4   Cement Board Construction

DUROCK Brand Cement Board products and installation procedures, including proper attachment, taping and finishing. Encompasses moisture and climatic considerations, proper framing, fasteners, and finishing options in baths, kitchens, floors and specialty uses.

5   Finishing Drywall Systems

Complete guide to proper joint treatment and surface preparation for drywall construction. Includes installation of corner beads, trim and control joints; hand and mechanical finishing with setting-type and drying-type compounds; addresses special environmental and lighting situations. Covers textures, resurfacing and redecorating.

6   Finishing Veneer Plaster Systems

In-depth instructions for selecting, preparing and installing veneer plaster systems. Outlines plaster finish performance, appearance and abuse resistance options. Encompasses one-coat and two-coat veneer plaster systems and specialty finishes.

7 Conventional Plaster Products

Describes full line of conventional plasters, laths and accessories for successful completion of plaster systems. Helps evaluate specific situations and end-use requirements to match plaster products to needs. Includes gypsum and plaster laths, beads and trims, clips and screws, framing components and specialty plasters.

8 Conventional Plaster Application

Comprehensive guide to plaster systems, including framing installation, base and lath application, accessories and control joints, plaster mixing and application and finishing options.

9   Acoustical Ceiling Design & Application

Complete information on selection and installation of acoustical ceiling systems, including design considerations. Also contains information on standards, building codes, sound control, lighting and light reflectance, fire safety, seismic considerations and HVAC.

10   System Design Considerations

Outlines methods for matching systems to specific performance criteria. Covers fire and sound criteria, wood and steel partitions, and sound control systems. Specialty systems include area separation walls, cavity shaft walls, fireproofing, curtain wall/fire containment systems, thermal insulation, air water and vapor control.

11 Planning, Execution & Inspection

Selection of materials, regulatory requirements, handling, job conditions, movement in structures, product quality and inspection.

12 Problems, Remedies & Preventive Measures

Trouble shooting for drywall, veneer plaster, conventional plaster and cement board problems. Cites problems and how to handle them.

13   Safety Considerations, Material Handling

Provides health and safety considerations relative to drywall and plaster applications.

14   Tools & Equipment

Defines tools and how to use them. Includes framing tools, board and lath tools, mixing equipment, finishing tools, hand and spray texturing equipment, machines, hoses, guns, nozzles, etc.

Appendix
Agencies, ratings, testing procedures, comparisons, standards, conversions, rating designations, company literature, plant locations.

Drywall and Veneer Plaster Products

Since their introduction over 60 years ago, SHEETROCK Brand Gypsum Panels from USG have dominated the drywall industry and have become the standard for quality interior walls and ceilings. With the addition of veneer plaster bases and finishes, USG has the nation's largest-selling, broadest line of gypsum products with the highest quality and the best performance.

The gypsum products described in this chapter conform to product standards recommended by USG and most applicable ASTM, government and commercial standards. These materials meet the essential requirements of economy, sound isolation, workability, strength, fire resistance and ease of decoration which are characteristic of quality construction.

USG continues to be at the forefront of technological advances in the industry. In recent years, the company's research and development staff has produced a series of materials that offer exceptional strength and durability. Those materials now are commercially available as abuse-resistant products and systems. These systems were initially developed for government buildings, commercial construction, schools, prisons and other structures where walls and ceilings are subject to exceptional traffic, and abusive wear and tear. They now also provide longer lasting quality in typical commercial and residential construction. You will find information on abuse-resistant products and systems throughout this text.

Our sales and technical representatives are ready to consult with tradespeople, contractors, architects, dealers and code officials on gypsum products and systems, and their application to individual job problems and conditions. For more in-depth information, contact your nearest USG sales office by calling (877) 874-6655, or our Architectural Services line (800) 874-4968, or our website (http://www.usg.com).

Gypsum Panel Products

SHEETROCK Brand continues to be the preferred and most widely used brand of gypsum panels in existence. These panels are available in more specialized forms than any other gypsum panel line. The high quality standards extend to other USG components, designed to provide high-performance walls and ceilings. Thus, one dependable source of supply offers unit responsibility for the system used.

The SHEETROCK Brand Panel is a factory-produced panel composed of a noncombustible gypsum core encased in a strong, smooth-finish paper on the face side and a natural-finish paper on the back side. The face paper is folded around the long edges to reinforce and protect the core, and the ends are square-cut and finished smooth. Long edges of panels have a choice of edge designs (including tapered), allowing joints to be reinforced and concealed with a USG joint treatment system.

Advantages

Interior walls and ceilings built with SHEETROCK Brand Panels have a durable surface suitable for most types of decorative treatment and for redecoration during the life of the building.

1

Dry Construction Factory-produced panels do not contribute moisture during construction. The joint finishing system contributes very little.

Fire Protection The gypsum core will not support combustion or transmit temperatures greatly in excess of 212°F until completely calcined (the water is chemically driven off). Fire-resistance ratings of up to 4 hours for partitions, 3 hours for floor-ceilings and 4 hours for column and shaft fireproofing assemblies are available with specific assemblies. (See Chapter 10 for specific ratings and related assemblies.)

Sound Control SHEETROCK Brand Gypsum Panels are a vital component in sound-resistive partition and floor-ceiling systems. (See Chapter 10 and appendix for specific rating data.)

Low In-place Cost The easily cut gypsum panels install quickly. Fixture attachment and installation of electrical and mechanical services are simplified.

Dimensional Stability Expansion or contraction under normal temperature and humidity changes is small and normally will not result in warping or buckling. With joints properly reinforced, SHEETROCK Brand Panels are exceptionally resistant to cracking caused by internal or external forces. (See Appendix for thermal and hygrometric coefficients of expansion.)

Availability Nearly 50 strategically located USG manufacturing plants produce gypsum board and related products described herein throughout North America. Special warehouse facilities, in addition to these plants, increase total distribution and service efficiency to major markets and rural areas from coast to coast. All standard gypsum board products are readily available upon short notice. Not all products are available from USG subsidiary plants in Mexico and Canada.

Gypsum Panel Limitations

1. Exposure to excessive or continuous moisture and extreme temperatures should be avoided. Not recommended for use in solar or other heating systems when board will be in direct contact with surfaces exceeding 125°F.

2. Must be adequately protected against wetting when used as a base for ceramic or other wall tile (see foil-back panel limitation, page 6). DUROCK Brand Cement Board or SHEETROCK Brand W/R Gypsum Panels are recommended for partitions in moisture-prone areas.

3. Maximum spacing of framing members: 1/2″ and 5/8″ gypsum panels are designed for use on framing centers up to 24″; 3/8″ panels are designed for use on framing centers up to 16″. In both walls and ceilings, when 1/2″ or 5/8″ gypsum panels are applied across framing on 24″ centers and joints are reinforced, blocking is not required. 1/4″ SHEETROCK Brand Panels are not recommended for single-layer applications on open framing.

4. Application of SHEETROCK Brand Panels over 3/4″ wood furring applied across framing is not recommended since the flexibility of the furring under impact of the hammer tends to loosen nails already driven. Furring should be nom. 2″ x 2″ minimum (may be nom. 1″ x 3″ if panels are to be screw-attached).

5. The application of gypsum panels over an insulating blanket that has first been installed continuously across the face of the framing members, is not recommended. Blankets should be recessed and flanges attached to sides of studs or joists.

6. To prevent objectionable sag in new gypsum panel ceilings, the weight of overlaid unsupported insulation should not exceed: 1.3 psf for 1/2" thick panels with frame spacing 24" o.c.; 2.4 psf for 1/2" panels on 16" o.c. framing (or 1/2" SHEETROCK Brand Interior Gypsum Ceiling Board, Sag-Resistant on 24" o.c. framing); 2.2 psf for 5/8" panels on 24" o.c. framing. 3/8" thick panels must not be overlaid with unsupported insulation. A vapor retarder should be installed in all exterior ceilings, and the plenum or attic space should be properly vented.

During periods of cold or damp weather, where a polyethylene or equivalent vapor retarder is installed on ceilings behind the gypsum board, it is important to install the ceiling insulation before or immediately after installing the ceiling board. Failure to follow this procedure may result in moisture condensation on the back side of the gypsum board, causing the board to sag.

Water-based textures, interior finishing materials and high ambient humidity conditions can produce sag in gypsum ceiling panels, if adequate vapor and moisture control is not provided. The following precautions must be observed to minimize sagging of ceiling panels:

a) Where vapor retarder is required in cold weather conditions, care must be taken to avoid moisture condensation. The temperature of the gypsum ceiling panels and vapor retarder must remain above the interior air dew point temperature during and after the installation of panels and finishing materials.

b) The interior space must be adequately ventilated and air circulation must be provided to remove water vapor from the structure.

Most sag problems are caused by the condensation of water within the gypsum panel. The placement of vapor retarders, insulation levels and ventilation requirements will vary by location and climate and should be reviewed by a qualified engineer if in question.

7. To produce final intended results, certain recommendations regarding surface preparation, and painting products and systems must be adhered to for satisfactory performance.

8. Precaution should be taken against creating a double vapor retarder by using gypsum panels as a base for highly water vapor-resistant coverings when the wall already contains a vapor retarder. Moreover, do not create a vapor retarder by such wall coverings on the interior side of exterior walls of air-conditioned buildings in hot-humid climates where conditions dictate a vapor retarder location near the exterior side of the wall. Such conditions require assessment by a qualified mechanical engineer.

Products Available

1

SHEETROCK **Brand Gypsum Panels, Regular** Have long edges tapered on the face side to form a shallow recess (nom. 0.050″ deep) to accommodate joint reinforcement. Made in three thicknesses for specific purposes:

- 1/2″, recommended for the finest single-layer construction in typical new construction and remodeling. The greater thickness provides increased resistance to fire exposure, transmission of sound, and sagging.

- 3/8″, lightweight, applied principally in repair and remodel work over existing surfaces.

- 1/4″, lightweight, low-cost, utility gypsum panel, used as a base layer for improving sound control in multilayer partitions and in covering old wall and ceiling surfaces. Also used for forming curved surfaces with short radii.

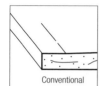

Conventional

SW

Types of Tapered Edges

SHEETROCK **Brand 54″ Gypsum Panels** Same as 1/2″ regular core SHEETROCK Brand Gypsum Panels, but 6″ wider. The added width reduces cutting, waste, joint finishing and labor costs for walls that are 8′6″ or 9′ tall.

SHEETROCK **Brand Gypsum Panels, SW** Have an exclusive tapered rounded edge design to help minimize ridging or beading and other joint imperfections. This edge produces a much stronger joint than regular tapered edge when finished with joint treatment. Except for the rounded edge, panels are tapered like, and otherwise identical to, regular tapered-edge gypsum panels. Made in 5/8″ and 1/2″ thicknesses. Panels are available in regular or FIRECODE Core (Type X and Type C) formulations.

SHEETROCK **Brand Gypsum Panels, FIRECODE Core** 5/8″ thick, combine all the advantages of regular panels with additional fire resistance—the result of a specially formulated core containing special additives that enhance the integrity of the core under fire exposure. Panels comply with ASTM requirements for Type X gypsum board.

SHEETROCK **Brand Gypsum Panels, FIRECODE C Core** Available in 1/2″ and 5/8″ thicknesses. Improved formulation exceeds ASTM requirements for Type X gypsum board. Based on tests at Underwriters Laboratories Inc. and other nationally recognized testing agencies, certain partition, floor-ceiling, and column fire-protective assemblies using these special products provide 1-hr. to 4-hr. fire-resistance ratings.

In order to attain fire-resistance ratings, the construction of all such assemblies must be consistent with the assembly tested.

SHEETROCK **Brand 1/4″ Flexible Gypsum Panels** Designed specifically for curved partitions, these panels are more flexible than standard SHEETROCK Brand Panels of the same thickness, making them ideal for use anywhere a tight radius is required for curved walls, arches and stairways. (See curved surface section, Chapter 3.)They make construction of curved surfaces easy and fast. Double-layer installation improves surface smoothness and fire protection. Meet ASTM C36.

Sʜᴇᴇᴛʀᴏᴄᴋ **Brand Gypsum Panels, Uʟᴛʀᴀᴄᴏᴅᴇ Core** 3/4″ thick, UL tested to provide a 2-hr. fire rating with single-layer construction and a 4-hr. fire rating with double-layer construction in certain specified systems (steel studs only). Because fewer layers are needed to meet fire ratings, Uʟᴛʀᴀᴄᴏᴅᴇ Core panel systems reduce labor material costs.

Gypsum Panels, Foil-Back

Sʜᴇᴇᴛʀᴏᴄᴋ Brand Gypsum Panels, Foil-Back, are made by laminating special kraft-backed aluminum foil to the back surface of regular, SW, Fɪʀᴇᴄᴏᴅᴇ or Fɪʀᴇᴄᴏᴅᴇ C Panels. Forms an effective vapor retarder where required in cold climates; for walls and ceilings when applied with foil surface next to framing on interior side of exterior wall in single-layer application; or as the base layer in multi-layer systems. Foil-Back Gypsum Panels provide a water vapor retarder to help prevent interior moisture from entering wall and ceiling spaces. In tests per ASTM E96 (desiccant method), 1/2″ foil-back panels showed a vapor permeability of 0.06 perms. The permeance of the total exterior wall is dependent on the closure of leaks with sealants at periphery and penetrations such as outlet boxes.

These panels are designed for use with furred masonry, or wood or steel framing. Thickness: 5/8″, 1/2″ and 3/8″. Sizes, edges and finish: same as for base panels.

Foil-Back Panel Limitations

1. Not recommended as a base for ceramic or other tile or as base layer for Sʜᴇᴇᴛʀᴏᴄᴋ Brand Vinyl-Faced Gypsum Panels in double-layer assemblies.

2. Not to be used in air conditioned buildings in climates having sustained high outside temperature and humidity, such as the Southern Atlantic and Gulf Coast areas. Under these conditions, a qualified mechanical engineer should determine vapor retarder location.

Foil-Back Panels applied to steel framing over the interior of exterior walls provide effective vapor retarder.

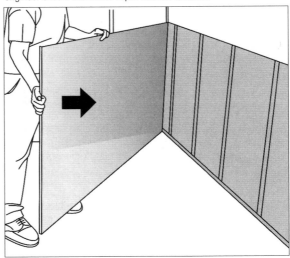

Gypsum Panels, Water Resistant

A proven water-resistant base for the adhesive application of ceramic and plastic tile and plastic-faced wall panels. Made water-resistant all the way through. The multilayered face and back paper are chemically treated to combat penetration of moisture. The gypsum core is made water-resistant with a special moisture-resistant composition. The panels are easily recognized because of their distinctive green faces.

These panels are designed for bathrooms, powder rooms, kitchens and utility rooms. In addition, they may be used in modernization work when the existing surfaces are removed and Water Resistant Panels are applied directly to framing. SHEETROCK Brand Gypsum Panels, Water-Resistant, FIRECODE C Core Panels also are used in fire-rated assemblies that may be exposed to moisture during construction. Panels comply with ASTM C630.

Available in four product types:

SHEETROCK Brand Gypsum Panels, Water-Resistant, Regular 1/2″ thickness for single-layer application in residential construction; 5/8″ thickness is also available.

SHEETROCK Brand Gypsum Panels, Water-Resistant, FIRECODE Core in 5/8″ thickness with a Type X core to provide fire resistance for required ratings.

SHEETROCK Brand Gypsum Panels, Water-Resistant, FIRECODE C Core in 1/2″ thickness with special core to provide fire resistance for required ratings.

FIBEROCK Brand Panels—Water Resistant (with AQUA-TOUGH) Finishing flexibility and superior water resistance in a single panel. Manufactured using USG's unique gypsum-fiber technology, these durable panels provide water resistance superior to conventional drywall, but can be installed and finished using basic drywall techniques. Uniform composition, without face paper, is based on a uniquely engineered gypsum/cellulose-fiber combination that won't weaken if the surface is penetrated by moisture. Panels comply with ASTM C1278, C79 and C630.

Because FIBEROCK Brand Panels—Water Resistant is a new product, see the current literature for the latest information about uses and application.

Water-Resistant Panel Limitations

1. Adherence to recommendations concerning sealing exposed edges, painting, tile adhesives, framing and installation is necessary for satisfactory performance.

2. Not recommended for ceilings with framing spacing greater than 12″ o.c. for 1/2″ board or 16″ o.c. for 5/8″ board, or for single-layer resilient attachment where tile is to be applied or in remodeling unless applied directly to studs.

3. Panels that would normally receive an impervious finish, such as ceramic tile, should not be installed over a vapor retarder nor on a wall acting as a vapor retarder.

4. Store in an enclosed shelter and protect from exposure to the elements.

5. Panels are not intended for use in areas subject to constant moisture, such as interior swimming pools, gang showers and commercial food processing areas—DUROCK Brand Cement Board is recommended for these uses. (See DUROCK applications, Chapter 4.)

Exterior Gypsum Ceiling Board

SHEETROCK Brand Exterior Gypsum Ceiling Board Weather-resistant board designed for use on the soffit side of eaves, canopies and carports and other commercial and residential exterior applications with indirect exposure to the weather. Noncombustible core is simply scored and snapped for quick application. Panels can be painted and provide good sag resistance.

Installed conventionally in wood and metal-framed soffits; batten strips or mouldings can be used over butt joints or joints can be treated; backing strips are required for small vent openings. Natural finish. Available in 1/2" thickness with regular core and in 5/8" thickness with fire-rated core—both with eased edges. Board complies with ASTM C931.

Sag-Resistant Ceiling Panels

SHEETROCK Brand Interior Ceiling Panels, Sag-Resistant Significantly lighter in weight than 5/8" gypsum panels (also lighter than standard 1/2" panels) and provide greater sag resistance. These panels also support sprayed textures and overlaid insulation better than 5/8" gypsum panels. Panels are 1/2" thick and are available in 8' or 12' lengths, 4' wide. Meet ASTM C1395.

Abuse-Resistant Panel Products

SHEETROCK Brand Abuse-Resistant Gypsum Panels Offer greater indentation and through-penetration resistance than standard gypsum panels. Available in 1/2" regular core or 5/8" FIRECODE Core. Abuse-resistant panels are made with strong face paper and a heavy-duty backing sheet, which improves the integrity of the board. As a result, the panels are able to withstand impact better than standard gypsum board and are less likely to allow penetrations or show indentations. Meets ASTM C36.

FIBEROCK Brand Gypsum Panels Deliver greater impact and puncture resistance that any other gypsum panel. Made with a unique gypsum/cellulose fiber core, the panels impede penetrations by sharp objects, including sharp blows from small objects, and exhibit more rigidity than standard gypsum panels. They also provide greater flexural strength and screw withdrawal properties than other gypsum panels. The 5/8" panels comply with ASTM C1278 for Type X gypsum board. Meets ASTM E136 for noncombustability. See the current literature for the latest application information.

FIBEROCK Brand VHI Gypsum Panels Are glass fiber mesh reinforced to provide extraordinary penetration resistance and rigidity for a single-layer gypsum panel. Available in 1/2" and 5/8" thicknesses. See the current literature for the latest application information.

Specifications—Gypsum Panel Products

	Thickness		Length	Approx. wt.	
	in.	mm	ft.(1)	lb./ft.²	kg/m²
SHEETROCK Brand Regular Panels(2)	1/4	6.4	8 and 10	1.2	5.9
	3/8	9.5	8, 9, 10, 12, 14	1.4	6.8
	1/2	12.7	8, 9, 10, 12, 14	1.7	8.3
FIRECODE Core Panels(2)	5/8	15.9	8, 9, 10,12, 14	2.2	10.7
Firecode C Core Panels(2)	1/2	12.7	8, 9, 10, 12, 14	1.9	9.3
	5/8	15.9	8, 9, 10, 12, 14	2.5	12.2
ULTRACODE Core Panels	3/4	19.0	8, 9, 10, 12	2.8	13.7
Water-Resistant Panels	1/2	12.7	8, 10, 12	1.8	8.8
	5/8	15.9	8, 10, 12	2.2	10.7
Water-Resistant FIRECODE Core Panels	5/8	15.9	8, 10, 12	2.2	10.7
Water-Resistant FIRECODE C Core Panels	1/2	12.7	10	1.9	9.3
FIBEROCK Brand Panels— Water Resistant	1/2	12.7	5, 8, 9,10	2.2	10.7
	5/8	15.9	5, 8, 9, 10	2.7	13.2
Exterior Ceiling Board Regular Board	1/2	12.7	8, 12	1.9	9.3
	5/8	15.9	8, 12	2.4	11.7
FIRECODE Board	5/8	15.9	8, 12	2.4	11.7
Interior Ceiling Panels Sag Resistant	1/2	12.7	8, 12	1.6	7.8
1/4" Flexible Panels	1/4	6.4	8 and 10	1.2	5.9
54" Panels	1/2	12.7	8, 9, 10, 12, 14	1.7	8.3
Abuse Resistant Panels	1/2	12.7	8, 9, 10, 12	2.2	10.7
	5/8	15.9	8, 9, 10,12, 14	2.7	13.2
FIBEROCK Brand Gypsum Fiber Panels	1/2	12.7	8, 9, 10	2.2	10.7
	5/8	15.9	8, 9, 10	2.7	13.2
FIBEROCK Brand VHI Gypsum Fiber Panels	5/8	15.9	8, 9, 10	2.7	13.2

(1) Metric lengths: 8 ft. = 2440 mm; 9 ft. = 2745 mm; 10 ft. = 3050 mm; 12 ft. = 3660 mm; 14 ft. = 4270 mm.
(2) Also available in Foil-Back Panels. NOTE: See page 13 for information on gypsum bases.

Veneer Plaster Gypsum Base Products

Square

Tapered

Type of Edge

Gypsum Bases finished with veneer plasters are recommended for interior walls and ceilings in all types of construction. For these interiors, a veneer of specially formulated gypsum plaster is applied in one coat (1/16" to 3/32" thick) or two coats (approximately 1/8" thick) over the base. The resulting smooth or textured monolithic surfaces are preferred for hard-wear locations where durability and resistance to abrasion are required.

IMPERIAL Brand Gypsum Bases are large-size gypsum board panels (4-ft. width) that are rigid and fire-resistant. A gypsum core is faced with specially treated, multilayered paper (blue) designed to provide a maximum bond to veneer plaster finishes. The paper's absorbent outer layers quickly and uniformly draw moisture from the veneer plaster finish for proper application and finishing; the moisture-resistant inner layers keep the core dry and rigid to resist sagging. The face paper is folded around the long edges. Ends are square-cut and finished smooth.

Gypsum Base Advantages

Gypsum bases, in conjunction with selected veneer plaster finishes provide the lasting beauty of plaster walls and ceilings at a lower cost and with less weight and residual moisture than conventional plaster.

Rapid Installation Construction schedules are shortened. Walls and ceilings can be completed in 3 to 4 days, from bare framing through decorated interiors.

Fire Resistance Ratings of up to 4 hours for partitions, 3 hours for floor-ceilings and 4 hours for column fire protection assemblies have been obtained.

Sound Control Gypsum base partitions faced with veneer plaster finishes on both sides have high resistance to sound transmission. Resilient attachment of base and use of THERMAFIBER SAFB Insulation further improve sound isolation.

Durability Hard, high-strength surfaces provide excellent abrasion resistance, resulting in minimum maintenance, even in high-traffic areas.

Easily Decorated Smooth-surfaced interiors readily accept paints, texture, fabric and wallpaper. Veneer plaster finishes also may be textured. If completely dry, finishes can be painted with breather-type paints the day following application.

Gypsum Base Limitations

1. Maximum frame and fastener spacing is dependent on thickness and type of base used.

2. Recommended for use with IMPERIAL Brand Basecoat Plaster, IMPERIAL Brand Finish Plaster, DIAMOND Brand Veneer Basecoat Plaster and DIAMOND Brand Interior Finish Plaster. Do not apply gauged lime-putty finishes or portland cement plaster directly to base; bond failure is likely.

3. Not recommended for use in areas exposed to excessive moisture for extended periods or as a base for adhesive application of ceramic tile in wet areas (SHEETROCK Brand Gypsum Panels, Water-Resistant, or DUROCK Brand Interior Cement Board are recommended for this use).

4. Gypsum base that has faded from the original light blue color, due to exposure to sunlight, should be treated with either USG Plaster Bonder or a solution of USG Accelerator—Alum Catalyst before DIAMOND Brand Interior Finish Plaster or any veneer plaster finish containing lime is applied. IMPERIAL Brand Basecoat and Finish Plaster, or DIAMOND Brand Basecoat Plasters, do not contain lime and are not susceptible to bond failure over faded base.

5. Joints and internal angles must be treated with SHEETROCK Brand Joint Tape and SHEETROCK Brand Setting-Type Joint Compound (DURABOND) or SHEETROCK Brand Lightweight Setting-Type Joint Compound (EASY SAND) when building temperature-humidity conditions fall in the "rapid-drying" area of the graph, or when metal framing is specified, or when 24" o.c. wood-frame spacing and a single layer gypsum base veneer system is specified (5/8" base with one-coat veneer finish and 1/2" or 5/8" base with two-coat veneer finish). Single layer 1/2" base is not recommended with 24" o.c. spacing and one-coat veneer plaster.

Plaster Drying Conditions

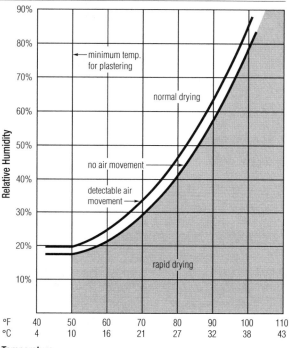

Products Available

IMPERIAL **Brand Gypsum Base** A special gypsum board that has been specifically engineered for use with IMPERIAL Brand Finish Plaster and DIAMOND Brand Interior Finish Plaster, or IMPERIAL Brand and DIAMOND Brand Basecoat Plasters. It provides the strength and absorption characteristics necessary for top-quality veneer plaster finishing performance. Large sheets minimize the number of joints and speed installation. The high-density, fire-resistant gypsum core has a superior controlled-absorption paper lightly tinted blue on the face side and a strong liner paper on the back side. Available in two thicknesses with square or tapered edges: 1/2" for single-layer application in new light construction; 5/8" recommended for the finest high-strength veneer plaster finish construction. The greater thickness provides increased resistance to fire exposure and sound transmission and allows 24" o.c. spacing of wood framing. IMPERIAL Brand Gypsum Base may be used with Diamond Brand Interior Finish Plaster to embed cables for radiant heat ceilings. Meets ASTM C588.

IMPERIAL **Brand Gypsum Base,** FIRECODE **and** FIRECODE **C** CORE IMPERIAL Brand Gypsum Base, FIRECODE Core, in 5/8" thickness, and FIRECODE C Core in 1/2" and 5/8" thicknesses, combine all the advantages of Regular IMPERIAL Brand Gypsum Base with additional resistance to fire exposure—the result of specially formulated mineral cores. UL Classified for fire resistance. Meets ASTM C588.

IMPERIAL **Brand Gypsum Base, ULTRACODE Core** IMPERIAL Brand Gypsum Base, ULTRACODE Core in 3/4″ thickness, has a fire-resistant core that permits fire ratings to be achieved with fewer layers of panels. Meets ASTM C588.

IMPERIAL **Brand Abuse-Resistant (AR) Gypsum Base** offers greater indentation and through-penetration resistance than standard gypsum panels. Available in 1/2″ regular core or 5/8″ FIRECODE Core.

Abuse-resistant panels are made with strong face paper and a heavy-duty backing sheet, which improves the integrity of the board. As a result, the panel is able to withstand impact better than standard gypsum board and is less likely to allow penetrations or show indentations. The face of the panel also has better natural abrasion resistance. Meets ASTM C588.

Foil-Back IMPERIAL **Brand Gypsum Base** Bright aluminum foil laminated to the back side acts as a vapor retarder. Available in Regular, FIRECODE and FIRECODE C Bases. Not available in all geographical areas.

Foil-Back Base Limitation: Do not use as a base for ceramic or other tile or as a face layer in multilayer systems.

Other Veneer Plaster Base Products

DUROCK **Brand Cement Board** A glass fiber-mesh reinforced aggregated portland cement panel that provides a high-strength substrate for improved abuse-resistance. Requires the use of USG Plaster Bonder. Available 1/2″ thick (5/8″ available under minimum order conditions) in 4′ x 8′ and 4′ x 10′ dimensions.

FIBEROCK **Brand Gypsum Fiber Panels and** FIBEROCK **Brand VHI Gypsum Fiber Panels** Provide improved indentation and penetration resistance. These panels deliver greater impact and puncture resistance than any other gypsum panel. Made with a unique gypsum/cellulose fiber core, the panels impede penetrations by sharp objects, including sharp blows from small objects, and exhibit more rigidity than standard gypsum panels. They also provide greater flexural strength and screw withdrawal properties than other gypsum panels. The 5/8″ panels comply with ASTM C1278 for Type X gypsum board. Requires the use of USG Plaster Bonder. Meets ASTM E136 for noncombustability. VHI Panels are glass fiber mesh reinforced to provide extraordinary penetration resistance and rigidity for a single-layer gypsum panel; available in 1/2″ and 5/8″ thicknesses. See the current literature for the latest application information.

Specifications—Gypsum Bases

Product	Thickness in.	mm	Length ft.(1)	Approx. wt lb./ft.²	kg/m²
IMPERIAL Brand Base(2)					
Regular	1/2	12.7	8, 9, 10, 12, 14	1.8	8.8
Regular	5/8	15.9	8, 9, 10, 12, 14	2.3	11.2
FIRECODE	5/8	15.9	8, 9, 10, 12, 14	2.3	11.2
FIRECODE C	1/2	12.7	8, 9, 10, 12, 14	2.0	9.8
FIRECODE C	5/8	15.9	8, 9, 10, 12, 14	2.5	12.2
ULTRACODE	3/4	19.0	8, 9, 10, 12, 14	3.0	14.6
Abuse-Resistant	1/2	12.7	8, 9, 10, 12, 14	2.0	9.8
Abuse-Resistant FIRECODE C	5/8	15.9	8, 9, 10, 12, 14	2.5	12.2
DUROCK Brand Cement Board	1/2	12.7	8, 9, 10, 12, 14	3.0	14.6
FIBEROCK Brand Gypsum Fiber Panels	1/2	12.7	8, 9, 10	2.2	10.9
	5/8	15.9	8, 9, 10	2.7	13.4
FIBEROCK Brand VHI Gypsum Panels	5/8	15.9	8, 9, 10	2.7	13.4

(1) Metric lengths: 8 ft. = 2440 mm; 9 ft. = 2745 mm; 10 ft. = 3050 mm; 12 ft. = 3660 mm; 14 ft. = 4270 mm.
(2) Also available in Foil-Back Base.

Gypsum Liner and Sheathing Products

Double Beveled

"V" T&G

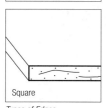

Square

Types of Edges

SHEETROCK **Brand Gypsum Liner Panels** A 1″ thick, special fire-resistant gypsum core encased in multilayered, moisture-resistant green paper. Panels are used in USG Cavity Shaft Walls, USG Area Separation Walls, select floor assemblies and infill panel systems for exterior curtain walls. Panels have beveled edges for easy insertion between the supporting flanges of steel C-H studs, E-studs or H-studs. Meets ASTM C442.

SHEETROCK **Brand Gypsum Coreboard** A 1″ thick gypsum core encased in strong liner paper on both sides. It is used in vent shaft and laminated gypsum partitions with additional layers of gypsum panels applied to the coreboard to complete the wall assembly. Manufactured with V-shaped T&G edges for use in solid partitions or with square edges and prescored 6″ or 8″ o.c. for use in semi-solid partitions. Coreboard strips are then easily snapped and separated from this coreboard panel. Coreboard complies with ASTM C442. Not available in all geographic areas.

SHEETROCK **Brand Gypsum Sheathing** A fire-resistant gypsum board, 1/2″ thick, with a water-resistant gypsum core encased in specially treated water-repellent paper on both sides and long edges. Its weather resistance, water repellency, fire resistance and low applied cost make it suitable for use in exterior wall construction of garden apartments and light commercial buildings as well as in homes. Also used in steel stud curtain wall construction.

SHEETROCK Brand Gypsum Sheathing is suitable for a wide range of exterior finishes such as, but not limited to, masonry veneer, wood, vinyl and aluminum siding, wood shingles and stucco—exterior finish attachment is limited to mechanical fastening through sheathing into the framing.

Made 1/2″ and 5/8″ thick in two economical types: 2′ wide, 8′ long with V-shaped T&G long edges for horizontal wall applications; 4′ wide, 8′ and 9′ long with square edges for vertical application. Meets ASTM C79.

FIBEROCK Brand Sheathing with AQUA-TOUGH New sheathing product manufactured using USG's unique gypsum-fiber technology. FIBEROCK Brand Sheathing panels outperform paper- or glass-mat-faced gypsum sheathing. They are strong, water-durable and provide a unique water-drainage capability. FIBEROCK Brand Sheathing has a unique engineered drainage design on its back surface to aid in removing water that has entered the system. Since the panels have no face paper or mesh, they serve as an effective substrate for expanded polystyrene (EPS) insulation board that is adhesively attached to them.

Meets ASTM C1278, C79 and C1177. Available 1/2″ and 5/8″ thick, in 32″ and 48″ widths and in 8′ length. They have square edges and weigh approximately 2.2 psf for 1/2″ thickness, 3.0 psf for 5/8″. See the current literature for the latest application information.

GYP-LAP Gypsum Sheathing A low-cost, weather and fire-resistant board designed to combine excellent performance with excellent economy. Noncombustible gypsum core adds fire safety not available with plywood or wood fiber sheathing. Clad in water-repellent paper on face and back surfaces, although core is not water resistant. Lightweight and easily handled by one worker. Panels are 2′ wide, 8′ long with V-shaped T&G long edges for horizontal application, and 4′ wide, 8′ long with square edges for vertical application. Thickness is 1/2″; Type X core available in 5/8″ thickness. Meets ASTM C79. Not available in all geographic areas.

USG Triple-Sealed Gypsum Sheathing Lowest cost sheathing available from U. S. Gypsum Company. Noncombustible gypsum core adds fire safety not available with plywood or wood-fiber sheathing. Clad in water-repellent paper on face, back and long edges; ends are coated with special waterproofing compound, but panels are not totally waterproof. Lightweight and easily handled by one worker, panels are 4′ wide, 8′ or 9′ long and 0.40″ thick. Square edges. Meets ASTM C79. Not available in all geographic areas.

Sheathing Limitations

1. Sheathing may be stored outside for up to one month, but must be stored off the ground and must have a protective covering.

2. Maximum stud spacing is 24″ o.c.

3. When applied to a structure, sheathing must not be left exposed to the elements for more than one month unless the procedure as outlined in limitation 5 (below) is followed.

4. Exterior finish systems applied over gypsum paper-faced sheathing must be applied with mechanical fasteners through the sheathing into the wall framing. Alternate methods of application are not endorsed and their performance and that of the substrate are solely the responsibility of the specifier. Direct application of paint, texture finishes and coatings over gypsum sheathing is not recommended.

5. For in-place exposure up to six months, all gaps resulting from cuts, corners, joints and machine end cuts of the sheathing should be filled with exterior caulk at time of erection, or wrapped with a suitable water barrier.

6. For curtain wall construction, cover the sheathing with No. 15 asphalt felt or other suitable water barrier within 30 days of sheathing installation. Felt should be applied horizontally with 2″ overlap and immediately anchored with metal lath, masonry ties or corrosion-resistant screws or staples. (See SA-923 Technical Folder for additional curtain wall details.)

7. Sheathing is not recommended for exterior ceilings and soffits, unless covered with metal lath and exterior portland cement stucco.

8. System should be designed to allow free movement of water out of the system where the sheathing is installed to allow it to dry.

Specifications—Liner and Sheathing Products

Product	Thickness in.	mm	Width in.	mm	Edges	Length ft.	Approx.wt. lb./ft.²	kg/m²
Sheetrock Brand Liner Panels	1	25.4	24	610	Bevel	up to 16	4.1	20.0
Sheetrock Brand Coreboard	1	25.4	24	610	"V"T&G	8, 9, 10, 12[1]	4.1	20.0
Sheetrock Brand Sheathing	1/2	12.7	24	610	"V"T&G	8	2.0	9.8
	1/2	12.7	48	1219	Square	8, 9	2.0	9.8
	5/8	15.9	48	1219	Square	8, 9	2.4	11.7
Sheetrock Brand Firecode Sheathing	5/8	15.9	48	1219	Square	8, 9	2.4	11.7
Fiberock Brand Sheathing	1/2	12.7	32, 48	815,1219	Square	8	2.2	10.7
	5/8	15.9	32, 48	815,1219	Square	8	3.0	13.2
Gyp-Lap Sheathing	1/2	12.7	24	610	"V"T&G	8	—	—
	1/2	12.7	48	1219	Square	8	—	—
USG Triple-Sealed Sheathing	4/10	10.2	48	1219	Square	8, 9	1.6	7.8

(1) Prescored coreboards available in 7′-8″ lengths only.

Predecorated Panel Products

Sheetrock **Brand Vinyl-Faced Gypsum Panels** Conventional gypsum board with factory-applied vinyl facings in a wide range of coordinated decorator colors. The facings provide a broad choice of color, texture and pattern for mix-and-match versatility. The tough vinyl covering is durable and easily cleaned. Panels have beveled long edges which form a shallow V-groove joint.

Sheetrock Brand Vinyl-Faced Panels, together with Sheetrock Brand Mouldings factory-wrapped in Sheetrock Brand Vinyl, fasteners, adhesives and other conventional drywall components, are used for predecorated permanent partitions, demountable partitions and in remodeling work. Not recommended for ceilings because end joints are difficult to conceal.

The rugged, scuff-resistant vinyl is embossed for texture and woodgrain effects.

Vinyl-Faced Panel Limitations

1. For adhesive application of Sheetrock Brand Vinyl-Faced Panels, only water-thinned adhesives are recommended. Other adhesives may not be compatible and could result in delamination and discoloration of vinyl surface.

2. If Sheetrock Brand Vinyl-Faced Panels, Firecode Core, are used in a fire-rated assembly, instead of a non-vinyl-faced product such as Sheetrock Brand Gypsum Panels, Firecode Core, the applicable fire test must permit exposed joints or battens.

3. Not recommended for use over foil-back panels or other vapor retarder in exterior walls.

4. Avoid exposure to excessive or continuous moisture and extreme temperatures.

5. Do not apply Sheetrock Brand Vinyl-Faced Gypsum Panels or field laminate nonpermeable vinyls over gypsum panels on exterior walls in hot, humid climates without suitable vapor control or dry air circulation behind the panels.

Technical Data:

Sheetrock Brand Vinyl-Faced Panels—meet ASTM C960; gypsum panels comply with ASTM C36. Light-reflectance values available on request. (See Surface Burning Characteristics below.)

Panels are manufactured 1/2″ thick, 4′ wide, and 8′, 9′ and 10′ long. They may also be specially ordered in 3/8″ and 5/8″ thicknesses, 2′ widths and custom lengths from 6′ to 14′. Sheetrock Brand Vinyl-Faced Panels, Firecode Core, with special core for fire-rated construction, are available in 1/2″ and 5/8″ thicknesses, 4′ wide. (See current Technical Folder SA-928 for pattern and color selections. Contact sales representative for custom colors and patterns also available.)

Vinyl covering of Sheetrock Brand Vinyl-Faced Panels is directly attached to gypsum panel without sheeting.

Specifications—Sheetrock Brand Vinyl-Faced Panel Vinyl

Panel surface burning characteristics[1] and vapor permeance[2]

Sheetrock Brand Vinyl-Faced Pattern	Film thickness or weight	Flame spread	Smoke dev.	Vapor perm.
Pumice	6 mils	20	25	0.8
Suede	6 mils	15	25	0.6
Presidio	6 mils	15	25	0.6
Granite	6 mils	15	25	0.6
Linen	8 mils	15	25	0.6
Country Weave	10 mils	20	35	0.8
Newstone (Type 1, Fabric-Backed)[3]	8 oz./yd.^{2}	5	20	N/A
Hatton (Type 1, Fabric-Backed)[3]	8 oz./yd.^{2}	5	20	N/A
Cutler (Type 1, Fabric-Backed)[3]	8 oz./yd.^{2}	5	20	N/A
Tahiti (Type 1, Fabric-Backed)[3]	8 oz./yd.^{2}	5	20	N/A
Washi (Type 1, Fabric-Backed)[3]	12 oz./yd.^{2}	5	20	N/A

(1) Tested in accordance with ASTM E84. (2) Tested in accordance with ASTM E96-90. (3) Comply with Federal Specification CCC-2-408C, Type 1.

SHEETROCK **Brand Vinyl Wallcovering** Provides a good match with SHEETROCK Brand panels on adjacent walls and columns. SHEETROCK Brand Wallcoverings are supported on cotton sheet backing and weigh 15 oz./yd.^{2} The cotton sheeting, whose primary purpose is to facilitate field installation, weighs 1.3 oz./yd.^{2} Available in rolls 54″ wide by 30 lin. yds.

Inside corner	End cap	Snap-on corner	Snap-on batten

RP series vinyl trim	*RP series vinyl trim*	*RP series vinyl trim*	*RP series vinyl trim*

SHEETROCK **Brand Mouldings** Cover joints and edges, protect corners. Available to match or contrast with SHEETROCK Brand Panels in 1/2″ and 5/8″ sizes, they are low-cost, precision-extruded vinyl mouldings in five shapes and two finishes. Available plain (RP series) in standard almond or ash blue colors, or factory-laminated with matching SHEETROCK Brand Vinyl (RPV series).

Specifications—SHEETROCK Brand Vinyl Mouldings

Product	Size in.(1)	Length ft.(1)	Approx. wt. lb./1000 ft.²	kg/100m²
RP-2, RPV-2 Inside Corner	1/2,5/8	8,9,10	77	11
RP-4, RPV-4 End Cap	1/2,5/8	8,9,10	66	10
RP-5, RPV-5 Snap-on Corner	(2)	8,9,10	184	27
RP-7, RPV-7 Snap-on Batten	(2)	8,9,10	95	14
RP-46, RPV-46 Ceiling Drive-in Trim	1/2	10	155	23

(1) Metric conversions: 1/2 in. = 12.7 mm; 5/8 in. = 15.9 mm; 8 ft. = 2440 mm; 9 ft. = 2745 mm; 10 ft. = 3050 mm; 12 ft. = 3660 mm. (2) One size fits all panel thicknesses.

Floor Underlayment Products

FIBEROCK **Brand Gypsum Fiber Underlayment** A fiber-reinforced panel for floor underlayment in residential construction. These panels resist indentation. They are free of resins, adhesives, solvents and dyes and are approved by major resilient-flooring and adhesive manufacturers. They have a surface coating that enhances bonding and workability. Available 1/4″ to 3/8″ thick. See current literature for the latest application information.

DUROCK **Brand Underlayment** A glass fiber-mesh reinforced aggregated portland cement panel for floors and countertops. Its nominal 5/16″ thickness helps eliminate transition trim when abutting carpet or wood flooring, and it helps minimize level variations with other finish materials. Its 4′ x 4′ size is easy to handle and helps cut down on waste. It may be applied directly over old substrate on countertops to save time. Regular 1/2″ DUROCK Brand Cement Board may also be used for underlayment applications.

Suspended Ceiling Products

Suspended ceilings offer the advantages of variable ceiling height and expanded plenum usage that are not always available with conventional ceiling construction. USG offers several products for suspended ceiling construction that provide superior performance in the areas of fire resistance and sound attenuation. See Chapter 9 for information on acoustical ceilings.

SHEETROCK Brand Lay-In Ceiling Tile

SHEETROCK Brand Lay-In Ceiling Tile, with CLIMAPLUS performance, are designed for use in standard ceiling suspension systems for exceptional economy, ease of installation and accessibility to the plenum. Panels also qualify for UL design fire-rated assemblies to 1-1/2 hours (UL design G222) and 2 hours (UL design G259) when used with fire-rated steel suspension systems such as DONN DXL, DXLA or ZXLA grid systems. SHEETROCK Brand Lay-In Ceiling Tile, with CLIMAPLUS performance, are made of 1/2″ FIRECODE C Core gypsum board in both 2′x2′ or 2′x4′ sizes. Both sizes are available with either laminated white vinyl facing or natural paper facing.

All *ClimaPlus* performance products carry a warranty to withstand conditions up to 104°F and 90% relative humidity without visible sag when used with DONN Brand Suspension Systems. The panels are guaranteed for 10 years against visible sag, or 15 years when used with DONN Brand Suspension Systems.

Vinyl facing is embossed in a stipple pattern for a soft, lightly textured look. It is 2 mils thick for toughness and durability, and can withstand repeated washings with no sign of abrasion. Natural paper facing can be left plain for utilitarian applications or can be painted to match room color scheme.

SHEETROCK Brand Lay-In Ceiling Tile, with CLIMAPLUS performance, are safe, sanitary and washable. They meet USDA requirements for kitchens, restaurants and other food service areas and suitable for hospitals, laboratories, nursing homes and other health care facilities. Attain interior finish classification Type III, Form A, Class 3; Class A (NFPA 101). Panels with white vinyl facing achieve light reflectance LR1. Panels also can be used in applications such as covered entryways and parking garages.

CLEAN ROOM CLIMAPLUS Vinyl Panels

CLEAN ROOM *ClimaPlus* Class 100 and Class 10M-100M Panels have embossed vinyl laminated aluminum facing and meet Federal Standard 209E; "Clean Room and Work Station Requirements Controlled Environment."

Advantages

Conventional Installation Tiles install quickly and easily in standard exposed grid.

Easy Maintenance Embossed vinyl facing is washable to keep surface bright and light-reflecting.

Outdoor Applications Excellent in protected areas when used with compatible suspension system, such as DONN Environmental ZXA grid, which features 25-gauge, hot-dipped galvanized steel with corrosion-resistant aluminum face. 4′ hanger spacing achieves intermediate-duty rating vs. 3′ spacing for aluminum grids.

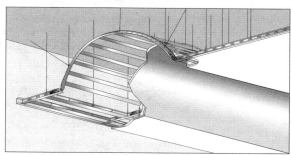

Sound Attenuation Tiles provide STC range of 45-49.

Performance Tiles qualify for fire-rated assemblies. Surface burning characteristics: Flame Spread 15, Smoke Developed 0. Class A rated on all products (ASTM E84 test procedure). Thermal performance up to R-0.45. Weight 2.00 lb./ft.[2]

Specifications—SHEETROCK Brand Lay-In Ceiling Tile

	Size	Edge	Regular			FIRECODE		
			Item No.	NRC Range	CAC Range	Item No.	NRC Range	CAC Range
Stipple Pattern SHEETROCK Brand Lay-In Ceiling Tile	2'x2'x1/2"	Square	N/A	—	—	3260	N/A	45-49
	2'x4'x1/2"	Square	N/A	—	—	3270	N/A	45-49
Unfinished Paper Facing SHEETROCK Brand Lay-In Ceiling Tile	2'x4'x1/2"	Square	N/A	—	—	3450	N/A	45-49
CLEAN ROOM *CLIMAPLUS* Vinyl Panels	2'x4'x1/2"	Square	N/A	—	—	3200	N/A	45-49

USG Drywall Suspension System

The USG Drywall Suspension System provides a fast and economical method of installing a gypsum panels ceiling while supplying support for lighting and air handling accessories. The system is designed for direct screw attachment of gypsum panels to produce either flat or curved surfaces. Single panels may be up to 5/8" thick. Double-layer panel applications may be up to 1-1/4" combined thickness.

The USG Drywall Suspension System is made of hot-dipped galvanized steel. Main tees are 1-1/2" high x 144" long with a rectangular top bulb and 15/16" or 1-1/2" wide flange. The system offers the option of using 1-7/16" wide-faced furring cross channels or 1-1/2" wide fur-

Vault Drywall Ceilings

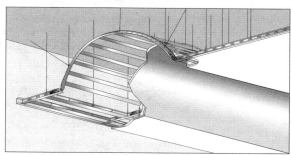

Flat Drywall Ceilings

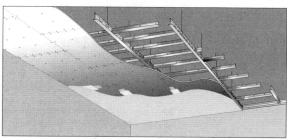

ring cross tees for gypsum panel attachment. Face of both cross channels and cross tees is knurled to improve fastening of drywall screws. Also available are tees with 15/16″ exposed flange to be used with lay-in light fixtures.

Direct-hung USG Drywall Suspension System is used in UL designs with fire ratings of 1, 1-1/2, 2 and 3 hours. 1-hour UL designs: L-502, L-525, L-526, L-529, P-508, P-509, P-510. 1-1/2-hour UL designs: G-528, P-506, P-507, P-510, P-513. 2-hour UL designs: G-523, G-526, G-529, J-502. 3-hour UL designs: G-523, G-529. Consult UL Fire Resistance Directory and revisions for further information and construction details.

Advantages

Labor Saving Factory-controlled module spacing and snap-lock connection of cross channels and cross tees with main tees cuts installation time.

Cost Saving Components are low in cost compared with conventional construction to achieve the same result.

Strength Strong metal components are designed with interlocking tabs and splicing mechanisms to resist twisting of assembly.

Accommodates Light Fixtures Accepts NEMA type G light fixtures.

System Components

Main Tee Conforms to ASTM C635 Heavy-Duty Main Tee Classification. Designed to support gypsum board ceiling with maximum deflection of 1/360 of the span. Double-web design, 1-1/2″ high x 144″ long, rectangular top bulb, 15/16″ wide flange, integral reversible end splice. Furring cross channel holes 4″ from ends, spaced 8″ o.c., hanger wire holes 4″ o.c.

DGCL Cross Channel Hat-shaped formed section, 1-7/16″ wide x 7/8″ high knurled screw surface, integral end locks stamped at each end. For fire-rated assemblies.

DGLW Cross Tee 1-1/2″ high, roll formed into double web design with rectangular bulb, 1-1/2″ knurled face and a steel cap, high-tensile-steel double-locking and self-indexing end clenched to web. For fire-rated assemblies.

DGL Cross Tee 1-1/2″ high, roll-formed into double-web design with rectangular top bulb, 15/16″ exposed flange, high-tensile-steel double-locking and self-indexing end clenched to web.

Channel Moulding U-shape, 1″ flange x 1-9/16″ or 1″ x 1-1/2″ angle.

Hanger Wire Galvanized carbon steel, soft temper, prestretched, yield stress load at least five times design load, but not less than 12-gauge wire.

USG Drywall Suspension System — Curved Surfaces

The USG Drywall Suspension System is uniquely engineered to take advantage of curved metal framing components and flexible gypsum panels to produce arched and/or wavy ceiling surfaces. Framing components are formed channels in a variety of standard radii. The system is designed for direct screw attachment of gypsum panels.

The suspension system includes 22 standard main tees with radii ranging from 2′6″ to 19′ in both vault and valley shapes. The system easily accommodates transferring from straight to curved members and from concave to convex directions. Tees can be field cut to specific arc or chord lengths. Main tees are 144″ long before bending. Spans from single sections vary. Main tees and cross channels both have knurled surfaces to aid screw attachment of gypsum panels.

The system is completed with attachment of SHEETROCK Brand Gypsum Panels. Joints are taped and finished with a SHEETROCK Brand joint treatment system. Fire-rated constructions are achievable with multiple layers of the gypsum panels.

Advantages

Labor Saving Components are factory prepared for easy installation of the main-tee and cross-tee assembly.

Accuracy Uniform arched components assure accurate fit of attached components, including gypsum panels.

Esthetic Appearance Dynamic arched or wavy surface is esthetically pleasing.

Curved System Components

Curved Main Tees Conform to ASTM C635 Heavy Duty Main Tee Classification. 1-1/2″ high, galvanized cold-rolled-steel tee with 15/16″ flange comes with various radius curvatures in either concave or convex direction. Tee length before bending is 144″. Tee web is punched 4″ from the end and thereafter at 8″ intervals to accept cross channels. Web also is punched at 3′ intervals with holes to accept hanger wire.

Cross Channel Hat-shaped, galvanized-steel channel has 1-7/16″ wide knurled screw surface for convenient attachment of gypsum panels.

Hanger Wire Galvanized carbon steel, soft temper, prestretched, yield stress load at least five times design load, but not less than 12-gauge wire.

USG Drywall Suspension System — Fascia Applications

A special feature of the USG Drywall Suspension System is the array of fascia trim designed to finish edges that do not abut walls, soffits, or adjacent ceilings. The trim strips, called COMPÄSSO Trim, are available either flat or curved (convex or concave) to meet design requirements. Trim system is designed for parallel, perpendicular or angled attachment to suspension system tees.

Advantages

Labor Saving Components are factory prepared for easy installation.

Cost Saving Trim is low in cost compared with conventional construction to achieve the same result.

Esthetic Appearance Flat or curved fascia trim is esthetically pleasing.

COMPÄSSO Fascia Trim Components

COMPÄSSO Trim Available flat or in a variety of radii to match design requirements. Widths available up to 8″.

COMPÄSSO Drywall Clip Provides ready attachment of COMPÄSSO Trim to main or cross tees, either parallel or perpendicular to the tee direction. Clip edges fit snugly inside trim edges; screw attach to tees.

Bead and Trim Accessories

USG sells and distributes construction, drywall and plastering steel products. These trim accessory products include corner reinforcements, beads, trims, control joints and decorative mouldings.

Paper Faced Metal Bead and Trim

SHEETROCK **Brand Paper Faced Metal Bead and Trim** Paper faced metal corner bead ensures durable reinforcement of drywall corner and delivers positive adhesion of the bead face paper to the face of the panel. As a result, edge cracking is virtually eliminated, reducing contractor callbacks. Bead is applied using setting type, taping or all-purpose joint compound instead of nails to bond the bead to gypsum panel surfaces. Then bead edge is finished with typical joint treatment system. SHEETROCK Brand Paper Faced Metal Bead and Trim is available in a full range of types and sizes, including outside corners in regular and bullnose profiles, offset corners, flexible metal corner tape, inside corners, inner cove, L-shaped trim, J-shaped trim and reveal trim.

SHEETROCK **Brand Paper Faced Metal Outside Corner, Tape On Bead (B1W, B1XW EL, B1 Super Side)** For 90° outside corners. Suitable for use on any thickness of wallboard. Comes in several flange/paper widths: B1W—regular width, B1XW EL—extra wide, B1 Super Wide—super wide.

SHEETROCK **Brand Paper Faced Metal Inside Corner, Tape On Trim (B2)** Designed to form a true inner 90° corner. For use with any thickness of wallboard.

SHEETROCK **Brand Paper Faced Metal Offset Outside Corner, Tape On Bead (B1 OS)** For 135° corners. Offset bead is designed to give a true offset corner with a smaller bead height for less compound fill. Can be used with any thickness of wallboard.

SHEETROCK **Brand Paper Faced Metal Offset Inside Corner, Tape On Bead (B2 OS)** Designed to provide a true offset angle on inside corners greater than 90°. Use on any thickness of wallboard.

SHEETROCK **Brand Paper Faced Metal 3/4″ Bullnose Outside Corner, Tape On Bead (SLOC)** Use to create a rounded 3/4″ radius 90° corner angle. For use with 1/2″ or 5/8″ gypsum panels.

SHEETROCK **Brand Paper Faced Metal Inner Cove, Tape On Trim (SLIC)** Creates a rounded 3/4″ radius 90° inside corner. For use with 1/2″ or 5/8″ gypsum panels.

SHEETROCK **Brand Paper Faced Metal Bullnose Offset Outside Corner, Tape On Bead (SLOC OS)** Forms a rounded 135° offset outside corner. Ideal for bay window offsets and similar applications.

Sᴍᴇᴇᴛʀᴏᴄᴋ Brand Paper Faced Metal Offset Inner Cove, Tape On Trim (SLIC OS) Forms a smooth cove for 135° inside corners.

Sᴍᴇᴇᴛʀᴏᴄᴋ Brand Paper Faced Metal 1-1/2" Bullnose Outside Corner, Tape On Bead (Danish) Broader and gentler corner than 3/4" radius bullnose. Use with 1/2" or 5/8" thick wallboard.

Sᴍᴇᴇᴛʀᴏᴄᴋ Brand Paper Faced Metal "L" Shaped Tape On Trim (B4 Series) For use where wallboard abuts suspended ceilings, beams, plaster, masonry and concrete walls, as well as untrimmed door and window jambs.

Sᴍᴇᴇᴛʀᴏᴄᴋ Brand Paper Faced Metal Outside Corner (Micro Bead) Reduced bead height results in less joint compound consumption. Extra wide flanges for maximum corner coverage.

Sᴍᴇᴇᴛʀᴏᴄᴋ Brand Paper Faced Metal Reveal, Tape On Trim (B4 NB) Modified tape-on "L" trim solves problems with reveals on soffits, wall offsets, ceilings, light boxes and other interior architectural features. B4 Reveal features a paper flange on both trim legs, eliminating the need to caulk the edge of reveal details and providing a cleaner, straighter line.

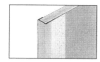

Sᴍᴇᴇᴛʀᴏᴄᴋ Brand Paper Faced Metal "J" Shaped Tape On Trim (B9) Used to finish rough drywall panel ends. Ideal for use at window and door openings and casements.

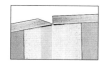

Sᴍᴇᴇᴛʀᴏᴄᴋ Brand Flexible Metal Corner Reinforcing Tape A flexible reinforcing tape that ensures straight, sharp corners on any angle (shown at left and below). Provides durable corner protection on cathedral and drop ceilings, arches and around bay windows. Tape is 2-1/16" wide and has 1/16" gap between two 1/2" wide galvanized steel strips. When folded, tape forms a strong corner bead. applied with standard joint compound feathered at the edges for a smooth wall surface. Also used to join drywall partition to plastered wall in remodeling and for repairing chipped and cracked corners. Available in convenient 100-ft. rolls in dispenser box.

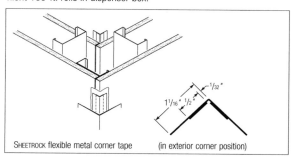

Sᴍᴇᴇᴛʀᴏᴄᴋ flexible metal corner tape   (in exterior corner position)

24

Metal Beads

Metal corner beads permit positive fastening to studs and construction of true, concealed external angles with gypsum base and panels. The exposed nose of the bead helps prevent damage from impact and provides a screed for finishing. Offered in the following styles, all part of the family of trim and moulding products available to complete SHEETROCK Brand and IMPERIAL Brand Gypsum Panel installation:

DUR-A-BEAD Corner Bead A specially galvanized steel reinforcement for protecting external corners in drywall construction. It is screwed or nailed to framing through the panels and concealed with USG joint compounds as a smooth, finished corner. Flanges also may be attached with a clinch-on tool. Available in 1-1/4″ x 1-1/4″ flange width (No. 103).

Expanded Flange Corner Bead No. 800 A galvanized steel external corner reinforcement with 1-1/4″ wide fine-mesh expanded flanges, tapered along outer edges to enhance concealment. It is easily nailed or stapled. Provides superior bond to panels and base with joint compound and veneer plaster finishes through approx. 90 keys per lin. ft. It also provides the proper 1/16″ grounds for one-coat veneer finishes.

Expanded Flange Corner Bead No. 900 Used with two-coat veneer plaster systems. It provides 3/32″ grounds and its 1-1/4″ fine-mesh flanges can be either stapled or nailed. Provides reinforcement equivalent to No. 800.

DUR-A-BEAD Corner Bead

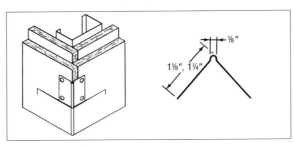

Expanded Flange Corner Bead, Nos. 800 and 900

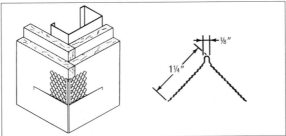

SHEETROCK Brand SPEED BEAD Corner Bead A unique metal corner bead with edge barbs to hold the bead firmly in place with a minimal use of fasteners. Installed with hand pressure or a rubber hammer, SPEED BEAD corner bead cuts application time, virtually eliminates nail pops, minimizes framing alignment problems, and helps avoid board fracturing and bead deformation that results from normal hammer-and-nail installation. Made of electrogalvanized steel. Meets ASTM C1047.

Metal Trim

Metal Trims provide maximum protection and neat finished edges to gypsum panels and bases at window and door jambs, at internal angles and at intersections where panels abut other materials. Easily installed by nailing or screwing through the proper leg of trim. Made in following types and sizes:

L-Trim & J-Trim Galvanized steel casing for gypsum panels, includes No. 200-A J-shaped channel in 1/2″ and 5/8″ sizes; No. 200-B L-shaped angle edge trim without back flange to simplify application, in 1/2″ and 5/8″ sizes. Both require finishing with USG joint compounds.

J-Stop Reveal type all-metal trim for drywall panels, requires no finishing compound, includes No. 401 in 1/2″ size, No. 402 in 5/8″ size.

No. 200-A Metal J-Trim

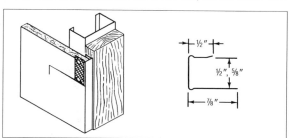

No. 200-B Metal L-Trim

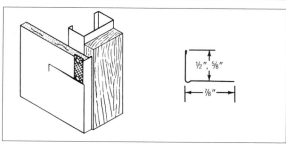

J-Stop

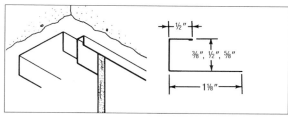

26

No. 701-A Metal Trim
No. 801-A Metal Trim

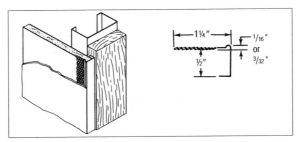

No. 701-B Metal Trim
No. 801-B Metal Trim

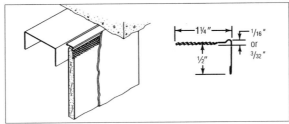

Expanded Flange L-Trim & J-Trim, No. 700 series All-metal trim provides neat edge protection for two-coat veneer plaster finishes at cased openings and ceiling or wall intersections. Fine-mesh expanded flanges strengthen veneer bond and eliminate shadowing. No. 701-A J-shaped channel-type, and No. 701-B L-shaped angle edge trim provide 3/32″ grounds; sizes for 1/2″ and 5/8″ thick gypsum base.

Expanded Flange L-Trim & J-Trim, No. 800 series All-metal trim companion to 700 series, but with 1/16″ grounds for one-coat veneer plaster finishes or finishing with joint compound in drywall applications. Fine-mesh 1-1/4″ expanded flanges strengthen veneer bond, eliminate shadowing, provide a superior key and are easily nailed or stapled. No. 801-A J-shaped channel-type, and No. 801-B L-shaped angle edge trim come in sizes for 1/2″ and 5/8″ thick panels and bases.

Vinyl Trim

USG Rigid Vinyl Trim (RP Series) Vinyl plastic in Almond and Ash Blue. Available for 1/2″and 5/8″ thick panels in 8′, 9′ and 10′ lengths. Shapes include: RP-2 Inside Corner, RP-4 End Cap, RP-5 Snap-on Corner, RP-7 Snap-on Batten, RP-46 Ceiling Drive-in Trim. RPV series trims also are available with factory laminates to match SHEETROCK Brand Vinyl-Faced Gypsum Panels. RP trims help to stop condensation damage where board terminates at exterior metal surfaces such as window mullions. Requires no finishing compound; paints easily.

Control Joints

Control Joints are used to relieve stresses induced by expansion and contraction in large ceiling and wall expanses in drywall and veneer plaster systems. Used from door header to ceiling; from floor to ceiling in long partitions and wall furring runs; from wall to wall in large ceiling areas. Made from roll-formed zinc to resist corrosion. The control joint is covered with a roll-formed zinc trim member with a 1/4″ slot protected by plastic tape which is removed after finishing.

Zinc Control Joint No. 093 For interior applications. Provides 3/32"
grounds for drywall and veneer finishes. Staple-applied to panel face.
Requires finishing. Limitation: Where fire and sound control are prime
considerations, a seal must be provided behind the control joint.

Control Joint No. 93

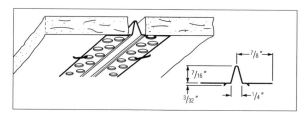

Specifications—Trim Accessories

Product	Size in.	mm	Length ft.[1]	Approx.wt. lb./1000 ft.	kg/m
Dur-A-Bead Corner Bead					
No. 103	1-1/4x1-1/4	31.8x31.8	8, 10	131	0.19
Expanded Flange Corner Bead					
No. 800 and 900	1-1/4x1-1/4	31.8x31.8	8, 10	83	0.12
Metal Trim					
J-Shaped	1/2	12.7	8, 10	103	0.15
No. 200-A	5/8	15.9	8, 10	110	0.16
L-Shaped	1/2	12.7	8, 10	80	0.12
No. 200-B	5/8	15.9	8, 10	87	0.13
J-Stop					
No. 401	1/2	12.7	8, 10	125	0.19
No. 402	5/8	15.9	8, 10	131	0.19
Expanded Flange					
J-Shaped	1/2	12.7	10	95	0.14
No. 801-A	5/8	15.9	10	103	0.15
L-Shaped	1/2	12.7	10	71	0.11
No. 801-B	5/8	15.9	10	77	0.11
USG Vinyl Trim					
RP-2 Inside Corner	1/2	12.7	8, 9, 10	100	0.15
	5/8	15.9	8, 9, 10	105	0.16
RP-4 End Cap	1/2	12.7	8, 9, 10	100	0.15
	5/8	15.9	8, 9, 10	105	0.16
R-5 Snap-on Corner	1/2	12.7	8, 9, 10	100	0.15
	5/8	15.9	8, 9, 10	105	0.16
R-7 Snap-on Batten	1/2	12.7	8, 9, 10	100	0.15
	5/8	15.9	8, 9, 10	105	0.16
R-46 Ceiling Drive-in Trim	1/2	12.7	8, 9, 10	100	0.15
	5/8	15.9	8, 9, 10	105	0.16
Zinc Control Joint					
No. 093	1-3/4x7/16	44.4x11.1	10	115	0.17

(1) Metric lengths: 6'8" = 2030 mm; 6'10" = 2080 mm; 7' = 2135 mm; 8' = 2440 mm; 9' = 2745 mm; 10' = 3050 mm.

Framing Components

USG pioneered the development of steel framing components for gypsum construction. They offer the advantages of light weight, low material cost, quick erection, and superior strength and versatility in meeting job requirements.

Today, steel studs and runners are available from a number of manufacturers. It is important to note that while manufacturers produce the same gauge of material, the steel properties and thicknesses can vary from manufacturer to manufacturer. To assure the best system performance, manufacturer specifications should be checked against the design and minimum thicknesses provided by USG. Failure to do so could result in excessive deflection, overstressed or even buckled steel studs.

USG does not sell common steel framing, but does sell framing components for its proprietary systems, and accessory products for high-performance systems. All components are noncombustible, made from corrosion-resistant steel.

It is important that light-gauge steel components such as steel studs and runners, furring channels and resilient channels be adequately protected against rusting in the warehouse and on the job site. In marine areas, particularly sea coasts, and especially such areas as the Caribbean, Florida and the Gulf Coast where salt-air conditions exist with high humidity, components which offer increased protection against corrosion should be used.

Steel Studs and Runners

Steel studs and runners are channel-type, roll-formed from corrosion-resistant steel, and designed for quick screw attachment of facing materials. They are strong, non-load bearing components of interior partitions, ceilings and column fireproofing and as framing for exterior curtain wall systems. Heavier thickness members are used in load-bearing construction. Limited chaseways for electrical and plumbing services are provided by punchouts in the stud web. Matching runners for each stud size align and secure studs to floors and ceilings, also functioning as headers.

25-ga. (18-mil) Studs and Runners Efficient, low-cost 25-ga. members for framing non-load bearing interior assemblies. Studs come in widths to match wood framing dimensions and are available in lengths up to 20-ft. Runners come in matching stud widths—10-ft. lengths. Not recommended for high-density board applications, such as for DUROCK Brand Cement Board or FIBEROCK Brand Abuse-Resistant Panels.

22-ga. (27-mil) Studs and Runners Heavier gauge, stronger studs in widths of 2-1/2″, 3-5/8″, 4″ and 6″. Runners come in widths to match studs. Not recommended for high-density board applications, such as for DUROCK Brand Cement Board or FIBEROCK Brand Abuse-Resistant Panels.

20-ga. (33-mil) Studs and Runners Heavier 20-ga. members used in framing interior assemblies requiring greater-strength studs, and reinforcement for door frames. Also used in curtain wall assemblies.

Studs available in 2-1/2", 3-5/8", 4", 6" widths—cut-to-order lengths up to 28 ft. Runners come in stud widths, 10-ft. lengths.

Studs and Runners should be hot-dip galvanized.

Load-Bearing Studs and Runners Used for framing load-bearing interior and exterior walls and non-load bearing curtain walls. These studs have stiffened flanges and are available in several sizes.

Typical Steel Thickness—Steel Studs and Runners[1]

Stud/Runner Gauge[3]	Design[2]		Minimum[2]	
	in.	mm	in.	mm
25	0.0188	0.48	0.0179	0.45
22	0.0283	0.72	0.0269	0.68
20	0.0346	0.88	0.0329	0.84
18	0.0451	1.15	0.0428	1.09
16	0.0566	1.44	0.0538	1.37
14	0.0713	1.81	0.0677	1.72
12	0.1017	2.58	0.0966	2.45

(1) Uncoated steel thickness; must meet ASTM A568. Studs and runners meet ASTM C645. Coatings are hot-dip galvanized per ASTM A653 or aluminum-zinc per ASTM A792 or ASTM A591(weight equivalent of A653). (2) Data is from Steel Stud Manufacturers Association (SSMA) catalog. (3) For information only; refer to limiting height tables and structural properties for design data.

There is a serious misconception within the construction industry regarding the substitution of one manufacturer's studs for those of another manufacturer. The assumption is that all studs of a given size and steel thickness are interchangeable. It is possible that the substitution can safely be made, but the decision should not be made until the structural properties of the studs involved are compared. Most reliable manufacturers publish structural property tables in their technical literature. USG includes recommended minimum thickness data in all architectural technical literature covering steel-framed systems.

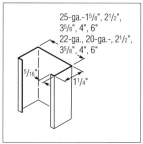

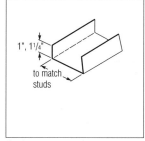

Steel stud
(25, 22, 20-ga.)

Steel runner
(25, 22, 20, 18, 16, 14-ga.)

Cavity Shaft Wall & Area Separation Fire Wall/Party Wall Components

These steel components are lightweight, versatile non-load bearing members of economical, fire and sound-barrier systems: (1) Area Separation Walls between units in multifamily wood-frame buildings; (2) Shaft Walls around elevator and mechanical shafts, return air ducts, stairwells and smoke shafts in multi-story buildings. Components are formed from corrosion-resistant steel: C-H Stud base metal meets structural performance standards in ASTM A446, Grade A. Components should be hot-dipped galvanized.

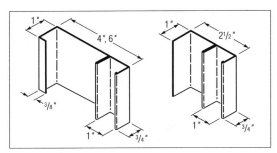

Steel E-studs

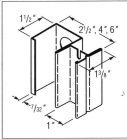

Steel C-H stud

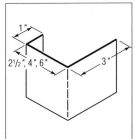

Steel jamb strut (20 ga.)

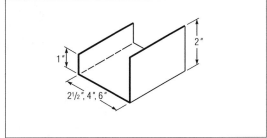

Steel J-runner

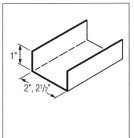

Steel C-runner

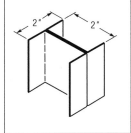

Steel H-stud (two piece)

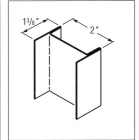

Steel H-stud (one piece)

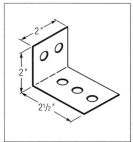

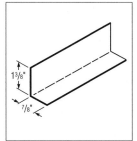

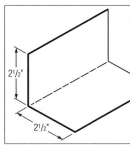

Breakaway clip • *Metal angle runner* • *Corner angle*

Thickness—Area Separation, Shaft Wall and Furring Components[1]

Component Designation	Design[2]		Minimum		
	in.	mm	in.	mm	Gauge[3]
CR, CH, ES25	0.0188	0.48	0.0179	0.45	25
JR24	0.0239	0.61	0.0227	0.58	24
Metal Angles	0.0239	0.61	0.0227	0.58	24
CH22	0.0310	0.79	0.0294	0.75	22
ES, JR, JS, CH20	0.0359	0.91	0.0341	0.87	20

(1) Uncoated steel thickness; meets ASTM A568. Studs and runners meet ASTM C645. Base metal meets ASTM A446 standards for structural performance. Min. yield strength 33 ksi, except C-H stud 40 ksi. Coatings are hot-dip galvanized per ASTM A525; aluminized per ASTM A463, or aluminum-zinc per ASTM A792. (2) Conforms to AISI Specification for the Design of Cold Formed Steel Structural Members, 1986 edition. (3) For information only; refer to limiting height tables and structural properties for design data.

Cavity Wall Components 2-1/2", 4" and 6" wide and designed for use with 1" thick SHEETROCK Brand Gypsum Liner Panels. USG Steel C-H Studs 2-1/2", 4" and 6" are non-load bearing sections installed between abutting liner panels. They have 1" holes spaced 12" to 16" from each end for easy installation of horizontal pipe and conduit. USG Steel E-Studs are 2-1/2", 4" or 6" wide, used singly to cap panels at intersections with exterior walls or back-to-back as studs in unusually high partitions. USG Steel J-Runners, made with unequal legs, are used at floor and ceiling in Shaft Walls. USG Steel C-Runners are used singly at terminals, top and bottom of wall and back-to-back between vertical liner panels at intermediate floors, in Area Separation Walls. USG Steel Jamb Struts (20-gauge), 2-1/2", 4" and 6" wide, are used in jamb framing for fire-rated elevator doors.

Solid Wall Components 2" wide and used with two thicknesses of 1" Gypsum Liner Panels. USG Steel H-Studs fit over and engage edges of adjacent liner panels. USG Steel C-Runners are used in area separation walls as floor and top runners and back-to-back between liner panels at intermediate floors. Also used singly to cap Area Separation Walls.

USG Aluminum Breakaway Clip A 2" wide angle clip made of 0.63" thick aluminum. Used to attach Area Separation Walls to intermediate floor and roof framing. Clips are designed to melt and break away when exposed to fire. 2-1/2" x 2"; approx. 60 lb./1,000 pcs.

Specifications—Area Separation Wall & Shaft Wall Components

Component Designation[1]	Section Depth in.	mm	Length ft.	mm	Approx. Weight lb./1000 ft.	kg/100 m
C-H Studs						
212CH25	2-1/2	63.5	8 to 24	2440 to 7315	519	77.2
212CH22	2-1/2	63.5	8 to 24	2440 to 7315	861	126.5
212CH20	2-1/2	63.5	8 to 24	2440 to 7315	1000	148.8
400CH25	4	101.6	8 to 24	2440 to 7315	612	91.1
400CH20	4	101.6	8 to 24	2440 to 7315	1245	185.3
600CH20	6	152.4	8 to 24	2440 to 7315	1366	203.3
E-Studs						
212ES25	2-1/2	63.5	8 to 28	2440 to 8530	358	53.3
212ES20	2-1/2	63.5	8 to 28	2440 to 8530	729	108.5
400ES25	4	101.6	8 to 28	2440 to 8530	472	70.2
400ES20	4	101.6	8 to 28	2440 to 8530	970	144.3
600ES25	6	152.4	8 to 28	2440 to 8530	689	102.5
600ES20	6	152.4	8 to 28	2440 to 8530	1285	191.2
J-Runners						
212JR24	2-1/2	63.5	10	3050	535	79.6
212JR20	2-1/2	63.5	10	3050	736	109.5
400JR24	4	101.6	10	3050	680	101.2
400JR20	4	101.6	10	3050	937	139.4
600JR24	6	152.4	10	3050	860	128.0
600JR20	6	152.4	10	3050	1191	177.2
C-Runners						
200CR25	2	50.8	10	3050	270	40.1
Metal Angles						
2-1/2" x 2-1/2"	2-1/2	63.5	10	3050	425	63.2
1-3/8" x 7/8"	1-3/8	34.9	10	3050	190	28.3
Jamb Strut						
212JS20	2-1/2	63.5	8 to 12	2440 to 3660	826	122.9
400JS20	4	101.6	8 to 12	2440 to 3660	1026	152.7
600JS20	6	152.4	8 to 12	2440 to 3660	1256	186.9

(1) All components shipped unbundled, additional charge for bundling.

Framing & Furring Accessories

Metal Angles Made of 24-ga. galvanized steel in two standard sizes. The 1-3/8" x 7/8" size is used to secure 1" coreboard or liner panels at floor and ceiling in laminated gypsum drywall partitions. Length: 10 ft.; Approx. wt./1000 ft: 190 lb. (1-3/8" x 7/8"), 425 lb. (2-1/2" x 2-1/2"). Angles in other sizes and gauges available on request.

Cold-Rolled Channels Made of 16-ga. steel. Used in furred walls and suspended ceilings. Available either galvanized or black asphaltum painted. Sizes 3/4" with 1/2" flange, 1-1/2" and 2" with 17/32" flange; lengths 16 and 20 ft.; approx. wt. 3/4"—300 lb./1,000 ft., 1-1/2"—500 lb./1,000 ft., 2"—590 lb./1000 ft. (see page 34).

RC-1 Resilient Channel Made of 25-ga. corrosion resistant steel. One of the most effective, lowest-cost methods of improving sound transmission loss through wood and steel-frame partitions and ceilings.

Used for resilient attachment of Sheetrock Brand Gypsum Panels and Imperial Brand Gypsum Bases. Prepunched holes 4″ o.c. in the flange facilitate screw attachment to framing; facing materials are screw-attached to channels. Size 1/2″ x 2-1/2″; length 12 ft.; approx. wt. 200 lb./1,000 ft. (see page 34).

Limitation: not for use beneath highly flexible floor joists; should be attached to ceilings with 1-1/4″ Type W or Type S Screws only—nails must not be used; see Framing Requirements, Chapter 2.

Z-Furring Channels Made of min. 24-ga. corrosion-resistant steel used to mechanically attach Thermafiber FS-15 Insulating Blankets, polystyrene insulation (or other rigid insulation) and gypsum panels or base to interior side of monolithic concrete and masonry walls. Sizes 1″, 1-1/2″, 2″, 3″; length 8′6″, approx. wt. (lb./1000 ft.): 224 (1″), 269 (1-1/2″), 313 (2″), 400 (3″) (see page 34).

Metal Furring Channels Roll-formed, hat-shaped sections made of 20 and 25-ga. corrosion resistant steel. They are designed for screw attachment of gypsum panels and gypsum base in wall and ceiling furring. Size 7/8″ x 2-9/16″; length 12 ft.; approx. wt.: lb./1,000 ft.: 276 (DWC-25), 515 (DWC-20) (see page 34).

Furring Channel Clips Made of galvanized wire and used in attaching metal furring channels to 1-1/2″ cold-rolled channel ceiling grillwork. For use with single-layer gypsum panels or base. Clips are installed on alternate sides of 1-1/2″ channels; where clips cannot be alternated, wire-tying is recommended. Size 1-1/2″ x 2-3/4″; approx. wt. 38 lb./1,000 pcs. (see page 35).

Adjustable Wall Furring Brackets Used for attaching 3/4″ cold-rolled channels and metal furring channels to interior side of exterior masonry walls. Made of 20-ga. galvanized steel with corrugated edges, brackets spaced not more than 32″ o.c. horizontally and 48″ o.c. vertically are attached to masonry and wire-tied to horizontal channel stiffeners in braced furring systems. Permits adjustment from 1/4″ to 2-1/4″ plus depth of channel. Approx. wt. 56 lb./1,000 pcs. (see page 35).

Hanger and Tie Wire Galvanized soft annealed wire available in three sizes: 8-ga. wire, used for hangers in suspended ceiling grill work, available in 50-lb. coils (approx. 730′); 12-ga. wire for the USG Drywall Suspension System; 18-ga. wire, used for wire-tying channels in wall furring and ceiling construction, available in 50-lb. coils (approx. 8,310′) and 25-lb. hanks (48″ straight lengths—4,148′ total) (see page 35).

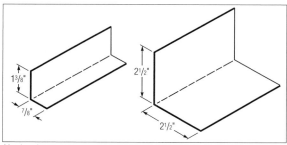

Metal angles

34

Cold-rolled channel

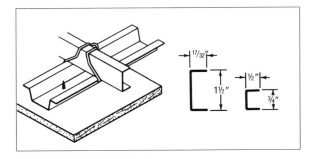

RC-1 resilient channel

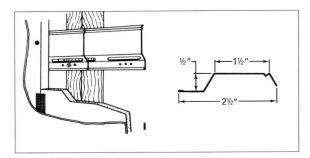

Z-furring channel

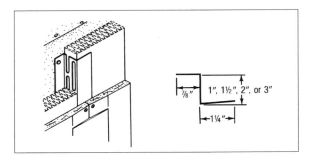

Metal furring channel

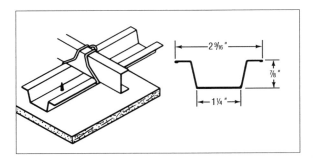

Furring channel clip

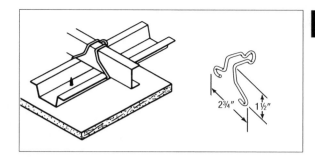

Hanger and tie wire

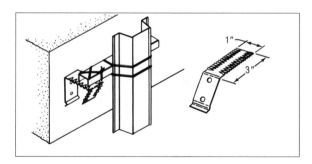

Adjustable wall furring bracket

Sound Control and Insulation Products

Adequate sound control and energy conservation are among the most important requirements in today's buildings. The public has become sufficiently aware of these factors to demand effective measures to control unwanted sound and heat transfer in both commercial and residential construction. With its advanced research, USG has been a leader in developing new systems and products for efficient, low-cost sound control and thermal insulation for new construction and remodeling.

THERMAFIBER Mineral Fiber Insulation products are manufactured by Thermafiber LLC and marketed by USG. They meet every important insulation need—thermal, acoustical and fire protection. They provide superior resistance to heat and sound transmission, resilience that assures full installed thickness and outstanding durability.

THERMAFIBER Insulation products consist of spun mineral fibers formed into mats of varying dimensions and densities, or into nodules for pouring or blowing into framing spaces.

The use of THERMAFIBER Insulation products increases fire ratings of certain partition assemblies—provides greater fire resistance than low-melt point, glass-fiber insulation. Products without facings are rated noncombustible as defined by NFPA 220 when tested per ASTM E136.

THERMAFIBER Insulation Blankets offer excellent sound-absorbing properties, in addition to providing thermal values. When used in partition cavities, THERMAFIBER Insulation improved STC ratings up to nine points. All THERMAFIBER Insulation products are asbestos-free. They resist decay, corrosion and moisture, and will not support vermin.

Products Available

SHEETROCK **Brand Acoustical Sealant** A highly elastic, water-based caulking compound for sealing sound leaks around partition perimeters, cutouts and electrical boxes. Easily applied in beads or may be worked with a knife over flat surfaces such as the outside of electrical boxes. Provides excellent adherence to most surfaces. Highly resilient, permanently flexible, shrink and stain-resistant, long life expectancy. Accepted for use in 1 to 3-hour fire-rated assemblies with no adverse effect on assembly fire performance. Complies with ASTM C919.

Coverage—SHEETROCK **Brand Acoustical Sealant**

Product	Bead size		Approx. coverage
	in.	mm	
SHEETROCK Brand Acoustical Sealant	1/4	6.4	392 ft./gal
	3/8	9.5	174 ft./gal.
	1/2	12.7	98 ft./gal.

SHEETROCK Brand Acoustical Sealant at partition perimeters seals leaks to help deliver tested sound attenuation.

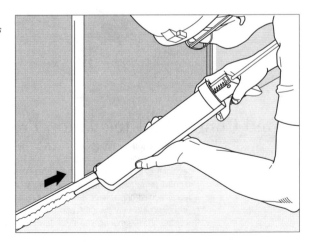

Insulation Blankets

THERMAFIBER Sound Attenuation Fire Blanket

THERMAFIBER Sound Attenuation Fire Blankets fit snugly between steel studs

USG sells and distributes insulation blankets that are compatible with the company's other products and meet the performance specification for the company's recommended and tested systems. The best fire protection and sound attenuation characteristics have been shown in tested systems using insulation blankets or batts produced by THERMAFIBER LLC. Those products include sound attenuation fire blankets, fire safety insulating blankets, curtain wall insulation, safing insulation and fire stop compounds.

THERMAFIBER Sound Attenuation Fire Blankets (SAFB) Paperless, semi-rigid spun mineral fiber mat which substantially improves STC ratings when used in stud cavities of USG partition assemblies. Each blanket has a dense, highly complex labyrinthine structure composed of fibers which produce millions of sound-retarding air pockets. Easily handled and cut; simple to install. Meet ASTM C665, Type I.

Creased THERMAFIBER Sound Attenuation Fire Blankets (SAFB) Creased THERMAFIBER SAFB offers the most economical drywall and veneer plaster sound systems in the 50 to 55 STC range. These fire-rated systems are ideal for party and corridor walls in hotels, motels, offices and multi-family dwellings.

The Creased THERMAFIBER SAFB system is a patented insulation blanket assembly that is 1″ wider than regular blankets. In the field, a 1″ deep vertical cut is made in the center and for the full length of the blanket. The cut enables the wider-than-normal insulating blanket to be buckled and the edges fitted into the partition stud cavity. Installation of SHEETROCK Brand Gypsum Panels on the creased side compresses the insulation blanket, applying pressure both to the studs and the drywall. The applied pressure dampens sound vibrations in the partition and boosts its STC rating. For example, a single-layer drywall partition with Creased THERMAFIBER SAFB has the same STC rating as an unbalanced drywall partition with standard THERMAFIBER SAFB.

Specifications—THERMAFIBER Blankets[1]

product	Thickness in.	mm	Width in.	mm	Length ft.	m	Nom. Density lb./ft.^{3}	kg/m^3	Thermal Resistance[2] R[3] °F-h-ft. Btu[4]	K-m^2 W[4]
Sound Attenuation Fire Blankets (SAFB)	1	25	16, 24	406, 610	4	1.22	4.0	0.25	4	0.7
	1-1/2	38	16, 24	406, 610	4	1.22	2.5	0.16	5.6	1.1
	2	51	16, 24	406, 610	4	1.22	2.5	0.16	7.4	1.4
	3	76	16, 24	406, 610	4	1.22	2.5	0.16	11.1	2.1

(1) Check local availability of package sizes.

(2) C factor = $\frac{1}{R}$; K factor = $\frac{1}{R/thickness}$

(3) "R" value at 75° F (24° C), without facing.

(4) Symbols: °F = degrees Fahrenheit; h = hour; Btu = British thermal units; K = Kelvins; W = watts.

Safing and Firestop Products

THERMAFIBER and USG Fire/Smoke Containment Products

Through-penetration openings—where metallic pipes and conduit pass through floors and walls—can also be passage points for fire and smoke to spread through the building. The THERMAFIBER Through-Penetration Fire/Smoke-Stop System restores the floor or wall as a fire barrier by preventing smoke and fire from passing through openings.

The THERMAFIBER Through-Penetration Fire/Smoke-Stop System is unsurpassed in protecting against fire. But it is also fast, economical and easy to use. No time is wasted mixing patching materials. There is no mess to clean up. No hidden labor or material costs. The principal components of the system are:

THERMAFIBER **Safing Insulation** An easy to handle forming/filling material, made from mineral fiber, with an ability to resist temperatures of up to 2,000°F.

THERMAFIBER SMOKE SEAL **Compound** A flexible sealant especially formulated to stop smoke, bond to the hole perimeter and keep the firestop in place. THERMAFIBER SMOKE SEAL Compound is a caulk-type material applied from a caulking tube or pail; it dries to form a flexible seal.

FIRECODE **Compound** A mortar-type material, it is applied wet over the forming material (where applicable). It then sets or dries to form a tough, curable seal. It is available in either a powder or ready-mixed form.

Both THERMAFIBER SMOKE SEAL Compound and FIRECODE Compound are UL-Classified and low in cost. Both products have been tested in a variety of penetration conditions.

THERMAFIBER **Safing Insulation** Fills the void between slab edges and curtain wall insulation to contain fire. Foil-faced insulation also impedes the passage of smoke and noxious gasses. THERMAFIBER Insulation also is the principal fire-resistant material used to fill through-penetration openings. Blankets come in batts 4″ thick by 24″ wide and are designed for field cutting and installation using special impaling clips or wire support brackets. Strips of insulation must be cut min. 1/2″ wider than the opening to assure a compression fit. See Chapter 10 for information on firestop systems.

THERMAFIBER SMOKE SEAL **Compound** A specially designed fire and smoke-resistant compound. Applied with a caulking gun to seal foil backing of curtain wall insulation to foil backing of safing insulation, and safing insulation to perimeter floor slab. Also can be trowel applied

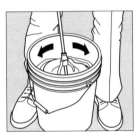

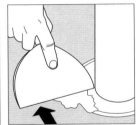

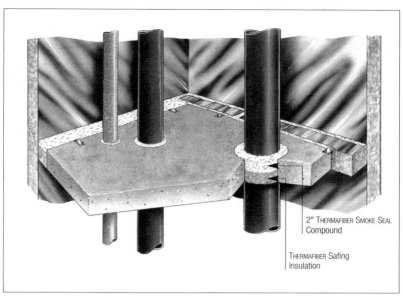

2″ THERMAFIBER SMOKE SEAL
Compound

THERMAFIBER Safing
Insulation

THERMAFIBER Through-
Penetration Fire/Smoke-Stop
System

to seal insulation-filled penetration holes with 2″ layer of SMOKE SEAL Compound. Effectively blocks particulate, smoke and air movement. Smoke Stop system carries UL Classification #165 for through-penetration firestops, 2-hr. and 3-hr. ratings. Comes in 30-oz. cartridges and 5-gal. pails.

FIRECODE Compound Non-toxic compound developed for use with THERMAFIBER Safing Insulation to provide wall and floor through-penetration fire stop systems that combine exceptional economy and performance. Rated non-combustible as defined by NFPA Standard 220 when tested in accordance with ASTM E136. Surface burning characteristics: flame spread 0, smoke developed 0, when tested in accordance with ASTM E84. Effectively seals openings around pipe and cable poke-through openings. Comes ready-mixed in 3-qt. or 4.5 gal. pails, or in 15-lb. bags to mix easily with water at the job site. More economical to use than tube products, especially in large-scale jobs. See Chapter 10 for Floor and Wall penetrations. Complies with ASTM E814, UL 1479, CAN-S115 and UL 2079.

Coverage—FIRECODE Compound

Dry Powder Compound	Approx. Water Additions (pts.)	Approx. Applied Firestop (cu. in.)*	Premixed Compound (qts.)	Approx. Applied Firestop (cu. in.)
1	0.5	33.6	1.0	57.8
5	2.5	172.5	4.0 (1 gal.)	231.0
7.5	3.8	257.6	18.0 (4.5 gal.)	1039.5
10	5.0	344.9	—	—
15	7.5	517.4	—	—

*Based on approximately 7.5 pints water per 15 lb. bag for wall penetrations. For floor penetrations, approximately 8.3 pints water per 15 lb. bag is recommended and yields approximately 537 cu. in. of applied firestop.

Fasteners

Gypsum Board Screws

BUILDEX Screws A complete line of special self-drilling, self-tapping steel screws, including types with a double-lead thread design which produces up to 30% faster penetration, less screw stripping, and greater holding power and pull-through resistance than conventional fasteners.

Screws are corrosion-resistant and all (except Hex Washer Head type) have a Phillips-head recess for rapid installation with a special bit and power-driven screw gun. The bugle head spins the face paper into the cavity under the screwhead for greater holding power and helps prevent damage to the gypsum core and face paper. Defects associated with improper nail dimpling are eliminated. Other head types are designed specifically for attaching metal to metal and installing wood and metal trim. Screws meet ASTM C1002 (TYPE S and Type W) and ASTM C954 (TYPE S-12).

TYPE S Screws have specially designed drill point and threads that minimize stripping, provide maximum holding power and pull-through resistance in steel studs and runners. TYPE S Screws are designed for use with steel up to .04″ thick; TYPE S-12 Screws for steel from .04″ to .07″ thick (see table, below). The special threads on Type G and Type W Screws offer superior holding power in attachment to gypsum boards and wood framing, respectively. TAPCON Anchors provide fast, safe attachment of steel components to poured concrete and concrete block surfaces. Special 1-15/16″ TYPE S-12 Bugle Head Pilot Point Screws are designed for attachment of plywood to steel joists and studs.

The superior pull-through resistance of Type W Screws has virtually eliminated loose panel attachment and nail pops in wood-frame construction. Tests have shown the Type W Screw to have 350% greater pullout strength than GWB-54 nails. Fewer screws than nails are generally required, and the speed of installation using electric screwguns compares favorably with nailing.

Secret to superiority of screw attachment is shown by comparative diagrams. Bugle-head (left) screw depresses face paper of gypsum panel without tearing; threads cut into and deform wood to hold tightly. Longer drywall nail (right) grips with friction, loosens hold as wood shrinks, which may pop nailhead above surface to create callback situation.

Selector Guide for Screws

Fastening Application	Fastener used	Fig[2]
Gypsum panels to steel framing[1]		
1/2″ single-layer panels to steel studs, runners, channels	1″ Type S bugle head	1
5/8″ single-layer panels to steel studs, runners, channels	1″ Type S bugle head 1-1/8″ Type S bugle head	1 1
3/4″ single-layer panels to steel studs, runners, channels	1-1/4″ Type S bugle head	1
1″ coreboard to metal angle runners in solid partitions	1-5/8″ Type S bugle head	1
1/2″ double-layer panels to steel studs, runners, channels	1-5/8″ Type S bugle head	1
5/8″ double-layer panels to steel studs, runners, channels	1-5/8″ Type S bugle head	2
3/4″ double-layer panels to steel studs, runners, channels	2-1/4″ Type S bugle head	2
1/2″ panels through coreboard to metal angle runners in solid partitions	1-7/8″ Type S bugle head	2
5/8″ panels through coreboard to metal angle runners in solid partitions	2-1/4″ Type S bugle head 3″ Type S bugle head	2 2
1″ double-layer coreboard to steel studs, runners	2-5/8″ Type S bugle head	2
Wood to steel framing		
Wood trim over single-layer panels to steel studs, runners	1″ Type S or S-12 trim head 1-5/8″ Type S or S-12 trim head	5 5
Wood trim over double-layer panels to steel studs, runners	2-1/4″ Type S or S-12 trim head	5
Steel cabinets, brackets through single-layer panels to steel studs	1-1/4″ Type S oval head	6
Wood cabinets through single-layer panels to steel studs	1-5/8″ Type S oval head	6
Wood cabinets through double-layer panels to steel studs	2-1/4″, 2-7/8″, 3-3/4″, Type S oval head	6
Steel studs to door frames, runners		
Steel studs to runners 25 & 22-ga.	3/8″ Type S pan head	9
Steel studs to runners		
Steel studs to door frame jamb anchors 20-ga.	3/8″ Type S-12 pan head 5/8″ Type S-12 low-profile head	10 11
Other metal-to-metal attachment (12-ga. max.)		
Steel studs to door frame jamb anchor clips (heavier shank assures entry in clips of hard steel)	1/2″ Type S-12 pan head 5/8″ Type S-12 low-profile head	10 11
Metal-to-metal connections up to double thickness of 12-ga. steel	3/4″ S-4 hex washer head Anticorrosive-coated	12
Gypsum panels to 12-ga. (max.) steel framing		
1/2″ and 5/8″ panels and gypsum sheathing to steel studs and runners; specify anticorrosive-coated screws for exterior curtain wall applications	1″ Type S-12 bugle head	3
Self-Furring Metal Lath and brick wall ties through gypsum sheathing to steel studs and runners; specify anticorrosive-coated screws for exterior curtain wall applications	1-1/4″ Type S-12 bugle head 1-1/4″ Type S-12 pancake head	4 13
1/2″ and 5/8″ double-layer gypsum panels to steel studs and runners	1-5/8″ Type S-12 bugle head	4

Selector Guide for Screws continued

Fastening Application	Fastener used	Fig[2]
Gypsum panels to 12-ga. (max.) steel framing		
Multilayer gypsum panels and other materials to steel studs and runners	1-7/8", 2, 2-3/8", 2-5/8", 3" TYPE S-12 bugle head	4
Cement board to steel framing		
DUROCK Brand Cement Board or Exterior Cement Board direct to steel studs, runners	1-1/4", 1-5/8" DUROCK Brand Steel Screws	17
Rigid foam insulation to steel framing		
Rigid foam insulation panels to steel studs and runners; Type R for 20- 25-ga. steel	1-1/2", 2, 2-1/2", 3" TYPE S-12 or R wafer head	15
Aluminum trim to steel framing		
Trim and door hinges to steel studs and runners (screw matches hardware and trim)	7/8" TYPE S-18 oval head anticorrosive-coated	7
Batten strips to steel studs in demountable partitions	1-1/8" TYPE S bugle head	1
Aluminum trim to steel framing in demountable and UTRAWALL partitions	1/4" TYPE S bugle head anticorrosive-coated	1
Gypsum panels to wood framing		
3/8", 1/2" and 5/8" single-layer panels to wood studs, joists	1-1/4" TYPE W bugle head	8
Cement board to wood framing		
DUROCK Brand Cement Board or Exterior Cement Board to wood framing	1-1/4",1-5/8", 2-1/4" DUROCK Brand Wood Screws, with anticorrosive coating	18
Resilient channels to wood framing		
Screw attachment required for both ceilings and partitions	1-1/4" Type W bugle head	8
	1-1/4" TYPE S bugle head	1
For fire-rated construction	1-1/4" TYPE S bugle head	1
Gypsum panels to gypsum panels		
Multilayer adhesively laminated gypsum-to-gypsum partitions (not recommended for double-layer 3/8" panels)	1-1/2" Type G bugle head	8
Plywood to steel joists		
3/8" to 3/4" plywood to steel joists (penetrates double thickness 14-ga.)	1-5/16" TYPE S-12 bugle head, pilot point	16
Steel to poured concrete or block		
Attachment of steel framing components to poured concrete and concrete block surfaces	3/16" x 1-3/4" acorn slotted HWH TAPCON Anchor	14

Notes: (1) Includes 25, 22 and 20-ga. steel studs and runners; metal angles; metal furring channels; resilient channels. If channel resiliency makes screw penetration difficult, use screws 1/8" longer than shown to attach panels to resilient channels. For other gauges of studs and runners, always use TYPE S-12 screws. For steel applications not shown, select a screw length which is at least 3/8" longer than total thickness of materials to be fastened. Use anticorrosive-coated screws for exterior applications. (2) Figures refer to screw illustrations on page 43.

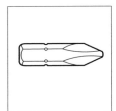

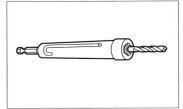

No. 1 Bit for trim and pancake heads

No. 2 Bit for bugle pan, wafer, low-profile & oval heads

CONDRIVE Tool/Bit for HWH TAPCON Anchors
Note: Hex-head bit not illustrated

Basic Types of Screws — Numbers refer to descriptions on pages 41-42.

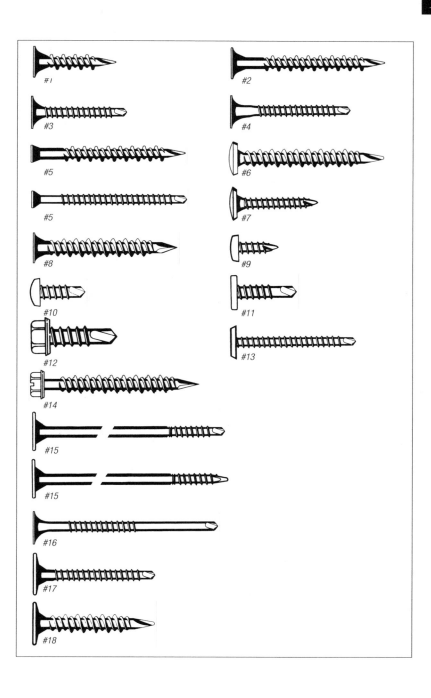

#1

#2

#3

#4

#5

#6

#5

#7

#8

#9

#10

#11

#12

#13

#14

#15

#15

#16

#17

#18

Specifications— Screws

Description	Length in.	mm	Type	Head
Base Screws	1	25.4	Type S	bugle
	1-1/8	28.6	Type S	bugle
	1-1/4	31.8	Type S	bugle
	1-5/8	41.3	Type S	bugle
	1-7/8	47.6	Type S	bugle
	2-1/4	57.2	Type S	bugle
	2-5/8	66.7	Type S	bugle
	3	76.2	Type S	bugle
Specialty Screws	3/8	9.5	Type S	pan
	3/8	9.5	Type S-12	pan
	1/2	12.7	Type S-12	pan
	1/2	12.7	Type S-12	pancake
	1/2	12.7	Type S-16	pan[1]
	5/8	15.9	Type S-12	low-profile
	3/4	19.1	Type S-4	hex washer[1]
	7/8	22.2	Type S-18	oval[1]
	1	25.4	Type S	trim
	1	25.4	Type S-12	trim
	1	25.4	Type S-12	bugle
	1-1/4	31.8	Type S-12	bugle
	1-1/4	31.8	Type S	bugle[1]
	1-1/4	31.8	Type W	bugle
	1-1/4	31.8	Type S-12	pancake
	1-1/4	31.8	Type S	oval
	1-1/2	38.1	Type G	bugle
	1-1/2	38.1	Type R	wafer
	1-1/2	38.1	Type S-12	wafer
	1-5/8	41.3	Type S	oval
	1-5/8	41.3	Type S	trim
	1-5/8	41.3	Type S-12	bugle
	1-5/8	41.3	Type S-12	trim
	1-7/8	47.6	Type S-12	bugle
	1-15/16	49.2	Type S-12	bugle, pilot pt.
	2	50.8	Type S-12	bugle
	2	50.8	Type R	wafer
	2	50.8	Type S-12	wafer
	2-1/4	57.2	Type S	trim
	2-1/4	57.2	Type S	oval
	2-1/4	57.2	Type S-12	trim
	2-3/8	60.3	Type S-12	bugle
	2-1/2	63.5	Type R	wafer
	2-1/2	63.5	Type S-12	wafer
	2-5/8	66.7	Type S-12	bugle
	2-7/8	73.0	Type S	oval
	3	76.2	Type S-12	bugle
	3	76.2	Type R	wafer
	3	76.2	Type S-12	wafer
	3-3/4	95.3	Type S	oval
Tapcon Screw	1-3/4	44.5	conc.	hex

(1) Anticorrosive-coated

Screw Applications

Application	Screw Size and Length (no. x Inches)
1″ (25.4 mm) Bugle Head Type S Attaches 1/2″ or 5/8″ single-layer gypsum panels and bases to steel framing.	6x1
1-1/8″ (28.6 mm) Bugle Head Type S Attaches 5/8″ gypsum panels and bases to resilient channels or other steel framing, also batten strips for demountable partitions.	6x1-1/8
1-1/4″ (31.8 mm) Bugle Head Type S Attaches 1″ coreboard to steel runners. Attaches 1/2″, 5/8″ and 3/4″ gypsum panels and bases to wood studs.	6x1-1/4
1-5/8″ (41.3 mm) Bugle Head Type S Attaches double-layer gypsum panels to steel framing.	6x1-5/8
2″ (50.8 mm) Bugle Head Type S **2-1/4″ (57.2 mm) Bugle Head** **2-1/2″ (63.5 mm) Bugle Head** **3″ (76.2 mm) Bugle Head** Attaches multiple layers of gypsum panels and other compatible materials to steel framing.	6x2 6x2-1/4 7x2-1/2 8x3
1-1/4″ (31.8 mm) Bugle Head (Type W) Attaches 1/2″ or 5/8″ single-layer gypsum panels, bases, or resilient channels to wood framing.	6x1-1/4
7/16″ (11.1 mm) Pan Head Attaches 25-ga. steel studs to runners.	6x7/16 7x7/16
1-1/2″ (38.1 mm) Bugle Head-Laminating Temporary attachment of gypsum to gypsum.	10x1-1/2
1-5/8″ (41.3 mm) Trim Head **2-1/4″ (57.2 mm) Trim Head** Attaches wood trim to 20 to 25-ga. steel framing.	6x1-5/8 6x2-1/4

Double Thread Screw Applications

Application	Screw Size and Length (no. x Inches)
Bugle Head Attaches gypsum board to 20 to 25-ga. steel framing.	6x1 6x1-1/8 6x1-1/4 6x1-5/8 6x2 6x2-1/4 7x2-1/2 8x3

Drill Tip Screw Applications

Application	Screw Size and Length (no. x Inches)
Bugle Head Attaches single-layer gypsum board to steel framing up to 14-ga.	6x1 6x1-1/8 6x1-1/4
Bugle-Head Attaches multilayer gypsum board to steel framing up to 14-ga.	6x1-5/8 6x1-7/8 8x2-1/8 8x2-5/8 8x3
Pan Head Attaches stud to runner up to 14-ga.	7x7/16 8x5/8
Hex Washer Head Attaches steel to steel up to 14-ga.	8x1/2 8x5/8 8x3/4 8x1
Modified Truss Head Attaches metal lath to steel framing up to 14-ga.	8x1/2 8x3/4 8x1 8x1-1/4

Gypsum Board Nails

The design of nails has vastly improved since the relationship of wood shrinkage to nail popping was discovered. Nails have been developed to concentrate maximum holding power over the shortest possible length—notably the annular ring type nail which has about 20% greater holding power than a smooth-shank nail of the same length and shank diameter. However, under lengthy, extreme drying conditions, such as a cold dry winter or in arid climates, resultant wood shrinkage may cause fastener pops even with the shorter annular ring nail.

As with screws, specification of the proper nail for each application is extremely important, particularly for fire-rated construction where nails of the specified length and diameter only will provide proper

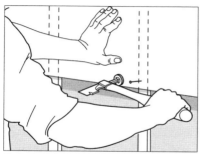

Hand pressure is applied to panel as nail is driven.

performance. When wood-frame gypsum panel systems are subjected to fire, nails on surface attain temperatures that tend to char the wood, thereby reducing their holding power. Nails used in gypsum construction should comply with performance standards of ASTM C514. Nails are not available from USG.

Selector Guide for Gypsum Board Nails[1]

Fastener description[2] in.	Fastener length in.	mm	Total thickness of surfacing materials[3] in. 1/4 mm 6.4	3/8 9.5	1/2 12.7	5/8 15.9	3/4 19.1	7/8 22.2	1 25.4	1-1/4 31.8	1-3/8 34.9	Approx Usage lb/1,000 ft²	kg/100m²
Annular Ring Drywall Nail 12-1/2 ga. (2.50 mm) 1/4″ (6.35 mm) diam. head, med. diamond point	1-1/4	31.8	X	X	X							4.50	2.20
	1-3/8	34.9			X							5.00	2.44
	1-1/2	38.1				X						5.25	2.56
	1-5/8	41.3					X					5.75	2.81
Same as above except 19/64″ (7.54 mm) diam. head	1-1/4	31.8	X	X	X							4.50	2.20
	1-3/8	34.9			X							5.00	2.44
	1-1/2	38.1				X						5.25	2.56
	1-5/8	41.3					X					5.75	2.81
	1-3/4	44.5						X				6.00	2.93
	2	50.8							X			7.00	3.42
12-1/2 ga. (2.50 mm) 19/64″ (7.54 mm) diam. head	1-1/4	31.8	X	X	X							4.50	2.20
	1-3/8	34.9			X							5.00	2.44
	1-1/2	38.1				X						5.25	2.56
	1-5/8	41.3					X					5.75	2.81
Same as above except 1/4″ (6.35 mm) diam. head													
14 ga. (2.03 mm)	1-3/8 (4d) 34.9			X								3.50	1.71
13-1/2 ga. (2.18 mm)	1-5/8 (5d) 41.3				X							4.50	2.20
13 ga. (2.32 mm)	1-7/8 (6d) 47.6						X					5.75	2.81
13-1/2 ga. (2.18 mm)	2-1/8 (7d) 54.0								X			7.50	3.66

(1) For wood framing 16″ o.c., nails 8″ o.c. for walls, 7″ o.c. for ceilings. (2) All nails treated to prevent rust with joint compounds or veneer plaster finishes. Fire-rated assemblies generally require greater nail penetration; therefore, for fire-rated assemblies, use exact nail length and diameter specified for rated assembly (see Fire Test Report). (3) In laminated double-layer construction, base layer is attached in same manner as single layer.

48

Adhesives

Drywall adhesives make an important contribution to gypsum panel attachment where the finest room interiors are desired. Their use greatly reduces the nail or screw fastening otherwise required, thus saving labor on spotting and sanding, as well as minimizing nail pops and other fastener imperfections.

USG offers reliable, field-tested adhesives designed for professional use. Each is formulated to produce superior attachment, freedom from fastener imperfections and high-quality results. Recommended for laminating gypsum panels in multilayer fire-rated or non-rated partitions and ceilings are SHEETROCK Brand Setting-Type (DURABOND) or Lightweight Setting-Type (EASY SAND) Joint Compounds—(dry powder products, applied by spreader, requiring mixing and temporary fastening in application) or SHEETROCK Brand Ready-Mixed Joint Compound—All Purpose or Taping. All provide tight bond when dry yet permit adjustment of panels after contact.

SHEETROCK Brand Setting-Type (DURABOND) or Lightweight Setting-Type (EASY SAND) Joint Compounds Dry, powder products to be mixed with water, used for laminating gypsum panels in multilayer fire-rated or non-rated partitions and ceilings. Spreader-applied, these compounds require temporary fastening in application. Provide tight bond when dry, yet permit panel adjustment after contact. Meet ASTM C475.

SHEETROCK Brand Ready-Mixed Joint Compound Taping or All Purpose Compounds formulated to a creamy smooth consistency for fast spreader application. Used for laminating gypsum panels in multilayer fire-rated or non-rated partitions and ceilings. Offer ready-to-use convenience, eliminate extensive mixing and waste. Provide good bond and strength when dry. Use above grade; keep from freezing. Meet ASTM C475.

Commercial Adhesives Available in drywall stud and construction types meeting ASTM C557; used in non-fire rated gypsum construction. These adhesives bridge minor irregularities in the base or framing, making it easier to form true joints and level surfaces. The use of adhesive adds strength to an assembly, reduces fasteners required, and helps eliminate loose panels and nail pops.

SHEETROCK Brand Lightweight Setting-Type (EASY SAND) Joint Compound

SHEETROCK Brand Ready-Mixed All Purpose Joint compound

Coverage—Laminating Adhesives

Product[1]	Type of laminating	2″ o.c.	1-1/2″ o.c.
SHEETROCK Brand Ready-Mixed Joint	sheet	340	465
Compounds—Taping or All Purpose	strip	170	230
SHEETROCK Brand Lightweight All Purpose	sheet	23.0	31.7
Ready-Mixed Joint Compound (PLUS 3)	strip	11.5	15.5
SHEETROCK Brand Setting-Type	sheet	184	246
Joint Compounds (DURABOND)	strip	93	123
SHEETROCK Brand Lightweight Setting-Type	sheet	134	179
Joint Compounds (EASY SAND)	strip	68	90

Approx. coverage[2] / Lam. blade notch spacing

(1) See Joint Compound Specifications for standard package sizes. (2) Coverage in lb./1000 ft.^{2} of packaged product, not including water, necessary to achieve working consistency. Exception: PLUS 3 is gal./1000 ft.^{2}.

Joint Compounds

Today's complete USG SHEETROCK Brand Joint Compound line includes both ready-mixed and powder products in drying and setting (hardening) types. In addition to conventional joint finishing and fastener spotting, some of these products are designed for repairing cracks, patching, spackling, back-blocking, texturing and for laminating gypsum panels in double-layer systems. Products comply with ASTM C475.

Advantages

Low Cost High-quality products reduce preparation time, save application labor and prevent expensive callbacks.

Versatility Job-tested compounds are available in specialized types to meet finishing requirements.

Safety Safe to handle and use; meet OSHA and Consumer Product Safety Standards.

Use of USG joint compounds brings the important added advantage of dealing with one manufacturer who is responsible for all components of the finished walls and ceilings—formulated in our laboratories, and manufactured in our plants for maximum system performance.

General Limitations

1. USG joint compounds are not compatible with and should not be intermixed with any other compounds.

2. For interior use only except for the use of SHEETROCK Brand Setting-Type (DURABOND) and SHEETROCK Brand Lightweight Setting-Type (EASY SAND) Joint Compounds with SHEETROCK Brand Exterior Gypsum Ceiling Board.

3. Not recommended for laminating except SHEETROCK Brand Setting-Type (DURABOND) and SHEETROCK Brand Lightweight Setting-Type (EASY SAND) Compounds and SHEETROCK Brand Ready-Mixed Compounds—All Purpose and Taping.

4. Protect bagged and cartoned products against wetting; protect ready-mixed products from freezing and extreme heat.

5. Each compound coat must be dry before the next is applied (except SHEETROCK Brand Setting-Type (DURABOND) and SHEETROCK Brand Lightweight Setting-Type (EASY SAND) Compounds); and completed joint treatment must be thoroughly dry before decorating.

6. Use only SHEETROCK Brand Setting-Type (DURABOND) 90 or SHEETROCK Brand Lightweight Setting-Type (EASY SAND 90) with 85-130 min. hardening time, or SHEETROCK Brand Setting-Type (DURABOND) 45 or SHEETROCK Brand Lightweight Setting-Type (EASY SAND 45) with 30-80 min. hardening time for treating joints of Water-Resistant Gypsum Panels to be covered with ceramic or plastic tile.

7. With regard to the following products: SHEETROCK Brand Lightweight All Purpose Joint Compound (PLUS 3), SHEETROCK Brand Topping Joint Compound Ready-Mixed and SHEETROCK Brand Lightweight All Purpose Joint Compound (AP LITE)— If smoothing by dry sanding, use nothing coarser than 150 grit sandpaper or 220 grit abrasive mesh cloth.

8. For painting and decorating, follow manufacturer's directions for materials used. All surfaces must be thoroughly dry, dust-free and not glossy before decorating. SHEETROCK Brand First Coat should be applied and allowed to dry before decorating.

9. Gypsum panel surface should be skim coated with joint compound to equalize suction before painting in areas where gypsum panel walls and ceilings will be subjected to severe artificial or natural side lighting and be decorated with a gloss paint (egg shell, semi-gloss or gloss).

10. If dry sanding is used to smooth the joint compound, avoid roughening the gypsum panel face paper.

11. Do not use topping compound for taping or as first coat over bead.

12. Not recommended for texturing by spray application.

13. Children can fall into joint compound bucket and drown. Keep children away from bucket with even a small amount of liquid. Do not reuse bucket.

SHEETROCK Brand Ready-Mixed Drying-Type Joint Compounds

SHEETROCK Brand Ready-Mixed Joint Compounds are drying-type products which are vastly superior to ordinary ready-mixed compounds and are preferred for consistently high-quality work. These vinyl-based formulations are specially premixed to a creamy, smooth consistency essentially free of crater-causing air bubbles. They offer excellent slip and bond, and easy workability. Available for hand or machine-tool applications.

Limitation: must protect wet joints and container from freezing.

Six specialized products:

Ready Mixed Taping

Ready Mixed Topping

Ready Mixed All Purpose

PLUS 3

Midweight

EASY SAND Ready Mixed

SHEETROCK **Brand Taping Joint Compound Ready-Mixed** A high-performance product for embedding tape and also as a first fill coat over metal bead, trim and fasteners in some areas. Check suitability of the formula with your local sales office. Also used for laminating.

SHEETROCK **Brand Topping Joint Compound Ready-Mixed** A low-shrinkage, easily applied and sanded product recommended for second and third coats over SHEETROCK Brand Taping and All Purpose Joint Compounds. Also used for simple hand-applied texturing in some geographic areas. Check suitability of the formula with your local sales office. Not suitable for embedding tape or as first coat over metal corners, trim and fasteners.

SHEETROCK **Brand All Purpose Joint Compound Ready-Mixed** Used for embedding, finishing, skim coating, simple hand-applied texturing and for laminating. Combines single-package convenience with good taping and topping characteristics. Recommended for finishing SHEETROCK Brand Gypsum Panels, SW Edge, joints over prefill of SHEETROCK Brand Setting-Type (DURABOND) or Lightweight Setting-Type (EASY SAND) Compound; also for repairing cracks in interior plaster and masonry not subject to moisture.

SHEETROCK **Brand Lightweight All Purpose Joint Compound Ready-Mixed (PLUS 3)** Offers all the benefits of an all purpose compound, plus three exclusive advantages: up to 35% less weight, less shrinkage, and exceptional ease of sanding. Usually needs only two coats over metal. Eliminates need for separate taping and topping compounds—sands with ease of topping compound, bonds like taping compound.

SHEETROCK **Brand All Purpose Joint Compound Ready-Mixed (Midweight)** A ready-mixed compound that weighs 15% less than conventional-weight compounds, offers excellent tape-embedding properties, easy workability and sandability. Works well for both taping and topping applications. Lower shrinkage means that only two coats typically are required over metal bead, trim and fasteners.

SHEETROCK **Brand Lightweight Setting-Type Joint Compound (EASY SAND, Ready-Mixed)** This lightweight ready-mixed joint compound offers the choice of drying-type or setting-type performance. When used directly from the container, the compound works as a conventional lightweight ready-mixed all purpose compound. When the special yellow activator powder (packed inside the pail) is thoroughly mixed into the compound, it works as a setting-type product similar to regular EASY SAND. Setting times are regulated by the amount of activator added to the mix, and may range from 20-210 minutes.

SHEETROCK Brand Powder Joint Compounds

SHEETROCK Brand Powder Joint Compounds are top-quality, non-asbestos, drying-type products providing easy mixing, smooth application and ample working time. Designed for embedding tape, for fill coats and finishing over drywall joints, corner bead, trim and fasteners. Included in product line:

SHEETROCK **Brand Taping Joint Compound** Designed for embedding tape and for first fill coat on metal corner beads, drywall trims and fasteners; also used for patching plaster cracks. Offers excellent bond and resistance to cracking.

SHEETROCK Brand Topping Joint Compound A smooth-sanding material for second and third coats over taping or all-purpose compound. Produces excellent feathering and superior finishing results.

SHEETROCK Brand All Purpose Joint Compound Incorporates good taping and topping characteristics in a single product, for use where finest results of the specialized compounds are not necessary. Also has good hand-applied texturing properties.

SHEETROCK Brand Lightweight All Purpose Joint Compound (AP LITE) All Purpose compound weighs 20% less than conventional compounds; offers lower shrinkage, better crack resistance, easier mixing, application and sanding.

SHEETROCK Brand Powder Setting-Type Joint Compounds

These setting-type powder products were developed to provide faster finishing of drywall interiors, even under slow drying conditions. Rapid chemical hardening and low shrinkage permit same-day finishing and usually next-day decoration. Features exceptional bond; virtually unaffected by humidity extremes. Ideal for laminating double-layer systems, particularly fire-rated assemblies, and for adhering gypsum panels to above-grade concrete surfaces. May be used for surface texturing and for filling, smoothing and finishing interior above-grade concrete. Also used to treat joints in exterior gypsum ceiling board; as prefill material for SHEETROCK Brand Gypsum Panels, SW Edge; for treating joints of SHEETROCK Brand Gypsum Panels, Water-Resistant; treating fastener heads in areas to receive ceramic or plastic tile; and (except for SHEETROCK Brand Lightweight Setting-Type Joint Compound) to embed tape and fill beads in veneer plaster finish systems when rapid drying conditions exist.

SHEETROCK Brand Lightweight Setting-Type Joint Compound (EASY SAND) Weighs 25% less than conventional setting-type compounds for easier handling, faster application and improved productivity on the job. Provides sanding ease similar to a ready-mixed, all purpose joint compound. Offers varied setting times of 8 to 12 min. (EASY SAND 5); 20 to 30 min. (EASY SAND 20); 30 to 80 min. (EASY SAND 45); 85 to 130 min. (EASY SAND 90); 180-240 min. (EASY SAND 210); and 240 to 360 min. (EASY SAND 300).

SHEETROCK Brand Setting-Type Joint Compound (DURABOND) Provides the strongest joint bond of all setting-type compounds. Available in a number of setting times to meet varying job requirements: 20 to 30 min. (DURABOND 20); 30 to 80 min. (DURABOND 45); 85 to 130 min. (DURABOND 90); 180 to 240 min. (DURABOND 210); 240 to 360 min. (DURABOND 300).

Setting-Type Joint Compound Limitations

1. Not to be applied over moist surfaces or surfaces likely to become moist, on below-grade surfaces, or on other surfaces subject to moisture exposure, pitting or popping.

2. SHEETROCK Brand Setting-Type Joint Compounds (DURABOND) are difficult to sand after drying and must be smoothed before complete hardening.

3. Before using over new interior concrete surfaces, concrete should age 60 days or more.

EASY SAND   *DURABOND*

Joint Compound Selection

Choosing the right joint compound for a specific job requires an understanding of a number of factors: job conditions, shop practices, applicators' preferences, types of available joint systems, characteristics of products considered and recommended product combinations.

Joint compound products are usually named according to function, such as taping, topping and all-purpose. Taping typically performs as the highest shrinking, strongest bonding, hardest sanding of the three compounds, and is used for embedding tape. Topping usually is the lowest shrinking, easiest applying and sanding of the compounds for use in second and third coats; may occasionally be designed for simple hand-applied texturing. Taping and topping are usually designed as companion products to give the highest quality workmanship. All-Purpose is generally a compromise of taping and topping and may be used as a simple hand-applied texturing material. Lightweight All Purpose Joint Compound is also an all-purpose compound, but is lighter, shrinks less and sands easier.

Types of Joint Compounds

Two-Compound Systems Formulated for superior performance in each joint finishing step. Separate taping compounds develop the greatest bond strength and crack resistance. Separate topping compounds have the best sanding characteristics, lower shrinkage and smoothest finishing.

All-Purpose Compounds Good performance in all joint finishing steps; do not have the outstanding bond strength, workability and sandability of separate taping and topping compounds. However, All-Purpose Compounds minimize inventories, avoid jobsite mix-ups and are especially good for scattered jobs.

Ready-Mixed Compounds Open-and-use convenience; save time and mistakes in mixing, leading to minimum waste. Require minimal water supply at the job. Ready-Mixed Compounds have the best working qualities of all compounds—excellent performance plus factory-controlled batch consistency.

These compounds do require heated storage. Should they freeze, they can be slowly thawed at room temperature, mixed to an even viscosity and used without damaging effect. However, repeated freeze/thaw cycles cause remixing to become more difficult.

Powder Compounds Have the special advantage of being storable (dry) at any temperature. If they are stored in a cold warehouse, however, they should be moved to a warm mixing room the day before they are to be mixed. Best results require strict adherence to proportioning of powder and water.

Specifications—SHEETROCK Brand Joint Compounds

Product	Container size	Approx. coverage
SHEETROCK Brand Ready-Mixed Joint Compound—Taping, Topping, All Purpose	12-lb. (5.4 kg), 42-lb. (19 kg) or 61.7-lb. (28 kg) pail; 48-lb. (21.8 kg), 50-lb. (22.7 kg) or 61.7-lb. (28 kg) carton	138 lb./1,000 ft.^{2} (67.4 kg/100 m^2)
SHEETROCK Brand Lightweight All Purpose Joint Compound, Ready-Mixed (PLUS 3)	1 gal, (3.8L) or 4.5 gal. (17L) pail; 4.5 gal. (17L) or 3.5-gal. (13L) carton	9.4 gal./1,000 ft.^{2} (38.3L/100 m^2)
SHEETROCK Brand All Purpose Joint Compound, Ready-Mixed (Midweight)	4.5 gal. (17L) pail; 4.5 gal. (17L) or 3.5-gal. (13L) carton	9.4 gal./1,000 ft.^{2} (38.3L/100 m^2)
SHEETROCK Brand Powder Joint Compound-Taping, Topping, All Purpose	25-lb. (11.3 kg) bag	83 lb./1,000 ft^2 (40.5 kg/100 m^2)
SHEETROCK Brand Lightweight All Purpose joint Compound (AP LITE)	20-lb. (9 kg) bag	67 lb./1,000 ft.^{2} (32.7 kg/100 m^2)
SHEETROCK Brand Setting-Type Joint Compound (DURABOND) 20, 45, 90, 210, 300	25-lb. (11.3 kg) bag	72 lb./1,000 ft^2 (35.2 kg/100 m^2)
SHEETROCK Brand Lightweight Setting-Type Joint Compound (EASY SAND) 20, 45, 90, 210, 300	18-lb. (8.1 kg) bag	52 lb./1,000 ft^2 (25.3 kg/100 m^2)

Concrete Finishing Compounds

COVER COAT Compound

COVER COAT Compound A vinyl-base product, formulated for filling and smoothing monolithic concrete ceilings, walls and columns located above grade—no extra bonding agent needed. Supplied in ready-mixed form (sand can be added), easily applied with drywall tools in two or more coats. Dries to a fine white surface usually making further decoration unnecessary. Not washable unpainted. Also can be used for embedding tape, for first coat over metal bead and trim, and for skim coating over gypsum panels.

Limitation: Not to be applied over moist surfaces or surfaces likely to become moist (from condensation or other source), on ceiling areas below grade, on surfaces that project outside the building, or any area that might be subject to moisture, freezing, efflorescence, pitting or popping.

SHEETROCK Brand Setting-Type (DURABOND) and Lightweight Setting-Type (EASY SAND) Joint Compounds These setting-type compounds are ideally suited to fill offsets and voids left in concrete. They produce a hard finish in various shades of white. Overpainting may be required.

Where deep fills are required, SHEETROCK Brand Setting-Type (DURABOND) and SHEETROCK Brand Lightweight Setting-Type (EASY SAND) Compounds are especially recommended for the first coat, then followed by COVER COAT Compound. This practice minimizes check cracking.

Limitations: same as for COVER COAT Compound.

Reinforcing Tapes

From the originator of modern joint finishing, USG reinforcing tapes add strength and crack resistance for smooth concealment at flat joints and inside corners. Two products—both quickly and easily applied—are available for specialized uses: paper tape for treatment with joint compounds; glass-fiber tape for veneer plaster finishes.

SHEETROCK **Brand Joint Tape** A special high-strength fiber tape for use with USG joint compounds in reinforcing joints and corners in gypsum drywall and veneer plaster finish interiors. Exceptional wet and dry strength; resists stretching, wrinkling and other distortions; lies flat and resists tearing under tools. The wafer-thin tape is lightly sanded for increased bond and lies flat for easy concealment on next coat. Precision-processed with positive center creasing, which simplifies application in corners; uniform winding provides accurate, trouble-free attachment to angles and to flat joints.

Preferred for its consistent high performance in gypsum drywall finishing, SHEETROCK Brand Joint Tape with SHEETROCK Brand Setting-Type (DURABOND) Joint Compounds is also used with veneer plaster finish systems. The regular SHEETROCK Brand Joint Tape is 1-31/32″ wide in 75′, 250′ and 500′ rolls. SHEETROCK Brand Joint Tape-Heavy provides added strength and crack-resistance in drywall joint treatment; it is

SHEETROCK Brand Joint Tape is designed for both embedding by hand (below) and application with mechanical taping tool (right). Joint is covered with thin layer of compound before taping.

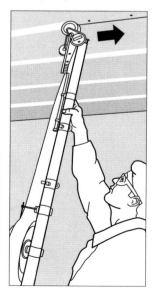
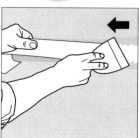

2-1/16″ wide in 250′ and 500′ rolls. Approx. coverage: 370 lin. ft. tape per 1,000 sq. ft. panels.

A joint treatment system (reinforcing tape and joint compound) must provide joints as strong as the gypsum board itself. Otherwise, normal structural movement in a wall or ceiling assembly can result in the development of cracks over the finished joint.

Repeated joint strength tests conducted at the USG Research Center have shown that joints taped and finished with conventional fiberglass leno-weave mesh tape and conventional joint compounds are more prone to cracking than joints finished with paper tape and conventional joint compounds. This is because fiberglass mesh tapes tend to stretch under load, even after being covered with joint compounds.

Permanent repair of these cracks is difficult. Accordingly, USG does not recommend using conventional fiberglass leno-weave mesh tape with conventional ready-mixed, powder or chemically setting compounds for general drywall joint finishing.

SHEETROCK **Brand Fiberglass Drywall Tape** Made with a unique cross-fiber construction to provide greater drywall joint strength than conventional fiberglass leno-weave mesh tapes. This self-adhesive tape goes on quickly, eliminating the bedding coat. Smooth, finished joints are accomplished in two coats by using SHEETROCK Brand Setting-Type Joint Compound (DURABOND or EASY SAND) for at least the first application. The setting-type joint compound also provides the added bond to provide desired joint strength. Second SHEETROCK Brand Joint Compound application can be either setting-type or drying-type (ready-mixed or powder) joint compound. Tape also is ideal for patching small holes and cracks.

IMPERIAL **Brand Tape** A strong, glass-fiber tape used in wood-frame construction to conceal and reinforce joints and interior angles of IMPERIAL Brand Gypsum Base prior to veneer plaster finishing with IMPERIAL Brand Basecoat, IMPERIAL Brand Finish Plaster, DIAMOND Brand Veneer Basecoat and DIAMOND Brand Interior Finish Plaster. High-tensile strength glass fibers are woven into an open mesh, coated with binder and slit to roll width.

The open weave of IMPERIAL Brand Tape (100 meshes per sq. in.) provides excellent reinforcing and keying of plaster to resist cracking. The glass fibers lay flat and minimize stretching for wrinkle-free attachment without springback or distortion. Spirally woven (leno) long strands and the binder coating reduce edge raveling and fraying, and keep loose threads from defacing finished surfaces. Tape flexes readily to permit fast application to flat joints and corners. Available in two types:

Type P with pressure-sensitive adhesive backing. Selected for quick, self-stick hand application; saves installation time and fastener cost.

Type S with plain back, fastened with staples. Lower in cost than Type P.

Availability: Type S in 300-ft.-rolls 2-1/2″ wide; Type P in 300-ft.-rolls 2″and 2-1/2″ wide; 12 rolls per ctn. Approx. coverage: 370 lin. ft. tape per 1,000 sq. ft. gypsum base.

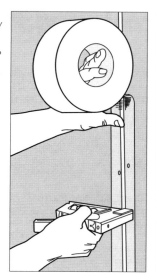
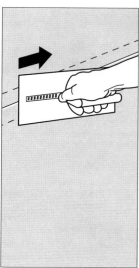

Both types of glass-fiber IMPERIAL Brand Tape are quickly applied—Type S with 3/8" staples at staggered 24" intervals (left), self-stick Type P by light hand pressure and bonding with finishing knife or trowel (right). Use of Type P Tape cuts taping time up to 50%, simplifies embedding and saves cost of staples.

Veneer Plaster Finishes

Veneer plaster finishes offer the opportunity to trim days from interior finishing schedules and provide strong, highly abrasion-resistant surfaces. These products are designed for one or two-coat work over gypsum bases or directly to concrete block or properly prepared monolithic concrete. Formulated for hand or machine application (IMPERIAL Brand Finish and DIAMOND Brand Interior Finish hand only), they provide a thin, lightweight veneer that sets rapidly.

Conventional plaster is the best system to attain a uniform, monolithic, blemish-free, smooth surface with excellent wear resistance. By contrast, veneer plaster systems have large-size gypsum panels to improve speed of installation, while providing more monolithic, harder, abrasion-resistant surfaces than are achievable with drywall. Plaster thickness is reduced from the standard 1/2" associated with conventional plaster to a mere 1/16" to 1/8" using high-strength gypsum in the product formulations. While RED TOP Keenes Cement-lime-sand provides the most universal texture finish in two-coat application, IMPERIAL Brand Finish Plaster and DIAMOND Brand Interior Finish Plaster provide better surface hardness abrasion resistance and wearability. Ready for final finish in as little as 48 hours if completely dry. (See "Comparing Plaster Systems" in Appendix.)

Advantages

Rugged, Abuse-resistant Surfaces High-strength IMPERIAL Brand Plaster Finishes (3,000 psi compressive strength) provide hard, durable interiors that require minimum maintenance.

Quicker Completion/Faster Occupancy Veneer plaster finishes apply rapidly, set fast, dry quickly to save days in finishing interior walls and ceilings. DIAMOND Brand Interior Finish Plaster can be decorated in 24 hrs. (if completely dry) with breather-type paint or left undecorated if desired.

When abraded 1000 cycles by 25-lb. weighted wire brush in laboratory test, IMPERIAL Brand Veneer Plaster Finish showed virtually no penetration—proof of outstanding abrasion resistance.

Competitive Costs Veneer plaster finishes are easily applied and cover more area per ton than conventional plasters. Joints and interior angles are pre-set with the same veneer plaster finish that goes on the walls and ceilings.

Easily Decorated Veneer plasters are readily finished in smooth-trowel, float or texture surfaces. The hard, smooth surface is decorated easily and economically with paint, fabric, wallpaper or texture.

Versatile A wide choice of assemblies is available to meet design requirements: Fire and sound-rated systems for wood or steel framing, hard and abuse-resistant surfaces for high-traffic areas, and electrically heated ceilings.

Products Available

IMPERIAL Brand Basecoat Plaster

IMPERIAL Brand Basecoat Plaster For use as a basecoat in two-coat veneer application finished with proper lime or gypsum finishes. Can be applied to either IMPERIAL Brand Gypsum Base, directly to concrete block, or over USG Plaster Bonder on monolithic concrete. Formulated as the basecoat for high-strength IMPERIAL Brand Finish Plaster, gauged lime putty, DIAMOND Brand Interior Finish Plaster, STRUCTO-GAUGE—lime—smooth trowel, or Keenes—lime—sand float finishes. Available in hand and machine-application formulations. Complies with ASTM C587. Available in 80-lb. bags.

IMPERIAL Brand Finish Plaster For single-coat application composed of scratch coat and immediate doubling back directly over special IMPERIAL Brand Gypsum Base, glass-fiber tape or SHEETROCK Brand Joint Tape or SHEETROCK Brand Setting-Type Joint Compound (DURABOND or EASY SAND). Also used over IMPERIAL Brand Basecoat Plaster in a two-coat system. Available for hand application—provides a smooth-trowel or float or spray-texture finish ready for decoration. Complies with ASTM C587. Available in 80-lb. bags.

Coverage—IMPERIAL Brand Basecoat and Finishes

| Product | ft.²/ton | | m²/ton (metric)[1] | |
	Gypsum base	Masonry	Gypsum base	Masonry
IMPERIAL Brand Basecoat	3250-4250	2700-3600	335-435	275-370
IMPERIAL Brand (1-coat) Finish	3500-4000	not recommended	360-410	not recommended
IMPERIAL Brand (2-coat) Finish	3200-3600	3200-3600	330-370	330-370

(1) Coverage rounded to nearest 5m² per metric ton.

DIAMOND Brand Veneer Basecoat Plaster Provides quality walls and ceilings for residential construction where superior strength of IMPERIAL Brand Basecoat Plaster is not essential. Offers superior workability, ease and speed of application. Formulated to receive a variety of finishes. Apply to IMPERIAL Brand Gypsum Base, concrete block or monolithic concrete. Complies with ASTM C587. Available in 80-lb. bags.

Coverage—DIAMOND Brand Basecoat

Product	ft.²/ton		m²/ton (metric)[1]	
	Gypsum base	Masonry	Gypsum base	Masonry
DIAMOND Brand Basecoat	4000-5000	3500-4500	410-510	360-460

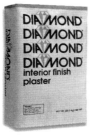

DIAMOND Brand Interior Finish Plaster

DIAMOND Brand Veneer Basecoat Plaster

DIAMOND Brand Interior Finish Plaster A white finish formulated for hand application directly to IMPERIAL Brand Gypsum Base or over USG Plaster Bonder on monolithic concrete. Also suitable in a two-coat system over IMPERIAL Brand or DIAMOND Brand Basecoat or a sanded gypsum basecoat. Applied to a nom. 1/16″ thickness, this finish is unaggregated for a smooth or skip-trowel finish; may be job aggregated with up to an equal part by weight of clean, fine silica sand for Spanish, swirl, float or other textures. Not recommended for use over portland cement basecoat or masonry surfaces. Complies with ASTM C587. Available in 50-lb. bags.

DIAMOND Brand Interior Finish Plaster should be applied only to IMPERIAL Brand Gypsum Base having blue face paper. Faded base must be treated with USG Accelerator—Alum Catalyst or USG Plaster Bonder before finish is applied to prevent possible bond failure. See page 228 for specific application instructions.

DIAMOND Brand Interior Finish Plaster is also suitable for use with electric cable ceilings. Allows higher operating temperatures than with other products, provides more heat transmission and greater resistance to heat deterioration. Finish is job-sanded and hand-applied 3/16″ thick to cover cable. A finish coat of the same material is applied 1/16″ to 3/32″ thick to bring the total plaster thickness to 1/4″. Applied over IMPERIAL Brand Base attached to wood joists, to metal furring channel or suspended metal grillage, or over USG Plaster Bonder directly to monolithic concrete ceilings (5/16″ fill coat plus finish coat for 3/8″ total thickness.)

Coverage—DIAMOND Brand Interior Finish Plaster
Conventional walls and ceilings

Surface applied to	Neat		Sand float finish sanded 1:2[1] (Sand:DIF)[1]		Heavy texture finish sanded 1:1[1] (Sand:DIF)[1]	
	ft.²/ton	m²/ton[2]	ft.²/ton	m²/ton[2]	ft.²/ton	m²/ton
IMPERIAL Brand Gypsum Base	6000	610	4660	475	3500	355
IMPERIAL Brand or DIAMOND Brand Basecoat	5500	560	4330	440	3250	330
Sanded RED TOP Basecoat	5000	510	4000	410	3000	305
Monolithic concrete[3][4]	5500	560	4330	440	3250	330
Veneer basecoat over monolithic concrete[3]	5500	560	4330	440	3250	330

Electric cable heat ceilings

Surface applied to	fill coat[5] sanded 1:1[1]		1/16″ finish coat sanded 1:4[1]		1/16″ finish coat sanded 1:1[1]	
	ft.2/ton	m2/ton[2]	ft.2/ton	m2/ton[2]	ft.2/ton	m2/ton[2]
IMPERIAL Brand Gypsum Base	2300	235	5000	510	3250	330
Monolithic concrete[3]	900	84	5500	560	4500	418

(1) Coverage based on one ton of aggregated mixture (combined weight of sand and DIAMOND Brand Interior Finish Plaster). (2) Coverage rounded to nearest km² per metric ton. (3) USG Plaster Bonder required. (4) Must be job sanded, minimum 1/2:1, sand to plaster. (5) Fill coat over gypsum base is 3/16″ thick—over monolithic concrete is 5/16″.

Primers

SHEETROCK *Brand First*
Coat—Ready-Mixed

SHEETROCK **Brand First Coat—Ready-Mixed** Decorating problems such as "joint banding" or "photographing" are usually caused by differences between the porosities and surface textures of the gypsum board face paper or concrete on one hand, and the finished joint compound on the other. SHEETROCK Brand First Coat is a flat latex basecoat paint-type product especially formulated to provide a superior first (prime) coat over interior gypsum board, wood and concrete surfaces.

In contrast to a sealer, SHEETROCK Brand First Coat does not form a film that seals the substrate surface. Instead, it minimizes porosity differences by providing a base that equalizes the absorption rates of the drywall face paper and the finished joint compound when painted. SHEETROCK Brand First Coat also provides the proper type and amount of pigments and fillers, lacking from conventional primers and sealers, that minimize surface texture variations between the gypsum board face paper and the finished joint compound.

SHEETROCK Brand First Coat is designed for fast, low-cost application. Applies with brush, roller or airless or conventional sprayer. Dries in less than 30 minutes under 72° F/50% R.H. conditions. White finish is ready for decoration in an hour. Not intended as a final coating—it should be overpainted when dry. The product comes ready-mixed in 5-gal. and 1-gal. pails.

SHEETROCK **Brand Wallcovering Primer—Ready-Mixed** Ideal basecoat product for wallcoverings. Also, the required primer for joint-treated areas of walls and ceilings to receive the USG Decorative Interior Finish System (see page 211); in these applications the primer is then covered with USG Plaster Bonder—Clear. For wallpaper applications, SHEETROCK Brand Wallcovering Primer prevents wallcovering adhesive from soaking into porous wall surfaces and improves adhesion and slip. Also, permits later removal of wallpaper. May be used on cured new or old plaster, stripped wallpaper, masonry and gypsum panels. Not recommended over lime-gauging or lime-containing plaster finishes. Available in 1-gal. and 5-gal. containers.

SHEETROCK *Brand*
Wallcovering Primer—
Ready-Mixed

Interior Texture Finishes

Texture finishes from USG offer a wide variety of possible texture patterns to provide distinctive interior styling. Fast, easy application; quick drying. Hide minor surface blemishes to reduce surface preparation needed. Save labor time to preserve job profits. All products are non-asbestos containing.

Powder Texture Products

SHEETROCK **Brand Ceiling Spray Texture (QT)—(Fine) (Medium) (Coarse)** A powder product with polystyrene aggregate, available in three finishes. Produces a handsome simulated acoustical ceiling finish but with no acoustical correction. Requires only addition of water and short soaking period at job site. Produces excellent bonding qualities for application to gypsum panels, concrete, plaster or wood. High wet and dry hide masks minor surface defects. Dries to a white finish, usually left unpainted but may be overpainted if desired. Not recommended for use where constant humid conditions exist.

Examples of high-style textures produced by SHEETROCK Brand Ceiling Spray Texture (QT): (1) Fine Finish for light effect; (2) Medium Finish for striking texture; (3) Coarse Finish for unusual decorating effect.

1   2

3

Surface designs available with SHEETROCK Brand Wall and Ceiling Spray Texture include Spatter Finish (left) and Spatter/Knockdown Finish (right).

SHEETROCK **Brand Wall and Ceiling Spray Texture** A product available in aggregated and unaggregated forms for texture variety on most interior wall surfaces. Produces light spatter, and light "orange peel" texture with spray application. Dries to a soft-tone white surface with good concealment. Should be overpainted when dry on walls. Can be left unpainted on ceilings if adequate amount of material is applied to provide sufficient hiding properties. Not washable unpainted.

SHEETROCK **Brand Wall and Ceiling Texture (TUF TEX)** An unaggregated texture coating. Produces a variety of texture patterns from bold spatter/knockdown to light orange peel. May be by spray applied and/or hand tooled with broad knife, brush or roller, depending on pattern desired. Dries to a hard, white finish. Helps conceal minor substrate defects. Not intended as a final coating—should be overpainted when dry. Not washable unpainted.

Distinctive medium stipple texture is achieved with SHEETROCK Brand Wall and Ceiling Texture (TUF-TEX).

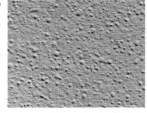

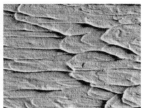

Variety of effects obtained with SHEETROCK Brand Wall and Ceiling Texture—Multi-Purpose include (clockwise from left) bold shadowing with roller application, medium-light finish applied by spray and lightly stippled surface applied with small brush or roller-stippler.

SHEETROCK Brand Wall and Ceiling Texture—Multi-Purpose An economical, unaggregated, powder product, to be mixed with water for desired texturing consistency. Excellent for producing fine to medium texture patterns (such as fine orange peel and crow's foot stipple finishes) on drywall or other interior surfaces. Textured effect obtained by brush, roller or spray application. Helps conceal minor surface defects; dries to a soft-tone white finish; should be overpainted on walls; can be left unpainted on ceilings when adequate material is applied. Not washable unpainted.

SHEETROCK Brand Wall and Ceiling Spray Texture Sand Finish Texture 12 A powder product that yields a fine sand finish on walls and ceilings. Combines easy mixing, fast drying, excellent coverage and good concealment. Spray apply only. Ideal base for wall paints. May be left unpainted on ceilings. Not washable unpainted.

Close-up view shows typical sand-effect finish obtained with aggregated SHEETROCK Brand Wall and Ceiling Spray Texture—Sand Finish Texture 12. In application, fan technique is used on walls, cross-spray on ceilings (left).

Simple roller-applied texture is obtained with vinyl-base SHEETROCK Brand Powder Joint Compounds. Same products can be used for joint finishing and texturing on job (right).

SHEETROCK **Brand Powder Joint Compound (All Purpose)** Easy-mixing, smooth-working products that can be used to produce attractive light to medium textures. Color is white but may vary in degree of whiteness. Surfaces should be painted. Applied with brush, roller or trowel. Not washable unpainted.

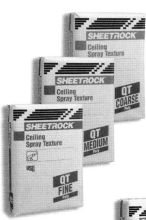

SHEETROCK Brand Ceiling Spray Texture (QT)— (Fine) (Medium) (Coarse)

SHEETROCK Brand Wall and Ceiling Spray Texture—(Unaggregated) (Aggregated)

SHEETROCK Brand Wall and Ceiling Texture (TUF TEX)

SHEETROCK Brand Wall and Ceiling Texture—Multi- Purpose

SHEETROCK Brand Wall and Ceiling Spray Texture Sand Finish Texture 12

Sound-Absorbing Plaster Finish

USG Acoustical Plaster Finish

USG Acoustical Plaster Finish An attractive spray plaster texture for application to gypsum basecoats, interior monolithic concrete, metal decks and gypsum panel ceilings. Chemically setting-type product gives a sound-absorbing, sound-rated decorative finish to gypsum panels, concrete and non-veneer-type plaster ceilings and other non-contact surfaces. Produces a handsome, natural-white, evenly textured finish. Requires no application of a bonding agent except over metal decking. Reduces surface preparation time and costs. For use on new or renovation construction. Surface burning characteristics: flame spread 10, smoke developed 25 per ASTM E1042-85. Sound rated: NRC 0.55 for concrete and conventional plaster at 1/2″ finish thickness; NRC 0.75 for concrete and conventional plaster at 1″ finish thickness, NRC 0.50 for gypsum panels at 1/2″ finish thickness. Use on noncontact surfaces only.

USG Acoustical Plaster Finish absorbs sound and gives dramatic appeal to ceilings and other noncontact surfaces (left).

Extra-thick finish applied in one coat provides eye appeal and decorative charm (right).

Ready-Mixed Texture Products

SHEETROCK **Brand Wall and Ceiling Texture** Offers unique super thickness with just one coat, plus the fast start of ready-mixed material. Massive thickness in just one pass eliminates doubling back. This white, latex-type finish develops a tough, durable surface with stubborn resistance to fissure cracks. Apply with trowel, roller, brush or spray, depending on pattern desired. Bonds well with excellent hide over many surfaces—gypsum panels, concrete, primed plaster, interior masonry and non-staining wood surfaces. Painting not required on non-contact surfaces. Overpaint if desired. Not washable unpainted.

SHEETROCK **Brand Wall and Ceiling Spray Texture** A ready-mixed vinyl formulation for texturing interior, above-grade surfaces. Ideal where moderate to bold texture patterns are desired. Designed for spray application over gypsum panel, concrete, and most other interior wall and ceiling surfaces. Formulated to create unique texture patterns such as spatter, spatter/knockdown, and orange peel designs. Dries to a white surface, but should be overpainted when dry. Not washable unpainted.

SHEETROCK **Brand Wall and Ceiling Texture Paint (Sand Finish Texture 1)** White; produces a sand finish on walls and ceilings. Sanded effect is obtained by brush, roller or spray application. Durable finish; may be left unpainted.

SHEETROCK **Brand Wall and Ceiling Texture Paint (Ripple Finish Texture 2)** Produces an orange peel to moderate ripple texture patterns

SHEETROCK Brand Wall and Ceiling Texture

SHEETROCK Brand Wall and Ceiling Spray Texture

SHEETROCK Brand Wall and Ceiling Texture Paint (Sand Finish Texture 1)

on ceilings and sidewalls; textured effect obtained by roller or spray, depending on the desired texture finish; may be left unpainted.

SHEETROCK **Brand Wall and Ceiling Texture Paint (**TEXOLITE **Sanded Paste Stipple)** White; produces a sand finish on ceilings and sidewalls. Texture effect is obtained by roller application that can be left as-is or brushed to create a sanded-swirl texture finish. Durable finish; may be left unpainted.

SHEETROCK **Brand Ceiling Texture Paint (Coarse Finish)** An easy-to-use aggregated (perlite) latex paint for creating dramatic effects on ceilings and other noncontact surfaces. May be applied over properly prepared drywall, plaster, concrete and previously painted ceiling surfaces. Dries to a white finish.

SHEETROCK **Brand Ready-Mixed Joint Compounds (Topping or All Purpose)** Virtually ready to use, these products will produce textures ranging from light to medium depending upon method of application. Color is white, but may vary. Surfaces should be painted. Applied with brush, roller or trowel. Not recommended for spray application. Not washable unpainted. Not recommended for texturing in all areas. Check local sales office for suitability of formulation for texturing in your area.

SHEETROCK Brand Wall and Ceiling Texture Paint (Ripple Finish Texture 2)

SHEETROCK Brand Wall and Ceiling Texture Paint (TEXOLITE Sanded Paste Stipple)

SHEETROCK Brand Ceiling Texture Paint (Coarse Finish)

SHEETROCK Brand Ready-Mixed Topping Joint Compound

SHEETROCK Brand Ready-Mixed All Purpose Joint Compound

Texture/Compound Selector

SHEETROCK Brand Textures

Product	SHEETROCK Brand Ceiling Spray Texture (QT) (Fine)	SHEETROCK Brand Ceiling Spray Texture (QT) (Medium)	SHEETROCK Brand Ceiling Spray Texture (QT) (Coarse)	SHEETROCK Brand Wall and Ceiling Spray Texture (Aggregated)
Surfaces prime coat required	yes	yes	yes	yes
ceilings	yes	yes	yes	yes
walls	no	no	no	yes
Properties type of aggregate	polystyrene	polystyrene	polystyrene	perlite
aggregate size	fine	medium	course	fine-med.
ability to hide substrate imperfections	good	excellent	excellent	very good
water dilution gal./lb.[4]	varies**	varies**	varies**	4-5/50, 3-4/40
Application solution time	very good	very good	very good	good
machine	yes	yes	yes	yes
hand	no	no	no	yes
Spray Equipment pole gun	yes	yes	yes	no
7E2 type texture gun	yes	yes	yes	yes
18D type texture gun	no	no	no	yes
hopper gun	yes	yes	yes	yes
aggregate fallout (bounce)	min. to. mod.	min. to. mod.	min. to. mod.	min.
abrasiveness on equipment	min.	min.	min.	mod.
Features drying time	slow-med.	slow-med.	slow-med.	very fast
bond of dry aggregate	mod.	mod.	mod.	good
dried whiteness	excellent	excellent	excellent	good
crack resistance	good	good	good	good
coverage ft.²/lb. -spray[1]	up to 8	up to 8	up to 8	up to 40
coverage ft.²/lb. -hand[1]	N/A	N/A	N/A	N/A

N/A—not applicable   * no primer required under painted walls.   ** Varies—see Chapter 5.. Also see footnotes.

(1) Coverage—Coverage, as considered here, is intended to provide a relative comparison between products when mixed and applied according to directions—not to provide a figure for job estimating. Coverage can vary widely depending on factors such as condition of substrate, amount of dilution, spray techniques and procedures, thickness and uniformity of coating and market preferences in texture appearance.

(2) Joint Compounds—Basically, joint compounds are designed for treating joints, fasteners, metal bead and trim. However, these products have been used in many markets for hand-applied textures and because of this trade practice, are included as texturing materials.

(3) SHEETROCK Brand Ready-Mixed Topping Joint Compound is not recommended for texturing in all areas. Check local sales office for suitability of joint compound in your area.

(4) Water dilution properties shown here are only approximate. Check product container for actual dilution requirements.

Texture/Compound Selector

SHEETROCK Brand Textures

Product	SHEETROCK Brand Wall and Ceiling Spray Texture (Unaggregated)	SHEETROCK Brand Wall & Ceiling Spray Texture (TUF TEX)	SHEETROCK Brand Wall and Ceiling Texture Multi-Purpose	SHEETROCK Brand Wall and Ceiling Spray Texture Sand Finish Texture 12
Surfaces prime coat required	yes	yes	yes	yes
ceilings	yes	yes	yes	yes
walls	yes	yes	yes	yes
Properties type of aggregate	N/A	N/A	N/A	perlite
aggregate size	N/A	N/A	N/A	fine
ability to hide sub-strate imperfections	good	good	good	good
water dilution gal./lb.[4]	4-5/50, 3-4/40	4-4.8/40	2-3/25, 3-4/40	2-1/2–3-1/4/25
Application solution time	good	good	good	good
machine	yes	yes	yes	yes
hand	yes	yes	yes	no
Spray Equipment pole gun	no	no	no	no
7E2 type texture gun	yes	yes	yes	no
18D type texture gun	yes	yes	yes	yes
hopper gun	yes	yes	yes	yes
aggregate fallout (bounce)	N/A	N/A	N/A	min.
abrasiveness on equipment	min.	min.	min.	mod.
Features drying time	fast	fast	fast	fast
bond of dry aggregate	N/A	N/A	N/A	excellent
dried whiteness	good	good	good	very good
crack resistance	good	good	good	good
coverage ft.²/lb. -spray[1]	up to 40	up to 40	up to 20	20-35
coverage ft.²/lb. -hand[1]	N/A	10-20	10-15	N/A

N/A—not applicable   * no primer required under painted walls.   ** Varies—see Chapter 5. Also see footnotes.

(1) Coverage—Coverage, as considered here, is intended to provide a relative comparison between products when mixed and applied according to directions—not to provide a figure for job estimating. Coverage can vary widely depending on factors such as condition of substrate, amount of dilution, spray techniques and procedures, thickness and uniformity of coating and market preferences in texture appearance.

(2) Joint Compounds—Basically, joint compounds are designed for treating joints, fasteners, metal bead and trim. However, these products have been used in many markets for hand-applied textures and because of this trade practice, are included as texturing materials.

(3) SHEETROCK Brand Ready-Mixed Topping Joint Compound is not recommended for texturing in all areas. Check local sales office for suitability of joint compound in your area.

(4) Water dilution properties shown here are only approximate. Check product container for actual dilution requirements.

68

Texture/Compound Selector

Texture Finishes

	Product	USG Acoustical Plaster Finish	USG Quick & Easy Ready-to-Use Wall & Ceiling Texture	USG Ready-Mixed Texture Compound	
Surfaces	prime coat required	yes	yes*	yes*	
	ceilings	yes	yes	yes	
	walls	no	yes	yes	
Properties	type of aggregate	polystyrene	N/A	N/A	
	aggregate size	fine-medium	N/A	N/A	
	ability to hide sub-strate imperfections	excellent	excellent	very good	
	water dilution gal./lb.[4]	3.5/30	up to 3 pts./ 3.5 gal.	1/2-2 / 50	
Application	solution time	good	N/A	N/A	
	machine	yes	yes	yes	
	hand	no	yes	yes	
Spray Equipment	pole gun	yes	yes	no	
	7E2 type texture gun	yes	yes	yes	
	18D type texture gun	no	yes	yes	
	hopper gun	no	yes	yes	
	aggregate fallout (bounce)	min. to. mod.	N/A	N/A	
	abrasiveness on equipment	min.	min.	min.	
Features	drying time	slow	slow-med.	slow-med.	
	bond of dry aggregate	very good	N/A	N/A	
	dried whiteness	good	very good	fair	
	crack resistance	excellent	good	good	
	coverage ft.²/lb. -spray[1]	1-1/2 – 3	70 ft.²/gal.	7-8	
	coverage ft.²/lb. -hand[1]	N/A	25-70 ft.²/gal.	4-6	

N/A—not applicable   * no primer required under painted walls.   ** Varies—see Chapter 5. Also see footnotes.

(1) Coverage—Coverage, as considered here, is intended to provide a relative comparison between products when mixed and applied according to directions—not to provide a figure for job estimating. Coverage can vary widely depending on factors such as condition of substrate, amount of dilution, spray techniques and procedures, thickness and uniformity of coating and market preferences in texture appearance.

(2) Joint Compounds—Basically, joint compounds are designed for treating joints, fasteners, metal bead and trim. However, these products have been used in many markets for hand-applied textures and because of this trade practice, are included as texturing materials.

(3) SHEETROCK Brand Ready-Mixed Topping Joint Compound is not recommended for texturing in all areas. Check local sales office for suitability of joint compound in your area.

(4) Water dilution properties shown here are only approximate. Check product container for actual dilution requirements.

Texture/Compound Selector

Texture Finishes

	Product	SHEETROCK Brand Powder All-Purpose[2]	SHEETROCK Brand Ready-Mixed Topping[3] or All-Purpose[2]	SHEETROCK Brand Lightweight All Purpose Joint Compound (PLUS 3)[2]
Surfaces	prime coat required	yes	yes*	yes*
	ceilings	yes	yes	yes
	walls	no	yes/no[3]	no
Properties	type of aggregate	N/A	N/A	N/A
	aggregate size	N/A	N/A	N/A
	ability to hide substrate imperfections	very good	very good	very good
	water dilution gal./lb.[4]	2-1/4–2-3/4 / 25	1–1-1/2 / 62	1–1-1/2 / 40
Application	solution time	good	N/A	N/A
	machine	no	no	no
	hand	yes	yes	yes
Spray Equipment	pole gun	no	no	no
	7E2 type texture gun	no	no	no
	18D type texture gun	no	no	no
	hopper gun	no	no	no
	aggregate fallout (bounce)	N/A	N/A	N/A
	abrasiveness on equipment	min.	min.	min.
Features	drying time	slow-med.	slow-med.	slow-med.
	bond of dry aggregate	N/A	N/A	N/A
	dried whiteness	good	good	fair
	crack resistance	good	good	good
	coverage ft.²/lb. -spray[1]	N/A	N/A	N/A
	coverage ft.²/lb. -hand[1]	4-7	6-11	9-17

N/A—not applicable   * no primer required under painted walls.   ** Varies—see Chapter 5. Also see footnotes.

(1) Coverage—Coverage, as considered here, is intended to provide a relative comparison between products when mixed and applied according to directions—not to provide a figure for job estimating. Coverage can vary widely depending on factors such as condition of substrate, amount of dilution, spray techniques and procedures, thickness and uniformity of coating and market preferences in texture appearance.

(2) Joint Compounds—Basically, joint compounds are designed for treating joints, fasteners, metal bead and trim. However, these products have been used in many markets for hand-applied textures and because of this trade practice, are included as texturing materials.

(3) SHEETROCK Brand Ready-Mixed Topping Joint Compound is not recommended for texturing in all areas. Check local sales office for suitability of joint compound in your area.

(4) Water dilution properties shown here are only approximate. Check product container for actual dilution requirements.

Interior Patch and Repair Products

Finished interior walls are subject to abuse and damage from time to time. USG has developed a line of repair products to deal with a variety of holes, cracks, dents and abrasions. Many of these products may be found in retail hardware and home center stores.

SHEETROCK **Brand Spackling Compound** An effective, low-shrinkage, vinyl-based compound for filling small holes.

SHEETROCK **Brand Lightweight Spackling Compound** A minimal shrinkage filling compound with half the weight of regular spackling compound for filling small holes.

SHEETROCK **Brand Spackling Powder** Easy-to-mix hole-filling compound.

SHEETROCK **Brand Plaster of Paris** Fast-setting plaster is excellent for first fill of large holes. Expands upon setting. Not sandable.

SHEETROCK **Brand Floor Patch/Leveler** A high-compressive-strength compound for leveling concrete floors or patching holes in concrete. Expands upon setting.

SHEETROCK **Brand Patching Plaster** A fiber reinforced plaster for patching larger holes in plaster or drywall walls. Expands upon setting. Not sandable.

SHEETROCK **Brand Patching Compound,** EASY SAND **5** An easy-to-mix, low-expansion compound for quick fills and rapid finishing of cracks and holes. Working time of 5-10 minutes.

SHEETROCK **Brand Popcorn Ceiling Patch** Ready-to-use texture for repairing popcorn ceiling finishes.

SHEETROCK **Brand Drywall Repair Clips** Metal clips that provide for ready attachment of a drywall patch to an existing wall. Use with replacement drywall to repair larger holes.

2

Framing

General Requirements

The choice and installation of framing depends on a number of factors. In the case of wood framing these include the species, size and grade of lumber used. In the case of steel framing, the cross-sectional shape of the frame member, size and the thickness and grade of steel must be considered. Equally important are height of the wall, the frame spacing and the maximum span of the surfacing material. Selection of steel stud size is usually derived from limiting height tables, based on the capacity of the steel and the allowable deflection of finish surfaces. The limiting heights tables included in the *Gypsum Construction Handbook* are from ASTM C754 and were developed by the Gypsum Association. USG presents these data as a reference, but is not responsible for performance of the wall based on them.

Loads Framing members and their installation must be selected according to their ability to withstand the loads to which they will be subjected. These include live loads (contributed by the occupancy and elements such as wind, snow and earthquake) and dead loads (weight of the structure itself). Minimum lateral load for interior partitions is 5 psf; for exterior walls 15 psf to 45 psf or greater depending on building height and geographic location.

Deflection Even though an assembly is structurally capable of withstanding a given load, its use may be restricted if the amount of deflection that would occur when the lateral load is applied exceeds that which the surfacing materials can sustain without damage. Obviously, this deflection factor influences the selection of surfacing materials.

For drywall assemblies it is desirable to limit deflection to L/240 (L = length of the span in inches) and to never exceed L/120 (L/180 in some codes). The preferred limit for veneer assemblies is L/360 and should not exceed L/240. Using L/240 as an example, and where the length of a span (distance between framing members) is 10', deflection is determined as follows:

Tip
For instructions on safety in the application of framing, see Chapter 13.

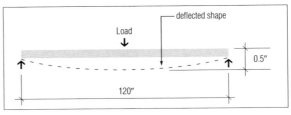

$$D = \text{Deflection Limit} = \frac{L}{240}$$

$$L = 10' \text{ or } 120''$$

$$D = \frac{120}{240}$$

$$D = 0.5''$$

Bending Stress Framing members also must withstand any unit force exerted that will break or buckle the stud, based on the capacity of the studs acting alone.

End Reaction Shear This factor is determined by the amount of force applied to the stud which will bend or shear the runner, or buckle the web of the stud.

2

Frame Spacing A factor in load-carrying capability and deflection, it also is a limiting factor for the finishing materials. Every finishing or surfacing material is subject to a span limitation—the maximum distance between frame members that a material can span without undue sagging. For that reason, "maximum frame spacing" tables for the various board products are included in this chapter. However, where frame spacing exceeds maximum limits, furring members can be installed to provide necessary sag resistance support for the surfacing material (covered in this chapter under wall and ceiling furring).

Insulation and Services Chase walls provide vertical shafts where greater core widths are needed for pipe runs and other service installations. They consist of a double row of studs with gypsum panel or metal cross braces between rows. Plumbing, electrical and other fixtures, and mechanicals within the framing cavities must be flush with or inside the plane of the framing. Fasteners used to assemble the framing must be driven reasonably flush with the surfaces.

In wood frame construction, the flanges of batt-type insulation must be attached to the sides of frame members and not to their faces. Any obstruction on the face of frame members that will prevent firm contact between the gypsum board and framing can result in loose or damaged board and fastener imperfections.

Wood Framing

Wood framing meeting the following minimum requirements is necessary for proper performance of all gypsum drywall and plaster base assemblies:

1. Framework should meet the minimum requirements of applicable building codes.

2. Framing members should be straight, true and of uniform dimension. Studs and joists must be in true alignment; bridging, fire stops, soil pipes, etc., must not protrude beyond framing.

3. All framing lumber should be the correct grade for the intended use, and 2″ x 4″ nominal size or larger should bear the grade mark of a recognized inspection agency.

4. All framing lumber should have a moisture content not in excess of 19% at time of gypsum board application.

Failure to observe these minimum framing requirements, which are applicable to screw, nail and adhesive attachment, will substantially increase the possibility of fastener failure and surface distortion due to warping or dimensional changes. This is particularly true if the framing lumber has greater than normal tendencies to warp or shrink after erection.

The moisture content of wood framing should be allowed to adjust as closely as possible to the level it will reach in service before gypsum drywall or plaster base application begins. After the building is enclosed, delay board application as long as possible (consistent with schedule requirements) to allow this moisture content adjustment to take place.

Framing should be designed to accommodate shrinkage in wide dimensional lumber such as is used for floor joists or headers. Gypsum wallboard and veneer plaster surfaces can buckle or crack if firmly anchored across the flat grain of these wide wood members as shrinkage occurs. With high uninterrupted walls, such as are a part of cathedral ceiling designs or in two-story stairwells, regular or modified balloon framing can minimize the problem.

Framing Corrections If joists are out of alignment, 2″ x 6″ leveling plates attached perpendicular to and across top of ceiling joists may be used. Toe-nailing into joists pulls framing into true horizontal alignment and ensures a smooth, level ceiling surface. Bowed or warped studs in non-load bearing partitions may be straightened by sawing the hollow sides at the middle of the bow and driving a wedge into the saw kerf until the stud is in line. Reinforcement of the stud is accomplished by securely nailing 1″ x 4″ wood strips or "scabs" on each side of the cut.

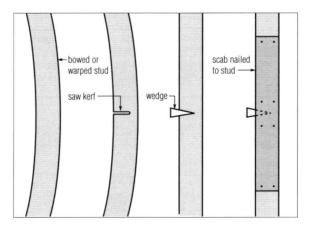

Framing Member Spacing

To assure adequate support for gypsum panels, and the integrity of walls and ceilings, attention must be paid to the distance between framing members. Minimum spacing requirements will depend on a number of variables, including the location of the paneled surface (ceiling or wall), the thickness of the gypsum panels, the number of panel layers on each side of the completed wall, and the orientation of the panels to the framing members. For thicker gypsum panels or double-layer applications, the distance between framing members can be increased. For wood framing installed in the conventional manner, with lumber meeting requirements outlined above, maximum frame spacing is as shown in the tables on the following pages:

Maximum Frame Spacing—Drywall Construction
Direct Application

Panel thickness[1]	Location	Application method[2]	Max. frame spacing o.c.	
Single-Layer Application			in.	mm
3/8" (9.5 mm)	ceilings[3]	perpendicular[4]	16	406
		parallel[4]	16	406
1/2" (12.7 mm)	ceilings	perpendicular	24[5][6]	610
		parallel[4]	16	406
	sidewalls	parallel or perpendicular	24	610
		parallel[4]	16	406
5/8" (15.9 mm)	ceilings[6]	perpendicular	24	610
	sidewalls	parallel or perpendicular	24	610
Double-Layer Application				
3/8" (9.5 mm)	ceilings[7]	perpendicular	16	406
	sidewalls	perpendicular or parallel	24[8]	610
1/2" & 5/8" (12.7 & 15.9 mm)	ceilings	perpendicular or parallel	24[8]	610
	sidewalls	perpendicular	24[8]	610

(1) 5/8" thickness is recommended for the finest single-layer construction, providing increased resistance to fire and transmission of sound; 1/2" for single-layer application in new residential construction and remodeling; and 3/8" for repair and remodeling over existing surfaces. (2) Long edge position relative to framing. (3) Not recommended below unheated spaces. (4) Not recommended if water-based texturing material is to be applied. (5) Max. spacing 16" if water-based texturing material is to be applied. (6) If 1/2" SHEETROCK Brand Interior Ceiling Board is used in place of gypsum panels, max. spacing is 24" o.c. for perpendicular application with weight of unsupported insulation not exceeding 1.3 psf., 16" o.c. with weight of unsupported insulation not exceeding 2.2 psf. (7) Adhesive must be used to laminate 3/8" board for double-layer ceilings. (8) Max spacing 16" o.c. if fire rating required.

Maximum Frame Spacing—Veneer Plaster Construction
Direct Application

Gypsum base thickness	Construction	Location	Application method[1]	Max. frame spacing o.c. in.	mm
1/2" (12.7 mm)	one layer, 1-coat finish	ceilings	perpendicular	16	406
		sidewalls	perpendicular or parallel	16	406
	one layer, 2-coat finish	ceilings	perpendicular	16 or 24[2]	406 or 610[2]
		sidewalls	perpendicular or parallel	16 or 24[2]	406 or 610[2]
	two layer, 1 & 2-coat finish	ceilings	perpendicular	24	610
		sidewalls	perpendicular or parallel	24	610
5/8" (15.9 mm)	one layer, 1-coat finish	ceilings	perpendicular	16 or 24[2]	406 or 610[2]
		sidewalls	perpendicular or parallel	16 or 24[2]	406 or 610[2]
	one layer, 2-coat finish	ceilings	perpendicular	24[2]	610[2]
		sidewalls	perpendicular or parallel	24[2]	610[2]
	two layer, 1 & 2-coat finish	ceilings	perpendicular	24	610
		sidewalls	perpendicular or parallel	24	610

(1) Perpendicular preferred on all applications for maximum strength. Where fire rating is involved, application must be identical to that in assembly tested. Parallel application not recommended for ceilings. (2) 24" o.c. frame spacing with either one or two-coat veneer application requires SHEETROCK Brand Joint Tape Reinforcement and SHEETROCK Brand Setting-Type (DURABOND or EASY SAND) Joint Compound.

Ceiling Insulation To prevent objectionable sag in ceilings, weight of overlaid unsupported insulation should not exceed 1.3 psf for 1/2" thick panels with frame spacing 24" o.c.; 2.2 psf for 1/2" panels on 16" o.c. framing and 5/8" panels 24" o.c.; 3/8" thick panels must not be overlaid with unsupported insulation. A vapor retarder should be installed in all exterior ceilings, and the plenum or attic space properly vented.

Resilient Application On ceiling assemblies of both drywall and veneer plaster, install resilient channels perpendicular to framing and spaced 24″ o.c. for joists 16″ o.c.; 16″ o.c. for joists 24″ o.c. For sidewalls, install at 24″ o.c. max. See single-layer sections in tables, preceding pages, for limitations for specific board thickness. Fasten channels to framing with screws only.

Cable Heat Ceilings Maximum frame spacing is 16″ o.c. for 1/2″ IMPERIAL Brand Gypsum Base; 24″ o.c. for 5/8″ base.

Spray-Textured Ceilings Where water-based texturing materials or any slow-drying surface treatment are used over single-layer panels, max. frame spacing is 16″ o.c. for 1/2″ panels applied perpendicular to framing. Parallel application is not recommended, nor is use of 3/8″ thick panels. For best results use SHEETROCK Brand Interior Ceiling Board, Sag-Resistant, with max. spacing 24″ o.c. Note: Airless spraying of latex paint in one heavy application (10 to 14 mil) also will sag ceilings. See "Ceiling Sag Precautions" in Chapter 10.

Water-based texturing materials applied to ceilings should be completely dry before insulation and vapor retarder are installed. Under most conditions, drying takes several days.

Partition Layout Properly position partitions according to layout. Snap chalk lines at ceiling and floor. Be certain that partitions will be plumb. Where partitions occur parallel to and between joists, ladder blocking must be installed between ceiling joists. Double joists are recommended beneath partitions.

Steel Framing

Steel stud framing for non-load bearing interior partitions is secured to floors and ceilings with runners fastened to the supporting structure.

Runner Installation Securely attach runners:

1. **To concrete and masonry** use stub nails, power-driven fasteners.

2. **To foam-backed metal (max. 14-ga.) concrete inserts** use 3/8″ TYPE S-12 Pan Head Screws.

3. **To suspended ceilings** use expandable hollow wall anchors, toggle bolts, screws or other suitable fasteners.

4. **To wood framing** use 1-1/4″ TYPE S Oval Head Screws or 8d nails.

Fastening channel runners

To all substrates, secure runners with fasteners located 2″ from each end and spaced max. 24″ o.c. (Tall walls require that fasteners be spaced closer together. Contact your local sales office for more detailed information.) Attach runner ends at door frames with two anchors when 3-piece frames are used. (One-piece frames should be supplied with welded-in-place floor anchor plates, pre-punched for two anchors into structure.)

At partition corners, extend one runner to the end of the corner and butt the other runner to it. Runners should not be mitered.

Fastening angles

Interior Framing Limiting Heights

Stud Depth (in.)	Stud Spacing (in.)	Design Limit (psf)	Allowable Deflection	25 Gauge (18 mil) 0.01799 min. (0.455 mm min.) ft.-in.	(mm)	20 Gauge (33 mil) 0.03299 min. (0.836 mm min.) ft.-in.	(mm)
1-5/8 (162S125-18/33)	24	5	L/120	9-9	(2970)	11-0	(3350)
1-5/8 (162S125-18/33)	24	5	L/240	7-11	(2410)	8-9	(2670)
1-5/8 (162S125-18/33)	24	5	L/360	7-1	(2160)	7-8	(2030)
1-5/8 (162S125-18/33)	16	5	L/120	10-7	(3230)	12-1	(3680)
1-5/8 (162S125-18/33)	16	5	L/240	8-4	(2540)	9-8	(2950)
1-5/8 (162S125-18/33)	16	5	L/360	8-2	(2490)	8-5	(2570)
2-1/2 (250S125-18/33)	24	5	L/120	11-10	(3610)	14-10	(4520)
2-1/2 (250S125-18/33)	24	5	L/240	10-7	(3230)	11-7	(3530)
2-1/2 (250S125-18/33)	24	5	L/360	9-3	(2820)	10-0	(3050)
2-1/2 (250S125-18/33)	16	5	L/120	13-3	(4040)	16-5	(5000)
2-1/2 (250S125-18/33)	16	5	L/240	11-3	(3430)	12-10	(3910)
2-1/2 (250S125-18/33)	16	5	L/360	9-10	(3000)	11-2	(3400)
3-5/8 (362S125-18/33)	24	5	L/120	13-9	(4190)	18-6	(5640)
3-5/8 (362S125-18/33)	24	5	L/240	13-5	(4090)	14-9	(4500)
3-5/8 (362S125-18/33)	24	5	L/360	11-7	(3530)	12-9	(3890)
3-5/8 (362S125-18/33)	16	5	L/120	15-4	(4670)	20-8	(6300)
3-5/8 (362S125-18/33)	16	5	L/240	14-4	(4370)	16-5	(5000)
3-5/8 (362S125-18/33)	16	5	L/360	12-4	(3760)	14-3	(4340)
4 (400S125-18/33)	24	5	L/120	15-1	(4600)	20-9	(6330)
4 (400S125-18/33)	24	5	L/240	14-2	(4320)	16-5	(5000)
4 (400S125-18/33)	24	5	L/360	12-4	(3760)	14-3	(4340)
4 (400S125-18/33)	16	5	L/120	17-2	(5230)	23-1	(7040)
4 (400S125-18/33)	16	5	L/240	15-4	(4670)	18-4	(5590)
4 (400S125-18/33)	16	5	L/360	13-4	(4060)	15-11	(4850)
6 (600S125-18/33)	24	5	L/120	16-9	(5110)	27-2	(8280)
6 (600S125-18/33)	24	5	L/240	16-9	(5110)	21-7	(6580)
6 (600S125-18/33)	24	5	L/360	16-9	(5110)	18-10	(5740)
6 (600S125-18/33)	16	5	L/120	19-9	(6020)	30-10	(9400)
6 (600S125-18/33)	16	5	L/240	19-9	(6020)	24-6	(7470)
6 (600S125-18/33)	16	5	L/360	17-11	(5770)	21-4	(6500)

Notes: The number following the stud depth is a new industry-wide product identification, created by the Steel Stud Manufacturers Association; the number identifies the member depth, style, flange width and material thickness in mils.

This limiting heights data is from ASTM C754. USG presents this information only as a reference, and will not be responsible for the performance of walls based on this table. Consult current information from ASTM C754 and SSMA (Steel Stud Manufacturers Association), and the stud manufacturers for limiting heights characteristics of their particular products.

Limiting heights apply to walls constructed with minimum 1/2" (12.7 mm) thickness of gypsum board and with a minimum of one full-height layer on both sides of the stud framing.

Limiting heights are based on tests conducted with gypsum board attached with screws spaced 12" (305 mm) o.c. to framing members.

Stud Installation

Insert floor-to-ceiling steel studs between runners, twisting them into position. Position studs vertically, with open side facing in same direction, engaging floor and ceiling runners and spaced 16" or 24" o.c. max. as required. Proper alignment will provide for proper bracing, utility runs and prevention of stepped or uneven joint surfaces. The recommended practice for most installations is to anchor only those studs adjacent to door and borrowed light frames. This would also be applicable to

Steel studs are positioned in floor and ceiling runners.

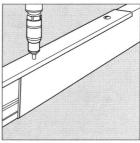

Splicing of steel studs.

partition intersections and corners. In cases where a significant slab live load deflection must be accommodated, the anchoring of these studs may restrict slab movement and cause partition cracking. In these cases, anchoring of these studs may need to be omitted. The services of a design professional is desirable to identify these instances and address them on a case-specific basis.

Place studs in direct contact with all door frame jambs, abutting partitions, partition corners and existing construction elements. Spot grouting of door frames is always suggested and is required where heavy or oversize doors are used. Contact door frame manufacturer for specific requirements and recommendations.

Where a stud directly abuts an exterior wall and there is a possibility of condensation or water penetration through the wall, place a No. 15 asphalt felt strip between stud and wall surface.

Over metal doors and borrowed light frames, place a section of runner horizontally with a web-flange bent at each end. Secure runner to strut-studs with two screws in each bent web. At the location of vertical joints over the door frame header, position a cut-to-length stud extending to the ceiling runner. (See section 'Door and Window Openings' later in this chapter.)

Steel studs may be conveniently spliced together when required. To splice two studs, nest one into the other forming a box section, to a depth of at least 8″.

Fasten together with two 3/8″ Type S Pan Head Screws in each flange. Locate each screw (shown above) no more than 1″ from ends of splice.

Resilient Channel Framing—Steel Framing

Stud System Installation Attach steel runners at floor and ceiling to structural elements with suitable fasteners located 2″ from each end and spaced 24″ o.c. Position studs vertically, with open side facing in same direction, engaging floor and ceiling runners, and spaced 24″ o.c. For non-fire rated resilient channel system, anchor studs to floor and ceiling runners on the resilient side of the partition. Fasten runner to stud flange with 3/8″ Type S Pan Head Screw.

Resilient Channel Installation Position resilient channel at right angles to steel studs, space 24″ o.c. and attach to stud flanges with 3/8″ TYPE S Pan Head Screws driven through holes in channel mounting flange. Install channels with mounting flange down, except at floor to accommodate attachment. A strip of gypsum panel is sometimes used at the base of a partition in lieu of the first inverted resilient channel. Locate channels 2″ from floor and within 6″ of ceiling. Splice channel by nesting directly over the stud, screw-attach through both flanges. Reinforce with screws located at both ends of the splice.

Chase Wall Framing

Align two parallel rows of floor and ceiling runners according to partition layout. Spacing between outside flanges of each pair of runners must not exceed 24″. Follow instructions above for attaching runners.

Position steel studs vertically in runners, with flanges in the same direction, and with studs on opposite sides of chase directly across from each other. Except in fire-rated walls, anchor all studs to floor and ceiling runner flanges with 3/8″ or 1/2″ TYPE S Pan Head Screws.

Cut cross-bracing to be placed between rows of studs from gypsum board 12″ high by chase wall width. Space braces 48″ o.c. vertically and attach to stud web with screws spaced 8″ o.c. max. per brace.

Bracing of 2-1/2″ min. steel studs may be used in place of gypsum board. Anchor web at each end of metal brace to stud web with two 3/8″ pan head screws. When chase wall studs are not opposite, install steel stud cross-braces 24″ o.c. horizontally, and securely anchor each end to a continuous horizontal 2-1/2″ runner screw-attached to chase wall studs within the cavity.

Methods of cross bracing

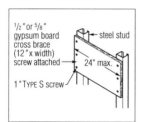

Gypsum brace

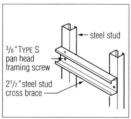

Steel stud brace

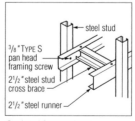

Steel stud & runner brace

Drywall and Plaster Ceiling Suspension Systems

Space metal furring channels 24″ o.c. at right angles to bar joists or other structural members. As an alternate, 1-5/8″ steel studs may be used as furring. Saddle-tie furring channels to bar joists with triple-strand 18-ga. tie wire at each intersection. Provide 1″ clearance between furring ends and abutting walls and partitions. At splices, nest furring channels with at least an 8″ overlap and securely wire-tie each end with triple-strand 18-ga. tie wire (see illustration). Frame around openings such as light troffers with additional furring channels and wire-tie to bar joists.

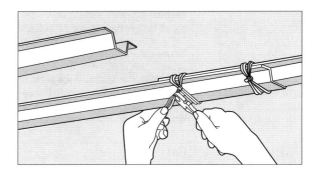

Max. allowable spacing for metal furring channel is 24″ o.c. for 1/2″ and 5/8″ thick gypsum panels or plaster base. See frame spacing tables for limiting spans.

For bar joist spacing up to 60″, steel studs may be used as furring channels. Wire-tie studs to supporting framing as shown. Position 1-5/8″ studs with open side up; position larger studs with opening to side. See table for stud spacings and limiting spans.

Limiting Span[1]—Metal Furring Members[2]

Type furring member	Member spacing (in. o.c.)	Single layer panels (2.5 psf max.)		Double layer panels (5.0 psf max.)	
		1-span	3-span	1-span	3-span
DWC-25-ga.	16	5′9″	7′1″	4′7″	5′8″
	24	5′0″	6′2″	4′0″	4′11″
DWC-20-ga.	16	6′11″	8′6″	5′5″	6′9″
	24	6′0″	7′5″	4′9″	5′11″
1-5/8″ stud, 25-ga.	16	7′2″	8′10″	5′8″	7′0″
	24	6′3″	7′9″	5′0″	6′2″

(1) For beams, joists, purlins, sub-purlins; not including 1-1/2″ cold rolled channel support spaced 4′0″ max. Check Manufacturer's literature to verify that the selected furring member is capable of the indicated span. (2) Limiting spans for 1/2″ and 5/8″ thick panels, max. L/240 deflection and uniform load shown. Investigate concentrated loads such as light fixtures and exhaust fans separately.

Metal furring channel

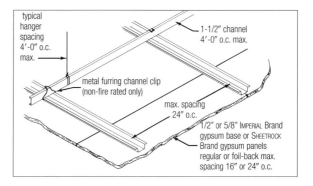

typical hanger spacing 4′-0″ o.c. max.

1-1/2″ channel 4′-0″ o.c. max.

metal furring channel clip (non-fire rated only)

max. spacing 24″ o.c.

1/2″ or 5/8″ IMPERIAL Brand gypsum base or SHEETROCK Brand gypsum panels regular or foil-back max. spacing 16″ or 24″ o.c.

Steel stud furring

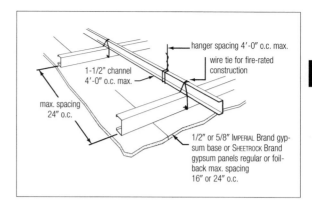

hanger spacing 4'-0" o.c. max.

wire tie for fire-rated construction

1-1/2" channel
4'-0" o.c. max.

max. spacing
24" o.c.

1/2" or 5/8" IMPERIAL Brand gypsum base or SHEETROCK Brand gypsum panels regular or foilback max. spacing
16" or 24" o.c.

Control joint

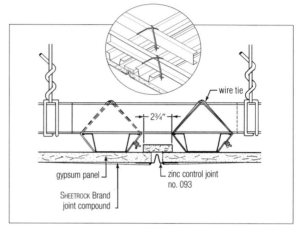

wire tie

2¾"

gypsum panel

zinc control joint
no. 093

SHEETROCK Brand
joint compound

Suspended Ceiling Grillage Erection

Space 8-ga. hanger wires 48" o.c. along carrying channels and within 6" of ends of carrying-channel runs. In concrete, anchor hangers by attachment to reinforcing steel, by loops embedded at least 2" or by approved inserts. For steel construction, wrap hanger around or through beams or joists. Do not attach components to air ducts.

Install 1-1/2" carrying channels 48" o.c. (spaced as tested for fire-rated construction) and within 6" of walls. Position channels for proper ceiling height, level and secure with hanger wire saddle tied along channels (see illustration). Provide 1" clearance between runners and abutting walls and partitions. At channel splices, interlock flanges, overlap ends 12" and secure each end with double-strand 18-ga. tie wire.

Erect metal furring channels at right angles to 1-1/2" carrying channels. Space furring within 6" of walls. Provide 1" clearance between furring ends and abutting walls and partitions. Attach furring channels to 1-1/2" channels with wire ties or furring channel clips installed on

82

Steel stud framing system

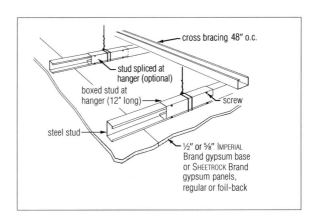

cross bracing 48″ o.c.

stud spliced at hanger (optional)

boxed stud at hanger (12″ long)

screw

steel stud

½″ or ⅝″ IMPERIAL Brand gypsum base or SHEETROCK Brand gypsum panels, regular or foil-back

Lighting fixture

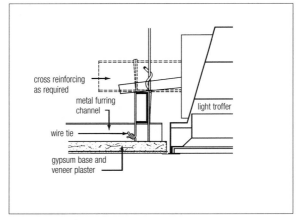

cross reinforcing as required

metal furring channel

light troffer

wire tie

gypsum base and veneer plaster

alternate sides of carrying channel. Saddle tie furring to channels with double-strand 18-ga. tie wire when clips cannot be alternated. At splices, nest furring channels with at least an 8″ overlap and securely wire tie each end with double-strand 18-ga. tie wire.

Where required, in fire-rated assemblies, install double furring channels to support gypsum panel ends and back block with gypsum board strip. When staggered end joints are not required, control joints may be used.

At light troffers or any openings that interrupt the carrying or furring channels, install additional cross-reinforcing to restore the lateral stability of grillage.

Single span   Double span   Triple span

Limiting Span-Steel Stud Ceiling System[1]

2

Stud Style		Stud Spacing (in.)	Single Span (ft.-in.) (uniform load-psf)				Double and Triple Span (ft.-in.) (uniform load-psf)			
			5	10	15	20	5	10	15	20
2-1/2"	25-ga.	12	10'11"	8'8"	7'7"	6'9"	13'6"	10'2"	8'2"	6'11"
		16	9'11"	7'11"	6'10"	5'4"	12'4"	8'8"	6'11"	5'9"
		24	8'8"	6'9"	4'9"	—	10'2"	6'11"	5'9"	4'4"
3-5/8"[2]	25-ga.	12	14'7"	11'7"	9'8"	7'3"	17'5"	11'2"	8'4"	6'8"
		16	13'3"	10'6"	7'3"	5'5"	14'8"	9'2"	6'8"	5'3"
		24	11'7"	7'3"	4'9"	—	11'2"	6'8"	4'9"	—
4"[2]	25-ga.	12	15'9"	12'6"	10'4"	9'0"	17'6"	11'0"	8'0"	6'3"
		16	14'4"	11'0"	9'0"	7'6"	14'7"	8'9"	6'3"	4'10"
		24	12'6"	9'0"	6'8"	5'0"	11'0"	6'3"	4'4"	—
2-1/2"	20-ga.	12	13'2"	10'5"	9'1"	8'3"	16'4"	12'11"	11'4"	10'0"
		16	11'11"	9'6"	8'3"	7'6"	14'10"	11'9"	10'0"	8'9"
		24	10'5"	8'3"	7'3"	6'4"	12'11"	10'1"	8'2"	7'1"
3-5/8"	20-ga.	12	17'6"	13'11"	12'2"	11'0"	21'9"	17'3"	15'0"	13'3"
		16	15'11"	12'8"	11'0"	10'0"	19'9"	15'8"	13'3"	11'6"
		24	13'11"	11'0"	9'8"	8'4"	17'8"	13'3"	10'10"	9'4"
4"	20-ga.	12	19'0"	15'0"	13'2"	11'11"	23'6"	18'8"	16'3"	14'3"
		16	17'3"	13'8"	11'11"	10'10"	21'4"	16'11"	14'3"	12'4"
		24	15'0"	11'11"	10'4"	9'0"	18'8"	14'3"	11'7"	9'9"
6"	20-ga.	12	26'3"	10'10"	18'2"	16'6"	32'6"	25'9"	20'3"	16'10"
		16	23'10"	18'11"	16'6"	14'9"	29'6"	21'10"	16'10"	13'10"
		24	10'10"	16'6"	13'11"	12'0"	25'9"	16'10"	13'10"	10'2"

(1) Based on L/240 allowable deflection. Bracing of top flanges is required and must not exceed 48" o.c. Check manufacturer's literature to verify that the selected framing member is capable of the indicated span. (2) Stud end stiffening required. Additional hangers are necessary when span area exceeds 16 ft.²

Light Fixture Protection Use over recessed lighting fixtures installed in direct suspension grid when required in fire-rated construction. Cut pieces of 1/2" or 5/8" SHEETROCK Brand Gypsum Panels or IMPERIAL Brand Gypsum Base with FIRECODE C Core to form a five-sided enclosure, trapezoidal in cross-section (see detail). Fabricate box larger than the fixture to provide at least 1/2" clearance between the box and the fixture, and in accordance with fire test report.

Light fixture fire protection

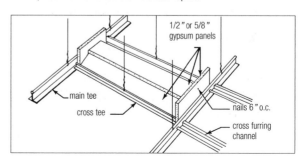

1/2" or 5/8" gypsum panels

main tee

cross tee

nails 6" o.c.

cross furring channel

Lighting fixture

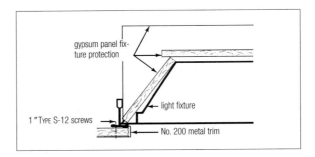

USG Drywall Suspension System

Flat Ceilings   Main tees shall be spaced a maximum of 48″ on center and supported by hanger wires spaced a maximum 48″ on center and as specified by UL Fire Resistance Directory, attaching hanger wires directly to structure above. Cross tees shall be spaced per manufacturers' recommendations and as specified by UL Fire Resistance Directory.

Curved Ceilings   Valley and Vault main tees shall be spaced a maximum 48″.

Hanger wires shall be spaced a maximum 48″ for Vault main tees. Hanger wires shall be spaced a maximum 24″ for Valley main tees. Cross tees shall be spaced as per manufacturers' recommendations. Additional hanger wires may be necessary to stabilize any curved ceiling during and after drywall attachment.

Transitions: Changes in Elevation in Soffit and Fascia Ceiling Applications   When constructing stepped soffits, bracing of the drywall suspension system and/or additional hanger wires may be necessary to ensure stability and structural performance during and after drywall attachment. The maximum vertical soffit height is 48″. (Maximum unsupported drywall area shall not exceed 48″ x 24″). Intermediate cross tees are not necessary when bulkhead dimensions do not exceed 24″.

Cross tee spacing in horizontal soffit plane is not to exceed 24″. Intermediate cross tees may be necessary to maintain visually acceptable drywall planes and drywall corners.

General Hanger Wire Notes   Hanger wires are required within 12″ on both sides of a pivoted splice clip. At least 1 hanger wire is required within 12″ of a transition clip.

Limitations   Do not support wires from mechanical and/or electrical equipment occurring above ceiling.

Accessories   Install accessories as applicable to meet project requirements.

Gypsum Panel Installation   Apply gypsum panels first to ceiling and then to walls. Position all ends and edges of gypsum panels at framing members. Extend ceiling board to corners and make firm contact with the wall angle, channel or top plate. To minimize end joints, use panels of maximum practical lengths. Fit ends and edges closely, but not forced together.

2

Cut ends, edges; scribe or make cutouts within the field of panels in a workmanlike manner. Cut gypsum board to size using a knife and straight edge.

Attach gypsum panels to the suspension system main runners, cross tees and cross channels with conventional gypsum panel fasteners (No. 6 Type S HiLo bugle head, self-drilling, self-tapping steel screws) spaced 8″ o.c. at periphery of gypsum panels and located 3/8″ in from panel edges and spaced 12″ o.c. in the field. Drive fasteners in field of panels first, working toward ends and edges. Hold panels in firm contact with framing while driving fasteners. Drive fastener heads slightly below surface of gypsum panels in a uniform dimple without breaking face paper. (See *Gypsum Panels and Accessories* Specification, SA927).

Install trim at all internal and external angles formed by the intersection of panel surfaces or other dissimilar materials. Apply corner bead to all vertical or horizontal external corners in accordance with manufacturer's directions.

Ceilings Note

See *Drywall/Steel Framed Systems* Specifications, SA923. Spacing of drywall grid is designed to support only the dead load. Heavy concentrated loads should be independently supported. Lighting fixtures or troffers, air vents and other equipment should be separately supported from the structure; gypsum panels will not support these items.

To prevent objectionable sag in new gypsum panel ceilings, the weight of overlaid unsupported insulation should not exceed 1.3 psf for 1/2″ thick gypsum panels with spacing of 24″ o.c.; 2.2 psf for 1/2″ thick gypsum panels 16″ o.c. framing. Where Sheetrock Brand Interior Gypsum Ceiling Panels, Sag-Resistant, are used, framing should be spaced 24″ o.c. for 1/2″ or 5/8″ panels. Note that 3/8″ thick gypsum panels must not be overlaid with unsupported insulation. A vapor retarder should be installed in exterior ceilings, and plenum or attic spaces should be properly vented.

During periods of cold or damp weather when a polyethylene vapor retarder is installed on ceilings behind the gypsum panels, it is important to install the ceiling insulation before or immediately after installing the gypsum panels. Failure to follow this procedure may result in moisture condensation in the back of the gypsum panels causing sag.

Spray-Textured Ceilings

Where water-based texturing materials or any slow-drying surface treatment are used over single-layer panels, maximum frame spacing is 16″ o.c. for 1/2″ panels applied perpendicular to framing.

Expansion Joints

Provide a separation in the suspension system at expansion joints as shown on the drawings and carry the joint through the gypsum panels. Expansion joints are installed between two main tees to separate the suspension system and allow for movement in large ceiling areas.

Control Joints

Provide control joint No. 093 which has a 3/32″ ground for drywall and veneer plaster. Ceiling areas should not exceed 50 ft. (2500 sq. ft.) with perimeter relief and 30 ft. (900 sq. ft.) without perimeter relief.

Wall Furring

Exterior walls are readily furred using steel or wood furring to which 1/2″ regular or foil-back gypsum panels are screw attached. Use of foil-back board can provide an effective, low-cost vapor retarder. In these systems, different framing methods may be used to provide for a vapor retarder, thermal insulation, and chase space for pipes, conduits and ducts. Vinyl wall coverings are not recommended in furred walls containing foil-back gypsum panels or plaster base. The need for and location of a vapor retarder should be determined by a qualified mechanical engineer.

Metal furring channels are fastened directly to interiors of exterior walls or monolithic concrete and virtually any type of masonry—brick, concrete block, tile. This economical system provides an excellent vapor retarder and a durable, easily decorated interior surface, when foil-back gypsum panels or plaster base is screw-attached to channels, and appropriate sealants are applied at periphery and penetrations.

Z-furring channels are used with insulating blankets or rigid plastic foam insulation on interiors of exterior walls. The insulation panels are applied progressively as Z-furring channels are attached to the wall. Gypsum panels are screw-attached to channel flanges to provide an interior surface isolated to a great degree from the brick, concrete or concrete masonry wall. In new construction and remodeling, this system provides a highly insulative self-furring solid backup for gypsum boards.

Steel studs erected vertically between floor and ceiling runners serve as free-standing furring for foil-back gypsum panels screw-attached to one side of studs. This free-standing system with 1-5/8″ studs provides maximum clear chase space and minimizes possibilities for photographing or shadowing to occur. When heights greater than 12′0″ are required, the stud framing is secured to the exterior wall with adjustable wall furring brackets at mid-height, in addition to the normal attachment of the studs at their head and base. Other furring providing greater height may be constructed with wider and heavier steel studs.

Wall elevation—furring

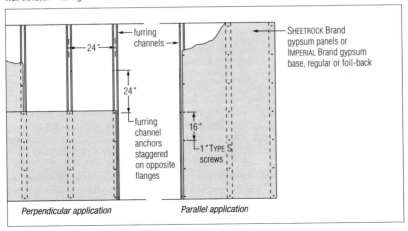

Perpendicular application *Parallel application*

Temperature differentials on the interior surface of exterior walls may result in collection of dust on the colder areas of the surface. Consequently, shadowing (accumulated dust) may occur at locations of fasteners or furring channels where surface temperatures usually are lowest. U.S. Gypsum cannot be held responsible for surface discoloration of this nature. Where temperature, humidity and soiling conditions are expected to cause objectionable blemishes, use free-standing furring with insulation against the exterior wall.

Furring Channel Erection — Direct Attachment Attach metal furring channels to masonry or concrete surfaces, either vertically (preferred) or horizontally (for spacing, see frame spacing tables). For channels positioned horizontally, attach a furring channel not more than 4″ from both the floor line and the ceiling line. Secure channels with fasteners placed on alternate channel flanges and spaced 24″ o.c. Use a 2″ cut nail in mortar joints of brick, clay tile or concrete block or in the field of lightweight aggregate block; 5/8″ concrete stub nail, or other power-driven fasteners in monolithic concrete.

Channels may be furred using adjustable wall furring brackets and 3/4″ cold-rolled channels to provide additional space for pipes, conduits or ducts.

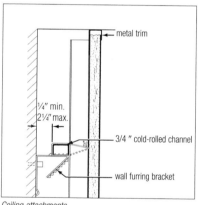

Ceiling attachments

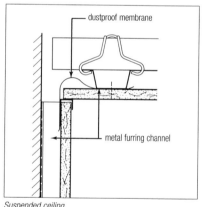

Suspended ceiling

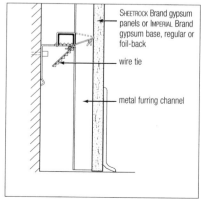

Floor attachments

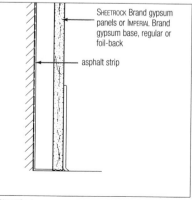

Direct furring

At window locations, attach furring channels horizontally over the substrate returns to support gypsum board at corners (see detail).

Free-standing Furring

Free-standing furring consists of 1-5/8″ steel studs in 1-5/8″ steel runners. To erect, plumb and align runners at the desired distance away from the exterior wall. Fasten runners to floor and ceiling with suitable anchors. Snap studs into place in runners (see framing spacing tables for required stud spacing).

If greater height is required than can be attained with 1-5/8″ studs, wider or heavier gauge studs can be used. However, if space is critical, heights greater than 12′0″ can be attained with 1-5/8″ studs by bracing them to the exterior wall at midheight or more frequently. For bracing, install adjustable furring brackets or sheet metal "L" pieces to the exterior wall and attach to the stud webs with 3/8″ pan head TYPE S screws.

Z-furring Channel Erection

Erect insulation vertically and hold in place with Z-furring channels spaced 24″ o.c. Except at exterior corners, attach narrow flanges of furring channels to wall with concrete stub nails or power-driven fasteners spaced 24″ o.c. At exterior corners, attach wide flange of furring channel to wall with short flange extending beyond corner. On adjacent wall surface, screw attach short flange of furring channel to web of attached channel. Start from this furring channel with a standard width insulation panel and continue in regular manner. At interior corners, space second channel no more than 12″ from corner and cut insulation to fit. Hold mineral-fiber insulation in place until gypsum panels are installed with 10″ long staple field-fabricated from 18-ga. tie wire and inserted through slot in channel. Apply wood or other appropriate blocking around window and door openings and as required for attachment and support of fixtures and furnishings.

Apply gypsum drywall or plaster base panels parallel to channels with vertical joints occurring over channels. Attach gypsum panels with 1″ TYPE S Screws spaced 16″ o.c. in field and at edges, and with 1-1/4″ TYPE S Screws spaced 12″ o.c. at exterior corners. For gypsum base,

Metal window—jamb

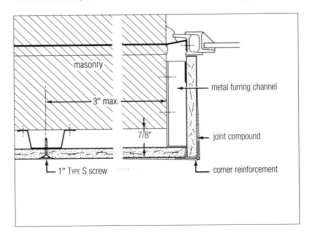

Z-furring application details

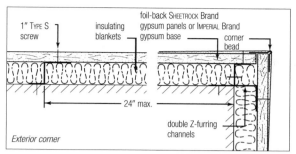

1″ Type S screw

insulating blankets

foil-back Sheetrock Brand gypsum panels or Imperial Brand gypsum base

corner bead

24″ max.

double Z-furring channels

Exterior corner

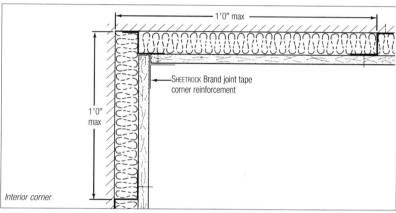

1′0″ max

1′0″ max

Sheetrock Brand joint tape corner reinforcement

Interior corner

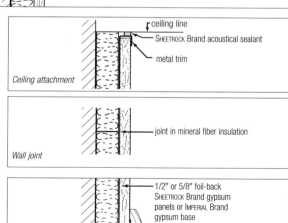

ceiling line

Sheetrock Brand acoustical sealant

metal trim

Ceiling attachment

joint in mineral fiber insulation

Wall joint

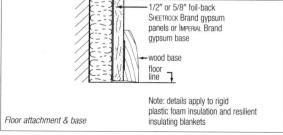

1/2″ or 5/8″ foil-back Sheetrock Brand gypsum panels or Imperial Brand gypsum base

wood base

floor line

Note: details apply to rigid plastic foam insulation and resilient insulating blankets

Floor attachment & base

2

Z-furring application details

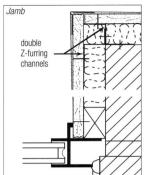

Jamb

double
Z-furring
channels

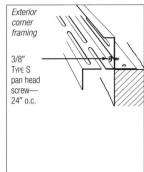

Exterior
corner
framing

3/8"
TYPE S
pan head
screw—
24" o.c.

Design of Z-furring channels helps prevent wicking of moisture to inside surfaces.

space screws 12" o.c. in the field and at edges. For double-layer application, apply first layer parallel to channels, face layer either perpendicular or parallel to channels with vertical joints offset at least one channel. Attach first layer with screws 24" o.c. and face layer with 1-5/8" screws 16" o.c.

Wood Furring Erection

Wood furring strips over wood framing must be 2" x 2" (nom.) min. size for nail-on application. Strips may be 1" x 3" (nom.) if gypsum board is to be screw-attached.

When panels are to be applied parallel to furring strips securely attached to masonry walls, use strips 2" x 3" or 1" x 3" (nom.) min. size; where long edges of board are to be applied across the furring, use strips 2" x 2" or 1" x 2" (nom.) min. size. Space furring strips as specified by frame spacing tables. For board application select a screw length that will not penetrate through furring.

Where there is a possibility of water penetration through the walls, install a layer of asphalt felt between furring strips and wall surface.

Note: Nail application of gypsum board over 1" (nom.) thickness wood furring applied across framing members is not recommended since the relative flexibility of undersize furring prevents proper fastening and tends to loosen nails already driven.

Resilient Framing—Wood Frame

Resilient attachment of gypsum board with RC-1 Resilient Channels provides low-cost, highly efficient, sound-rated drywall and veneer-partitions and floor-ceilings. The steel channels float the panels away from the studs and joists and provide a spring action that isolates the gypsum board from the framing. This spring action also tends to level the panel surface when installed over uneven framing. Additional features include excellent fire resistance (from the total assembly) and simple, fast installation for overall economy. For fire- and sound-resistant assemblies, refer to *USG Construction Selector*, SA-100.

Resilient Channels Partitions

Attach RC-1 Resilient Channels attachment flange down and at right angles (perpendicular) to wood studs. Position bottom channel with attachment flange up for ease of attachment. Use 1-1/4" Type W

Screws driven through the flanges for attachment. Nails are not rec-ommended. Fasten channels to studs at each intersection with the slotted hole directly over a framing member.

Locate channels 2" max. up from floor, within 6" of the ceiling and at no more than 24" intervals. (For some veneer assemblies max. chan-nel spacing is 16" o.c. Refer to frame spacing tables earlier in this chapter.) Extend channels into all corners and attach to corner fram-ing. Splice channels directly over studs by nesting (not butting) the channels and driving fastener through both flanges into the support.

Where cabinets are to be installed, attach RC-1 Channels to studs directly behind cabinet hanger brackets. When distance between hangers exceeds 24" o.c., install additional channel at midpoint between hangers.

For cabinet installation with resilient framing, refer to section on Fixture Installation, Chapter 3.

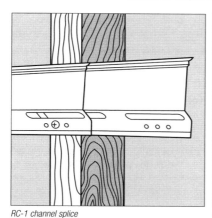

RC-1 channel splice

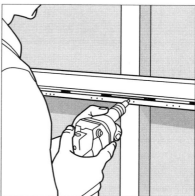

Channel attachment to stud

Resilient Channels Ceilings

Attach RC-1 Resilient Channels at right angles to wood joists. Use 1-1/4" Type W or 1-1/4" Type S Screws driven through channel attachment flange for single-layer construction. Fasten channels to joists at each intersection. Do not use nails to attach channels to joists in either sin-gle or double-layer assemblies. For the channels to function acousti-cally, they should be held away from adjacent walls a minimum of one inch. Thermafiber SAFB is required when sound control is needed.

A 2-hr. floor/ceiling system with STC ratings as high as 60 is achiev-able with a ceiling of double-layer 5/8" Sheetrock Brand Gypsum Panels, Firecode C Core, attached to RC-1 Channels mounted across joists and 3" Thermafiber SAFB in the cavity. The same fire rating applies to the system using Imperial Firecode or Firecode C Gypsum Base and any USG veneer plaster finish.

For fire-rated, double-layer assembly, apply RC-1 Channels over base layer and attach with 1-7/8″ Type S Screws driven through channel flange and base layer into joist (see UL Des L511—**not recommended when sound control is a major consideration**).

Framing—Partition Corners

Framing for partition corners must assure firm fastening of the gypsum panels to vertical studs and allow enough room from the inside corner to do so. Studs should be attached to runners a minimum of 2″ but not more than 6″ from where the runners intersect. While the edges of the panels will extend slightly beyond these corner studs, the edge of the second-applied panel will overlap the plane of the first enough to assure good taping of the inside corner. Outside corners of partition intersections require firm attachment of panels to perpendicular edges of the outside corner stud.

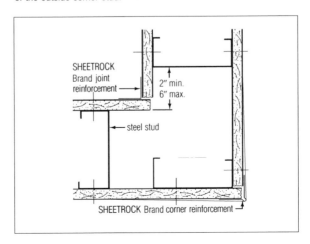

SHEETROCK Brand joint reinforcement
2″ min.
6″ max.
steel stud
SHEETROCK Brand corner reinforcement

Framing—Door and Window Openings

Rough framing for most door and window openings is the same for gypsum panels and gypsum base veneer systems.

Wood Framing

Install additional cripple studs above header and 1/2″ from bearing studs where control joints are required. Do not anchor cripple stud to bearing stud, header or plate.

In long runs, treat window openings in same manner as shown for doors.

Steel Framing

Door and borrowed light openings should be rough-framed with steel studs and runners. The recommended practice for most installations is to position floor to ceiling height strut studs vertically, adjacent to frames, and anchor them securely to the top and bottom runners with screws. However, in cases where significant slab live-load deflection must be accommodated in the vicinity of the door, the anchoring of these studs may need to be omitted in order to accommodate the slab movement. The services of a design professional is desirable to identify these instances and address them on a case-specific basis. Where heavy or oversize doors are used, install additional strut-stud at jambs. Fabricate sill and header sections from steel runners and install over less-than-ceiling-height door frames and above and below borrowed light frames. Fabricate from a section of runner cut-to-length approx. 6″ longer than rough opening. Slit flanges and bend web to allow flanges to overlap adjacent vertical strut-studs. Securely attach to jamb-studs with screws. For frames with jamb anchor clips, fasten clips to strut-studs with two 3/8″ Type S Pan Head Screws. Install cripple studs in the center above the door opening and above and below borrowed light openings spaced 24″ o.c. max.

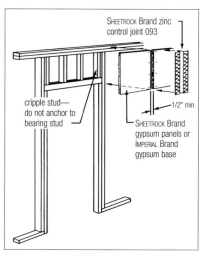

Wood frame door opening

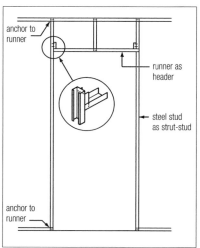

Door frame with steel runner as header

94

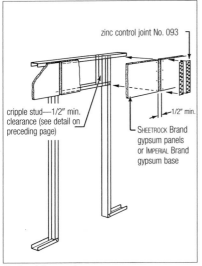

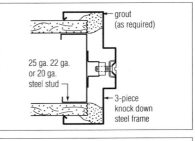

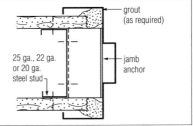

Steel stud door opening

Jamb standard door

Where control joints in header panels are required, install cripple studs away from strut-studs but do not attach cripple to runners or strut-studs.

Note: Three-piece frames are recommended for drywall and veneer plaster construction since these frames are installed after drywall or plaster base is in place. One-piece frames, which must be installed before the gypsum panels, are more difficult to use because the panels must be inserted under the frame returns as it is installed.

Framing for Heavy and Oversize Doors

The steel framing method described above is suitable for standard doors up to 2'8" wide, weighing not more than 100 lb. max. Use 25-ga. steel studs and runners for framing the opening. For wider or heavier doors, the framing must be reinforced.

For solid-core doors and hollow-core doors 2'8" to 4'0" wide (200 lb. max.), rough framing should be 20-ga. steel studs and runners. For heavy doors up to 4'0" wide (300 lb. max.), two 20-ga. studs should be used. For doors over 4'0" wide, double doors and extra-heavy doors (over 300 lb.), framing should be specially designed to meet load

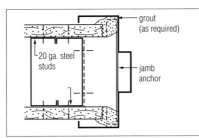

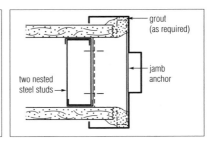

Cross-section through frame (heavy doors)

conditions. Rough framing for all doors in fire-rated partitions should be 20-ga. studs and runners.

For added door frame restraint, grouting of the frame is recommended and often is required for solid-core doors and doors over 2'8" wide. To do so, apply SHEETROCK Brand Setting-Type Joint Compound (DURABOND or EASY SAND) or RED TOP Gypsum Plaster (job-aggregated) just before inserting board into frame. Do not terminate gypsum panel against trim return.

Door Frame Installation

The following general recommendations apply to one-piece and three-piece door frames and are basic considerations for satisfactory performance.

Rough framing and rough frame reinforcement for these frames should be installed as previously described.

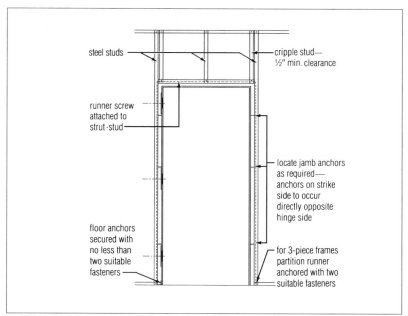

Frame for standard door

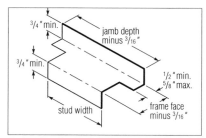
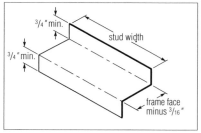

Jamb anchors (furnished with frame)

Installation One-piece metal door (and borrowed light) frames used with gypsum panel and gypsum base partitions must be constructed and installed properly to prevent twisting or movement. Basic considerations for satisfactory performance are:

1. Frames must be securely anchored. If frames are free to twist upon impact, or trim returns are free to vibrate, movement of the frame will tend to pinch gypsum board face paper and crush core, resulting in unsightly cracks in the finish and loose frames.

2. Partition must fit securely in frame so that wall and frame work as a unit. Impact stresses on frame will then be dissipated over entire partition surface and local damage minimized.

3. The frame must have a throat opening between trim returns that accurately fits the overall thickness of the partition. The face-layer panels should be enclosed by the trim and not butted against the trim return. This throat opening measurement is critical, as too large a tolerance between panels and trim return will cause door frame to twist and vibrate against the panels. Too small a tolerance will prevent the panels from fully entering frame opening; as a result, the door frame will not be held securely by the partition.

4. One-piece metal door (and borrowed light) frames should be formed from 18-ga. steel min., shop-primed. Floor anchor plates for door frames should be 16-ga. steel min., designed with two anchor holes to prevent rotation, and shop-welded to frame rabbets to dampen door impact vibrations. Floor anchorage should be by two power-driven anchors or equivalent per plate. Jamb anchors should be formed of 18-ga. steel min., fit tightly in jambs, and screw-attached to the stud. A minimum of three anchor clips per jamb is recommended with locations at approximate hinge points.

5. Spot grouting of one-piece door jambs will increase the rigidity of the frame and improve resistance to frame rotation caused by the weight of the door. To spot grout, apply Sheetrock Brand Setting-Type Joint

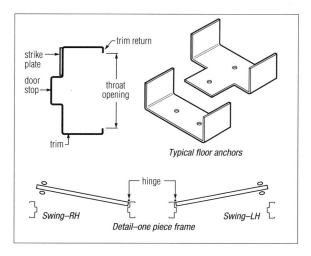

Typical floor anchors

Detail—one piece frame

Compound (Durabond) mixed in accordance with bag instructions to each jamb anchor filling the inside face of the jamb at each point. Immediately insert the gypsum panels into the jamb and attach to framing. Do not terminate the gypsum board against the trim.

Full grouting of the jambs flush with the jamb anchors prior to installation of framing may be used as an option to spot grouting. Red Top Gypsum Plaster (job-aggregated) or Structo-Lite Gypsum Plaster (mill-mixed) is recommended for this purpose.

To improve the sound seal around door frames, apply a continuous bead of Sheetrock Brand Acoustical Sealant to the return of the jamb at the intersection with the gypsum board. Tool the bead of sealant smooth and allow to dry before finishing the door jamb.

6. Door closers and bumpers are required on all doors where door weight (including attached hardware) exceeds 50 lb., or where door width exceeds 36″. These doors require grouting.

7. When installing a three-piece knock-down door frame, secure runner ends with two floor anchors and allow space in the rough framing for the adjustment shoes in the frame.

8. When ordering metal door frames, the factors to be considered include: Gauge of frame; width and height of door; swing direction of door; type and thickness of door; stud size, and overall thickness of partition.

Metal Window Framing

In climates where extremes in summer or winter temperatures may result in condensation on metal frames, gypsum board (drywall and veneer) should be isolated from direct contact with the frame.

By placing metal trim (No. 200-B, No. 801-A and B and No. 400 for drywall assemblies No. 801-A and B for veneer plaster assemblies) between the gypsum board and window frame, protection against moisture damage is provided.

Waterproof insulating tape, 1/4″ thick and 1/2″ wide, or a waterproof acrylic caulk is required to separate metal sash and metal trim and will provide some measure of insulation between the two different metals. Direct contact of an aluminum frame and steel trim in the presence of condensation moisture may cause electrolytic deterioration of aluminum frame.

Detail—window trim

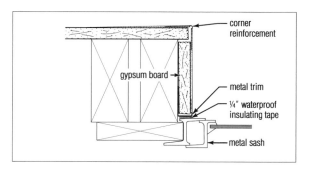

corner reinforcement

gypsum board

metal trim

1/4″ waterproof insulating tape

metal sash

3

Cladding

General Planning Procedures

In most instances, job planning requirements and the application techniques used for the installation of gypsum board apply equally to gypsum panels and gypsum bases. For that reason the term "gypsum board" is used throughout this chapter wherever the recommendations apply to both types of products. Where the requirements differ, the products are treated separately.

Various organizations provide information about recommended standards or tolerances for installation of drywall systems. See page 467 and 474 in the Appendix for information about standards and tolerances.

For instructions on the safe use of gypsum panels, gypsum base and other products, see Chapter 13, Safety Considerations, Material Handling.

Planning the Job

Advance planning by the wall and ceiling contractor can mean savings in time and material cost and result in a better-appearing job. It also helps assure that the intended purpose of the walls is matched with the proper materials.

Since the last edition of this handbook, a number of new gypsum board products and systems have been developed that either speed the construction process, or improve the abuse resistance and performance of the finished wall. Wider gypsum board, for example, reduces the number of joints that need to be taped on walls between 8' and 9' tall. And gypsum boards with heavy-duty face paper and backing sheets (SHEETROCK Brand Abuse Resistant Panels) or cellulose or glass fiber reinforcement in the core (FIBEROCK Brand Panels or FIBEROCK Brand VHI Panels) improve the overall impact and abuse resistance of the finished wall system. In addition, panels have been developed to reduce ceiling sag (SHEETROCK Brand Interior Gypsum Ceiling Board, Sag-Resistant). Performance factors should be revisited at this time to make sure that the cladding products used are the best suited to meet the project's performance requirements.

Note that installation of FIBEROCK Brand products sometimes varies from the procedures used to install conventional drywall panels and gypsum base. See the most current literature on FIBEROCK Brand Panels for the latest installation information.

Proper planning achieves the most effective use of materials, elimination of unnecessary joints, and the placement of necessary joints in the least conspicuous locations. One gypsum board should span the entire length or width of the wall or ceiling, if possible. By using the longest practical board lengths obtainable, end joints are kept to a minimum. Where they do occur, end joints should be staggered.

In double-layer construction, end joints in the face layer must be offset at least 10″ from parallel joints in the base layer. Layout of the base layer must be planned to accommodate this offset and still provide optimum joint-finishing conditions and efficient use of materials in the face layer.

Fire-rated designs stipulate framing, fastener spacing, use of adhesive, joint details, etc. and those factors must be included in the planning stage.

3

Estimating Materials

Gypsum Board From practical experience, professional estimators have developed methods for determining footage required to complete various types of jobs. Basically, these methods stem from the simple principle of "scaling a plan," and determining the length and width and ceiling height of each room on the plan. Frequently, door and window openings are "figured solid" with no openings considered. Exceptions may be large picture windows and large door openings. From these dimensions the estimator determines the square footage of each room. The footage of each room is added to determine total footage required. From these figures the number of gypsum boards needed may be determined. (Refer to Chapter 1 for available lengths of each panel.)

Screws For single-layer wall application to 16″ o.c. framing, approx. 1,000 Type W Screws are required for wood or TYPE S or TYPE S-12 for steel per 1,000 ft.^{2} of gypsum board; approx. 850 for 24″ o.c. framing. See pages 467-468 in Appendix for complete information on estimating screws.

Fastener usage for other assemblies varies with the construction and spacing. Refer to specific system descriptions for fastener requirements.

Nails Usage for nails is shown in the Selector Guide for Gypsum Board Nails, page 47.

Acoustical Sealant The approximate lin. ft. of bead realized per gal. of SHEETROCK Brand Acoustical Sealant is: 392 for 1/4″ bead, 174 for 3/8″ bead, 98 for 1/2″ bead.

Adhesive The following table shows the amount of adhesive needed per 1000 ft.^{2} of laminated board surface:

Coverage — Adhesives for Lamination

Product	Application	Approx. quantity			
		lb./1000 ft.^{2}		kg/100 m^2	
		Lam. blade 1/4″ notch spacing			
		2″	1-1/2″	50 mm	38 mm
SHEETROCK Brand Ready-Mixed Joint Compound	Strip lam.	170	230	83	112
	Sheet lam.	340	465	166	227
SHEETROCK Brand Setting Type (DURABOND) Joint Compound	Strip lam.	93	123	45	60
	Sheet lam.	184	246	90	120
SHEETROCK Brand Lightweight Setting Type (EASY SAND)	Strip lam.	68	90	33	44
	Sheet lam.	134	179	66	87
		gal./1000 ft.^{2}		L/100 m^2	
		2″	1-1/2″	50 mm	34 mm
SHEETROCK Brand Lightweight All Purpose Ready-Mixed (PLUS 3)	Strip lam.	11.5	15.5	45.6	63
	Sheet lam.	23.0	31.7	93.5	129

Joint Treatment–Gypsum Panels Approximate quantities required for finishing 1,000 ft.^{2} of gypsum panels: 370′ of SHEETROCK Brand Joint tape; 83 lb. of conventional drying-type powders, 67 lb. of lightweight drying-type powder (AP LITE), 72 lb. of conventional setting type powders, 52 lb. of lightweight setting-type powder (EASY SAND); 138 lb.

of SHEETROCK Brand All Purpose Ready-Mixed or 9.4 gal. of SHEETROCK Brand Lightweight All Purpose Ready-Mixed compound (PLUS 3).

Joint Treatment–Veneer Plaster Gypsum Base For regular application, approx. 370' of either Type "P" or Type "S" IMPERIAL Brand Tape is required per 1,000 ft.^{2} of base surface.

For application over metal framing, approx. 370' SHEETROCK Brand Joint Tape and 72 lb. of SHEETROCK Brand Setting Type (DURABOND) Joint Compound are required per 1,000 ft.^{2} of surface. This application also is required for certain spacing requirements and when building temperature-humidity conditions fall in the rapid drying area of the graph on page 214.

Handling and Storage

When drywall and veneer construction moved into high-rise buildings, it brought with it the new challenge of moving large gypsum boards from ground level to the point of use, stories above. Inefficient materials handling at the job site can add cost and reduce profit. Time and money savings can be substantial when correct handling procedures are used.

Tip
See Chapter 13,
Safety Considerations,
Material Handling for
more information on the
safe use of gypsum
panels and base.

Gypsum board products should be ordered for delivery several days in advance of installation. Materials stored on the job for a long period of time are subject to damage. Gypsum boards, like millwork, must be handled with care to avoid damage. Since joint compounds and veneer finishes are subject to aging, they must not be stored for extended periods.

Board should be placed inside under cover and stacked flat on a clean floor in the centers of the largest rooms. It is often desirable to place the necessary number of boards in the location where they will be used. All materials used on the job should remain in their packaging until ready for actual use.

When stacking heavy loads, it may be preferable to scatter smaller amounts of panels and distribute them around the perimeter of the room. See pages 411-413 of Chapter 13 more more information on the safe handling of gypsum panels and base.

Gypsum boards intended for use on ceilings should be placed on top of pile for removal first. Avoid stacking long lengths atop short lengths.

All successful veneer plaster finish jobs require adequate equipment: power mixers, mortar boards, scaffolding and tools. Ample scaffolding should be provided. Rather than ship all veneer plaster finish to the job at one time, fresh material should be sent to the job every few days as needed. Plaster stored for long periods is subject to damage, variable moisture conditions and aging that probably will produce variations in setting time and create performance problems.

Store veneer plaster products inside, in a dry location and away from heavy traffic areas. Stack bags on planks or platforms away from damp floors and walls. Protect metal corner beads, casing beads and trim from being bent or damaged. All materials used on the job should remain in their packages until used.

| **Environmental Conditions** | In cold weather (outdoor temperature less than 55°F), controlled heat in the range of 55° to 70°F must be provided. This heat must be maintained both day and night, 24 hours before, during and after entire gypsum board joint finishing and until the permanent heating system is in operation or the building is occupied. Minimum temperature of 50°F should be maintained during gypsum board application. |

Methods for Applying Drywall and Veneer Bases

Gypsum panels and gypsum bases may be applied in one or two layers directly to wood framing members, to steel studs or channels, or to interior masonry walls with adhesive. Use of stilts will provide convenience in application. See Chapter 13 for safety precautions.

Single Layer vs. Double Layer

Nailing technique for single-layer application

Single-Layer Application This basic construction is used to surface interior walls and ceilings where economy, fast erection and fire resistance are required. It is equally suitable for remodeling, altering and resurfacing cracked and defaced areas.

Double-Layer Application Consists of a face layer of gypsum board applied over a base layer of gypsum board that is directly attached to framing members. This construction can offer greater strength and higher resistance to fire and to sound transmission than single-layer applications. Double-layer construction when adhesively laminated is especially resistant to cracking and provides one of the finest, strongest walls available. Also, these adhesively laminated constructions are highly resistant to sag and joint deformation. In double-layer application, always apply all base-layer board in each room before beginning face-layer application.

Attachment Methods

Gypsum boards are attached to framing by several methods depending on the type of framing and the results desired.

Single Nailing Conventional attachment for wood framing.

Double Nailing Minimizes defects due to loose board. See page 110 for a more detailed description of double nailing.

Screw Attachment Screws are excellent insurance against fastener pops caused by loosely attached board. Screws are recommended for wood frame attachment, and required for attachment to steel framing and resilient channels. When mounting to resilient channels, take care not to locate screws where they will also penetrate studs, thereby 'shorting out' or negating the resiliency.

Screw attachment along vertical edges of face-layer board in double-layer application

Adhesive Attachment A continuous bead of drywall stud adhesive applied to wood framing plus supplemental nail or screw attachment improves bond strength and greatly reduces the number of face nails or screws needed.

Adhesive Lamination (Double Layer) Produces the finest interior surfaces. Adhesive attachment of face layer to base layer in double-layer construction and of single-layer board to interior masonry walls usually requires only supplemental mechanical fastening until adhesive attains full bond. Reduces nails or screws required, saves finishing labor and minimizes fastener pops and joint ridging. A SHEETROCK Brand Setting-Type (DURABOND) or Lightweight Setting-Type (EASY SAND) Joint Compound or SHEETROCK Brand Ready-Mixed Joint Compound—Taping or All Purpose is required for adhesive lamination with fire-rated assemblies.

Perpendicular vs. Parallel Application

Gypsum board may be applied perpendicular (long edges of board at right angles to the framing members) or parallel (long edges parallel to framing). Fire-rated partitions may require parallel application (see Chapter 10 for specific information on fire-rated systems).

Perpendicular application generally is preferred because it offers the following advantages:

1. Reduces the lineal footage of joints to be treated up to 25%.

2. Strongest dimension of board runs across framing members.

3. Bridges irregularities in alignment and spacing of frame members.

4. Better bracing strength—each board ties more frame members together than does parallel application.

5. Horizontal joints on wall are at a convenient height for finishing.

For wall application, if ceiling height is 8′1″ or less, perpendicular application of standard 4′ wide panels results in fewer joints, easier handling and less cutting. If ceiling height is greater than 8′1″ or wall is 4 ft. wide or less, parallel application is more practical.

Walls ranging in height from 8′1″ to 9′ 1″ can be clad with perpendicular 54″ wide panels, to eliminate the addition of more joints. See SHEETROCK Brand Gypsum Panels—54″ in Chapter 1.

For ceiling application, use whichever method—parallel or perpendicular— results in fewer joints, or is required by frame spacing limitations.

For double-layer ceiling application, apply base-layer boards perpendicular to frame members; apply face layer parallel to framing with joints offset. On wall, apply base layer parallel with long edges centered on framing; apply face layer perpendicular. Exception: when using SHEETROCK Vinyl-Faced Gypsum Panels for face layer, apply base-layer boards at right angles to studs.

Starting at ceiling line, horizontal board is screw-attached (left). Parallel application (right) is used in special situations.

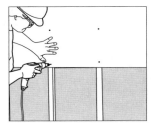
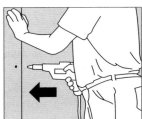

Gypsum Drywall and Plaster Base Application

General Recommendations

General Recommendations for gypsum panels applied to wood and steel framing:

1. Apply ceiling boards first.

2. Cut boards so that they slip easily into place.

3. Butt all joints loosely. Never force panels into position.

4. Whenever possible, place tapered or wrapped edges next to one another.

5. Wherever possible, apply boards perpendicular to framing and in lengths that will span ceilings and walls without creating end (butt) joints. If butt joints do occur, stagger and locate them as far from the center of walls and ceilings as possible.

6. Support all ends and edges of gypsum board on framing, except long edges at right angles to framing and where end joints are to be floated between frame members and back-blocked. Back-blocking is covered later in this chapter on pages 115-116.

7. When fastening, apply hand pressure on panel next to fastener being driven to insure panel is in tight contact with framing member.

8. If metal or plastic trim is to be installed around edges, doors, or windows, determine if trim is to be installed before panel application. Refer to Chapter 1 for description of products.

9. Do not anchor panel surfaces across the flat grain of wide dimensional lumber such as floor joists and headers. Float panels over these members or provide a control joint to compensate for wood shrinkage.

10. To insure level surfaces at joints, arrange board application so that the leading edge of each board is attached to the open or unsupported edge of a steel stud flange. To do this, all studs must be placed so that their flanges point in the same direction. Board application is then planned to advance in the direction opposite to flange direction. When this simple procedure is followed, attachment of each board holds the stud flange at the joint in a rigid position for attachment of the following board.

If the leading edge of gypsum board is attached to the web edge of a flange, the open edge of the flange can deflect under the pressure of attachment of the following gypsum board. Friction between the tightly abutted board edges can then cause them to bind, preventing return of the second board to the surface plane of the first. A stepped or uneven joint surface results.

This recommended application procedure is absolutely essential for good results in steel-framed veneer and drywall assemblies. (See drawings following for correct methods.)

Measurements All measurements must be accurate. Make two measurements as a check. This procedure will usually warn of partitions or

Correct application

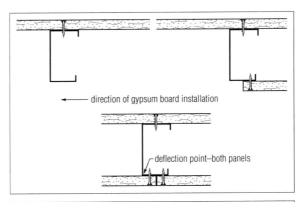

← direction of gypsum board installation

deflection point—both panels

Incorrect application

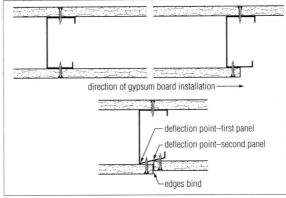

direction of gypsum board installation →

deflection point—first panel

deflection point—second panel

edges bind

Cut edges of board are smoothed with a rasp, coarse sandpaper or piece of metal lath stapled around wood block (top), Measurements for cutouts are carefully made with flexible rule (bottom).

door openings that are out of plumb or out of square. Then, framing corrections can be made before the board is hung. A 12′ to 25′ steel power tape is recommended. Tools for measuring and cutting are shown in Chapter 14.

Cutting Make straight-line cuts across full width or length of board by scoring the face paper, snapping the board core and then cutting the back paper. The common tool used to score and cut gypsum board is a utility knife with replaceable blade. Regardless of the type knife used, its blade should be kept sharp so that score will be made through paper without tearing or rolling it up, and into the gypsum core. For FIBEROCK Brand Panels, several cuts may be required on panel surface and into core; no cut on panel back is required, unless cutting Very High Impact (VHI) panels.

Note that installation of FIBEROCK Brand products sometimes varies from the procedures used to install conventional drywall panels and gypsum base. See the most current literature on FIBEROCK Brand Panels for the latest installation information.

For cuts across the board width, a straightedge is recommended. An aluminum 4′ drywall T-square, ruled on both edges, facilitates clean, straight cuts. For cuts along the long length of the board, use a steel

Left to right, gypsum board is cut by scoring with utility knife against drywall T-square, then snapping toward back (top), cutting back paper with same knife and separating sections (bottom)—quick method to obtain clean edges and precise fit.

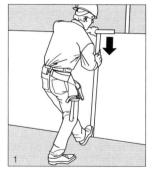
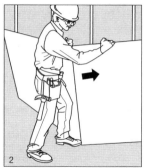
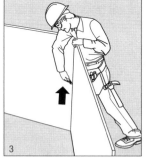

Adjustable cutting tool makes quick work of circular holes, as cutter wheel on calibrated shaft rotates from center pin (top). Edges are trimmed with hook-bill knife (bottom). Stiff drywall saw and other tools are used to make odd-shaped cuts.

tape with an adjustable edge guide and a tip that accepts the utility knife blade. With this tape the edge guide is set for the desired width and placed against the board edge. The knife blade is then inserted into the slotted tape tip, and by moving both hands together the tool is drawn down the full length of the board to make a smooth and accurate cut. (See manufacturer instructions for proper use and any safety precautions.)

Cut and fit board neatly for pipes, electrical outlet boxes, medicine cabinets, etc. Holes for electrical outlet boxes can be made with a special outlet box cutting tool. For circular holes, an adjustable circular cutting tool or drywall router is available. Keyhole saws and similar cutting tools can be used for any type of cutout. After cutting hole, remove any loose face paper at cut. Refer to Chapter 14, Tools and Equipment, for examples of appropriate tools.

Screw Application

Screws are applied with a positive-clutch electric power tool, commonly called an electric screwgun, equipped with adjustable screw-depth control head and a Phillips bit. The use of screws provides a positive mechanical attachment of gypsum board to either wood or steel framing.

Adjust Screwgun Set adjustment for proper screw depth. For gypsum panels (drywall), screwhead must be driven slightly below face of panel (max. 1/32"), but not deep enough to break the paper. For gypsum bases (veneer plaster), screwhead is set flush with the base surface. To adjust depth, rotate control head to provide proper screw depth. When proper adjustment has been made, secure control head to maintain adjustment.

Secure control head to
maintain adjustment.

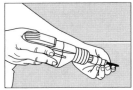

Phillips-head tip holds drywall
screw for driving.

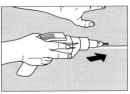

Hold screwgun as shown (not by pistol
grip) to avoid stress on wrist.

Place Screw Phillips head tip holds drywall screw for driving (above, center). Bit tip does not rotate until pressure is applied to gypsum board during application.

Start Screw Straight Firm hand grip on electric screwgun is important for straight line of entry. To avoid stress on wrist, hold gun as shown (above), not by the pistol grip. Screw must enter perpendicular to board face for proper performance. Drive screws at least 3/8" from ends or edges of board.

Operate electric screwgun constantly during usage. When the screwhead is driven solidly against the board, the screwgun head will automatically stop turning as the positive clutch disengages.

The electric screwgun technique is relatively simple and a proficiency with the tool can be developed after a few hours of use. For description of screws, see Chapter 1; for screw spacing, see the fastener spacing table on the next page.

Staple Application

Staples are recommended only for attaching base layer boards to wood framing in double layer assemblies. Staples should be 16-ga. flattened galvanized wire with 7/16" wide crown, divergent points and leg lengths to provide min. 5/8" penetration into supports. Drive staples with crown perpendicular to gypsum board edges except where edges fall on supports. Drive staples so crown bears tightly against board but does not cut paper.

Single-Nailing Application

1. Begin nailing from abutting edge of board and proceed toward opposite ends or edges. Do not nail perimeter before nailing field of board. Ceiling application may cause board to deflect or sag in center and prevent firm fastening.

2. Position nails on adjacent ends or edges opposite each other.

3. Drive nails at least 3/8" from ends or edges of gypsum board.

4. Apply hand pressure on board adjacent to nail being driven to insure that board is in tight contact with framing member.

5. Drive nails with shank perpendicular to face of board.

6. Use a drywall hammer with crowned head for gypsum panels.

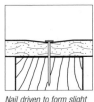

Nail driven to form slight
dimple in drywall panel.

7a. For gypsum panels (drywall), seat nail so head is in a shallow, uniform dimple formed by last blow of hammer. Do not break paper or crush core at nailhead or around circumference of dimple by over-driving.

Never use a nail set. Depth of dimple should not exceed 1/32" for gypsum panels.

    b. For gypsum bases (veneer plaster) nail heads should be driven flush with the board surface without dimpling.

Maximum Fastener Spacing—Constructions Using Drywall, Gypsum Base and Similar Products[1]

				Maximum Fastener Spacing			
				Drywall Assemblies		Veneer Plaster Assemblies	
				SHEETROCK Brand Gypsum Panels or FIBEROCK Brand Abuse-Resistant Panels		IMPERIAL Brand Gypsum Base or FIBEROCK Brand Abuse-Resistant Panels	
Framing	Type const.	Type Fastener	Location	in	mm	in	mm
wood	single layer[2]—mechanically attached	nails	ceilings	7	178	7	178
			sidewalls	8	203	8	203
		screws	ceilings	12	305	12	305
			sidewalls	16[3]	406	12	305
		screws—with RC-1 channels	ceilings	12	305	12	305
			sidewalls	12	305	12	305
	single layer—adhesively attached	nails/screws	ceilings (perpendicular)	16" or 406 mm o.c. at ends, edges—1 field fastener per frame member at mid-width of board		same as for gypsum panels	
			ceilings (parallel)	16" or 406 mm o.c. along each edge and 24" or 610 mm o.c. along intermediate framing		same as for gypsum panels	
			walls (perpendicular)	16" or 406 mm o.c. at ends, edges—1 field fastener per frame member at mid-width of board		same as for gypsum panels	
	base layer of double layer—both layers mechanically attached	nails	ceilings	24	610	24	610
			sidewalls	24	610	24	610
		screws	ceilings	24	610	24	610
			sidewalls	24	610	24	610
		staples	ceilings	16	406	16	406
			sidewalls	16	406	16	406
	face layer of double layer—both layers mechanically attached	nails	ceilings	7	178	7	178
			sidewalls	8	203	8	203
		screws	ceilings	12	305	12	305
			sidewalls	16	406	12	305
	base layer of double layer—face layer adhesively attached	nails	ceilings	7	178	7	178
			sidewalls	8	203	8	203
		screws	ceilings	12	305	12	305
			sidewalls	16	406	12	305
		staples	ceilings	7	178	7	178
			sidewalls	7	178	7	178
	face layer of double layer—face layer adhesively attached	nails/screws	ceilings	16" or 406 mm o.c. at ends, edges—1 field fastener per frame member at mid-width of board		same as for gypsum panels	
			sidewalls	fasten top and[4] bottom as required		same as for[4] gypsum panels	

Maximum Fastener Spacing—Constructions Using Drywall, Gypsum Base and Similar Products[1]

				Maximum Fastener Spacing			
				Drywall Assemblies		Veneer Plaster Assemblies	
				SHEETROCK Brand Gypsum Panels or FIBEROCK Brand Abuse-Resistant Panels		IMPERIAL Brand Gypsum Base or FIBEROCK Brand Abuse-Resistant Panels	
Framing	Type const.	Type Fastener	Location	in	mm	in	mm
steel	single layer	screws	ceilings	12	305	12	305
			sidewalls	16[3]	406	12	305
	base layer of double layer— both layers mechanically attached	screws	ceilings	16	406	16	406
			sidewalls	24	610	24	610
	face layer of double layer— both layers mechanically attached	screws	ceilings	12	305	12	305
			sidewalls	16	406	12	305
	base layer of double layer— face layer adhesively attached	screws sidewalls	ceilings	12[4] 16[4]	305[5] 406[5]	12[5] 12[5]	305[5] 305[5]
	face layer of double layer— face layer adhesively attached	screws	ceilings	16" or 406 mm o.c. at ends and edges— 1 field fastener per frame member at mid-width of board		same as for gypsum panels	
			sidewalls	fasten top and[4] bottom as required		same as for[4] gypsum panels	

(1) Fastener spacings based on wood framing 16" o.c., steel framing 24" o.c. Spacings are not for fire-rated assemblies; see test listing for fastener spacing for specific fire-rated assemblies. (2) See page 113 for fastener spacing using adhesive. (3) Water-resistant board spacing is 12" o.c. (4) When board has been prebowed. For flat boards, use temporary nails or Type G screws called for in sheet or strip lamination section. (5) Spacing is 8" (203mm) o.c. at joint edges.

Double-Nailing Application (Walls and Ceilings)

In the double-nailing method for attaching gypsum board to wood framing, space the first nails 12" o.c. along the supports in the field of the board and around the perimeter spaced 7" o.c. for ceilings and 8" o.c. for walls. Drive second nails about 2" from first in field of board and make sure first nails are properly seated.

This application method helps prevent loose panels and resultant nail pops that may occur when boards are not applied correctly and drawn tightly to framing. This method will not reduce the incidence or severity of nail pops due to wood shrinkage.

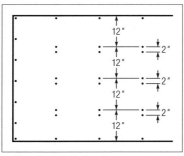

Double-nailing in field of board

Adhesive Application

In the adhesive method, a continuous bead of drywall stud or construction adhesive is applied to the face of wood framing. Adhesives should meet ASTM C557 standards. Gypsum boards are applied and attached with only a minimum number of supplementary fasteners compared to conventional fastening methods (see preceding table for fastener spacing required).

Spacing of framing members is the same as that used for conventional attachment.

Advantages of attachment with adhesives are:

1. Reduces up to 75% of the number of fasteners used, and consequent problems.

2. Stronger than conventional nail application—up to 100% more tensile strength, up to 50% more shear strength.

3. Unaffected by moisture, high or low temperature.

4. Fewer loose panels caused by improper fastening.

5. Bridges minor framing irregularities.

6. Will not stain or bleed through most finishes.

Adhesives are readily available in 29-oz. cartridges and applied with hand or powered-guns.

General Directions

The following recommendations will help explain the proper use of adhesives and the conditions which may affect the quality of the finished job.

1. Select the proper adhesive for specific job requirements. Read container directions carefully.

2. Make sure that all substrates are clean, sound and free from oil, dirt or contamination.

3. Exercise care regarding open flames when using flammable solvent adhesives in poorly ventilated areas.

4. Prevent freezing of adhesives.

5. Apply adhesives at temperatures between 50°F and 100°F except as directed by the manufacturer. Extremely high temperatures may cause solvent-base products to evaporate rapidly, shortening open time and damaging bond characteristics.

6. Close containers whenever adhesive is not in use. Evaporation (or escape) of vehicle can affect adhesive's wetting, bonding and application properties.

7. Do not exceed open time specified by manufacturer. Disregarding directions may cause poor bonding.

8. Follow manufacturer's recommendation on proper amounts of adhesive to be applied. Too small or too large a bead will lead to performance problems or waste.

9. Apply adhesive with proper tools and as recommended by the manufacturer.

Cartridge Preparation

Cut the cartridge tip in two different ways: for walls, make a chevron or 'V' cut in order to produce a round, uniform bead. The cut edge of the nozzle then rides along the stud easily.

For ceilings, use a single, angled slash across the nozzle. This gives a wipe-on effect on the ceiling joist to minimize dripping.

With a 3/8″ bead, approx. 3 to 5 gal. of adhesive will prepare framing for 1,000 sq. ft. of gypsum board. See adhesive manufacturer information for specific product coverage.

Proper nozzle opening and gun position (see sketches) are required to obtain the right size and shape of bead for satisfactory results. Initial height of bead over framing should be 3/8″ and of sufficient volume to provide 1/16″ thickness of adhesive over the entire support when compressed.

Apply adhesive in a continuous 3/8″ bead in center of attachment face (below) and to within 6″ of ends of all framing members. Where two gypsum boards meet on a framing member, apply two continuous 3/8″ beads to framing members at extreme edges of face, to insure adequate contact with paper on back of board. Do not apply adhesive to members such as bridging, diagonal bracing, etc. into which no supplemental fasteners will be driven. Adhesive is not required at inside corners, top and bottom plates or bracing and is not ordinarily used in closets.

Place gypsum boards shortly after adhesive bead is applied and fasten immediately, using proper screws or nails. After board has been fastened, impact by hand along each stud or joist to insure good contact at all points.

Where fasteners at vertical joints are objectionable (such as with pre-decorated panels), boards may be prebowed and adhesively attached with fasteners at top and bottom only.

Prebow boards by stacking face up with ends resting on nominal 2″ x 4″ lumber or other blocks and with center of boards resting on floor. Allow to remain overnight or until boards have a 2″ permanent bow. (Under very humid conditions, board may be too flexible to assume stiff bow needed to provide adequate pressure against framing.)

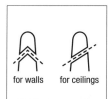
for walls / for ceilings

Nozzle cuts

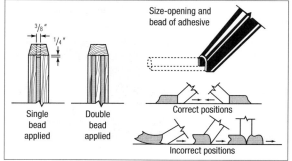

To insure good bond, no more adhesive should be applied than can be covered in 15 minutes. If adhesive is left exposed to the air for longer periods, the volatile materials will evaporate, causing surface hardness or skimming that prevents a full bond. Remove excess adhesive from board and other finished surfaces and tools with a solvent-base cleaner before adhesive dries. Follow solvent manufacturer's safety procedures.

Allow adhesive to dry at least 48 hours before treating drywall joints or applying veneer finishes.

3

Fastener Spacing Using Adhesive

Ceilings–Long Board Edges Across Framing Fasten board at each framing intersection and 16" o.c. at each end. Install one temporary field fastener per framing member required at midwidth of board.

Ceilings–Long Board Edges Parallel to Framing Space fasteners 16" o.c. along board edges and at each framing intersection on ends. Space fasteners 24" o.c. on intermediate supports.

Walls–Long Board Edges Across Framing Application Same as 'Ceilings'—above, except that no field fasteners are required.

Walls–Long Board Edges Parallel to Framing Same as 'Ceilings'—above, except that no fasteners are required on intermediate supports. Where fasteners at the vertical joints are objectionable, prebow the gypsum board and apply fasteners 16" o.c. only at the top and bottom of the board.

Note: If using vinyl foam tape as a temporary supplementary fastener, follow manufacturer's directions for additional fasteners required.

Gypsum Board Ceiling Installation

The size and weight of standard gypsum boards makes them somewhat cumbersome for ceiling installation, even with two people doing the work. Installation typically is made easier if the installers wear stilts or erect temporary platforms to position their heads and hands so that initial fasteners can be easily driven. Marking the panel face for anticipated joist locations also is helpful for some installers.

For reasons of safety, ease of adjustment and more secure panel attachment, use of aids such as panel lifters or T-jacks are recommended. Panel lifters are essentially scissor jacks that lift panels into position and enable accurate alignment with ceiling joists. They also can hold the panels firmly in place so that fasteners can secure the gypsum board directly to the framing. T-jacks are simply bars on adjustable poles. They do a good job of holding the panels in place once they are in position, but do not facilitate alignment in the same manner as panel lifters. Nevertheless, either equipment addition can make ceiling installation easier and safer. (See Chapter 13 and equipment manufacturer instructions for safety precautions.)

Wood Frame Single-Layer Application

This basic construction provides economical, quickly completed walls and ceilings with wood framing; also usable for wall furring. All types of gypsum boards, including predecorated vinyl-faced panels, may be used in the assembly. For measuring and cutting, perpendicular or parallel application, framing requirements and fastening, refer to sections found earlier in this chapter. For complete information on fire and sound-resistant assemblies, refer to USG publication, *Construction Selector,* SA-100.

114

Installation

Wood Studs and Joists Apply gypsum boards so that ends and edges occur over framing members, except when joints are at right angles to the framing members as in perpendicular application or when the end joints are to be back-blocked (see section following).

To minimize end joints, use boards of maximum practical lengths. When end joints occur, they should be staggered. Arrange joints on opposite sides of a partition so they occur on different studs.

Apply gypsum boards first to the ceiling and then to the walls. If foil-back gypsum boards are used, apply foil side against framing. Fit ends and edges closely but do not force boards into place. Cut boards accurately to fit around pipes and fixtures.

Fasteners are placed at least 3/8" from edges and ends.

Usually two mechanics are required to install long-length board on ceilings. Fasten boards with screws or nails starting from abutting edges and working toward the opposite ends and edges. While fasteners are being driven, the boards must be held in firm contact with the framing or joists. When single fasteners are used, attach boards to framing with screws or nails spaced as shown in the Fastener Spacing Table on pages 109-110. Drive fasteners at least 3/8" from edges and ends of board.

Apply gypsum boards to the sidewalls after ceilings are erected. Where long panel edges are across studs (perpendicular application), apply top wall board first, butted against ceiling. When long edges are parallel to studs (parallel application), span sidewall from ceiling to floor with a single length of board. For situations where ceiling height is greater than 8'1" but less than 9'1", SHEETROCK Brand Gypsum Panels—54" provide the added board width needed to avoid additional joint finishing. Use parallel application where ceiling height is over 9'1" or where this method reduces waste and joint treatment.

On sidewalls, space screws 16" o.c. max. for gypsum panels, 12" o.c. max. for gypsum base. Space nails 8" o.c. (If wall is fire-rated, follow specific design specifications.)

Wherever possible, use board of sufficient length to span wall areas. If joints occur near an opening, apply boards so vertical joints are centered, if possible, over opening. Keep vertical joints at least 8" away from external corners of windows, doors, or similar openings except at interior or exterior angles within the room or when control joints are used.

After installation, exert hand pressure against wall and ceiling surfaces to detect loose fasteners. If loose fasteners are found, drive them tight. Whenever nails or screws have punctured paper, hold board tight against framing and install another fastener properly, about 1-1/2" from screw or nailhead which punctured paper. Remove the faulty fasteners. When nailing boards to second side of a partition, check opposite side for nails loosened by pounding and drive them tight again.

With platform framing and sidewall expanses exceeding one floor in height, fur the gypsum boards over floor joists using RC-1 Resilient Channels (see detail).

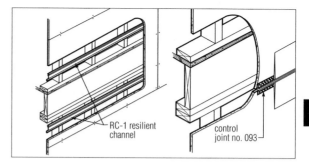

RC-1 resilient
channel

control
joint no. 093

As an alternate, install a horizontal control joint between gypsum
boards at the junction of the bottom of top plates and the first-floor
studs (see detail). Do not fasten gypsum boards to the side face of
joists or headers.

**Acoustical
Sealant
Application**

To prevent flanking and loss of the sound-control characteristics of
sound-rated partitions, SHEETROCK Brand Acoustical Sealant must be
used at all wood and steel floor runners (detailed below) to seal bottom
edge of gypsum board and at wall angles where dissimilar materials
meet. Caulking at possible leaks in all sound-rated systems is required
to obtain comparable sound reduction to that obtained in the laboratory.

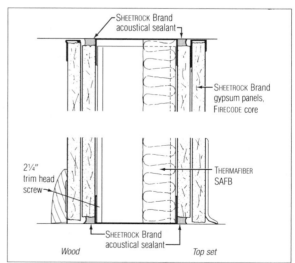

SHEETROCK Brand
acoustical sealant

SHEETROCK Brand
gypsum panels,
FIRECODE core

2¼"
trim head
screw

THERMAFIBER
SAFB

SHEETROCK Brand
acoustical sealant

Wood

Top set

**Back-Blocking
Application**

Back-Blocking is a system designed to minimize an inherent joint
deformation "ridging" in single-layer gypsum board construction,
which sometimes occurs under a combination of adverse job and
weather conditions. The Back-Blocking System, developed by USG,
enables floating of end joints between studs or joists and makes it easier to form a good surface over a twisted stud or joist. The system has
been widely used for years and produces outstanding results.

Back-Blocking consists of laminating cut-to-size pieces of gypsum board to the back surface of boards directly behind joints to provide resistance to ridging. To install the system, follow these steps:

a. Cut backing blocks 8″ wide and long enough to fit loosely between framing.

b. Install separate gypsum strips along sides of studs, set back enough to accommodate block thickness and keep face of blocks flush with or slightly behind stud faces.

c. Spread the surface of the blocks with SHEETROCK Brand Setting-Type (DURABOND) or Lightweight Setting-Type (EASY SAND) Joint Compound or SHEETROCK Brand Ready-Mixed Joint Compound—Taping or All Purpose. Apply the compound in beads 1/2″ high, 3/8″ wide at the base, spaced 1-1/2″ o.c.

d. Apply gypsum boards horizontally with long edges at right angles to joists. Place backing blocks along full length of edge and ends of board.

e. Immediately after all blocks are in place, erect the next board, butting ends loosely.

f. Upon fastening the abutting board, install a block and bracing as shown in the cross-section illustration. This method forms a taper that remains after bracing strips are removed.

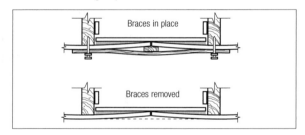

Double-Layer Adhesive Lamination

In adhesive application, face-layer gypsum boards or predecorated SHEETROCK Brand Vinyl-Faced Gypsum Panels are job-laminated to a base layer of gypsum board or interior masonry partitions.

In multilayer adhesive systems, the base layer must be attached with the same fastener, fastener spacing, and framing spacing as for a single-layer assembly of the same thickness as the base layer.

In fire-rated assemblies, permanent fasteners and the type of board used must be the same as in the particular tested assembly (see specific design for complete description).

Application of the base layer may have long edges either parallel or perpendicular to the framing. Plan the layout of the face layer so that all joints are offset a minimum of 10″ from parallel base-layer joints. It is preferable to apply the face layer perpendicular to the base layer. At inside vertical angles, only the overlapping base layer should be attached to the framing to provide a floating corner. Omit all face-layer fasteners within 8″ of vertical angles.

Application — Laminating Adhesive

Apply laminating adhesive in strips to center and along both edges of face layer board. Apply strips with a notched metal spreader having four 1/4"x1/4" minimum notches spaced max. of 2" o.c. Position face layer against base layer; fasten at top and bottom (vertical application) as required. For laminated ceilings, space fasteners 16" o.c. along edges and ends, with one permanent field fastener per framing member installed at mid-width of board. Press board into place with firm pressure to insure bond; reimpact within 24 hr. if necessary.

3

Application — Joint Compound (used as laminating adhesive)

All SHEETROCK Brand Setting-Type (DURABOND) and Lightweight Setting-Type (EASY SAND) Joint Compounds and SHEETROCK Brand Ready-Mixed Joint Compounds—All Purpose and Taping may be used for two methods of lamination: sheet lamination and strip lamination.

When using SHEETROCK Brand Setting-Type Compounds, supplemental or temporary fasteners or supports are required until compound has hardened (minimum three hours depending on which type of compound is used). Because the compound is of heavy consistency, it provides a leveling action not obtainable with thinner-bodied adhesives. When using SHEETROCK Brand Ready-Mixed Joint Compounds for laminating, temporary nailing or permanent Type G Screws are needed until the compound is dry (usually overnight). In cold weather, provide heat to keep compound from freezing until adhesive is dry.

Corner detail

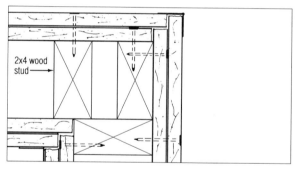

2x4 wood stud

Mixing — SHEETROCK Brand Setting-Type Compounds

1. Mix in a clean plastic container.

2. Use only clean, potable water.

3. Mix according to bag directions, making sure compound is uniformly damp.

4. Do not contaminate with previously mixed SHEETROCK Brand Setting-Type Joint Compound (DURABOND) or Lightweight Setting-Type (EASY SAND) Joint Compound or other compounds or dirty water as it will affect the setting time.

5. Mix only as much compound as can be used within the time period indicated on the bag— usually one hour for SHEETROCK Brand Setting-Type (DURABOND) or Lightweight Setting-Type (EASY SAND) 90 and two hours for 210, for example.

6. The addition of extra water (retempering) will not prevent set or increase working time with SHEETROCK Brand Setting-Type Joint Compounds.

In sheet lamination (right), notched spreader is used to spread compound over entire back surface of face-layer board. In strip lamination of vertical sidewall boards (above), adhesive can be applied to either base surface or face panel. Mechanical tool used is Ames Laminating Spreader.

Mixing— SHEETROCK Brand Ready-Mixed Compounds

Use the compound at package consistency for best leveling action. If a thinner adhesive is desired, add cool water in half-pint increments to avoid overthinning. Remix lightly with a potato masher-type mixer and test apply after each water addition. If compound becomes too thin, add thicker compound from another container and remix.

See Chapter 13, Safety Considerations, Material Handling, for more information on the safe use of joint compounds.

On all laminated ceilings, face layer must be permanently attached with fasteners spaced 16″ o.c. max. at ends and edges, plus one field fastener in each frame member at midwidth of board. Nails must penetrate wood framing a minimum of 3/4″. Screws must penetrate steel framing a minimum of 3/8″

On walls, permanently attach top and bottom of the face layer with fasteners driven 24″ o.c. max. (except prebowed boards). Provide temporary support fasteners, or Type G Screws 24″ o.c. max. in the field of the board.

1. **Temporary Nailing** Use double-headed scaffold nails driven through wood or gypsum board scraps so that nail penetrates framing a minimum of 3/4″.

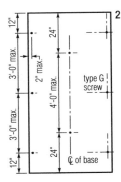

2. **Type G Screws** Permanently attach face layer with screws driven into base layer to avoid framing. Apply compound just prior to face board erection to prevent wetting of base layer that would reduce holding power of screws. Press face layer firmly against base layer when driving screw. Compound should be thin enough to spread as screw is driven. Type G Screws should not be used with base-layer boards less than 1/2″ thick.

Strip Lamination (vertical face layer, sidewalls only) This method is often preferred because it requires less compound and improves sound attenuation. Apply strips (four beads, each 3/8″ wide by 1/2″ high spaced 1-1/2″ o.c.) 24″ o.c. max. Place permanent fasteners 24″ o.c. max. at each end of face layer. Drive Type G Screws as shown in diagram.

Application —
Liquid Contact
Adhesive

Apply liquid contact adhesive according to manufacturer's directions. Use a short nap paint roller to cover both contact surfaces. Let adhesive air dry to the touch. Apply boards as soon as possible after drying occurs. On walls, fasten 16″ o.c. at top and bottom (vertical application) as required. In ceiling lamination, apply permanent supplementary fasteners at each corner of board, and along edges spaced max. 48″ o.c. Press board into place with firm pressure to ensure bond.

Resilient Board
Application

Gypsum Board —
Sidewalls

Apply gypsum boards perpendicular to framing with long dimension of boards parallel to resilient channels. (Assure that resilient channels are oriented with attachment flange down except for baseboard channel which should be oriented with attachment flange up for easier board attachment.) To avoid compromising sound insulation, lift panels off floor and assure 1/8″ relief around perimeter to be filled later with SHEETROCK Brand Acoustical Sealant. Attach boards with 1″ TYPE S screws spaced 12″ o.c. along channels. Center horizontal abutting edges of boards over screw flange of channel, and screw-attach. Take particular care that these screws do not penetrate the resilient channels and enter studs since this "grounding" will nullify the resilient properties of the channels. For vertical applications, butt joints should be centered over the RC-1 Channels. Where fire rating is required, board must be applied with long dimension vertical.

For two-layer application of gypsum board, apply base layer vertically and attach to resilient channels with 1″ TYPE S screws spaced 24″ o.c. Apply face layer with long dimension at right angles to long edges of base layer and fasten with TYPE S screws spaced 16″ o.c., and of sufficient length to penetrate channels 3/8″ min.

Gypsum Board —
Ceilings

Single Layer Apply boards of maximum practical length with long dimension at right angles to resilient channels and end joints staggered. To avoid compromising sound insulation, assure 1/8″ relief around perimeter to be filled later with SHEETROCK Brand Acoustical Sealant. End joints may occur over resilient channels or midway between channels with joint floated and back-blocked with sections of RC-1 Channels. Fit ends and edges closely, but not forced together. Fasten boards to channels with 1″ TYPE S screws spaced 12″ o.c. in field of boards and along abutting ends. Cut boards neatly and provide support around cutouts and openings.

Two-Plane Assembly Provides two layers of gypsum panels for a specific fire-endurance rating, with resilient channel between layers. Base layer of gypsum board is applied with long edges across joists and end joints staggered. Attach resilient channels perpendicular to framing with 1-7/8″ TYPE S screws through the base layer. Face layer of gypsum boards is applied in the same manner as for single layer but at right angles to base layer. Fasten boards to resilient channels with 1″ TYPE S Screws. (See specific fire-rated assembly design for board type, fastener requirements and fastener spacing.)

Double Layer Assembly Provides two layers of gypsum panels with resilient channel between panels and framing. RC-1 Channel is applied 16″ o.c. perpendicular to joists. Base layer of 5/8″ gypsum boards is attached to RC-1 Channel with 1″ TYPE S screws. Face layer is attached at right angles to base layer. For added sound control and fire protection, install 3″ THERMAFIBER SAFB in cavity. (See specific fire-rated assembly design for board type, fastener requirements and fastener spacing.)

Steel Frame Single-Layer Partition Application

This noncombustible assembly has won wide acceptance because of its sound attenuation, low cost, speed of erection and light weight—only 4 to 6 lb./ft.[2]. Partitions are ideal for space division within units. Ceilings, both suspended and furred, conceal overhead structural and mechanical elements and provide a surface ready for either final decoration or adhesively applied acoustical tile.

Gypsum Board Erection

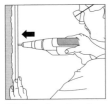

With long edges of panels applied parallel to steel framing, workman places screws at 16″o.c. intervals for drywall, 12″ o.c. for gypsum base.

Apply gypsum boards with long dimension parallel or perpendicular to framing. (See Frame Spacing Tables on page 75 for limitations.) Use maximum practical lengths to minimize end joints. Position boards so all abutting ends and edges (except edges with perpendicular application) will be located in center of stud flanges. Plan direction of board installation so that lead edge or end of board is attached to open end of stud flange first. Be certain that joints are neatly fitted and staggered on opposite sides of the partition so they occur on different studs. Cut boards to fit neatly around all outlets and switch boxes.

For single-layer application, fasten boards to supports with 1″ TYPE S screws spaced according to Fastener Spacing Table. Stagger screws on abutting edges or ends.

For fire-rated construction, apply gypsum boards and fasten as specified in the fire-tested assembly (see specific design).

Steel Frame Double-Layer Partition Application

Double-layer construction using steel studs offers some of the best performances in both fire and sound resistance—up to 2-hr. fire ratings and 55 STC sound rating. These economical, lightweight partitions are adaptable as party walls or corridor walls in virtually every type of new construction.

In these assemblies a face layer of gypsum board is job-laminated to the base layer or screw-attached through the base-layer gypsum board to steel studs. The installation of steel studs and runners is the same as for single-layer application.

Base-Layer Erection

Apply gypsum board with long dimension parallel to studs. Position board so that abutting edges will be located in the center of stud flanges. Be certain joints are neatly fitted and staggered on opposite sides of partition so they occur on different studs. For double-layer screw attachment (both layers screw-attached), fasten panels to studs with TYPE S screws spaced 24″ o.c. Use 1″ screws for 1/2″ and 5/8″ thick board. For double-layer adhesively laminated construction, fasten board with 1″ screws spaced 8″ o.c. at joint edges and 12″ o.c. in field for panels and gypsum base. For fire-rated construction, fasten board as specified in the fire-tested design being erected (see specific design).

Face-Layer Erection

Apply gypsum board with long dimension parallel to studs. Position board so abutting edges will be located in center of stud flanges. Stagger joints from those in base layer and on opposite sides of partition. For double-layer screw attachment (both layers screw-attached), fasten face layer to studs with TYPE S screws spaced 16" o.c. for gypsum panels, 12" o.c. for gypsum base. Use 1-5/8" screws for 1/2" and 5/8" thick board. (As a rule of thumb, screws should be a min. 3/8" longer than the total thickness of material to be attached to steel studs.) For double-layer laminated construction, attach face layer using adhesive lamination described earlier in this chapter. For fire-rated construction, fasten gypsum boards with screws as specified in the fire-tested design (see specific design).

Steel Frame— Multilayer Application

Multilayer construction, using steel studs, 1-1/2" or greater THERMAFIBER SAFB Insulation and 1/2" or 5/8" SHEETROCK Brand Gypsum Panels, FIRECODE C Core, SHEETROCK Brand Abuse Resistant Gypsum Panels, SHEETROCK Brand Gypsum Panels, ULTRACODE Core or 1/2" IMPERIAL Brand Gypsum Base, FIRECODE C Core, offers 3 and 4-hour fire ratings and up to 65 STC sound rating. These superior assemblies are low cost, much lighter weight and thinner than concrete block partitions offering equivalent performance.

3-Layer Application

Apply gypsum panels vertically with long dimension parallel to studs (except face layer may be applied horizontally across studs). Position base so abutting edges are located in center of stud flanges. Stagger joints from those in adjacent layers and on opposite sides of the partition.

Fasten first layer to studs with 1" TYPE S screws spaced 48" o.c. Fasten second layer to studs with 1-5/8" TYPE S screws spaced 48" o.c. Fasten face layer to studs with 2-1/4" TYPE S screws spaced 12" o.c. Horizontally applied face layer requires 1" Type G screws in base between studs and 1-1/2" from horizontal joints.

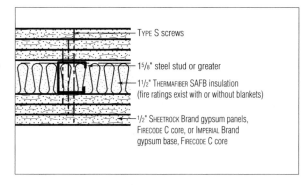

TYPE S screws

1⁵/₈" steel stud or greater

1¹/₂" THERMAFIBER SAFB insulation
(fire ratings exist with or without blankets)

¹/₂" SHEETROCK Brand gypsum panels,
FIRECODE C core, or IMPERIAL Brand
gypsum base, FIRECODE C core

4-layer Application

Apply gypsum boards vertically with long dimension parallel to studs (except face layer may be applied horizontally across studs). Position base so abutting edges are located in center of stud flanges. Stagger joints from those in adjacent layers and on opposite sides of the partition.

Fasten first layer to studs with 1″ Type S screws spaced 48″ o.c. Fasten second layer to studs with 1-5/8″ Type S screws spaced 48″ o.c. Fasten third layer to studs with 2-1/4″ Type S screws spaced 12″ o.c. Fasten fourth layer to studs with 2-5/8″ screws spaced 12″ o.c. Horizontally applied face layer requires 1-1/2″ Type G screws in base between studs and 1″ from horizontal joints.

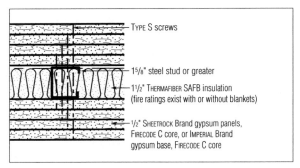

Type S screws

1⁵/₈″ steel stud or greater

1¹/₂″ Thermafiber SAFB insulation (fire ratings exist with or without blankets)

¹/₂″ Sheetrock Brand gypsum panels, Firecode C core, or Imperial Brand gypsum base, Firecode C core

Furred Framing Board Application

Apply gypsum board of maximum practical length with long dimension at right angles to furring channel. Center end joints over channel web; fit joints neatly and accurately; stagger end joints from those in adjacent rows of board. Fasten boards to furring channels with Type S screws spaced according to Fastener Spacing Table. Use 1″ screw length for 1/2″ or 5/8″ thick boards.

Masonry Single-Layer Direct Application

Gypsum boards adhesively applied directly to interior, above-grade monolithic concrete or unit masonry are laminated using a Sheetrock Brand Setting-Type (Durabond) or Sheetrock Brand Lightweight Setting-Type (Easy Sand) Joint Compound or Sheetrock Brand Ready-Mixed Joint Compound (All Purpose or Taping) or an appropriate subfloor plywood construction adhesive. Either regular or predecorated Sheetrock Brand Vinyl-Faced Gypsum Panels may be applied. Use the Metal Furring Channels or Z-Furring Channels system for gypsum board application to interior of exterior and below-grade wall surfaces. If cavity walls have been erected inside of exterior walls and have a continuous (1″ min.) clear air space, and the masonry wall surface is well dampproofed, the wall surfaces may be considered here as an interior wall surface.

Note: Gypsum panels should not be installed where they will be in continuous contact with moisture.

Preparation

Mortar joints on surface of unit masonry to which gypsum boards are to be bonded should be cut flush with the masonry to provide a level surface. The wall surface should be plumb and true. Grind off rough or protruding areas before lamination is started. Fill pockets or holes greater than 4″ in diameter and 1/8″ deep with grout, mortar, or SHEETROCK Brand Setting-Type (DURABOND) or SHEETROCK Brand Lightweight Setting-Type (EASY SAND) Joint Compound. Allow to dry before laminating.

The masonry surface must have all form oils, grease and other release agents removed. It must be dry and free of dust, loose particles and efflorescence. If masonry has been coated or painted, test by attaching a small section of board to surface. Pull from surface after allowing sufficient time for adhesive to bond. If attachment fails at bond line to masonry, the surface coating must be removed or a furring system used.

If wood base is used, attach a wood nailer to the wall with mechanical fasteners before laminating gypsum boards. Nailer should be equal to the board thickness and at least 1-1/2″ high (or 3/4″ less than wood base height).

Board Installation With Adhesive

Cut face boards to allow continuous clearance (1/8″ to 1/4″) at floor. Apply SHEETROCK Brand Setting-Type (DURABOND) or SHEETROCK Brand Lightweight Setting-Type (EASY SAND) Joint Compound, SHEETROCK Brand Ready-Mixed Joint Compound—All Purpose or Taping at center and near each board edge in strips consisting of 4 beads, 3/8″ wide by 1/2″ high and spaced 1-1/2″ to 2″ o.c. Position boards vertically over wall surface, press into place and provide temporary support until adhesive is hardened.

Trim and Finishing

Upon mounting the board, walls and ceilings are ready for trims and corner beads in preparation for finishing. Information regarding correct application of beads and trims is covered in Chapter 5. See page 169.

Predecorated Panel Application

The use of predecorated gypsum panels takes full advantage of the real economy of fire-resistant gypsum panels in providing highly serviceable, quickly installed decorative walls. With SHEETROCK Brand Vinyl-Faced Gypsum Panels, walls resist stains and minor scuffs, are readily washable and colorfast. They also resist dimensional change. (See Appendix for hygrometric and thermal coefficients.)

SHEETROCK Brand Vinyl-Faced Gypsum Panels are applied vertically to the walls so that ends occur at floor and ceiling lines. The beveled edges form an attractive joint not requiring joint treatment. Panels are not practical as a ceiling finish, as end joints are difficult to conceal. They can be used with wood or steel studs in single- or double-layer application in new construction or over plaster or gypsum panel surfaces in remodeling; may also be applied to furring attached to masonry. Not recommended for use over foil-back panels in exterior walls. For additional information, fire-rated construction and technical data, see USG technical folders WB-1330 and SA-928.

Panel Installation

When installing patterns other than one-color patterns, place panels against wall, inverting alternate panels, and rearrange to obtain the best match in pattern and tone; there will be a slight variation from panel to panel. Number backs of panels for proper installation sequence. Panels used in the same area should be of the same lot number for best color match (lot numbers are imprinted on panel backs).

Apply panels vertically. Position less-than-full-width panels with cut edge at corner where the raw edge can be overlapped by the abutting panel or covered with a corner mould. Use USG Color-Matched Nails for nail-on application. Drive nails with plastic-headed hammer or rawhide mallet. Space 1-3/8″ nails at least 3/8″ from ends and edges, 8″ o.c.

Cut SHEETROCK Brand Vinyl-Faced Panels with a sharp knife. Cut through vinyl film into core; then snap board and cut back paper.

SHEETROCK Brand Mouldings in matching colors and patterns are available to finish edges and conceal fasteners in Vinyl-Faced Panel installations.

Prebowing Where fasteners at the vertical joints are objectionable, panels may be prebowed, adhesively applied and fastened at top and bottom only. Prebow by stacking panels face up with ends resting on 2" x 4" lumber on edge or gypsum panel slitters and center of panel resting on floor. Allow to remain overnight or until panels show at least a 2" permanent bow. During high humidity, it may be necessary to elevate ends as much as 8" to achieve desired permanent bow.

Adhesives Generally, most water-based adhesives and some solvent-based adhesives may be used to install vinyl-covered SHEETROCK Brand Vinyl-Faced Panels. However, many solvent-based adhesives may not be compatible and could result in delamination and/or discoloration of the vinyl surface. It is recommended that 24 hours before installation, a small piece of SHEETROCK Brand Vinyl-Faced Gypsum Panel be test-laminated to the actual framing or backing with the actual adhesive. If results are acceptable after 24 hours, the job can begin. Also, check the adhesive manufacturer's recommendations before use with vinyl-covered panels.

The following commercially available adhesives may be used for applying SHEETROCK Brand Vinyl-Faced Gypsum Panels in non-fire rated assemblies: drywall stud adhesive (meeting ASTM C557) for application to wood or steel studs; laminating adhesive for bonding panels to monolithic concrete, concrete block, wood and mineral-fiber sound deadening board, polystyrene and urethane rigid-foam insulation and most other wall surfaces; contact adhesive for laminating SHEETROCK Brand Vinyl-Faced Panels to gypsum base-layer panels. Vinyl foam

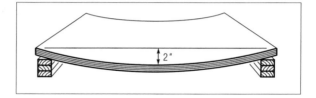

tape may be used with adhesive for supplemental attachment (in lieu of prebowing or temporary shoring) until permanent adhesive attains ultimate strength.

A SHEETROCK Brand Setting-Type (DURABOND) or SHEETROCK Brand Lightweight Setting-Type (EASY SAND) Joint Compound or SHEETROCK Brand Ready-Mixed Joint Compound-All Purpose or Taping and mechanical fasteners are required for fire-rated construction (see page 116, "Double Layer Adhesive Application").

Adhesive Application to Wood or Steel Studs Apply 8"-long strip of vinyl foam tape to face of each stud, positioned at midpoint of studs up to 8' long, at third-points on studs up to 12' long and quarter-points on studs over 12'. Where no mechanical fasteners are to be used at top or bottom of stud, apply an 8"-long strip of tape. Apply a continuous 3/8" bead of drywall stud adhesive to the entire face of studs between vinyl foam tape. Immediately apply SHEETROCK Brand Vinyl-Faced Gypsum Panels vertically and apply sufficient pressure to ensure complete contact with both tape and adhesive.

Adhesive Application to Base Layer of Gypsum Panels Apply liquid contact adhesive to back of SHEETROCK Brand Vinyl-Faced Panels and face of base layer according to manufacturer's directions. Allow adhesive to air dry, then bring panels in contact. Impact entire surface to assure complete contact.

Adhesive Application to Base Layer of Masonry, Gypsum Board or Mineral Fiber Board For interior masonry walls and gypsum board, apply continuous strips of vinyl foam tape to entire width of SHEETROCK Brand Vinyl-Faced Panel back at midpoint and 3/8" from each end. Spread laminating adhesive over entire area of panels between tape using notched metal spreader with 1/4" x 1/4" notches spaced 2" o.c. Position panel and immediately apply sufficient pressure to assure complete contact over entire surface. (Mechanical fasteners may be substituted for tape at ends of panels.)

For application of SHEETROCK Brand Vinyl-Faced Gypsum Panels to wood or mineral board, prebow panels and apply laminating adhesive over entire back surface. Use mechanical fasteners at top and bottom of panel.

Moulding Installation

Rigid vinyl trim and mouldings are available in solid and matching colors to finish SHEETROCK Brand Vinyl-Faced Gypsum Panel installations. Refer to page 17 for product description and colors available.

Installation

General Store mouldings at room temperature for 24 hr. before installation. Start installation from corner or door. Be sure that starting points are plumb and level. Fasten mouldings with flat-head wire nails, staples or drywall screws 12" o.c. Fasten snap-on mouldings with nails or screws driven through holes in retainer. Use a fine-toothed hacksaw to cut mouldings. For mitering, use the same procedures as with wood moulding. Cut mouldings 1/16" short for a loose fit to allow for thermal expansion; never force mouldings into place.

RP-2 and RPV-2 Inside Corner Install first panel so that vertical edge aligns with framing. Apply moulding over first panel, fastening exposed flange to framing. Insert opposite panel into moulding.

RP-4 and RPV-4 End Cap Align and fasten end cap to framing. Insert panel into moulding and apply panel to wall.

RP-5 and RPV-5 Snap-on Corner Apply panels, then place retainer strip over joint and fasten with nails or screws through holes provided. Snap corner face over retainer strip.

RP-7 and RPV-7 Snap-on Batten Apply panels, then place retainer strip over joint and fasten with nails or screws through holes provided. Snap batten face over retainer strip.

RP-46 and RPV-46 Ceiling Drive-in Trim Use only with steel stud partitions. Install after panels are applied. Insert grooved flange between runner and ceiling; tap trim into place. (Not recommended where perimeter must be acoustically sealed.)

Painting If mouldings other than SHEETROCK Brand Vinyl-Faced Mouldings are used, they should be decorated prior to application over panels. Avoid applying masking tape to mouldings or predecorated panels when decorating.

RP-series mouldings should be used when painting is required. A good quality alkyd enamel or acrylic latex paint is recommended. Apply according to manufacturer's directions.

SHEETROCK Vinyl Mouldings

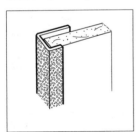

RP-4, RPV-4 End Cap

RP-46, RPV-46 Ceiling Drive-in Trim

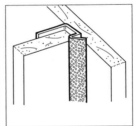

RP-2, RPV-2 Inside Corner

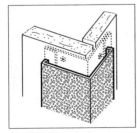

RP-5, RPV-5 Snap-On Corner

RP-7, RPV-7 Snap-On Batten

Water-Resistant Gypsum Panel Application

SHEETROCK Brand Gypsum Panels, Water Resistant, Water Resistant FIRECODE Type X and Water Resistant FIRECODE C Core, are specially designed to minimize moisture problems and serve as a base for the adhesive application of ceramic tile. For use in new construction in wet areas such as bathrooms, powder rooms, kitchens and utility rooms. They install quickly and easily to wood or steel framing or furring using standard attachment methods. Minimum framing spacing for ceiling framing is 12" o.c. for 1/2" water-resistant board and 16" o.c. for 5/8" water-resistant board. Also do not use for single-layer resilient attachment where tile is to be applied.

Exposed edges and joints in areas to be tiled are treated with a coat of thinned down ceramic tile mastic or an approved waterproof flexible sealant. Joints are treated with SHEETROCK Brand Setting-Type (DURABOND 45 or 90) or SHEETROCK Brand Lightweight Setting-Type (EASY SAND 45 or 90) Joint Compound and SHEETROCK Brand Joint Tape.

Where water resistant panels are used in remodeling, old wall surfaces must be removed and water resistant panels applied to exposed studs as in new construction. Refer to page 7 for other limitations.

Installation **Framing** Check alignment of framing. If necessary, fur out studs around shower receptor so that inside face of lip of fixture will be flush with gypsum panel face.

Install appropriate blocking, headers, or supports for tub and other plumbing fixtures, and to receive soap dishes, grab bars, towel racks or similar items. SHEETROCK Brand Gypsum Panels, Water Resistant are designed for framing 16" o.c. but not more than 24" o.c. When framing is spaced more than 16" o.c., or when ceramic tile more than 5/16" thick will be used, install suitable blocking between studs. Place blocking approx. 1" above top of tub or receptor and at midpoint between base and ceiling. Blocking is not required on studs spaced 16" o.c. or less. Vapor retarders must not be installed between water resistant panels and framing.

Store panels in an enclosed shelter and protect from exposure to the elements.

Panels are not intended for use in areas subject to constant moisture, such as interior swimming pools, gang showers and commercial food processing areas. DUROCK Cement Board is recommended for such purposes. See Chapter 4.

Receptors Install receptors before panels are erected. Shower pans, or receptors, should have an upstanding lip or flange at least 1" higher than the water dam or threshold at the entry to the shower.

Gypsum Panels After tub, shower pan or receptor is installed, place temporary 1/4" spacer strips around lip of fixture. Cut panels to required sizes and make necessary cut-outs. Before installing panels, apply thinned ceramic tile mastic to all cut or exposed panel edges at utility holes, joints and intersections.

Install panels perpendicular to studs with paper-bound edge abutting top of spacer strip. Fasten panels with nails 8″ o.c. max., or screws 12″ o.c. max. Where ceramic tile more than 5/16″ thick will be used, space nails 4″ o.c. max. and screws 8″ o.c. max.

For tile 5/16″ thick or less, panels may be installed with stud adhesive (meeting ASTM C557) to wood framing. Apply 3/8″ bead to stud faces—two beads on studs where panels join. Do not apply adhesive to blocking where no fasteners will be used. Position panel and drive nails or screws at 16″ intervals around perimeter, 3/8″ from edges.

For double-layer applications, both face and base layer must consist of SHEETROCK Brand Gypsum Panels, Water Resistant.

In areas to be tiled, treat all fastener heads with SHEETROCK Brand Setting-Type (DURABOND 45 or 90) or Lightweight Setting-Type (EASY SAND 45 or 90) Joint Compound. Fill tapered edges in gypsum panel completely with compound, embed SHEETROCK Brand Joint Tape firmly, and wipe off excess compound. When hardened, apply a second or skim coat over the taping coat, being careful not to crown the joint or to leave excess compound on panel (some setting-type compounds are difficult to sand and remove when dry). For butt joints and interior angles, embed SHEETROCK Brand Joint Tape with SHEETROCK Brand Setting-Type (DURABOND 45 or 90) or SHEETROCK Brand Lightweight Setting-Type (EASY SAND 45 or 90) Joint Compound without crowning the joints. A fill coat is not necessary. Spot fastener heads at least once with SHEETROCK Brand Setting-Type (DURABOND) or SHEETROCK Brand Lightweight Setting-Type (EASY SAND) Compound.

Fill and seal all openings around pipes, fittings and fixtures with a coat of thinned-down ceramic tile mastic or an approved waterproof flexible sealant. To thin water-based mastic, add one-half pint of water per quart of mastic to make a paint-like viscosity. With a brush, apply the thinned compound onto the raw gypsum panel core at cut-outs. Allow areas to dry thoroughly prior to application of tile. Before compound dries, wipe excess material from surface of gypsum panels. Remove spacer strips but do not seal gap at bottom edge of panels. Install tile down to top edge of shower floor or tub and overlapping lip or return of tub or receptor.

For areas not to be tiled, embed tape with SHEETROCK Brand Setting-Type (DURABOND 45 or 90) or SHEETROCK Brand Lightweight Setting-Type (EASY SAND 45 or 90) Joint Compound in the conventional manner. Finish with at least two coats of a USG joint compound to provide a treated surface for painting and wallpapering.

Fill all tile joints with grout. Apply nonsetting caulking compound, such as tub caulk, between wall surfacing material and shower floor, curb or tub rim. Weeps may be required in some applications.

Where SHEETROCK Brand Gypsum Panels, Water Resistant, are to be painted with a gloss enamel and subject to critical lighting, it is recommended that the panel surface be skim coated with a conventional joint compound prior to painting.

Single-Layer application

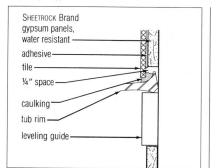

SHEETROCK Brand
gypsum panels,
water resistant
adhesive
tile
¼" space

caulking
tub rim

leveling guide

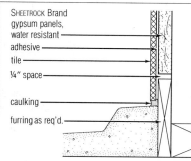

SHEETROCK Brand
gypsum panels,
water resistant
adhesive
tile
¼" space

caulking

furring as req'd.

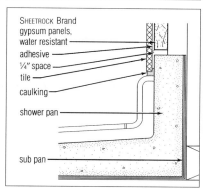

SHEETROCK Brand
gypsum panels,
water resistant
adhesive
¼" space
tile
caulking

shower pan

sub pan

Double-Layer application

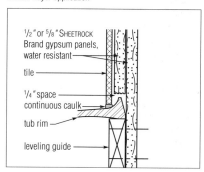

¹/₂" or ⁵/₈" SHEETROCK
Brand gypsum panels,
water resistant
tile
¼" space
continuous caulk
tub rim

leveling guide

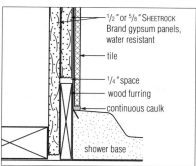

¹/₂" or ⁵/₈" SHEETROCK
Brand gypsum panels,
water resistant
tile
¼" space
wood furring
continuous caulk

shower base

Note that ceiling framing must be 12″ o.c. Panels should not be installed over a vapor retarder or on a wall acting as a vapor retarder.

FIBEROCK Brand Panels, Water Resistant (with AQUA-TOUGH) are now available for water-resistant applications. However, note that installation of FIBEROCK Brand products sometimes varies from the procedures used to install conventional drywall panels and gypsum base. See the most current literature on FIBEROCK Brand Panels for the latest installation information.

3

Gypsum Sheathing Application

Paper-faced gypsum sheathing is not intended for use where the subsequent building materials (such as expanded polystyrene foam insulation) are to be adhesively applied with no mechanical fasteners. Sheathing should be covered with a continuous water barrier over its face. Refer to page 14 for other limitations.

Installation
SHEETROCK **Brand Gypsum Sheathing** Apply 1/2″ x 2′ x 8′ SHEETROCK Brand Gypsum Sheathing horizontally with face side out (paper on back is lapped at edges). With tongue-and-groove edge, place tongue edge up to prevent water penetration at joints. Use diagonal bracing where necessary. Space 1-3/4″ 11-ga. galvanized nails 8″ o.c. at each stud.

Apply 4′ x 8′ or 9′ (1/2″ or 5/8″) square-edge SHEETROCK Brand Gypsum Sheathing vertically with face side out. Space nails 8″ o.c. on framing members. Sheathing may also be installed horizontally.

For staple or screw application, use same fastener spacing as for nails. Drive staples parallel to long dimension of framing, heads flush with sheathing surface but not breaking face paper.

GYP-LAP **Gypsum Sheathing** Apply 2′-wide GYP-LAP Gypsum Sheathing horizontally with tongue edge up, or 4′ wide sheathing vertically, to braced framing. Use 11-ga. galvanized roofing nails 1-3/4″ long, spaced 8″ o. c.

SHEETROCK **Brand Triple-Sealed Gypsum Sheathing** Apply 4′-wide SHEETROCK Brand Gypsum Sheathing vertically to braced framing. Use 11-ga. galvanized roofing nails 1-3/4″ long, spaced 8″ o.c.

The sheathing products above are not designed to perform as shear or racking braces. Install diagonal corner braces, or equal, at all external corners as required by applicable code.

Refer to USG folder GS-116 for complete data on gypsum sheathing. Refer to separate Technical Folder SA-923 for sheathing application to exterior steel framing systems.

FIBEROCK Brand Sheathing with AQUA-TOUGH is now available for exterior applications. However, note that installation of FIBEROCK Brand products sometimes varies from the procedures used to install conventional drywall panels and gypsum base. See the most current literature on FIBEROCK Brand Panels for the latest installation information.

Interior Gypsum Ceiling Panels Application

1/2″ SHEETROCK Brand Interior Gypsum Ceiling Panels, Sag-Resistant, are specially formulated to support water-based spray texture paints and overlaid insulation with the same sag resistance as regular 5/8″ gypsum board. Can be substituted for regular 1/2″ board in other applications, such as on sidewalls, reducing waste and lowering in-place cost. Ideal for new construction or renovation over wood or steel framing.

Handling Store and handle 1/2″ SHEETROCK Brand Interior Gypsum Ceiling Panels, Sag-Resistant, in the same manner as other gypsum board. Stack flat and store under cover.

Installation Apply 1/2″ Sheetrock Brand Interior Gypsum Ceiling Panels, Sag-Resistant, to ceilings before applying gypsum boards to walls. Joists must be spaced 24″ o.c. or less. Board may be cut by scoring and snapping in the same manner as other gypsum board.

Sheetrock Brand Interior Ceiling Panel, Sag-Resistant, is designed for parallel or perpendicular application to framing components spaced up to 24″ o.c. with a maximum 2.2 lb./ft.² insulation loading and wet texturing for ceiling application. For single-layer wood-framed ceilings, nails are spaced 7″ o.c.; 1-1/4″ Type W screws are placed 12″ o.c. Adhesive/nail-on fastening improves bond strength and reduces face nailing. Finish with a USG joint treatment system.

In new construction or renovation applications, steel furring channels can be used (RC-1 Resilient Channels or metal furring channels spaced a maximum of 24″ o.c., fastened to bottom of joists). For complete information on application to steel framing, consult publication SA923, *Drywall/Steel Framed Systems.*

Caution: Careful attention should be paid to framing construction and alignment. Problems will "telegraph" through the board if the framing is not true. Excessively long drying times may also cause problems with the ceiling finish, such as joint banding and staining. Ensure proper ventilation to remove excess moisture during and after finishing. Supplemental heat or dehumidification may be required.

Surface Preparation Before texturing, apply a high-quality, undiluted latex or alkyd primer/sealer. Follow manufacturer's directions for application.

Sagging To prevent objectionable sag in new gypsum panel ceilings, the weight of overlaid unsupported insulation should not exceed 1.3 psf for 1/2″ thick panels with frame spacing 24″ o.c.; 2.2 psf for 1/2″ panels with frame spacing 16″ o.c. (or 1/2″ Sheetrock Brand Interior Gypsum Ceiling Panels, Sag-Resistant, with framing 24″ o.c.) and 5/8″ panels 24″ o.c. 3/8″ thick panels must not be overlaid with unsupported insulation. A separate vapor retarder should be installed where required in roofed ceilings, and the plenum or attic space vented with a minimum one sq. ft. of free vent area per 150 sq. ft. of horizontal space, or per local code.

See "Ceiling Sag Precautions" on page 353 for more information on the application of water-based textures and interior finishing materials.

Exterior Ceiling Board Application

Sheetrock Brand Exterior Gypsum Ceiling Board embodies a specially treated gypsum core encased in chemically treated paper. The result is an ideal surface material for sheltered exterior ceiling areas such as covered walkways and malls, large canopies, open porches, breezeways, carports and exterior soffits.

Weather and fire-resistant, 1/2″ or 5/8″ thick Sheetrock Brand Exterior Gypsum Ceiling Board may be applied directly to wood framing or to cross-furring of wood or metal furring channels attached to main supports.

Special Conditions

Where frame spacing exceeds 16" o.c. for 1/2" board or 24" o.c. for 5/8" board, furring is required to provide support for gypsum board.

Wood Framing Requirements 1" x 3" wood furring may be used for screw application where support member spacing is 24" o.c. max. Furring of 2" nom. thickness should be used for nail application of board or where framing spacing is from 24" to 48" max. o.c.

Steel Framing Requirements Installation of grillage should be the same as for "Steel Frame Single-Layer Application" previously described in this chapter on page 120.

Ventilation Where the area above the ceiling board opens to an attic space above habitable rooms, the space should be vented to the outside in accordance with local building codes. Where the ceiling board is applied directly to rafters or to roof-ceiling joists (as in flat roof construction) that extend beyond habitable rooms, vents are required at each end of each rafter or joist space. Vents should be screened and be a minimum of 2" wide x full length between rafters (or joists). Vents should be attached through the board to minimum 1" x 2" backing strips installed prior to board application. Vent openings should be framed and located within 6" of the outer edge of the eave.

Soffit ventilation

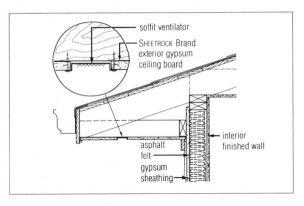

Weather Protection At the perimeter and at vertical penetrations, the exposed core of panels must be covered with No. 401 Metal Trim or securely fastened mouldings.

In areas subject to freezing temperatures and other severe weather conditions, shingled roofs should be installed in accordance with good roofing practices.

Exterior Ceiling Board application showing wall intersection (top), and control joint.

Fascia boards should extend at least 1/4" below the Ceiling Board or adjacent trim mouldings, whichever is lower to provide a drip edge.

Intersections Where Ceiling Board expanse exceeds 4', a space of at least 1/4" should be provided between edge of Exterior Ceiling Board and adjacent walls, beams, columns and fascia. This space may be screened or covered with moulding but must not be caulked.

Control Joints SHEETROCK Brand Exterior Gypsum Ceiling Board, like other building materials, is subject to structural movement, expansion and contraction due to changes in temperature and humidity.

Install a Control Joint No. 093 or a control joint consisting of two pieces of No. 401 Metal Trim back-to-back in Ceiling Board where expansion or control joints' occur in the exterior wall or roof.

Long narrow areas should have control joints spaced no more than 30′ apart. Wings of "L", "U" and "T"-shaped areas should be separated with control joints. Also, intersections of dissimilar materials should be separated with control joints. These joints usually are placed to inter- sect light fixtures, vents, etc. to relieve stress concentrations. Canopy must be designed to resist uplift.

Fixtures Provide backing or blocking for electrical boxes, vents and heavy fixtures. Cut board neatly and accurately to fit within 1/4″ of fix- tures and vents. Cover openings with trim.

Steel frame canopy (commercial)

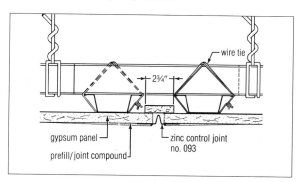

wire tie

2¾″

gypsum panel — ⌐ zinc control joint no. 093

prefill/joint compound⌐

Steel frame furred canopy

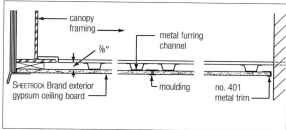

canopy framing →

metal furring channel

⅞″

SHEETROCK Brand exterior gypsum ceiling board — moulding   no. 401 metal trim —

Installation

Apply Exterior Ceiling Board with long dimension across supports. For 1/2″ board, max. support spacing is 16″ o.c.; for 5/8″ board, 24″ o.c. max. Position end joints over supports. Use maximum practical lengths to minimize end joints. Allow 1/16″ to 1/8″ space between butted ends of board. Fasten board to supports with screws spaced 12″ o.c. or nails spaced 8″ o.c.

For steel framing, use 1″ TYPE S corrosion-resistant screws. (TYPE S-12 for 20-ga. and thicker steel). For wood framing, use 1-1/4″ Type W Screws or 1-1/2″ galvanized box nails or 1-1/2″ aluminum nails. Treat

Hotel entrance canopy, faced with S<small>HEETROCK</small> *Brand Exterior Ceiling Board.*

fasteners and joints using a S<small>HEETROCK</small> Brand Setting-Type (D<small>URABOND</small>) or S<small>HEETROCK</small> Brand Lightweight Setting-Type (E<small>ASY</small> S<small>AND</small>) Joint Compound. If desired, panel joints may be concealed with batten strips or by installing panels with ends inserted into aluminum H-mouldings (by others). After joint compound has dried, apply one coat of oil-based primer-sealer and one coat exterior oil or latex paint or other balanced finishing system recommended by paint manufacturer to all exposed surfaces.

Gypsum Board Suspended Ceilings

Gypsum board applications for suspended ceilings provide excellent fire protection and appearance with exceptional economy. Applications include S<small>HEETROCK</small> Brand Ceiling Lay-In Tiles in standard D<small>ONN</small> suspension grid or surface mounted S<small>HEETROCK</small> Brand Gypsum Panels on USG Drywall Suspension System.

Lay-In Tiles S<small>HEETROCK</small> Brand Ceiling Lay-In Tiles have a F<small>IRECODE</small> C Core and square-cut edges. They are available in 2′ x 2′ or 2′ x 4′ sizes and either natural paper facing or a laminated white vinyl facing with stipple pattern. Tiles may be installed in D<small>ONN</small> Brand DX, DXL or DXLA suspension systems for most interior applications or ZXA, ZXLA or AX suspension systems for exterior applications or high humidity areas (see USG ceilings catalogs for complete information).

Install tiles beginning at one corner of the room and work one row at a time. Tilt tiles up through opening and lower it to rest squarely on all four tees. Snap firmly in place. Where partial tiles are required, use a straight edge and cut face of tiles with utility knife, snap at score and cut through backing. Trim rough edges as necessary to fit.

Surface Mounted Panels S<small>HEETROCK</small> Brand Gypsum Panels provide a monolithic ceiling when mounted to USG Drywall Suspension System. System offers 1, 1-1/2, 2 and 3-hr. fire ratings when constructed with S<small>HEETROCK</small> Brand Gypsum Panels, F<small>IRECODE</small> C or Type X formulations (consult UL Fire Resistance Directory).

Beginning at one corner of room, mount panels parallel to main tees with butt ends meeting in center of cross channels. hold panels firmly in place against channels and secure with 1-1/4″ Type S screws. Complete assembly in the same manner as conventional gypsum board ceiling construction. Finish with a USG joint treatment system and caulk perimeter with Sheetrock Brand Acoustical Sealant.

Mineral Fiber Blanket Application

3

Many USG drywall and veneer partitions have been developed to meet the demand for increased privacy between units in residential and commercial construction. Designed for wood stud, steel stud or laminated gypsum board construction, these assemblies offer highly efficient sound-control properties, yet are more economical than other partitions offering equal sound isolation. These improved sound-isolation properties and ratings are obtained by using Thermafiber Sound Attenuation Fire Blankets and decoupling the partition faces. Decoupling is achieved with resilient application or with double rows of studs on separate plates. General application procedures for these products follow. See Chapter 1 for product descriptions and SA-100, *Construction Selector* for sound ratings.

Installation

Install blankets to completely fill stud cavity from bottom to top and with the vapor retarder oriented according to job specifications. If necessary to tightly fill height, cut stock-length blankets with a serrated knife for insertion in the void. Tightly butt ends and sides of blankets within a cavity. Cut small pieces of Thermafiber Blankets for narrow stud spaces next to door openings or at partition intersections. Fit blankets carefully behind electrical outlets, bracing, fixture attachments, medicine cabinets, etc.

In ceilings, insulation should be carefully fitted around recessed lighting fixtures. Covering fixtures with insulation causes heat to build up which could possibly result in fire.

Creased Thermafiber Sound Insulation Systems

Creased Thermafiber application—Thermafiber SAFB 1″ wider than stud cavity is field cut with utility, carpet or hook-blade knife. Crease will press against gypsum panel to dampen sound vibrations.

Creased Thermafiber assemblies are non-load bearing, steel-framed, 1-hr. fire-rated systems that offer high sound ratings (50-55 STC) plus the lower in-place cost of lightweight single-layer gypsum board. The systems consist of 5/8″ Sheetrock Brand Gypsum Panels, Firecode C Core; 3- 5/8″ steel studs spaced 24″ o.c. and set in runners; and Thermafiber Sound Attenuation Fire Blankets, 25″ wide.

Since the blanket is 1″ wider than the cavity, it is installed with a slit that is field cut down the center and partially through the blanket. This allows the blanket to flex or bow in the center, easing the pressure against the studs and transferring it to the face panel, thereby dampening sound vibrations more effectively. Gypsum panels may be screw attached directly or resiliently to the steel framing.

Perimeter Isolation

Perimeter relief should be provided for gypsum construction surfaces where (a) partition or furring abuts a structural element (except floor) or dissimilar wall or ceiling; (b) ceiling or soffit abuts a structural element, dissimilar partition or other vertical penetration; (c) ceiling, partition or furring run exceeds 30′ in either direction; (d) expansion or control joints occur throughout the building itself.

In addition, less-than-ceiling-height frames should have control joints extending to the ceiling from both corners. Ceiling-height door frames may be used as control joints. Treat window openings in the same manner as doors.

Isolation is important to reduce potential cracking in partitions, ceilings, wall, column, and beam furring, and reduces the likelihood of sound flanking in rated construction. Generally, methods for isolating surfaces are detailed and specified according to the job. The typical intersection application described below may be adapted as required.

Gypsum Board Edge Treatment Where boards intersect dissimilar materials or structural elements, appropriate trim should be applied to the face-layer perimeter and SHEETROCK Brand Acoustical Sealant applied to close the gap. P-1 Vinyl Trim may be used without sealant or joint treatment.

Partition-Structural Ceiling Attach steel runner to structural ceiling to position partition. Cut steel stud 3/8″ min., 1/2″ max. less than floor-to-ceiling height. Attach gypsum board to stud at least 2-1/2″ down from ceiling. Allow 3/8″ min. clearance atop gypsum boards; finish as required. Also, special detailing may be required to meet fire ratings. Check UL listings for specifications.

Partition-Radiant Heat Ceiling Allow at least 1/8″ clear space between radiant-heated ceilings and walls or partition framing. Finish ceiling angle with P-2 Vinyl Trim or wood moulding fastened to wall members only.

Partition-Exterior Wall or Column Attach steel stud to exterior wall or column to position partition. Attach gypsum board only to second steel stud erected vertically at max. 6″ from wall. Allow at least 3/8″ clearance between partition panel and wall. Caulk as required with SHEETROCK Brand Acoustical Sealant.

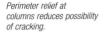

Perimeter relief at columns reduces possibility of cracking.

Furring-Exterior Wall Allow 1/4″ min. clearance between acoustical trim and intersecting exterior wall or column. Apply Sheetrock Brand Acoustical Sealant as required.

Ceiling-Exterior Wall On suspended or furred ceilings, locate supports for gypsum board within 6″ of abutting surfaces but do not allow

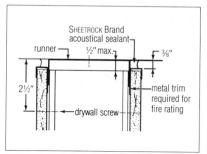

Partition-structural ceiling

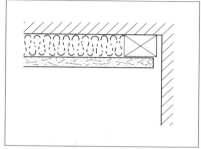

Partition-radiant heat ceiling

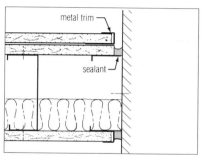

Partition-exterior wall

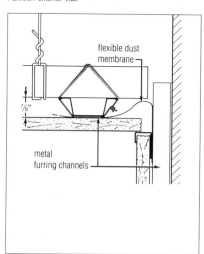

Furring-exterior wall

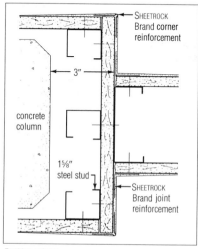

main runner or furring channels to be let into or come into contact with abutting masonry walls.

Partition-Column Fur gypsum board away from concrete column using vertical steel studs. Attach stud in intersecting partition to stud within free-standing furring.

Floating Interior Angle Application

The floating interior angle method of applying gypsum board effectively reduces angle cracking and nail pops resulting from stresses at intersections of walls and ceilings. Fasteners are eliminated on at least one surface at all interior angles, both where walls and ceilings meet and where sidewalls intersect. Follow standard framing practices for corner fastening. Conventional framing and ordinary wood back-up or blocking must be provided where needed at vertical and horizontal interior angles. Apply gypsum board to ceilings first.

Ceilings

Use conventional single nail or screw application. Apply the first nails or screws approx. 7″ from the wall and at each joist. Use conventional fastening in the remainder of the ceiling area.

Sidewalls

Apply gypsum board on walls so that its uppermost edge (or end) is in firm contact with and provides support to the perimeter of the board already installed on the ceiling. Apply the first nails or screws approx. 8″ below the ceiling at each stud. At vertical angles omit corner fasteners for the first board applied at the angle. This panel edge will be overlapped and held in place by the edge of the abutting board. Nail or screw-attach the overlapping board in the conventional manner. Use conventional fastening for remainder of sidewall area.

Double Nailing

When double nailing is used with a floating interior angle, follow above spacing on first nail from intersection and use double nailing in rest of area. Conventional framing and ordinary wood back-up or blocking at vertical internal angles must be provided.

Detail—floating interior angle

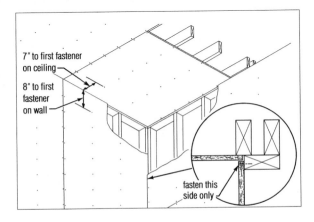

7″ to first fastener on ceiling

8″ to first fastener on wall

fasten this side only

Fixture Installation

Electrical Fixtures

After electrical services have been roughed in and before gypsum board is installed, cut necessary openings in base and face layers of board to accept switches, outlet and fixture boxes, etc. Cut out openings with a keyhole saw or with specially designed cutting tools which produce more precise openings. (See Tools and Equipment, Chapter 14.)

On SHEETROCK Brand Vinyl-Faced Gypsum Panels, holes made with a special outlet cutter should be cut from back of panel to avoid loosening vinyl around the cut. Erect panel in the usual manner.

Sealant Where the partition is used as a sound barrier, do not install boxes back-to back or in the same stud cavity. Apply SHEETROCK Brand Acoustical Sealant around all boxes to seal the cutout. See typical sealant application, earlier in this chapter. Electrical boxes having a drywall ring or device cover for use as a stop in caulking are recommended.

Fixture Attachment

Gypsum board partitions can provide suitable anchorage for most types of fixtures normally found in residential and commercial construction. To ensure satisfactory job performance it is important to have an understanding of particular fixture attachment so that sound-control characteristics will be retained and attachment will be within the allowable load-carrying capacity of the assembly.

In wood-frame construction, fixtures are usually attached directly to the framing or to blocking or supports attached to the framing. Blocking or supports should be provided for plumbing fixtures, towel racks, grab bars and similar items. Fixture supports used with DUROCK Brand Cement Board are shown in Chapter 4. Single or double-layer gypsum boards are not designed to support loads imposed by these items without additional support to carry the main part of the load.

The attachment of fixtures to partitions may impair the sound-control characteristics. Only lightweight fixtures should be attached to resilient wall surfaces constructed with RC-1 Resilient Channel unless special framing is provided (see Cabinet Attachment System, following). Refrain from attaching fixtures to party walls so as to provide a direct flow path for sound. Gypsum boards used in the ceiling are not designed to support light fixtures or troffers, air vents or other equipment. Separate supports must be provided.

Fixture Attachment Types

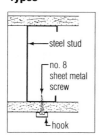

Loading capacities of various fasteners and fixture attachments used with gypsum board partitions appear in load table on page 466. Fasteners and methods follow:

No. 8 Sheet Metal Screw Driven into 25-ga. min. sheet metal plate or strip, laminated between face board and base board in laminated gypsum partitions. Also may be driven through gypsum board into a steel stud. Ideal for planned light fixture attachment.

Continuous Horizontal Bracing Back-up for fixture attachment is provided with notched runner attached to steel studs with two 3/8″ TYPE S pan head screws.

steel stud

no. 8 sheet metal screw

hook

Bolt and Nested Channels Bolt welded to nested 1-1/2″ channels for use in mounting hanger brackets for heavy fixtures. Suitable for use in laminated gypsum partitions, provided that fixture attachments do not contact opposite coreboard.

Hollow Wall Anchors 1/4″ hollow wall anchors installed in gypsum boards only. One advantage of this fastener is that threaded section

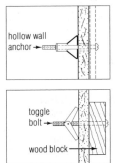

hollow wall anchor →

toggle bolt →

wood block →

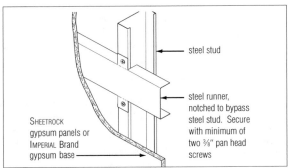

steel stud

steel runner, notched to bypass steel stud. Secure with minimum of two ⅜″ pan head screws

SHEETROCK gypsum panels or IMPERIAL Brand gypsum base

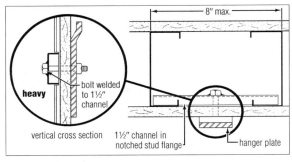

8″ max.

heavy

bolt welded to 1½″ channel

vertical cross section   1½″ channel in notched stud flange

hanger plate

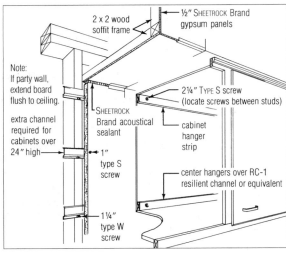

2 x 2 wood soffit frame

½″ SHEETROCK Brand gypsum panels

Note:
If party wall, extend board flush to ceiling.

extra channel required for cabinets over 24″ high →

SHEETROCK Brand acoustical sealant

1″ type S screw

2¼″ TYPE S screw (locate screws between studs)

cabinet hanger strip

center hangers over RC-1 resilient channel or equivalent

1¼″ type W screw

remains in wall when screw is removed. Also, widespread spider support formed by the expanded anchor spreads load against wall material, increasing load capacity.

Anchor Inserts Inserted into drilled holes, these anchors spread when a fastener is inserted, gripping the inside of the hole. Good for fastening small objects.

Screw Anchors Also inserted into a drilled hole, these anchors have broad screw planes for more positive attachment to the gypsum board. The screw attachment improves pull-out resistance capacity.

Toggle Bolt 1/4″ Toggle Bolt installed in gypsum board only. One disadvantage of toggle bolt is that when bolt is removed, wing fastener on back will fall down into hollow wall. Another disadvantage is that a large hole is required to allow wings to pass through wall facings.

Bolt and 1-1/2″ Channel Bolt welded to single 1-1/2″ channel and inserted in notches cut in steel stud for use in mounting hanger brackets for heavy fixtures.

Fixture Attachment Load Data—Drywall and Veneer Plaster Construction

fastener type	size in.	mm	base[1]	allowable withdrawal resistance lb.	N[2]	allowable shear resistance lb.	N[2]
Toggle Bolt or	1/8	3.18	1/2″ gypsum board	20	89	40	178
Hollow Wall Anchor	3/16	4.76		30	133	50	222
	1/4	6.35		40	178	60	267
	1/8	3.18	1/2″ gypsum board and	70	311	100	445
	3/16	4.76	25-ga. steel stud	80	356	125	556
	1/4	6.35		155	689	175	778
No. 8 sheet metal screw			1/2″ gypsum board and 25-ga. steel stud or	50	222	80	356
Type S bugle head screw			25-ga. steel insert	60	267	100	445
Type S-12 bugle head screw			1/2″ gypsum board and 20-ga. steel stud or 20-ga. steel insert	85	378	135	600
3/8″ Type S pan head screw			25-ga. steel to 25-ga. steel	70	311	120	534
Two bolts welded to steel insert	3/16	4.76	1/2″ gypsum board, plate and steel stud	175	778	200	890
	1/4	6.35	1/2″ gypsum board, plate and steel stud	200	890	250	1112
Bolt welded to 1-1/2″ chan.	1/4	6.35	(see drawing)	200	890	250	1112

(1) Comparable information is available for FIBEROCK Brand Panels. See the most current literature on FIBEROCK Brand Panels for data. (2) Newton.

Cabinet Attachment Method Detailed below, allows kitchen, bathroom and other cabinets and fixtures (except lavatories and wall-mounted toilets) of moderate weight, and "Hollywood" style headboards on party walls using RC-1 Resilient Channel to be mounted without reducing the sound rating. Recommended only for residential and light commercial wood-frame construction. Suitable for loads including cabinet weight of 67-1/2 lb. for studs spaced 16″ o.c. and 40 lb. for studs 24″ o.c. Loads are max. per lin. ft. of RC-1 Channel installed for cabinet attachment. Mounting cabinets back-to-back on a partition should be avoided since this practice creates a flanking path that increases sound transmission.

In this system, 5/8″ gypsum board is installed with long dimension parallel to channels and fastened with 1″ Type S Screws spaced 12″ o.c. along channels. Cabinets are attached to channels with 2-1/4″ Type S Screws spaced 12″ o.c. and located between studs. Screws must be driven between studs. Screws which penetrate the stud cause a significant loss in the partition's sound rating.

Curved Surfaces

Versatile Sheetrock Brand Gypsum Panels and Imperial Brand Gypsum Base can be formed to almost any cylindrically curved surface. Boards can be applied either dry or wet depending on the radius of curvature desired and the thickness and flexibility of the board. To prevent flat areas between framing, shorter bend radii require closer than normal stud and furring spacing.

Sheetrock Brand 1/4″ Flexible Gypsum Panels are specifically designed for this purpose. These 1/4″ panels are more flexible than standard gypsum panels of the same thickness and adapt quickly to the curved framing for walls, archways and circular stairways. Multiple layers may be applied.

Boards are horizontally or vertically applied, gently bent around the framing, and securely fastened to achieve the desired radius. When boards are applied dry, the minimum radius of curvature meets many applications (see table for dry gypsum boards). By thoroughly moistening the face or back paper prior to application, and replacing in the stack for at least one hour, the board may be bent to still shorter radii (see table for wetted gypsum board). When the board dries thoroughly, it will regain its original hardness.

Minimum Bending Radii of Dry Gypsum Board[1]

Board Thickness		Board Applied With Long Dimension Perpendicular to Framing		Board Applied with Long Dimension Parallel to Framing	
in.	mm	ft.	m	ft.	m
1/4	6.4	3	0.9	5	1.8
3/8	9.5	6	1.8	9	2.7
1/2	12.7	12[1]	3.7	—	—
5/8	15.9	18	5.5	—	—

(1) Comparable information is available for Fiberock Brand Panels. See the most current literature on Fiberock Brand Panels for data.
(2) Bending two 1/4″ pieces successively permits radii shown for 1/4″ gypsum board.

Minimum Radii of Sheetrock Brand 1/4″ Flexible Gypsum Panels

Application	Condition	Lengthwise Bend Radii		Max. Stud Spacing		Widthwise Bend Radii		Max. Stud Spacing	
		in.	mm	in.	mm	in.	mm	in.	mm
Inside (concave)	Dry*	32	813	9	229	45	1143	9	229
Outside (convex)	Dry*	34	864	9	229	20	508	6	152

*@75°F/50% relative humidity.

Minimum Bending Radii of Wetted Gypsum Board[1]

Board Thickness	Radius	Inside Length of Arc[2]	Outside Length of Arc[2]	No. of Studs on Arc Including at Tangents[3]	Approx. Stud Spacing c. to c.[4]	Max. Stud Spacing c. to c.[4]	Oz. of Water Required per Panel One Side—oz[5]
1/4"	2'0"	3.14'	44.0"	9	5.50"	6"	30
1/4"	2'6"	3.93'	53.4"	10	5.93"	6"	30
3/8"	3'0"	4.71'	62.8"	9	7.85"	8"	35
3/8"	3'6"	5.50'	72.2"	11	7.22"	8"	35
1/2"	4'0"	6.28'	81.6"	8	11.70"	12"	45
1/2"	4'6"	7.07'	91.1"	9	11.40"	12"	45

(1) For gypsum board applied horizontally to a 4" thick partition (2) Arc length $= \frac{3.14 \cdot R}{2}$ (for a 90° arc).

(3) No. studs = outside arc length/maximum spacing +1 (rounded up to next whole number). (4) Stud spacing = outside arc length/no. of studs -1 (measured along outside of runner). (5) Wet only the side of board that will be in tension. Water required per board side is based on 4' x 8' sheet.

Installation

Framing Cut one leg and web of top and bottom steel runner at 2" intervals for the length of the arc. Allow 12" of uncut steel runners at each end of arc. Bend runners to uniform curve of desired radius (90° max. arc). To support the cut leg of runner, clinch a 1" x 25-ga. steel strip to inside of leg. Select the runner size to match the steel studs; for wood studs, use a 3-1/2" steel runner. Attach steel runners to structural elements at floor and ceiling with suitable fasteners as previously described.

Position studs vertically, with open side facing in same direction and engaging floor and ceiling runners. Begin and end each arc with a stud and space intermediate studs equally as measured on outside of arc. Secure steel studs to runners with 3/8" Type S pan head screws; secure wood studs with suitable fasteners. On tangents, place studs 6" o.c. leaving last stud free standing. Follow directions previously described for erecting balance of studs.

Panel Preparation Select length and cut board to allow one unbroken panel to cover the curved surface and 12" tangents at each end. Outside panel must be longer than inside panels to compensate for additional radius contributed by the studs. Cutouts for electrical boxes are not recommended in curved surfaces unless they can be made after boards are installed and thoroughly dry.

When wet board is required, evenly spray water on the surface which will be in tension when board is hung. Apply water with a conventional garden sprayer using the quantity shown in the table. Carefully stack boards with wet surfaces facing each other and cover stack with plastic sheet (polyethylene). Allow boards to set at least one hour before application.

Panel Application Apply panels horizontally with the wrapped edge perpendicular to the studs. On the convex side of the partition, begin installation at one end of the curved surface and fasten panel to studs as it is wrapped around the curve. On the concave side of the partition, start fastening panel to the stud at the center of the curve and work outward to the ends of the panel. For single-layer panels, space screws 12" o.c. Use 1" Type S screws for steel studs and 1-1/4" Type W screws for wood studs.

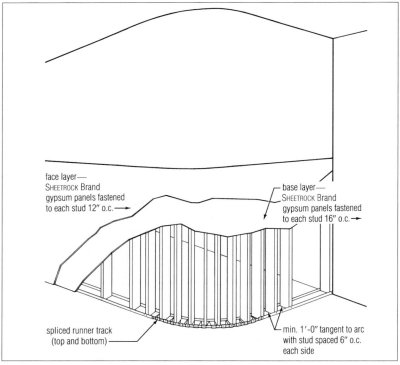

face layer—
SHEETROCK Brand
gypsum panels fastened
to each stud 12″ o.c. →

base layer—
SHEETROCK Brand
gypsum panels fastened
to each stud 16″ o.c. →

spliced runner track
(top and bottom) —

min. 1′-0″ tangent to arc
with stud spaced 6″ o.c.
each side

Board application

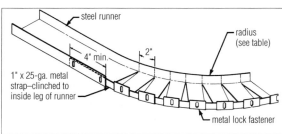

steel runner

radius
(see table)

4″ min.

2″

1″ x 25-ga. metal
strap–clinched to
inside leg of runner

metal lock fastener

Runner installation

For double-layer application, apply base layer horizontally and fasten to stud with screws spaced 16″ o.c. Center face layer panels over joints in the base layer and secure to studs with screws spaced 12″ o.c. Use 1″ TYPE S screws for base layer and 1-5/8″ TYPE S screws for face layer. Allow panels to dry completely (approx. 24 hrs. under good drying conditions) before applying joint treatment.

Arches

Arches of any radii are easily faced with gypsum panels or base and finished with a USG joint system, or veneer plaster finish. Score or cut through back paper of panels at 1″ intervals to make them flexible. The board should previously have been cut to desired width and length of arch.

Curved stairwell, faced with drywall, forms attractive design element in a shopping mall (right). Radius of curved gypsum board, joints treated, is shown in construction view (below).

3

After board has been applied to arch framing with nails or screws, apply tape reinforcement (SHEETROCK Brand Joint Tape for drywall panels or IMPERIAL Brand Type P or S for plaster base). Crease tape along center. Make scissor cuts half-way across tape and 3/4″ apart to make tape flexible. Apply uncut half to curved surface, and fold cut half of tape onto wall surface. Finish as appropriate for drywall or veneer plaster construction.

Soffits

Gypsum board soffits provide a lightweight, fast and economical method of filling over cabinets or lockers and of housing overhead ducts, pipes or conduits. They are made with wood framing or with steel stud and runner supports, faced with screw-attached gypsum board. Braced soffits up to 24" deep are constructed without supplementary vertical studs. Select components for the soffit size desired from table following. Unbraced soffits without horizontal studs are suitable for soffits up to 24" x 24". To retain fire protection, partitions and ceilings are finished with gypsum board before soffits are installed.

Installation

Braced Soffit Attach steel runners to ceiling and sidewall as illustrated on page 146, placing fasteners close to outside flange of runner. On stud walls, space fasteners to engage stud. Fasten vertical gypsum face board to web of face corner runner and flange of ceiling runner with TYPE S screws spaced 12″ o.c. Place screws in face corner runner at least 1″ from edge of board. Insert steel studs between face corner runner and sidewall runner and attach alternate studs to runners with screws. Attach bottom face board to studs and runners with TYPE S screws spaced 12″ o.c. Attach corner bead and finish. Where sound control is important, attach RC-1 Resilient Channel to framing before attaching gypsum board.

Unbraced Soffit Attach steel studs and runners to ceiling and side-wall, placing fasteners to engage wall and ceiling framing. Cut gypsum board to soffit depth and attach a soffit-length stud with TYPE S screws spaced 12″ o.c. Attach this preassembled unit to ceiling stud flange with screws spaced 12″ o.c. Attach bottom panel with TYPE S screws spaced 12″ o.c. Attach corner bead and finish.

Braced Soffit Design Maximum Dimensions[1]

Gypsum Board Thickness[2]		Steel Stud Size		Maximum Vertical[3]		Max. Horizontal for Max. Vertical Shown	
in.	mm	in.	mm	in.	mm	in.	mm
1/2	12.7	1-5/8	41.3	60	1525	48	1220
1/2	12.7	2-1/2, 3-5/8	63.5, 92.1	72	1830	36	915
5/8	15.9	1-5/8	41.3	60	1525	30	760
5/8	15.9	2-1/2, 3-5/8	63.5, 92.1	72	1830	18	455

(1) The construction is not designed to support loads other than its own dead weight. (2) Double-layer applications and 3/8″ board are not recommended for this construction. (3) Widths shown are based on construction having no supplemental vertical studs.

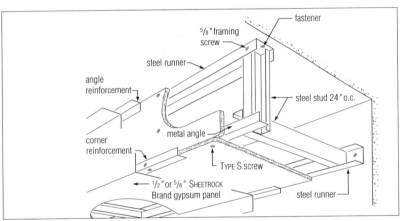

Braced soffit

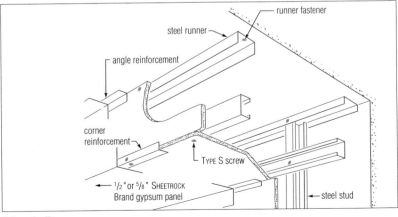

Unbraced soffit

Cement Board
Construction

Cement Board Products

Durock Brand Cement Board offers architects, builders and tile contractors a strong, water-durable base for ceramic and stone tile in tub and shower areas. It also serves as an ideal abuse-resistant and fire-resistant substrate for veneer plaster in walls, and ceramic tile, quarry tile, lugged tile, thin stone tile, thin brick, glass and ceramic mosaics, or aggregate in both walls and floors.

The board is readily applied over load-bearing or nonload-bearing wood or steel framing to produce extraordinary, high-performance systems.

A panel product, Durock Brand Cement Board is formed in a continuous process that consists of an aggregated portland cement core reinforced with polymer-coated, glass-fiber mesh embedded in both surfaces and wrapped around the edges. Its composition also makes it noncombustible and dimensionally stable.

Durock Brand Cement Board products are highly versatile. In addition to interior applications, panels are available for exterior applications such as fences, mobile home skirting, agricultural buildings, wall shields, floor protectors, exterior chimneys and garage wainscot, to name a few. See Chapter 6 for veneer plaster applications over Durock Brand Cement Board.

Various organizations provide information about recommended standards or tolerances for installation of cement board systems. See pages 467 and 474 in the Appendix for information about standards and tolerances.

For instructions on the safe use of cement board and related products, see Chapter 13, Safety Considerations, Material Handling.

Cement Board Sizes[1] and Packaging

Type	Thickness	Width	Lengths	Shipping Units[2]
Cement Board	1/2"	32"	5'	50
	1/2"	3'	4', 5', 6'	50
	1/2"	3'	8'	30
Exterior Cement Board	1/2"	4'	8'	30
	5/8"	4'	8'	24
Underlayment	5/16"	4'	4'	40
	5/16"	3'	5'	40

(1) Other lengths available. Contact your USG Representative.
(2) Stretch wrapped and shipped in packaging units as shown.

Durock **Brand Cement Board** Especially sized and formulated for use in interior areas that may be subject to water or high moisture/humidity conditions, such as bathtub or shower enclosures, gang showers, bathroom floors, bath and kitchen counter tops and steam rooms.

Aggregated portland cement core resists water penetration and will not deteriorate when wet.

Durock Brand Cement Board is a superior substrate for ceramic tile, slate and quarry tile on all interior surfaces. Panels are manufactured in three widths for minimum cutting and easy handling and installation. Use larger panel sizes for larger projects such as commercial kitchens and gang showers. Smaller panels are designed to fit typical tub and shower enclosures. Also UL-listed as a wall shield and floor protector for room heaters and stoves.

DUROCK Brand Cement Board exceeds the ANSI Standards for cementitious backer units (CBU). See ANSI A 118.9 for Test Methods and Specifications for CBU; and ANSI A 118.9 for Interior Installation of CBU. The ASTM designation for DUROCK Brand Cement Board is C1325 and for DUROCK Brand Exterior Cement Board is C1186. See National Evaluation Service Reports No. 259 and No. 396 for fire-resistant designs and/or conditions of use. Reports are subject to re-examination, revisions and possible changes. All DUROCK Brand Cement Board Products meet ASTM Standard E136 for noncombustibility. UL listed 34L2.

DUROCK Brand Cement Board Limitations

1. Steel framing must be 20-ga. or heavier.

2. Systems using DUROCK Brand Exterior Cement Board are designed for positive or negative uniform loads of up to 30 psf with studs spaced max. 16″ o.c. (See publication SA700 for design recommendations on systems requiring uniform loads up to 40 psf.)

3. Maximum stud spacing: 16″ o.c. (24″ o.c. for cavity shaft wall assembly, requires intermediate adhesive bead); maximum allowable deflection, L/360. Maximum fastener spacing: 8″ o.c. for wood and steel framing on floors and walls; 6″ o.c. for ceiling applications.

4. Maximum dead load for ceiling system is 7.5 psf, including cement board.

5. Do not use drywall screws or drywall nails, as they do not provide adequate holding capacity.

6. Not recommended for vinyl flooring.

7. 5/16″ thickness should not be used for walls or ceilings.

8. Drywall joint compounds must not be used directly over cement board unless it is properly sealed; see page 161.

Note: An exterior cement board product is also available for use in exterior soffits, walls, privacy fences and chimney enclosures. It also has proved to be an excellent substrate for exterior insulation and finish systems (EIFS) as well as direct-applied exterior finish systems. That product, DUROCK Brand Exterior Cement Board, is not covered in this text. Contact your USG Representative or Sales Office and request USG publication SA700 for detailed information.

DUROCK Brand Underlayment A strong, thin substrate designed for use under ceramic or thin-cut stone tile floors and countertops. DUROCK Brand Underlayment is similar in composition to DUROCK Brand Cement Board. Because its primary use is for overlaid ceramic tile floors, it comes in convenient 4′ x 4′ and 3′ x 5′ panels and is 5/16″ thick. This slimmer thickness reduces the variation in level between the ceramic tile floor and abutting carpet or wood floors. The reduced thickness also eliminates the need to cut down entry doors in threshold applications and allows easier installation of kitchen appliances

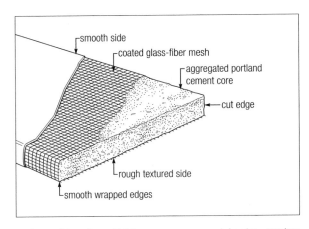

Durock Brand Cement Board features.

such as dishwashers. Not for use over exposed framing; requires underlaid substrate material such as plywood for structural support. May be applied directly over old substrate on countertops to save time.

Durock Brand Cement Board

Typical Physical Properties

Property	ASTM Test reference	Cement board value	Underlayment value
Flexural strength—psi	C947	750	1250
Indentation strength— psi 1″ dia. disc @ 0.02″ indent.	D2394	2300	2300
Uniform load—psf studs 16″ o.c.	—	30 max,	—
Water absorption-% by wt. 24 hrs.	C473-84	10	10
Nail pull resistance—lb. 0.4″ head diameter (wet or dry)	C473-84	125	—
Weight-psf	C473-84	3	2
Freeze/thaw resistance—Procedure B number of cycles with no deterioration	C666-84	100	100
Surface burning characteristics— flame/smoke	E84	5/0	5/0
Thermal "R"/k value	C177	0.26/1.92	—
Standard method for evaluating ceramic floor tile installation systems	C627	Residential	Residential
Min. bending radius[1]—ft.	—	8	—

Durock Brand Accessory Products

Durock Brand Wood (above) and Steel Screws (below)

Durock Brand Wood and Steel Screws developed especially for use with Durock Brand Cement Boards. All Durock Brand Screws are made with a special corrosion resistant coating that is superior to cadmium plating or zinc. Wafer head design with countersinking ribs allows flush seating while preventing strip-outs. Increased bearing surface provides greater pull-through resistance. Drywall screws do not provide adequate pull-through resistance and must not be used. For 14 to 20-ga. steel framing, use 1-1/4″ and 1-5/8″ Durock Brand Steel Screws. For wood framing, use 1-1/4″, 1-5/8″ or 2-1/4″ Durock Brand Wood

Hot-Dipped Galvanized Roofing Nails

Galvanized Staples

Durock Brand Alkali-Resistant Tape

Screws. Packaging: 1-1/4" screws, 5,000 pieces per carton, or twenty 150-pc. boxes; 1-5/8" screws, 4,000 pieces per carton; 2-1/4" screws, 2,000 pieces per carton. Assure minimum thread penetration of 3/4" into steel framing and 1/2" into wood framing.

Nails 1-1/2" hot-dipped galvanized roofing nails may be used for Durock Brand Cement Board or Durock Brand Underlayment to wood framing.

Staples 1/4" x 7/8" galvanized staples may be used only for Durock Brand Underlayment attachment to wood framing.

Durock Brand Interior Tape A specially designed, alkali-resistant tape for use with Durock Brand Cement Board. Tape is 2"-wide, polymer-coated, open glass-fiber mesh. Packaging: 2" (nom.) x 75' rolls; 24 rolls per carton.

Adhesives, Mortars and Grout Use only adhesive products compatible with alkaline or portland cement-based substrates. Multipurpose adhesive for subfloor attachment to framing must meet ASTM C557-73; ceramic tile adhesive must be Type I, (such as Durock Brand Ceramic Tile Adhesive), meeting ANSI A136.1; dry-set mortar mixed with acrylic latex additive must meet ANSI A118.1; latex portland cement mortar must meet ANSI A118.4; and grout must meet ANSI A118.6.

4

Job Preparation and Design Considerations

Estimating

Estimate material requirements for Durock Brand Cement Board applications in much the same manner used for estimating gypsum drywall applications. There are, however, certain important differences.

Measure surface area "solid," ignoring cutouts for doors and windows. Use 1/2" or 5/8" Durock Brand Cement Board as necessary to match adjacent gypsum panel thickness. Both panel thicknesses may be used for wall and ceiling applications. 5/8" Durock Brand Cement Board may be substituted for 1/2" Durock Brand Cement Board to meet surface dimension requirements without diluting the fire-rated performance of fire-rated assemblies that call for 1/2" Durock Brand Cement Board.

Fastener spacing requirements are 8" for walls and floors and 6" for ceilings—considerably more frequent than for drywall construction. Plan for fasteners accordingly. Average usage—1,600 pcs./1,000 sq. ft.

A water barrier, not a vapor retarder, may be required behind cement board in many applications. Water barrier must be Grade D building paper, No. 15 asphalt felt or equivalent. Ensure that total square footage of water barrier exceeds total square footage of cement board to take into account material overlaps required to prevent moisture penetration.

To estimate quantities of mortars, grouts and adhesives, consult packaging and coverage information for those products.

Environmental Conditions

All materials should be delivered and stored in their original unopened packages and stored in an enclosed shelter providing protection from damage and exposure to the elements. Even though the stability and durability of Durock Brand Cement Board is unaffected by the elements, moisture and temperature variations may have an effect on the bonding effectiveness of basecoats and adhesives.

Various humidity and temperature conditions may require a vapor retarder. A qualified engineer should be consulted to determine the proper location of the retarder to prevent moisture condensation within the wall.

Control Joints

Certain interior wall surface constructions should be isolated with surface control joints (sometimes referred to by the industry as expansion joints) or other means where: (a) a wall abuts a structural element or dissimilar wall or ceiling; (b) construction changes within the plane of the wall; (c) tile and thin brick surfaces exceed 16′ in either direction. Surface control joint width should comply with architectural specifications. Location and design of building control joints must be detailed by a professional architect. Steel framing at building control joints that extend through the wall (with top and bottom runner tracks broken) should have 1-1/2″ cold-rolled channel alignment stabilizers spaced a maximum of 5′0″ o.c. vertically. Channels should be placed through holes in the stud web of the first two adjacent studs on both sides of the joint and securely attached to the first adjacent stud on either side of the joint. (See Durock Brand Cement Board Systems publication SA932 for further information.)

Cement board should be separated at all surface and building control joints. Where vertical and horizontal joints intersect, the vertical joint should be continuous and the horizontal joint should abut it. Splices, terminals, and intersections should be caulked with a sealant complying with architectural specifications and sealant manufacturer recommendations. Do not apply tile or finishes over caulked, sealed expansion joints.

High Moisture Areas

Pool Enclosures Cement board systems may be used for the walls and ceilings around indoor swimming pools. In areas of high moisture and chlorine content, adequate consideration should be given for ventilation to protect against deterioration of metal hangers and framing members.

Steam Rooms and Saunas Where temperatures exceed 120°F for extended periods, use dry-set or latex-portland cement mortar; do not use organic adhesive.

Leaching and Efflorescence

Latex leaching and efflorescence are natural phenomena which occur with the use of latex modified mortars and grouts through no fault in the products. To help protect against their occurrence, follow current manufacturer guidelines and recommendations.

Applications

Framing

Frame spacing for Durock Brand Cement Board attachment must not exceed 16″ o.c. (24″ o.c. for UL Design U459). Studs of freestanding furred walls must be secured to exterior wall with furring brackets or laterally braced with horizontal studs or runners spaced 4′ o.c. max. Laterally brace all steel-framed walls prior to application of joint treatment. If necessary for tub or shower surround applications, fur out studs to allow fixtures and components to be flush with ceramic tile face. Install appropriate blocking or headers to support tub and other plumbing fixtures and to receive soap dishes, grab bars, towel racks and other accessories and hardware.

Ceiling framing must be capable of supporting the total ceiling dead load, including insulation, ceramic tile, bonding materials and tile-backer board, with deflection not exceeding L/360.

Floor framing must be covered with min. 3/4″ exterior grade plywood subfloor firmly attached to assure stability. Apply 3/8″ bead of multi-purpose adhesive to center of top flange of joists. Place plywood panels with long dimension across or parallel to wood or steel joists spaced max. 16″ o.c. Fasten to steel joists with 1-15/16″ pilot point Type S-12 screws spaced 16″ o.c. Fasten plywood to wood joists with suitable nails or screws spaced 12″ o.c. or as required by code.

For countertops, install min. 3/4″ exterior grade plywood base across wood cabinet supports spaced 16″ o.c. Position ends and edges over supports.

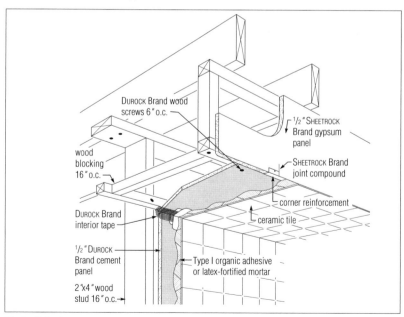

Wood soffit framing

154

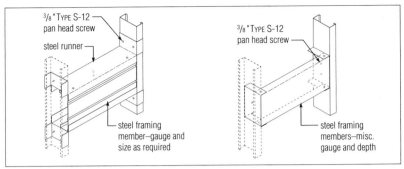

Fixture attachment—steel framing

Fixture Attachment

Framing and bracing must be capable of supporting the partition elements and fixture additions within L/360 allowable deflection limit. Install bracing and blocking flush with the face of the framing to keep the stud faces smooth and free of protrusions.

Heavy gauge metal straps mounted on the studs are not recommended supports because the metal thickness and/or screwheads used to attach them cause bowing in the board and interfere with the flat, smooth application of the cement board and ceramic tile. When heavy anchor plates must be used, fur out studs with a metal strap or wood shim to provide an even base for the cement board.

If required, the board may be ground or drilled to provide relief for projecting bolts and screwheads.

Fixture Attachment Load Table—Cement Board

Fastener type	size in.	mm	Base assembly	Allowable withdrawal resistance lb.	N[1]	Allowable shear resistance lb.	N[1]
toggle bolt or hollow wall anchor	1/8	3.18	1/2" cement board & steel stud	70	311	100	445
	3/16	4.76		80	356	125	556
	1/4	6.35		155	689	175	778
3/8" Type S-12 pan head screw	3/8	9.5	20-ga. steel to 20-ga. steel	53	236	133	680
two bolts welded to steel insert	3/16	4.76	1/2" cement board, plate and steel stud	175	778	200	890
	1/4	6.35		200	890	250	1112
bolt welded to 1-1/2" chan.	1/4	6.35	See "Bolt and 1-1/2" Channel," page 141	200	890	250	1112

(1) Newtons

Panel Fabrication

Cutting and shaping of Durock Brand Cement Board panels is similar to cutting and shaping gypsum panels. A utility knife or cement board cutting tool is used to cut through the glass-fiber mesh scrim on both sides of the board. Then it is snapped in the same manner used for gypsum board. Cutouts for penetrations must be made on both sides of the board and then may be tapped out with a hammer. To ensure

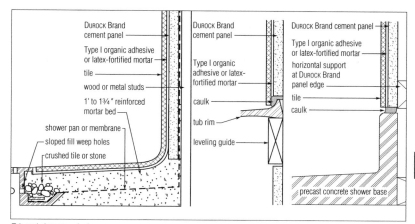

DUROCK Brand cement panel
Type I organic adhesive or latex-fortified mortar
tile
wood or metal studs
1' to 1¾" reinforced mortar bed
shower pan or membrane
sloped fill weep holes
crushed tile or stone

DUROCK Brand cement panel
Type I organic adhesive or latex-fortified mortar
caulk
tub rim
leveling guide

DUROCK Brand cement panel
Type I organic adhesive or latex-fortified mortar
horizontal support at DUROCK Brand panel edge
tile
caulk
precast concrete shower base

Tub and shower—single layer board

Tip
See Chapter 13, for safety considerations.

that the cuts occur at the right locations on both sides, it is often useful to drive nails through the board at key locations such as the center or corners of required penetration locations. A wood rasp is useful for shaping cutouts and board edges. For Safety: Wear eye protection while cutting or shaping; gloves are recommended when handling.

Panel Application

For Floors Laminate 5/16" DUROCK Brand Underlayment to subfloor using Type I ceramic tile adhesive, latex fortified mortar or thin-set mortar mixed with acrylic latex additive. Apply it to subfloor with 1/4" square-notched trowel for thin set mortar, 5/32" V-notched trowel for mastic. DUROCK Brand Underlayment has both a rough and a smooth surface. Typically, the smooth side is used for mastic applications of tile; the rough side for mortar applications. Place underlayment with joints staggered from subfloor joints. Fit ends and edges closely but not forced together. Fasten to subfloor with 1-1/4" DUROCK Brand Wood Screws or 1-1/2" galvanized roofing nails spaced 8" o.c. in both directions with perimeter fasteners at least 3/8" and less than 5/8" from ends and edges; or with 1/4"x 7/8" galvanized staples spaced 4" o.c. in both directions.

Floors, wood or steel joists

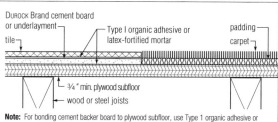

DUROCK Brand cement board or underlayment
tile
Type I organic adhesive or latex-fortified mortar
padding
carpet
¾" min. plywood subfloor
wood or steel joists

Note: For bonding cement backer board to plywood subfloor, use Type 1 organic adhesive or latex-fortified mortar that is suitable for this kind of application. For application of various types of tiles to cement backer board on floors or countertops, contact the tile manufacturer for the appropriate type of tile-setting mortar.

1/2″ Durock Brand Cement Board may be used instead of Durock Brand Underlayment. Use the same procedure, except fastening with staples is not recommended.

Note: for bonding cement backer board to plywood subfloor, use Type I organic adhesive or latex-fortified mortar that is suitable for this kind of application. For application of various types of tiles to cement backer board on floors or counter tops, contact the tile manufacturer for the appropriate type of tile-setting mortar.

Tile/carpet underlayment

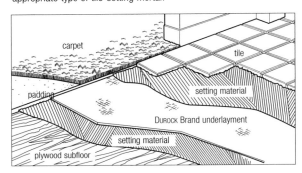

carpet
tile
padding
setting material
Durock Brand underlayment
setting material
plywood subfloor

For Walls After tub, shower pan or receptor is installed, place temporary 1/4″ spacer strips around lip of fixture. Installation of a water barrier over studs and overlapping the vertical flange of the fixture is highly recommended.

Durock Brand Cement Board has both a rough and a smooth surface. Typically, the smooth side is used for mastic applications of tile; the rough side for mortar applications. Cut the cement board to required sizes and make necessary cut-outs. Fit ends and edges closely, but not forced together. Install board abutting top of spacer strip. Stagger end joints in successive courses. Fasten boards to wood studs spaced max. 16″ o.c. and bottom plates with 1-1/4″ Durock Brand Wood Screws or 1-1/2″ galvanized roofing nails spaced 8″ o.c. Fasten boards to steel studs spaced max. 16″ o.c. and bottom runners only with 1-1/4″

Durock Brand steel or wood screw 8″ o.c.

tile

Type I organic adhesive or latex-fortified mortar

Durock Brand interior tape

setting material

Durock Brand cement panel

membrane (if required)

wood or steel studs 16″ o.c. max.

Walls, interior—wood or steel studs

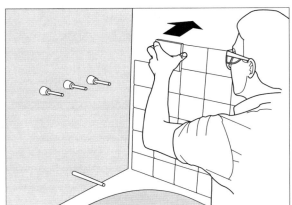

DUROCK Brand Steel Screws spaced 8″ o.c. with perimeter fasteners at least 3/8″ and less than 5/8″ from ends and edges. Do not fasten to, or within 1″ of, top runner. In double-layer walls where cement board is installed over base-layer gypsum boards, apply a water barrier (not a vapor retarder) between gypsum board and cement board. If water barrier was installed, trim overlap back so that it can be concealed by tile and caulk application.

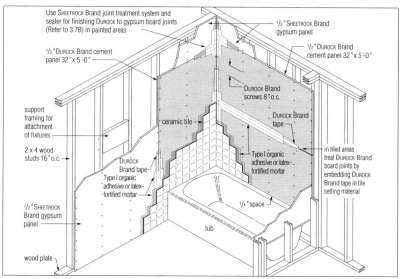

Typical bathtub installation

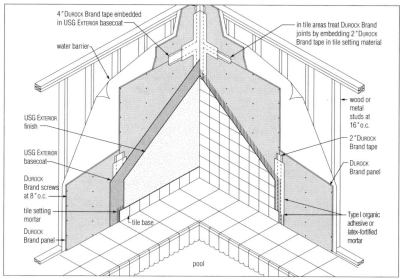

Typical swimming pool installation (tile or exterior finish)

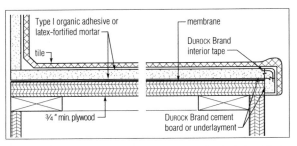

For Countertops Staple-attach 15-lb. felt or 4-mil polyethylene film to 3/4″ exterior plywood base with galvanized staples. Laminate 5/16″ Durock Brand Underlayment to membrane using ceramic tile mastic, latex fortified mortar or thin-set mortar mixed with acrylic latex additive applied to felt-covered plywood with 1/4″ square-notched trowel for thin set mortar, 5/32″ V-notched trowel for mastic. Fasten to plywood with 1-1/4″ Durock Brand Wood Screws or 1-1/2″ galvanized roofing nails spaced 8″ o.c. in both directions and around edges; or with 1/4″ x 7/8″ galvanized staples spaced 4″ o.c. in both directions and around edges.

1/2″ Durock Brand Cement Board may be used instead of Durock Brand Underlayment. use the same procedure, except fastening with staples is not recommended. In each case, select the rough or smooth side of the board for tile application depending on whether mortar or mastic will be used.

For Ceilings Assure that ceiling joists, furring channels or strips are spaced max. 16″ o.c. and are capable of supporting the total ceiling system dead load, including insulation, ceramic tile, bonding materials and cement board, with deflection not exceeding L/360 of the span.

Suspended ceiling

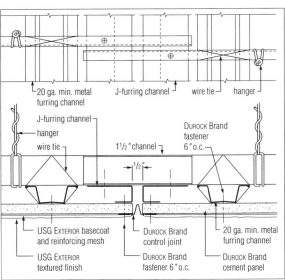

When steel is used, min. 20-ga. is required. Apply 1/2″ DUROCK Brand Cement Board to framing with long dimension across framing. Center end or edge joints on framing and stagger joints in adjacent rows. Fit ends and edges closely, but not forced together. Fasten boards to steel framing with 1-1/4″ DUROCK Brand Steel Screws spaced 6″ o.c. and to wood framing with 1-5/8″ DUROCK Brand Wood screws spaced 6″ o.c. with perimeter fasteners at least 3/8″ and less than 5/8″ from ends and edges. If necessary, provide additional blocking to permit proper attachment. Make sure edges or ends are continuously supported.

For Wall Shield Cut 1/2″ DUROCK Brand Cement Board into furring strip sizes using a carbide scoring tool or a circular saw with a carbide-tipped blade. Attach a double layer of furring strips to wall framing with 2-1/4″ DUROCK Brand Wood Screws or 2-1/4″ galvanized roofing nails with 3/4″ minimum framing penetration. Then attach 1/2″ DUROCK Brand Cement Board panels through furring strips to wall framing with 2-3/4″ galvanized roofing nails with 3/4″ minimum framing penetration.

Wall shield and floor protector

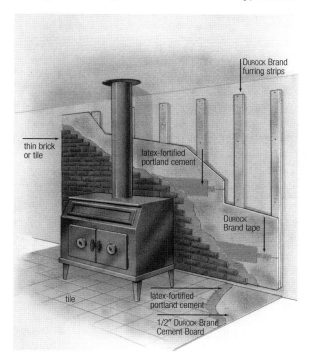

For Floor Protectors and Hearth Extensions

For Floor Protectors and Hearth Extensions Apply 1/8″ to 1/4″ thick latex-fortified portland cement to solid surface—never on top of carpeting or padding. Attach 1/2″ DUROCK Brand Cement Board with 1-1/4″ DUROCK Brand Wood Screws or 1-1/2″ galvanized roofing nails at 8″ o.c. both directions and with 3/4″ minimum flooring penetration. See the illustration on page 160 for minimum wall shield or floor protector extensions beyond the room heater or stove.

160

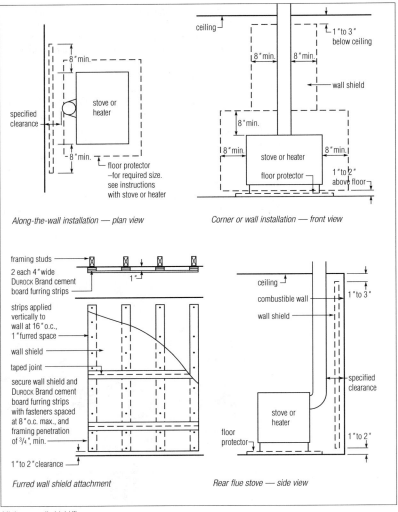

Along-the-wall installation — plan view

Corner or wall installation — front view

framing studs
2 each 4" wide
Durock Brand cement
board furring strips
strips applied
vertically to
wall at 16" o.c.,
1" furred space
wall shield
taped joint
secure wall shield and
Durock Brand cement
board furring strips
with fasteners spaced
at 8" o.c. max., and
framing penetration
of ³/₄", min.
1" to 2" clearance

Furred wall shield attachment

Rear flue stove — side view

Minimum wall shield/floor
protector extensions

Hearth Extensions Extend hearths with Durock Brand Cement Board in accordance with local building codes and fireplace manufacturer recommendations. The thickness of cement board panels is determined using the following formula:

$$\frac{\text{k-value Durock}}{\text{k-value specified}} \times \begin{array}{l}\text{Hearth extension}\\ \text{thickness}\\ \text{(specified)}\end{array} = \begin{array}{l}\text{Thickness of Durock}\\ \text{Brand Cement Board}\\ \text{(not less than hearth}\\ \text{extension specified)}\end{array}$$

For example, if the fireplace manufacturer or code requires one layer of 0.75-in. millboard with a k-value of 0.84, use the formula as follows to determine the required layers of cement board panels:

$$\frac{1.92}{0.84} \times 0.75 \text{ in.} = 1.71 \text{ in. of D\textsc{urock} Brand Cement Board, or 4 layers.}$$

Joint Treatment

Fill joints with tile-setting mortar or adhesive and then immediately embed tape and level joints.

For small areas where the D\textsc{urock} Brand Cement Board will not be tiled, such as a board extending beyond the tiled area and abutting another surface, treat joints as follows: Seal D\textsc{urock} Brand Cement Board with Type I Ceramic Tile Adhesive. (Mix four parts adhesive with one part water.) E\textsc{mbed} S\textsc{heetrock} Brand Joint Tape over joints and treat fasteners with S\textsc{heetrock} Brand Setting-Type Joint Compound (D\textsc{urabond} 45 or 90) applied in a conventional manner. Flat trowel S\textsc{heetrock} Brand Setting-Type Joint Compound over board to cover fasteners and fill voids to a smooth surface. Finish joints with at least two coats of S\textsc{heetrock} Brand Ready-Mixed Joint Compound. Do not apply ready-mixed or setting-type joint compound over unsealed board.

Panel Surfacing

Install tile or thin brick and grout in accordance with ANSI A108.4 for Type I organic adhesive or ANSI A108.5 for dry-set or latex portland cement mortar and ANSI A108.10 for grouts. Before tile application begins, the moisture content of the D\textsc{urock} Brand Cement Board should be allowed to adjust as closely as possible to the level it will reach in service. Avoid extreme changes in environmental conditions during the curing of the tile setting material. Provide adequate ventilation to carry off excess moisture. Note: D\textsc{urock} Brand Cement Board used in floor-protector applications will still perform its protective function unfinished, so long as the integrity of the board surface is not compromised.

Abuse-Resistant Walls

In addition to its use as a moisture-resistant backing for interior ceramic tile, D\textsc{urock} Brand Cement Board has also become a suitable substrate for veneer plaster to produce rugged, fire-rated, abuse resistant walls. The extraordinary strength and durability of D\textsc{urock} Brand Cement Board offers uncommon advantages for walls in high-traffic and abuse-prone areas. Combined with a two-coat veneer plaster application, the wall system looks as good as it performs. It is particularly well suited for institutional and commercial applications.

In this two-coat veneer plaster system, D\textsc{iamond} Brand Veneer Basecoat Plaster and I\textsc{mperial} Brand Finish Plaster are applied over D\textsc{urock} Brand Cement Board attached to framing spaced 16″ o.c. Apply panels with long edges either parallel or perpendicular to the framing and with the rough side of the panels exposed. Attach board with D\textsc{urock} Brand Screws or galvanized roofing nails spaced max. 8″ o.c. Prior to treatment of joints, apply USG Plaster Bonder in a continuous film to the joint area in accordance with application directions. Treat joints with SHEETROCK Brand Setting-Type Joint Compound (DURABOND or EASY SAND) and SHEETROCK Brand joint Tape.

Joint surfaces must be treated with a separate coat of joint compound to fully conceal the paper tape. When joints are completely dry, treat entire wall surface with USG Plaster Bonder according to application directions. Then apply DIAMOND Brand Veneer Basecoat Plaster from 1/16″ to 3/32″ thickness using a scratch and double-back technique. This is accomplished by applying a tight, thin coat over the entire area, and immediately doubling back with plaster from the same batch to achieve full thickness. When basecoat plaster is firm, broom the surface to leave it rough and open for finish. With basecoat set and partially dry, apply IMPERIAL Finish Plaster using a scratch and double-back technique. Complete finishing when material is firm. Leave finished surface smooth and dense for decorating.

DUROCK Brand Cement Board also may be employed as the base layer in two-layer wall systems that use SHEETROCK Brand Gypsum Panels for the top layer. These systems, too, are exceptionally durable and provide fire-rated protection.

Finishing Drywall Systems

Levels of Gypsum Finishing

The finished appearance of a drywall wall or ceiling is largely dependent upon the quality of the framing job and the care exercised in applying the drywall panels. The better the framing and cladding, the easier it is to have a near-perfect wall. Once that is accomplished, the last remaining challenge is to finish the joints to meet your appearance expectations. This chapter helps you determine the level of quality you need in your finish and shows you how to obtain it.

Note that various organizations provide information about recommended standards or tolerances for finishing of drywall joints. See pages 467 and 474 in the Appendix for information about standards and tolerances.

For instructions on the safe use of joint compounds, texturing materials and related products, see Chapter 13, Safety Considerations, Material Handling.

Contract documents traditionally have used nonspecific terms such as 'industry standards' or 'workmanlike finish' to describe how finished gypsum board walls and ceilings should look. This practice often has lead to misunderstanding about the degree of finishing sophistication required for any particular job.

A collective effort of four industry trade associations—Association of the Wall and Ceiling Industries-International (AWCI), Ceilings and Interior Systems Construction Association (CISCA), Gypsum Association (GA) and Painting and Decorating Contractors of America (PDCA)—has resulted in the adoption of industry-wide recommended specifications on levels of gypsum board finish. The work identifies five specific levels of finishing, enabling architects to more closely identify the sophistication required and allowing for better competitive bidding among contractors. ASTM recognized this specification by including the levels of gypsum board finishing in ASTM C840.

Key factors used in determining the sophistication level required include the location of the work to be done, type and angle of surface illumination (both natural and artificial lighting), orientation of the panels during installation (see page 104), type of paint or wall covering to be used and method of application. Critical lighting conditions, gloss paints and thin wall coverings require a high level of finish, while heavily textured surfaces or surfaces that will be decorated with heavy-gauge wall coverings require less sophistication.

Definitions of the five levels of finishing are provided below, together with a matrix that helps detail how each level of finishing is achieved, using Sheetrock Brand joint treatment and finishing products, and the appearance of the finished wall that may be anticipated for each level.

Applications of Sheetrock Brand joint treatment products to joints, beads, trims and corners is described on pages 169-175. The number of layers of compound and the degree of finishing advances to meet the requirements of each level.

Finishing Level Definitions

The following finishing level definitions are based on GA-214-96, "Recommended Levels of Gypsum Board Finish," and are intended to provide an industry standard for drywall finishing.

Level 0 Used in temporary construction or wherever the final decoration has not been determined. Unfinished. No taping, finishing or corner beads are required. Also could be used where non-predecorated panels will be used in demountable-type partitions which are to be painted as a final finish.

Level 1 Frequently used in plenum areas above ceilings, in attics, in areas where the assembly would generally be concealed or in building service corridors and other areas not normally open to public view. Some degree of sound and smoke control is provided; in some geographic areas, this level is referred to as "fire-taping," although this level of finish does not typically meet fire-resistant assembly requirements. Where a fire resistance rating is required for the gypsum board assembly, details of construction should be in accordance with reports of fire tests of assemblies that have met the requirements of the fire rating imposed.

All joints and interior angles shall have tape embedded in joint compound. Accessories are optional at specifier discretion in corridors and other areas with pedestrian traffic. Tape and fastener heads need not be covered with joint compound. Surface shall be free of excess joint compound. Tool marks and ridges are acceptable.

Level 2 May be used with setting-type compound for areas where water-resistant gypsum backing board, specification ASTM C630, is used as a substrate for tile. It may also be specified for standard gypsum board surfaces in garages, warehouse storage or other similar areas where surface appearance is not of primary importance.

All joints and interior angles shall have tape embedded in joint compound and shall be immediately wiped with a joint knife or trowel, leaving a thin coating of joint compound over all joints and interior angles. Fastener heads and accessories shall be covered with a coat of joint compound. Surface shall be free of excess joint compound. Tool marks and ridges are acceptable.

Level 3 Typically used in areas which are to receive heavy texture (spray or hand applied) finishes before final painting, or where commercial-grade (heavy duty) wallcoverings are to be applied as the final decoration. This level of finish should not be used where smooth painted surfaces or where lighter weight wallcoverings are specified. The prepared surface shall be coated with a drywall primer prior to the application of final finishes.

All joints and interior angles shall have tape embedded in joint compound and shall be immediately wiped with a joint knife or trowel, leaving a thin coating of joint compound over all joints and interior angles. One additional coat of joint compound shall be applied over all joints and interior angles. Fastener heads and accessories shall be covered with two separate coats of joint compound. All joint compounds shall be smooth and free of tool marks and ridges. The prepared surface shall be covered with a drywall primer prior to the application of the final decoration.

Level 4 This level should be used where residential grade (light duty) wall coverings, flat paints or light textures are to be applied. The prepared surface shall be coated with a drywall primer prior to the application of final finishes. Release agents for wall coverings are specifically formulated to minimize damage if coverings are subsequently removed. The weight, texture and sheen level of the wallcovering material selected should be taken into consideration when specifying wallcoverings over this level of drywall treatment. Joints and fasteners must be sufficiently concealed if the wallcovering material is lightweight, contains limited pattern, has a glossy finish or has any combination of these features. In critical lighting areas, flat paints applied over light textures tend to reduce joint photographing. Gloss, semigloss and enamel paints are not recommended over this level of finish.

All joints and interior angles shall have tape embedded in joint compound and shall be immediately wiped with a joint knife or trowel, leaving a thin coating of joint compound over all joints and interior angles. In addition, two separate coats of joint compound shall be applied over all flat joints and one separate coat of joint compound applied over interior angles. Fastener heads and accessories shall be covered with three separate coats of joint compound. All joint compounds shall be smooth and free of tool marks and ridges. The prepared surface shall be covered with a drywall primer prior to the application of the final decoration.

Level 5 The highest quality finish is the most effective method to provide a uniform surface and minimize the possibility of joint photographing and of fasteners showing through the final decoration. This level of finish is required where gloss, semigloss or enamel are specified. or when flat joints are specified over an untextured surface, or where critical lighting conditions occur. The prepared surface shall be coated with a drywall primer prior to the application of final decoration.

All joints and interior angles shall have tape embedded in joint compound and immediately wiped with a joint knife or trowel, leaving a thin coating of joint compound over all joints and interior angles. Two separate coats of joint compound shall be applied over all flat joints and one separate coat of joint compound applied over interior angles. Fastener heads and accessories shall be covered with three separate coats of joint compound. A thin skim coat of joint compound shall be trowel applied to the entire surface. Excess compound is immediately sheared off, leaving a film or skim coating of compound completely covering the paper. As an alternative to a skim coat, a material manufactured especially for this purpose may be applied. The surface must be smooth and free of tool marks and ridges. The prepared surface shall be covered with a drywall primer prior to the application of the final decoration.

The following matrix helps define the expected appearance of each level and basic requirements for achieving that level. Additional guidelines are offered for meeting the specified finish level using SHEETROCK Brand products and application techniques.

Finishing Level Matrix

Finishing Level	Final Appearance	How To Achieve Result		
		Joints & Interior Angles	Accessories & Fasteners	Surface
5	No marks or ridges. Entire surface covered with skim coat of compound and ready to prime before decorating with gloss, semigloss or enamel, or flat joints over an untextured surface.	As in Level 4	As in Level 4	Skim coat plus prime with SHEETROCK Brand First Coat primer before painting or texturing
4	No marks or ridges. Ready for priming, followed by wallcoverings, flat paints or light textures.	Two separate coats of compound over Level 2	Three separate coats of compound	Joints filled and smoothed again. Shall be primed with SHEETROCK Brand First Coat before painting or texturing
3	No marks or ridges. Ready for priming, to be followed by heavy texture.	One separate coat of compound over Level 2	Two separate coats of compound	Joints filled and smooth. Shall be primed with SHEETROCK Brand First Coat before painting or texturing
2	Tool marks and and ridges okay. Thin coating of compound covers tape; one one coat compound over fastener heads.	Tape embedded in compound and immediately wiped to leave a thin coating of compound over tape	One coat of compound	Free of excess compound
1	Tool marks and ridges acceptable.	Tape embedded in compound	Optional— One coat of compound	Free of excess compound
0	Unfinished	None		

Recommended Levels of Paint Finish Over Gypsum Board

The recommended level of paint finish over gypsum board wall and ceiling surfaces varies depending on location in the structure, the type of paint applied, the finish achieved on the gypsum board substrate prior to final decoration and the type of illumination striking the surface. The following recommendations from the Drywall Finishing Council Incorporated describe various levels of paint finish as the final decoration over new interior gypsum board surfaces.

Level 0

No painting required. Note that this is recommended where final decoration is not required.

Level 1

a. When final decoration is undetermined, all appropriately prepared gypsum board surfaces shall have one coat of drywall primer applied. Drywall primer shall be applied to the mil film thickness and application conditions specified by the primer manufacturer.

or

b. When wallcoverings are to be applied, all appropriately prepared gypsum board surfaces shall have one coat of wallcovering primer applied.

Wallcovering primer shall be applied to the mil film thickness and application conditions specified by the primer manufacturer.

Level 2

All appropriately prepared gypsum board surfaces shall have one coat of topcoat material applied to yield a uniform surface. Paint shall be applied to the mil film thickness and application conditions specified by the paint manufacturer. Note that the painted surface may not achieve uniform appearance, color or sheen, but shall be absent of defects caused by the painting contractor's workforce. This level is recommended where economy is of primary concern.

Level 3

All appropriately prepared gypsum board surfaces shall have two separate coats of topcoat material applied to yield a properly painted surface. Paint shall be applied to the mil film thickness and application conditions specified by the paint manufacturer. Note that this is typically recommended for areas having textures (spray or hand applied) over a primed gypsum board surface and the area is not subject to critical lighting. Refer to Drywall Finishing Council document titled, "Recommended Specification For Preparation of Gypsum Board Surfaces Prior To Texture Application." When subjected to critical lighting, a Level 5 gypsum board finish as defined in GA-214-96 ("Recommended Levels of Gypsum Board Finish") is recommended.

Level 4

All appropriately prepared gypsum board surfaces shall have one coat of drywall primer applied to yield a properly painted surface and one separate coat of topcoat material applied to a properly painted surface over the drywall primer. Paint shall be applied to the mil film thickness and application conditions specified by the paint manufacturer. Note that this is typically recommended for smooth surfaces not subject to critical lighting and areas having light to medium texture finishes (spray or hand applied over a primed gypsum board surface). Refer to Drywall Finishing Council document titled, "Recommended Specification For Preparation of Gypsum Board Surfaces Prior To Texture Application." When subjected to critical lighting, a Level 5 gypsum board finish as defined in GA-214-96 is recommended.

Level 5

All appropriately prepared gypsum board surfaces shall have one coat of drywall primer applied to yield a properly painted surface. Two separate coats of topcoat material shall be applied over the drywall primer to yield a properly painted surface. Paint shall be applied to the mil film thickness and application conditions specified by the paint manufacturer. Note that this level is recommended where the best paint finish is required, such as under critical lighting conditions or when paints that have a glossy surface are used. Recommended with a Level 5 gypsum board finish as described in the "Recommended Levels of Gypsum Board Finish" (GA-214-96). This system, when combined with the Level 5 gypsum board finish is the most effective method to minimize joint and fastener photographing and provides the most uniform final finish.

Trim Accessory Application

Trim accessories simplify and enhance the finishing of gypsum board assemblies. The accessories are low in cost, easily applied and designed to work together for long-lasting, trouble-free construction. All are suitable for steel-frame and wood-frame construction.

Corner Bead Application

SHEETROCK Brand corner reinforcements provide strong, durable protection for outside angle corners, uncased openings, pilasters, beams and soffits. The exposed nose of the bead resists impact and forms a screed for finishing. Corner bead should be installed in one piece unless the length of corner exceeds stock bead lengths. Install as noted for each product.

SHEETROCK **Brand Paper Faced Metal Corner Bead** is a solid-flange corner bead with a specially formulated paper laminated to its surface. The combination of materials assures strong corner protection plus an extraordinary bonding mechanism that eliminates edge cracking problems commonly experienced with conventional bare metal bead. The bead is affixed by applying a laminating layer of joint compound between the rough corner and the bead. This is accomplished by 1) hand applying compound to the gypsum board with a 4″ drywall knife, or 2) using a mechanical angle applicator to apply compound to the wall surface, or 3) hopper-applying joint compound to the back of the bead. Once the joint compound is uniformly applied, the bead is simply pressed in place by hand or with a bead roller, then finished in a normal fashion.

 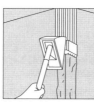

Hand Application *Mechanical Application* *Hopper Application* *Press in Place*

 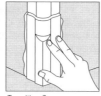

If paper-faced bullnose corner bead is used, transition corners and transition caps are available to assure smooth transitions around corners and from bullnose wall corners to square baseboard corners.

Transition Corner *Transition Cap*

There are also a variety of paper-faced trim products. In general, these are installed in the same way as the beads. Among these are the following special trim products:

- SHEETROCK Brand Paper Faced Metal Inside Corner, Tape On Trim (B2), forms true inner 90-degree corner angles.

- SHEETROCK Brand Paper Faced Metal Offset Inside Corner, Tape On Trim (B2 OS), is designed for 135-degree inside corner offset angles.

- SHEETROCK Brand Paper Faced Metal Inner Cove, Tape On Trim (SLIC), creates smooth, rounded inside corners.

- SHEETROCK Brand Paper Faced Metal Offset Inner Cove, Tape On Trim (SLIC OS), is a softline (bullnose) inside corner for 135-degree offset angles.

- SHEETROCK Brand Paper Faced Metal "L" Shaped, Tape On Trim (B4 Series), is a trim used where wallboard abuts suspended ceilings, beams, plaster and concrete walls; also used at untrimmed door and window jambs; available with and without bead.

- SHEETROCK Brand Paper Faced Metal Reveal, Tape On Trim (Reveal NB), is a modified tape-on "L" trim which can be used to create reveals on soffits, walls and ceilings, around light boxes and other architectural components.

- SHEETROCK Brand Paper Faced Metal "J" Shaped, Tape On Trim (B9), is a J-trim that completely surrounds the rough edge of wallboard, providing a strong, clean corner.

- SHEETROCK Brand Paper Faced Metal Premasked L-Shaped, Tape On Trim (Premasked L), provides a serrated paper strip that protects the adjacent surfaces of ceiling or wall intersections. Simply tear away the protective strip after the job is completed, leaving virtually no clean up of the adjacent surface.

More information about these and related products is available in J1424, *Interior Finishing Products Catalog,* and additional installation information may be found in J1124, SHEETROCK *Brand Paper Faced Metal Bead and Trim Installation Guide.*

SHEETROCK **Brand Flexible Metal Corner Tape** is a flexible reinforcement that ensures straight, sharp corners on any angle. It provides durable corner protection on cathedral and drop ceilings, arches and around bay windows. The tape is available in two widths: 2-1/16″ and 4″. The 2-1/16″ width has a 1/16″ gap between two 7/16″-wide galvanized, rust-resistant steel strips and the 4″ width has two 7/8″-wide galvanized, rust-resistant steel strips. When folded, the tape forms a strong corner bead. It is applied with standard joint compound, feathered at the edges for a smooth wall surface. It is also useful for joining drywall partitions to plastered walls in remodeling and for repairing chipped and cracked corners. Available in convenient 100′ rolls in dispenser box.

To install: Cut tape to length desired with snips or score with knife and bend. Notch or angle cut for arches and window returns. Do not overlap at intersections or corners. Apply joint compound to both sides of corner angle, fold tape at its center to form a bead and press the metal strip side into joint compound. Follow immediately with a thin coat of compound over the tape and let dry. Finish the corner in the conventional manner with additional coats of joint compound.

Cut tape with snips.　*Embed in joint compound.*　*Finish corner.*

Dur-A-Bead Corner Bead is a galvanized solid-flange corner bead designed for protecting external corners. It may be nailed through the board to wood framing or staple attached with 9/16" galvanized staples to the board alone in either wood- or steel-framed construction. A special clinch-on tool also may be used for flange attachment. Bead should be attached at 9" intervals in both flanges with fasteners placed opposite one another. Flange widths available: No. 103, 1-1/4" x 1-1/4"; No. 104, 1-1/8" x 1-1/8".

Clinch-on tool crimps solid-flange beads into place.

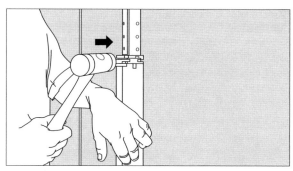

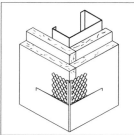 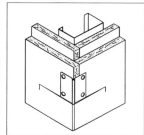

No. 800 Corner Bead　*Dur-A-Bead Corner Bead*

Sheetrock Brand No. 800 Corner Bead is a galvanized fine-mesh, expanded-flange corner bead. The mesh flange provides exceptional joint compound bond and reinforcement. It may be attached with nails or staples directly opposite one another at 9" intervals, just as Dur-A-Bead is applied. Finishing with three coats of a Sheetrock Brand Joint Compound is recommended.

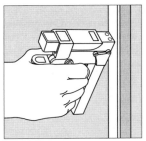 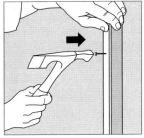

Stapling is the standard way to attach SHEETROCK Brand No. 800 Corner Bead.

For wood studs, nails in both bead flanges are also satisfactory.

SHEETROCK Brand SPEEDBEAD Corner Bead is a unique metal corner bead with edge barbs that hold the bead in place with minimal use of fasteners. Press SPEEDBEAD onto outside corners, using hand pressure or a rubber mallet to ensure adequate penetration of barbs into gypsum panel surface. Supplemental fasteners may be used near each end and at midpoints of each bead section, making sure the fasteners are driven below the anticipated finished joint compound surface.

Metal Trim Application

SHEETROCK Brand Metal Trim serves to protect and finish gypsum panels at window framing and door jambs; they are also used at ceiling-wall intersections and partition perimeters to form a recess for acoustical sealant. Also serve as a relief joint at the intersection of dissimilar constructions, such as gypsum board to concrete.

Metal trims provide maximum protection and neat finished edges to gypsum panels at window and door jambs, at internal angles and at intersections where panels abut other materials. The trim pieces are easily installed by nailing or screwing through the proper leg of trim. Various configurations are available depending on the required application.

No. 200-A SHEETROCK Brand Metal Trim (J-shaped channel, 1/2″ and 5/8″ size)–Apply gypsum panels, omitting fasteners at framing member where trim is to be installed. Leave a space 3/8″ to 1/2″ wide between edge of panel and face of jamb. This provides space for installation of hardware. Slip trim over edge of panel with wide knurled flange on room side and fasten trim and panel to framing. Use same type fasteners used to attach panels; space fasteners 9" o.c. max. Finish with three coats of conventional joint compound; only two coats are required with SHEETROCK Brand Lightweight All Purpose (PLUS 3) Ready-Mixed Joint Compound.

No. 200-B SHEETROCK Brand Metal Trim (L-shaped channel, 1/2″ and 5/8″ size)–Apply gypsum panels the same way as for No. 200-A Trim, omitting fasteners and leaving 3/8″ to 1/2″ space at jamb. Place trim over edge of panel with knurled flange exposed. Attach trim and panel to framing with fasteners spaced 9″ o.c. max. Finish with three coats of conventional joint compound; only two coats are required with SHEETROCK Brand Lightweight All Purpose (PLUS 3) Ready-Mixed Joint Compound.

Nos. 401 and 402 Sʜᴇᴇᴛʀᴏᴄᴋ Brand Metal Trim (J-stop, 1/2" and 5/8" size)–Apply the trim to the wall before the gypsum panels go up, by nailing through trim flange into framing; board is held firmly in place by short leg of trim. No additional edge fastening is necessary. Space fasteners 9" o.c. Requires no finishing compound.

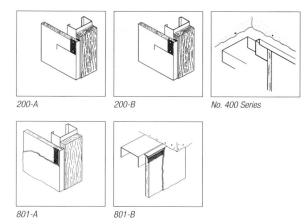

200-A *200-B* *No. 400 Series*

801-A *801-B*

No. 801-A and 801-B Sʜᴇᴇᴛʀᴏᴄᴋ Brand Metal Trim (1/2″ and 5/8″ size)–Slip channel-type 801-A Trim over the edge of the board, or position L-shaped 801-B Trim on the edge of the board with the expanded flange on the room side. Fasten with staples or nails 9″ o.c. max. for drywall applications. Finish with three coats of conventional joint compound (only two coats are required with Sʜᴇᴇᴛʀᴏᴄᴋ Brand Lightweight [Pʟᴜs 3] All Purpose Ready-Mixed Joint Compound).

Vinyl Trim Application

P-1 Vinyl Trim

For structural relief and effective sound control, Sʜᴇᴇᴛʀᴏᴄᴋ Brand Vinyl Trim finishes edges of gypsum panels and acts as a seal where the panel adjoins dissimilar structural surfaces. Install as follows:

Sʜᴇᴇᴛʀᴏᴄᴋ Brand P-1 Vinyl Trim (P-1A, 1/2″ size; P-1B, 5/8″ size)-Apply trim to edges of gypsum panels that will abut ceilings or walls. Slip trim over edges of panels for friction fit. Position panels, press trim edges against abutting surfaces for a snug contact and attach in conventional manner. Use the same procedure for P-1A and P-1B.

Control Joint Application

Proper installation of control joints in wall and ceiling membranes should include breaking the gypsum boards behind the control joint. In ceiling construction, the framing should also be broken, and in partitions, separate studs should be used on each side of the control joints. Control joints should be positioned to intersect light fixtures, air diffusers, door openings and other areas of stress concentration.

Gypsum construction should be isolated with control joints where (a) partitions or ceilings of dissimilar construction meet and remain in the same plane; (b) wings of "L", "U" and "T" shaped ceiling areas are joined; and (c) expansion or control joints occur in the base wall construction and/or building structure. Just as important, control joints should be used in the face of gypsum partitions and ceilings when the size of the surface exceeds the following control-joint spacings; Partitions, 30 ft. maximum in either direction; Interior Ceilings (with perimeter relief), 50 ft. maximum in either direction; Interior Ceilings (without perimeter relief), 30 ft. maximum in either direction; and Exterior Ceilings, 30 ft. maximum in either direction.

Ceiling-height door frames may be used as vertical control joints for partitions; however, door frames of lesser height may only be used as control joints if standard control joints extend to the ceiling from both corners of the top of the door frame. When planning locations for control joints in the ceiling, it is recommended that they be located to intersect column penetrations, since movement of columns can impose stresses on the ceiling membrane.

Control Joints, when properly insulated and backed by gypsum panels, have been fire-endurance tested and are certified for use in one- and two-hour-rated walls.

Installation   At control joint locations:

1. Leave a 1/2" continuous opening between gypsum boards for insertion of surface-mounted joint.

2. Interrupt wood floor and ceiling plates with a 1/2" gap, wherever there is a control joint in the structure.

3. Provide separate supports for each control joint flange.

4. Provide an adequate seal or safing insulation behind control joints where sound and/or fire ratings are prime considerations.

   Control Joint No. 093—Apply over the face of gypsum board where specified. Cut to length with a fine-toothed hacksaw (32 teeth per in.). Cut end joints square, butt together and align to provide a neat fit. Attach the control joint to the gypsum board with Bostitch 9/16" Type G staples, or equivalent, spaced 6" o.c. max. along each flange. Remove the plastic tape after finishing with joint compound.

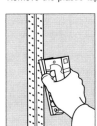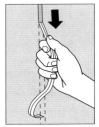

Control Joint No. 093 stapled, finished, tape removed.

Fire-Rated Control Joints

**47 STC
(SA-860302);
2-hr. Fire Rating**

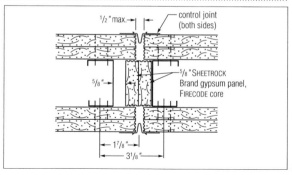

**47 STC
(SA-860217);
2-hr. Fire Rating**

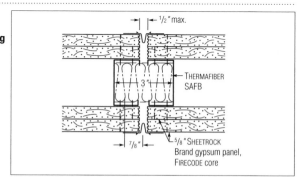

1-hr. Fire Rating

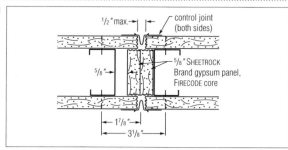

Maximum Spacing–Control Joints

Construction & Location	Max. Single Dimension		Max. Single Area	
	ft.	m	ft².	m²
Partition-interior	30	9	–	–
Ceiling-interior				
with perimeter relief	50	15	2500	230
without perimeter relief	30	9	900	85
Ceiling-exterior gypsum	30	9	900	85

Control Joint No. 093

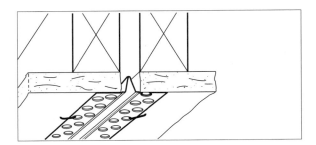

Joint Treatment for Drywall Construction

Application Conditions

In cold weather during joint finishing, temperatures within the building should be maintained within the range of 55° to 70°F and adequate ventilation should be provided. Also see "Quality Drywall Finishing in All Kinds of Weather," USG folder J-75.

Check Working Surfaces

Gypsum panels must be tightly fastened to framing members without breaking the surface paper or fracturing the core. Make certain panel joints are aligned. When one panel is higher than another it becomes difficult to leave sufficient compound under the tape covering the high panel. Blisters, bond failure and cracks can easily develop in these areas.

Open spaces between panels of 1/4" or more should be filled with compound at least 24 hours prior to embedding or first-coat work. SHEETROCK Brand Setting-Type (DURABOND) and SHEETROCK Brand Lightweight Setting-Type (EASY SAND) Joint Compounds, which are hardening types, are recommended for these large fills. With these setting-type compounds as a fill, joint treatment may begin as soon as the compound has hardened, eliminating the typical 24-hr. drying period. Good planning prior to hanging panels eliminates unnecessary joints.

Care of Equipment

Applicators must keep tools and equipment clean and in good repair to secure satisfactory results. With mechanical tools, parts must be replaced when they show signs of wear.

Mixing joint compounds in dirty buckets or failure to wash down the exposed container sides as material is used causes lumps, scratches and usually creates hard working material. With setting-type materials such as SHEETROCK Brand Setting-Type (DURABOND) and SHEETROCK Brand Lightweight Setting-Type (EASY SAND) Joint Compounds, a residue of dry compounds will shorten setting time of the new batch.

The hardening action of SHEETROCK Brand Setting-Type (DURABOND) and SHEETROCK Brand Lightweight Setting-Type (EASY SAND) Joint Compounds requires that all tools, mixing containers, mud pans, etc., used for application be thoroughly cleaned. Flush and clean these compounds from equipment and brush before the setting action takes place. Immersion of equipment in water will not prevent hardening of the compound.

Mechanical tool application is not recommended with fast-setting SHEETROCK Brand Setting-Type (DURABOND) and SHEETROCK Brand Lightweight Setting-Type (EASY SAND) Joint Compounds.

Mixing Joint Compounds

1. Mix powder joint compounds in a clean 5-gal. container—(preferably plastic for SHEETROCK Brand Setting-Type (DURABOND) and SHEETROCK Brand Lightweight Setting-Type (EASY SAND) Joint Compounds. A hand mixer resembling a commercial potato masher makes a convenient mixing tool. Power mixing saves considerable time, particularly where mixing in a central location is convenient. Power mixing is highly recommended. Power may be supplied by a 1/2" heavy-duty electric drill operating at 450 to 650 rpm. Drills operating at high speeds whip air into the compound, and also accelerate setting of setting-type compounds. (See page 432 for information about mixing paddles.) Small amounts of powder joint compounds may be mixed in a small bowl or mud pan. Keep mixing buckets and tools clean at all times. Containers having any residue of joint compounds in them may cause premature hardening, scratching and incompatibility problems.

2. Pour proper amount of clean drinkable water into a container. Use room-temperature water, as very cold or hot water will affect the set time. The amounts for type of application and product used are shown in the directions on the package. Dirty water (such as that used to clean tools) will contaminate compound and cause erratic setting of SHEETROCK Brand Setting-Type (DURABOND) and SHEETROCK Brand Lightweight Setting-Type (EASY SAND) Compounds.

3. Sift powder joint compound into water, allowing complete wetting of the powder.

4. Mix as shown below:

a. For powder SHEETROCK Brand Setting-Type (DURABOND) and Lightweight Setting-Type (EASY SAND) Joint Compounds, follow mixing directions on the bag. Do not overmix; this may speed up hardening time. Note: Keep compound from being contaminated by any other materials such as other type joint compounds, dirty water or previously mixed SHEETROCK Brand Setting-Type (DURABOND) and SHEETROCK Brand Lightweight Setting-Type (EASY SAND) Joint Compounds. Contamination will affect the hardening time and properties of the compound. Do not remix if product has started to set. Overmixing or retempering of setting-type joint compounds will affect the set time and reduce strength development.

Mix only as much SHEETROCK Brand Setting-Type (DURABOND) and SHEETROCK Brand Lightweight Setting-Type (EASY SAND) Joint Compound as can be used within time period shown on bag (usually about 30 minutes for DURABOND 45, 1 hour for DURABOND 90, for example).

The compound will harden chemically after this time period, even under water. Do not attempt to hold wet mix or immerse joint compound-coated tools in water to hold back hardening. Retempering the compound is not recommended.

An accelerator may be used to alter the set time of the compound. USG Gypsum Accelerator-High Strength is an accelerator that was developed for use in conventional basecoat plaster products, but can be used to reduce the setting time of Sheetrock Brand Setting-Type (Durabond or Easy Sand) Joint Compounds. The following chart shows the amounts of accelerator per unit of joint compound and the resulting set times.

Set Time Chart For the Addition of USG High Strength Gypsum Accelerator To Setting-Type Joint Compounds

Accelerator Amounts		Approximate Set Time (minutes)*		
Tbls. per Bag	Tbls. per Bread Pan (Approx. 1/4 bag)	Easy Sand/ Durabond 90 Joint Compound	Easy Sand/ Durabond 45 Joint Compound	Easy Sand/ Durabond 20 Joint Compound
1.0	0.22	40	20	10
2.0	0.44	30	10	—
6.0	1.33	20	—	—

* Actual set times may vary due to mixing procedures, temperature, water and other job conditions. When set time is critical, a small test batch should be made to determine required amounts of accelerator.

b. For Sheetrock Brand Powder Joint Compounds (drying type), sift powder into water and stir until the powder is uniformly damp, then after approx. 15 min., remix vigorously until smooth. Note: Do not add extra water. Use specified amounts of water, as Sheetrock Brand Joint Compounds will retain their original mixed consistency over extended periods. On occasions, some slight liquid separation or settlement of compound may take place in the bucket, but a remix will restore the compound to its original consistency.

c. For Sheetrock Brand Ready-Mixed Compounds (drying type), mix contents and use at package consistency for fasteners and corner beads. Should be thinned for taping and finishing and for use with mechanical tools. Add water in half-pint increments to avoid overthinning. Remix and test apply after each water addition. Either hand mixer or drill mixer can be used to mix compounds.

Use cool to lukewarm (not hot) water. If compound should accidentally be overthinned, simply add more Ready-Mixed Compound to thicken, then remix.

To hold the wet mix in a container for prolonged periods, wash down the exposed container sides, cover the material with a wet cloth or a thin layer of water and put the lid back on the pail. When needed, pour off water and adjust to a working viscosity.

Ready-mixed compound is sensitive to cold weather and must be protected from freezing. If material freezes in container, allow it to thaw at room temperature (do not force the thawing process). Do not pour off any liquid that has separated from the compound. Remix using a power drill mixer until smooth and creamy. Usually it will again be usable, unless it has been subjected to several freeze-thaw cycles.

Ready-mixed compound can be used in tools and containers previously used for powder compound after normal cleaning.

Joint Compounds for Manufactured Housing

USG has formulated special joint compounds for manufactured housing. These are setting-type compounds designed for the industry's controlled manufacturing environment and the strength characteristics required for over-the-road transit of the factory-built home. For information about these products, recommended applications and instructions for their use, contact your local USG sales office.

Hand Tool Application

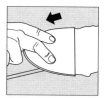

Prefilling 'V' joint of SHEETROCK Brand Gypsum Panels

Prefilling Joints This step is necessary with SW Edge board. Prefilling is desirable when large gaps are present between panels. Fill the 'V' groove between SHEETROCK Brand Gypsum Panels, SW (see diagram) with SHEETROCK Brand Setting-Type (DURABOND 45 or 90) or Lightweight Setting-Type (EASY SAND 45 or 90) Joint Compound. Apply compound directly over 'V' groove with a flexible 5" or 6" joint finishing knife. Wipe off excess compound that is applied beyond the groove. Allow fill compound to harden.

Embedding Tape Make sure no fasteners protrude above the gypsum panel surface. Using a broad steel finishing knife, apply a continuous coat of taping, all-purpose or setting-type joint compound to fill the channel formed by the tapered edges of the panels. Center and lightly press SHEETROCK Brand Joint Tape into fresh joint compound. Working within a convenient arms-reach area, embed tape by holding knife at an angle to panel. Draw knife along joint with sufficient pressure to remove excess compound above and below tape and at edges (see illustration).

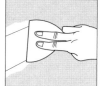

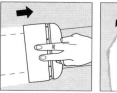

Apply a thin coat of taping compound, above; press joint tape into compound; draw knife over tape to remove excess compound, right.

Apply a thin coat of joint compound over tape, above; apply taping compound, all-purpose or setting-type, over fasteners, right.

Leave sufficient compound under tape for proper bond but not over 1/32" under edge. While embedding, apply a thin coat of joint compound over the tape (above). This thin coat reduces edge wrinkling or curling and makes the tape easier to conceal with following coats. Allow to dry completely. (See drying and setting time guides on pages 183 and 186.) Do not use topping compound for embedding tape.

For interior corners, apply compound to each side of the 90° inside corner. Crease SHEETROCK Brand Joint tape down the center with fingers and embed into joint compound. Use knife to embed tape into compound, first on one side of the angle, then the other.

Apply all-purpose or setting-type taping compound, at least 6" wide, over all corner beads and trims that are to receive joint compound.

Spotting Fastener Heads Use ready-mixed compounds at package consistency or powder compounds mixed per bag directions. Do not add excess water. Apply all-purpose or setting-type joint compound over all fasteners (above, right) immediately before or after embedding tape. Fill only the fastener depression. Apply enough pressure on knife to level compound with panel surface. Allow each coat to dry. Repeat application until fastener depressions are flush with panel surface (normally two or three applications).

Filling Beads Use ready-mixed compounds at package consistency or powder compounds mixed per bag directions. Apply all-purpose or setting-type compound at least 6″ wide over all corner beads (below) and to trims that are to receive compound. Allow each coat to dry. Apply following coats approximately 2″ wider than preceding coats. For smoother finishing, the final coat of joint compound may be thinned slightly.

Paper-faced metal drywall bead is applied quickly by applying joint compound to the bead with an installation hopper. Bead is then pressed onto corner.

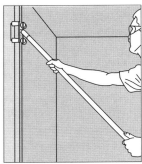

Paper-Faced Metal Beads and Trims Paper-faced metal beads and trims perform the same function as bare metal or vinyl beads and trims, but are applied at the taping stage rather than at the cladding stage of the drywall job. SHEETROCK Brand Paper-Faced Metal Bead and Trim are preferred because the paper bonds with the joint compound and drywall surface to provide superior resistance to edge cracking and chipping despite the stresses of normal building movement and everyday wear and tear.

Unlike conventional metal or vinyl, which are mechanically attached to the board surface, paper-faced metal beads and trims are adhesively applied using SHEETROCK Brand Setting-Type (DURABOND or EASY SAND), or SHEETROCK Brand Ready-Mixed (Taping or All Purpose) Joint Compounds. Topping compounds are not recommended for embedding bead. The paper facing assures excellent adhesion of joint compounds, textures and paints for a strong, smooth finish.

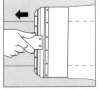

After tape embedding coat is dry, apply topping coat 7″ to 10″ wide over joints, beads and trim.

Apply the joint compound by hand or mechanically to the wallboard and then press the bead in place, or apply joint compound by hopper to the inside of the bead (see illustrations above), then mount in position on board corners. The bead is then finished in the same manner as other beads.

Fill Coat Application After the tape embedding coat is dry, apply a topping or all-purpose compound fill (second) coat approx. 7″ to 10″ wide over taped joints (shown below), beads and trim. Feather edge of second coat approx. 2″ beyond edge of first coat. Spot fasteners with second coat. Allow to dry.

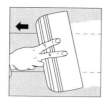

Apply topping compound over joints, fasteners, beads and trim with edges 2" wider than previous coat.

Bevel edges of butt ends of drywall panels before applying joint compound.

Finish Coat Application After second coat is dry, smooth tool marks and other protrusions with a finishing knife. Apply a thin finish (third) coat of ready-mixed, topping or all-purpose compound over joints, fasteners, beads and trim. Finish compound should be applied at a slightly thinner consistency. Feather edges of third coats at least 2" wider than second coats (left). SHEETROCK Brand Lightweight All Purpose (PLUS 3) Joint Compound requires only two coats over metal corner beads and fasteners. Joints, fasteners, beads and trim should be finished as smooth as possible to minimize sanding. Go over the whole job to smooth and touch up with joint compound all scratches, craters, nicks and other imperfections in the dried finish coat.

End Joints Because ends of gypsum panels are flat and have no taper like panel edges, end joints are difficult to conceal. Also, exposed paper on ends may cause visible ridging or beading. The following steps are recommended for joint treatment to minimize crowning and/or ridging of end joints:

1. Before attachment, bevel panel ends approx. 1/8" at a 45° angle using a sharp utility knife. This keeps the paper ends apart and reduces expansion problems caused by the raw paper edge. Also, peel back and remove any loose paper from the end.

2. Gypsum panel ends should be loosely butted together. Ends should be separated slightly and not touching.

3. Prefill the recess with compound and allow to set or dry.

4. Apply compound and paper reinforcing tape over the joint in the same manner as for tapered joints. Embed tape tightly to minimize joint thickness but leave sufficient compound under tape for continuous bond and blister prevention.

5. Finish the end joint to a width at least twice the finish width of a recessed edge joint. This will make the joint less apparent after decoration as the crown will be more gradual.

Finishing Inside Corners Fold tape along center crease. Apply joint compound to both sides of corner and press folded tape into angle. Tightly embed tape into both sides of angle with finishing knife and let dry. Next, apply a thin coat to one side of angle only. Allow to dry before applying finish coat to other side of angle.

Dry Sanding Sand joint compounds to prepare gypsum drywall surfaces for decoration. Sand as necessary to remove excess joint compound from tool marks, lap marks and high crowned joints. Scratches, craters and nicks should be filled with joint compound, then sanded. Do not try to remove these depressions by sanding only.

Select sandpaper or abrasive-mesh cloth with grit as fine as possible. Excessively coarse sandpapers leave scratches that are visible after decoration. For conventional-weight all-purpose compounds, use #120 grit or finer sandpaper (#200 grit or finer mesh cloth or 100 micron or less polyester film-back abrasive sheets). For lightweight, midweight and topping compounds, use #150 grit or finer sandpaper (#220 grit or finer mesh cloth or 80 micron or less polyester film-back abrasive

182

sheets). Only sand surfaces coated with joint compound to avoid scuffing gypsum panel paper. Remove sanding dust before decorating.

Ventilate or use a dust collector to reduce dust in work areas. Use a NIOSH-approved respirator specified for mica and talc when air is dusty. Use of safety glasses is recommended.

Wet Sanding Wet sanding or sponging finished joints, bead, trim and fasteners is suggested rather than dry sanding to avoid creating dust. The best material to use for wet sanding is a high density, small celled, polyurethane sponge. This type of sponge material resembles high quality carpet padding. When only a touch-up is required, a general purpose sponge or smooth, soft cloth will work.

Wet sanding avoids creating dust.

To wet sand, saturate the sponge with clean water containing no soap or additives. Water temperature should be cool to lukewarm, not hot. Wring out sponge only enough to eliminate dripping. To remove high spots, moisten the joint compound with the sponge, then pull a joint knife across. Use as few strokes as possible. Excessive rubbing will groove joints. Clean sponge frequently.

Mechanical Tool Application

Several types of mechanical and semi-mechanical tools are available. Tools used in the following sequence illustrate typical procedures.

1, 2   Using compound of suitable consistency, mechanically tape all joints; wipe down with broad knife. Allow to dry.

3, 4   Mechanically apply tape and compound to the interior angles. Smooth the tape and compound in the angles with corner roller and corner finisher. Touch up with broad knife as necessary. Apply first coat to fastener heads and metal accessories. Allow to dry.

5   Apply fill coat of compound over tape on flat joints using a flat finishing box (above). Using compound of thicker consistency, spot fastener heads and apply second coat to metal accessories. Allow to dry.

Apply finish coat of compound to flat joints with a wider finishing box. Apply finish coat to the interior corner angles with the corner applicator box. Apply finish coat to metal accessories and fastener heads. Allow to dry and smooth lightly as required. Remove all dust before decoration. Do not scuff face paper by oversanding.

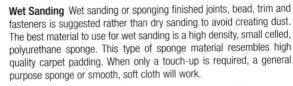

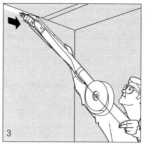

5

**Setting-Type
Joint Compounds—
System
Applications**

SHEETROCK Brand Setting-Type (DURABOND) and SHEETROCK Brand Lightweight Setting-Type (EASY SAND) Joint Compounds are chemical hardening products with varied working (setting) times for finishing interior gypsum panels and exterior gypsum ceiling boards. These specialized products provide short setting times for fast one-day finishing and extended times (up to 6 hours) to suit individual needs. The following application guide will help you choose the proper product to meet your requirements.

Application Guide—Setting-Type Joint Compounds

Compound Type	Setting Time-Min.	Working Time-Min.	Recommended Application
20	20-30	15	application needing very short working time
45	30-80	20	prefill SW panels spot fastener heads embed metal beads
90	85-130	60	all applications
210	180-240	150	embed tape embed metal beads
300	240-360	210	application needing longer working time

For One-Day Finishing Use the techniques shown for hand application; mechanical tool application is not recommended for Sheetrock Brand Setting-Type (Durabond) and Sheetrock Brand Lightweight Setting-Type (Easy Sand) Joint Compounds because these compounds may harden in the tools, making them inoperable. If mechanical tool application is required, caution must be taken in selection of product set time to ensure enough working time exists for application and thorough cleanup of tools. In the following sequence, Steps 1 through 4 should be completed by mid-day. Planning and scheduling according to the setting times of the compounds are essential. For best results, use compound that will set within 1-1/2 to 2 hours.

(Where Sheetrock Brand Gypsum Panels, SW Edge, are used, the first step is to fill the 'V' grooves between panels.)

1. Embed Sheetrock Brand Joint Tape over all joints and angles.

2. Apply compound over corner reinforcement. For best results use compound that will set within 1-1/2 to 2 hours.

3. Spot fastener heads.

4. As soon as taping coat has set (hardened even though not dry), apply second (fill) coat over all joints and angles.

5. After the second (fill) coat application has hardened, apply finishing coat of selected finishing compound to completely cover all joints, angles, corner bead and fasteners.

For Sheetrock Brand Exterior Ceiling Board Surfaces Use hand application techniques and a Sheetrock Brand Setting-Type (Durabond) or Sheetrock Brand Lightweight Setting-Type (Easy Sand) Joint Compound to treat joints and fasteners in USG Exterior Ceiling Board applications. During periods of near-freezing temperatures, check weather forecast before beginning work. Minimum air, water, mix and surface temperatures of 45°F must be assured until compound is completely dry. Apply Sheetrock Brand Setting-Type (Durabond) or Sheetrock Brand Lightweight Setting-Type (Easy Sand) Joint Compound in the following sequence:

1. Prefill joints of Sheetrock Brand Exterior Gypsum Ceiling Board with compound. After prefill has set, tape all joints and angles in the ceiling with compound and Sheetrock Brand Joint Tape. When compound sets (hardens), immediately apply a fill coat of compound; allow to harden before finishing.

2. Apply compound over flanges of control joints, metal beads and trim. Spot all fastener heads.

3. After fill coat has set, apply compound finishing coat. Completely cover all joints, angles, beads, control joints and fasteners.

4. After the joint compound has dried, apply one coat of a good-quality latex flat exterior primer to equalize the joint and wallboard surfaces. Then follow with at least one coat of a balanced, good-quality alkyd or latex exterior finishing system as specified by the paint manufacturer.

For Use with SHEETROCK Brand Gypsum Panels, W/R In areas to be tiled, for tapered edge joints, embed SHEETROCK Brand Joint Tape with SHEETROCK Brand Setting-Type (DURABOND) 45 or 90 or SHEETROCK Brand Lightweight Setting-Type (EASY SAND) 45 or 90 Joint Compound. When set, apply a fill coat of the same joint compound. Take care not to crown the joint. Wipe excess joint compound from the water resistant panel surface before it sets. For end joints and interior angles, embed SHEETROCK Brand Joint Tape with SHEETROCK Brand Setting-Type (DURABOND) or SHEETROCK Brand Lightweight Setting-Type (EASY SAND) Joint Compound. A fill coat is not necessary. Again, take care not to crown the joint. For fasteners, spot fastener heads at least once with setting-type joint compound. Chapter 4 provides instructions for tile work and substrates for areas subjected to constant moisture.

Fill and seal all openings around pipes, fittings and fixtures with a thinned down coat of a good quality tile adhesive. For best results, use tile adhesive both as a sealer and to set the tile. Thin to a paint-like viscosity and apply the thinned compound with a small brush onto the raw gypsum panel core at the cutouts and allow areas to dry thoroughly prior to application of tile. Before adhesive dries, wipe excess material from the surface of gypsum panels.

For areas not to be tiled, embed tape with SHEETROCK Brand Setting-Type (DURABOND) or SHEETROCK Brand Lightweight Setting-Type (EASY SAND) Joint Compound 45 or 90 in the conventional manner. Finish with at least two coats of a SHEETROCK Brand Joint Compound to provide joint finishing for painting and wallpapering.

Note: SHEETROCK Brand Gypsum Panels, WR are not intended for use in areas subject to constant moisture, such as interior swimming pools, gang showers and commercial food processing areas. DUROCK Cement Boards are recommended for these uses.

Drying Time — Joint Compound Under Tape

Standard drying times are based on evaporation of 10 lb. water per 250 ft. reinforcing tape, corresponding to 1/16″ to 5/64″ wet compound thickness under the tape. The drying times for thicker (or thinner) coats of wet compound between tape and panels will increase (or decrease) in proportion to the wet compound thickness.

These drying times apply when the exposed surface of tape is bare or nearly bare, and when adequate ventilation is provided. A heavy compound coat over tape lengthens drying time.

Drying Time—Joint Compound Under Tape

Temp. °F	60°	70°	80°	90°	100°
Temp. °C	16°	21°	27°	32°	38°
98%	18 D	12 D	9 D	6 D	4-1/2 D
97%	12D	9 D	6 D	4-1/2 D	3-1/4 D
96%	10 D	7 D	5 D	3-1/2 D	2-1/2 D
95%	8 D	6 D	4 D	2-3/4 D	2 D
94%	7 D	5 D	3-1/4 D	2-1/4 D	41 H
93%	6 D	4 D	2-3/4 D	2 D	36 H
92%	5 D	3-1/2 D	2-1/2 D	44 H	32 H
91%	4-3/4 D	3-1/4 D	2-1/4 D	40 H	29 H
90%	4-1/2 D	3 D	49 H	36 H	26 H
85%	3 D	2 D	34 H	25 H	18 H
80%	2-1/4 D	38 H	27 H	19 H	14 H
70%	38 H	26 H	19 H	14 H	10 H
60%	29 H	20 H	14 H	10 H	8 H
50%	24 H	17 H	12 H	9 H	6 H
40%	20 H	14 H	10 H	7 H	5 H
30%	18 H	12 H	9 H	6 H	4-1/2 H
20%	16 H	11 H	8 H	5-1/2 H	4 H
10%	14 H	10 H	7 H	5 H	3-1/2 H
0	13 H	9 H	6 H	4-1/2 H	3 H
RH	RH = Relative Humidity	D = Days (24 hr.)	H = Hours		

Finishing

Gypsum drywall provides smooth surfaces that readily accept paint, texture finishes and wall coverings. For satisfactory finishing results, care must be taken to prepare surfaces properly to eliminate possible decorating problems commonly referred to as 'joint banding' and 'photographing.' These problems are usually caused by differences between the porosities and surface textures of the gypsum panel face paper and the finished joint compound, and magnified by the use of gloss paints. Then, when viewed in direct natural lighting, the joints and fasteners in painted walls and ceilings may be visible.

Skim Coating

The best method to prepare any gypsum drywall surface for painting is to apply a skim coat of joint compound. This leaves a film thick enough to fill imperfections in the joint work, smooth the paper texture and provide a uniform surface for decorating. Skim coating is currently recommended when gloss paints are used. It is also the best technique to use when decorating with flat paints.

Skim Coat Application

Finish joints and fasteners in the conventional three-coat manner. After joints are dry, mix joint compound—preferably SHEETROCK Brand All Purpose, SHEETROCK Brand All Purpose (Midweight) or COVER COAT Compound—to a consistency approximating that used for hand taping. Using a trowel, broad knife, or long-nap texture roller, apply only sufficient amounts of joint compound to cover the drywall surface. Then immediately wipe the compound as tightly as possible over the panel surface using a trowel or broad knife. Note: Do not use setting-type joint compound for thin skim coats. If setting-type compound dries before it sets, bond failure may result.

Finishing and Decorating Tips

1. When sanding joint compound applied over joints, fasteners, trim and corner bead, take care to avoid roughening the panel face paper. Any paper roughened during sanding has raised fibers which are conspicuous after painting.

2. All surfaces (including applied joint compound) must be thoroughly dry and dust free before decorating.

3. After conventional finishing of gypsum panel joints and fasteners, apply a skim coat of joint compound over the entire surface. This is the best technique for minimizing surface defects that will show through after painting if critical lighting conditions exist and/or glossy paints are used. Skim coating fills imperfections in joint work, smooths the paper texture and provides a uniform surface for decorating. After skim coat has dried, apply a prime coat of SHEETROCK Brand First Coat for best results.

4. If skim coating is not done, the next best technique for minimizing decorating problems is to apply a prime coat of SHEETROCK Brand First Coat. This paint-like product equalizes joint and wallboard surfaces to help avoid texture or suction variations when the finished paint coats are applied. This procedure minimizes problems with concealment of joints and fasteners.

5. A ceiling or wall texture finish is an excellent method for masking imperfections and diffusing light across wall and ceiling surfaces.

6. Frequent job inspections forestall potential problems and help insure project specifications are being met. Wall and ceiling surfaces should be inspected after the gypsum panels are installed, when the joints are being treated and after the joints are finished before the surface is decorated. These checks will reveal starved and crowned joints which always show up under critical lighting.

Priming

Surface Preparation Proper preparation is essential for producing the best possible painted finish. Surfaces must be dry, clean, sound and free of oil, grease and efflorescence. Glossy surfaces must be dulled. Metal: Exposed metal should be primed with a good rust-inhibitive primer. Concrete: New concrete should age 60 days or more before covering. Fill cracks and level any offsets and voids to the same level as adjacent surfaces with SHEETROCK Brand Setting-Type (DURABOND) or SHEETROCK Brand Lightweight Setting-Type (EASY SAND) Joint Compound or COVER COAT Compound. Apply as many coats as are needed to provide a crack-free fill without edge joinings that show through decoration. Exercise special care to provide a smooth surface free of irregularities in areas exposed to sharply angled lighting. Drywall: Treat drywall joints and nailheads with a SHEETROCK Brand Joint Treatment System.

Also important for a superior paint job is the equalization of both the porosity and texture of the surface to be painted. The best way to achieve this is to skim coat the entire surface with SHEETROCK Brand All Purpose, SHEETROCK Brand All Purpose (Midweight) or COVER COAT

Compound as described above, followed by a prime coat of SHEETROCK Brand First Coat. If skim coating is not done, the next best technique for minimizing decorating problems is to apply a prime coat of SHEETROCK Brand First Coat.

SHEETROCK **Brand First Coat Application**

Specially formulated, fast drying SHEETROCK Brand First Coat equalizes surface texture and porosity to minimize decorating problems.

SHEETROCK Brand First Coat is a specially formulated flat latex paint product with exceptionally high solids content that provides a superior first (prime) coat over interior gypsum board.

In contrast to sealers or vapor barrier paints, SHEETROCK Brand First Coat does not provide a film that seals the substrate surface. Instead, it minimizes porosity differences by providing a base that equalizes the surface absorption and texture of the substrate to minimize 'joint banding', 'photographing' and other decorating problems. SHEETROCK Brand First Coat also provides the proper type and amount of pigments and fillers, that are lacking in many conventional primers and sealers, to equalize the surface textures.

SHEETROCK Brand First Coat is designed for fast, low-cost application. It dries to a hard, white finish in less than 30 minutes and can be top-coated within one hour. Not intended as a final coating, it should be overpainted when dry. The product comes ready-mixed in 5-gal. and 1-gal. pails.

Mixing Ready-mixed SHEETROCK Brand First Coat should be stirred gently. Do not thin for brush or roller application. For spray application, if necessary, add water in half-pint increments up to a maximum 1 qt. of water per gallon. May be tinted.

Application (Walls and Ceilings) Apply a full coverage coat. Material dries to touch in under 30 min. Maintain minimum air, product mix and surface temperature of 55°F during application and until surface is dry. Brush, roller, airless or conventional spray gun may be used.

Brush Use a high-quality, professional paint brush.

Roller Use a high-quality roller with 1/8″ to 1/4″ nap on smooth and semi-smooth surfaces. For any surface, maximum nap length should not exceed 1/2″.

Conventional Spray Gun Use Binks Model 2001 gun, pressurized external, with #565 fluid needle, #66 fluid nozzle and #65 PR air nozzle; or Binks Model 18, pressurized external, with #65 fluid needle, #66 fluid nozzle and #65 PR air nozzle; or Binks model 18, pressurized internal, with #68 fluid needle, #68 fluid nozzle and #206 air nozzle; or Binks Model 18D gun, pressurized internal with #54-1209 fluid needle, #57 fluid nozzle and R-27 air nozzle; or similar equipment. Air hose is typically 3/8″ i.d. with 1/2″ fluid hose i.d.

Airless Spray Gun Use professional equipment that meets or exceeds the following when spraying through 50' of 1/4″ i.d. airless spray hose: output at least 3/4 gal. per minute; pressure at least 2700 psi; and accommodates a spray tip of 0.021″ at 2000 psi. Recommended equipment includes Graco Ultra 1500, 1000 or 750 models with a suitable spray gun that will accommodate a RAC IV 519 (0.019) or RAC IV 521 (0.021) tip, a RAC IV Dripless Guard, and a 30-mesh filter.

Note: Adjust atomizing air pressure and fluid flow rate so that full coverage rate can be achieved by overlapping preceding application with one-quarter to one-half the fan width at a distance of 18″ from the surface. Air pressures and flow rates will vary with hose size and length and paint consistency.

SHEETROCK Brand First Coat contains a high level of select pigments and fillers like conventional latex flat paints. When these paints are used in spray equipment previously used to spray PVA sealers which contain high levels of resin, clogging at the spray gun tip may result. The use of clean or new hoses is recommended to avoid this problem when spraying SHEETROCK Brand First Coat.

Coverage Approx. 300-500 ft.^{2} per gal. of wet-mixed material depending upon factors such as application equipment and technique, condition of the substrate, amount of dilution and thickness and uniformity of coating.

Adding to Wall and Ceiling Textures If slightly better spray properties, wet hide, improved bond, whiteness and surface hardness of texture are desired, SHEETROCK Brand First Coat may be added to wet-mixed SHEETROCK Brand Wall and Ceiling Textures at a rate of up to 1-gal. SHEETROCK Brand First Coat per 30, 32, 40 or 50-lb. bag of texture. Reduce water quantity to account for addition of SHEETROCK Brand First Coat based on 1:1 replacement basis. Surface priming recommendations on texture bag still apply.

SHEETROCK Brand Wallcovering Primer Application

Ready-mixed SHEETROCK Brand Wallcovering Primer prepares and seals most wall and ceiling surfaces for decoration. It is an ideal basecoat for wallcoverings and the USG Decorative Interior Finish System. It may be used on cured new or old plaster, stripped wallpaper, masonry and gypsum panels. It prevents wallcovering adhesive from soaking into porous wall surfaces. Improves adhesion and slip. SHEETROCK Brand Wallcovering Primer is not recommended over lime-gauging or lime-containing plaster finishes. When used in the USG Decorative Interior Finish System it is applied over all joint-treated surfaces prior to the application of USG Plaster Bonder-Clear. It dries quickly to a smooth working surface. It permits later removal of wallpaper.

Preparation Surface must be smooth, clean and dry. Strip old wallcovering. Patch and sand where necessary. Wash walls with a strong detergent, such as a TSP wall cleaner. Rinse and let dry.

Application, Mixing SHEETROCK Brand Wallcovering Primer is ready to use right out of the container. However, if thinning is necessary, add up to 4 oz. water per gallon of primer. Stir well before using. Overthinning will reduce sealing properties.

Application, Joint Treatment When used with the USG Decorative Interior Finish System, tape the joints of the drywall substrate and fill the fasteners with joint compound; apply one additional coat of joint compound on flat joints.

Application, Primer Apply full, uniform coat with brush or roller. Make sure entire surface is covered, especially base and corner areas. One coat is usually sufficient but two coats may be needed over surfaces with excessive suction. Let dry thoroughly between coats and before hanging wallcovering. For USG Decorative Interior Finish System, Sheetrock Brand Wallcovering Primer is applied to the joint compound surfaces only.

Coverage-Approximately 250-350 ft.^{2} per gal. Coverage depends on surface and method of application. Dries in approximately 60 minutes under normal conditions (75°F/50% R.H.). High humidity and cold temperature will slow drying.

Concrete Coating Application

Cover Coat Compound

With ready-mixed Cover Coat Compound, drywall contractors are able to offer smooth or textured, white, ready-to-decorate surfaces on concrete ceilings and columns located above grade. Smooth application and excellent bonding strength make Cover Coat Compound ideal for filling small holes and crevices and for second and following covering applications with drywall methods and tools.

Cover Coat Compound should not be applied over moist surfaces or surfaces likely to become moist (by condensation or otherwise), on ceiling areas below grade, on surfaces which project outside the building, or on other areas which might be subject to moisture, freezing, efflorescence, pitting or popping, movement, or other abnormal condition.

Application

For best results, apply Cover Coat Compound before interior partitions are erected. Use the compound at package consistency to minimize shrinkage. If a thinner material for roller application is desired, the compound may be thinned by adding clean water (up to 1 to 1-1/2 gal. per 61.7 lb. carton or pail) and mixing to desired consistency using a hand mixer or low-speed drill-type mixer. If applicator should inadvertently overthin, simply add additional compound to thicken and remix.

Protect Cover Coat Compound from freezing. During entire application, maintain temperature at or above 55°F, and provide heat and ventilation when necessary.

Prepare the concrete surfaces by removing any major protrusions or ridges. New concrete should age 60 days or more. Remove any form or parting oils, grease or efflorescence. All surfaces must be dry, clean and sound. Prime any exposed metal with a good, rust-inhibitive primer. Fill cracks and holes and level any offsets and voids to the same level as adjacent surfaces with Sheetrock Brand Setting-Type (Durabond) or Sheetrock Brand Lightweight Setting-Type (Easy Sand) Joint Compound. Apply in as many coats as are needed to provide a crack-free fill without edge joinings that show through decoration. Then apply a skim coat of Cover Coat Compound over these areas after setting-type joint compound has hardened but not necessarily dried. Mix compound lightly and test-apply. Add small amounts of water if required. Exercise special care to provide a smooth surface, free of irregularities in areas that will be exposed to sharply angled lighting.

Cover Coat Compound can be applied over joints and ridges left by concrete forms with a flat finisher, broad knife or trowel. Fill in and/or level out small holes and lumps, ridges, lips, etc. with compound. Allow to dry.

Using two workers, apply first coat of compound to entire surface area of ceiling, beam, or column with flat finisher, long nap roller or broad knife. Keep moving in one direction, making sure that each application overlaps the previous one. Follow application with wide rubber squeegee or long-handle drywall blade, 24″ or wider, to smooth out fresh application, leaving a minimum of ridges and imperfections. Apply SHEETROCK Brand No. 800 Corner Bead or SHEETROCK Brand Paper Faced Metal Bead on angles and corners as required, embedding and covering both flanges with a smooth fill of COVER COAT Compound 3″ to 4″ wide. Allow to dry (under good drying conditions, 24 hr.).

Before second-coat application, sand and dust first coat. Apply second coat in manner described above or texture at this point if desired. Allow to dry. Sand to ultimate smoothness with fine sandpaper, if necessary. For texturing second coat, simply add water and/or sand. Use very fluid mix for fine texture, less fluid for coarse effects.

A very rough or uneven concrete surface may require three or more coats applied in the same manner.

COVER COAT Compound may be left undecorated, but it is not washable unpainted. If decoration is specified, follow directions on container of decorating product

More detailed directions, spray application and special-use information are available. Ask for USG Technical Data Sheet J-59.

Note: Check cracking may occur in excessively deep fills. For this reason successive coats are recommended for deep fills using a SHEETROCK Brand Setting-Type (DURABOND) or SHEETROCK Brand Lightweight Setting-Type (EASY SAND) Joint Compound for the first coat.

SHEETROCK Brand Setting-Type Joint Compounds

A SHEETROCK Brand Setting-Type (DURABOND) or SHEETROCK Brand Lightweight Setting-Type (EASY SAND) Joint Compound is equally suitable for filling form offsets and voids left in interior concrete. As with COVER COAT Compound, SHEETROCK Brand Setting-Type (DURABOND) and SHEETROCK Brand Lightweight Setting-Type (EASY SAND) Joint Compounds should not be applied over moist surfaces or surfaces subject to moisture, or any abnormal condition.

Application

Grind off high plane differences in concrete level with adjacent area; remove any form oil, efflorescence or greasy deposits.

Prime exposed metal with a good rust-inhibitive primer.

Mix SHEETROCK Brand Setting-Type (DURABOND) or SHEETROCK Brand Lightweight Setting-Type (EASY SAND) Joint Compound according to bag directions.

Use compound to fill cracks and holes and level any offsets and voids to the same level as adjacent surfaces. Apply as many coats as are needed to provide a crack-free fill without edge joinings that show through decoration. Exercise special care to provide a smooth surface, free of irregularities in areas that will be exposed to sharply angled lighting.

Apply additional coats of SHEETROCK Brand Setting-Type (DURABOND) or SHEETROCK Brand Lightweight Setting-Type (EASY SAND) Joint Compound as required after each coat has set, but not necessarily dried.

Apply a thick skim coat of SHEETROCK Brand Setting-Type (DURABOND) or SHEETROCK Brand Lightweight Setting-Type (EASY SAND) Joint Compound over entire surface. Skim coat must be thick enough to prevent dryout before setting, or bond failure may result. If an easier-sanding surface is desired, apply final skim coat of COVER COAT Compound or SHEETROCK Brand All Purpose Ready-Mixed Joint Compound instead of SHEETROCK Brand Setting-Type (DURABOND) Joint Compound.

Before decorating with paint or texture, apply coat of SHEETROCK Brand First Coat or a good quality, undiluted interior latex flat wall paint over entire surface and allow to dry.

For textured ceiling, apply SHEETROCK Brand Ceiling Spray Texture QT in uniform coat at rate up to 10 ft.^{2}/lb.

Sealant Application (Caulking)

If gypsum board assemblies are to effectively reduce the transmission of sound, they must be airtight at all points. To achieve this, perimeters must be sealed with SHEETROCK Brand Acoustical Sealant, a caulking material that remains resilient. Also, penetrations for electrical outlets, medicine cabinets, plumbing, heating and air-conditioning ducts, telephone and intercom hookups and television antenna outlets must be effectively sealed. (Sealant is not to be used as a fire stopping material for through-penetrations and head-of-wall construction joints.)

Sealing or caulking for sound-control is so important that it must be covered in the specifications, understood by the workers of all related trades, supervised by the foremen, and inspected carefully during construction.

Acoustical sealant application has proven to be the least expensive, most cost effective way to seal assemblies and prevent sound leaks. SHEETROCK Brand Acoustical Sealant is approved for use in all UL fire-rated assemblies without affecting fire ratings. However, sealant is not intended for use as a fire stopping material for through penetrations and head-of-wall construction joints. All references herein to "caulk" or "caulking" indicate use of SHEETROCK Brand Acoustical Sealant.

SHEETROCK Brand Acoustical Sealant effectively seals perimeters and openings in walls and ceilings, increasing sound ratings.

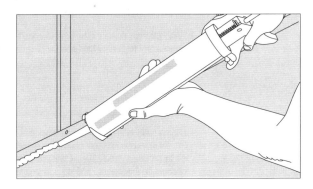

Proper caulking of outlet box (left), and double-layer partition (right).

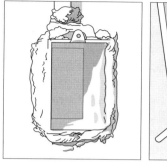
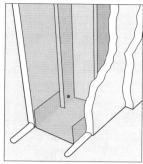

SHEETROCK Brand Acoustical Sealant applied around pipes and ducts effectively seals the wall to reduce sound transmission. Note: Sealant is not to be used as a fire stopping material for through penetrations and head-of-wall construction joints.

5

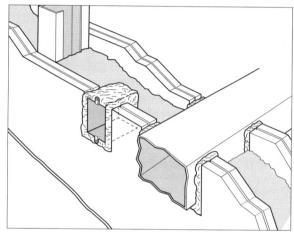

Tests conducted at the USG Research Center demonstrate that reliability of the perimeter seal is increased if perimeter relief does not exceed 1/8″. When such a gap, around the base-layer perimeter, is caulked with a 1/4″ bead of sealant, installation of face panels compresses the sealant into firm contact with all adjacent surfaces to form a permanent airtight seal.

To be effective, sealant must be properly placed. Placement is as important as the amount used. The technical drawings below indicate correct and incorrect applications of acoustical sealant.

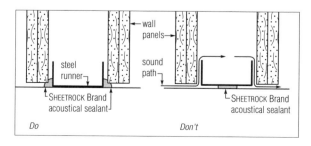

The assemblies tested consisted of 2-1/2″ steel studs 24 o.c., double-layer Sheetrock Brand Gypsum Panels, SW each side; and 1-1/2″ Thermafiber Sound Attenuation Blankets between studs. Results of sealant conditions are shown below.

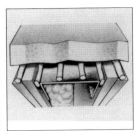

29 STC Unsealed

53 STC Both base layers sealed. No relief on face layers.

53 STC Sealed beneath and on edge of runner track. Base layer not relieved. Face layer relieved and sealed.

Installation	**Partition Perimeter** Cut gypsum boards for loose fit around partition perimeter. Leave a space no more than 1/8″ wide. Apply a 1/4″ min. round bead of sealant to each leg of runners, including those used at partition intersections with dissimilar wall construction. Immediately install boards, squeezing sealant into firm contact with adjacent surfaces. Fasten boards in normal manner. Gypsum panels may have joint treatment applied in normal manner over sealed joints, and gypsum base may be finished normally with veneer plaster. Or, panels may be finished with base or trim as desired.

For caulking application with metal trim over edge of boards where boards intersect dissimilar materials or cracking due to structural movement is anticipated, refer to "Perimeter Isolation" section on page 136.

Control Joints Apply sealant beneath control joint to reduce path for sound transmission through joint.

Partition Intersections Seal intersections with sound-isolating partitions that are extended to reduce sound flanking paths.

Openings Apply sealant around all cutouts such as at electrical boxes, plumbing, medicine cabinets, heating ducts and cold air returns to seal the opening. Caulk sides and backs of electrical boxes to seal them. (Sealant is not to be used as a fire stopping material.)

Door Frames Apply a bead of sealant in the door frame just before inserting face panel.

Details—
use of SHEETROCK Brand
Acoustical Sealant

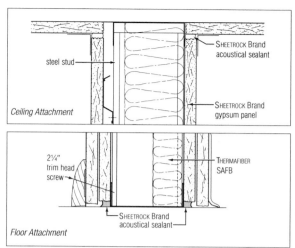

steel stud

SHEETROCK Brand
acoustical sealant

SHEETROCK Brand
gypsum panel

Ceiling Attachment

2¼"
trim head
screw

THERMAFIBER
SAFB

SHEETROCK Brand
acoustical sealant

Floor Attachment

5

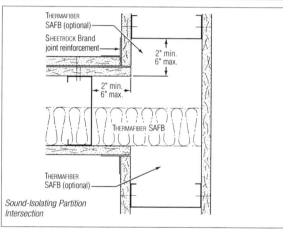

THERMAFIBER
SAFB (optional)

SHEETROCK Brand
joint reinforcement

2" min.
6" max.

2" min.
6" max.

THERMAFIBER SAFB

THERMAFIBER
SAFB (optional)

Sound-Isolating Partition
Intersection

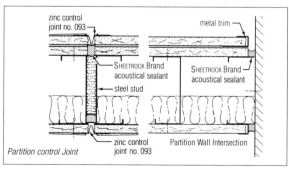

zinc control
joint no. 093

metal trim

SHEETROCK Brand
acoustical sealant

SHEETROCK Brand
acoustical sealant

steel stud

zinc control
joint no. 093

Partition Wall Intersection

Partition control Joint

Details—
use of SHEETROCK *Brand*
Acoustical Sealant
(continued)

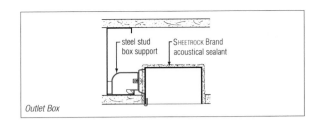

Outlet Box

Texture Finish Application

Textured finishes for gypsum board surfaces are desired for their decorative beauty and ability to obscure minor surface imperfections with economical spray application. USG offers a full line of products to create fine, medium or coarse simulated acoustic texture finishes, as well as sand finishes. Also available is a sound-rated texture finish. Interesting wall patterns can be created by using texture finish products with stipple brushes, pattern devices, rollers, floats, trowels and finishing knives.

Note: Textured surfaces also can be created with veneer plaster finishes. See veneer application section in Chapter 6.

General Limitations

1. Not recommended below grade or in high-humidity areas.
2. Heavy, water-based texturing materials may cause sag in gypsum panel ceilings under the following adverse conditions: high humidity, improper ventilation, panels applied parallel to framing and panels having insufficient thickness to span the distance between framing. The following table gives max. framing spacing for panels that are to be covered with water-based texturing materials.

Frame Spacing—Textured Gypsum Panel Ceilings

| Board Thickness | | Application Method | Max. Framing Spacing o.c. | |
in.	mm	(long edge relative to frame)	in.	mm
3/8	9.5	not recommended	—	—
1/2	12.7	perpendicular only	16	406
1/2*	12.7*	perpendicular only*	24*	610*
5/8	15.9	perpendicular only	24	610

* 1/2″ SHEETROCK Brand Interior Gypsum Ceiling Board provides the strength and sag resistance of 5/8″ standard board without the added thickness. Note: For adhesively laminated double-layer applications with 3/4″ or more total thickness, 24 o.c. max.

3. The following surface preparation directions apply to new drywall and concrete surfaces. When redecorating an old, existing surface with a water-based texture, migrating stains or contaminants from the substrate may leach to the finished surface, resulting in discoloration and staining. See preparation directions for 'Redecorating Ceilings' on pages 209-211 for more information on the proper surface preparation of existing surfaces prior to redecorating with a water-based texture.

See "Ceiling Sag Precautions" on page 353 for more information on the application of water-based textures and interior finishing materials.

Preparation   All surfaces must be dry, clean and sound. Dull glossy surfaces. Metal: Prime metal with a good rust inhibitive primer. Wood: Fill and seal surfaces. New concrete: Age 60 days or more before covering; remove form oils, grease, efflorescence; grind down plane differences and remove grinding dust and sludge; fill cracks and holes and level any offsets and voids to the same level as adjacent surfaces with SHEETROCK Brand Setting-Type (DURABOND) or SHEETROCK Brand Lightweight Setting-Type (EASY SAND) Joint Compound or COVER COAT Compound. Apply as many coats as are needed to provide a crack-free fill without edge joinings that show through decoration. Exercise special care to provide a smooth surface free of irregularities in areas that will be exposed to sharply angled light. New drywall: reinforce and conceal drywall joints using SHEETROCK Brand Joint Tape and a SHEETROCK Brand joint compound; fill all fastener depressions with joint compound; smooth surface scratches and scuffs. Correct plane irregularities, as these are accentuated by sharp, angular lighting.

When prepared surfaces are dry and free of dust, apply a prime coat of SHEETROCK Brand First Coat. This product equalizes porosity variations between the gypsum board face paper and the finished joints, minimizing decorating problems such as "joint banding." As a less effective substitute, a good quality, white, interior latex flat wall paint with high solids content may be used. Apply undiluted and allow to dry before decorating.

Note: Application of a prime coat is to equalize the surface porosity and to provide a uniform color. Primers are not intended to reduce sag potential or to prevent migrating stains or contaminants from leaching to the finished surface.

Note: For redecorating old ceilings, see pages 209-211 for proper surface preparation and application of decorating materials.

Powder Texture Finishes

SHEETROCK Brand Ceiling Spray Textures (QT) (Fine), (Medium) (Coarse)

Mixing Use clean vessel equipped with variable-speed power agitator. Sift texture finish into the recommended amount of water, agitating water during powder addition. Allow to soak for at least 15 min.— longer in cold water. Remix until a creamy (but aggregated) lump-free mix is obtained. Adjust spray consistency by adding small amounts of powder or water. Do not overthin, as poor adhesion, lack of hide and texture variation may result.

Equipment Use professional spray equipment such as a 10-to-1 ratio, double-action piston pump with 7-1/2-in. stroke, equipped with 4-ft. pole gun having 3/8- to 1/2-in. round orifice, or Binks 7E2 or equivalent hand gun with 3/8-in. round opening. Use 3/4-in. to 1-in. material hose, 3/8-in. atomizing hose and 1/2-in. air line from compressor to pump; or rotor-stator pump (L3 or L4) with 5/16″ to 3/8″ round orifice. Compressor must be adequate for length and size of hose. Keep pressure as low as possible. Plaster mixers or hopper-type applicators also may be used.

Application Apply at rate up to 10 ft.^{2} per lb. Do not exceed recommended coverage, as subsurface defects, variations in base suction or color differences may show through, or lighter texture may result.

Surfaces with uneven suction may require two coats. Let first coat dry before applying second. Remove splatters immediately from woodwork and trim. Maintain 55°F minimum air, water, product mix and surface temperature of the substrate during application and until surface is dry. Not washable, but can be painted (spray application is recommended) when redecoration is needed.

SHEETROCK Brand Wall and Ceiling Spray Texture (Unaggregated)

Mixing Use a clean vessel equipped with variable-speed power agitator. In initial mix, stir powder into recommended amount of water per bag directions. Agitate during powder addition. Allow to soak for at least 15 min.—longer in cold water. Remix until a creamy, lump-free mix is obtained. If additional hardness and bond are desired, add up to 1 gal of SHEETROCK Brand First Coat or 1/4 gal (2 pts) of USG Latex Additive per bag of SHEETROCK Brand Wall and Ceiling Spray Texture. Do not overthin, as poor adhesion, lack of hide and texture variation may result.

Equipment Use equipment similar to Binks No. 7D gun with #57 fluid nozzle, R-27 air nozzle combination, 1/2-in. fluid hose, 3/8-in. air hose, air-powered 4-to-1 ratio materials pump (minimum requirement) with double regulators, 1/2-in. main line air hose and 7-1/2 to 9-hp gasoline compressor.

Application Apply with suitable spray equipment at rate of 10-25 ft.^{2}/lb. for spatter and spatter/knockdown patterns, 20-40 ft.^{2}/lb. for orange peel pattern. Spray using 16″ to 20″ fan. Hold gun 16″ to 18″ from surface. Overlap preceding application with 1/2 to 2/3 of fan width. With 75 to 125 ft. of 1/2″ hose, use 30 to 40 lb. fluid pressure and 50 to 60 lb. atomizing pressure. Then texture with roller or other tool if required for desired pattern. Flatten raised portions of wet material or sand it when dry to provide further variation. Maintain 55°F minimum air and surface temperature during application and until surface is dry. Avoid drafts while applying, but provide ventilation after application to aid drying. Do not use unvented gas or oil heaters. May be painted after overnight drying. Not washable unpainted.

SHEETROCK Brand Wall and Ceiling Texture (TUF TEX)

Mixing Use a clean mixing vessel equipped with a variable speed power agitator. Using drinkable water and clean mixing equipment, slowly add dry powder texture to the recommended amount of water (see directions on bag) and mix to a heavy but lump-free consistency. Allow to soak for at least 15 min.—longer in cold water. Remix until mixture has a wet, smooth and creamy appearance. Adjust to desired spray consistency by adding small amounts of water to the wet mix. Do not overthin, as poor adhesion, lack of hide, or texture variation may result. Do not intermix with any materials other than those recommended.

Application Apply by machine or hand to create the desired effect. Application rates will vary depending on the texture pattern of choice. Generally, apply at 10-ft^2/lb for crowsfoot, swirl and stipple patterns; 20-40 ft^2/lb. for orange peel pattern; and 10-25 ft^2/lb. for spatter and knockdown patterns. Maintain 55°F minimum air, water, product mix and surface temperature during application and until surface is dry. Avoid drafts while applying product but provide ventilation after application to aid drying. Do not use unvented gas or oil heaters. May be painted after overnight drying. Not washable unpainted.

SHEETROCK Brand Wall and Ceiling Texture (Multipurpose)

Mixing Use a clean mixing vessel equipped with variable-speed power agitator. In initial mix, stir powder into recommended amount of water. (See directions on bag.) Agitate during powder addition. Allow to soak for at least 15 min.—longer in cold water. Remix until creamy, lump-free mix is obtained, then stir in up to 1 gal. water. To obtain suitable consistency for texturing as desired, do not use more than recommended amount of water. Do not overthin as poor adhesion, lack of hide and texture variation may result. Do not intermix with other materials.

Application Apply with brush, roller or with suitable spray equipment at rate of 10-20 ft.²/lb. for crowsfoot, swirl and stipple patterns; 10-40 ft.²/lb. for fine orange peel pattern; then texture with roller or other tool if necessary for desired pattern. For finer textures and designs, use small brush, roller-stippler, whisk broom, comb or similar items. Flatten raised portions of wet material or sand it when dry to provide further variation. Maintain 55°F minimum air, water, product mix and surface temperature during application and until surface is dry. Avoid drafts while applying, but provide ventilation after application to aid drying. Do not use unvented gas or oil heaters. May be painted after overnight drying. Not washable unpainted.

SHEETROCK Brand Texture 12 Wall and Ceiling Spray Texture

Mixing Place recommended amount of water in suitable mixing container. Gradually add powder to water. Stir thoroughly with mechanical mixer until completely mixed and lump-free. Soak mix for 15 min.—longer in cold water; remix. Gradually add under agitation up to 1-3/4 gal. of water to reach desirable spraying consistency. Overthinning may result in poor adhesion, lack of hide, texture variation and inability to compensate for base suction variations. Do not exceed 3-1/4 gal. total water per bag. Use within 24 hours.

Equipment Spray equipment: Binks Model 7D gun with #68 stainless-steel fluid nozzle, orifice size .110; air nozzle #101 carbide; atomizing pressure at gun 40-50 psi; air-hose size 3/8-in. i.d. with 3/8-in. swivel; fluid hose size 1/2-in. i.d. with 1/2-in. swivel; control-hose size 3/16-in. with 1/4-in. swivel. Air-driven pump sizes: 4-1/2:1 ratio for hose lengths up to 125 ft.; 7-1/2:1 for lengths up to 200 ft.; 10:1 for lengths over 200 ft.

Application Apply with spray gun using 24-in. fan. Hold gun 18-in. from surface and move parallel to surface. Avoid curved, sweeping strokes. Overlap preceding application with 1/2 to 2/3 of fan width. Apply a full coat in one direction, then immediately cross-spray in opposite direction. Use 1/2-in. fluid hose with fluid-pressure variable depending on hose length. Air and surface temperatures should be 55°F or higher during application and until surface is dry. Avoid drafts while applying, then provide adequate circulating ventilation to aid drying. Do not use unvented gas or oil heaters. May be painted after overnight drying. Not washable unpainted.

Texture Additives— Optional

a. Adding latex emulsion to powder texture—If increased bond and surface hardness are desired, SHEETROCK Brand Latex Additive for texture may be added to the wet-mix at a rate of 1 to 2 pints per bag of texture. The more latex additive used, up to 2 pints, the greater the bond and hardness of the dried surface. Surface-priming recommendations still apply.

b. Adding paint to powder textures—If better wet and dry hide, improved surface hardness, wider spray fan, and faster spray application are desired, SHEETROCK Brand First Coat or a good-grade, compatible polyvinyl acetate, vinyl-acrylic, or acrylic-type paint in white, off-white or pastel colors only may be added to ceiling texture. For SHEETROCK Brand First Coat, or a compatible paint product, wet-mix at a rate of 1 gal. per 32 or 40 lb. bag of texture by substituting 1 gal. paint for 1 gal. water. When adding 1 gal. paint to a fully diluted mix, the above properties remain appreciably the same but somewhat sparser aggregate surface may also result. Also, if aggregate is accidentally brushed off, a lighter colored surface can result. Interior flat, eggshell or semigloss paint products can be used. Compatibility of paints to be used with SHEETROCK Brand texture products should be carefully checked before use. Surface priming recommendations still apply.

Sound-Rated Texture Finish

USG Acoustical Plaster Finish

Mixing Read mixing and spray application directions completely before proceeding with mixing. Use a 7 cu. ft. or larger paddle-type plaster mixer with rubber-tipped blades (Anchor mixer) or a self-contained integral mixing/pumping spray texture tank with horizontal shaft and plaster or texture rig-type paddles mounted on a horizontal shaft. To insure uniform product performance, mix a minimum of two bags. Add powder to clean, room-temperature water in quantity specified on bag. Mix approx. 5 minutes until lump-free, and a thick, foamy consistency is generated (initial mix will appear dry and heavy). **Note:** If material is over-mixed, excessive foam will occur. Add more powder to break down foam and remix until proper foam level is reached. Additional mixing may be necessary during application to maintain foam consistency. Note that this is a chemically setting material; use mixed material within 3-4 hours.

Spray Application All pumps and hoses must be cleaned initially with water followed by approximately one gallon of SHEETROCK Brand Ready-Mixed Joint Compound prior to spray application to prevent severe aggregate separation or clogging by the clean-out water.

For combined mixing/pumping units: Initially fill mixing hopper with necessary water to flush hoses. Pump all water from hopper, then drop joint compound into material reservoir of pump. Start pumping until compound feeds into hose. Immediately stop pump. Add water and powder in mixing hopper following mixing directions. When USG Acoustical Plaster Finish is properly mixed, pump out and discard joint compound. Turn on atomizing air, material valve and pump (in that order).

For pump units only: Add previously mixed finish to material hopper after pumping joint compound into hose. Then follow the start-up procedure as stated for combined mixing/pumping units.

Recommended spray pattern is 1-1/2 ft. to 3 ft. in diameter. The spray gun should be held 2 ft. to 4 ft. from the surface, depending upon material density and atomizer pressure. Apply USG Acoustical Plaster Finish evenly, holding pole gun perpendicular to the surface being sprayed and slowly waving it from side to side until area is covered. Then immediately double back, crosshatching prior coat. Repeat same procedure as necessary until desired thickness is reached.

Elimination of spray lines and section seams is essential in producing an acceptable finish. Do not spray a portion of a ceiling in one day and the final portion on another day as a noticeable seam will result. If entire ceiling area cannot be sprayed to the final thickness in one day, spray the entire surface with a material coat of uniform thickness (min. 1/4 in.). Complete to final thickness the following day using a crosshatch application. Use natural breaks and boundaries to "frame" pattern edges and conceal seams. To measure average thickness, mark desired thickness on a blunt-tipped object (head of pencil or finishing nail) and insert into finish.

For a different surface color, use a good quality, flat latex paint (white or pastel) and spray apply over dried finish. There will be a minimal loss in NRC value.

Ready-Mixed Texture Finishes

Sheetrock Brand Ready-Mixed Wall and Ceiling Texture

Product Preparation Although Sheetrock Brand Ready-Mixed Wall and Ceiling Texture is virtually ready to use, slight mixing will increase creaminess of the product.

If remixing by drill is desired, use a heavy-duty drill; 400-600 RPM under load is best, with an open-blade mixer paddle. Faster drills also may be used, but they tend to whip air bubbles into the mix. Plunge the mixer paddle up and down in the mix several times before switching on drill, then mix until smooth and uniform (about 1 to 2 min.).

Thinning Experiment with small amount of mixed material prior to use, adjusting water proportions to match product viscosity to individual requirements. For thickest finish (heavy trowel, roller or brush application), use as is. For thinnest finish (light roller or spray application), add no more than 1 qt. of water per 2 gal. pail.

Coverage

1. For unthinned texture, up to 51 ft.^{2}/2-gal. pail.
2. For thinned texture, up to 142 ft.^{2}/2-gal. pail.
3. Actual coverage may vary depending on factors such as the condition of the substrate surface, dilution, application techniques, uniformity of the coating, thickness and texture pattern applied.

Aggregate Additions

Perlite Up to 1.6 lbs. /2-gal. pail.

White Silica Sand Up to 8.6 lbs. /2-gal. pail.

Note: Water is not to exceed 2/3 gal./2-gal. pail.

Application Apply finish with trowel, roller or brush; troweling provides best results. Protect from freezing in containers during application and in place until dry. Maintain 55°F min. air, product mix and surface temperature during application and until texture is dry. Avoid drafts, but provide good circulating ventilation. Do not use unvented gas or oil heaters.

For spray application, use professional spray equipment such as a 10-to-1 ratio, double-action pump with 7-1/2-in. stroke, equipped with 4-ft. pole gun having 3/8- to 1/2-in. round orifice, or Binks 7E2 or equivalent hand gun with 3/8-in. round opening. Use 3/4- to 1-in. material hose, 3/8-in. atomizing hose and 1/2-in. air line from compressor to pump. Compressor must be adequate (85 cfm) for length and size of hose. Keep pressure as low as possible. Hopper-type applicators, rotorstator and diaphragm pumps also may be used.

Do not exceed recommended coverage, as subsurface defects, variations in base suction or color differences may show through, or lighter texture may result. Remove splatters immediately from woodwork and trim. Maintain 55°F minimum air and surface temperature during application and until surface is dry.

New surface must be primed and may be optionally painted after drying. All walls must be painted after texturing except for noncontact areas. Not washable unpainted.

SHEETROCK Brand Ready-Mixed Wall and Ceiling Spray Texture

Product Preparation Use a heavy-duty drill fitted with a suitable mixing paddle, and operate it at 400-600 rpm. Excessive or high-speed mixing may produce voids in finished appearance. Mix until consistency is smooth and uniform. Do not mix with other materials in wet or dry form.

Thinning Thinning of texture with water will vary considerably, depending on the finished appearance desired and the method of application to be employed. Applicator should experiment with some of the mixed material prior to use, then adjust water proportions to suit the job. Overthinning may cause poor bond, pinholes, and cracking.

Coverage Up to 115 ft.^{2}/gal. or 400 ft.^{2} for each 3.5-gal. carton is an estimate. Actual coverage will vary depending on factors such as the type of texture design, the condition of the substrate surface, the amount of dilution of the product, application technique, and the uniformity of the coating.

Application Apply with brush, roller or with suitable professional spray equipment. For spray application, spray using a 16-in. to 20-in. fan. Overlap preceding application with 1/2 to 2/3 of fan, applying first in one direction and then in cross direction. Texture must be evenly spread and free from runs, sags, and other blemishes. Allow texture to dry before applying paint. Maintain 55°F minimum air, texture, and surface temperatures within working area until texture is completely dry. Texture color may not match color of other texture products. May be painted after overnight drying. Not washable unpainted.

SHEETROCK Brand Ready-Mixed Joint Compound (All Purpose)

Mixing and Thinning Product is ready to use but slight mixing will increase creaminess of the product. To mix, transfer contents into a suitable vessel. Use an open-blade mixer paddle on a heavy-duty drill, preferably at 450-600 RPM under load. Higher speeds tend to whip air bubbles into the product. Plunge the mixer paddle up and down in the mix about 10 times before switching on drill. Mix, adding water as recommended, until smooth and uniform, always keeping paddle completely immersed to avoid whipping in air bubbles.

Experiment with small amount of mixed material prior to use, adjusting water proportions to match product viscosity to individual requirements. For brush or roller/crow foot pattern, dilute with 1 to 1-1/2 gal. of water per 50 lb.

If large areas are being textured, prevent shade differences by sorting out enough boxes bearing identical manufacturing codes to cover entire area. Also, be sure to add exactly the same amount of water to each 50-lb. batch of ready-mixed compound.

Application Material may be brush, roller or trowel applied. Finishes must be evenly spread and free from runs, sags and other blemishes. Some cracking may occur upon drying. Allow each coat to dry before applying following coat. Coverage depends on amount of dilution and method of application to achieve desired effect.

Ready-Mixed Texture Paints

SHEETROCK Brand Wall and Ceiling Texture Paint

Product Preparation Wall and Ceiling Texture Paint comes in three formulations to produce a sand finish (Texture 1), ripple finish (Texture 2), or sanded paste stipple finish (TEXOLITE). These textured products in a paint base may be used from the container as supplied. Stir well before applying, but avoid excessive agitation that will entrain air. Thinning with water is not required, and will affect the coating's appearance. If thinning is necessary, add one or two ounces of water per gallon and stir. Can be tinted using universal colorants; incomplete mixing may result in color streaks.

Coverage 150-200 ft.^{2} per gallon, depending on substrate, application method and texture desired.

Application Maintain minimum air, product and surface temperature of 55°F during application and until surface is dry. Can be roller or spray applied. Apply a full coverage coat. Provide ventilation after application to encourage drying.

For roller application, cut in corners and trim using a trim brush. Roll surface immediately with a 3/4″ nap roller cover. Generously apply in long strokes, keeping the roller cover filled to obtain texture effect. Cross roll area to prevent ridging and framing.

For spray application, use a Binks 7D gun having a #57 fluid nozzle and an A-27 fan cap, or similar equipment. Air hose is typically 3/8″ i.d. with 1/2″ i.d. material hose. The spray gun should be approximately 18″ from the surface. Adjust atomizing air pressure and material flow rate so that a full coverage rate can be achieved by overlapping the preceding application by 1/4 to 1/2 the fan width.

Dries to the touch in approximately 60 min. at 72°F/50% RH. Allow overnight to dry hard.

SHEETROCK Brand Ceiling Texture Paint, Coarse Finish Texture

Product Preparation Stir until consistency is smooth and uniform. Up to 1 pt. per gallon of water may be added if necessary to adjust consistency. Excessive water will cause cracking and poor bonding. Do not mix with other materials. 2 gallons cover approximately 100 ft.^{2} on smooth, hard surfaces.

Application Stain blocking sealer may be required on stained or previously decorated surfaces. Maintain surface and air temperature above 55°F. Using a roller, apply texture generously in long strokes. Cross-roll adjoining areas to prevent ridging. Avoid applying in one direction; random spreading will create a more natural appearance. Allow to dry at least overnight before painting.

Creating Texture Patterns

Texture finishes and compounds offer opportunities for a variety of patterns and appearances. The number of patterns that can be created is limitless, but several patterns are particularly popular. Here are some commonly used patterns and information about how to achieve them.

Spatter and Light Orange Peel

Material for Light Orange Peel and Spatter
· SHEETROCK Brand Wall and Ceiling Spray Texture
· SHEETROCK Brand Wall and Ceiling Texture (TUF TEX)
· SHEETROCK Brand Wall and Ceiling Spray Texture Ready-Mixed

Application Spray

Equipment Binks 7D gun or equivalent, equipped with a #57 fluid nozzle and A-27 fan cap.

Procedure Mix products to a thin, latex-paint consistency. For a light orange peel, which is always the first application, atomizing air should be approximately 60 psi and material feed pressure approx. half the atomizing pressure. When spraying, apply in long even strokes with no wrist action, holding gun perpendicular to surface and approx. 18 in. from surface. Apply material as uniformly as possible avoiding lap marks.

Spatter Coat After fog coat has been applied, allow about 10-15 min. for surface to partially dry, then apply spattering by removing the A-27 fan cap and reducing atomizing air to approx. 15 psi and material feed to approx. 10 psi. While applying spatter coat, move spray gun in a rapid random fashion standing about 6 ft. from surface. Size of spatters depends on pressures used. Amount (or density) of spatters on surface depends on personal preference.

Orange Peel

Material for Orange Peel

- SHEETROCK Brand Wall and Ceiling Spray Texture
- SHEETROCK Brand Wall and Ceiling Texture (TUF TEX)
- SHEETROCK Brand Wall and Ceiling Texture (Multi-Purpose)
- SHEETROCK Brand Wall and Ceiling Texture Paint (Ripple Finish Texture 2)
- SHEETROCK Brand Ready-Mixed Wall and Ceiling Spray Texture

Application Spray

Equipment Same as for light orange peel except atomizing air pressure should be approximately 40 psi and material feed pressure approx. 20 psi. Degree of orange peel pattern depends on amount of material applied to surface.

Knock-Down and Skip-Trowel

Material for Knock-Down and Skip-Trowel

- SHEETROCK Brand Wall and Ceiling Spray Texture
- SHEETROCK Brand Wall and Ceiling Texture (TUF TEX)
- SHEETROCK Brand Ready-Mixed Wall and Ceiling Texture
- SHEETROCK Brand Ready-Mixed Wall and Ceiling Spray Texture

Application Spray

Equipment Pole gun, hopper, or Binks 7D or Binks 7E2 gun

Knock-Down Procedure Apply as spatter as described except use material at heavy latex-paint consistency. After spattering surface, wait about 10-15 min., then very lightly flatten only tops of spatters with flat blade or flat hand trowel. Again, size of spatters depends on pressures used.

Skip-Trowel Procedure Mix in #30 mesh silica sand (2 cups silica sand/5 gallons of texture). Apply as spatter coat but at very low pressures to allow for large spatters on surface. Wait approx. 10 to 15 min., then use blade as in the knock-down procedure, but applying more pressure.

Stipple Texture

Material for Stipple Texture
- SHEETROCK Brand Wall and Ceiling Texture (Multi-Purpose)
- SHEETROCK Brand Wall and Ceiling Texture (TUF TEX)
- SHEETROCK Brand Ready-Mixed Wall and Ceiling Texture
- SHEETROCK Brand Wall and Ceiling Texture Paint (Ripple Finish Texture 2)

Application Hand

Equipment Paint pan or large pail, paint roller 1/4-in. to 1-in. nap. Short nap produces lower stipple—fine pattern. Long nap produces higher stipple—coarse pattern.

Procedure for Hand Texturing Mix product to a consistency similar to spatter/knockdown. Completely wet out roller with material, then apply to surface as evenly as possible, covering entire surface. Let partially dry to a "dull wet" appearance, then roll again for desired texture effect.

Crow's Foot Use same material, equipment and application as for stipple texture, then use texture brush instead of paint roller to texture surface.

Procedure is the same as for roller texture, except that after material has partially dried to dull wet finish, stamp surface with texture brush prewetted with texture material for desired stipple finish.

Swirl Finish **Material for Swirl Finish**
· SHEETROCK Brand Wall and Ceiling Texture (Multi-Purpose)
· SHEETROCK Brand Wall and Ceiling Texture (TUF TEX)
· SHEETROCK Brand Ready-Mixed Wall and Ceiling Texture

Application Hand

Equipment Same as for stipple texture, plus wallpaper-type brush.

Procedure Apply as a roller texture. Let surface dry to dull wet finish, then use wallpaper brush to achieve desired swirl texture, rotating brush in circular motion on the wet surface.

Brocade or **Material for Brocade or Travertine**
Travertine · SHEETROCK Brand Wall and Ceiling Texture (Multi-Purpose)
· SHEETROCK Brand Wall and Ceiling Texture (TUF TEX)
· SHEETROCK Brand Ready-Mixed Wall and Ceiling Texture

Application Hand

Equipment Same as for crow's foot texture, plus flat blade.

Procedure Same as for crow's foot. After crow's foot texture has been achieved, wait 10-15 min., then knock down tips only by lightly drawing a flat blade across surface.

Other Hand Textured effects cited above are only a few of the many imaginative
Textured textures possible. Other effects can be achieved using different texturing
Effects tools.

A string-wrapped roller produces an attractive striated stone effect while cross-rolling gives an additional interesting squared pattern. For finer designs and textures, use a small brush, roller-stippler, whisk broom, crumpled paper, comb, sponge or similar items. Flattening raised portions of wet material or sanding when dry provides further variations. Material also may be scored to represent block, tile or cut stone outlines.

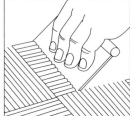

Interior Patching and Repairing

Finishing of drywall systems often requires patches and repairs of existing walls, or corrections to errors made in erecting new ones. A number of products are available to handle problems ranging from small holes to large breaks and cutouts. Problems in finishes and textures also can be corrected. Following are a few steps for solving several patch and repair problems:

Small Holes

SHEETROCK Brand Spackling Compound fills small holes, cracks, and covers nailheads. Used directly from the container, the compound should be stirred with a putty knife before application. Spread the compound into holes or cracks with a putty knife. Wipe away ridges and let dry approximately 2 hrs. Apply second fill and let dry. Sand lightly to smooth before painting.

SHEETROCK Brand Lightweight Spackling Compound is formulated for low-shrinkage, one-application fills. Stir lightly to assure uniform consistency, then spread into small holes and cracks with putty knife and smooth. Allow to dry. Sand lightly before painting.

SHEETROCK Brand Spackling Powder is a fast-setting, non-shrinking patching compound. Thoroughly mix 1 lb. of powder into approximately 8 oz. clean, cool water in a clean vessel. Stir until heavy paste is achieved. Press into cracks and holes with putty knife, or use a heavy paint brush to brush into hairline cracks. Use two applications in cracks more than 1/4″. Let dry thoroughly and sand lightly before painting.

Larger Holes

SHEETROCK Brand Plaster of Paris has a working time of about 15 minutes after mixing, then sets hard in 20-30 minutes. Mix 1 lb. of plaster into approximately 6 oz. of clean, cool water in a clean vessel and stir until smooth. Let stand one minute, then remix 1 min. Wet hole edges with a sponge, then apply compound with putty knife. For holes more than 1″ wide and/or more than 1/4″ deep, apply first coat to fill opening to within 1/16″ to 1/8″ of level. Let set, then apply second coat to level.

SHEETROCK Brand Patching Compound, EASY SAND 5 also is a setting-type compound. Mix 2 lb. into approximately 16 oz. of clean, cool water in a clean vessel. Mix until smooth, let soak 1 min., then remix 1 min. Add water in small increments, if desired, to achieve working consistency. Apply with putty knife. For large cracks, fill with compound, cover with SHEETROCK Brand Joint Tape, embed tape and let harden. Apply second coat (third if necessary) and let set. Sand and prime when dry. For medium holes up to 2″, apply compound around edges and coat perimeter of hole. Crisscross tape over hole and embed. Apply second coat (third if necessary) and let set. Sand and prime when dry.

SHEETROCK Brand Drywall Repair Clips enable damaged drywall to be cut away and replaced. After damaged piece has been eliminated, clips are mounted midway on each of the four cut edges. Screw attach to assure permanent connection. Measure and cut new panel of the same size and screw attach to other end of each repair clip. Remove tabs used for temporary mounting. Finish as with fresh panels.

5

SHEETROCK Brand Drywall Repair Kit contains drywall clips, SHEETROCK Brand Fiberglass Drywall Tape, SHEETROCK Brand Setting-Type Joint Compound (EASY SAND 90), and plastic spreader. Follow instructions above for drywall clips.

SHEETROCK Brand All-In-One Drywall Repair Kit contains 5″ x 8″ x 1/2″ drywall, drywall clips, drywall screws, SHEETROCK Brand Fiberglass Drywall Tape, SHEETROCK Brand Setting-Type Joint Compound (EASY SAND) complete with mixing tray and stick, and plastic saw/spreader.

Floor Surfaces SHEETROCK Brand Floor Patch/Leveler repairs and levels substrates before applying new floor covering. May be applied to plywood, hardboard or masonry/concrete surfaces inside and above grade. Surface should be between 40°F and 80°F. Coverage: 0.75 lb. floor patch covers 1 ft.^{2} at 1/8″ thickness; 1.5 lb. covers 1 ft.^{2} at 1.4″; 2.25 lb. covers 1 ft.^{2} at 3/8″.

Mix 2 parts powder into 1 part water. Stir thoroughly and apply flush with surface using a concrete trowel. Feather into surrounding areas and let dry 4 hours before sanding.

Additive SHEETROCK Brand Sand Finish Paint Additive may be added to your favorite paint or varnish to produce a sand-textured finish. Stir in approximately 8 oz. of additive to one gal. of paint. Mix 2-3 hours before painting and let stand. Roller or brush apply paint in normal fashion.

Resurfacing

Where ceilings or sidewalls are so badly disfigured that an entirely fresh surface is desirable, they may be resurfaced using a layer of 1/4″ or 3/8″ SHEETROCK Brand Gypsum Panels or predecorated SHEETROCK Brand Vinyl-Faced Panels. Ceilings may also be redecorated with texture finishes. For resurfacing masonry walls, see application of gypsum board to wall furring, described in Chapter 3.

Preparation Remove all trim (this may not be necessary if 1/4″ panels are used). To remove trim easily, drive all nails completely through the trim with a pin punch. Remove all loose surfacing material. Fill small holes with joint compound or patching plaster. Patch large holes to the surrounding level with single or multiple layers of gypsum board nailed to framing and shimmed out as required.

Electrical outlet boxes for switches, wall receptacles and fixtures should be extended outward to compensate for the added gypsum panel thickness.

Locate joists and studs by probing or with a magnetic "stud finder." Snap a chalk line to mark their full length and mark their location on the adjacent wall or ceiling. Where great irregularities of surface exist, apply furring strips not over 16″ o.c., using wood shingles to shim out to a true, even plane.

Installation Apply SHEETROCK Brand Gypsum Panels with long dimension placed horizontally or vertically. Fasten with gypsum board nails or drywall screws, spaced 7" o.c. on ceilings, 8" o.c. on walls. Nails or screws must be long enough to penetrate into framing members at least 5/8". Nail SHEETROCK Brand Vinyl-Faced Gypsum Panels over existing walls and ceilings with matching color nails using a plastic-headed hammer.

Gypsum panels may be adhesively applied over sound, existing walls (see directions, Chapter 3, page 117) with SHEETROCK Brand Setting-Type (DURABOND) or SHEETROCK Brand Lightweight Setting-Type (EASY SAND) Joint Compound.

Finish SHEETROCK Brand Panels with metal corner reinforcement and joint treatment as necessary, and replace all trim.

Redecorating Ceilings

5

Redecorating cracked, discolored or damaged ceilings with texture can make old ceilings look like new. Spray-applied texture finishes cover minor surface cracks and imperfections and provide beautiful surfaces. Redecorating surfaces previously decorated with a large-aggregate texture (e.g., SHEETROCK Brand Ceiling Spray Texture [QT]) is especially effective since these surfaces normally are not easily cleaned, rolled or brush-painted. Yet they are easily spray-painted with texture. These modernized ceilings add value and beauty. Best of all, most jobs can be done in one day without removing rugs, furniture or light fixtures.

Preparation Surface cracks larger than hairline size should be treated with a drywall joint compound and tape, and thoroughly dried, prior to redecorating. Tobacco smoke stains require predecorating attention and treatment with special stain-blocking sealer. Remove grease stains using mild detergent. Seal water-stained surfaces with primer specifically recommended by the manufacturer. Remove soot or dirt by "air dusting" surfaces. Wash mildew-contaminated surfaces with a solution of 1 qt. household bleach such as Clorox (sodium hypochlorite) to 3 qt. water. Cover all furniture, rugs, etc. with drop cloths and wear gloves and protective clothing as well as eye protection. For heavy mildew deposits, two applications of the bleach solution may be necessary. On textured ceilings, heavy coats of bleach are not recommended. Mist-coat surface with bleach solution using an aerating device such as a trigger-type household sprayer. No rinsing of the bleach solution is necessary since this would rewet the texture and cause serious bond problems. Let bleach dry thoroughly, then respray surface with SHEETROCK Brand Ceiling Spray Texture.

On previously painted mildew-contaminated surfaces, apply bleach solution with a scrub brush. When dry, rinse the painted surface to remove bleach, dry, and then spray-apply desired texture finish.

Caution. Treatment for mildew will not necessarily prevent its recurrence if humidity, temperature and moisture conditions are favorable for further mildew growth.

Redecorating with Texture

Painted Surfaces Ceilings that have been painted with pastel flat alkyd or latex flat paints can be sprayed with no special pretreatment if free of grease, dirt, smoke stains or other contaminants. Glossy surfaces must be dulled by lightly sanding to develop "tooth" for good bond. Wash surface with a strong solution of TSP (tri-sodium phosphate). Stained surfaces require application of a stain-blocking sealer. Spot prime bare metal with a good rust-inhibitive primer. After prepared surfaces have thoroughly dried, apply SHEETROCK First Coat.

Previously Textured Surfaces Priming a ceiling previously decorated with a large-aggregate texture (e.g., SHEETROCK Brand Ceiling Spray Texture [QT]) with a paint primer is not necessary if the surface is not stained and is free of grease, dirt, smoke stains or other contaminants. Use only SHEETROCK Brand Ceiling Spray Texture (QT Coarse) to redecorate an aggregated texture surface.

Wallpaper or Vinyl Wall Covering Remove material and prime ceiling surface with appropriate primer prior to texturing.

Plaster Ceilings Surface must be in paintable condition. Prior to texturing, cover with primer-sealer specifically recommended by paint manufacturer.

Mask surfaces by covering floors and walls with 0.85 to 1-mil-thick polyethylene sheeting, available in 8 to 12-ft. widths, folded and rolled in half for easier handling. Spread polyethylene sheeting on floor, making sure that all areas are completely covered. Next, apply wide masking tape to wall-ceiling intersection, fastening only top of tape to wall and leaving bottom hanging free. Fasten one edge of folded poly sheeting to loose edge of tape, then unfold film to full width. Press tape into firm contact with both wall and sheeting.

Cover Furniture, Cabinets, Light Fixtures Anything that will remain in the room during spraying operation. Lower ceiling light fixtures so they can be quickly and completely covered.

For information on mixing, equipment and application, see pages 197-198.

Equipment Use professional spray equipment such as a hand-held hopper or 10:1 ratio, double-action piston pump with 7-1/2-in. stroke, equipped with 4-ft. pole gun having 3/8 to 1/2-in. round orifice, or Binks 7E2 hand gun or equivalent with 3/8-in. round opening. Use 3/4 to 1-in. material hose, 3/8-in. atomizing hose and 1/2-in. air line from compressor to pump. Compressor must be adequate (85 cfm) for length and size of hose. Keep pressure as low as possible. Plaster mixers or hopper-type applicators also may be used.

Application Apply SHEETROCK Brand Ceiling Spray Texture at a rate of up to 10 ft²/lb. Do not exceed recommended coverage, as subsurface defects, variations in base suction or color differences may show through, or lighter texture may result. Maintain 55°F minimum air and surface temperature during application and until surface is dry.

Redecorating an Aggregated Textured Surface with Paint
After properly preparing the surface as described on pages 209-210, redecorate a previously aggregated textured surface with paint following the guidelines below.

Brush application of paint over an aggregated textured ceiling is not recommended. Spray application is preferred. In redecorating by hand, use a long-nap paint roller with 1/2 to 3/4-in. nap. Any good-quality interior latex or vinyl acrylic paint in flat, egg-shell or semigloss can be used. Slight dilution of paints with water, particularly high-viscosity types, may be necessary for smoother, easier spreading. Apply paint by rolling in one direction, immediately followed by cross rolling. Use light pressure and avoid over-rolling and saturating the surface to minimize loosening of surface aggregate.

Whether spraying or rolling, avoid drafts while applying, but provide adequate circulation and ventilation to aid drying.

Precautions   Ventilate or use a dust collector to avoid creating dust in the workplace. A NIOSH-approved respirator should be used if the air is dusty. The use of safety glasses is recommended. Do not take internally. Keep out of reach of children.

Decorative Interior Finish System   5

USG Decorative Interior Finish System is a gypsum-based finish system that puts color and texture together on interior drywall or basecoat plaster surfaces in a single application. The finish surface can be semismooth or finished with nearly any texture you can imagine. System is applied with trowel, similar to veneer plaster. The system is less expensive to use and apply than other specialty colored finish materials. Colors can be mixed using a standard tint machine and COLORTREND 888 Universal Machine Colorants. USG recommends using only COLORTREND 888 Universal Machine Colorants. Colorants from other manufacturers are not recommended since they may not be compatible with USG materials, they may cause color variations and they may interfere with the intended product application. We recommend only the use of COLORTREND 888 Universal Machine Colorants, the basic USG color formulas with these colorants and custom colors created using the COLORTREND AMBIANCE Fan Deck Selector.

For standard colors using COLORTREND 888 Universal Machine Colorants, the formula selected will produce a five-gallon batch size. To create a custom color, select a color and formula from the fan deck and color formula book that represents a color somewhat darker than the color you desire as the finished, dried, surface color. Note that the shade of finished colors is dependent on many factors. Each color formula yields a slightly different degree of color lightness compared to the color swatch depicted in the fan deck selector. The texture applied and the consistency of the mixed mortar also effect the appearance of the finished surface, and therefore the color. Even the plaster product chosen (DIAMOND Brand Interior Finish, IMPERIAL Brand Basecoat Plaster, DIAMOND Brand Veneer Basecoat Plaster or IMPERIAL Brand Finish Plaster) for the mix can vary the resulting shade. Depending on these factors, the final dried finish can be up to several shades lighter than the color swatch depicted in the fan deck selector. Note also that when wet, the wet mixed mortar appears darker than the selected color swatch, but will lighten in color when set and dry.

Preparation   Embed tape over drywall joints and apply one coat of joint compound over joints, fasteners and beads/trims. Pretreat joint-treated surfaces with SHEETROCK Brand Wall Covering Primer to minimize absorption differences between joint compound and face paper. After primer has dried, apply USG Plaster Bonder—Clear to all wall and ceiling surfaces.

Mixing USG Decorative Interior Finish usually consists of DIAMOND Brand Interior Finish mixed with colorants and water, but IMPERIAL Basecoat Plaster, DIAMOND Brand Veneer Basecoat Plaster or IMPERIAL Brand Finish Plaster also may be used. Mix in 5-gal. pail (14″ high, 10-1/4″ bottom, 11-1/4″ top). Use 6-1/2″ of water per batch for DIAMOND Brand Interior Finish, 4-1/2″ for DIAMOND Brand Veneer Basecoat Plaster, 4″ for IMPERIAL Brand Basecoat Plaster, and 5″ for IMPERIAL Brand Finish Plaster. Add the predetermined amount of colorant (COLORTREND Formula) to the water. The plaster is added to the water in three stages. First, fill the bucket with plaster and stir lightly with an on-and-off action using a 450 RPM 1/2″ drill and blade-type (joint compound) mixing paddle. Add plaster to the top of the bucket and repeat stirring with on-and-off action. Add plaster a third time and mix completely, ensuring that no colored water splashes out of mixing container. Mix approximately 40-45 lbs. of DIAMOND Brand Interior Finish with the water, or 60 lbs. of DIAMOND Brand Veneer Basecoat Plaster or IMPERIAL Brand Basecoat Plaster, or 50 lbs. of IMPERIAL Brand Finish Plaster. These quantities should fill the container to about 1 to 1-1/2 inches from its top. Finish should be slightly thicker than normal. To ensure color uniformity, each batch must be mixed exactly the same way, by volume and to the same fluidity in a volume-specific container.

Application Each wall or ceiling must be covered in a continuous application, always continuing joinings of separate mixes prior to either mix setting. Work walls and vaulted ceilings from top to bottom; ceilings from angle to angle. For one-coat semi-smooth texture, apply plaster in random, 1′ to 2′ strokes at a nominal 1/16″ to 1/8″ thickness, leaving lap marks as desired. After approx. 20 minutes from initial application, draw a trowel, held almost flat, lightly over the surface with short strokes in various directions. Trowel again as initial set begins (approx. 45 minutes). For two-coat heavy texture, apply first coat to a nominal thickness of approx. 1/8″, covering the entire surface. When surface has firmed slightly, apply second coat in short strokes as described above. Two-coat thickness should vary from 1/8″ to 1/4″. Additional troweling of second coat should be as described above for one-coat finish.

Sealing After finish has set and dried (approx. 24 hr.), apply USG Decorative Finish Sealer and maintain min. 55°F temperature. Do not shake or box-mix sealer. Apply using brush, roller or sprayer with 0.015″ to 0.023″ tip. Initially, sealer will appear milky, but will dry clear and colorless. When appearance changes to clear, wipe or roll drips and puddles, then recoat.

Finishing Veneer
Plaster Systems

6

Advances of Veneer Plaster

Veneer plaster has been growing in popularity as a wall finishing system. The speed of application for one-coat systems make it cost competitive with drywall, and the added smoothness of two-coat veneer provides a look of luxury and adds ease to decorating. With either system, the toughness of veneer plaster makes walls more durable and resistant to scuffs, gouges and impact damage.

Note that various organizations provide information about recommended standards or tolerances for finishing of veneer plaster systems. See pages 467 and 474 in the Appendix for information about standards and tolerances.

For instructions on the safe use of veneer plaster and related products, see Chapter 13, Safety Considerations, Material Handling.

Veneer Plaster Finishes

Veneer plaster finishes can be used in one or two-coat applications and can be given smooth or textured surfaces. Each method has its particular advantage.

Plaster Drying Conditions

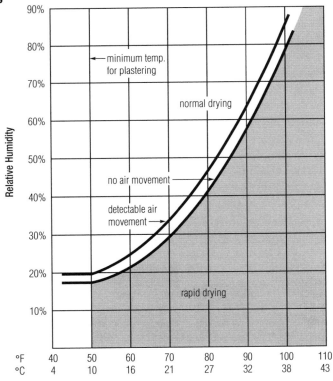

Two-Coat Veneer Finish Compared to many other finishes, two-coat veneer provides a more durable, abrasion-resistant surface and can be finished to a truer plane than one-coat applications. These finishes can be used with steel or wood framing wherever the ultimate in appearance is desired. Ready for next-day decorating, provided complete dryness has been reached. Assemblies with these monolithic gypsum surfaces offer excellent fire and sound ratings.

One-Coat Veneer Finish Provides a hard monolithic surface at low cost. Complete application—from bare studs to decorated walls and ceilings—takes no more than 48 to 72 hr., provided complete dryness has been reached. Assemblies with one-coat veneer plaster application meet fire and sound requirements, and shorten construction schedules for added profit.

Job Environment

Maintain building temperature in comfortable working range, above 55°F. Keep air circulation at minimum level prior to, during and following application until finish is dry.

If possible, maintain building temperature-humidity combination in the "normal drying" area of the graph. When dry conditions exist, relative humidity often can be increased by wetting down the floor periodically. During these periods, make every effort to reduce air movement by closing windows and deflecting heater blower and duct output away from the surfaces being plastered.

Selection of Joint Treatment System

Under normal working conditions, joints of veneer plaster systems may be treated by applying Imperial Brand Type P (pressure-sensitive) or Type S (staple) to the joints and then applying the veneer plaster basecoat or finish to preset the tape. However, there are a number of special situations that require the use of a setting-type joint treatment system.

— High room temperature, low humidity or excessive evaporation conditions fall in the "rapid drying" area of the graph.

— Metal framing is specified.

— Wood-framing spacing of 24″ o.c. and a single-layer gypsum base veneer system is specified (5/8″ base with one-coat veneer finish and 1/2″ or 5/8″ base with two-coat veneer finish).

Under any of these conditions, use Sheetrock Brand Joint tape and Sheetrock Brand Setting-Type (Durabond) or Lightweight Setting-Type (Easy Sand) Joint Compound to treat all joints and internal angles. Allow joint treatment to set and dry thoroughly before plaster application.

Grounds

Correct thickness of veneer plaster finish is one of the most important factors in obtaining good results. To insure proper thickness, all corner beads, trim and expansion joints must be of the recommended type and be properly set.

Accessories must provide grounds for the following minimum plaster thicknesses:

1. Over veneer gypsum base, one coat... 1/16 in. (1.6 mm)

2. Over veneer gypsum base, two coats... 3/32 in. (2.4 mm)

Trim Accessory Application

Trim accessories simplify and enhance the finishing of veneer plaster assemblies. The accessories are low in cost, easily applied and designed to work together for long-lasting, trouble-free construction. All are suitable for steel-frame and wood-frame construction.

Corner Bead Application

SHEETROCK Brand Corner Reinforcements provide strong, durable protection for outside angle corners, uncased openings, pilasters, beams and soffits. The exposed nose of the bead resists impact and forms a screed for finishing. Corner bead should be installed in one piece unless length of corner exceeds stock bead lengths. Install as noted for each product following.

SHEETROCK **Brand No. 800 and No. 900 Corner Beads** are galvanized fine-mesh, expanded-flange corner beads especially designed for veneer plaster construction. Apply No. 800 or No. 900 Corner Bead with nails through the board into wood framing or to board alone in wood or steel-framed assemblies with 9/16″ galvanized staples spaced 12 o.c. through both flanges. Fasteners should be placed opposite one another in both flanges. Both beads provide superior reinforcement with veneer plaster finishes through approximately 90 keys per lin. ft.

Use No. 800 for one-coat applications. It provides the proper 1/16″ ground height for one-coat finishing.

Use No. 900 for two-coat applications. It provides the 3/32″ ground height needed for two-coat applications.

On masonry corners, hold bead firmly against the corner and grout both flanges with IMPERIAL Brand Plaster Finish. On monolithic concrete apply a high-grade bonding agent, such as USG Plaster Bonder, over the corner before placing the bead and grouting. Preset all beads with a veneer finish.

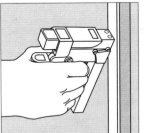 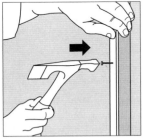

Stapling is the standard way to attach No. 800 Corner Bead.
For wood studs, nails in both bead flanges are also satisfactory.

Metal Trim Application

SHEETROCK Brand Metal Trim serves to protect and finish gypsum base at window framing and door jambs; also used at ceiling-wall intersections and partition perimeters to form a recess for acoustical sealant. Also serves as a relief joint at the intersection of dissimilar constructions, such as gypsum board to concrete.

No. 800 & 900 Corner Bead.

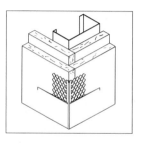

Metal trims provide maximum protection and neat finished edges to gypsum bases at window and door jambs, at internal angles and at intersections where panels abut other materials. They are easily installed by nailing or screwing through the proper leg of trim. Various configurations are available depending on the required application.

No. 701-A and 701-B SHEETROCK **Brand Metal Trim (1/2″ and 5/8″ size)** Slip channel-type 701-A Trim over the edge of the base or position L-shaped 701-B Trim on the edge of the base with the expanded flange on the room side. Fasten with staples or nails 12″ o.c. max. Both trims are designed for two-coat veneer finish applications.

No. 801-A and 801-B SHEETROCK **Brand Metal Trim (1/2″ and 5/8″ size)** Slip channel-type 801-A Trim over the edge of the base, or position L-shaped 801-B Trim on the edge of the base with the expanded flange on the room side. Fasten with staples or nails 12″ o.c. max. for veneer assemblies. Finish with one-coat veneer plaster.

Nos. 401 and 402 SHEETROCK **Brand Metal Trim (J-stop, 1/2″ and 5/8″ size)** Apply the trim to the wall before the gypsum base goes up, by nailing through the trim flange into the framing; the base is held firmly in place by the short leg of the trim. No additional edge fastening is necessary. Space fasteners 9″ o.c. Requires no finishing compound.

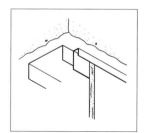

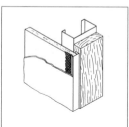

No. 400 Series   *701A, 801-A*   *701-B, 801-B*

Control Joint Application

Proper installation of control joints in wall and ceiling membranes should include breaking the gypsum base behind the control joint. In ceiling construction, the framing should also be broken, and in partitions, separate studs should be used on each side of the control joints. Control joints should be positioned to intersect light fixtures, air diffusers, door openings and other areas of stress concentration.

Gypsum construction should be isolated with control joints where (a) partitions or ceilings of dissimilar construction meet and remain in the same plane; (b) wings of "L", "U" and "T" shaped ceiling areas are joined; and (c) expansion or control joints occur in the base wall construction and/or building structure. Just as important, control joints should be used in the face of gypsum partitions and ceilings when the size of the surface exceeds the following control-joint spacings;

Partitions, 30 ft. maximum in either direction; Interior Ceilings (with perimeter relief), 50 ft. maximum in either direction; Interior Ceilings (without perimeter relief), 30 ft. maximum in either direction; and Exterior Ceilings, 30 ft. maximum in either direction.

Ceiling-height door frames may be used as vertical control joints for partitions; however, door frames of lesser height may only be used as control joints if standard control joints extend to the ceiling from both corners of the top of the door frame. When planning locations for control joints in the ceiling, it is recommended that they be located to intersect column penetrations, since movement of columns can impose stresses on the ceiling membrane.

Control Joints, when properly insulated and backed by gypsum base panels, have been fire-endurance tested and are certified for use in one- and two-hour-rated walls.

Installation   At control joint locations:
1. Leave a 1/2″ continuous opening between gypsum boards for insertion of surface-mounted joint.

2. Interrupt wood floor and ceiling plates with a 1/2″ gap, wherever there is a control joint in the structure.

3. Provide separate supports for each control joint flange.

4. Provide an adequate seal or safing insulation behind control joints where sound and/or fire ratings are prime considerations.

Control Joint No. 093 Apply over the face of gypsum base where specified. Cut to length with a fine-toothed hacksaw (32 teeth per in.). Cut end joints square, butt together and align to provide a neat fit. Attach the control joint to the gypsum base with Bostitch 9/16″ Type G staples, or equivalent, spaced 6″ o.c. max. along each flange. Remove the plastic tape after finishing with veneer plaster.

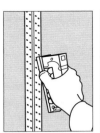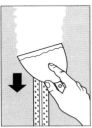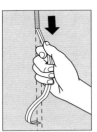

Control Joint No. 093 stapled, finished, tape removed.

Fire-Rated Control Joints

**47 STC
(SA-860217);
2-hr. Fire Rating**

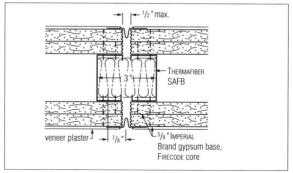

**47 STC
(SA-860302);
2-hr. Fire Rating**

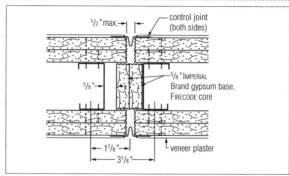

6

1-hr. Fire Rating

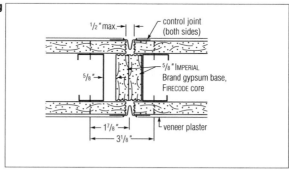

Control Joint No. 093

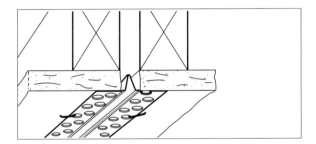

Maximum Spacing-Control Joints

Construction & Location	Max. Single Dimension ft.	m	Area ft².	Max. Single m²
Partition-interior	30		9	–	–
Ceiling-interior					
with perimeter relief	50		15	2500	230
without perimeter relief	30		9	900	85
Ceiling-exterior gypsum	30		9	900	85

SHEETROCK **Brand Control Joint No. 75** Apply to the bottom of the double row of wood joists in radiant-heated ceilings before IMPERIAL Brand Gypsum Base is applied. Attach control joint to joists with Bostitch 9/16″ Type G staples or nails spaced 6″ o.c. max. along each flange. Splice end joints with two pieces 16-ga. galvanized tie wire inserted in the sections. Apply gypsum base over control joint attachment flange and fasten to joist with proper fastener (see fastener selector guide in Chapter 1). Space nails 7″ o.c., screws 12″ o.c. Use control joint as a screed for applying DIAMOND Interior Finish. Remove plastic tape after veneer application.

Joint Treatment and Surface Preparation for Veneer Plaster Construction

For Wood-Framed Assemblies and Normal Drying Conditions
Align IMPERIAL Brand Type P (pressure-sensitive) Tape over joint and press into place over entire length. Eliminate wrinkles and assure maximum adhesive bond by pressing entire length of tape with steel finishing knife or trowel. Press tape into corners with corner tool; do not overlap.

Or, attach IMPERIAL Brand Type S Tape with spring-driven hand stapler using 3/8″ staples. Use two staples at each end of tape; staple remainder at staggered 24″ intervals. At wall-ceiling angles, staple every 18″ to 24″ along ceiling edge only. For wall-to-wall interior angles, staple every 18″ to 24″ on one edge only, working from top to bottom. Position tape to bridge the joint at all interior corners without overlapping.

Embed tape and fill beads with a coat of veneer plaster being used, and allow to set–but not dry–prior to veneer plaster application. Slightly underfill in the bead by screeding along the bead with edge of trowel after setting the bead. (Best results are obtained by planning the finishing to permit continuous application from angle to angle.)

Simplified, wrinkle-free attachment of self-stick Type P IMPERIAL Brand Tape speeds joint reinforcing, boosts production.

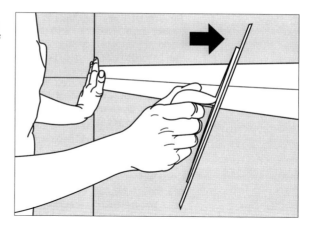

For Steel-Framed Assemblies and Rapid Drying Conditions With steel framing and/or when building temperature-humidity conditions fall in the 'rapid drying' area of the graph for steel or wood framing (see page 214), SHEETROCK Brand Joint Tape embedded with a SHEETROCK Brand Setting-Type Joint Compound (DURABOND or EASY SAND) is recommended.

Mix the compound in a clean 5-gal. container (plastic is preferred for setting type compounds). Use a commercial handmixer (commonly called a potato masher) or a 1/2" heavy-duty 200 to 300-rpm electric drill with a drywall blade-type mixing paddle. Drill speed must not exceed 400 rpm. Use the amount of water shown on the bag and always sift the powder into the water to ensure complete wetting. Stir according to directions on bag.

Note: Do not contaminate compound with other materials, dirty water or previous batches. Do not retemper batches.

Butter joints with compound using a trowel or steel finishing knife to force compound into the joints. Center SHEETROCK Brand Joint Tape over joint and press it into the fresh compound with trowel held at a 45° angle. Draw trowel along joint with sufficient pressure to remove excess compound.

After tape is embedded, apply a thin coat of joint compound to reduce possibility of edge wrinkling or curling. Allow thin coat to harden, then apply a fill coat completely covering the tape and feathering 3" to 4" beyond edges of tape. Allow to harden before finishing. Plaster prefill is not required over SHEETROCK Brand Setting-Type Joint Compound (DURABOND or EASY SAND).

Note: Under the following conditions a SHEETROCK Brand Setting-Type Joint Compound (DURABOND or EASY SAND) and SHEETROCK Joint Tape must be used: (1) where two-coat finish is applied over 1/2" or 5/8" base on 24" o.c. framing; (2) where one-coat DIAMOND Brand Interior Finish Plaster or IMPERIAL Brand Finish Plaster is applied over 5/8" base on 24" o.c. framing; where IMPERIAL Brand Gypsum Base and veneer plaster is used over steel framing.

For Cement Board Substrate Prior to treatment of Durock Brand Cement Board panel joints, apply USG Plaster Bonder in a continuous film to the joint area according to application directions. Joints should then be treated with Sheetrock Brand Joint Tape and Sheetrock Brand Setting-Type Joint Compound (Durabond or Easy Sand). Mix and apply following directions on the bag. When the joints are completely dry, treat the entire wall surface with USG Plaster Bonder according to application directions. Then apply Diamond Brand Veneer Basecoat Plaster and Imperial Brand Finish Plaster in a two-coat application.

For Gypsum Fiber Bases This assembly provides added abuse-resistant characteristics when completed. Joints of Fiberock Brand Gypsum Panels must be treated with Sheetrock Brand Joint Tape and Sheetrock Brand Setting-Type Joint Compound (Durabond or Easy Sand) following directions on the bag. When the joints are completely dry, treat the entire wall surface with USG Plaster Bonder according to application directions. Then apply Diamond Brand Veneer Basecoat Plaster and Imperial Brand Finish Plaster in a two-coat application.

For Improved Bond Several products are available to help setting-type joint compounds and veneer plasters work better. USG Plaster Bonder, used on concrete, cement board, gypsum fiber panels and dry setting-type joint compound surfaces, enhances the plaster's ability to bond to those surfaces. USG Plaster Accelerator-Alum Catalyst also can be used in a solution applied to the substrate surface to help lime-containing veneer plaster adhere to sun-faded plaster base surfaces or setting-type compound at joints (see page 392).

For Changing Working Time To alter the setting time of Sheetrock Brand Setting-Type Joint Compounds (Durabond or Easy Sand) USG High Strength Accelerator also may be used as a mix additive to reduce the setting time, or USG High Strength Retarder to extend the setting and working time.

Veneer Plaster Finish Applications

Veneer Plaster Product Compatibility Selector

	Substrate				Finish Plaster							
Basecoat Plaster	**CMU**	**Mono. Concrete(1)**	**Durock(1) Brand Cement Board**	**Imperial Brand Veneer Base**	**Red Top Finish**	**Structo Gauge/ Lime**	**Keenes/ Lime**	**Gauging/ Lime**	**Keenes/ Lime/Sand**	**Gauging/ Lime/Sand**	**Diamond/ Imperial Brand Finish**	**Decorative Interior Finish**
Imperial Brand Basecoat	√	√		√	√	√	√	√	√	√	√	√
Diamond Brand Veneer Basecoat	√	√	√	√	√	√	√	√	√	√	√	√
Imperial Brand Finish				√								
Diamond Brand Interior Finish		√(2)		√								
Diamond Brand Interior Finish (Electric Cable)		√(2)		√								

Notes: (1) Fiberock Brand Gypsum Panels may also be used. In both cases, USG™ Plaster Bonder must first be applied.
(2) Job sanded. √ = Acceptable

Mixing and Proportioning

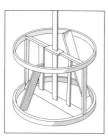

Cage-type mixing paddle is designed to draw material into and through paddle blades to disperse and blend ingredients by shear action rather than folding action of conventional mixers.

All veneer finishes require the addition of water on the job. Water should be clean, fresh, suitable for human consumption, and free from mineral and organic substances that affect the plaster set. Water used for rinsing or cleaning is not suitable for mixing because it accelerates the plaster set.

Mechanical mixing is mandatory for veneer finish plasters. Mix no more material than can be applied before set begins. Since veneer finishes set more rapidly than most conventional plasters, always consult bag directions for specific setting times.

Veneer plasters will produce mortar of maximum performance and workability when the correct equipment is used and mixing directions carefully followed. Proper mixing is one of the most important factors in producing mortar of maximum workability.

Use a cage-type mixer paddle driven by heavy-duty 1/2″ electric drill with a no-load rating of 900 to 1,000 rpm. Do not use propeller-type paddle or conventional mortar mixer. (For details of the cage-type mixing paddle and available electrical drills, see pages 432-433 and PM19, *Mixing Equipment for Veneer Plasters*).

Mix plaster in 16 or 30-gal. smooth-sided container strong enough to withstand impacts that could cause gouging. Do not use brittle containers for mixing.

Correct mixing—rapid and with high shear action—is essential for proper dispersion of plaster ingredients. Slow mixing can reduce plasticity of material. Overmixing can shorten working time. Operated at correct speed, the cage-type design paddle mixes thoroughly without introducing excess air into the mix.

Mixing IMPERIAL Brand Plasters

Water requirements for IMPERIAL Brand Veneer Plasters:
IMPERIAL Brand Basecoat Plaster—8 to 10 qt./80 lb. bag.
IMPERIAL Brand Finish Plaster—11 to 13 qt./80 lb. bag.

Place water in a 12 to 16-gal. smooth-sided container. Start mixer, slowly add plaster and mix at least 2 min. to disperse lumps completely. Do not mix more than 5 min.

For sand float finish, add up to 20 lb. clean silica sand per 80-lb. bag of IMPERIAL Brand Plaster to achieve desired texture. The use of more than 20 lb. of sand per bag will decrease hardness of surface. (Apply plaster in normal manner but omit final troweling. After surface has become firm, float to desired texture, using sponge, carpet or other float. Use water sparingly.)

Mixing DIAMOND Brand Plasters

Water requirements for DIAMOND Brand Veneer Plasters:
DIAMOND Brand Veneer Basecoat—12 to 14 qt./80-lb. bag
DIAMOND Brand Interior Finish Plaster—12 to 15 qt./50-lb. bag.

Place all but 1 or 2 qt. of water into mixing container; then with mixer operating, slowly add one bag of material. If a texture finish is desired, up to 50 lb. clean silica sand may be added per 50-lb. bag of DIAMOND Brand Interior Finish Plaster. For electric cable heat systems, clean, sharp, fine silica sand must be added as follows: fill coat, 50 lb. but no less than 25 lb. per 50-lb. bag Diamond Brand Interior Finish Plaster; finish coat, at least 12-1/2 lb. per 50-lb. bag plaster. When material is wetted, add more water (1 to 2 qt.) to obtain desired consistency. Mix for minimum of two minutes, but no longer than five minutes.

When Diamond Brand Finish Plaster is job-aggregated, one table spoon Cream of Tartar or 1/4 to 1/2 teaspoon of USG Retarder for Lime Containing Plaster Products should be added for each bag of plaster to retard set and allow sufficient working time.

Application

Maintain temperature in all work areas at min. 55 to 60°F. Keep air circulation at minimum level during and after application until finish is dry.

Imperial Brand Plasters

Hand Application—Embed Imperial Brand Tape, Type P or S, and fill beads with a tight, thin coat of Imperial Brand Plaster; allow to set, then plaster (See "Selection of Joint Treatment System" on page 215.)

Plaster Finishing

Imperial Brand Plasters offer a wide range of finish options with three distinct systems:

1. Imperial Brand Finish Plaster (one-coat)

2. Imperial Brand Basecoat Plaster with selected hand-applied or spray finish (two-coat).

3. Imperial Brand Basecoat MA (special application equipment required) with selected hand-applied or spray finish (two-coat).

Imperial Brand Finish Plaster (one-coat) Scratch in a tight, thin coat of Imperial Brand Finish Plaster over entire area, immediately doubling back with plaster from same batch to full thickness of 1/16″ to 3/32″. Fill all voids and imperfections. Final trowel after surface has become firm, holding trowel flat and using water sparingly. Do not overtrowel.

For texture finished surfaces, with or without the addition of job-added sand, final troweling is omitted. The surface is textured naturally as the material firms and water is removed into the base.

Best results are obtained by planning the plastering to permit continuous application from angle to angle. Where joining is unavoidable, use trowel to terminate unset plaster in sharp clean edge—do not feather out. Bring adjacent plaster up to terminated edge and leave level. Do not overlap. During finish troweling, use excess material to fill and bridge joining.

Imperial Brand Basecoat Plaster (two-coat) Scratch in a tight, thin coat of Imperial Brand Basecoat Plaster over entire area, immediately doubling back with plaster from same batch to full thickness of 1/16″ to 3/32″. Fill all voids and imperfections. Leave surface rough and open by cross-raking with a fine-wire rake or broom. Allow basecoat to set to provide proper suction for finish coat.

Finish coat materials are applied by scratching in and doubling back with selected finish—Imperial Brand Finish Plaster, Diamond Brand Interior Finish Plaster, gauged lime-putty, Structo-Gauge Gauging-lime, Red Top Finish Plaster or Red Top Keenes Cement-lime-sand finishes—to achieve a smooth, dense surface for decoration, free of surface blemishes. For textured finishes, floating on textures with additional material is conducted once the surface has become firm, using water sparingly.

For spray-applied finish, mix Keenes Cement-lime-sand in proportion of 50 lbs. Keenes Cement to 100 lbs. dry double-hydrated lime, and up to 400 lb. but not less than 200 lb. clean, properly graded silica sand with sufficient water to form a smooth consistency for hand application. Apply this mix evenly over a properly prepared IMPERIAL Brand Basecoat surface by first applying a well-ground-in scratch coat, then immediately double back with sufficient material to cover the basecoat to a total thickness of 1/16″ to 1/8″. When the surface has become firm by water removal, float the surface to a uniform blemish-free flat texture. After floating, and while the application is still wet, but totally firm, prepare additional finish material with the consistency adjusted for spray application. With either a hand-held hopper gun or machine-application equipment without catalyst, spray apply the texture to provide a uniform texture appearance. Vary aggregate grading, aggregate proportion, number of passes over the surface, air pressure and nozzle orifice as necessary to achieve the desired appearance.

IMPERIAL Brand Basecoat MA Plaster (two-coat) Machine application of IMPERIAL Brand Basecoat MA Plaster requires special equipment that provides for automatic catalyst injection. The machine should be operated in strict accordance with the manufacturer's directions. Successful results require advance job planning and operator training.

The plaster base should be protected from overspray or contamination by lime or casein materials. Such materials adversely affect the bonding characteristics of plaster. Mask all areas to be protected from plaster overspray with plastic sheeting or paper secured with masking tape.

Mix two to six 1.5-lb. bags of USG Accelerator Alum Catalyst in 3 gal. of clean water in a plastic pail. The amount of catalyst used will be determined by the desired setting time. Stir until material dissolves, let residue settle and pour solution into accelerator tank of the machine.

Mix basecoat plaster as previously described and pour into the machine through the 8 x 8-mesh screen hopper. Adjust water in mix until 75% to 90% will pass the screen without shaking.

Caution: Clean mixing equipment after each batch. Clean hopper and screen free of set plaster to avoid acceleration. Machine should be completely cleaned after each four hours of use.

Adjust the setting time by controlling the catalyst flow at the machine. Test the setting time by spraying plaster on a scrap of gypsum base.

With setting time adjusted to 30 min, spray joints and corner bead and trim flanges in a pattern wide enough to cover the tape and flanges. Immediately trowel level, completely embedding tape and covering flanges. Leave no voids. Allow to set before plastering. This initial spraying is not required over SHEETROCK Brand Setting-Type Joint Compound (DURABOND or EASY SAND).

Adjust set for 20-30 min., spray IMPERIAL Brand Basecoat Plaster (MA) over entire area to a thickness of 1/32″, then immediately cross spray to a total thickness of 1/16″. Allow to set and dry sufficiently to provide proper suction for the finish coat.

For hand-applied finish plaster, scratch in and double back with selected finish–IMPERIAL Brand Finish Plaster, DIAMOND Brand Interior Finish Plaster, gauged lime-putty, STRUCTO-GAUGE Gauging-lime, RED TOP Finish Plaster or RED TOP Keenes Cement-lime-sand finishes–to achieve a smooth, dense surface for decoration, free of surface blemishes, to a full plaster thickness of 1/8". Trowel after surface has become firm, holding trowel flat and using water sparingly. Do not overtrowel. Texturing with desired finish is started once initial scratch and double-up application has become firm.

For spray-applied finish, mix and apply finish as described above for IMPERIAL Brand Basecoat Plaster (two-coat).

Spray Texture Finish Mix RED TOP Keenes Cement-lime-sand in proportion of 100 lb. Keenes to 50 lb. dry hydrated lime and 400 lb. clean white silica sand, with sufficient water to form a smooth consistency. Alternative finish coat materials for this application may consist of high-strength gauging/lime putty finish, regular gauging/lime putty finish, or various mill-manufactured products. Apply this mix over IMPERIAL Brand Basecoat surface, which is free of ridges or other imperfections, with either a hand-held hopper gun or machine application equipment without catalyst. Vary aggregate grading, number of passes over the surface, air pressure and nozzle orifice as necessary to achieve desired texture. Limitations: While this method of achieving a textured surface by spraying is expedient, it is not normally recommended because 1) the properly roughened basecoat may not be uniform in appearance and any irregularities will photograph through the finish coat, and 2) providing sufficient air pressure and viscosity to achieve proper bond minimizes the degree of texture attainable.

When spray texture is desired, the following recommendation should be followed: Using the selected finish-coat material, mixed for hand-application consistency, apply a tight scratch coat over the properly prepared, set and partially dry basecoat, then double back. When the surface has become firm, float to a uniform, blemish-free flat texture. Apply selected spray finish material while scratch coat is firm, but not set. Spray texture to a uniform thickness and appearance.

This same procedure can be used with the application of IMPERIAL Brand Finish Plaster or DIAMOND Brand Interior Finish Plaster direct to IMPERIAL Brand Gypsum Base.

Other IMPERIAL Brand Basecoat Applications

Concrete Block Surface must be porous for proper suction or be roughened/face-scored to provide adequate mechanical bond. Lightly spray walls with water to provide uniform suction. Fill and level all voids, depressions and joints with IMPERIAL Brand Basecoat Plaster and allow to set; then apply a subsequent coat, as with gypsum base application, leaving final surface rough and open to provide proper bonding of the finish coat.

Monolithic Concrete Prepare surface with USG Plaster Bonder applied according to application directions. Fill all voids and depressions with IMPERIAL Brand Basecoat Plaster and allow to set and partially dry. Then apply IMPERIAL Brand Basecoat Plaster as with gypsum base or concrete block. Important: It is essential that the applied basecoat surface be raked or broomed once the material has become firm for a rough and open surface in order to provide for proper suction for the finish material. Failure to do this may result in delamination of the finish material.

Integral Plaster Chalkboards

Plaster chalkboards offer maximum freedom in design. There is no limiting sheet size as is the case with fabricated boards; therefore, entire walls can be utilized as chalkboards. Maintenance is accomplished as easily as with conventional fabricated chalkboards. (Requirements for control joints in chalkboard surfaces are the same as for other gypsum surfaces.)

Chalkboard with Steel-Stud IMPERIAL Brand Gypsum Base Partitions

Follow directions for system construction. Locate floor and ceiling runners and position studs 16" o.c. Attach IMPERIAL Brand Gypsum Base using 1" TYPE S Screws spaced 16" o.c. When chalkboard area does not extend from floor to ceiling, use 701-A or 801-A Metal Trim to frame the IMPERIAL Brand Gypsum Base face layers that will be used as chalkboard. (All chalkboard surfaces must have two layers of IMPERIAL Brand Gypsum Base.) Miter corners of the metal trim to form a neat joint. Attach chalkboard using 1-5/8" TYPE S Screws, driven through IMPERIAL Brand Gypsum Base layer into the studs.

Veneer Plaster Application: use one or two-coat plaster for chalkboard surface. With one-coat work, apply IMPERIAL Brand Finish Plaster to 1/16" to 3/32" thickness. Cover entire area with a tight, thin coat, then double back to full thickness. After surface has become firm, final-trowel to a smooth surface, using water sparingly.

For two-coat application, apply IMPERIAL Brand Basecoat Plaster to 1/16" to 3/32" thickness as described for single-coat application. Allow basecoat to set and partially dry; then apply IMPERIAL Brand Finish Plaster or STRUCTO-GAUGE-lime smooth-trowel finish plaster. Leave surface very hard and polished.

Plaster chalkboard

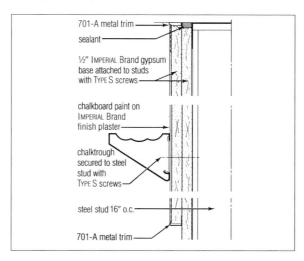

701-A metal trim

sealant

½" IMPERIAL Brand gypsum base attached to studs with TYPE S screws

chalkboard paint on IMPERIAL Brand finish plaster

chalktrough secured to steel stud with TYPE S screws

steel stud 16" o.c.

701-A metal trim

When dry, paint chalkboard with one coat primer-sealer and two coats chalkboard paint.

Install chalk trough with 1-5/16″ Type S Screws, driven through the two layers of Imperial Brand Gypsum Base and into the steel studs.

Diamond Brand Plasters

Diamond Brand Interior Finish Plaster

All finish materials and finish surfaces must be protected from contact with Diamond Brand Interior Finish Plaster. This includes glass, ceramic materials, metal and wood. Apply wood, plastic or other exposed trim after plaster application.

Diamond Brand Interior Finish Plaster should be applied to Imperial Brand Gypsum Base having unfaded blue face paper. However, under abnormal conditions where there is no alternative to using gypsum base faded from excessive exposure to sunlight or ultra-violet radiation, precautions should be taken to prevent delamination. Degraded gypsum base is indicated if face paper is not blue or grayish blue. When face paper color has become gray to tan (or if questionable), treat paper with a solution of USG Accelerator—Alum Catalyst or USG Plaster Bonder.

Degrading may occur when gypsum base has been installed long before the finish is applied.

When used with lime-containing plaster, such as Diamond Brand Interior Finish Plaster, sunfaded Imperial Brand Gypsum Base face paper should be treated with USG Accelerator—Alum Catalyst or USG Plaster Bonder. This precaution is unnecessary when applying products that do not contain lime (Imperial Brand Finish Plaster, Imperial Brand Basecoat Plaster and Diamond Brand Veneer Basecoat Plaster).

For alum catalyst solution treatment, pour 3 pounds of alum catalyst slowly into one gallon of water and mix thoroughly. Allow the solution to stand until any undissolved material has settled, then strain the solution into tank-type sprayer (such as a garden sprayer). Spray the solution onto the faded Imperial Brand Base face paper so that it is wet but not soaked. One gallon of solution should treat 750 sq. ft. of Imperial Brand Gypsum Base. Begin finish plaster application before face paper treated with alum solution is completely dry. Caution: Alum treatment shortens the setting time of Diamond Brand Interior Finish Plaster.

Begin application only after joints have been reinforced with glass fiber tape and preset with an application of Diamond Brand Interior Finish Plaster or treated with Sheetrock Brand Joint Tape and Sheetrock Brand Setting-Type) Joint Compound (Durabond or Easy Sand). Apply a thin, tight scratch coat of this finish over entire working area. Immediately double back with material from same batch to a full 1/16″ to 3/32″ thickness.

Start the finish troweling as soon as material has become sufficiently firm to achieve a smooth trowel finish free from trowel marks, voids and other blemishes. Smooth and level the surface with trowel held flat; use water sparingly to lubricate. Final hard troweling should be accomplished prior to set as indicated by darkening of the surface.

A variety of textures ranging from sand float to heavy Spanish can be achieved with DIAMOND Brand Interior Finish Plaster when job-aggregated with silica sand. Application is the same as for neat DIAMOND Brand Interior Finish Plaster except that once the surface has been leveled and sufficient take-up has occurred, begin floating material from the same batch with trowel, float, sponge or by other accepted local techniques.

DIAMOND Brand Interior Finish Plaster also may be textured by skip-troweling. When applying in this manner, eliminate final troweling. When surface has become sufficiently firm, texture with material from same batch prior to set.

Painting or further decoration of DIAMOND Brand Interior Finish Plaster is recommended and should be specified. However, in many residential applications, DIAMOND Brand Interior Finish Plaster provides a uniform white color and may satisfy a job's specific acceptance criteria if skip-trowel and float-finish textured finishes are utilized. DIAMOND Brand Interior Finish Plaster is formulated to allow quick drying and can be decorated when thoroughly dry using a latex base or breather-type paint. Under ideal conditions, painting can take place in as little as 24 hours, which minimizes costly delays and speeds occupancy.

6

Graceful, wavelike swirl texture

Unique, skip trowel

Sand-aggregated float finish

Luxurious Spanish texture

DIAMOND Brand Veneer Basecoat Plaster

DIAMOND Brand Veneer Basecoat Plaster provides quality walls and ceilings for residential construction where the superior strength of IMPERIAL Brand Basecoat Plaster is not essential. DIAMOND Brand Veneer Basecoat Plaster produces a base that esthetically enhances the finish by providing regulated suction, resulting in exceptional integral bond. Once basecoat is applied and has become firm, surface is raked or broomed to provide a rough and open surface for the finish coat.

Over Gypsum Base Apply DIAMOND Brand Veneer Basecoat Plaster from 1-16" to 3/32" thickness. When IMPERIAL Brand Gypsum Base is used, reinforce all joints and interior angles with IMPERIAL Brand Type P or Type S Tape. Embed tape and fill beads with DIAMOND Brand Veneer Basecoat Plaster and allow to set, but not dry. After beads and joints have been properly prepared (rough and open), apply a tight, thin coat of DIAMOND Brand Veneer Basecoat Plaster over the entire area, immediately doubling back with plaster from the same batch to full thickness. Fill all voids and imperfections. Leave surface rough and open by cross raking with a fine wire rake, sponge or fine broom once the surface has become somewhat firm. Allow basecoat to set to provide proper suction for finish coat.

Over Concrete Block Surface must be porous and develop proper suction to provide adequate mechanical bond. Lightly spray walls with water to provide uniform suction. Fill and level all voids, depressions and joints with DIAMOND Brand Veneer Basecoat Plaster and allow to set; then apply subsequent coats as with gypsum base application, leaving final surface rough and open to provide proper bonding of the finish coat.

Over Monolithic Concrete Prepare surface with USG Plaster Bonder applied according to application directions. Fill all voids and depressions with DIAMOND Brand Veneer Basecoat Plaster and allow to set and partially dry. Then apply DIAMOND Brand Veneer Basecoat Plaster as with gypsum base or concrete block. Important: It is essential that the applied basecoat surface be raked or broomed once the material has become firm for a rough and open surface to provide proper suction for the finish coat. Failure to do so may result in delamination of the finish material.

Painting of Veneer Plaster

No matter what paint or decoration is used, it is essential that the plaster be completely dry. Typically, veneer plasters may be dry in as little as 24 hours. Use a high-quality, undiluted acrylic latex, vinyl or alkali-resistant alkyd paint. Prior to the installation of an applied finish, such as epoxy-based finish systems, the veneer plaster must be properly sealed. Quick-drying vinyl acrylic latex or alkali-resistant alkyd primer-sealers are recommended. Polyvinyl acetate (PVA) based primers should not be used over wet plaster of any kind, including lime-containing plasters. The PVA film is subject to rewetting and will almost certainly cause bond loss and subsequent paint delamination.

Trowel job-sanded DIAMOND Brand Interior Finish Plaster over electric cable.

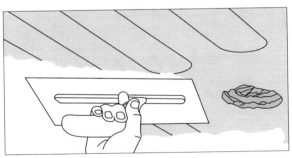

Radiant Heat Plaster System—DIAMOND Brand Interior Finish Plaster

Application-Radiant Heat Cable After IMPERIAL Brand Gypsum Base and joint reinforcement tape have been applied, install electric radiant heating cable in accordance with design requirements and cable manufacturer's specifications. Attach cable to ceiling in such a manner that it is kept taut and does not sag away from the base. All cable connectors and non-heating leads should be embedded (countersunk) into, but not through, the gypsum base so they do not project below the heating wire.

Fill Coat Application Apply job-sanded DIAMOND Brand Interior Finish Plaster in sufficient thickness to completely cover cable. Trowel plaster parallel to direction of cable but do not use cable as a screed. Level with a trowel, rod or darby to fill any low spots or to remove any high ridges, etc. Use a serrated darby or lightly broom the plaster surface prior to set to provide a key for the finish coat. Average thickness of fill coat should be 3/16".

Finish Coat Application Apply finish coat after fill coat has developed sufficient suction—in good drying weather, about two hours after the fill coat has set; in damp or cold weather usually overnight unless good supplementary heat and ventilation are provided. Use job-sanded DIAMOND Brand Interior Finish Plaster 1/16" to 3/32" thick, to bring total plaster thickness to 1/4".

Scratch in a tight thin coat over the entire area, immediately doubling back to full thickness. Fill all voids and imperfections. Scratch and double-back with the same mix of DIAMOND Brand Interior Finish Plaster. When surface has become firm, hold trowel flat and final-trowel using water sparingly. Best results are obtained by continuous application of an entire ceiling. Always work to a wet edge to avoid dry joinings.

Texture Finish When finish coat has become sufficiently firm, but not set, float surface to desired texture using a sponge, carpet, or other float. Use water sparingly. For heavier texture, additional material from the same batch may be applied to the firm surface to achieve a skip-trowel, Spanish, or other texture.

Simulated Acoustical Finish Spray-apply max. 1/8" thickness of SHEETROCK Brand Ceiling Texture Finish or similar product over a full 1/4" thickness of sanded DIAMOND Brand Interior Finish Plaster. Follow manufacturer's specifications.

Use of this finish, at the maximum 1/8" thickness, will slightly decrease heating system efficiency since simulated acoustical finishes are formulated with insulating-type aggregates.

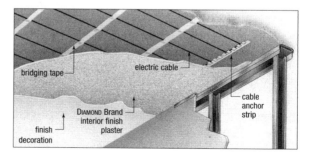

bridging tape

electric cable

DIAMOND Brand interior finish plaster

finish decoration

cable anchor strip

Radiant Heat Systems to Monolithic Concrete

Surface Preparation Concrete surface must be structurally sound and clean, free of dirt, dust, grease, wax, oil or other unsound conditions. Treat exposed metal with a rustproof primer. When corrosion due to high humidity and/or saline content of sand is possible, the use of zinc alloy accessories is recommended.

Remove form ridges to make surfaces reasonably uniform and level. Locate uneven ceiling areas and bad gravel pockets, which require filling prior to installing electric cable and filler.

After treating entire surface with USG Plaster Bonder, according to application directions, leveling may be done with fill-coat mix of DIAMOND Brand Interior Finish Plaster. Minor leveling may be done with a SHEETROCK Brand Setting-Type Joint Compound (DURABOND or EASY SAND).

Caution: Temperature of concrete ceiling with bonding agent applied must be above 32°F before filler and finish applications are started, with air temperature above 55°F.

Radiant Heat Cable Application After ceiling surface has been leveled, apply electric radiant heating cable according to design requirements and cable manufacturer's specifications. Attach cable to the ceiling so that it is kept taut and does not sag away from the ceiling. All cable connectors and non-heating leads must be securely attached to concrete ceiling.

Finishing Mix and apply job-sanded fill coat DIAMOND Brand Interior Finish Plaster according to directions in previous section. Apply 5/16" basecoat parallel to direction of cable, completely covering cable and anchor devices.

Mix and apply finish coat after fill coat has developed sufficient suction. Use job-sanded DIAMOND Brand Interior Finish Plaster 1/16" to 3/32" thick, to bring total plaster thickness to 3/8". Apply finish coat in same manner described in previous section.

Do not energize heating cable until plaster is thoroughly dry. When either or both the completed radiant heat ceiling and room temperature are below 55°F, the temperature should be increased in 5°F increments for each 24-hr. period until a room temperature of 55°F is attained.

If completed radiant heat ceiling and room temperature are 55°F or higher, thermostat may be set at desired temperature.

Special Abuse Resistant Systems

Veneer Plaster Over DUROCK Brand Cement Board

For improved impact strength and abrasion resistance, a two-coat veneer plaster system consisting of DIAMOND Brand Veneer Basecoat Plaster and IMPERIAL Brand Finish Plaster is applied over DUROCK Brand Cement Board attached to framing. This construction is particularly useful for commercial and institutional applications such as schools and high-traffic retail locations.

Space wood or steel framing 16" o.c. and install DUROCK Brand Cement Board with long edges either parallel or perpendicular to the framing and with the rough side of panels exposed. Fasteners are spaced a maximum of 8" o.c.

Prior to treatment of panel joints, apply USG Plaster Bonder in a continuous film to the joint areas according to application directions. Joints should then be treated with SHEETROCK Brand Joint Tape and SHEETROCK

Brand Setting-Type Joint Compound (DURABOND or EASY SAND). Joint surfaces must be treated with a separate coat of joint compound to fully conceal the paper tape.

When the joint is completely dry, treat the entire wall surface with USG Plaster Bonder. Then apply DIAMOND Brand Veneer Basecoat Plaster from 1/16" to 3/32" thickness using a scratch and double-back technique. When basecoat plaster is firm, broom the surface to leave it rough and open for a finish application. With basecoat set and partially dry, apply IMPERIAL Brand Finish Plaster using a scratch and double-back technique. Complete finishing when material is firm. Leave finished surface smooth and dense for decorating.

Veneer Plaster Over FIBEROCK Brand Abuse-Resistant Panels

The abuse resistant characteristics of already tough FIBEROCK Brand Abuse-Resistant Panels are enhanced with the application of a two-coat veneer plaster system. Panels are applied in the same fashion as for cement board above, then joints are treated using SHEETROCK Brand Joint Tape and SHEETROCK Brand Setting-Type Joint Compound (DURABOND or EASY SAND). When the joints are completely dry, treat the entire wall surface with USG Plaster Bonder according to the application directions. Then apply DIAMOND Brand Veneer Basecoat Plaster and IMPERIAL Brand Finish Plaster as described above for cement board.

6

Resurfacing Walls and Ceilings

Veneer plasters may be used to resurface walls that are damaged or walls that can benefit from a more abuse-resistant surface. However, care must be taken to prepare the wall surface for plaster application.

Make sure old wall coverings and their adhesives have been removed. Wash surface thoroughly. Scrape away any loose paint and remove and repair any damaged drywall or plaster surface with appropriate patching material. (See patch and repair products, page 70.) Fill all cracks or holes with SHEETROCK Brand Setting-Type Joint Compound (DURABOND or EASY SAND) and SHEETROCK Brand Joint Tape if necessary.

Once joint compound has set and dried, apply USG Plaster Bonder–Clear over entire wall and ceiling area to be resurfaced.

Mix DIAMOND Brand Veneer Basecoat and Interior Finish Plaster as described on pages 223-224 and trowel-apply over surface using a scratch and double-back technique with each coat. Do not overtrowel.

Decorating with Pigmented Finish Plaster

Decorative Interior Finish System

The USG Decorative Interior Finish System is applied to IMPERIAL Brand Gypsum Base, or other approved substrate. If SHEETROCK Brand Gypsum Panels or other approved substrate are used, the surface must be prepared with SHEETROCK Brand Wallcovering Primer and then with USG Plaster Bonder to assure a consistent bond.

USG Decorative Interior Finish consists of DIAMOND Brand Interior Finish Plaster mixed with pigments that will not affect plaster set. The system must be sealed upon completion.

Color is thoroughly mixed into the finish, providing a deep tinted layer that effectively hides mars, chips and scratches from appearing. High-quality colorants are used to assure color consistency and UV resistance. System identifies 12 basic colors that can be mixed using a standard tint machine and COLORTREND 888 Universal Machine Colorants. USG recommends using only COLORTREND 888 Universal Machine Colorants. Colorants from other manufacturers are not recommended since they may not be compatible with USG materials, they may cause color variations and they may interfere with the intended product application. We recommend only the use of COLORTREND 888 Universal Machine Colorants, the basic USG color formulas with these colorants and custom colors created using the COLORTREND AMBIANCE™ Fan Deck Selector.

For standard colors using COLORTREND 888 Universal Machine Colorants, the formula selected will produce a five-gallon batch size. To create a custom color, select a color and formula from the fan deck and color formula book that represents a color somewhat darker than the color you desire as the finished, dried, surface color. Note that the shade of finished colors is dependent on many factors. Each color formula yields a slightly different degree of color lightness compared to the color swatch depicted in the fan deck selector. The texture applied and the consistency of the mixed mortar also effect the appearance of the finished surface, and therefore the color. Even the plaster product chosen (DIAMOND Brand Interior Finish, IMPERIAL Brand Basecoat Plaster, DIAMOND Brand Veneer Basecoat Plaster or IMPERIAL Brand Finish Plaster) for the mix can vary the resulting shade. Depending on these factors, the final dried finish can be up to several shades lighter than the color swatch depicted in the fan deck selector. Note also that when wet, the wet mixed mortar appears darker than the selected color swatch, but will lighten in color when set and dry.

Mixing USG Decorative Interior Finish usually consists of DIAMOND Brand Interior Finish mixed with colorants and water, but IMPERIAL Brand Basecoat Plaster, DIAMOND Brand Veneer Basecoat Plaster or IMPERIAL Brand Finish Plaster also may be used. Mix in 5-gal. pail (14″ high, 10-1/4″ bottom, 11-1/4″ top). Use 6-1/2″ of water per batch for DIAMOND

Brand Interior Finish, 4-1/2″ for DIAMOND Brand Veneer Basecoat Plaster, 4″ for IMPERIAL Brand Basecoat Plaster, and 5″ for IMPERIAL Brand Finish Plaster. Add the predetermined amount of colorant (COLORTREND Formula) to the water.

The plaster is added to the water in three stages. First, fill the bucket with plaster and stir lightly with an on-and-off action using a 450 RPM 1/2″ drill and blade-type (joint compound) mixing paddle. Add plaster to the top of the bucket and repeat stirring with on-and-off action. Add plaster a third time and mix completely, ensuring that no colored water splashes out of mixing container.

Mix approximately 40-45 lbs. of DIAMOND Brand Interior Finish with the water, or 60 lbs. of DIAMOND Brand Veneer Basecoat Plaster or IMPERIAL Brand Basecoat Plaster, or 50 lbs. of IMPERIAL Brand Finish Plaster. These quantities should fill the container to about 1 to 1-1/2 inches from its top. Finish should be slightly thicker than normal. To ensure color uniformity, each batch must be mixed exactly the same way, by volume and to the same fluidity in a volume-specific container. Note that graded white silica sand may be used for float finishing.

Application Each wall or ceiling must be covered in a continuous application, always continuing joinings of separate mixes prior to either mix setting. Work walls and vaulted ceilings from top to bottom; ceilings from angle to angle. For one-coat semi-smooth texture, apply plaster in random, 1′ to 2′ strokes at a nominal 1/16″ to 1/8″ thickness, leaving lap marks as desired. After approx. 20 min. from initial application, draw a trowel, held almost flat, lightly over the surface with short strokes in various directions. Trowel again as initial set begins (approx. 45 min.). For two-coat heavy texture, apply first coat to a nominal thickness of approx. 1/8″, covering the entire surface. When surface has firmed slightly, apply second coat in short strokes as described above. Two-coat thickness should vary from 1/8″ to 1/4″. Additional troweling of second coat should be as described above for one-coat finish.

Sealing After finish has set and dried (approx. 24 hr.), apply USG Decorative Finish Sealer and maintain min. 55°F temperature. Do not shake or box-mix sealer. Apply using brush, roller or sprayer with 0.015″ to 0.023″ tip. Initially, sealer will appear milky, but will dry clear and colorless. When appearance changes to clear, wipe or roll drips and puddles, then recoat.

For complete information on selecting and applying the appropriate system over drywall, plaster or an existing substrate, see the following USG submittal sheets: P797 (drywall), P808 (existing substrate) or P809 (plaster).

Conventional Plaster Products

7

Quality Delivers Performance

A completed plaster job can be no better than the basecoat or finish materials used and the base to which they are applied. USG plastering products have gained their superiority on one basis: performance.

This record of performance extends through the complete USG line–broadest in the industry–of plaster and lime products, plaster bases and accessories, designed to work together in a wide range of wall and ceiling systems.

The basic materials recommended by USG for quality plaster walls and ceilings are described on the following pages. All meet the essential requirements of function, economy and speed of installation.

The USG trademark on a product is assurance of consistent high quality and proven performance to meet your construction needs.

USG sales representatives are ready to consult with contractors, architects and dealers on plastering materials, systems and special job conditions. They may be reached by contacting the nearest USG Sales Office at (877) 874-6655.

Plaster Bases

Proper use of USG plaster bases and plasters provides the secure bond necessary in order to develop surface strength and resistance to abuse and cracking. These characteristics are common to both metal lath and gypsum plaster bases.

Gypsum Plaster Base

ROCKLATH FIRECODE Plaster Base is a gypsum lath that provides a rigid, fire-resistant base for the economical application of gypsum plasters. ROCKLATH FIRECODE Base requires less basecoat plaster than does metal lath. The specially formulated core of this plaster base is made with mineral materials that enhance the board's resistance to fire exposure. ROCKLATH Base is made only in the FIRECODE formulation.

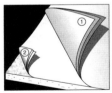

ROCKLATH multi-ply face paper

The gypsum core of this lath is faced with multilayer laminated paper engineered by a USG process to provide proper absorption, check plaster slide and resist lath sag. As illustrated, the three outer layers (1) are highly absorbent to draw moisture from the plaster mix uniformly and quickly so that the plaster takes on anti-slump strength before it can slide; the inner layers (2) are chemically treated to form a barrier against moisture penetration, thus reduce softening of the gypsum core and consequent sag after the board is in place. Face paper is folded around the long edges and the ends are square-cut.

ROCKLATH FIRECODE Base is made 3/8" thick and 16" wide. It comes in 48" lengths and is packaged in bundles of six. It weighs 1.4 lb./ft².

ROCKLATH FIRECODE Plaster Base complies with ASTM C37. Other features are:

Fire Resistance When used with gypsum plaster, gypsum plaster bases provide assemblies with fire ratings of up to 2 hrs. for partitions, ceilings and column fireproofing.

Strength When securely attached, gypsum plaster bases add lateral stability to the assembly.

Sound Resistance Partitions faced with gypsum plaster bases and plaster on both sides have excellent resistance to sound transmission; resilient attachment further improves ratings, makes assemblies suitable for party walls.

Bonding Gypsum plaster bonds to these gypsum plaster bases with a safety factor far higher than required to meet usual construction standards.

Durability Not harmfully affected by decay, dry rot, or normal humidity levels; will not attract vermin.

General Limitations: (1) To be used with gypsum plaster only. Bond between lime or portland cement plaster and ROCKLATH Base is inadequate; (2) Should not be used in areas that are exposed to excessive moisture for extended periods or as a backing for ceramic tile or other similar surfacing materials commonly used in wet areas; galvanized metal lath and portland cement-lime plaster or DUROCK Brand Cement Board systems are recommended; (3) ROCKLATH Base is unsuitable for veneer plasters and finishes.

Note: Gypsum basecoat plasters have slightly greater dimensional stability than gypsum lath. Therefore, the stability of the lath would govern in design considerations. Refer to Appendix for coefficients of expansion, and data on drying shrinkage.

Note: See Appendix for Thermal Resistance Values (R).

Specifications—ROCKLATH FIRECODE Plaster Base

ROCKLATH product	Thickness		Width		Length			Approx.wt.	
	in.	mm	in.	mm	in.	mm	pc/bdl	lb./ft.²	kg/m²
FIRECODE	3/8	5.9	16	406	48	1.2	6	1.4	6.8

Metal Lath

Metal Lath Mesh material formed from sheet steel that has been slit and expanded to form a multitude of small openings. It is made in Diamond Mesh and Riblath types and in two different weights for most applications. Diamond mesh and 3/8″ Riblath are also available in galvanized steel. They comply with ASTM C847.

Ends of bundles of metal lath are often spray painted in different colors for various weights, thus simplifying stocking and handling. Check the manufacturer's coding system to avoid confusion.

Metal lath offers these features:

Strength Metal lath embedded within the plaster provides reinforcement.

Flexibility Readily shaped to ornamental contours to a degree not possible with other plaster bases.

Fire Resistance When used with gypsum plaster, metal lath provides excellent fire-resistant construction; up to 2 hrs. for partitions and 4 hrs. for ceilings and column fireproofing (See Plaster Systems, Chapter 10).

Security Metal lath and plaster surfaces are extremely difficult to penetrate; provide excellent protection against penetration or forced entry.

Available in following types and styles:

Diamond Mesh Lath

Self-Furring Diamond Mesh Lath

Paper-Back Lath

Flat Riblath

3/8″ Riblath

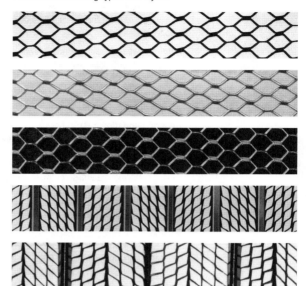

Metal Lath General Limitations

1. Metal lath products should not be used with magnesium oxychloride cement stuccos or stuccos containing calcium chloride additives.
2. In ceiling assemblies, certain precautions concerning construction, insulation and ventilation are necessary for good performance. A min. of 1/2 sq. in. net free vent area is recommended per sq. ft. of horizontal surface in plenum or other space.

Diamond Mesh Lath A small diamond mesh metal plaster base (approx. 11,000 meshes per sq. yd.). A general all-purpose lath; it is best for ornamental, contour plastering. The small mesh openings conserve plaster and reduce droppings. Also available in self-furring type having 1/4″ dimple indentations spaced 1-1/2″ o.c. each way, for use as exterior stucco base over sheathing, column fireproofing and for replastering over old surfaces.

Paper-Backed Metal Lath Asphalt paper-backed Diamond Mesh Lath. Regular or Self-Furring type. Asphalt-impregnated paper is factory-bonded to the back. Paper is vapor permeable; complies with Federal Specification UU-B-790a, Type I, Grade D, Style 2.

Paper-backed painted lath is recommended for lath and plaster back-up of interior tile work and other inside work. Paper-backed galvanized lath is a recommended base and reinforcement for some exterior wall construction, including stucco and other machine or hand applied exterior surfacing materials.

Flat Riblath A 'flat rib' type of lath with smaller mesh openings. More rigid than diamond mesh, excellent as nail-on lath, and for tie-on work on flat ceilings. Not recommended for contour lathing.

3/8″ Riblath A herringbone mesh pattern with 3/8″ V-shaped ribs running lengthwise of the sheet at 4-1/2″ intervals, with inverted intermediate 3/16″ ribs. The heavy ribs provide exceptional rigidity. Used when supports are spaced more than 16″ o.c. and not more than 24″, and for 2″ solid studless metal lath and plaster partitions. Also used as a centering lath for concrete floor and roof slabs. Unsuitable for contour plastering. Min. ground thickness must be 1″.

Metal Lath Selector

| Type of lath | Recommended Applications | | | | | |
	Ornamental contour	Over int. substrate	Over ext. substrate[1]	Nail-on/tie-on flat ceiling	Solid partitions	Concrete centering
Diamond Mesh	X			X[3]	X[5]	
Self-Furring		X	X[2]	X[4]		
Flat Riblath				X		
3/8″ Riblath					X	X

(1) For example: gypsum sheathing, replastering existing work, column fireproofing. (2) 3.4 lb./yd.² galvanized lath. (3) For tie-on only: supports 16″ o.c. max. (4) For nail-on only: supports 16″ o.c. max. (5) Supports 16″ o.c. max.

Trim Accessories

Corner beads should be used on all external plaster corners to provide protection, true and straight corners, and grounds for plastering; casing beads are used as plaster stops around wall openings and at intersections of plaster with other finishes.

Limitation: Galvanized steel accessories are recommended for interior use only. For exterior application and where corrosion due to high humidity and/or saline content of aggregates is possible, the use of zinc alloy accessories is recommended. Should not be used with magnesium oxychloride cement stucco or portland cement stucco containing calcium chloride additives.

Corner and Casing Beads

1-A Expanded Corner Bead A general-purpose corner bead, economical and most generally used. Has wide expanded flanges that are easily flexed. Preferred for irregular corners. Provides increased reinforcement close to nose of bead.

4-A Flexible Corner Bead A special utility, solid-punch-pattern bead. By snipping flanges, this bead may be bent to any curved design (for archways, etc.)

Double-X Corner Bead Has full 3-1/4″ flanges easily adjusted for plaster depth on columns. Ideal for finishing corners of structural tile and rough masonry. Has perforated stiffening ribs along expanded flange.

Casing Beads Used as a plaster stop and exposed to eliminate the need for wood trim around window and door openings; also recommended at junction or intersection of plaster and other wall or ceiling finishes, and as a screed. May be used with metal lath, ROCKLATH FIRECODE Plaster Base, DUROCK Brand Cement Board or masonry construction. In order to ensure proper grounds for plastering, 3/4″ casing beads are recommended for use with metal lath, 5/8″ beads with all masonry units, 7/8″ beads when solid flange is applied under gypsum plaster base, 1/2″ beads when flange is applied over veneer gypsum base. Available in galvanized steel, or zinc alloy for exterior applications.

1-A Expanded Corner Bead

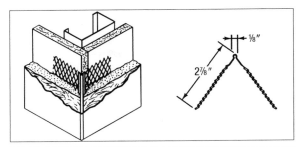

4-A Flexible Corner Bead

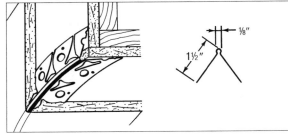

Double-X Corner Bead

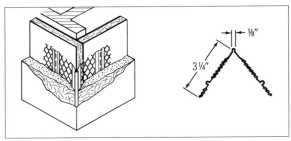

Cornerite and Striplath

These products are strips of painted or galvanized Diamond Mesh Lath used as reinforcement. Cornerite, bent lengthwise in the center to form a 100° angle, should be used in all internal plaster angles where metal lath is not lapped or carried around; over gypsum lath, anchored to the lath, and over internal angles of masonry constructions. Also used in the floating angle method of applying gypsum lath to wood framing in order to reduce plaster cracking. Striplath is a similar flat strip, used as a plaster reinforcement over joints of gypsum lath and where dissimilar bases join; also used to span pipe chases, and as reinforcement of headers over openings.

Control Joints

Zinc Control Joint Designed to relieve stresses of both expansion and contraction in large plastered areas. Made from roll-formed zinc alloy, it is resistant to corrosion in both interior and exterior uses with gypsum or portland cement plaster. An open slot, 1/4" wide and 1/2" deep, is protected with plastic tape which is removed after plastering

#66 Square Edge Casing Beads
(expanded or short flange)

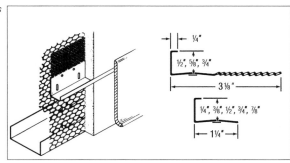

Cornerite

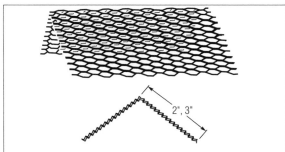

Striplath

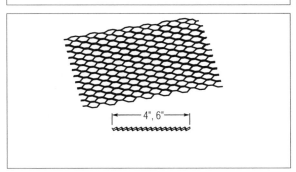

7

is completed (see page 244). The short flanges are perforated for keying and attachment by wire-tying to metal lath or by stapling to gypsum lath. Thus the plaster is key-locked to the control joint, which not only provides plastering grounds but can also be used to create decorative panel designs. Sizes and grounds: No. 50, 1/2"; No. 75, 3/4"; No. 100, 1" (for uses such as exterior stucco).

Maximum Spacing–SHEETROCK Brand Control Joints for Interior Plaster Assemblies

System	Location	Max. single dimension		Max. single area	
		ft.	m	ft.²	m²
Metal Lath & Plaster	Partition	30	9	–	–
	Ceiling	50⁽¹⁾	15	2500	230
		30⁽²⁾	9	900	83.6
Gypsum Lath & Plaster	Partition	30	9	–	–
	Ceiling	50⁽¹⁾	15	2500	230
		30⁽²⁾	9	900	83.6

(1) With perimeter relief. (2) Without perimeter relief.

For exterior application where wind pressure exceeds 20 psf, back control joints with 2″ wide butyl tape applied to the sheathing. Install joints with flanges under self-furring lath and attach with Bostitch 9/16″ "G" staples or equal, spaced 6″ apart on each side. Positive attachment of flange to framing through the lath is required using fasteners 12″ o.c. Break supporting members, sheathing and metal lath behind control joints. When vertical and horizontal joints intersect, vertical joint should be continuous; horizontal joint should abut it. Apply sealant at all splices, intersections and terminals.

SHEETROCK Brand
Control Joint Nos. 50,
75, 100

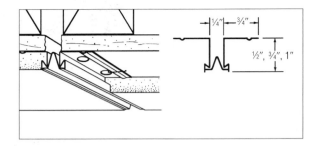

Limitation: Where sound and/or fire ratings are prime considerations, adequate protection must be provided behind the control joint. Functions only with transverse stresses. Should not be used with magnesium oxychloride cement stucco or portland cement stucco containing calcium chloride additives.

Double-V Expansion Joint Provides stress relief to control cracking in large plastered areas. Made with expanded flanges of corrosion-resistant galvanized steel, or zinc for exterior use in 1/2″ or 3/4″ grounds.

Double V Expansion Joint

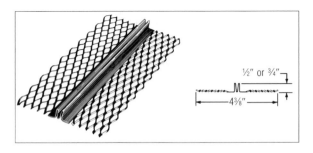

Specifications–Typical Plaster Trim Accessories

Product	Depth or grounds		Flange width		Finish
	in.	mm	in.	mm	
1-A Expanded Corner Bead	–	–	2-7/8	73.0	Galv. or Zinc Alloy
4-A Flexible corner Bead	–	–	1-1/2	38.1	Galv.
Double-X Corner Bead	–	–	3-1/4	82.6	Galv.
#66 Square Expanded Flange Casing Bead[2]	1/2	12.7	3-1/8	79.4	Galv. or Zinc Alloy
	5/8	15.9	3-1/8	79.4	Galv. or Zinc Alloy
	3/4	19.1	3-1/8	79.4	Galv. or Zinc Alloy
	7/8	22.2	3-1/8	79.4	Galv. or Zinc Alloy
	1	22.2	3-1/8	79.4	Galv. or Zinc Alloy
	1-1/4	22.2	3-1/8	79.4	Galv. or Zinc Alloy
#66 Square Short Flange Casing Bead	1/2	12.7	1-1/4	31.7	Galv. or Zinc Alloy
	3/4	19.1	1-1/4	31.7	Galv. or Zinc Alloy
	7/8	22.2	1-1/4	31.7	Galv. or Zinc Alloy
Cornerite	–	–	2	50.8	Paint or Galv.
	–	–	3	76.2	Paint or Galv.
Striplath	–	–	4	101.6	Paint or Galv.
	–	–	6	152.4	Paint or Galv.
SHEETROCK Brand Zinc Control Joint No. 93	1/2(#50)	12.7	3/4	19.1	Zinc Alloy
	3/4(#75)	19.0	3/4	19.1	Zinc Alloy
	1(#100)	25.4	3/4	19.1	Zinc Alloy
Double-V Expansion Joint	1/2	12.7	2-3/16	76.7	Galv.
	3/4	19.1	2-3/16	76.7	Galv.

(1) Available in zinc, special order only.

Clips and Screws

A specially formed steel clip and self-drilling screws are available for positive attachment and rapid erection of gypsum plaster bases and metal lath.

BRIDJOINT **Field Clip B-1** Used to support and align end joints which do not fall on framing members; designed for use with 3/8″ ROCKLATH FIRECODE Base. Approximate usage is 350 clips per 100 yd.² of lath, based on 16″ o.c. stud spacing. Shipped 500 pc./package; 19 lb./1000 pcs.

Specifications–Lath Attachment Clips

Product	Clips per 100 yd.² (84 m²) lath[1]	Shipping unit (pc)	wt./1000 pc	
			lb.	kg
BRIDJOINT Clip B-1	350	500	19	8.6

(1) Quantity based on stud spacing of 16" o.c. unless otherwise noted.

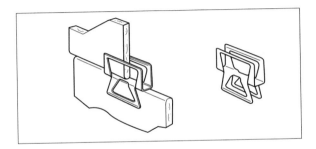

Screws The result of continuing development aimed at producing the best possible attachment of gypsum boards to steel, wood or gypsum supports simply and quickly. A complete line of self-drilling, self-tapping steel screws is available to improve construction systems and simplify installation methods. All screws are highly corrosion-resistant and have a Phillips head recess for rapid installation with a special bit and power-driven screw gun. (For complete data and Screw Selector Guide, see Chapter 1.)

Bugle head, high and low threads, slotted point of screws.

Economical SUPER-TITE Screws with specially designed drill point for steel studs.

Framing Components

Steel framing members offer the advantages of light weight, low material cost and quick erection, superior strength and versatility in meeting job requirements. All are noncombustible.

Steel Studs and Runners Channel-shape and roll-formed from galvanized or corrosion-resistant steel. Used in non-load and load-bearing interior partition and exterior curtain wall systems. Limited chaseways are provided by punchouts in the web. Assemblies using these studs are low in cost with excellent sound and fire-resistance characteristics. Available in various styles and widths to meet functional requirements:

For data on framing components see Chapter 1. For installation, see Chapter 2.

Cold-Rolled Channels Formed from 16-ga. steel, black asphaltum painted or galvanized. Used for furring, suspended ceilings, partitions and ornamental lathing. Sizes: 3/4″, 1-1/2″, 2″.

Metal Furring Channels Roll-formed, hat-shaped section of galvanized steel, this 25-ga. channel may be attached with furring clips or tie wire to the main carrying channels and spaced 16″ o.c. for economical screw attachment of ROCKLATH FIRECODE Base as a base for either adhesively applied acoustical tile or a basecoat plaster. Also available made from 20-ga. galvanized steel for heavier loads and longer spans. The furring channel also provides noncombustible furring for exterior walls, may be spaced up to 24″ o.c. Face width 1-1/4″, depth 7/8″. (See Chapter 1 for data on Z-Furring Channels.)

Adjustable Wall Furring Brackets Used for attaching 3/4″ furring channels to exterior masonry walls. Made of galvanized steel with corrugated edges. Brackets are attached to masonry and act as supports for horizontal channels 24″ o.c. in braced furring systems.

Tie Wire 18-ga. galvanized soft annealed wire for tying metal lath to channels and furring to runner channels.

Hanger Wire 8-ga. for suspended ceiling channel runners when spaced not more than 4 ft. o.c.

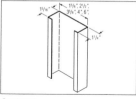

Cold-rolled channel

Cold-rolled channel

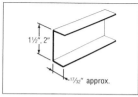

Steel stud

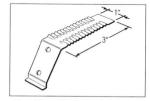

Z-furring channel

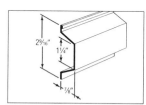

Furring channel

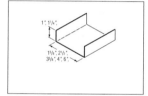

Adjustable wall furring bracket

Tie wire

Steel runner

Specifications–Structural Accessories[1]

Product	Size in./ga.	mm
Cold Rolled Channel[2] [3]	3/4"	19.1
	1-1/2"	38.1
	2"	50.9
Tie Wire/Hanger Wire[3]	8-ga. Coil	4.1
	18-ga Coil	1.2
	8-ga. Bdl.	4.1
	18-ga Hank	1.2
	18-ga.Hank	1.2

Notes: (1) See Chapter 1 for other structural accessories; (2) Painted; (3) Galvanized

STRUCTOCORE **Security Wall Components** Highly specialized security wall systems incorporate uniquely formed steel sheets as reinforcement within gypsum cementitious fireproofing materials. Complete information about STRUCTOCORE Security Walls and their system components is available from your USG sales representative or sales office. Request technical publication SA1119.

Plasters

The main ingredient of all gypsum plasters is gypsum rock–hydrous calcium sulfate–which has a water content of about 20% in chemical combination. During processing, about 3/4 of this chemically combined water is removed from the gypsum rock by means of a controlled heating process called calcination. When water is added at the job, the material crystallizes (sets), reverting to its original chemical composition.

USG plasters are specifically formulated to control setting time and other important characteristics. These depend upon the intended use and method of application, the climatic conditions of the area and job conditions.

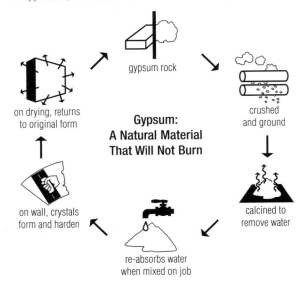

gypsum rock

on drying, returns to original form

crushed and ground

Gypsum: A Natural Material That Will Not Burn

on wall, crystals form and harden

calcined to remove water

re-absorbs water when mixed on job

Abuse Resistance

Abuse resistance has become a key wall system selection factor as designers and their clients have realized that it is often less expensive from a life-cycle perspective to address abuse resistance in critical areas in the initial project stage than to pay the high on-going costs of maintaining and repairing regular drywall partitions.

Abuse resistance may be defined as the ability of a system to resist three levels of damage: (1) Surface damage from abrasion and/or indentation; (2) Penetration through to the wall cavity from sharp or blunt impact; (3) Security breach through the entire assembly from ballistics or forced entry. For more detailed information on abuse resistance, see USG *Abuse Resistant Systems,* publication SA 929.

A table describing the categories of abuse resistance and a table of products and systems organized by category of abuse resistance is in the Appendix.

Basecoat Plasters

RED TOP Gypsum Plaster

RED TOP Two-Purpose Gypsum Plaster

RED TOP Wood Fiber Plaster

To take advantage of all the beauty and durability plaster can offer, the required number of coats must be applied in each of the following situations:

Three coats are required on all metal lath and are desirable on all gypsum lath.

Two coats are acceptable on gypsum lath and on interior face of rough concrete block, clay tile or porous brick.

Furring is required over the interior surface of outside masonry prior to plastering to prevent damage from seepage and condensation.

In preparing for plastering, consideration should be given to the selection of materials not only for compatibility but also for the quality of the structure to be plastered. It is wise to upgrade plastering specifications when possible.

RED TOP Gypsum Plaster Preferred for its low cost and excellent workability; must be job-aggregated. Three types: Regular—for sand aggregate, hand application; LW—for lightweight aggregate, hand application (not recommended over metal lath when smooth-trowel lime/gauging finish is used); Machine Application—for sand or lightweight aggregate. Perlite aggregate is not recommended when vertical lift exceeds 30' or hose length is over 150'. Meets ASTM C28. Available in 100-lb. bags.

RED TOP Two-Purpose Plaster—Suitable for machine or hand application; reduces inventory requirements. Must be job-aggregated, perlite aggregate not recommended when vertical lift exceeds 30 ft. or hose length is over 150 ft. Meets ASTM C28. Available in 100-lb. bags.

RED TOP Wood Fiber Plaster Contains selected wood fiber and can be used with the addition of water only. When used over masonry bases or for machine application, 1 cu. ft. of sand per 100 lb. of plaster must be added. When used as a scratch or brown coat, 1 cu. ft. of sand can be added.

STRUCTO-BASE Gypsum Plaster

STRUCTO-LITE Pre-Mixed Perlited Gypsum Plaster

RED TOP Wood Fiber Plaster can be applied to all standard lath and masonry surfaces and is recommended as a scratch coat for metal lath.

Wood Fiber Plaster, neat, weighs approx. 1/4 less than a sanded gypsum basecoat and generally provides greater fire resistance than normally sanded gypsum plaster at a slightly higher cost. Complies with ASTM C28. Available in 100-lb. bags.

STRUCTO-BASE **Gypsum Plaster** Develops higher strength than conventional plasters. Designed for use in STRUCTOCORE Security Wall Systems. Ideal for handball courts, hospital corridors, schools, etc., requiring high-strength basecoat. Superior as sanded scratch and brown coat over metal lath. Meets ASTM C28. Available in 100-lb. bags. Available in Regular and Machine Application.

STRUCTO-LITE **Gypsum Plaster** Contains mill-mixed perlite aggregate and is preferred in cold weather when aggregate may freeze, or when suitable aggregate is not readily available. Lighter weight and greater insulation value than sanded basecoats. Two types (not available in all areas; consult U. S. Gypsum representative): Regular–for gypsum or metal lath; Masonry–for high-suction unit masonry. Not recommended over metal lath when smooth-trowel lime finish is used or machine application when vertical lift exceeds 30 ft. or hose length is over 150 ft. Meets ASTM C28. Available in 80-lb. bags.

Coverage and Technical Data–Gypsum Basecoat Plasters

Plaster product	Mix	Ratio: aggregate (vol.)/ Basecoat (wt.) ft.³/100 lb. m³/ton[3]		Approx. compressive strength dry[1] lb./in.² (psi)	MPa[4]	Approx. coverage per ton of gypsum basecoat[2] Gypsum lath yd.²/ton	m²/ton[3]	Metal lath yd.²/ton	m²/ton[3]	Unit masonry yd.²/ton	m²/ton[3]
RED TOP Gypsum and Two-Purpose Plasters	sand	2.0	1.24	875	6.00	180	165	114	104	140	129
	sand	2.5	1.55	750	5.17	206	190	131	121	160	147
	sand	3.0	1.86	650	4.48	232	213	148	136	181	167
	perlite	2.0	1.24	700	4.82	176	162	112	103	137	126
	perlite	3.0	1.86	525	3.62	224	206	143	132	174	160
	vermiculite	2.0	1.24	465	3.21	171	157	109	100	133	123
	vermiculite	3.0	1.86	290	2.00	215	198	137	126	168	154
STRUCTO-BASE Gypsum Plaster	sand	2.0	1.24	2800 min.[5]	19.30	154	142	99	91	120	110
	sand	2.5	1.55	1900 min.[5]	13.10	185	170	118	109	144	132
	sand	3.0	1.86	1400 min.[5]	9.65	214	197	136	125	167	154
STRUCTO-LITE Gypsum Plaster	regular	–	–	700	4.82	140	129	89[6]	82[6]	109	100
RED TOP Wood Fiber Plaster	neat	–	–	1750	12.06	85	78	54	49	66	60
RED TOP Wood Fiber Plaster	sand	1.0	0.62	1400	9.65	135	124	86	79	105	97

(1) Average laboratory results when tested in accordance with ASTM C472. Figures may vary slightly for products from individual plants.
(2) Grounds (including finish coat): gypsum lath (face of lath), metal lath 3/4″ (back of lath), unit masonry 5/8″. (3) Metric ton.
(4) Megapascals (MN/m²). (5) Laboratory evaluations for sanded plaster are based on use of graded Ottawa silica sand. (6) Lightweight aggregated plasters are not recommended over metal lath when the finish coat is to be smooth troweled.

Basecoat Plaster Limitations

1. Where sound isolation is prime consideration, use sand aggregate only.

2. Do not use where water or excessive moisture is present. May be applied to exterior soffits equipped with suitable drips and casings and protected from direct exposure to rain and moisture.

3. Not recommended for masonry or concrete walls or ceilings coated with bituminous compounds or waterproofing agents. Interior of exterior walls shall be furred and lathed prior to plastering to prevent seepage and condensation.

4. The only USG plaster recommended for embedding electric heat cables is job-sanded DIAMOND Brand Interior Finish Plaster applied directly to properly prepared monolithic concrete or IMPERIAL Brand Gypsum Base (See pages 230-232 for more information). If IMPERIAL Brand Gypsum Base and job-sanded DIAMOND Brand Interior Finish are used for a radiant heat system, the cable-sheath operating temperatures must never exceed 125°F.

5. Basecoats containing job-mixed lightweight aggregate or STRUCTO-LITE Gypsum Plaster must be finished with an aggregated finish plaster.

Portland Cement Plaster

This mix is used for interior applications where high-moisture conditions exist, or for exterior stucco. Prepared as follows:

Job-Mixed Stucco Mix BONDCRETE or MORTASEAL Mason's Lime with portland cement and sand in accordance with ASTM C926. Type L basecoat, Type FL finish coat. Suggested proportions: scratch coat—1 bag portland cement, 1 bag lime, 8 cu. ft. sand; brown coat—1 bag portland cement, 1 bag lime, 10 cu. ft. sand; finish—1 bag portland cement, 1-1/2 bags lime, 9 cu. ft. sand.

Prepared Finish—ORIENTAL Exterior Finish Stucco (see page 257).

Portland Cement Plaster Limitations

1. Scratch, brown and finish coats of portland cement plasters require curing with water after set.

2. Must not be applied directly to smooth, dense surfaces or gypsum lath. Self-furring metal lath must be secured to such surfaces before plaster is applied.

3. Control joints should be provided to compensate for shrinkage during drying.

4. A Keenes cement-lime putty finish must never be used over a portland cement basecoat.

Finish Plasters

Conventional plaster walls are finished with gauging plasters and finishing limes or with prepared finishes. USG provides a range of products with a variety of characteristics, depending upon performance requirements. From the standpoint of workability, productivity and ease of achieving surface smoothness, the conventional finish plasters that follow are superior to the veneer finish plasters that are known best for their surface hardness. See page 469 in the Appendix for a comparison of various finish plasters.

Finish Coat Plaster General Limitations

1. A smooth trowel finish should not be used over lightweight aggregate gypsum basecoat applied over metal lath. Only sand float finishes are recommended over metal lath.

2. Where the gypsum basecoat is STRUCTO-LITE plaster or contains lightweight aggregate (perlite or vermiculite) and a smooth trowel finish is used over any plaster base except metal lath, the finish coat should be RED TOP Gauging Plaster (regular) and lime: a) with addition of 1/2 cu. ft. of perlite fines, or, b) with addition of 50 lb. of No. 1 white silica sand per 100 lb. gauging plaster, or, c) use Quality Type (RED TOP, CHAMPION or STAR) factory aggregated gauging plaster.

3. Gypsum or lime-based finishes, including Keenes cement, should not be used directly over a portland cement basecoat or over concrete block or other masonry surfaces.

4. Smooth-trowel high-strength finishes, such as STRUCTO-GAUGE Gauging Plaster and Keenes Cement, must not be used over STRUCTO-LITE Plaster or a basecoat with a lightweight aggregate.

5. Gauged-lime putty and RED TOP Finish applied over conventional basecoat plasters must age 30 days, be thoroughly dry and properly sealed before decorating. Quick-drying vinyl acrylic latex or alkali-resistant alkyd primer-sealers are recommended.

6. Primers containing polyvinyl acetate (PVA) are not recommended and should not be specified for use over wet plaster of any kind, over lime-gauging or lime-containing plasters. The PVA film is subject to rewetting and will almost certainly result in bond loss and subsequent paint delamination. In view of these precautions, strictly follow the specific lime-locking product recommendations of paint manufacturers for painting lime-gauging putty finishes and for lime-containing veneer plaster finishes.

Gauging Plasters

RED TOP Gauging Plaster Quick Set

RED TOP Gauging Plaster Slow Set

Lime, when used alone as a finish plaster, does not set, is subject to shrinkage when drying, and lacks a hard finish. Gauging plaster is blended into the lime putty in the proper proportions to provide controlled set, early hardness and strength, and to prevent shrinkage cracks.

Gauging plasters are carefully ground and screened to proper particle sizes to make the plasters quick-soaking and easily blended with lime putty.

High-strength RED TOP Keenes Cement and STRUCTO-GAUGE Gauging Plaster are to be used only over sanded or wood fiber or veneer basecoat plasters. Over lightweight aggregated basecoats, use white or regular gauging plaster that is properly aggregated.

RED TOP Gauging Plaster Blends easily with lime putty for durable smooth-trowel or sand-float finishes. Provides high strength, hardness and abrasion resistance superior to many other surfaces. Easily painted or decorated. Applied over a gypsum basecoat. Available in Regular, unaggregated; Quality, with perlite fines for lightweight-aggregated basecoats. Two types: Quick Set (30-40 min); Slow Set (50-70 min.). Meets ASTM C28. Available in 100-lb. bags.

CHAMPION *Gauging Plaster White Quick Set*

STAR *Gauging Plaster White Slow Set*

STRUCTO-GAUGE *Gauging Plaster Slow Set*

RED TOP *Keenes Cement*

CHAMPION **and** STAR **Gauging Plasters** Selected for their whiteness, they provide for smooth-trowel or sand-float lime-putty finishes. Effectively resist cracking, provide hardness and abrasion resistance required for normal interior walls and ceilings. Applied over a gypsum or veneer plaster basecoat. Job-aggregated, sand-float finish may be job colored. Available in Regular, unaggregated; Quality, with perlite fines for lightweight-aggregated basecoats. When mixed with recommended proportions of lime putty, CHAMPION Plaster sets in 20-30 min.; STAR Plaster in 40-60 min. Meet ASTM C28. Available in 50 and 100-lb. bags.

STRUCTO-GAUGE **Gauging Plaster** Mixed with lime putty, produces high-strength, durable white smooth-trowel finish for high-traffic areas. Excellent hardness and abrasion resistance to withstand abuse. Faster and easier to apply than Keenes Cement. Used over high-strength sanded, veneer plaster or wood fiber gypsum basecoats. Not for use over lightweight-aggregated or portland cement basecoats or masonry. Two types: Slow Set (60-75 min.) for regular sanded basecoats; Quick Set (30-40 min.) for low-suction veneer basecoats. Meets ASTM C28. Under equivalent application conditions will provide a harder finish than RED TOP, CHAMPION or STAR Gauging Plasters. Available in 100-lb. bags.

RED TOP **Keenes Cement** The only retemperable gauging plaster; provides best gauging for lime-sand float finishes; also suitable for job color. Can be used as a smooth-trowel finish, offering strong, hard surfaces when densified by extensive troweling through set. Permits mixing large batches for job-colored finishes. Requires high-strength gypsum basecoat. Two types: Regular (3-6 hr. set); Quick Trowel (1-2 hr. set.) Meets ASTM C61. Available in 100-lb. bags.

7

IVORY *Double-Hydrated Finish Lime*

SNOWDRIFT *Double-Hydrated Finish Lime*

GRAND PRIZE *Hydrated Finish Lime*

Finish Limes

The purpose of finish lime is to provide bulk, plasticity and ease of spread for the finish coat. There are two types of finish lime: (1) double hydrate (Type S), (2) normal or single hydrate (Type N). Each requires different preparation in order to produce a good finish-lime putty.

IVORY and SNOWDRIFT **Finish Limes** Autoclaved (double-hydrate) limes that immediately develop high plasticity when mixed with water and do not require overnight soaking. Virtually eliminate the possibility of future expansion within the finish coat because of unhydrated magnesium oxides. These limes are easy to apply and have excellent spreading qualities. Comply with ASTM C206, Type S. Available in 50-lb. bags.

GRAND PRIZE **Finish Lime** Single-hydrate lime that is economical, easy working, uniform, white and plastic. Requires soaking at least 16 hrs. to develop proper plasticity and the degree of hydration for use. Complies with ASTM C206, Type N. Available in 50-lb. bags.

Prepared Finishes

IMPERIAL **Brand Finish Plaster** Provides the ultimate in surface hardness and abrasion resistance. Available for hand application. Provides a smooth-trowel or float or spray-texture finish ready for decoration. Used as finish coat in STRUCTOCORE Security Wall Systems. Complies with ASTM C584. Available in 80-lb. bags.

DIAMOND **Brand Interior Finish Plaster** Offers a strong, hard white surface for construction where the extra hardness of IMPERIAL Brand Finish Plaster is not required. Extremely adaptable to textured finishes. Complies with ASTM C587. Available in 50-lb. bags.

IMPERIAL Brand
Finish Plaster

IMPERIAL Brand Finish
Plaster Special White

RED TOP Finish Plaster-
Regular Set

DIAMOND Brand Interior
Finish Plaster

DIAMOND Brand Interior
Finish Plaster Type F

DIAMOND Brand Interior
Finish Plaster Type F
Sanded

Rᴇᴅ Tᴏᴘ **Finish** Mill-mixed gauged interior finish requiring addition of water only. Has stabilized set, excellent troweling characteristics. Two formulations available: Regular Set, for use over conventional sanded gypsum basecoat, and Quick Set for use over Iᴍᴘᴇʀɪᴀʟ and Dɪᴀᴍᴏɴᴅ Brand Basecoats. Not for use over lightweight aggregate gypsum basecoat. Available in 50-lb. bags.

Coverage–Finish Plasters[1]

	Ratio of Mix (dry wt.)			Approx. Coverage[2]	
Product	Lime	Gauging	Sand[3]	yd.²/ton	m²/t[4]
Iᴍᴘᴇʀɪᴀʟ Brand Finish Plaster	–	–	–	360	330
Dɪᴀᴍᴏɴᴅ Brand Interior Finish Plaster	–	–	–	550	510
Rᴇᴅ Tᴏᴘ Finish	–	–	–	390	360
Cʜᴀᴍᴘɪᴏɴ, Sᴛᴀʀ and Rᴇᴅ Tᴏᴘ Gauging Plaster	2	1	–	390	360
	2	1	8	280	260
Rᴇᴅ Tᴏᴘ Keenes Cement	2	1	8	270	250
	2	1	–	430	400
	1	1	–	370	345
Sᴛʀᴜᴄᴛᴏ-Gᴀᴜɢᴇ Gauging Plaster	1	1	–	380	350
	2	1	–	430	400

(1) Over conventional basecoat plasters; over veneer basecoats, coverage is increased. (2) 1/16″ (1.6mm) thickness.
(3) Natural, uniformly graded, clean silica sand. (4) Metric ton.

7

Ornamental Plasters

USG Moulding Plaster Used for specialized work such as ornamental trim or running cornices. The plaster grain is very fine, ideal for sharp detail when used neat for cast work. Controlled set provides uniform workability. For running cornice work, add a small amount (max. 50%) of lime putty to add plasticity and to act as a lubricant for the template. Provides approx. 1.5 cu. ft. per 100 lbs. Complies with ASTM C28. Available in 50- and 100-lb. bags.

Hʏᴅʀᴏᴄᴀʟ **White Gypsum Cement** Has exceptional strength and is recommended for ornamental work having thin sections and for castings made with intricate latex molds where its high green strength minimizes breakage. In 50 and 100-lb. bags.

Hʏᴅʀᴏᴄᴀʟ **FGR 95 Gypsum Cement** Unique high-strength product used with glass fibers or a glass fiber mat for fabricating lightweight fire-resistant decorated shapes, architectural elements, column covers,

USG Moulding Plaster

Hydrocal White Gypsum Cement

cornices and trims. Adapts to most patterns, accepts most coatings. Safe and non-toxic; zero flame spread, zero smoke contribution material. In 50- and 100-lb. bags.

For additional information, contact Dept. 440, Industrial Gypsum Division, USG, Chicago, Illinois, 60606; phone: (800) 487-4431.

Special Plasters–Approximate Yield

Product	Bag size	Approx. volume dry		
	lb.	kg	ft.³/100 lb.	m³/t[1]
USG Moulding Plaster	50 & 100	22.7 & 45.4	1.5	0.94
HYDROCAL White Cement	50 & 100	22.7 & 45.4	1.3	0.81
HYDROCAL FGR 95 Gypsum Cement	100	45.4	1.0	0.62

(1)Metric ton

Special Additives

Plaster Retarders

USG Standard Strength Retarder Recommended for slight to moderate (30 to 45 min.) lengthening of set times of conventional and veneer plasters. Available for use with plaster when required by job or climate conditions. Available in 1-1/2-lb. package.

USG High Strength Retarder Extends setting time of plaster 1 to 3 hours. Especially suitable for conventional plasters where machine application set time alteration is required. Available in 1-1/4-lb. package.

USG Retarder for Lime Containing Plaster Products Especially formulated for use with lime/finish plasters, such as RED TOP Finish, DIAMOND Brand Interior Finish and gauging/lime plaster finishes.

Retarder Limitations: Avoid use of too much retarder, which can weaken the plaster finish. When used in excess, "dry-out" may occur–a condition where the water required for the chemical set reaction evaporates before adequate setting can take place. USG Retarders should never be added directly to the plaster mix. Pre-mixing with water assures faster and more uniform dispersion for better batch control.

Plaster Accelerators

USG Standard Strength Gypsum Plaster Accelerator Provides slight adjustments in setting time (10 to 30 min.) for conventional and veneer plasters. Available for use with plaster when required by job or climate conditions. When used in excess, setting and drying problems can arise. Available in 1-1/2-lb. package.

USG High-Strength Gypsum Accelerator Provides more substantial adjustments to setting times (30 min. to 2 hr.) for conventional plasters. Also may be used to alter set times for setting-type (DURABOND or EASY SAND) joint compounds. Available in 1-1/2-lb. package.

USG Plaster Accelerator–Alum Catalyst This accelerator helps correct plaster performance in dry-out conditions. In addition to shortening working times for plaster, this accelerator also may be used to treat sun-faded IMPERIAL Brand Gypsum Base when a lime-containing plaster is to be applied to it. It is used to improve the bond of alkaline veneer plaster to gypsum bases with faded face paper. Available in 1-1/2-lb. package.

Accelerator Limitations: Never add USG Standard Strength or High Strength Accelerator directly to the mixing water or mix it with water to form a solution before adding it to the plaster mix. When used in this manner, its ability to accelerate is significantly reduced. Instead, the accelerator should be sprinkled in dry form into the mixer after the plaster has been added. For hand mixing, dry accelerator can be added either to the dry mix or the plaster slurry.

Plaster Bonder

USG Plaster Bonder Vinyl acetate homopolymer emulsion for enhancing adhesion of new plaster to any structurally sound interior surface. Clear or tinted pink to allow visual confirmation of application where desired. May be brush, roller or spray applied. Dries to a film that rewets when plaster is applied. Compatible with gypsum plaster, cinder block, stone, gypsum drywall panels and other similar materials. Should not be used around swimming pools or in exceptionally moist areas. Do not apply to underside of concrete roof decks. Required for applications of plaster over DUROCK Brand Cement Board, FIBEROCK Brand Abuse-Resistant Gypsum Fiber Panels and monolithic concrete. Available in 1- and 5-gal. containers.

Acrylic Additive

USG ACRI-ADD 100% Acrylic Add-Mix Fortifier Water-based acrylic polymer emulsion admixture designed for interior use with gypsum-based products and for interior or exterior use with portland cement-based products. It enhances performance of gypsum plasters, mortars and cement plasters by improving bond strength and water resistance, it minimizes shrinkage cracking, and it improves overall durability. It also enhances curing qualities, imparts abrasion resistance and reduces cracking due to tensile and impact stresses. Low odor and color fast. Substitute the fortifier for a portion of the normal amount of mixing water, typically 1:3, but sometimes 1:2 or 1:1 depending on application end product, jobsite conditions and substrates selected. Available in 1- and 5-gal. containers.

7

Prepared Exterior Finish

ORIENTAL Exterior Finish Stucco A white, water-resistant finish for exterior portland cement-lime basecoats. Mill-prepared; requires water only. Easily hand or spray-applied as float, splatter-dash and other texture finishes; not designed for smooth-trowel finish. One ton covers 150-200 sq. yd. in 1/8" thickness. Available in 15 additional colors (Southwest only). In 100-lb. bags.

Masons and Stucco Lime

BONDCRETE Air-Entraining Masons and Stucco Lime A fine-grind, white, high-purity dolomitic lime, pressure-hydrated for immediate use in portland cement-lime plaster for interior and exterior use. Recommended for use in scratch, brown and finish coats. It produces a stucco that is free-flowing for spray application or easily spread with light trowel pressure. Excellent water retention allows the cement-lime plaster to resist suction and allow sufficient time for finishing. Not recommended for use with gypsum gauging plaster in gauged lime-putty finish. BONDCRETE Lime meets ASTM C207, Type SA. Available in durable, 3-ply, weather-resistant 50-lb. bags.

MORTASEAL Autoclaved Masons Lime A pressure-hydrated, high-purity, immediate-use dolomitic lime for use where non-air-entrained products are desired. Lacking air-entraining additive, it gives mortar greater compressive strength; exceeds minimum values of all ASTM C270 mortar types in both 7 and 28-day tests. High water retention reduces need for retempering mortar during use. Reduces water permeance. No soaking required. Meets ASTM C207, Type S for mason's lime. Available in durable, 3-ply, weather-resistant 50-lb. bags.

Sound-Absorbing Plaster Finish

USG Acoustical Plaster Finish An attractive spray plaster texture for application to gypsum basecoats, interior monolithic concrete, metal decks and gypsum panel ceilings. Chemically setting-type product gives a sound-absorbing, sound-rated decorative finish to gypsum panels, concrete and non-veneer-type plaster ceilings and other non-contact surfaces. Produces a handsome, natural-white, evenly textured finish. Requires no application of a bonding agent, except over metal decks. Reduces surface preparation time and costs. For use on new or renovation construction. Surface burning characteristics: flame spread 10, smoke developed 25 per ASTM E1042-85. Sound rated: NRC 0.55 for concrete and conventional plaster at 1/2" finish thickness; NRC 0.75 for concrete and conventional plaster at 1" finish thickness, NRC 0.50 for gypsum panels. Use on noncontact surfaces only.

Conventional Plaster Application

8

General Planning Procedures

Two ingredients are required for a quality plaster job—quality products and skilled craftsmen employing correct lathing and plastering procedures.

USG plaster bases, plasters and plastering accessories are top quality, job-proven products designed to work together. But without proper planning and correct installation by the contractor, these products cannot be expected to produce the desired results.

This chapter deals with the basic recommendations and installation procedures to follow in completing the best possible job. It describes wood and steel framing, applications of conventional plaster bases in fire and sound-rated assemblies, and includes frame-spacing and fastener-selector charts.

Various organizations provide information about recommended standards or tolerances for installation of plaster products and systems. See pages 467 and 474 in the Appendix for information about standards and tolerances.

For instructions on the safe use of plaster and related products, see Chapter 13, Safety Considerations, Material Handling.

Good lathing and plastering practices can give the contractor (1) greater profit through fewer callbacks, less waste and lower job costs, and (2) high quality results that produce quicker sales and a favorable business reputation.

Planning the Job

Advance planning by the plastering contractor can mean savings in time and materials cost and a better-appearing job.

Two areas of planning deserve special attention. In high-rise work it is essential to determine availability and charges for use of hoisting equipment on the job well in advance of the time when it will be needed. Failure to do so can result in costly delays while the hoist is tied up by other trades.

In all types of jobs it is wise to plan for clean-up as the work proceeds, not when the job is finished. Contractors who have adopted this practice affirm that it reduces job costs. They have discovered that it is easier, faster and cheaper to remove drop cloths of roofing paper than to scrape up set plaster. And stuffing electrical boxes with paper before plastering begins is far less costly than digging out set plaster when they are accidentally filled. When machines are shut down, they should be hosed off and thoroughly cleaned—made ready for a fresh start. The benefits from these good working practices add up to faster completions, less down time and equipment maintenance, and more profit.

Estimating Materials

Accurate take-off and estimating quantities of materials are an essential part of job planning. Underestimating causes expensive job delays while quantities are refigured and orders placed. Overestimating invariably results in damage or loss of at least part of the surplus materials.

The tables in Chapter 7 contain data needed for accurate estimating: packaging, coverage of various cementitious materials, and number of accessories needed per 100 sq. yd. of finished surface. Similar data on steel studs, runners and screws can be found in Chapter 1.

General Job Conditions

Handling and Storage

All successful plaster jobs require adequate equipment: power mixers, mortar boards, scaffolding and tools. Ample scaffolding should be provided to permit continuous application of both basecoat and finish plasters for a complete section of wall or ceiling. Obtain clean water for washing all mixing tools.

Lath and plaster products should be ordered for delivery to the job just prior to application. Materials stored on the job for longer periods are liable to damage and abuse.

Rather than ship all plaster to the job at one time, fresh plaster should be delivered as needed. Plaster stored for long periods is subject to variable moisture conditions and aging that can produce variations in setting time and performance problems.

Store plastering products inside, in a dry location and away from heavy-traffic areas. Stack plaster bags on planks or platforms away from damp floors and walls. Store gypsum plaster bases flat on a clean dry floor; vertical storage may damage edges or deform board. Protect metal corner beads, casing beads and trim from being bent or damaged. All materials used on the job should remain in their wrappings or containers until used.

Warehouse stocks of plaster products should be rotated to assure a supply of fresh materials and to prevent damage to plaster through aging and contact with moisture.

Environmental Conditions

1. When outdoor temperatures are less than 55°F, the temperature of the building must be maintained in the uniform range of 55° to 70°F both day and night for an adequate period prior to the erection of gypsum plaster base, the application of plaster, while the plastering is being done, and until the plaster is dry. The heat should be well distributed in all areas, with deflection or protective screens used to prevent concentrated or irregular heat on plaster areas near the source.

2. Ventilation must be provided to properly dry the plaster during and subsequent to its application. In glazed buildings, this should be accomplished by keeping windows open sufficiently to provide air circulation; in areas lacking normal ventilation, moisture-laden air must be mechanically removed.

3. To develop proper performance characteristics, the drying rate of plastering materials must be strictly controlled during and after application. Plaster should not be allowed to dry too slowly or too fast. If possible, maintain building temperature-humidity combination in the "normal drying" area of the graph on next page. Excessive ventilation or air movement should be avoided to allow plaster to properly set.

8

Plaster Drying Conditions

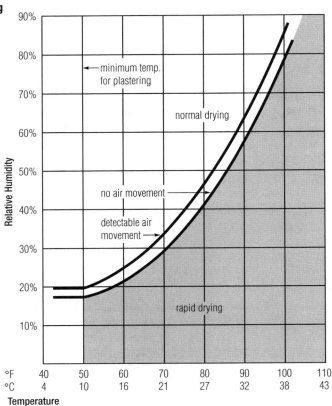

Framing Installation

Requirements for framing with wood and steel studs are the same for plaster and drywall construction and are covered in Chapter 2 of this Handbook. Maximum frame spacing for plaster base is as follows:

Frame Spacing—Gypsum Base (Ceilings & Sidewalls)

Type Framing	Base Thickness in.	mm	Max. Frame Spacing o.c. in.	mm
Wood	3/8	9.5	16	406
Steel Stud	3/8	9.5	16	406
	3/8	9.5	24[1]	610
3/4 (19.1 mm) Channel Metal Furring	3/8	9.5	16	406
	3/8	9.5	16	406

(1) Three-coat plastering.

Reinforcing

Openings in a gypsum lath-and-plaster system, such as door frames, borrowed lights, etc., cause a concentration of stresses in the plaster, typically at intersection of head and jamb. The use of additional reinforcement (channels, runners, Striplath, self-furring diamond mesh lath) can be used at the weakened area to distribute concentrated stresses.

Wood or metal inserts used as reinforcing or for attachment of cabinets and shelving on nonresilient surfaces should always be applied behind the plaster base to prevent unnecessary damage to the plaster surface. Heavy fixtures such as water closets and lavatories should be supported by separate carriers and not by the lath and plaster surface. (See page 293 and "Fixture Attachment" in Appendix.)

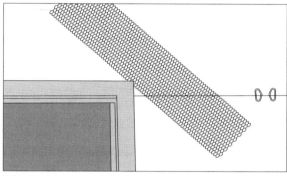

Reinforcing at door

8

Wall Furring

Exterior wall furring provides a way of spacing the plaster base and plaster away from masonry walls to produce an air space, a chase for services and space for insulation. By furring, uneven walls can be changed to true, even surfaces. Plaster base can be quickly attached, and the uniform plaster base saves plastering material and labor.

Exterior masonry walls should be furred out and a vapor retarder provided if necessary. Several systems are available; each provides structural and cost advantages for special furring conditions.

A properly designed wall furring system should provide:

1. Protection from moisture seepage.

2. Insulation and vapor retarder.

3. Some isolation from structural movement. Exterior walls are subject constantly to changing dimensions due to temperature changes and wind loads.

Wood Strip— ROCKLATH Base furring

For masonry wall furring, ROCKLATH Plaster Base and gypsum plaster over wood furring strips is an economical assembly. The wood furring is usually 1" x 2" or 2" x 2" strips spaced 16 o.c. for 3/8" lath, 24" o.c. max. for 1/2" lath. Apply furring vertically and securely attach to the masonry. If necessary, use small wooden wedges to shim strips to a plumb surface.

*Wood furring—
direct attachment*

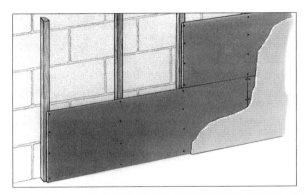

*Steel stud—
free-standing furring*

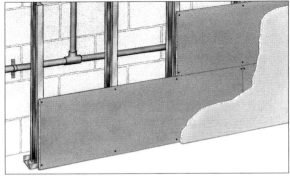

Installation Apply 16″ x 48″ Rocklath Plaster Base at right angles to furring strips with end joints occurring between strips using 1″ nails. When Rocklath Base has been installed, reinforce inside corners with Cornerite.

**Steel Stud—
Rocklath Base
Furring**

This free-standing furring assembly consists of Rocklath Plaster Base screw-attached to steel studs and finished with gypsum plaster. The assembly offers a maximum of free space for encasing pipes, ducts or conduits.

With a 6-mil polyethylene film installed under the Rocklath Base, the assembly provides an effective vapor retarder.

Installation Align floor and ceiling runners parallel to wall and positioned to provide required chase space. Attach to concrete slabs with concrete stub nails or power-driven anchors 24″ o.c., to suspended ceilings with toggle bolts or hollow metal fasteners 16″ o.c., or to wood framing with 1-1/4″ Type W screws 16″ o.c.

Studs should be selected to limit deflection to L/360 and satisfy applicable stress criteria. Position steel studs vertically in runners, 16″ o.c. for 3/8″ lath, with all flanges in same direction. The recommended practice for most installations is to anchor only those studs adjacent to door and borrowed light frames. This would also be applicable to partition intersections and corners. In cases where a significant slab live

Metal furring

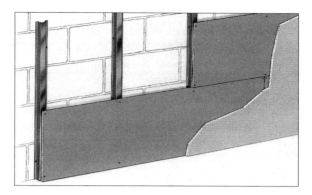

load deflection must be accommodated, the anchoring of these studs may restrict slab movement and cause partition cracking. In these cases, anchoring of these studs may need to be omitted. The services of a design professional is desirable to identify these instances and address them on a case-specific basis. Attach ROCKLATH Base to studs with three 1″ TYPE S Screws at each stud and BRIDJOINT B-1 Clips at ends. Apply 1/2″ sanded basecoat plaster, lime putty finish.

Metal Channel— ROCKLATH Base furring

For direct attachment with metal furring channels, ROCKLATH Plaster Base is screwed to furring channels that are attached directly to an exterior masonry wall. When a 6-mil polyethylene film is included, the system provides an excellent vapor retarder.

Installation Apply channels vertically to masonry not more than 16″ o.c. Fasten each channel with hammered or power-driven stud fasteners. If there is a possibility of water penetration, install an asphalt felt protection strip between the furring channel and wall surfaces.

8

Frame Spacing and Attachment

For Furred Ceilings Fasten 3/4″ cold-rolled channel or 3/8″ pencil rods directly to bottoms of framing members. On concrete joists, 8-ga. galvanized wire can be put in place before the concrete is poured. Space furring members as shown in the following cross-furring member spacing table. For joists spaced about 25″ o.c., attachment of 3/4″ channels may be on alternate joists; if greater than 25″ o.c. but not more than 48″ o.c., place attachment at every joist.

On steel joists or beams, place 3/4″ cold-rolled channels at right angles to joists; attach with 3 strands 18-ga. galvanized wire.

For Suspended Ceilings Space 8-ga. wire hangers not over 4′ o.c. in direction of 1-1/2″ carrying channels and not over 3′ o.c. at right angles to direction of carrying channels. If hanger wires are 3′ o.c. in direction of 1-1/2″ channels, then channels at right angles may be 4′ o.c. Place hangers within 6″ of ends of carrying channel runs and of boundary walls, girders or similar interruptions of ceiling continuity. Position and level carrying channel and saddle tie securely with hanger wire.

Position 3/4″ cold-rolled channel (cross-furring) across carrying channels, spacing them 12″ to 24″ depending on type of metal lath to be used, and saddle tie carrying channels with three strands of 18-ga. tie wire.

Apply 3.4-lb. DIAMOND Mesh Lath, Flat Riblath or 3/8″ Riblath as specified with long dimension of sheets across the supports. Details on lathing procedures and control joints follow later in this chapter.

Frame and Fastener Spacing—ROCKLATH Plaster Base

Type Framing	Base Thickness in.	mm	Fastener[1]	Max. Frame Spacing in.	mm	Max. Fastener Spacing in.	mm
Wood stud	3/8	9.5	Nails 13 ga., 1-1/8″ long, 19/64″ flat head, blued	16	406	5	127
			Staples—16-ga. galv. flattened wire, flat crown 7/16″ wide, 1″ divergent legs				
Steel stud	3/8″	9.5	1″ TYPE S Screws	16	406	12	305
Metal furring	3/8″	9.5	1″ TYPE S Screws	16	406	12	305

(1) Metric fastener dimensions: 19/64″=7.5mm; 7/16″=11.1mm; 1″=25.4mm; 1-1/8″=28.6mm.

Maximum Frame Spacing—Metal Lath[1]

Product	Weight lbs./yd.²	kg/m²	Spacing in.	mm
DIAMOND Mesh[2]	2.5	1.4	12[3]	305[3]
	3.4	1.8	24	406
3/8″ (9.5mm) Riblath	3.4	1.8	19	610
Flat Riblath	2.75	1.5	16[4]	406
	3.4	1.8	19[5]	483

(1) For spacing on fire-rated constructions, see test reports. (2) 2.5-lb. lath should not be used for ceilings. (3) 16 o.c. permitted with wood framing and 2″ solid partition. (4) Spacing of metal ceiling grills 12″ o.c. (5) 24″ spacing with solid partition.

Support Area—Hangers

Hanger Size and Type	Max. Ceiling Area per Hanger ft.²	m	Allowable Tensile Load lbs.[3]
9-ga. galvanized wire	12.5	1.2	340
8-ga. galvanized wire	16	1.5	408
3/16″ (4.8 mm) mild steel rod [1)(2]	20	1.9	546
1/4″ (6.4 mm) mild steel rod [1)(2]	22.5	2.1	972
3/16″ x 1″ (4.8mm x 25.4mm) mild steel flat[1)(2]	25	2.3	3712

(1) Where severe moisture conditions may occur, rods galvanized or painted with rust-inhibitive paint, or galvanized straps are recommended. (2) Not manufactured by USG. (3) Based on minimum yield 33,000 psi.

Maximum Spacing—Main Runner—Carrying Channels

Main Runner C. R. Channel Size in.	mm	Max c. to c. Spacing of Main Runners ft.	mm	Max. Spacing of Hangers Along Runners ft.	mm
3/4	19.1	3	914	2	610
3/4	19.1	2-1/4	686	3[1]	914
1-1/2	38.1	4	1219	3	914
1-1/2	38.1	3-1/2	1067	3-1/2	1067
1-1/2	38.1	3	914	4	1219
2	50.8	4	1219	5	1524
2	50.8	2-1/2	762	6	1829
2	50.8	2	610	7	2134

(1) For concrete joist construction only—where 8-ga. wire may be inserted in joist before concrete is poured.

Maximum Spacing—Cross-Furring Members

Cross-Furring Size	Max. c. to c. Spacing of Cross-Furring		Main Runner or Support Spacing	
	in.	mm	ft.	mm
3/4″ (19.1 mm) C. R. Channel	24	610	3	914
3/4″ (19.1 mm) C. R. Channel	19	483	3-1/2	1067
3/4″ (19.1 mm) C. R. Channel	16	406	4	1219

Plaster Base Application

Plaster bases may be classified as gypsum base, metal lath base or masonry base. These materials provide a surface for plastering and add reinforcement to the plaster. As such, they must be rigid enough to accept plaster and produce a secure bond between plaster and base—both necessary to develop strength and resistance to abuse and cracking.

To ensure adequate rigidity of plaster constructions, recommendations for the spacing of supports and fasteners must be strictly followed.

Apply plaster bases to ceilings first and then to partitions, starting at the top and working down to the floor line.

ROCKLATH **Plaster Base** An ideal high-suction rigid base for gypsum plasters, should be applied face out with long dimension across supports and with end joints staggered between courses. Cut lath accurately so it slips easily into place without forcing and fits neatly around electrical outlets, openings, etc. Install any lengthwise raw cut edges at bottom strip or wall-ceiling angle. Apply Cornerite to all interior angles and staple to the lath only.

Metal Lath Should be applied with long dimension across supports and with end joints staggered between courses. Apply Riblath with the rib against supports. Lap ends of metal lath 1″ and sides at least 1/2″. Lap Riblath by nesting outside ribs. If end laps occur between supports, they should be laced or tied with 18-ga. tie wire. Secure lath to all supports at intervals not exceeding 6″. At all interior angles, metal lath should be formed into corners and carried out onto abutting surface.

Clay Tile and Brick Frequently used for plaster bases. Care should be taken to make sure that surfaces are sufficiently porous to provide suction for the plaster and are scored for added mechanical bonding. Smooth-surfaced clay tile that is glazed or semi-glazed does not offer sufficient bond for plaster.

Concrete Block A satisfactory base for plaster. The surface should be porous, for proper suction, or face-scored for adequate mechanical bond. Units must be properly cured to minimize dimensional changes during and subsequent to plastering.

Monolithic Concrete Ceilings, walls, beams and columns should have a complete and uniform application of USG Plaster Bonder before plastering. This surface treatment produces an adhesive bond suitable for direct application of gypsum plasters.

8

Plastering Direct to Exterior Masonry Walls Not recommended. Exterior walls are subject to water seepage and moisture condensation that may wet the plaster and damage interior decoration.

Bituminous Waterproofing Compounds Do not provide a good plaster base. Gypsum plasters should not be applied to surfaces treated with these compounds.

Rigid Foam Insulations Such insulations have not proven to be satisfactory bases for direct application of gypsum plaster because of rigid foam insulation's low suction characteristics and low structural strength which may result in cracking of the plaster.

USG does not recommend direct application of plaster to rigid foam insulation. However, some rigid foam insulation manufacturers have specific directions for application when direct plastering is to be used, as well as detailed specifications for plaster mixes and methods of application to be employed. Confirm local fire code compliance prior to installation.

USG has designed various furring systems (covered earlier in this chapter) that avoid the need to apply plaster to these unsuitable surfaces and do provide high-quality plaster finishes over the inside of exterior walls.

Fastener Application

Correct fastener selection and adherence to fastener spacing are extremely important to good plastering performance and absolutely essential in meeting the requirements of specific fire-rated constructions.

Gypsum Plaster Bases Attached to framing with screws, nails, staples or special clips. Nails, screws and staples should be driven so that the fastener head or crown bears tightly against the base but does not cut the face paper. To prevent core fracturing, they should be driven at least 3/8″ away from ends and edges. Staples should be of flattened wire driven so the crown is parallel to wood framing. Screws should be used to attach gypsum plaster bases to steel studs, furring channels or RC-1 Resilient Channels.

For screw attachment of single-layer 3/8″ ROCKLATH Base to steel studs or furring channel, 1″ TYPE S Bugle Head Screws are used.

Nail Application Begin from center of base and proceed toward outer ends or edges. When nailing, apply pressure adjacent to nail being driven to insure base is secured tightly on framing member. Position nails on adjacent ends or edges opposite each other and at least 3/8″ from ends and edges. Drive nails with shank perpendicular to plaster base. The nail heads should be driven flush with paper surface but not break paper.

Metal Lath Attach to cold-rolled channel framing with tie wire (min. 18 ga.) and to wood framing with fasteners engaging two strands or a rib and providing at least 3/4″ penetration.

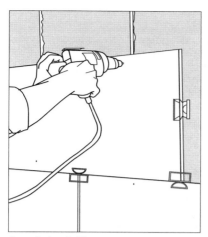

Screw attachment of ROCKLATH Base to steel studs

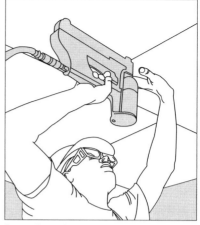

Power nailer used to attach ROCKLATH Plaster Base to ceiling

8

Gypsum Lath—Steel Studs

Screw Attachment Fasten to studs spaced 16″ o.c. with three 1″ TYPE S Screws per stud spaced 2″ from edge of lath. TYPE S-12 Screws are required for heavier gauges. Drive screws with an electric screwgun. Secure corners of 3/8″ lath falling between studs and midpoint of lath ends with BRIDJOINT B-1 Clips.

Gypsum Lath—Wood Framing (direct)

Nail ROCKLATH Plaster Base with face out and long dimension across framing members. Stagger end joints in successive courses with ends of lath falling between framing members. Butt all joints together and cut lath to fit neatly around electrical outlets and other openings. Secure ends to abutting and adjacent panels with BRIDJOINT B-1 Clips.

For ROCKLATH Plaster Base with 16″ o.c. stud spacing, use four fasteners, 5″ o.c. per 16″ width of lath. Place fasteners at least 3/8″ from edges and ends of lath. Make all interior plaster angles the floating type and space first fasteners at least 10″ from corner. Reinforce angle with Cornerite stapled to lath surface.

Metal Lath—Wood Framing (direct)

Apply metal lath with long dimension of sheet across supports. Lap ends of lath at least 1″ and if laps occur between supports, lace or tie with 18-ga. tie wire. Attach with fasteners 6″ o.c. so fastener engages two strands or a rib and provides at least 3/4″ penetration.

On walls, place metal lath so that the lower sheets overlap upper sheets and, where possible, stagger ends of lath in adjacent courses.

At all interior angles, form lath into corners and carry out onto abutting surface. Secure lath to joists with 1″ galvanized nails, to studs with nails or staples providing min. 3/4″ penetration.

Control Joint Application

Lath and plaster surfaces will not resist stresses imposed by structural movement. Additionally, plaster assemblies are subject to dimensional changes caused by fluctuations in temperature and humidity. (See thermal and hygrometric coefficients of expansion in Appendix.) Such surfaces should be isolated from the following structural elements by zinc control joints, casing beads or other means where:

a. A partition or ceiling abuts any structural element other than the floor, a dissimilar wall or partition assembly, or other vertical penetration.

b. The construction changes within the plane of a partition, or ceiling and wings of "L-," "U-" and "T-" shaped ceilings are joined.

In long partition runs, control joints should be provided at max. 30′ o.c. Door frames extending from floor to ceiling may serve as control joints. For less-than-ceiling-height doors, control joints extending from center or both corners of frame to ceiling is an effective application. If control joints are not used, additional reinforcement is required at corners to distribute concentrated stresses. (Door frame details appear later in this chapter.) In exterior wall furring systems, control joints must be provided at the same locations where control joints in the exterior walls are located and at max. 30′ o.c.

Control joints will not accommodate transverse shear displacement on opposing sides of a joint. A joint detail comprising casing beads each side of the joint opening is typically used to accommodate expansion, contraction and shear. Such joints require special detailing by the designer to control sound and fire ratings, where applicable, as well as dust and air movement. In exterior walls, particular attention is required to resist wind, driving rain, etc., by adequate flashing, backer rod, sealants and gaskets as required.

Large interior ceiling areas with perimeter relief should have control joints spaced at max. 50′ o.c. in either direction; without perimeter relief, 30′ o.c. maximum in either direction. The continuity of both lath and plaster must be broken at the control joints. Control joints should be positioned to intersect light fixtures, heating vents, or diffusers, etc., which already break ceiling continuity, and are points of stress concentration.

Maximum Spacing—SHEETROCK Brand Control Joints for Interior Plaster Assemblies

System	Location	Max. Single Dimension		Max. Single Area	
		ft.	mm	ft.²	m²
Metal Lath & Plaster	Partition	30	9144	—	—
	Ceiling	50[1]	15240	2500	230
		30[2]	9144	900	83.6
Gypsum Lath & Plaster	Partition	30	9144	—	—
	Ceiling	50[1]	15240	2500	230
		30[2]	9144	900	83.6

(1) With perimeter relief (2) Without perimeter relief

Sheetrock Brand Control Joint Nos. 50, 75, 100

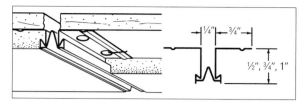

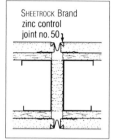

SHEETROCK Brand zinc control joint no. 50

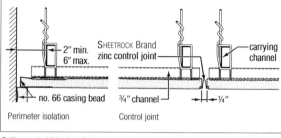

2" min.
6" max.
SHEETROCK Brand zinc control joint

carrying channel

no. 66 casing bead
¾" channel
¼"

Perimeter isolation

Control joint

Wall control joint installation

Ceiling control joint installation

Installation Provide a break in the lath at location of control joint. At this location install double framing members, one on each side of the break and 1/2" to 3/4" apart. Place control joints over all control or relief joints within structural frame of building. Staple or wire tie perforated flanges of control joint to lath. Plaster flush to grounds. Remove factory-applied protective tape after completion of finished surface.

Zinc control joints must be properly insulated or otherwise protected when used in fire-rated assemblies.

8

Basecoat Plaster Application

For the beauty and durability of which plaster is capable, certain requirements should be followed regarding the number of coats applied. Three-coat work is necessary on all metal lath and on edge-supported gypsum lath used in ceilings; three-coat work is desirable on all gypsum lath but two-coat work is acceptable when gypsum lath is properly supported and on masonry plaster bases (rough concrete block, clay tile, porous brick).

In preparing for plastering, consideration should be given to the selection of materials not only for compatibility but for the quality of the structure to be plastered. It is wise to upgrade plastering specifications when possible.

The "Plaster Product Compatibility Selector" table on page 272 will help you determine which basecoat plaster is appropriate for each possible substrate and which finish plasters may be used with each basecoat plaster. The table on "Basecoat Plasters for Conventional Plaster Systems" provides a numeric scale comparing the performance of various basecoat plasters over various substrates and for various properties. The table on "Basecoat Plaster (Over Metal Lath)" provides mixing proportions of sand to plaster.

Plaster Product Compatibility Selector

Basecoat Plaster	Substrate				Finish Plaster								
	CMU	Mono. Conc.(1)	ML CH-FMG	ML C-Studs	Rocklath Plaster Base	Red Top Finish	Structo-Gauge/Lime	Keenes/Lime	Gauging/Lime	Keenes/Lime/Sand	Gauging/Lime/Sand	Imperial Brand Finish	Diamond Brand Interior Finish
Red Top & Red Top Two Purpose(2)	✓	✓	✓		✓	✓	✓	✓	✓	✓	✓		✓
Red Top & Red Top Two Purpose (Lightweight)	✓	✓	✓		✓				✓(3)	✓	✓		
Red Top Wood Fiber(2) Plaster	✓	✓	✓		✓	✓	✓	✓	✓	✓	✓	✓	✓
Structo-Base Gypsum Plaster(2)	✓	✓	✓	✓	✓	✓	✓	✓	✓	✓	✓	✓	✓
Structo-Lite Gypsum Plaster	✓	✓	✓		✓				✓(3)	✓	✓		

Notes: (1) USG Plaster Bonder must first be applied .(2) Job sanded. (3) Quality Gauging/not over metal lath. Monolithic concrete to be treated with USG Plaster Bonder. ✓ = Acceptable

Basecoat Plasters for Conventional Plaster Systems

Product	Substrate			Machine		
	Metal Lath	Concrete Masonry Unit	Gypsum Lath	Application	Hardness	Productivity
Structo-Base Gypsum Plaster	1	2	1	yes*	1	3
Structo-Lite Gypsum Plaster	4	1	2	yes*	4	1
Red Top Gypsum Plaster	3	3	2	yes*	3	3
Red Top Wood Fiber Plaster	2	2	3	no	2	4

*Must request MA Formulation. 1 = Excellent 2 = Very Good 3 = Good 4 = Acceptable

Basecoat Plaster (Over Metal Lath)

Scratch Coat	Brown Coat
1. Structo-Base Plaster, sanded 100 lbs. : 2 cu. ft.	Structo-Base Plaster, sanded 100 lbs. : 3 cu. ft.
2. Wood Fiber, neat, or sanded up to 100 lbs. : 1 cu. ft.	Wood Fiber Plaster, sanded up to 100 lbs. : 1 cu. ft.
3. Wood Fiber, neat, or sanded up to 100 lbs. : 1 cu. ft.	Red Top Gypsum Plaster, sanded 100 lbs. : 2 cu. ft.
4. Red Top Gypsum Plaster, sanded 100 lbs. : 2 cu. ft.	Red Top Gypsum Plaster, sanded 100 lbs. : 3 cu. ft.
5. Wood Fiber, neat, or sanded up to 100 lbs. : 1 cu. ft.	Structo-Lite Plaster (Sand float finish only)
6. Wood Fiber, neat, or sanded 100 lbs. : 1 cu. ft.	Red Top Gypsum Plaster, perlited 100 lbs. : 2 cu. ft. (sand float finish only)

The architect's specifications and the plaster base used will determine the plastering method, either two-coat or three-coat.

Two- and Three-Coat Plastering

Two-Coat Plastering with Conventional Plasters Generally accepted for plaster application over gypsum lath and masonry. The base (first) coat should be applied with sufficient material and pressure to form a good bond to the base and to cover well; then be doubled back to bring plaster out to grounds, straightened to true surface with rod and darby without use of additional water, and left rough and open to receive the finish (second) coat.

Three-Coat Plastering Required over metal lath and edge-supported gypsum lath used in ceilings. It is preferred for other bases because it develops a harder, stronger basecoat. The scratch (first) coat should be applied with sufficient material and pressure to form good full keys on metal lath, and a good bond on other bases, and then cross-raked. The brown (second) coat should be applied after scratch (first) coat has set firm and hard, brought out to grounds and straightened to true surface with rod and darby without use of additional water, and left rough and open to receive the finish (third) coat.

To obtain the full hardness, high strength and superior performance available in gypsum basecoat plasters, water, aggregates and setting time must be carefully controlled. In addition, proper mixing and drying of the plaster are required to obtain these superior functional characteristics.

Grounds

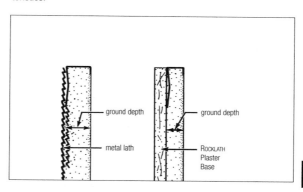

ground depth

ground depth

metal lath

ROCKLATH
Plaster
Base

8

Grounds

The thickness of conventional basecoat plaster is one of the most important elements of a good plaster job. To ensure proper thickness, grounds should be properly set and followed.

Grounds may be defined as wooden strips, corner beads (plumbed and aligned) or metal casing beads applied at the perimeter of all openings and other locations.

In addition to these, and especially on walls with no openings and on ceilings, plaster screeds should be installed to ensure plumb and level surfaces. Plaster screeds are continuous strips of plaster, approximately 4″ wide, applied either vertically or horizontally and plumb with the finish wall line, allowing for 1/16″ finish coat.

Grounds should be set to obtain the following minimum plaster thicknesses:

1. Over gypsum lath   1/2″ (12.7mm)

2. Over brick, clay tile, or other masonry   5/8″ (15.9mm)

3. Over metal lath, measured from face of lath   5/8″ (15.9mm)

274

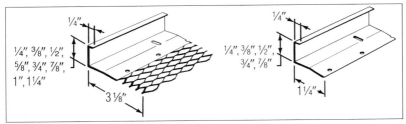

#66 Square Edge Casing Beads
(expanded or short flange)

Mixing

Use of the proper type of mechanical mixer assures that the plaster aggregate and water are evenly mixed. Keep the mixer continually clean—a most important precaution because partially set material is a powerful accelerator.

Proportioning is *Weight* of Gypsum to *Volume* of Aggregate A No. 2 shovel used to add sand to the plaster mix generally carries 15 lb., or approx. one-sixth cubic foot. Thus, a 100:1 mix would use 6 shovels of sand to 100 lb. of gypsum plaster, a 100:2 mix 12 to 13, and a 100:3 mix 18 to 19 shovels of sand.

Perlite is generally packaged in bags containing 3 or 4 cu. ft. for easy proportioning.

Prepare only one hour's supply of plaster at one time and do not remix if plaster has started to set. All such plaster should be discarded.

Water All gypsum plasters require addition of water on job. Water should be clean, fresh, suitable for domestic consumption, and free from mineral and organic substances which affect plaster set. Water used earlier for rinsing or cleaning containers and tools should not be used, as it accelerates plaster set.

Only enough water should be used to provide a plaster of workable consistency. Too much water in machine-applied plasters (in excess of 10% more than for hand-applied mixes) or over-aggregated plasters will cause weak, soft walls and ceilings. Excessive water reduces plaster strength and hardness.

Aggregates

Added to conventional gypsum plasters to extend coverage, reduce shrinkage, and lower cost. Aggregates recommended are: (1) sand, which is denser, stronger and dampens sound transmission better than lightweight aggregates, and (2) perlite, a lightweight aggregate that generally offers better fire resistance, insulation values and reduced weight. For sand-float finishes the aggregate should be a fine silica sand.

All aggregates used should have proper gradation of size as outlined in ASTM C35. Improperly sized aggregates will produce weak walls. Sand should be clean and free of dirt, clay and foreign matter that might affect the setting time of plaster. Perlite-aggregated plasters should not be machine-applied when vertical lift is over 30 ft. or hose length exceeds 150 ft. Maximum recommended proportions for aggregates are shown in following table.

Maximum Aggregate Quantity—Gypsum Plasters

Base	No. Coats[1]	Coat	Under Smooth Trowel Finishes				Under Texture Finishes			
			Sand[2]		Perlite[3]		Sand[2]		Perlite[3]	
			ft.³/ 100 lb.	m³/t	ft.³/ 100 lb.	m³/t	ft.³/ 100 lb.	m³/t	ft.³/ 100 lb.	m³/t
Gypsum Lath	3	Scratch	2	1.24	2	1.24	2	1.24	2	1.24
		Brown	3	1.86	2	1.24	3	1.86	3[4]	1.86[4]
	2	Basecoat[5]	2.5	1.55	2	1.24	2.5	1.55	2	1.24
Metal Lath	3	Scratch	2	1.24	—	—	2	1.24	2	1.24
		Brown	3	1.86	—	—	3	1.86	2	1.24
Unit Masonry	3	Scratch	3	1.86	3	1.86	3	1.86	3	1.86
		Brown	3	1.86	3	1.86	3	1.86	3	1.86
	2	Basecoat[5]	3	1.86	3	1.86	3	1.86	3	1.86

(1) Includes finish coat. (2) Approx. 6 No. 2 shovels of sand equal 1 cu. ft. (0.028 m³). (3) In a construction with metal lath as the plaster base, perlite aggregate is not recommended for use in the basecoat plaster, except under a float finish. For a smooth trowel finish over a perlite aggregated basecoat on any plaster base except metal lath, add 1/2 ft.³ of fine silica sand per 100 lb. of gauging plaster, or use aggregated gauging. (4) Only if applied 1″ thick, otherwise 2 ft.³. (5) Basecoat applied scratch and double-back.

Setting Time

The proper setting time for conventional basecoat plasters is generally from 2 to 4 hours after mixing, and this should be checked for close conformity on both the scratch coat and brown coat operations. Normally, plaster shipped to the job will fall in this range. If conditions exist that affect normal setting time, retarders or accelerators may be used.

Retarders The danger of "quick set" plaster is insufficient time to get the plaster from mixer to walls without retempering on mortar board, and such retempering will produce a plaster of lower than normal strength. The correction for "quick set" is to add the minimum required amount of retarder in solution with water in the mixer.

Good job practice for retarder use involves mixing a trial batch of formulated product and determining the set time. Once the set time is known, a measured amount of USG retarder and water mixture is added to adjust the set. Any available container (wax cup, coffee can, measuring cup, etc.) can be used to measure the retarder/water mixture. Keeping mixing equipment clean between batches helps prevent quick-setting action in subsequent mixes.

Retarder selection will depend on the length of time extension required to handle the job appropriately, and the type of plaster being used. USG Standard Strength Retarder is recommended for slight to moderate lengthening of set times and can be used with conventional and veneer plasters. Mix one teaspoon of dry USG Standard Strength Retarder with 5 oz. water to extend the set time of a 100-lb. batch of gypsum plaster by 30-40 minutes or more.

USG High Strength Retarder is used to extend setting times 2 hours or more and is especially suitable for conventional gypsum plasters where machine application set time alteration is required. Mix one teaspoon of dry USG High Strength Retarder with 5 oz. water to extend the set time of a 100-lb. batch of conventional gypsum plaster by 1-3 hours.

8

For larger quantities, premix 1 lb. of retarder to 2 gal. of water. Stir to make sure retarder is completely dispersed. Screen out any lumps that may have formed, as they will cause soft discolored spots in the plaster surface. Note that retarder is dispersed in the water, not dissolved. Stir thoroughly before each use.

USG Retarder for Lime Containing Plaster Products is used with such plasters as DIAMOND Brand Interior Finish, RED TOP Finish and gauging/lime finishes. This retarder may be added directly to the mixing water prior to addition of plaster. As little is 1/4 to 1/2 teaspoon per 50-lb. bag of lime-containing plaster will extend setting time by 20 minutes.

Accelerators If plaster does not set for 5 to 6 hr., no harm will be done to the resulting plaster surfaces, but a "slow set" of the plaster (generally one taking more than 6 hr.) should be avoided by adding accelerator at the mixer, as such plaster may be subject to a "dryout," particularly in hot, dry weather, and will have a lower than normal strength when finally set. A choice of accelerators is available depending on the degree of acceleration required and the type of plaster being used.

USG Standard Strength Gypsum Plaster Accelerator is used to slightly modify setting times of veneer and conventional plasters. To maximize the ability of the accelerator, sprinkle 4 oz. of USG Standard Strength Gypsum Plaster accelerator in dry form into the mixer for each bag of product after the plaster has been added. This amount of accelerator will reduce set time by 30 minutes.

USG High Strength Gypsum Accelerator is used to reduce setting time of conventional basecoat plaster by 1-1/2 to 2 hours. For best results, sprinkle 2 oz. of USG High Strength Gypsum Accelerator in dry form into the mixer for each bag of product after the plaster has been added.

USG Accelerator—Alum Catalyst is used to correct "dryout" conditions. Accelerating the set of the plaster surface eliminates dry-out shrinkage fissures that occur when the material dries faster than the normal setting time. The same result can be accomplished by fog-spraying the plaster with water from a garden hose to saturate the plaster and then floating the surface with a wooden float to fill in any already formed fissures, however the alum catalyst accelerator can help avert the problem. Mix 1/2 to 1 lb. of USG Accelerator—Alum Catalyst into 3 gal. of water in a garden sprayer. Spray solution onto the damp plaster surface. Applying the solution in combination with rewetting quickens the set time to prevent a recurrence of the dry-out condition.

Heating and Ventilation

Plaster must not be applied to surfaces that contain frost. A min. temperature of 55° F should be maintained for adequate period prior to, during, and after application of plaster. In cold, damp or rainy weather, properly regulated heat should be provided but precautions must be taken against rapid drying before set has occurred. This prevents 'dryouts.'

As soon as set occurs in conventional plasters, free circulation of air should be provided to carry off excess moisture. Heating should be continued to ensure as rapid drying as possible. In hot, dry weather, protect plaster from wind and from drying unevenly or too rapidly before set has taken place. If windows or curtain walls are not in place, exterior openings in the building should be screened.

Finish Plaster Application

Finish plasters applied to basecoats provide the surface for final wall or ceiling decoration. Finish coats should be applied only to properly prepared basecoats which are rough and open and partially dry.

Trowel Finishes Used where a smooth, easily maintained surface is desired, often as a base for paint or wall coverings. The degree of hardness, porosity, and polish is determined by the materials and application techniques used. When a smooth-trowel gauged lime putty finish is used over a basecoat containing lightweight aggregate on any plaster base except metal lath, three options are available. Either add at least 50 lb. of fine silica sand or 1/2 cu. ft. of perlite fines per 100 lb. of gauging plaster or use a mill-aggregated "Quality" gauging plaster.

Trowel finish

Float finish

Spray finish

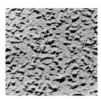
Texture finish

Finish Plasters for Conventional Plaster Systems

		Easy to Achieve Smooth Surface	Surface Hardness	Productivity	Texture Capability	
					Unsanded	Sanded
Veneer plaster finishes over conventional basecoat	IMPERIAL Brand Finish Plaster*	4	1	4	3	2
	DIAMOND Interior Finish Plaster*	3	3	2	3	2
Lime-gauging finishes over veneer basecoat or conventional basecoat	IVORY/SNOWDRIFT/GRAND PRIZE Finish Lime and STRUCTO-GAUGE Gauging Plaster*	2	3	2	4	2
	RED TOP Finish*	1	4	1	4	2
	Lime–Keenes Cement (Smooth)*	2	3	3	4	N/A
	Lime–Sand-Keenes Cement (Texture)	N/A	3	2	N/A	1
	IVORY/SNOWDRIFT/GRAND PRIZE Lime Finish and RED TOP, STAR or CHAMPION Gauging Plaster	1	4	3	4	2

*Not recommended for use over lightweight aggregate basecoats.
1 = Excellent 2 = Very Good 3 = Good 4 = Acceptable N/A = Not Applicable

Application To avoid blistering, allow basecoat to dry sufficiently or use a quick-set gauging plaster. Use 50-lb. bag of IVORY or SNOWDRIFT Lime with 5-1/2 to 6 gal. water. Machine-mix for immediate use. For a medium-hard finish, mix 100 lb. STRUCTO-GAUGE Gauging Plaster or 200 lb. CHAMPION, STAR or RED TOP Gauging Plaster to each 200 lb. dry lime (approx. 400 lb. putty). For extremely hard finish, mix one part Structo-Gauge Plaster to one part lime.

Scratch in thoroughly, then immediately double-back to a thickness of not more than 1/16″ and trowel to a smooth, dense surface ready for decoration.

Float or Spray Texture Finishes Provide attractive, durable finishes where surface textures are desired. They are recommended for use over all types of gypsum basecoats and are the most desirable finishes from the standpoint of crack resistance. The surface texture is easily controlled and can be produced by spray application, or a variety of hand tools.

Application, Sand Float Finish Machine-mix finish in proportion of 100 lb. Red Top Keenes Cement, 200 lb. lime, approx. 400-800 lb. sand and water to produce a mixture with smooth, plastic consistency.

Scratch in thoroughly over dry basecoat, then immediately double-back to a thickness of not more than 1/8″. Hand float to produce a uniform texture free of blemishes. Use water sparingly during floating.

Application, Machine Spray Texture Finish Acceptable finishes can be achieved using either a hand-held hopper gun or other machines specifically designed for spray-applying plaster.

The aggregate size, number of passes over the surface, air pressure and nozzle orifice can be varied to achieve the desired texture. When spraying, it is best to spray first in one direction and then in another direction crossing the first direction at right angles.

Before beginning spray application, test the pattern and make the necessary adjustments to give the desired appearance. There are many things that affect the pattern including the following:

1. **Orifice Size** The smaller the orifice or nozzle tip, the finer the spray.

2. **Air Pressure** If no other changes are made, the higher the air pressure, the finer the spray.

3. **Liquid State** The liquid state of the material should be like medium thick cream. the condition is obtained by taking the regular mix and adding more water until it comes to the desired consistency. It is good practice to pass the mix through a screen that will trap all particles larger than the aggregate being sprayed.

Basecoat must be free of ridges or other surface imperfections. Spraying texture finish directly onto basecoat is not normally recommended. The preferred method is to hand-apply a scratch coat before spray-applying finish. Finish materials for this method include gauging plaster, either regular or high-strength; Keenes cement job mixed with lime and silica sand; or various single component prepared finishes designated for two-component systems.

With finish coat material mixed for hand application, apply a well ground-in scratch coat over properly set and partially dry brown coat. After scratch coat is applied, double back with sufficient material to cover the basecoat completely. When the surface has become firm by water removal, float it to a uniform, blemish-free flat texture. After scratch and double-back set, and while material is in a wet state, spray material should be prepared using the same proportions as the finish material and mixed to proper fluidity for achieving the final texture finish. Spray texture to a uniform thickness and appearance.

Other Texture Finishes Many pleasing and distinctive textures are possible using various techniques in finishing. Finishes may range from an extremely fine stipple to a rough, heavy or coarse texture. Variety is limited only by the imagination of the designer or the ingenuity of the applicator.

Finish Plaster Limitations Certain precautions must be observed when applying finish coat plasters over various basecoats:

1. A smooth-trowel finish should not be used over lightweight aggregate gypsum basecoat applied over metal lath. A sand-float finish is recommended.

2. Where the gypsum basecoat over any plaster base except metal lath is STRUCTO-LITE or contains lightweight aggregate and a smooth-trowel finish is used, the finish coat should be RED TOP Gauging Plaster and lime, with addition of 1/2 cu. ft. of perlite fines or 50 lb. of No. 1 white silica sand per 100 lb. gauging plaster or mill-aggregated "Quality" Gauging Plaster.

3. Gypsum or lime-base finishes, including Keenes Cement, should not be used directly over a portland cement basecoat or over concrete block or other masonry surfaces.

4. In smooth trowel finishes, gauging plasters providing an extremely hard surface, such as STRUCTO-GAUGE and Keenes Cement, must not be used over STRUCTO-LITE Plaster or a basecoat with a lightweight aggregate.

5. Lime putty cannot be used without the addition of gauging plasters. When used alone as a finish plaster, lime does not set, is subject to shrinkage when drying and lacks hard finish.

Gauging Plasters

CHAMPION, STAR and RED TOP **Gauging Plasters** Gauging plaster (see following pages for full description) is blended into the lime putty in the proper proportions to provide controlled set, early hardness and strength, and to prevent shrinkage cracks.

Mixing Add gauging plaster to lime putty in proportion of 1 part dry gauging plaster by weight to 2 parts dry lime by weight or 1 part dry gauging by volume to 3 parts lime putty by volume. To mix, form a ring of lime putty on mixing board. The volume of putty used depends on wall or ceiling area to be covered. A hod of lime putty weighs approx. 100 lb., a 12-qt. bucket of lime putty about 35 lb. (50 lb. dry lime equals 100 lb. lime putty). After forming the putty ring, pour clean water into center of ring in correct proportions: 6 qt. water to 100 lb. lime putty; 2 qt. water to each 12-qt. bucket of lime putty. Next, sift Slow or Quick Set gauging plaster into water; 25 lb. gauging plaster to one hod of lime putty. Thoroughly wet gauging plaster and blend materials thoroughly to prevent gauging "streaks" and provide uniform density.

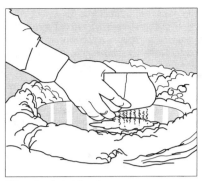

Sift gauging plaster into water   *Mix to blend thoroughly*

To protect against finish coat check or map-cracking, add 1/2 cu. ft. per-lite fines or 50 lb. fine silica sand to every 100 lb. of gauging used. This addition is necessary when applying smooth troweled finishes over light-weight aggregate basecoats. Mill-aggregated "Quality" gauging plasters are generally available and eliminate the need for on-the-job measuring.

Application Apply the gauged lime putty over a partially dry basecoat. Scratch in a thin coat, well ground into the basecoat, and double-back with a second coat, filling imperfections. After basecoat has absorbed most of excess water from finish, trowel to densify surface. As final set takes place, water-trowel surface to provide a dense, smooth surface.

STRUCTO-GAUGE Gauging Plaster This high-strength gypsum finishing plaster is used with lime putty to produce an easily applied finish of extreme hardness.

Finish hardness may be altered by adjusting the proportions of lime putty and STRUCTO-GAUGE Plaster. Since the material cannot be retempered, use of regular Keenes Cement is recommended when retempering is a factor. STRUCTO-GAUGE Plaster is not recommended for use where excessive or continued moisture conditions exist. Application must be over high-strength sanded or wood-fibered gypsum basecoats.

Mixing For a hard finish, mix proportions of 100 lb. dry hydrated lime (200 lb. of lime putty) to 100 lb. STRUCTO-GAUGE Plaster. For a medium hard finish, mix proportions of 200 lb. dry hydrated lime (400 lb. of lime putty) to 100 lb. STRUCTO-GAUGE Plaster. For best results, machine-mix.

Application Apply like regular finish over a partially dry gypsum basecoat. Scratch in thin coat, well ground into base, and immediately double-back with second coat, filling imperfections. Water-trowel to a smooth, hard finish, free of all blemishes. Continue troweling until final set has taken place. Clean tools and equipment after each mix.

RED TOP Keenes Cement A high-strength white gypsum plaster used with finish lime putty for extremely hard, dense surfaces. It is the only gypsum plaster that can be retempered. Made in two types: Regular (3-6 hr. set) and Quick Trowel (1-2 hr. set). Quick-troweling Keenes must be used with a min. of 25 lb. dry hydrated lime per 100 lb. of Keenes.

Keenes Cement-Lime Finish is similar in many respects to a lime gauged finish except that Keenes Cement, instead of gauging plaster, is used in varying proportions depending on the hardness required and is generally used as a float finish. If a smooth-trowel hard finish is desirable, use Structo-Gauge Gauging Plaster. Keenes Cement is for interior use over sanded or wood-fibered gypsum basecoats. Do not apply smooth-trowel finish over lightweight aggregate basecoats.

Application, Sand Float Finish Commonly used, hard float finish which may be satisfactorily colored. Mix in proportions of 100 lb. Keenes Cement to 200 lb. dry lime and 400-800 lb. sand, with or without limeproof colors. Apply in same manner as for Keenes Cement-Lime Finish but instead of final troweling, use a wood, cork, sponge or felt-covered float to bring sand particles to surface to produce a pleasing, durable sand finish.

Application, Keenes Cement-Lime Finish For medium hard finish, mix proportion of 200 lb. lime putty (100 lb. of dry hydrated lime) to 100 lb. Keenes Cement. For a hard finish, use 200 lb. lime putty (100 lb. dry hydrated lime) to 50 lb. Keenes Cement. Apply finish coat over a set high-strength basecoat that has been broomed and is partially dry. Spray with water if surface is too dry but do not soak. Scratch in thin coat and then double-back with second coat to a true surface. Trowel with water to a smooth, glossy finish, free from blemishes, until finish has set.

(See Chapter 7, Conventional Plaster Products, for lime-gauging ratios and coverage.)

Gauging Plasters—Technical Data

	Set Time with Lime Putty Product (min.)
Champion (white)	20-30
Star (white)	40-60
Red Top Gauging (local-gray)	slow set 50-75 / quick set 30-40
Red Top Keenes Cement (white)	regular 180-360 / quick set 60-120
Structo-Gauge (white or light gray)	slow set 60-75./ quick set 30-40

Finish Limes

The two types of finish lime are: (1) Type S (also called autoclaved, pressure or double hydrate); (2) Type N (also called normal or single hydrate). Both produce a good finish lime putty, but their preparation differs. Weather precautions:

In Cold Weather A few precautions will result in improved quality and easier working. Where weather and water are cold, lime develops better plasticity when soaked overnight. Best conditions are a warm room and water temperature above 50° F.

It is important to note that in cold weather the lime putty-gauging mixture requires a longer time to set. Therefore, gauging content should be increased or quick-set gauging added to offset the slower setting time.

Proper heat and ventilation are extremely important. Windows should be opened slightly so that moisture-bearing air moves out of the building. Fast drying after setting is essential to a hard finish.

Many cold-weather problems with finish lime are a direct result of improper basecoat conditions. Finish should go over a set, fairly dry basecoat. The basecoat will dry slowly in winter, so heat and ventilation are needed. The water retentivity of lime putty, plus a cold, "green" base, does not provide enough suction to remove excess moisture. Blistering and cracking can occur due to slow set.

In Hot Weather Precautions include proper soaking of lime putty. When the sun is hot, hydrated lime requires 1/2 to 1 gal. more water per 50 lb. The water should be cool. Soaking of putty in shade prevents undue water evaporation and helps to prevent curdling and loss of spreading properties. Avoid soaking for periods longer than two or three days.

For application of lime putty-gauging finish plaster, make sure that basecoat is set and partially dry. If applied over a dried-out basecoat, water will be drawn from the finish coat, resulting in severe check-cracking. Spray the basecoat before finish coat application and trowel coat until final set.

IVORY and SNOWDRIFT Finish Lime Autoclaved (double-hydrate)

Mixing Machine equipment must be clean. Place 5-1/2 to 6 gal. clear water per 50-lb. bag of lime in mixer. Using a motor-driven, propeller-type mixer, the complete mixing of lime putty takes 2 to 3 min. and results in a high-quality, easy-working putty. Machine-mixed putty is plastic and coverage is increased from 10% to 15%. With a paddle-type mixer, the mixing time is about 15 min. Hand Mixing—For immediate use, place 5-1/2 to 6 gal. water per 50 lb. IVORY or SNOWDRIFT Finish Lime in mixing box. Add finish lime to water and hoe sufficiently to eliminate lumps. Screen putty through 8-mesh screen before using. Overnight Soak—Place water hose in bottom of a level soaking box. Sift lime through screen into box. When full, run water slowly, but continuously, until a small amount of excess water is visible over top of lime. If excess water remains on the surface the following morning, absorb excess water by screening in additional IVORY or SNOWDRIFT Lime, allow to soak a few minutes, then blend into putty by hoeing. For use, if necessary, screen through 8-mesh hardware cloth and mix with gauging plaster that meets job requirement. Application—follows directions for Gauging Plasters.

RED TOP and GRAND PRIZE Finish Limes Single or Normal Hydrate

Machine Mixing Produces a smoother, more plastic putty, easier to use and with better coverage. Use approx. 6 gal. water to each 50-lb. bag of RED TOP or GRAND PRIZE Finish Lime. Hand Mixing—Slowly sift RED TOP or CHAMPION Lime into water in soaking box. Allow material to take up water for about 20 or 30 min. and then hoe briskly to mix thoroughly.

Let mix soak for min. of 16 hrs. to develop full workability and plasticity. For use, screen through 8-mesh hardware cloth and mix with gauging plaster that meets job requirements. Application follows directions for Gauging Plasters.

Prepared Finishes

USG Offers Several Prepared Finishes IMPERIAL Brand Finish Plaster, DIAMOND Brand Interior Finish Plaster and RED TOP Finish—to shorten construction time and provide hard, abrasion-resistant surfaces. The type of plaster finish used will depend to a large degree on the level of abuse resistance required from the final assembly (See Appendix for Categories of Abuse Resistance).

Allow basecoat plaster to set but not completely dry before application of prepared finishes. If basecoat plaster has dried, complete misting of the surface is required before applying finish.

Mixing Prepared finishes require the addition of water on the job. Water should be clean, fresh, suitable for human consumption, and free from mineral and organic substances that affect the plaster set. Water used for rinsing or cleaning is not suitable for mixing because it accelerates the plaster set.

Mechanical mixing is mandatory for prepared finishes. Mix no more material than can be applied before set begins. Since prepared finishes set more rapidly than most conventional plasters, always consult bag directions for specific setting times. Prepared finishes will produce mortar of maximum performance and workability when the correct equipment is used and mixing directions carefully followed. proper mixing is one of the most important factors in producing mortar of maximum workability.

Use a cage-type mixer paddle driven by a heavy-duty 1/2" electric drill with a no-load rating of 900-1,000 rpm. Do not use a propeller-type paddle or conventional mortar mixer. (For details on the cage-type mixing paddle and available electric drills, see pages 432-433 or PM19, *Mixing Equipment for Veneer Plasters.*)

8

Mix plaster in 16- or 30-gal. smooth-sided container strong enough to withstand impacts that could cause gouging. Do not use brittle containers for mixing.

Correct Mixing Rapid and with high shear action—is essential for proper dispersion of plaster ingredients. Slow mixing can reduce plasticity of the material. Overmixing can shorten working time. Operated at correct speed, the cage-type design paddle mixes thoroughly without introducing excess air into the mix.

IMPERIAL Brand Finish Plaster Scratch in a tight, thin coat of IMPERIAL Brand Finish Plaster over the entire area, immediately doubling back with plaster from the same batch to full thickness of 1/16" to 3/32". Fill all voids and imperfections. Final trowel after surface has become firm, holding trowel flat and using water sparingly. Do not overtrowel.

Best results for IMPERIAL Brand Finish Plaster are obtained by planning the plastering to permit continuous application from angle to angle. Where joining is unavoidable, use trowel to terminate unset plaster in sharp, clean edge—do not feather out. Bring adjacent plaster up to terminated edge and leave level. Do not overlap. During finish troweling, use excess material to fill and bridge joining.

Diamond **Brand Interior Finish Plaster** Scratch in a tight, thin coat of Diamond Brand Interior Finish Plaster over the entire area, immediately doubling back with plaster from the same batch to full thickness of 1/16" to 3/32". Fill all voids and imperfections. Final trowel after surface has become firm, holding trowel flat and using water sparingly. Do not overtrowel.

A variety of textures ranging from sand float to Spanish can be achieved with Diamond Brand Interior Finish Plaster when job-aggregated with silica sand. (When Diamond Brand Interior Finish Plaster is job-aggregated, one tablespoon of cream of tartar or 1/4 teaspoon of USG Retarder for Lime Containing Plaster Products should be added for each bag of finish to retard plaster and allow sufficient working time.) Application is the same as for neat Diamond Brand Interior Finish Plaster except that once the surface has been leveled and sufficient take-up has occurred, begin floating material from the same batch with trowel, float, sponge or by other accepted local techniques.

Diamond Brand Interior Finish Plaster also may be textured by skip troweling. When applying in this manner, eliminate final troweling. When surface has become sufficiently firm, texture with material from the same batch prior to set.

Red Top **Finish** Scratch in a tight, thin coat of Red Top finish over entire area, immediately doubling back with plaster from the same batch to full thickness of not more than 1/16". Final trowel to a smooth, dense surface ready for decoration.

Ornamental Plasters

Ornamental plasters are used to add decorative treatments such as crown mouldings, rails, lintels and wall and ceiling details. These features are often screeded in place. More intricate forms are molded, either on the job site or at an off-site location where the forms may be better controlled. In the latter case, the formed pieces are later mounted in place.

For complete information on the use of ornamental plasters, contact Dept. 440, Industrial Gypsum Division, USG, Chicago, Illinois, 60606; phone: (800) 487-4431.

Special Additives

USG offers a number of special additives to improve plaster bond or enhance its abuse resistance or performance characteristics. Among those additives are USG Plaster Bonder and USG Acri-Add 100% Acrylic Add-Mix Fortifier.

USG Plaster Bonder is a vinyl acetate homopolymer emulsion that helps bond new plaster to virtually any structurally sound interior surface. Structurally sound surfaces should be clean and free from loose material, dust, dirt, oi, grease, wax, loose paint, mildew, rust or efflorescence. Glossy painted surfaces should be dulled by an abrasive and adjacent surfaces should be protected using masking tape, soap powder emulsion or other commercially available protective product. Bonder should be hand stirred and applied as is with brush, roller or spray.

USG ACRI-ADD 100% Acrylic Add-Mix Fortifier is an additive that improves bond strength, water resistance, shrink/crack resistance and durability of gypsum or cement-based plaster products. Mix USG ACRI-ADD with water at a ratio of 1:3, 1:2 or 1:1 and substitute for water in mix of plaster material depending on end use. May be used as an additive for plaster patching, setting-type joint compound patching, mortar and grout fortification, and cement patching. Especially useful in areas subject to vibration and heavy traffic.

Prepared Exterior Finish

ORIENTAL Exterior Finish Stucco requires addition of water only. Do not add waterproofing or antifreeze compounds, sand, or other materials. All tools and equipment must be clean.

Measure water accurately. To ensure color uniformity, use the same amount of water for each batch mixed.

Do not overtrowel, as this may cause color to concentrate unevenly on the surface.

Mixing For mechanical mixing, add 100 lb. ORIENTAL Finish to 3 gal. water and mix for approx. 3 min. If more than one mixer load can be applied within three hours, mix entire amount, dump into box and blend to uniform color.

For hand mixing, add 100 lb. ORIENTAL Finish to 3 gal. water and allow to soak for approx. 15 min. Then hoe thoroughly to smooth consistency. If more than one batch can be applied within three hours, blend several batches together.

Hand Application Apply ORIENTAL Finish only over a portland cement-lime and sand basecoat that is level but left rough under the darby, or broomed and properly cured.

Water-spray basecoat to provide a uniformly damp surface. Remove loose and projecting particles from basecoat. Then apply a thin coat well ground into the base and completely covering it. Double-back and fill out to uniform thickness of about 1/8″. Cover total area in one operation to eliminate joinings. Trowel three or four times before texturing.

For a float finish, use a cork, wood, carpet or sponge-rubber float and work surface to an even texture, free from blemishes, as the material stiffens and starts to set. Floating must be done without use of additional water.

Machine Application ORIENTAL Exterior Finish Stucco may be applied in a single or two-coat operation. Excessive mixing water should not be used as this may result in "lime bloom." For one-coat application, spray-apply material to basecoat to uniform thickness of approx. 1/8″. Work from wet edges to complete an entire unbroken area in one continuous operation to eliminate joinings. For two-coat application, apply first coat with a trowel as in hand application. After troweling uniformly level, apply textured second coat, machine-spraying to total thickness of approx. 1/8″.

8

Solid keying of ORIENTAL Exterior Stucco in machine-spray application ensures high strength of finish.

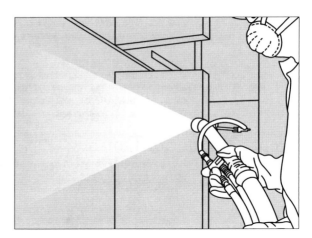

Sound-Absorbing Plaster Finish

USG Acoustical Plaster Finish

Mixing Read mixing and spray application directions completely before proceeding with mixing. Use a 7 cu. ft. or larger paddle-type plaster mixer with rubber-tipped blades (Anchor mixer) or a self-contained integral mixing/pumping spray texture tank with horizontal shaft and plaster or texture rig-type paddles mounted on a horizontal shaft. To insure uniform product performance, mix a minimum of two bags. Add powder to clean, room-temperature water in quantity specified on bag. Mix approx. 5 minutes until lump-free, and a thick, foamy consistency is generated. (Initial mix will appear dry and heavy). **Note:** If material is over-mixed, excessive foam will occur. Add more powder to break down foam and remix until proper foam level is reached. Additional mixing may be necessary during application to maintain foam consistency. Use wet-mixed material within 3-4 hours.

Spray Application All pumps and hoses must be cleaned initially with water followed by approximately one gallon of SHEETROCK Brand Ready-Mixed Joint Compound prior to spray application to prevent severe aggregate separation or clogging by the clean-out water.

For combined mixing/pumping units: Initially fill mixing hopper with necessary water to flush hoses. Pump all water from hopper, then drop joint compound into material reservoir of pump. Start pumping until compound feeds into hose. Immediately stop pump. Add water and powder in mixing hopper following mixing directions. When USG Acoustical Plaster Finish is properly mixed, pump out and discard joint compound. Turn on atomizing air, material valve and pump (in that order).

For pump units only: Add previously mixed finish to material hopper after pumping joint compound into hose. Then follow the start-up procedure as stated for combined mixing/pumping units.

Recommended spray pattern is 1-1/2 ft. to 3 ft. in diameter. The spray gun should be held 2 ft. to 4 ft. from the surface, depending upon

USG Acoustical Plaster Finish absorbs sound and gives dramatic appeal to ceilings and other noncontact surfaces.

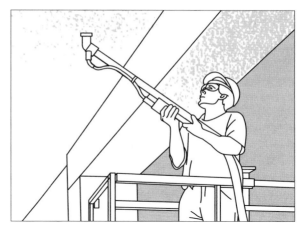

material density and atomizer pressure. Apply USG Acoustical Plaster Finish evenly, holding pole gun perpendicular to the surface being sprayed and slowly waving it from side to side until area is covered. Then immediately double back, crosshatching prior coat. Repeat same procedure as necessary until desired thickness is reached.

Elimination of spray lines and section seams is essential in producing an acceptable finish. Do not spray a portion of a ceiling in one day and the final portion on another day as a noticeable seam will result. If entire ceiling area cannot be sprayed to the final thickness in one day, spray the entire surface with a material coat of uniform thickness (min. 1/4 in.) Complete to final thickness the following day using a cross-hatch application. Use natural breaks and boundaries to "frame" pattern edges and conceal seams. To measure average thickness, mark desired thickness on a blunt-tipped object (head of pencil or finishing nail) and insert into finish.

For a different surface color, use a good quality, flat latex paint (white or pastel) and spray apply over dried finish. There will be a minimal loss in NRC value.

Masons and Stucco Lime

Portland Cement-Lime Plaster Used for interiors where high moisture conditions exist such as in steam rooms, dairies, showers, etc. It also is used as basecoat for exterior stucco. (Portland cement is not manufactured by USG.)

Surface Preparation Monolithic concrete surfaces should be brush-cleaned of all dust, loose particles and other foreign matter. Remove all laitance and efflorescence by washing with a 10% solution of commercial muriatic acid and water, then rinsing well with clear water. Remove grease or form oil by wiping with naphtha spirits. USG Plaster Bonder should be applied to all surfaces according to application directions.

Limitations

1. Brown coat requires curing with water after set.

2. Must not be applied directly to smooth, dense surfaces, gypsum lath or gypsum block. Self-furring metal lath must be secured to such surfaces before plaster is applied.

3. Control joints should be provided to compensate for shrinkage during drying.

4. A Keenes Cement-Lime Putty Finish must never be used over a portland cement basecoat.

Job-Mixed Stucco Mix mason's lime such as Bondcrete or Mortaseal Lime with portland cement and sand in accordance with ASTM C926 and in the following proportions:

Stucco Proportions (Job Mixed)

	Mix					
	Portland Cement		Bondcrete or Mortaseal Lime		Sand[2]	
Coat	lb.	kg	lb.	kg	ft.³	m³
Scratch	94	43	40-50[1]	18-23[1]	5-6[1]	0.14-0.17
Brown	94	43	50	23	6-7[1]	0.17-0.20
Finish	94	43	100	45	7-10	0.20-0.28

(1) Upper end of range for use over concrete block where greater water retention and plasticity are required; lower end of range for use over metal reinforcing mesh with exterior sheathing or building paper. (2) Quantity used varies, depending on shape and size of local sand particles.

Replastering Old Plaster Surfaces

In plastering over old plaster surfaces, certain precautions should be exercised to ensure a satisfactory result. Often, the old surface is lime mortar plaster on wood lath, is badly cracked, and usually has been covered with canvas and/or multiple coats of paint.

The following suggestions for lathing and plastering over such old surfaces are listed in order of preference for best results:

1. If the old plaster and lath are removed, 3/8″ Rocklath Plaster Base may be applied to the framing and plastered in the same manner as for new work, following all applicable specifications.

2. If the old lath and plaster are left in place, the following methods may be used, after determining that the framing is of adequate size to carry the additional weight of a new plaster finish (average 8 lb./ft.²).

(a) Apply 1″ x 3″ furring strips 16″ o.c. with 9-ga. nails, 3-1/4″ long or of sufficient length to achieve 1-3/4″ min. penetration into framing. Then apply 3/8″ Rocklath Base and plaster in same manner as specified for new work.

(b) Apply 3.4-lb. self-furring Diamond mesh metal lath over old surface by nailing through into framing, using 2″ 11-ga. 7/16″-head barbed-shank galvanized roofing nails, 6″ o.c. Wire tie side and end laps. Apply plaster in three coats. Red Top Gypsum Plaster can be used with max. 2 cu. ft. of sand for scratch coat, max. 3 cu. ft. of sand for brown coat, or with 2-1/2 cu. ft. of sand for scratch and brown coats. Lightweight aggregate should not be used in replastering when using metal lath.

3. If the old plaster is removed and wood lath left in place, all loose laths should be renailed and the lath repeatedly sprayed with water over a period of several hours in order to wet thoroughly. Then replaster as specified in 2(b). Note: If wood lath is not thoroughly nailed and wetted, cracking of the plaster may occur. Finish coat may be smooth trowel or sand float, as desired, mixed and applied per applicable specifications.

Integral Plaster Chalkboards

Plaster chalkboards offer definite design advantages. There is no limiting sheet size as is the case with fabricated boards; therefore, entire walls can be utilized as chalkboards. Maintenance is accomplished as easily as with conventionally fabricated chalkboards. Plaster chalkboards may be used with most plastered partition systems.

Chalkboard with Steel Stud Partitions Follow general directions for system construction. Fasten floor and ceiling runner tracks in place and set studs 16″ o.c. Toggle bolts installed after plastering may be used for chalk and eraser-trough clips. Attach Rocklath Plaster Base or metal lath and install No. 66 Expanded Flange Casing Bead, stapling to plaster base or wire-tying to metal lath, 8″ o.c. Plumb and level all casing bead installations.

Cross-section through chalkboard

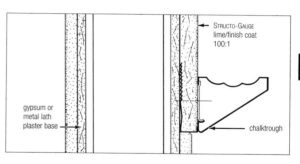

Mix Structo-Base Plaster in proportion of 2 cu. ft. sand per 100 lb. plaster; apply to 1/2″ grounds. Finish with Structo-Gauge Gauging-lime mixed 100 lb. gauging per 100 lb. lime; apply to max. 1/16″ thickness.

Paint chalkboard when dry, with one coat primer-sealer and two coats of quality chalkboard paint.

Door Frames

Hollow metal door frames are shop-fabricated of 16-ga. and 18-ga. primed steel. Floor anchor plates of 16-ga. steel, with two anchor holes to prevent rotation, are welded to trim flanges to dampen door impact vibrations. Jamb anchor clips should be formed of 18-ga. steel, welded in the jamb and head.

Frames used with various plaster systems must be rigidly secured to the floor and partition construction to prevent twisting or other movement.

Door frame

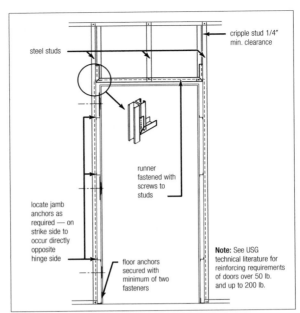

steel studs

cripple stud 1/4" min. clearance

runner fastened with screws to studs

locate jamb anchors as required — on strike side to occur directly opposite hinge side

floor anchors secured with minimum of two fasteners

Note: See USG technical literature for reinforcing requirements of doors over 50 lb. and up to 200 lb.

Elevation cross section

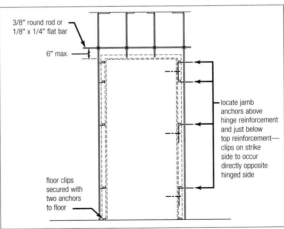

3/8" round rod or 1/8" x 1/4" flat bar

6" max.

locate jamb anchors above hinge reinforcement and just below top reinforcement— clips on strike side to occur directly opposite hinged side

floor clips secured with two anchors to floor

Jamb details

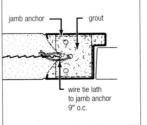

jamb anchor

grout

wire tie lath to jamb anchor 9" o.c.

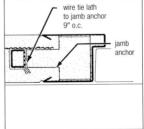

wire tie lath to jamb anchor 9" o.c.

jamb anchor

If door frames are free to twist upon impact, cracking of plaster will result and eventually the frames will loosen. In addition to the framing specifications described, door closers are recommended on all over-size doors where the weight, including hardware, is over 50 lb.

Grouting of Door Frames Always recommended, and required where heavy or oversize doors are used. As a grout, use a 100:2 RED TOP Gypsum Plaster-sand mix, adding enough water so that the material is stiff but workable.

Under no condition should the lath and plaster terminate against the trim of the door frame. Grouting of exterior door frames with gypsum plasters is not recommended.

Control Joints Also help prevent cracking of plaster at door frames. To break continuity of framing for control joint location, install door frame and place friction-fit cripple studs next to frame uprights. Allow 1/4″ clearance for Zinc Control Joints Nos. 50, 75 and 100. Continue with plaster base application using required control joint at break in framing above door frame.

Door Frames with Studless Metal Lath Partitions Follow general directions for fabricating door frames. Use four jamb anchors on each jamb and wire tie to support frame. Use temporary bracing to hold frame until plaster has set.

Door Frames with Stud-Metal Lath Solid Partitions Fabricate as previously described with four jamb anchors welded to trim returns. Anchor frame to floor with power-driven fasteners.

Insert studs into steel door frame. Nest studs in notches of jamb anchor clips and wire tie. Install a 3/8″ round rod or a 1/8″ x 1-1/4″ flat bar across head of door, extending to engage first stud beyond frame. Wire tie bar at each channel intersection.

Grout steel door frames solid with mortar when scratch coat of plaster is applied.

Caulking Procedures

Where a plaster partition is used as a sound barrier, SHEETROCK Brand Acoustical Sealant should be used to seal all cutouts and all intersections with the adjoining structure. Caulking at runners and around the partition perimeter between gypsum lath and/or plaster and the structure is required to achieve sound transmission class (STC) values on the job that approximate those determined by test. Caulking has proven to be the least expensive way to obtain better sound control.

The surfaces to be caulked should be clean, dry and free of all foreign matter. Using an air-pressure-activated or hand caulking gun, apply SHEETROCK Brand Acoustical Sealant in beads about 3/8″ round.

Partition Perimeters When gypsum lath is used, leave a space approx. 1/4″ wide between lath and floor, ceiling and dissimilar walls. Appropriate metal edge-trim or casing beads applied to the lath may be used to create this space. Fill space with SHEETROCK Brand Acoustical Sealant.

When conventional plaster is applied to metal lath, rake out plaster to form a 3/8″ groove at partition perimeter, and fill groove with acoustical sealant. Finish over groove with base or trim as desired.

Openings Apply a 3/8″ min. round bead of acoustical sealant around all cutouts such as at electrical boxes, medicine cabinets, heating ducts and cold air returns to seal the opening.

Electrical Fixtures Apply caulking to the backs of electrical boxes and around all boxes to seal the cutout. Avoid cutting holes back to back and adjacent to each other. Electrical boxes having a plaster ring or device cover for use as a stop for caulking are recommended.

Outlet box caulked with SHEETROCK Brand Acoustical Sealant

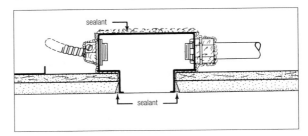

Fixture Attachment

Plaster partitions provide suitable anchorage for most types of fixtures normally found in residential and commercial construction. To ensure satisfactory job performance, evaluation of load requirements of unusual or heavy fixtures and preconstruction planning are needed so that attachments will be within the load-carrying capacity of the construction.

The carrying capacity of a given attachment depends upon the strength of the plaster used. Plaster having a compressive strength of at least 900 lb./in.^{2} was used to develop the data shown in the Fixture Attachment Load Table on page 466 in the Appendix.

The attachment of fixtures to sound-barrier partitions may impair the sound-control characteristics desired. Refrain from attaching fixtures to party walls so as to avoid a direct path for sound flow. Plastered ceilings are not designed to support light fixtures or troffers, air vents or other equipment. Separate supports should be provided.

In wood-frame construction, fixtures are usually attached directly to the framing or to blocking supports attached to the framing. Blocking or supports should be provided for plumbing fixtures, towel racks, grab bars and similar items. Lath and plaster membranes are not designed to support loads imposed by these items without additional support to carry the main part of the load.

To provide information for proper construction, an investigation of loading capacities of various fasteners and fixture attachments used with plaster partitions was conducted at the USG Research & Technology Center. These fasteners and attachments were tested:

Picture Hooks A flattened wire hook attached to the wall with a nail driven diagonally downward. Depending on size, the capacity varies from 5 to 50 lbs. per hook. Suitable for hanging pictures, mirrors and other lightweight fixtures from all plaster partitions.

Fiber and Plastic Expansion Plugs A sheet metal or wood screw driven into a fiber or plastic plug. Annular ribs are provided on outside of plastic plug to assure a positive grip in wall. As screw is inserted, rear end of plug expands and holds assembly in place. Suitable for attaching lightweight fixtures in all partitions (see below).

Fixture attachments

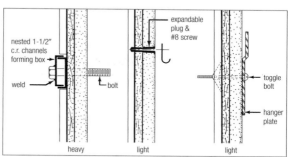

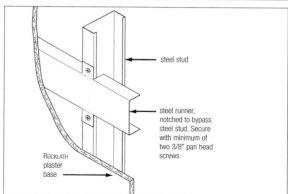

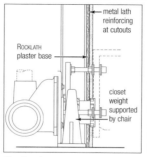

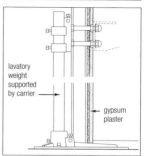

Closet carrier   *Lavatory carrier*

Toggle Bolts Installed in lath and plaster only. Disadvantages of toggle bolt are that when bolt is removed, wing fastener on back will fall down into a hollow wall and a large hole is required to allow wings to pass through wall facings (see page 293 for detail).

Hollow Wall Fasteners Installed in lath and plaster only. One advantage of this type fastener is that threaded section remains in wall when screw is removed. Also, widespread spider support formed by the expanded anchor spreads load against wall material, increasing load capacity.

Bolts and 1-1/2″ Channels Two 5/16″ bolts welded to 1″ channels for use in mounting hanger brackets for heavy fixtures. Two nested channels are securely attached to back of studs in steel-framed partitions (see page 293 for detail).

Angle Brackets Standard 10″ x 12″ shelving brackets spaced 24″ o.c. and fastened to wall with three-hole anchorage. Fastened to steel studs with sheet metal screws or to lath and plaster with toggle bolts or hollow wall fasteners.

Continuous Horizontal Bracing Back-up for fixture attachment is provided with notched runner attached to steel studs with two 3/8″ pan head screws (see page 293 for detail).

Slotted Standards With adjustable shelf brackets, are fastened 24″ o.c. to steel studs with sheet metal screws or to lath and plaster with toggle bolts or hollow wall fasteners. Normal standard spacing: 24″ o.c. for 24″ stud spacing, and 32″ o.c. for 16″ stud spacing. Limited to six shelves per partition height.

Separate Supports Individual carriers or chairs placed in the core wall, recommended where heavy bathroom fixtures such as lavatories and water closets without floor supports are required (see page 293 for detail).

Insulating Blankets

See page 135 for data on THERMAFIBER Sound Attenuation Fire Blankets for use in sound-rated assemblies.

Acoustical Ceiling
Design & Application

9

The development of suspended ceiling systems in the early 1950s produced a shift in thinking about the function of a ceiling in construction. A ceiling simply had been regarded as a single-plane, fire-protective, finished element overhead. Suddenly, with the introduction of a suspension system, the ceiling also offered access to plumbing, electrical and mechanical components in overhead runs.

Today's suspended ceiling systems offer even more advantages for building construction, including a range of acoustical control options, fire protection, esthetic appearance, flexibility in lighting and HVAC delivery, budget control and optional use of overhead space.

Note that various organizations provide information and recommended standards or tolerances for installing ceiling suspension systems and acoustical panel and tile products. See pages 467 and 474 in the Appendix for information about standards and tolerances.

For instructions on the safe use of ceiling suspension systems and acoustical panel and tile products, see Chapter 13, Safety Considerations, Material Handling.

Suspended Acoustical Ceiling Products

Key components for suspended acoustical ceilings are suspension grid and acoustical panels. Composition of each can vary depending on the end-use application. Acoustical tile (12″ x 12″) is also an acoustical ceiling product, but unlike larger panels (24″ x 24″ and larger), the tiles are typically glued or stapled to an existing ceiling surface. They also may be assembled like puzzle pieces on a special concealed grid suspension system.

Grid Systems

USG offers four primary grid systems. The systems all perform the same function of suspending panels in a single plane from the overhead building structure. Differences are in the design and compatibility with certain styles of panels, and the resulting appearance of the finished ceiling.

Acoustical suspension (grid) systems from USG Interiors are fast and easy to install. Acoustical panels simply drop into the suspension system.

DONN DX

DONN CENTRICITEE

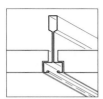

DONN FINELINE

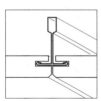

DONN DX Concealed

DONN DX Suspension System is an exposed 15/16″ wide face grid. It is the most commonly used suspension system. Note that exposed face grid products are typically differentiated by the width of the exposed portion and/or by reveals in the exposed portion.

DONN CENTRICITEE Suspension System is an exposed 9/16″ wide face grid. The narrower face fits reveal-edge panels and square-edge panels.

DONN FINELINE Suspension System is an exposed 9/16″ slotted grid. It features either a 1/4″ or 1/8″ slot in the center of the exposed face that adds an attractive feature. The face of this grid fits flush with the face of reveal-edge panels. Mitered intersections provide a clean, tailored appearance.

DONN DX Concealed Suspension System is designed for use with kerfed ceiling tile. In this application, the 15/16″ grid surface is completely concealed by the tile.

These grid systems are available either fire-rated or non-rated. Fire-rated versions are made with a special fire expansion relief notch in each main tee to compensate for the significant expansion of the grid if exposed to the extreme temperatures of a fire. This expansion relief notch absorbs the expansion to keep the grid modules intact, thus preventing ceiling panels from falling out.

In addition to the four primary grid systems, USG offers a range of special function products for controlled environment applications as follows:

DONN AX, a noncorrosive aluminum 15/16″ exposed grid system, ideal for high-humidity environments or wet-cleaned areas.

DONN DXLA, an aluminum-capped 15/16″, fire-rated, exposed grid system, offering maximum economy and design simplicity with UL designs.

DONN CE, a 1-1/2″ exposed, pre-gasket, heavy duty grid system, designed for controlled environment rooms that require a clean, particulate-free, sealed ceiling system.

DONN ZXA/ZXLA, a 15/16″ exposed, hot-dipped galvanized grid system with an aluminum cap, ideal for use in exterior and severe environments.

DONN DXSS, a 15/16″ Type 316 stainless steel grid system, designed for industrial and other extreme environments.

Structural Implications

The grid system becomes a structural component in the ceiling. It must carry the loads of lighting, air distribution and ceiling panels in a safe manner. Through the hanger wires that suspend the ceiling, these loads are transferred to the building structure. The performance of the grid system is dependent upon the integrity of the product as well as its proper installation.

There are two standards that must be met in order to assure the integrity of the installed ceiling. ASTM Standard C-635 governs the structural and quality standards of the grid. ASTM Standard C-636 provides for proper installation to assure the load-carrying and general structural integrity of the ceiling.

9

Ceiling Panels

The most commonly used panel sizes measure 2' x 2' or 2' x 4' and are typically 5/8" or 3/4" thick. Although this is the nominal reference, the dimensions actually refer to the module size of the ceiling. Panel sizes, in fact, are 1/4" less than the module size in both directions.

2' x 4' Radar Illusion Eight/12 panel (left) uses face cuts to simulate smaller grid modules. Lightly textured 2' x 2' Frost pattern panel is available with square-cut, Shadowline-cut or Fineline-cut edges.

USG offers a full line of acoustical panels to achieve any functional or esthetic need. Selection can be based on varied parameters—texture, budget, acoustical performance, functional requirements, color, etc. For a complete guide, call your USG representative, 1-800-874-6655, and ask for catalog information, or visit the USG web site at www.usg.com.

Ceiling Panel Types and Manufacturing Processes

Manufacturing Process	Product Pattern	Features/Benefits
XX-Technology Ceiling Panels	Eclipse ClimaPlus Mars ClimaPlus Millennia ClimaPlus Orion 210 ClimaPlus Orion 270 ClimaPlus	X-Technology Acoustical Ceiling Panels are manufactured using a unique process that maximizes sound and environmental performance, and provides the following: · Smooth surface with high noise reduction coefficient (NRC) and ceiling attenuation class (CAC) performance · Superior sag resistance and outstanding dimensional stability · Easy maintenance—surface cleans easily with soft brush or vacuum · Applications—Hotels, office and conference areas, transportation terminals, reception and lobby areas, room-to-room privacy areas, high sound absorbancy areas

Ceiling Panel Types and Manufacturing Processes (continued)

Manufacturing Process	Product Pattern	Features/Benefits
Cast Ceiling Panels	"F" FISSURED FROST GLACIER SANDRIFT	Cast ceiling panels are made with a process that enhances the surface appearance, orients fibers for excellent sound absorption and durability, and provides the following: · Attractive surface appearance plus high noise reduction coefficients (NRC) · Clear-through color masks nicks and scratches · Long-lasting, abuse resistant surface · Foil backing acts as a sound barrier and resists "breathing" (air passing through the surface), so surface stays cleaner longer · Easy maintenance—surface cleans easily with soft brush or vacuum · Applications—Traffic areas, conference/speech privacy areas, hospitality areas, entertainment, retail stores
Water-Felted	Aspen Fissured Olympia Micro *CLIMAPLUS* Omni Pebbled RADAR RADAR *CLIMAPLUS* ROCK FACE Touchstone *CLIMAPLUS*	Water-felted ceiling panels are manufactured by a process that orients mineral fibers for excellent sound attenuation and provides the following: · Good ceiling attenuation class (CAC) performance · Available in a variety of surface textures · Surface of panel has perforations to aid in sound absorption · Easy maintenance—surface cleans easily with soft brush or vacuum · Applications—General purpose areas, texture/light-sensitive areas, high design areas
Fiber Glass	MARS *CLIMAPLUS* High NRC Premier Hi-Lite *CLIMAPLUS* Premier Nubby *CLIMAPLUS*	Fiber glass panels offer superior sound control performance and provide the following: · High noise reduction coefficients (NRC) · Light weight · Extraordinary ease of maintenance—vinyl surface is washable · Applications—Open floor plans, retail stores, gymnasiums and auditoriums, conference rooms and executive offices
Gypsum	CLEAN ROOM Vinyl Faced Lightweight Natural Paper-Faced	SHEETROCK Brand Gypsum Lay In Panels, *CLIMAPLUS* all have a gypsum core and feature the *CLIMAPLUS* designation and provide the following: · Superior fire protection · Extraordinary dimensional stability · Exceptional foundation for added treatments/processes · Applications— Clean rooms 　　　　　　　Food preparation areas 　　　　　　　Mobile conveyances

9

Examples of specialty ceilings include Paraline (left) and Celebration (right) Ceilings.

Ceiling Panel Types and Manufacturing Processes (continued)

Manufacturing Process	Product Pattern	Features/Benefits
Metal/Cast Plaster Specialties	See Below	In addition to conventional acoustical suspension systems, USG offers many innovative specialty solutions for use in high-visibility spaces such as lobbies, retail environments, restaurants, entertainment complexes or any space where dramatic focus in important. The company has pioneered affordable and installable "systematized" metal and "curvalinear" products such as the following:
Cast Plaster	CADRE	Fiber reinforced cast gypsum panels offer the look of classic coffered architecture with complete accessibility to above-ceiling utilities. Designs include Contemporary, Historical, Executive and Concepts.
	QUADRA	Four-sided coffer frames give the appearance of moulded plaster with accessibility and sound control.
Roll Forming	CURVATURA	Imaginative ceiling system uses curved metal to enable free-flowing, three-dimensional designs that offer unique combinations of shape and texture.
	GRIDWARE	Open-cell suspension system comprised of main tees and cross tees.
	PARALINE	Decorative and functional linear metal ceiling system.
Metal Stamping/Forming	COMPÀSSO	Metal suspension trim allows the creation of free-form ceiling islands or fascias incorporating any standard DONN grid and USG Interiors panel.
	CELEBRATION	Metal ceiling panels produce a contemporary ceiling surface, by snapping into DONN FINELINE suspension and concealing the grid.
	PANZ	Standard steel or aluminum panels provide durability, accessibility, easy maintenance and sound control.
Welded Assembly	WIREWORKS	Open-cell ceiling solution of powder-coated wire mesh that is compatible with GRIDWARE Ceiling System, COMPÀSSO Suspension Trim

Unusual ceiling looks can be achieved with QUADRA Coffer Frames (left) and WIREWORKS Wire Mesh Grid (right).

Design Considerations for Suspended Acoustical Ceilings

The modern suspended acoustical ceiling makes both a functional as well as an esthetic contribution to overhead space. Selection of the ceiling that's right for a particular application requires careful consideration of a number of factors.

Function vs. Esthetics

Functional considerations include acoustical performance, durability, accessibility to the plenum, etc. Esthetics, on the other hand address texture, light enhancement, design, configuration and the like. Most often, both parameters can be met with a single system. Occasionally, however, one or both parameters must be compromised to accommodate the other.

9

Budget

Depending on the type of space, a larger or smaller percentage of the overall interior budget will be allocated for the ceiling system. If the ceiling simply needs to close off the plenum, without regard to looks, special functions, or acoustical performance, very inexpensive grid and tile products will be employed. "High End" applications, such as hotel lobbies, reception areas or top quality retail establishments command more attention and require greater budgets.

Acoustical Requirements

Acoustical performance sometimes is the primary criterion, especially in open plan spaces where conversations lose privacy and people can be disrupted in adjacent areas. NRC (Noise Reduction Coefficient) is the most important factor in a ceiling designed for an open office, and the most cost-effective material for maximum sound absorption is fiber glass. (See product selections, pages 298-300.) These products perform at 0.75 NRC to 0.95 NRC range. Other products in the cast and X-technology lines offer similar NRC ratings and are much more attractive.

If the acoustical objective is to attenuate or contain sound to the area of origin, hard-surfaced panels such as gypsum or metal face panels will do a better job. These products have CAC ratings as high as 45-49.

Purpose of the Space

Sound control typically is the most prominent purpose for ceiling selection, and the panels chosen for the sake of appearance then come from the selection that meets the acoustical criteria. There are times, however, when appearance criteria can far outweigh acoustical needs. USG offers several ceiling options for esthetic appearance if acoustical control value is of secondary importance.

For example, in a restaurant a designer may want to incorporate the sophisticated high-tech look that can be offered by the CURVATURA Ceiling System, including the system's 3-dimensional vaulted or wavy ceiling designs. It can incorporate metal panels or, for some sound control, poly-bagged fiber glass overlays. COMPÀSSO Trim systems can provide islands of overhead sound absorption, or be left with open grid.

If acoustical control remains a key consideration, there are several options for attaining it. One is to install a standard acoustical ceiling above the focal point ceilings. Another option for localized sound control is to use perforated metal panels with floppy poly-bagged fiber glass inserts above the panels. In any case, the trade-offs need to be carefully evaluated.

CURVATURA Ceiling System

Selection Criteria

While function and esthetics are important, there are other selection criteria, including durability, installed cost, textures, colors, type of grid system, fire ratings and cleanability/scrubbability. Of course, the reliability of the supplier and manufacturer is among the best reasons to select ceiling systems from USG Interiors.

USG catalog and data sheets provide information about each of these selection criteria in an easy-to-use, easy-to-compare format.

Step-By-Step Ceiling Design

Three simple steps can guide specifiers to the ceiling selection of their choice. It's as easy as one, two, three.

1. Find the predominant selection criteria in USG literature (SC2000). These pages are designed to narrow the search to products that apply. The selectors include acoustics, price or budget, color, textures, etc. The products that survive the screening can be evaluated in greater detail by going to their product pages.

2. Every product in each selector is described by its most common trade name. Information about things like tile and panel sizes, thickness, NRC values, fire rated designs, and color availability is provided to further narrow down the product choice.

3. Additional technical information is readily available for all products. Each product has a complete Technical Data and Specification Guide which is available by calling 1-800-USG-4YOU. These guides give important additional information such as installation details, application information, structural load carrying information and performance data on air handling or lighting where appropriate. More complex products such as CURVATURA Ceiling System or COMPÀSSO Trim System, offer complete design portfolios to aid in the design and specification process. As the name implies, the Technical Data and Specification Guides have complete three-part specifications for easy inclusion into project specs.

Standards for Suspended Acoustical Ceilings

The most common source for voluntary standards is the American Society for Testing and Materials (ASTM). ASTM standards are widely referenced in all major building codes (The Uniform Building Code created by ICBO, the BOCA National Building Code created by BOCA, the Standard Building Code created by SBCCI, and the International Building Code and the International Residential Code created by ICC). ASTM is a not-for-profit organization that provides a forum for industry, consumer and regulatory body representatives, as well as other interested parties, to meet on a common ground and develop standards for products, installations and product testing methods. See the Appendix for explanations of the various ASTM Standards.

9

Building Codes Applicable to Suspended Acoustical Ceilings

There are three major building codes that have been established as appropriate to certain segments of the country. These are the "Uniform Building Code (UBC)" published by the International Conference of Building Officials (ICBO), the "BOCA National Building Code (BOCA)" published by the Building Officials & Code Administrators International, Inc. (BOCA), and the "Standard Building Code (SBC)" published by the Southern Building Code Congress International, Inc. (SBCCI). The map on page 315 outlines appropriate areas of influence.

Regional building code authorities generally have adopted a form of one of the three major codes. Several city and/or state code authorities, such as the State of New York, City of New York, City of Los Angeles, State Architects Office for State of California, and the California State Fire Marshal, have added requirements for acoustical ceilings and their suspension systems, based on specific local needs.

In addition, there are several other codes that may have some influence over suspended ceiling construction, depending on the application. They include: The "National Electric Code (NEC)" written by a committee of the National Fire Protection Association, Inc., the "Life Safety Code—NFPA 101" written by a committee of the National Fire Protection Association, Inc., and the "Uniform Mechanical Code (UMC)" written by the International Conference of Building Officials (ICBO).

Product Specifications for Suspended Acoustical Ceiling Systems

Project specifications for the domestic building industry have almost entirely become coordinated with the use of standardized, organized systems for writing project manuals and specifications. Both the American Institute of Architects (AIA) and the Construction Specifications Institute (CSI) promote specification standardization. AIA adopted MASTERSPEC as a primary specification system. CSI developed MASTERFORMAT as the guideline in its Manual of Practice for a complete system of construction documentation.

Standard construction documents, particularly project and product specifications, streamline the bidding process while defining product and project quality. The project manual includes bid forms, contract conditions, drawings and specifications, addenda and modifications.

Sound Control

Acoustical sound control performance characteristics are referenced in three different ways: Noise Reduction Coefficient (NRC), Ceiling Attenuation Class (CAC) and Articulation Class (AC). These characteristics are expressed as ratings that can be used to compare products. See the Appendix for explanations of these ratings.

Qualified architects and interior designers use these acoustical rating values to determine which acoustical products will work best to satisfy the requirements of a certain installation. For detailed information about the acoustical performance of particular products, refer to USG acoustical ceilings literature or contact the nearest sales representative for individual product data sheets. The acoustical performance values (CAC, NRC and AC) of USG Interiors ceiling tile and panel products are independently verified under the Underwriters Laboratories Classification and Follow-Up Services Program.

Designing for Acoustical Performance

The key to controlling sound is to design ceiling solutions with products that meet specific sound control performance levels. For areas requiring excellent sound absorption, USG Interiors has panels rated as "High NRC" with noise reduction ratings of .70 up to 1.00+. Open or perforated steel specialty products such as PARALINE, CELEBRATION, and

Curvatura can also obtain high sound absorption ratings by adding a fiberglass backer to the panels in the plenum area. Perforated Panz Metal Ceiling Panels achieve sound absorption through a unique integral backer called Acoustibond Backer. Using high NRC-rated ceiling systems in combination with wall and floor coverings, furniture, window treatments and other sound absorbing materials can help to create an ambient acoustic environment free from echoes and reverberations.

"High CAC" panels are also available with CAC values of up to 45. These do an excellent job of stopping sound transmission through the plenum. Sound attenuation is even better with the addition of acoustical barriers in the plenum between rooms, as well as acoustical sealant at room perimeters, to stop sound from moving around the ceiling plane.

Reducing speech intelligibility is typically the key objective in open plan facilities. This can require baffles, such as USG Silent Baffles, and other sound attenuation measures in addition to noise reduction components. Additional measures can help to "mask" sound through the use of air diffusers, speakers, waterfalls or other methods of creating "white" noise.

Lighting and Light Reflectance

Lighting is one of the most important factors to consider in the design of interior spaces. To handle lighting situations correctly, the anticipated use or purpose of the space must be clearly understood first. Then, the illumination expectations for that space must be well defined. Of course, electrical service capacity should be sufficient to meet current needs as well as plans for future expansion.

Lighting should meet the esthetic and visual comfort criteria of the occupants and type of area. The amount of light, the types of sources and their placement affect the overall mood. Lighting can either be dramatic or subdued. It can be part of a general design or fulfill a specific task. Lighting designers and engineers can help determine what artificial light sources work best to complement ambient lighting and meet specific objectives.

Suspended acoustical ceilings play an important role in interior lighting. The suspension system is designed to support the mounting of lighting fixtures, and adds flexibility to the placement and relocation of those fixtures. Further, the panel selection can impact light reflectance and diffusion.

Many common lighting terms are defined in the Glossary in the Appendix.

Lighting Calculations

Interior general lighting calculations are generally used to determine how many luminaires are required to provide an average given illumination level in an interior space and how the luminaires should be arranged to provide uniform illumination throughout the space. A qualified lighting designer or engineer can be a valuable asset to your design team. Using the rated light output at the source and the source-to-surface distance, the engineer can calculate the number, type and placement of the luminaires.

$$\text{Illumination (footcandles)} = \frac{\text{lumens}}{\text{area (sq. ft.)}} \quad \text{or} \quad fc = \frac{\text{lumens}}{\text{sq. ft.}}$$

Determining the number and placement of luminaires is not as simple as the direct relationship above would suggest. It also is important to take into account absorption of light by wall, ceiling and floor surfaces, the interreflection of light, the efficiency or distribution of the luminaires, the shape of the room, etc. Those considerations result in a utilization factor that modifies the light-source-to-useful-light relationship.

$$\text{Illumination (footcandles)} = \frac{\text{lumens X Coefficient of Utilization}}{\text{area (sq. ft.)}}$$

Light Reflectance

Light reflectance is an important factor in determining the amount of source illumination that will be required. Acoustical panels will have different degrees of whiteness, surface pattern and texture, all of which affects the amount of light they reflect.

USG tests and measures panel reflectance in accordance with ASTM E-1477, Method for Luminous Reflectance Factor of Acoustical Materials by Use of Integrating-Sphere Reflectometers.

High light reflectance (High LR) ceiling panels enable architects and designers to use indirect light effectively. Pendulum, sconce and trim lighting directed at the ceiling produces a wash of light with three specific advantages:

1. Indirect lighting reduces glare against computer terminals, eyeglasses, and windows in an office space, creating a more enjoyable and productive work space.

2. Indirect lighting reduces up-front expenses as fewer fixtures are used in initial construction.

3. Indirect lighting also saves on energy costs over time.

   Applications especially well suited for High LR panels include open office space, medical facilities, educational settings, libraries and computer rooms. Using light reflectance effectively can bring value to architects and owners by reducing glare, reducing initial construction costs and reducing energy costs.

Dramatic or Theatrical Lighting

Direct, indirect and spot lighting for dramatic effect can be facilitated with the use of curved or undulating ceiling treatments. USG introduced Compässo and Curvatura Ceiling Systems to provide just such an avenue for creative expression. These products open up creative design options well beyond the office environment.

Retail space, entertainment complexes, restaurants and lobbies can be designed with very upbeat, upscale lighting. The use of both up-lighting and spot lighting with halogen light sources has become very popular in today's interior design. In these specialized spaces, it is even more important to acquire the services of a professional lighting designer.

Environmental Considerations

The typical environment for a suspended ceiling system is an enclosed and watertight building with all permanent heating and cooling systems in operation. All residual moisture from plaster, concrete or terrazzo has been dissipated. Temperatures remain in a range from 60-80° F, with relative humidity not exceeding 80%. Climatic conditions from outside these boundaries may have adverse effects on the panels and grid.

Typical Interior Environment: In some instances, ceiling systems can be specified to be used in some "non-standard" installations. USG feels that the standard suspension systems and tiles should be installed in conditions that meet certain environmental requirements.

Higher Humidity Environments

When the ceiling system will be exposed to constant high temperatures and humidity, special panels and grid can be specified. USG Interiors offers panels that will withstand high levels of humidity and temperature without sagging. These panels, categorized as *CLIMAPLUS*, are standard panels formulated with an added ingredient that remains stable in temperatures up to 104° F, and relative humidity up to 95%.

CLIMAPLUS Panels may be used in standard and typical environments as well. The technology allows for flexibility during and after construction, giving the installers the option to install before a building is entirely enclosed. *CLIMAPLUS* panels, when used with DONN Grid Systems, carry a lifetime warranty.

In addition to *CLIMAPLUS* Panels, USG offers a number of other special performance panels that can be used in situations such as swimming pools, kitchens, clean room areas, areas prone to abuse, and other non-standard installations.

Certain grids also are designed for unique situations. DONN AX Suspension Grid is an aluminum grid that stands up especially well in areas such as over swimming pools and other areas of high moisture content. AX is rated as a light-duty system but its load capacity can be increased to reach intermediate levels by decreasing the hanger wire spacing to 3' o.c.

Steel-bodied grid also is available with aluminum caps (DONN DXLA), as well as environmental grid with hot-dipped-galvanized bodies and aluminum caps (DONN ZXA and ZXLA) that are available in heavy and intermediate duty ratings. USG also offers special performance panels that can be used in situations such as swimming pools, kitchens, clean room areas, areas requiring abuse resistant panels, and other non-standard installations.

For extreme environments, DONN DXSS Stainless Steel Grid may be appropriate. A metallurgist should review its use in particularly corrosive environments.

9

Exterior Applications

Exterior applications are subject to environmental extremes. Suspended ceilings in exterior applications must be horizontal covered, and protected. Typically these are exterior conditions such as parking decks, walkways, soffits or protected drive-thrus and building entrances.

These are applications that must address some new areas of concern when installing suspended ceilings. Outside forces such as wind, moisture and fluctuating temperatures must be dealt with. USG offers a variety of products that can perform well in these environments, from standard grid and panel systems to specialty ceilings.

For a standard suspension system in an exterior application, USG recommends using the ZXA/ZXLA environmental grid. The hot-dipped galvanized body, aluminum cap and stainless steel attachment clips make it a non-corrosive system. In conjunction with this grid, USG provides SHEETROCK Brand Ceiling Lay-In Tile. These tiles consist of a FIRECODE gypsum core and white stipple vinyl facing. The tiles are durable, cleanable and stain resistant, making them an ideal choice for exterior applications.

The ZXA Grid/Gypsum Lay-In Tile system has been tested in actual wind tests to sustain winds of up to 120 mph. These tests were performed by an independent testing lab using compression posts at each hanger wire location (4' o.c.), and hold down clips (nails) on each panel. USG recommends this type of installation in exterior conditions, subject to review by a structural engineer for each project on an individual basis. To assure long-term integrity of the system and the structure, the plenum should be well ventilated.

Other specialty ceilings also perform well in protected exterior situations. USG manufactures the PARALINE Linear Pan Ceiling System and the CELEBRATION 2' x 2' Pan Ceiling System. Both may be used in sheltered exterior applications.

PARALINE Aluminum Pans used with the aluminum symmetrical carrier and compression posts have been tested in winds of up to 120 mph (37 psf). CELEBRATION Aluminum Ceiling Panels have also been tested in winds up to 120 mph, snapped into a galvanized FINELINE Grid with SHEETROCK Brand Ceiling Lay-In Tiles, compression posts and holddown clips. Both of these systems give architects the opportunity to specify a system that can be used as a continuous transition from indoors to outdoors. These systems also provide new and interesting alternatives for covered exterior projects.

Fire Safety

Combustibility Versus Fire-Rated Assemblies

Fire safety properties of suspended acoustical ceilings are widely misunderstood, largely because there are several terms with similar but different meanings. Flame Spread, Class A, non-combustible, fire resistance rating, and fire-rated assembly all mean different things. Sorting out the differences can help.

Non-combustible simply means that the material will not burn. Class A designation on products means that the material can be ignited, but will not sustain a flame, and the fire will extinguish itself. Flame spread is a measure of the material's self-extinguishing characteristics. Both the characteristics of flame spread and smoke developed are measured in accordance with ASTM E-84, and the measurement will determine whether the material can be considered Class A.

None of these terms should be mistaken or substituted for fire-rated assemblies or fire resistance ratings.

Fire Resistance Rating and Fire-Rated Assemblies

Fifteen to twenty percent of all suspended ceilings are sold and installed as fire-rated designs. "Fire resistance ratings" is the terminology that long has been used by Underwriters Laboratories to reference the performance of various constructions. The ratings relate to fire-tests designed to measure the time it takes for a fire to raise the temperature above the ceiling to unacceptable levels.

The very phrase "fire-resistance" causes one to think immediately of the characteristics discussed earlier, i.e. non-combustible. This causes an unfortunate misconception that, if Class A materials are used in a grid ceiling, it will stop a fire from spreading or that it is a "fire-rated" ceiling. That is not necessarily so.

Fire rated ceilings (or fire-rated assemblies) are tested and certified in their entirety. This includes everything included in the construction from the type of bar joists used to the type and size of acoustical panels. The entire design that was tested is identified in the *UL Fire Resistance Directory*, which is updated every year.

Because the intense heat of a fire affects different materials in different ways, the materials need to be tested in context, or relative to one another. So a fire-rated ceiling assembly duplicates as closely as possible a small portion of the entire building including, but not limited to, concrete, bar joists, light fixtures, grid type, ceiling panel type, floor type, roof type, etc.

The *Underwriters Laboratories Fire Resistance Directory* lists all of the types of constructions that have been tested in an actual fire environment. Although we are concerned primarily with ceilings in this chapter, the tests contained in the book also cover beams, columns, floors, roofs and wall constructions. It bears repeating, a fire rated assembly is the total construction as it was built and tested with all of the above. Any deviation from the construction tested leaves serious doubt as to the performance of the rest of the materials in the assembly.

Procedures for a Fire Test

The general method of testing a design for a fire-rated suspended ceiling is to actually build a room that will represent the typical construction and install a suspended ceiling in it. Depending on the type of construction, this room might include an actual concrete slab representing the floor above, bar joists if it is a roof construction, appropriate wall construction, fire-rated DONN Brand Grid System, and FIRECODE Ceiling Board. If the ceiling has light fixtures and air diffusers, these are included too.

All of the UL fire tests are conducted in accordance with ASTM E-119. The assembly passes if no openings occur in the ceiling where flames can get through or the temperatures in the plenum or of key structural components stay below a prescribed limit for the duration of the test.

Every building material that is used in a fire-rated, tested design is listed in the test report in the UL Directory. Any deviation of the individual materials listed or in the manner it is installed, brings the performance of the final construction into question. The ultimate authority on any substitutions or changes rests with of the local building official.

Types of Construction Tested

The primary types of fire tests for DONN Brand fire-rated grid and USG ceiling panels are based on the type of construction used for the structure. The UL test designation is keyed to those ceiling designs based on the prefix letter of the test:

A - Floor/Ceiling designs comprised of concrete cellular deck with cellular steel floor units and beam support.

D - Floor/Ceiling designs comprised of concrete with steel floor units and beam support.

G - Floor/Ceiling designs comprised of concrete and steel joists.

J or K - Floor/Ceiling designs comprised of precast and field-poured concrete.

L - Floor/Ceiling designs comprised of wood or combination wood and steel joists assemblies.

P - Roof/Ceiling designs.

These letter designations followed by three digit numbers are the designs called out in the *UL Directory* and written into the specifications. USG has over 100 tested ceiling designs. Tests that incorporate DONN Brand fire-rated grid and FIRECODE tile and panels are listed on the following pages. For specific information, refer to the latest *UL Fire Resistance Directory*.

Note: The following tests are correct as of the writing of this text. Both the tests and the construction specifications shown for them are subject to change from time to time. As a result, see the current USG literature and the current *UL Fire Resistance Directory* to determine the status of a fire-rated design before specifying it.

Fire-Rated Ceilings

Construction Designs	UL Design No.	Assembly Rating	Approved Ceiling Tiles/Panels	Grid System	Maximum Fixture Size— % of Ceiling Area	Duct Area Per 100 Sq. Ft. of Ceiling Area	Assembly Construction Details
A. Floor-Ceiling—Concrete with Cellular Steel Floor Units and Beam Support							
Exposed Grid System and Lay-In Panels	A204	2 hr. R; 2 hr. UR; 2 hr. URB	GR-1; FR-81; FR-83; FR-4; M; FR-X1	2′ x 4′ By Others	Florescent type, 2′ x 4′—24%	113 in.²	3″ concrete; Cellular deck; W8 x 28 beam
Additional UL designs are A203, A207, A003, A010							
D. Floor-Ceiling—Concrete with Steel Floor Units and Beam Support							
Exposed Grid System and Lay-In Panels	D201	2 hr. R; 2 hr. UR; 3 hr. URB	GR-1; FR-81; FR-83; FR-4; M; FR-X1	2′ x 2′; 2′ x 4′; 20″ x 60″ DXL, ZXLA, DXLZ, SDXL, DXLA, DXLZA, SDXLA	Florescent type, 2′ x 4′—24%, 20″ x 48″/60″	576 in.²	1-1/2″ concrete; Cellular deck; W8 x 31 beam
Additional UL designs are D209, D219							
G. Floor-Ceiling—Concrete and Steel Joist							
Exposed Grid System and Lay-In Panels	G204	2 hr. R; 2 hr. UR; 2 hr. URB	GR-1; FR-81; FR-83; FR-4; M; FR-X1 DXL, DXLA, DXLZ, SDXL, DXLZA, SDXLA	24″ x 24″ to 30″ x 60″	Florescent type, 24″ x 24″; 24″ x 48″; 24″ x 60″; 24%; 2′ x 2′ HID; Incandescent type, 6- 1/2″ diam.	113 in.² (576 in.²)	2-1/2″ concrete; Metal lath or deck; 10″ bar joists 30″ o.c. W6 x 12 Beam
	G262	1-1/2 hr. R; 1-1/2 hr. UR	GR-1; FR-83; FR-X1	2′ x 2′; SQ, ILT edge DXLT, DXLTA	Florescent type, 2′ x 4′—24%	113 in.²	2-1/2″ concrete; Steel deck; 8″ bar joists 24″ o.c.
	G264	1-1/2 hr. R; 1-1/2 hr. UR	GR-1; FR-X1; FR-83	2′ x 2′; FL edge DXLF	Florescent type, 2′ x 4′—24%; Incandescent type, 6-1/2″ diam.	113 in.²	2-1/2″ concrete; Steel deck; 89 bar joists 24″ o.c.
Additional UL designs are G203, G211, G213, G202, G215, G222, G227, G228, G230, G231, G265, G259, G201, G017, G002, G007, G008, G011, G018, G037, G040, G020							
J or K. Floor-Ceiling—Precast and Field Poured Concrete							
Exposed Grid System and Lay-In Panels	J201	2 hr. R; 2 hr. UR	GR-1; FR-81; FR-83; FR-4; M; FR-X1	2′x 2′; 2′ x 4′; 20″ x 60″ DXL, DXLT, DXLZ, SDXL, DXLTZ	Florescent type, 2′ x 4′—24%; Incandescent type, 6-1/2″ diam.	576 in.²	2-1/2″ concrete floor with 6″ concrete stems
Additional UL designs are J202							
L. Floor-Ceiling—Wood or Combination Wood and Steel Joist Assemblies							
Exposed Grid System and Lay-In Panels	L206	1 hr. UR Finish Rating: 17 min.	3/4″ GR-1; 3/4″ FR-83; FR-X1	2′ x 2′; 2′ x 4′ DXL, DXLA, DXLZ, SDXL, DXLZA, SDXLA	Florescent type, 2′ X 4′—8%; Incandescent type, 6-1/2″ diam. —0.5%	110 in.²	Wood floor; 2″ x 10″ wood joists 16″ o.c.
Additional UL designs are L211, L202, L206, L212, L003, L006							

9

Fire-Rated Ceilings (continued)

Construction Designs	UL Design No.	Assembly Rating	Approved Ceiling Tiles/Panels	Grid System	Maximum Fixture Size— % of Ceiling Area	Duct Area Per 100 Sq. Ft. of Ceiling Area	Assembly Construction Details
P. Roof Ceiling							
Exposed Grid System and Lay-In Panels	P237	2 hr. R; 2 hr. UR; 2 hr. URB	FR-4; FR-83; DW (for drywall), DXL, DXLA, ZXLA, DXLZ, SDXL, DXLZA, SDXLZ (for panels)	2' x 4'	Florescent type, 1' x 4'—16%; 2' x 2'—20%; 2' x 4'—24%; Incandescent type, 6-1/2" diam.	144 in.² Linear air returns	Unlimited insulation; Steel deck; 8" bar joists 72" o.c.; 1/2" FIRECODE C Gypsum Panel Ceiling w/6" fiber glass insulation
	P230	1-1/2 hr. R; 1-1/2 hr. UR; 1-1/2 hr. URB	GR-1; FR-4; FR-83; FR-X1	2'x2', 2'x4'; 20" x 60" DXL, DXLA, DXLP, ZXLA, DXLZ, SDXL, DXLZA, SDXLA	Florescent type, 2' x 4'—24%; Incandescent type, 6-1/2" diam.; 2' x 2' HID	255 in.² (576 in.² for 1-hr.)	Unlimited insulation; Gypsum panels or DUROCK on steel deck; 10" bar joists 72" o.c.; 6 x 12 beam
	P254	1 hr. R; 3/4 hr. UR; 3/4hr. URB	3/4" GR-1; 3/4" FR-81; 3/4" FR-83	2' x 2' FL edge DXLF	Florescent type, 2' x 2' or 2' x 4'—24%; Incandescent type, 6-1/2" diam.	113 in.²	Unlimited insulation; Gypsum wallboard; Steel roof deck, 10" bar joists 48" to 72" o.c.
	P268	1-1/2 hr. R; 1-1/2 hr. UR; 1-1/2 hr. URB	3/4" GR-1; 3/4" FR-81; 3/4" FR-83; FR-X1	2' x 2' DXL, DXLA, ZXLA, DXLZ, SDXL, DXLZA, SDXLA	Florescent type, 2' x 4'—24%	576 in.²	Metal roof deck panels; glass fiber insulation; steel roof purlins 60" o.c.; ceiling panels backloaded w/6" fiber glass

Additional UL designs are P213, P241, P201, P202, P214, P267, P235, P238, P245, P246, P255, P257, P269, P203

Product Codes for Fire Tests

FIRECODE ACOUSTONE Tile

G=FROST, GLACIER, "F"-FISSURED ceiling tile

W=FROST, GLACIER, "F"-FISSURED ceiling tile

AP=FROST, GLACIER, "F"-FISSURED ceiling tile

FIRECODE ACOUSTONE Panels

AP=SANDRIFT, FROST, GLACIER, "F"-FISSURED ceiling panels

AP-1=SANDRIFT, FROST, GLACIER, "F"-FISSURED ceiling panels

FIRECODE Special Function Gypsum Lay-In Panels CLIMAPLUS

FC-CB=Gypsum Lay-In ceiling panels

FIRECODE AURATONE, Special Function ORION CLIMAPLUS, MILLENNIA CLIMAPLUS and ECLIPSE CLIMAPLUS Panels

GR-1+Illusion, Aspen, Omni, Fissured ceiling panels

FR-X1=ORION CLIMAPLUS, ECLIPSE CLIMAPLUS, MILLENNIA CLIMAPLUS (clay back) ceiling panels

FR-X2=ECLIPSE CLIMAPLUS, MILLENNIA CLIMAPLUS (foil-back) ceiling panels

FR-83=Omni, Fissured, Pebbled, ROCK FACE CLIMAPLUS, CLEAN ROOM CLIMAPLUS ceiling panels

FR-4=RADAR CERAMIC CLIMAPLUS ceiling panels

General Notes for DXL/DXLA fire-rated systems

1. Hanger wire should be located between the main tee splice and the expansion relief notch and a maximum 48" o.c., or per the requirements of the specific UL design.

2. All 60" cross tees are to have hanger wires at their midpoint.

3. Assemblies are tested with the method and criteria established in Standard UL 263, also known as A2.1, ASTM E-119 and NFPA 251.

4. Hold-down clips are required when the fire-rated board used weighs less than 1.0 lb./ft.².

5. % Fixtures column indicates 24″ x 48″ fixture only, unless noted. Check for suspension requirements.

6. Some designs pertain for DXL only. Contact *UL Fire Resistance Directory* and revisions to confirm all information listed in these tables.

7. DXLR and ZXLA are also listed by UL.

8. DXL has been used in many other industry fire tests and listed in reports such as the National Evaluation Reports, for example, NER-148 and NER-399 (wood truss constructions).

9. Check UL Designs for deck options.

Additional DXL fire-rated assemblies

3 hr.: G-229

2 hr.: A-202, D-208, G-208, G-209, G-218, G-229, G-236, G-243, G-250, G-258 [Concealed systems D-010, G-022]

1-1/2 hr.: A-210, G-229, G-241, G-243, L-208, P-207, P-225, P-227, P-231, P-251

1 hr.: G-241, L-206, L-209, L-210, L-212, P-206, P-210, P-225, P-227, P-244, P-245, P-257, P- 509, P-513

3/4 hr.: P-204

Seismic Requirements for Suspended Acoustical Ceilings

Although most people are familiar with earthquakes on the west coast, every area of the world experiences seismic activity of some degree. Because of this, some areas of the U.S. require buildings to have extra structural support to resist these imposed seismic forces. The challenge to the U.S. architect is to determine if the building and/or installation needs extra lateral (horizontal) bracing, and if so, how much. The first step in determining the seismic bracing requirements for a building is to determine the building code that governs the area where the building will be located. The map on page 315 shows the approximate geographic usage for the three major code organizations: Uniform Building Code (UBC) by ICBO, Basic Building Code by BOCA, and the Standard Building Code (SBC) by SBCCI. As this map is only a general representation of acceptance and usage, it is up to the installing contractor to contact the general contractor, architect and/or local building officials regarding the applicable code for a project.

These three major codes each have sections on seismic load design. The requirements of each of these sections are nearly identical except for slightly differing formulas used for calculating Fp. Fp is the minimum horizontal (lateral) force that a ceiling must be able to resist. Lateral seismic load must be calculated using the formula from the appropriate building code.

Resisting Seismic Disturbance

Areas subject to seismic disturbance have added requirements for suspended ceilings. Extra bracing for ceilings in these areas is required primarily to prevent injury and keep the ceiling moving along with the building during seismic activity.

DONN Suspension Systems are continuously tested for minimum tension and compression strength at all connections (based on ASTM E580 requirements). In addition, taut, splayed hanger wires that resist horizontal movement (next page, top), and compression posts to resist vertical movement (next page, bottom) are common installation practices in seismic construction and are covered in two basic standards, UBC 25-2 and ASTM E-580.

The building codes can be used to determine the need and amount of bracing, but often these two standards are used as defaults. ASTM E-580 is either specified by itself or in conjunction with SBC and BOCA as the governing code body for splay wire bracing and seismic installation, in their respective regions. UBC 25-2 is the only standard created by a major code body for installation and default splay locations.

Local communities and state agencies are free to adopt all or part of any code or standard they choose. Some communities adopt only portions, or they may modify or adopt a code. Local officials have the final say as to what seismic bracing requirements and construction details must be used. Each job may have unique seismic requirements as well as varying factors depending on location, type of building, and construction details. It is advised that a local professional structural engineer review each installation to ensure adequate planning for the necessary seismic bracing. In addition, each code contains various exemptions from the seismic requirements, which may exclude some buildings and assemblies from providing seismic bracing.

Splayed tie wires restrict lateral movement.

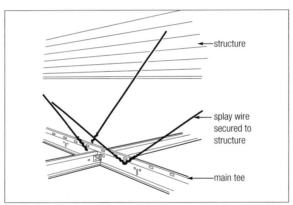

Compression post restricts vertical movement.

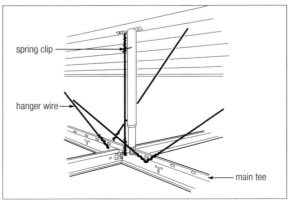

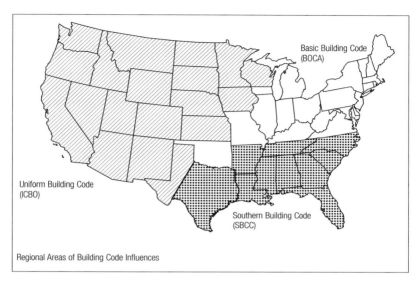

Basic Building Code
(BOCA)

Uniform Building Code
(ICBO)

Southern Building Code
(SBCC)

Regional Areas of Building Code Influences

Heating, Ventilation and Air Conditioning

Air distribution is an integral part of many suspended ceiling systems. The delivery of heated and air conditioned air to the areas below the ceiling is a major factor in the design of any ceiling system. The architect or designer must consider the amount of air flow and the distribution of the air from the HVAC equipment which is required to service a particular area. Typically, the air is delivered through diffusers in the ceiling system and is controlled by the amount of pressure produced by the HVAC equipment.

The movement and discharge of air into a conditioned space has a direct effect on the quality of the acoustical environment within the space. The acceptability of the sound caused by air movement depends on its loudness, its sound spectrum and its relationship to other sounds existing within the space.

Loudness of the air supply being delivered through an air diffuser is measured in decibels and the air diffusers are rated based on noise criteria (NC) for a given air flow in cubic feet per minute (CFM). In most cases, the loudness of the sound caused by air movement must be kept low so as to not interfere with necessary communication sounds. Sometimes, however, a relatively higher level can be used to mask or cover other undesirable sounds and/or to provide for conversational privacy.

The acoustical design should be based on a thorough analysis of the practical requirements of the of the conditioned space. This, generally, will be a balance between the sound caused by the air movement and other existing sounds, such as necessary communication sounds, sounds penetrating from the building exterior, and sounds intruding from adjacent spaces. The typical benchmark for noise produced by an air diffuser is a maximum of 35 NC in an office environment.

9

USG offers standard 2' x 2' air diffusers for 9/16" grid ceilings as well as linear air boots for the PARALINE Linear Metal Ceiling System. The air diffuser interface with the ceiling surface must maintain visual appeal and provide a clean, discreet slot for air flow. These diffuser units offer four-way air flow capability for optimum directional control and are available in one, two, three or four-slot versions for maximum flexibility in air delivery requirements.

The chart below lists design ranges for noise criteria (NC) for various indoor spaces:

Sound Control Guidelines for Air Handling Systems

Type of Area		Noise Criteria Range
Residences	Apartment houses, 2 and 3 family units	30-40
Hotels	Ballrooms, Banquet rooms	30-40
	Halls and corridors, Lobbies	35-45
	Garages	40-50
Hospitals and Clinics	Operating rooms, Wards	30-40
	Laboratories, Halls and corridors, Lobbies and waiting rooms	35-45
Offices	Conference rooms	25-35
	Reception rooms	30-40
	General open office, Drafting rooms	35-50
	Halls and corridors	35-55
Auditoriums	Multi purpose halls	25-30
	Semi-outdoor amphitheaters, Lecture halls, Planetarium	30-35
	Lobbies	35-45
Schools	Libraries	30-40
	Classrooms	30-40
	Laboratories	35-45
	Recreation halls	35-50
	Corridors and halls	35-50
Public Buildings	Public libraries, Museums, Court rooms	30-40
	Post offices. General banking areas, Lobbies	35-45
	Washrooms and toilets	40-50
Restaurants, Cafeterias	Restaurants	35-45
	Cafeterias	40-50
Stores, Retail	Clothing stores	35-45
	Department stores, Small retail stores	40-50
	Supermarkets	40-50
Sports Activities, Indoor	Coliseums	30-40
	Bowling alleys, Gymnasiums	35-45
	Swimming pools	40-55
Transportation	Ticket sales office	30-40
	Lounges and waiting rooms	35-50

Source: American Society of Heating, Refrigerating and Air-Conditioning Engineers, Inc.
Noise Criteria (NC) is important to the design of the HVAC system and selection of the proper air diffuser.

Donn Air Diffuser

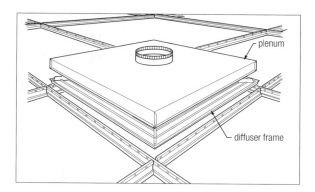

plenum

diffuser frame

Installation of Suspended Acoustical Ceilings

The appearance of a suspended acoustical ceiling is dependent both on the materials used and on the quality of the installation. USG manufactures components to meet ASTM C635, assuring that the material, structural and quality standards are as prescribed. Installation must meet ASTM 636, assuring proper level and secure attachment as prescribed.

Measuring and planning are key first steps in the installation process. Measurement and placement of the tees will be on center (o.c.), meaning from the center of one to the center of the next. Several components are involved:

Wall Angle is L- shaped metal strips that provide a continuous finished edge around the perimeter of the ceiling, where it meets the wall.

Main Tees are the metal framing members. They run the full length or width of the room (preferably perpendicular to joists) between the wall angles, and perform as the primary support for the ceiling's weight. They are hung by hanger wire from joists or other supports above.

Cross Tees snap into main tees at right angles, and serve as secondary support members for individual ceiling panels. They generally come in two lengths: 4', used for both 2'x 4' and 2'x 2' grid patterns; and 2' for 2'x 2' only. Some suspension systems offer 3', 5' and 8' cross tees for off-module applications.

Ceiling Panels lay in the open areas once the grid is assembled. Panels are supported by the grid along all four edges.

Hanger Wire typically is 12 gauge, specified by most local Building Codes to support the main runners, every 4' o.c., along the entire length of each main runner.

Planning

Start with a drawing of the room that shows all walls, including bays, alcoves beams and stairwells. Note which direction the joists are running, then determine the center line of the room's long direction. (If the center line is perpendicular to the joists, installation of the tees will be easier.)

Locate the main tees by starting at the center line and marking 4' intervals to each side wall. If more than 2' remain between the last mark and the side wall, place the main tees at these locations. If less than 2' remain, locate the first two main tees 2' either side of the center line and place all other main tees at 4' intervals. This procedure assures symmetrical border panels of the largest possible cut size.

Locate cross tees at 2' intervals perpendicular to the main tees. Follow the same procedure as above to be sure border panels are the same size. For a 2'x 2' grid pattern, indicate additional 2' cross tees by bisecting each 2'x 4' module.

Tools

See Chapter 14, Tools & Equipment, for information about applicable tools.

Step-By-Step Installation

Good construction conditions are very important to the success of a finished ceiling. It is recommended that the temperature and humidity range be 60-85° F and 75% relative humidity. Store materials in a protected area.

1. Choose the desired ceiling height, maintaining at least 3" clearance below the lowest duct, pipe or beam. Measure and mark the walls at corners 7/8" above desired ceiling height.

2. Snap a chalk line and test for level. Measuring down from joists or up from floor is not recommended, since either might not be level.

3. Install wall angle with top edge of angle at the chalk line, spacing nails 2' o.c. or closer.

4. Cut inside angles at 90° and miter outside angles at 45°, fitting them snugly together.

5. Stretch a string taught along positions main tees will occupy to assure level. Inserting a nail between the wall and the wall angle at marked locations serves as a good anchor for this purpose.

6. Stretch another string across the room where first row of cross tees will be located. This identifies where the first prepunched slots need to fall. Check to be sure the cross tee string is at 90° to the main tee string via the 3-4-5 method.

7. Install lag screws or screw eyes tightly into joists or suitable substrate at 4' intervals, attach hanger wire (18-ga. for residential, 12-ga. for commercial). The wires should extend 6" below the string line.

8. Bend wires 3/4" above string line with a pliers.

9. In each row, trim the main tee so that the cross-tee slot will line up with the cross-tee string.

10. Mount main tees, resting the cut end of the main tee on the wall angle and attaching wires by pulling them through the round hanger holes in the main tees. After checking the string line to be sure the tee is level, bend the wire up and around, twisting the wire tightly at least 3-1/2 turns to secure it. If the nearest hanger hole is not directly below the screw eye, adjust hanger length accordingly or punch new holes at those locations.

11. Install cross tees, assuring that they are adequately connected to main tees (they "click" in place when properly seated). Where two cross tees intersect in the same slot, insert second cross-tee end to the left of the first. Where a cross-tee is installed without an opposing cross-tee, a nail must be slipped into the opening of the cross-tee clip to maintain the pull-out value for the cross-tee. This is known as an Ashlar Condition.

12. Lay in panels, beginning at one corner and completing row by row. Tilt each panel up through the opening and lower it to rest squarely on all four tees.

Other tips Install light fixtures and wiring before installing ceiling. Cut tees with aviation snips, first the stem and then the flanges. Cut panels with utility knife and straight edge, cutting the face first. Cut panels should be 3/4" larger than the opening. To install panels around obstructions, draw their exact locations on the panels and cut out; cut panel from hole to side to enable fitting. To trim for Shadowline edge, use a utility knife to cut panel, first at face, then from edge, to same depth as Shadowline. If windows, stairwells, etc., extend above ceiling plane, build suitable valances and attach wall angle.

9

System Design Considerations

System Technical Data

USG leads the industry in developing high-performance systems to meet specialized requirements for modern building design and in documenting their performance at recognized testing laboratories. These systems provide fire resistance, sound control, structural capacity and esthetics for improved function and utility while reducing construction time and cost. All are constructed of quality products and released only after thorough testing and field trial.

In most instances, fire resistance and often sound-attenuation performance applies equally to systems constructed with gypsum panels and gypsum bases. Gypsum base with veneer plaster finish provides an acceptable alternative to gypsum panels. Therefore, the term "gypsum board" is used throughout this chapter to refer to both types of products. Only where performance differs greatly are the products treated separately.

Structural Criteria

Design of any structure must take into account the kinds of conditions that will exist and the resulting stresses and movements. Load-bearing walls include the exterior walls of a building and some interior walls, too. These structures must be designed to carry the weight of the structure, its components and other loads that occur once the building is occupied.

The amount of axial load that structural members can bear will vary with the amount of lateral load (pressure from wind or other horizontal stresses) that the final assembly may incur.

Manufacturers of structural components, particularly steel framing (studs, runners, joists) provide tables that identify the maximum allowable loads for various components under specific conditions. These tables typically start at 5 psf lateral loads and increase in 5 or 10 psf increments to about 40 psf. Interior partitions are typically designed for 5 psf lateral loads.

Interior non-bearing partitions are not designed to carry axial loads. Limiting heights are based on stress or deflection limits for given lateral loads. Height limitations depend on the gauge of the steel used, dimensions of the stud, stud spacing and the allowable deflection limit.

Curtain walls are not regarded as load-bearing walls and are not designed to carry axial loads. However, finished curtain wall assemblies do need to withstand wind loads within certain stress or deflection limits. Limiting height tables from the framing manufacturer should be consulted.

Load-span capacity of steel studs are based on the following factors as applicable:

1. AISI Specifications for the Design of Cold-Formed Steel Structural Members.

2. Yield strength of the steel.

3. Structural and physical properties of members.

4. Bending stress of the steel stud.

5. Axial load on the stud.

6. Shear stress of the stud.

8. Allowable deflection of the stud.

9. Web crippling of stud at supports.

10. Lateral bracing.

Stud Selection

Selection of a stud gauge and size must take into account a number of factors. The key consideration is whether the assembly is for a load-bearing, nonload-bearing or curtain wall application. Other variables include anticipated wall height, weight and dimensions of mounted fixtures, fire rating desired, sound attenuation needed, anticipated wind loads, insulation requirements, deflection allowance and desired impact resistance.

In general, stronger or heavier studs are needed to accommodate taller walls. Stronger studs also reduce deflection and vibration from impacts such as slamming doors. Wider studs may be required to handle insulation requirements. Fire-rated systems are usually designed, tested and classified based on using the lightest gauge, shallowest stud depth and maximum stud spacing as indicated in the assembly description. Stud gauge and depth may be increased without affecting the fire-resistance rating of the assembly.

Strength and performance characteristics can be achieved in a variety of ways. Wall strength can be increased by using heavier gauge material, stronger stud designs, narrower stud spacing or larger web dimensions. Studs typically are selected to maintain cost control and design integrity. Increased strength requirements generally are met by first increasing steel gauge or stud style before increasing stud dimensions.

Steel studs are typically manufactured in two different styles:

– Studs designed for nonload-bearing interior drywall partition applications have a minimum 1-1/4″ flange width on both sides. The web design incorporates a cutout for bracing and for electrical, communication and plumbing lines.

– Studs designed for load-bearing drywall partition applications have a flange width of 1-5/8″. Cutouts in the web accommodate bracing, utility service and mechanical attachments.

For specific stud design and assembly information, consult USG Technical Folder SA923, *Drywall/Steel Framed Systems.*

Fire and Sound Tests

Fire and sound test data aid in comparing and selecting materials and constructions. In addition, these data frequently are essential for securing acceptance by the building code or agency having jurisdiction. The USG *Construction Selector* SA100 provides tested fire resistance and acoustical performance for various systems.

Fire resistance refers to the ability of an assembly to serve as a barrier to fire and to confine its spread to the area of origin. Spread of fire from one area to another occurs because (a) the barrier collapses, (b) openings in the barrier allow passage of flame or hot gases or (c) sufficient heat is conducted through an assembly to exceed specified temperature limitations. These characteristics form the basis for judging when an assembly no longer serves as a barrier in a test.

A fire-resistance rating denotes the length of time a given assembly can withstand fire and give protection from it under precisely controlled laboratory conditions. All tests are conducted in accordance with the Standard, Fire Tests of Building Construction and Materials, ASTM E119. The standard is also known as ANSI/UL 263 and NFPA 251. The ratings are expressed in hours and apply to walls, floor- and roof-ceiling assemblies, beams and columns.

For assemblies tested at Underwriters Laboratories Inc. (UL), ratings are specific to the designs tested. Unless described in the design, insulation may not be added to floor- or roof-ceiling assemblies under the assumption that the rating either will remain the same or improve. Addition of insulation in the concealed space between the ceiling membrane and the floor or roof structure may reduce the hourly rating of an assembly by causing premature disruption of the ceiling membrane and/or higher temperatures on structural components under fire exposure conditions.

Sound control refers to the ability to attenuate sound passing through a partition.

The Sound Transmission Class (STC) is a widely used rating of sound attenuation performance—accurate for speech sounds but not for music, mechanical equipment noise or any sound with substantial low-frequency energy. It is tested per ASTM E90 and rated per ASTM E413.

The Impact Insulation Class (IIC) is a numerical evaluation of a floor-ceiling assembly's effectiveness in retarding the transmission of impact sound, also determined from laboratory testing. IIC is tested per ASTM E492 and rated per ASTM E989.

The Noise Reduction Coefficient (NRC) is a measure of sound absorption. This is an important consideration for controlling acoustics within a confined area.

The Ceiling Attenuation Class (CAC) applies to acoustical ceilings and is tested per ASTM E1414 for horizontally adjacent spaces.

Fire and sound tests are conducted on USG products assembled in a specific manner to meet requirements of established test procedures. Substitution of materials other than those tested or deviation from the specified construction may adversely affect performance and result in failure. For complete information on test components and construction, see the test report.

Additional information about fire and sound testing can be found in the Appendix.

Typical Fire Systems

A large number of systems have been designed and tested for fire resistance. The systems vary greatly in both design and performance. Nevertheless, certain basic system designs are commonly used. As a frame of reference, several typical designs and their accompanying fire ratings are shown below for wood-frame and steel-frame assemblies.

Also, in most tests, there are options that make them more versatile. Also, there are certain limitations that should be considered. Below are a series of notes that apply to many of the fire tests:

1. Two recent tests permit SHEETROCK Brand Gypsum Panel products and IMPERIAL Brand Gypsum Base products to be applied horizontally or vertically in partitions without compromising the fire rating. These tests are UL Design U419 for non-load-bearing partitions and UL Design U423 for load-bearing partitions. When either of these tests are listed with a USG system, it means that the system can now be built with the panels oriented in either direction.

2. The two fire tests indicated above also demonstrated that when FIRECODE or FIRECODE C Core products are used, the horizontal joints on opposite side of the studs need not be staggered (as was previously required).

3. In partitions indicating the use of 1/2″ DUROCK Brand Cement Board it is permissible to substitute 5/8″ DUROCK Brand Cement Board without compromising the fire rating.

4. In partition and ceiling systems indicating the use of 5/8″ SHEETROCK Brand Gypsum Panels, FIRECODE Core, or 1/2″ SHEETROCK Brand Gypsum Panels, FIRECODE C Core, it is permissible to substitute 5/8″ FIBEROCK Brand Abuse-Resistant Panels without compromising the fire rating.

5. Where thermal insulation is shown in assembly drawings, the specific product is required to achieve the stated fire rating. Glass fiber insulation cannot be substituted for THERMAFIBER Insulation.

6. In fire-rated nonload-bearing partitions, steel studs should not be attached to floor and ceiling runners.

Wood Frame Partitions

1-hr. Rating
UL Design U305
Drywall System

4¾″

10

Studs:	Wood 2″X4″ (nom.).
Stud spacing:	16″ o.c.
Gypsum panel:	5/8″ SHEETROCK Brand Gypsum Panel, FIRECODE Core, or 5/8″ SHEETROCK Brand Gypsum Panel, Water Resistant, FIRECODE Core, each side.
Panel orientation:	Vertical or horizontal.
Attachment:	1-7/8″ cement-coated nails spaced 7″ o.c.
Joints:	Exposed or taped and treated according to edge configuration.

Insulation:	Thermafiber SAFB (Optional).
Perimeter:	May be caulked With Sheetrock Brand Acoustical Sealant.

Veneer Plaster System

Studs:	Wood 2″x4″ (nom.).
Stud spacing:	16″ o.c.
Gypsum panel:	5/8″ Imperial Brand Gypsum Base Firecode Core, each side.
Panel orientation:	Vertical or horizontal.
Attachment:	1-7/8″ cement-coated nails spaced 7″ o.c.
Joints:	Taped.
Finish:	3/32″ Diamond Brand or Imperial Brand Plaster finish both sides.
Insulation:	Thermafiber SAFB (Optional).
Perimeter:	May be caulked with Sheetrock Brand Acoustical Sealant.

2-hr. Rating
UL Design U301
Drywall System

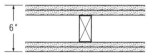

Studs:	Wood 2″x4″ (nom.).
Stud spacing:	16″ o.c.
Gypsum panel:	Two layers of 5/8″ Sheetrock Brand Gypsum Panel, Firecode Core, or 5/8″ Sheetrock Brand Gypsum Panel, Water Resistant, Firecode Core, each side.
Panel orientation:	Horizontal or vertical—joints of face layer staggered over joints of base layer.
Attachment:	Base layer—1-7/8″ cement-coated nails spaced 6″ o.c. Face layer—2-3/8″ nails 8″ o.c.
Joints:	Exposed or taped and treated.
Perimeter:	May be caulked with Sheetrock Brand Acoustical Sealant

Veneer Plaster System

Studs:	Wood 2″x4″ (nom.).
Stud spacing:	16″ o.c.
Gypsum panel:	Two layers of 5/8″ Imperial Brand Gypsum Base Firecode Core.

Panel orientation:	Horizontal or vertical—joints of face layer staggered over joints of base layer.
Attachment:	Base layer—1-7/8″ cement-coated nails spaced 6″ o.c. Face layer—2-3/8″ nails 8″ o.c.
Joints:	Taped.
Finish:	3/32″ DIAMOND Brand or IMPERIAL Brand Plaster finish both sides.
Perimeter:	May be caulked with SHEETROCK Brand Acoustical Sealant.

Steel Frame Partitions

1-hr. Rating
UL Design U419 or U465
Drywall System

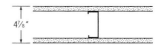

4⅞″

Studs:	Steel 3-5/8″ x 25-ga. (min.).
Stud spacing:	24″ o.c.
Gypsum panel:	5/8″ SHEETROCK Brand Gypsum Panel, FIRECODE Core, or 5/8″ SHEETROCK Brand Gypsum Panel, Water Resistant, FIRECODE Core, each side.
Panel orientation:	Vertical or horizontal.
Attachment:	TYPE S screws 8″ o.c.
Joints:	Taped and treated.
Insulation:	THERMAFIBER SAFB (Optional).
Perimeter:	May be caulked with SHEETROCK Brand Acoustical Sealant.

Veneer Plaster System

10

Studs:	Steel 3-5/8″ x 25-ga. (min.).
Stud spacing:	24″ o.c.
Gypsum panel:	5/8″ IMPERIAL Brand Gypsum Base FIRECODE Core, each side.
Panel orientation:	Vertical or horizontal.
Attachment:	TYPE S screws 8″ o.c.
Joints:	Taped (paper) and treated.
Finish:	3/32″ DIAMOND Brand or IMPERIAL Brand Plaster finish both sides.
Insulation:	THERMAFIBER SAFB (Optional).
Perimeter:	May be caulked with SHEETROCK Brand Acoustical Sealant.

328

2-hr. Rating
UL Design U411, U412 or U419
Drywall System

$4\frac{1}{2}$″
5″

Studs:	Steel 2-1/2″ x 25-ga.
Stud spacing:	24″ o.c.
Gypsum panel:	Two layers of 5/8″ SHEETROCK Brand Gypsum Panel, FIRECODE Core, or 1/2″ SHEETROCK Brand Gypsum Panel, FIRECODE C Core, each side.
Panel orientation:	Vertical or horizontal—joints of face layer staggered over joints of base layer.
Attachment:	Base layer—1″ TYPE S screws 8″ o.c. Face layer—laminated with joint compound or attached with 1-5/8″ TYPE S screws 12″ o.c.
Joints:	U411, exposed or taped and treated; U412, outer layer taped and treated.
Perimeter:	May be caulked with SHEETROCK Brand Acoustical Sealant.

Veneer Plaster System

Studs:	Steel 2-1/2″ x 25-ga.
Stud spacing:	24″ o.c.
Gypsum panel:	Two layers of 5/8″ IMPERIAL Brand Gypsum Base, FIRECODE Core, or 1/2″ IMPERIAL Gypsum Base, FIRECODE C Core.
Panel orientation:	Vertical or horizontal—joints of face layer staggered over joints of base layer.
Attachment:	Base layer—1″ TYPE S screws 8″ o.c. Face layer—laminated with joint compound or attached with 1-5/8″ TYPE S screws 12″ o.c. Face layer—2-3/8″ nails 8″ o.c.
Joints:	Taped (paper) and treated.
Finish:	3/32″ DIAMOND Brand or IMPERIAL Brand Plaster finish both sides.
Perimeter:	May be caulked with SHEETROCK Brand Acoustical Sealant.

2-hr. Rating
UL Design U484
Lath & Plaster System

$5\frac{7}{8}$″

Studs:	Steel 2-1/2″ x 25-ga.
Stud spacing:	16″ o.c.

Gypsum lath:	3/8″ Rocklath Plaster Base, each side.
Metal lath:	3.4 lb. self-furring Diamond Mesh Lath, each side.
Panel orientation:	Gypsum lath applied horizontally.
Attachment:	Gypsum lath and metal lath attached with1″ Type S screws 8″ o.c.
Finish:	3/4″ scratch and brown coat 100:2 gypsum sand plaster.

Wood Floor/ Ceilings

**1-hr. Rating
UL Design L501 or L512
Drywall System**

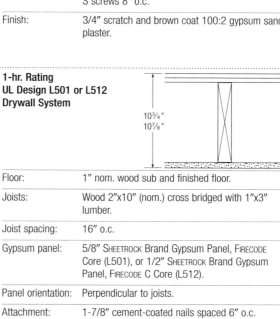

10³⁄₄″
10⁷⁄₈″

Floor:	1″ nom. wood sub and finished floor.
Joists:	Wood 2″x10″ (nom.) cross bridged with 1″x3″ lumber.
Joist spacing:	16″ o.c.
Gypsum panel:	5/8″ Sheetrock Brand Gypsum Panel, Firecode Core (L501), or 1/2″ Sheetrock Brand Gypsum Panel, Firecode C Core (L512).
Panel orientation:	Perpendicular to joists.
Attachment:	1-7/8″ cement-coated nails spaced 6″ o.c.
Joints:	Taped and treated.

Veneer Plaster System

Floor:	1″ nom. wood sub and finished floor.
Joists:	Wood 2″x10″ (nom.) cross bridged with 1″x3″ lumber.
Joist spacing:	16″ o.c.
Gypsum panel:	5/8″ Imperial Brand Gypsum Base, Firecode Core (L501), or 1/2″ Imperial Brand Gypsum Base, Firecode C Core (L512).
Panel orientation:	Perpendicular to joists.
Attachment:	1-7/8″ cement-coated nails spaced 6″ o.c.
Joints:	Taped.
Finish:	3/32″ Diamond Brand or Imperial Brand Plaster finish both sides.

10

**Steel Floor/
Ceilings**

**3-hr. Rating
UL Design G512
Drywall System**

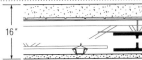

16"

Floor:	2-1/2" concrete on corrugated steel deck or riblath over bar joist—includes 3-hr. unrestrained beam.
Joists:	Type 12J2 min. size, spaced 24" o.c. (riblath); Type 16J2 min. size, spaced 24" o.c. (corrugated steel deck).
Furring channel:	25-ga. spaced 24" o.c. perpendicular to joists; 3" on each side of wallboard end joints—double-strand saddle tied.
Gypsum panel:	5/8" SHEETROCK Brand Gypsum Panel, FIRECODE C Core.
Panel orientation:	Perpendicular to furring.
Attachment:	1" TYPE S screws 12 " o.c.
Joints:	End joints backed with wallboard strips and attached to double channels.

Veneer Plaster System

Floor:	2-1/2" concrete on corrugated steel deck or riblath over bar joist—includes 3-hr. unrestrained beam.
Joists:	Type 12J2 min. size, spaced 24" o.c. (riblath); Type 16J2 min. size, spaced 24" o.c. (corrugated steel deck).
Furring Channel:	25-ga. spaced 24" o.c. perpendicular to joists; 3" on each side of wallboard end joints—double-strand saddle tied.
Gypsum panel:	5/8" IMPERIAL Brand Gypsum Base, FIRECODE C Core.
Panel orientation:	Perpendicular to furring.
Attachment:	1" TYPE S screws 12 " o.c.
Joints:	End joints backed with wallboard strips and attached to double channels.
Finish:	3/32" DIAMOND Brand or IMPERIAL Brand Plaster finish both sides.

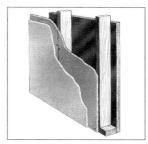 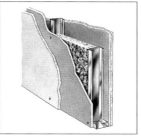

Wood Stud Partitions   *Steel Stud Partitions*

Wood Stud Partitions

Suitable for residential and light-commercial construction where combustible framing is permitted, these designs include single and double-layer gypsum board facings, single- and double-row studs, those with insulating blankets, and those with resilient attachment. Performance values of up to 2-hr. fire resistance and 59 STC can be obtained.

Steel Stud Partitions

Suitable for all types of construction, these designs include single and multi-layer gypsum board facings, with and without THERMAFIBER Sound Attenuation Fire Blankets. Performance values of up to 4-hr. fire resistance and 62 STC can be obtained.

Sound Control Systems

USG fire-rated partition systems offer a range of assemblies that are highly effective in isolating all types of sound. In both wood-framed and steel-framed construction, resilient channel systems offer improved sound attenuation to direct attachment systems.

In steel-framed construction, USG systems provide economical sound isolating systems without the excessive weight or space required of masonry construction. Systems are designed to control not only the mid and high frequencies, but also the low frequencies prevalent in music and mechanical equipment environments. Partition systems include both load-bearing and nonload-bearing designs.

For assistance with specific project requirements, contact your local USG sales representative or the Company's product information department (800-USG-4YOU [874-4968]).

10

Creased THERMAFIBER Sound Insulation System

Creased THERMAFIBER assemblies are steel-framed, 1-hour fire-rated systems that offer high sound ratings (50-55 STC), plus the lower in-place cost of lightweight single-layer gypsum board. The systems consist of 5/8" SHEETROCK Brand Gypsum Panels, FIRECODE Core; 3-5/8" steel studs spaced 24" o.c. and set in runners; and THERMAFIBER Sound Attenuation Blankets (SAFB), 25" wide.

Since the blanket is 1" wider than the stud cavity, it is installed with a slit field-cut down the center and partially through the blanket. This

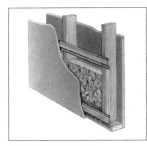

*50 STC, UL Design U311,
BBN-760903*

*55 STC, UL Design U412 or
U419, SA800421*

allows the blanket to flex or bow in the center, thereby damping sound vibrations more effectively. Panels screw-attach directly or resiliently to the steel framing.

Area Separation Fire Wall/Party Wall Systems

USG Area Separation Fire Walls/Party Walls are used for constructing common walls with fire-resistive protection for adjacent properties. These lightweight, nonload-bearing gypsum drywall assemblies are designed as vertical fire barriers for fire walls and party walls separating occupancies in wood-frame apartments and townhouses.

Large-size gypsum panels used in conjunction with steel studs and runners quickly become thin, space-saving walls offering excellent privacy. Their engineered performance and low labor and material costs make these systems superior to the usual masonry construction.

USG Area Separation Fire Walls/Party Walls are available in two basic systems, both providing fire-resistant walls from ground level to roof:

Solid Type, with independently framed interior gypsum panel surfaces both sides of fire wall or party wall.

Cavity Type, with integral interior gypsum panel surfaces for commonly shared party walls between apartments.

These systems may be used in buildings up to four stories high (44′) and with all common floor-ceiling heights found in multi-family housing. Both cavity and solid types are suitable for exterior walls with

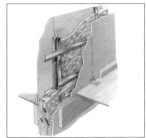

Solid-Type Separation Wall

Cavity-Type Separation Wall

appropriate weather-resistant cladding when building offsets are desired.

Fire Resistance: Both types of separation walls offer 2 hr. and 3 hr. fire ratings.

Sound Isolation: STC ratings up to 60 with the solid system and 57 with the cavity system are available.

Lightweight: These drywall assemblies weigh at least 50% less than masonry walls. This fact speeds installation.

Space-Saving: Use of these assemblies gains valuable floor space. Thickness is 3-1/2" to 4" for cavity-type walls, compared to 8" to 12" for a masonry wall without interior finish.

Weather Resistance: Moisture-resistant components permit installation in any weather; eliminate many costly winter construction delays.

Code Compliance: In compliance with fire resistance requirements under evaluation reports of BOCA Report No. 89-13 and SBCCI PST ES Report No. 9834.

Solid-Type Separation Wall

The solid-type wall consists of two 1" thick SHEETROCK Brand Gypsum Liner Panels installed vertically between 2" USG Steel C-Runners. Panel edges are inserted in 2" USG Steel H-Studs spaced 24" o.c. C-runners are installed at top and bottom of wall and back-to-back between vertical panels at a convenient height above each intermediate floor. H-Studs are attached on both sides to adjacent wood framing at intermediate floors, the bottom chords of attic trusses, and at the roof

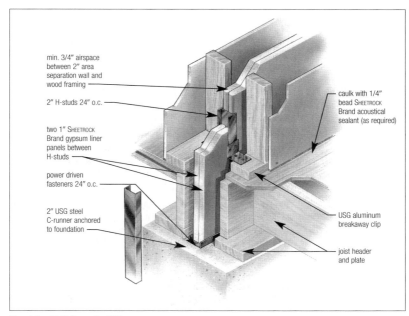

min. 3/4" airspace between 2" area separation wall and wood framing

2" H-studs 24" o.c.

two 1" SHEETROCK Brand gypsum liner panels between H-studs

power driven fasteners 24" o.c.

2" USG steel C-runner anchored to foundation

caulk with 1/4" bead SHEETROCK Brand acoustical sealant (as required)

USG aluminum breakaway clip

joist header and plate

Foundation–Solid Separation Wall

Foundation—
solid separation wall

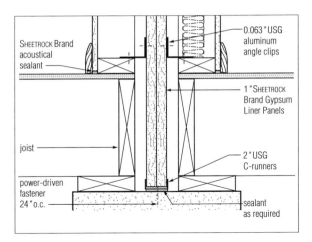

SHEETROCK Brand acoustical sealant

0.063″ USG aluminum angle clips

1″ SHEETROCK Brand Gypsum Liner Panels

joist

2″ USG C-runners

power-driven fastener 24″ o.c.

sealant as required

line with 0.063″ USG Aluminum Angle Clips designed to break away when exposed to fire, thus permitting a fire-damaged structure to fail while the fire barrier remains intact. Refer to the architectural specifications in SA925, *USG Area Separation Fire Walls/Party Wall Systems,* for exact clip placement.

With aluminum angle clips attached on both sides of 25-gauge H-Studs, the assemblies are suitable for spans (between clip angle supports) up to 10′ under 5 psf lateral load and up to 8′ as an exterior wall under 15 psf wind load without exceeding L/240 allowable deflection (see section 3.1 of the specifications).

With 2″ THERMAFIBER Sound Attenuation Fire Blankets (SAFB) stapled each side of liner panels, the assembly has obtained a 3-hr. fire resistance rating allowing separate selection and construction of tenant walls.

Installation

Layout A minimum 3/4″ clearance must be maintained between area separation wall and wood framing . A three-inch space is required to accommodate insulation thickness (for the 3-hr. wall). THERMAFIBER Insulation fire blocking at intermediate platforms is required in all cases.

Foundation Position 2″ C-Runner at floor and securely attach to foundation with power-driven fasteners at both ends and spaced 24″ o.c. Space adjacent runner sections 1/4″ apart. When specified, caulk under runner at foundation with min. 1/4″ bead of acoustical sealant.

First Floor Install H-studs and liner panels to a convenient height (max. 2′) above the floor line. Install two thicknesses of 1″ liner panels vertically in C-Runner with long edges in H-Stud. Erect H-Studs and liner panels alternately until wall is completed. Cap top of panels with horizontal C-Runner. Fasten C-Runner flanges at all corners both sides with two 3/8″ TYPE S Screws.

Intermediate Floors and Bottom of Trusses Cap top of liner panels and H-Studs with C-Runner. Attach C-Runner for next row of panels to the C-Runner below with end joints staggered at least 12″.

Details - UL Design U336

Note: As required by code, ⁵/₈ " Sheetrock Brand gypsum panels, FIRECODE core, may be used as underlayment to untreated roof sheathing with panels extending 4 ' on both sides of area separation wall and possibly roof side at rake end. Clip placement below is for typical construction.

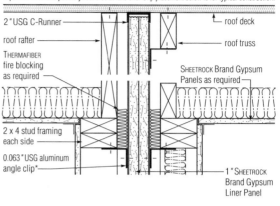

Intersection at roof

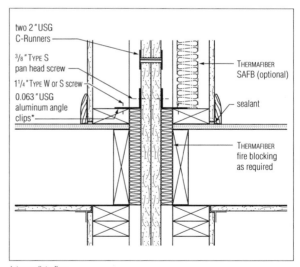

Intermediate floor

*Note: When installing the solid-type wall and its height is over 23 feet, up to a maximum height of 44 feet, the aluminum clips shall be vertically spaced a maximum of 10 feet on center for the upper 23 feet of the wall and 5 feet on center for the remaining portion of the wall below the 23 foot increment.

Fasten the C-Runners together with double 3/8″ screws at ends and 24″ o.c. Attach all H-Studs to adjacent framing with an aluminum breakaway clip. Clips attaching H-Studs and vertical C-Runners to adjacent wood framing on both sides require attachment to the H-Stud and C-Runner with one 3/8″ TYPE S Screw. Clips attaching H-Studs and vertical C-Runners to adjacent wood framing on only one side and with exterior exposure on the other side require attachment to the H-Stud and C-Runner with two 3/8″ TYPE S Screws. Attachment to the wood framing is with one 1-1/4″ Type W or TYPE S Screw. Locate horizontal C-Runner joint within 2′ of the intermediate floor. Install fire blocking between the solid wall system and adjacent framing at floor lines, bottom of truss line, and any other locations required by the applicable code. Note that for walls with exterior exposure on opposite side, the clips should be spaced maximum 4′ o.c. vertically.

Roof Continue erecting H-Studs and liner panels for succeeding stories as described. Cut the liner panels and H-Studs to roof pitch and length as necessary to follow the roof pitch. At roof, cap liner panels and H-Studs with C-Runner. Attach all H-Studs to adjacent framing with an aluminum breakaway clip. Clips attaching H-Studs and vertical C-Runners to adjacent wood framing on only one side and with exterior exposure on the other side require attachment to each vertical framing member with two 3/8″ TYPE S Screws.

Sound Attenuation Fire Blankets For direct attachment to 1″ liner panels, install blankets with joints staggered and attach blankets with seven staples driven through each blanket. Blanket installation within cavities is friction fit between stud framing.

Interior Finish Apply specified gypsum panels to wood studs and joists with screws or nails in conventional manner.

Cavity-Type Separation Wall

Cavity-Type Wall consists of steel C-H Studs and SHEETROCK Brand Gypsum Liner Panels set in steel runners and faced both sides with SHEETROCK Brand Gypsum Panels, Water-Resistant, Firecode C Core. Liner panels, 1″ thick, are erected vertically with ends set into 2-1/2″ USG C-Runners and edges inserted into specially formed 2-1/2″ USG Steel C-H Studs. C-runners are installed singly at top and bottom of wall and back-to-back between vertical liner panels on a line above each intermediate floor, the bottom chords of attic trusses, and at roof line. Aluminum clips, which attach the C-H Studs on both sides to adjacent wood framing, break away in the same fashion as with solid-type walls. To improve sound transmission loss, THERMAFIBER SAFB are inserted in the stud cavity and RC-1 Resilient Channels or equivalent may be used to isolate the face layer on the cavity side.

With aluminum angle clips attached on both sides of 212CH25 steel studs, the assemblies are suitable for spans (between clip angle supports) up to 10′ under 5 psf lateral load and up to 8′ as an exterior wall under 15 psf wind load without exceeding L/240 allowable deflection (see the specifications).

Components used in these systems are designed to permit temporary exposure to inclement weather during construction.

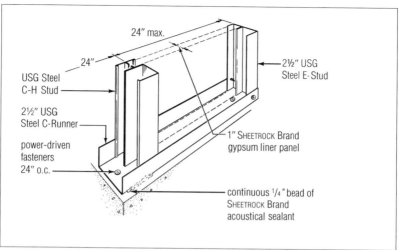

Foundation—cavity wall

Installation

Foundation Position 2-1/2″ C-Runner at floor and attach to foundation with power-driven fasteners at both ends and spaced 24″ o.c. When specified, caulk under runner at foundation with min. 1/4″ bead of SHEETROCK Brand Acoustical Sealant.

First Floor Install 1″ liner panels and steel studs to a convenient height (max. 2′) above floor line. Erect liner panels vertically in C-Runner with long edges in groove of C-H stud. Install C-H Studs between panels. Cap top of panels with horizontal C-runner, and cap ends of the wall with C-Runner. Fasten C-Runner flanges at all corners on both sides with two 3/8″ TYPE S Screws both sides.

Intermediate Floors and Bottom of Trusses Cap top of liner panels and C-H Studs with C-Runner and fasten C-H Studs to the C-Runner flanges on alternate sides with 3/8″ TYPE S Screws. Attach C-Runner for next row of panels to the C-Runner below with end joints staggered at least 12″ o.c. Fasten the C-Runners together with double 3/8″ screws at ends and 24″ o.c. Attach all C-H Studs to adjacent framing with an aluminum breakaway clip. Clips attaching C-H Studs to adjacent wood framing on both sides require attachment to the C-H Stud (not the resilient channel) with one 3/8″ TYPE S Screw. Clips attaching C-H Studs and vertical C-Runners to adjacent wood framing on only one side and with exterior exposure on the other side require attachment to the C-H Stud and C-Runner (not the resilient channel) with two 3/8″ TYPE S Screws. Attachment to the wood framing is with one 1-1/4″ Type W or TYPE S Screw. Locate horizontal C-Runner joint within 2′ of the intermediate floor. As required by the applicable code, install fire blocking in the wall cavity at floor lines, bottom-of-truss line, and any other required locations.

Roof Continue erecting C-H Studs and liner panels for succeeding stories as described. Cut the liner panels and C-H Studs to roof pitch and

10

length as necessary to follow the roof pitch. At roof, cap liner panels and C-H Studs with C-Runner. Attach all C-H Studs and vertical C-Runners to adjacent framing with an aluminum breakaway clip. Clips attaching C-H Studs and C-Runner to adjacent wood framing on only one side and with exterior exposure on the other side require attachment to the C-H Stud and vertical C-Runner (not the resilient channel) with two 3/8" Type S Screws.

Sound Attenuation Fire Blankets When specified, install blankets in cavity butting blankets closely and filling all voids.

Resilient Channels When specified, install RC-1 Resilient Channels or equivalent horizontally to face side of studs, 6" below ceiling joists and maximum 24" o.c. Attach channels to C-H Studs with 3/8" Type S Screws driven through holes in mounting flange. Extend channels to ends of runs and attach to C-Runners. Splice channel by nesting directly over stud; screw-attach through both flanges. Reinforce with screws at both ends of splice.

Gypsum Panels Apply 1/2" Sheetrock Brand Gypsum Panels, Water-Resistant, Firecode C Core, vertically to both sides of C-H Studs. Stagger joints on opposite partition sides. Fasten panels with 1" Type S Screws spaced 12" o.c. in field and along edges and runner flanges.

Resilient Single-layer Apply 1/2" Sheetrock Brand Gypsum Panels, Firecode C Core vertically to resilient channels and fasten with 1-1/4" Type S Screws placed 6" from C-H Studs and 12" o.c. Do not place screws directly over C-H Studs.

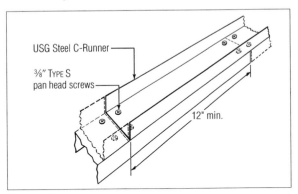

C-runner splice

Good Design Practices

Clip Attachment Both solid and cavity systems with adjacent wood framing on both sides require an aluminum breakaway clip to the wood framing on both sides of the H-Stud or the C-H Stud. Clips are attached to the H-Studs or C-H Studs and vertical C-Runners (not to the resilient channels) with one 3/8" Type S Screw, and to the wood framing with one 1-1/4" Type W or Type S Screw (3-hole leg of clip).

Both solid and cavity systems with exterior exposure and with adjacent wood framing on only one side require an aluminum breakaway clip on the side of the H-Stud or C-H Stud toward the wood framing. Clips are attached to each vertical framing member (not to the resilient channels) with two 3/8″ TYPE S Screws, and to the wood framing with one 1-1/4″ Type W or TYPE S Screw (3-hole leg of clip). Exterior exposure is limited to 15 psf wind load, and requires vertical clip spacing of 4′ o.c. maximum. For use with the solid system, these clips may be attached to adjacent wood framing. For the cavity system, supplementary framing may be required in order to install the clips at this reduced spacing.

Sound Control Construction For maximum sound control with both the solid and cavity wall systems, seal the entire perimeter and between the horizontal, back-to-back C-Runners at the intermediate levels with a minimum 1/4″ bead of SHEETROCK Brand Acoustical Sealant. Carefully seal around all gaps and cutouts for lights, cabinets, pipes, ducts, electrical boxes, etc. to minimize sound leakage. Back-to-back penetrations of the gypsum panel diaphragm and flanking paths should be eliminated.

Cavity Type Walls 1/2″ SHEETROCK Brand Gypsum Panels, FIRECODE C Core, may be used when partitions will not be exposed to moisture or inclement weather during construction. If weather exposure is expected, panels must be 1/2″ SHEETROCK Brand Gypsum Panels, FIRECODE C Core, Water-Resistant.

USG Shaft Walls

Cavity Shaft Walls

USG Cavity Shaft Walls are nonload-bearing, fire-resistant gypsum board partition systems for enclosing shafts, air ducts and stairwells. Designed for erection from one side, USG Shaft Walls offer superior performance and greater economy than other designs.

The engineered design of the strong, rigid USG C-H Stud system provides a simpler, thinner, lighter-weight assembly. It offers faster installation and lower material costs which reduce total in-place costs. It also saves on structural framing costs. For example, masonry shaft enclosures in high-rise buildings can weigh up to 45 psf, whereas lightweight USG Shaft Walls range from 9 psf (2-hour assembly) to 16 psf (3-hr. assembly).

10

USG Shaft Walls provide up to 4-hr. fire resistance and sound ratings to 51 STC. Designs are available for intermittent lateral loads up to 15 psf. For sustained pressure in air returns, design uniform pressure loads should not exceed 10 psf.

Maximum partition heights depend on expected pressures. For elevator shafts, the applied pressure load is selected by the designer based on elevator cab speed and the number of elevators per shaft. Instead of using only deflection criteria, USG design data considers several additional factors in determining limiting partition heights. These include:

Bending Stress the unit force that exceeds the stud strength.

End Reaction Shear determined by the amount of force applied to the stud (at the supports) that will bend or shear the J-Runner or cripple the stud.

Deflection the actual deflection under a load. Allowable deflection is based on the amount of bowing under load that a particular wall can accommodate without adversely affecting the wall finish.

A wide range of product and installation combinations is available to meet performance requirements: Intermittent air pressure loading of 5, 7-1/2, 10, 15 psf; vertical heights in three stud sizes and four steel thicknesses to accommodate lobbies and mechanical rooms. Assemblies can be constructed with fire-resistance ratings from 2-hr. to 4-hr. For more information, consult USG Technical Folder SA-926, *USG Cavity Shaft Wall Systems.*

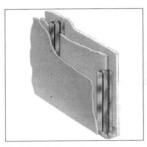

Single-layer both sides
(UL Designs U415 and U467)

Double-layer one side
(UL Designs U415 and U438)

Horizontal Shaft Walls

USG Cavity Shaft Walls installed horizontally provide economical construction for fire-resistive duct protection, corridor and other ceilings and stairway soffits. Also ideal for ceilings over office areas in pitched-roof buildings and in modular buildings where ceiling framing is independent of the floor above. With 1″ liner panels inserted into USG C-H Studs 24″ o.c. and triple–layer 1/2″ SHEETROCK Brand Gypsum Panels, FIRECODE C Core, screw attached to studs, the system provides greater spans and 2-hr. protection from fire either inside or outside the duct.

With double-layer 1/2″ SHEETROCK Brand Gypsum Panels, FIRECODE C Core, screw attached to studs, the assembly provides suitable 2-hr. fire-resistive ceiling construction for corridors and stairs. One-hour fire-rated construction is offered with single-layer 1/2″ SHEETROCK Brand Gypsum Panels, FIRECODE C Core.

Installation of Vertical Shaft Walls

Studs and Liner Panels Position USG J-Runners at the floor and ceiling with the the short leg toward the finish side of the wall. Securely attach the runners to the structural supports with power-driven fasteners at both ends and max. 24″ o.c. With steel-frame construction, install floor and ceiling runners and USG J-Runners or USG E-Studs on columns and beams before they are fireproofed. Remove spray fireproofing from the runners and the USG E-Studs before installing the gypsum line panels (2-hr. steel fireproofing). For other structural steel fireproofing requirements, use Z-shaped stand-off clips secured to the structural steel before the fireproofing application.

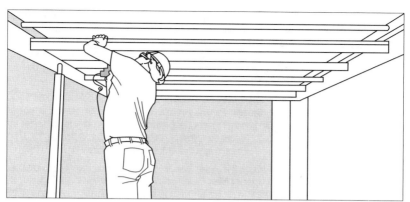

No other drywall shaft assembly provides such an economical horizontal application.

Cut the liner panels 1″ less than floor-to-ceiling height and erect vertically between USG J-Runners. Where the shaft walls exceed the maximum available panel height, position the liner panel end joints within the upper and lower third points of the wall. Stagger joints top and bottom in adjacent panels. Screw studs to runners on walls over 16′.

Use steel USG C-H Studs 3/8″ to not more than 1/2″ less than floor-to-ceiling height, and install them between liner panels with the liner inserted in the groove. Install full-length steel USG E-Studs or J-Runners vertically at T-intersections, corners, door jambs and columns. Install full-length USG E-Studs over gypsum liner panels on both sides of closure panels. For openings, frame them with vertical USG E-Studs or J-Runners at edges, horizontal USG J-Runners at head and sill, and reinforcing as specified. Suitably frame all openings to maintain structural support for the wall.

Install floor-to-ceiling steel USG E-Studs on each side of steel-hinged door frames and jamb struts on each side of elevator door frames to act as strut studs. Attach strut studs to floor and ceiling runners with two 3/8″ TYPE S-12 Pan-Head Screws. Attach strut studs to jamb anchors with 1/2″ TYPE S-12 Screws. Over steel door frames, install a cut-to-length section of USG J-Runner and attach it to the strut stud with 3/8″ TYPE S-12 Pan-Head Screws.

10

Gypsum Panel Attachment

For a single-layer one-side, one-hour wall, apply 5/8″ SHEETROCK Brand Gypsum Panels, FIRECODE Core, to the "C" side of the C-H studs. Position the gypsum panels vertically and fasten them to the studs and runners with 1″ TYPE S Screws 12″ o.c. (UL Design U415 or U469).

For a double-layer one side, two-hour wall, apply the base layer of 1/2″ SHEETROCK Brand Gypsum Panels, FIRECODE Core, or 5/8″ SHEETROCK Brand Gypsum Panels, FIRECODE Core, vertically or horizontally to the studs with 1″ TYPE S Screws 24″ o.c. along the edges and in the field of the panels. For vertical application, apply the face layer of 1/2″ SHEETROCK Brand Gypsum Panels, FIRECODE C Core, vertically and fasten it to the studs and J-runners with 1-5/8″ TYPE S Screws 12″ o.c. along the edges and in the field of the panels, staggered from the screws of the base layer. Joints between the base and face layers should be staggered. For horizontal applications, apply the face layer horizontally and attach it over the base layer with 1-5/8" Type S Screws 12" o.c. in the field, along the vertical edges and to the floor and ceiling runners. Attach the face layer to the base layer with 1-1/2" long Type G screws midway between the studs and 1" from the horizontal joint (UL Design U415 or U438).

For a single-layer both sides, two-hour wall, apply 1/2" Sheetrock Brand Gypsum Panels, Firecode C Core, or 5/8" Sheetrock Brand Gypsum Panels, Firecode Core, vertically or horizontally to both sides of the studs. Fasten the gypsum panels with 1" Type S Screws 12" o.c. along the vertical edges and in the field (UL Design U415 or U467).

For a single 3/4" layer one side, two-hour wall, apply 1" Sheetrock Brand Gypsum Liner Panels on one side, between 4" USG Steel C-H Studs, 24" o.c., install 3" Thermafiber SAFB in the cavity, and 3/4" Sheetrock Brand Gypsum Panels, Ultracode Core, on the other side. Position the panels vertically or horizontally, and fasten them to the studs and runners with 1-1/4" Type S Screws 8" o.c. (UL Design U415 or U492).

For a double-layer, two-hour wall, with Durock Brand Cement Board, install 1-1/2" Thermafiber SAFB in the stud cavity. Apply a base layer of 5/8" Sheetrock Brand Gypsum Panels, Firecode Core, vertically or horizontally, and attach with 1" Type S Screws 24" o.c. along the vertical edges and in the field of the panels. Install the face layer of 1/2" Durock Brand Cement Board by lamination to the gypsum panels with 4" wide strips of organic adhesive applied with a 3/4" notched trowel midway between the studs and fasten to the studs with 1-5/8" Durock Brand Screws 6" o.c. (UL Design U415 or U459).

For a double-layer, two-hour resilient wall, apply a base layer of 1/2" Sheetrock Brand Gypsum Panels, Firecode C Core, to resilient channels with end joints staggered; fasten with 1" Type S Screws 12" o.c. Apply face layer of 1/2" Sheetrock Brand Gypsum Panels, Firecode C Core, vertically with joints staggered; fasten to channels with 1-5/8" Type S Screws 12" o.c. (UL Design U415).

For triple-layer, three-hour wall, install three layers of 5/8" Sheetrock Brand Gypsum Panels, Firecode C Core, vertically or horizontally on corridor side of studs. Use 1" Type S self-drilling, self-tapping bugle-head screws, spaced 24"/16" o.c. (vertical/horizontal orientation) for the first layer; mid-layer 1-5/8" Type S Screws, spaced 24"/16" o.c. (vertical/horizontal orientation). Apply the third layer using 2-1/4" Type S Screws, spaced 16" (vertical board application) or 12" o.c. (horizontal board application). Finish joints with paper tape and joint compound (UL Design U415).

For horizontal shaft wall installation, two-hour assembly, install three layers of 1/2" Sheetrock Brand Gypsum Panels, Firecode C Core, to horizontally installed USG C-H and/or E-Studs. Install the base layer with the edges parallel to the studs and attached with 1" Type S Screws 24" o.c.; apply the middle layer in the same manner with joints offset 2' and attached with 1-5/8" Type S Screws 24" o.c.; and apply the face layer perpendicular to the studs and attached with 2-1/4" Type S Screws 12" o.c. Place the face-layer end joints between the studs and secure them with 1-1/2" Type G screws 8" o.c.

Vent Shaft

USG Vent Shaft System provides a 2-hr. fire-rated enclosure (UL Design U505 or U529) for vertical shafts in apartments and other types of multi-story buildings. The assembly is particularly suited for relatively small and widely separated mechanical, service and ventilator shafts. USG Shaft Walls are preferred where service and mechanical lines and equipment are consolidated within the building core.

Installation

Support Member Attachment Install 1″ X 2″ X 25-ga. galvanized steel angles as runners on floor and sidewalls by fastening through their short legs. Steel angles may be used as ceiling runners. Install side angle runners 30″ long and centered for attachment of horizontal bracing angles.

Bracing Angle Attachment (UL Design U505) Install 1″ X 2″ X 25-ga. galvanized steel bracing angles horizontally at quarter-points between the floor and ceiling and spaced max. 5′ o.c. Position the long leg vertically for board attachment and fasten to sidewall angles with 1″ TYPE S Screws.

Gypsum Panel and Liner Application Install 5/8″ SHEETROCK Brand Gypsum Panels, FIRECODE Core, or 1/2″ SHEETROCK Brand Gypsum Panels, FIRECODE C Core, vertically on the shaft side and fasten to angles and runners with 1″ TYPE S Screws 16 o.c. Apply SHEETROCK Brand Setting-Type (DURABOND) or SHEETROCK Brand Lightweight Setting-Type (EASY SAND) Joint Compound or SHEETROCK Brand Ready-Mixed Joint Compound—Taping or All Purpose on the back side of the liner panels and strip or sheet-laminate to the shaft-side board. Install a second set of floor and sidewall angle runners (and ceiling angles, if required) with their long legs against the liner panels. Attach the liner to the runners and angles with 2-1/4″ TYPE S Screws 12″ o.c. and at

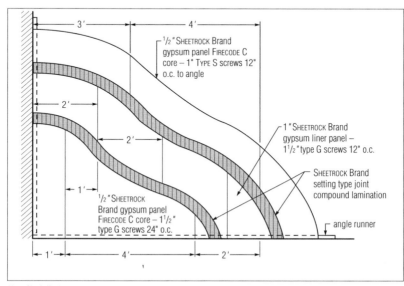

Vent Shaft Enclosure

10

least 6″ away from the liner edges. Laminate the floor-side face board to liner panels with joint compound and install vertically. Joints should be offset 12″ from one layer to the next and moderate pressure should be applied to ensure good adhesive bond. Fasten to the liner panels with 1-1/2″ Type G Screws. Drive the screws approx. 24″ from the ends of the board and 36″ o.c. along lines from vertical edges. Temporary bracing may be used instead of screws to maintain bond until adhesive is hard and dry. Caulk the perimeter with Sheetrock Brand Acoustical Sealant to prevent air infiltration. Complete the assembly with the appropriate drywall or veneer finish application.

Floor/Ceiling Assemblies

Wood Frame Floor/Ceilings

These designs, which are suitable for all types of wood-framed residential and commercial buildings, include those with single and double-layer gypsum board facings, and other assemblies with Thermafiber Sound Attenuation Blankets and resilient attachment.

Performance values of up to 2-hr. fire resistance, STC 60 and IIC 69 can be obtained as well as a nonfire-rated assembly with STC 57 and IIC 53.

Wood-frame—direct attachment.

Wood-frame—with resilient attachment and Thermafiber SAFB.

USG publishes data for more than 20 tests conducted on resilient wood-frame ceiling assemblies including the only 1-hr. residential gypsum board system for 48″ joist spacing. For complete listings, refer to Technical Folder SA924, *Drywall/Steel Framed Systems,* and the USG *Construction Selector* SA100.

Sound Control Floor/Ceilings

Several floor/ceiling systems have been developed to provide exceptional sound control as well as fire resistance in wood-framed assemblies. The systems require two layers of 5/8″ Sheetrock Brand Gypsum Panels, Firecode Core, applied over RC-1 Resilient Channels and 3″ batts of Thermafiber Sound Attenuation Fire Blankets (SAFB) installed within the cavity. More detailed information is provided in Technical Folder SA924, *Drywall/Steel Framed Systems*, or Technical Data Sheets WB1868 and WB1869.

Noncombustible Floor/Ceilings

Noncombustible ceilings with steel furring channels conceal and protect structural and mechanical elements above a lightweight fire-resistant layer of gypsum board. The furring channels, to which gypsum board is screw-attached, are wire-tied to bar joists, or wire-tied to suspended

1-1/2″ main runner channel grillage. Panels are also screw-attached below a direct suspension system (USG Drywall Suspension System). Plaster systems consisting of ROCKLATH Plaster Base or expanded metal lath may also be specified.

Furred Ceiling

Suspended Ceiling

For long-span suspension beneath large ducts or pipes, steel studs are substituted for furring channels. With foil-back gypsum board, the ceiling is effective as a vapor retarder. Also, the board provides a firm base for adhesively applied acoustical tile.

Performance values of up to 3-hr. fire resistance (3-hr. beam) and STC 43 and IIC 60 have been obtained on certain specified systems.

Beam and Column Fire Protection

Beam Fire Protection

Beam fire protection consists of double or triple layers of 5/8″ gypsum board (FIRECODE Core and FIRECODE C Core) screw-attached to framework of steel runners and metal angles. These are lightweight, easily and economically installed assemblies that provide 2-hr. and 3-hr. beam protection.

Installation

Framing System Install ceiling runners parallel to and at least 1/2″ away from the beam. Position metal angles with 1-3/8″ leg vertical. Fasten ceiling runners to steel floor units with 1/2″ TYPE S-12 Pan Head Screws spaced 12″ o.c.

Fabricate channel brackets from 1-5/8″ steel runners; space brackets to provide the clearance shown in the specific design selected (see illustrations on pages 346-347). When steel runners are used for corner runners, cope or cut away legs of the runner used for brackets to allow insertion of the corner runner. When metal angles are used for corner runners, slit the channel bracket runner legs and bend the runner to a right angle. Install channel brackets 24″ o.c. along the length of the beam and fasten them to ceiling runner with 1/2″ TYPE S-12 Pan Head Screws.

Install lower corner runners parallel to the beam. Set steel runner corner runners in coped channel brackets. Apply metal angles to the outside of the channel brackets with the 7/8″ leg vertical, and fasten with 1/2″ TYPE S-12 Pan Head Screws.

Gypsum Board For 2-hr. assemblies, apply the vertical base-layer board and attach it to the ceiling and corner runners with 1-1/4″ TYPE S Screws spaced 16″ o.c. Install the base layer to the beam soffit

10

overlapping vertical side panels and fasten with 1-1/4" Type S Screws 16" o.c. Apply face-layer boards so the soffit board supports the vertical side boards. Fasten the face layer to runners with 1-7/8" Type S Screws spaced 8" o.c.

For 3-hr. assemblies, apply base-layer boards and attach them to ceiling and corner runners with 1" Type S Screws spaced 16" o.c. Apply the middle layer over the base layer and attach it to the brackets and runners with 1-5/8" Type S Screws spaced 16" o.c. Install hexagonal mesh over the middle layer at the beam soffit. Extend the mesh 1-1/2" up the sides of the beam and hold it in place with the 1-5/8" screws used to attach middle layer. Apply the face layer over the middle layer and wire mesh, and fasten it to brackets and runners with 2-1/4" Type S Screws spaced 8" o.c. Apply all layers so soffit panels support vertical side boards.

Finishing Construction Apply corner bead to bottom outside corners of face layers and finish with joint treatment as directed in Chapter 5 or with veneer plaster finish described in Chapter 6.

UL Design N501 (beam only)

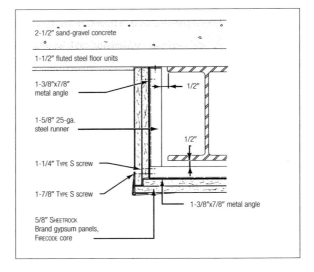

2-1/2" sand-gravel concrete

1-1/2" fluted steel floor units

1-3/8"x7/8" metal angle — 1/2"

1-5/8" 25-ga. steel runner

1/2"

1-1/4" Type S screw

1-7/8" Type S screw

1-3/8"x7/8" metal angle

5/8" Sheetrock Brand gypsum panels, Firecode core

*UL Design N505
(beam only)*

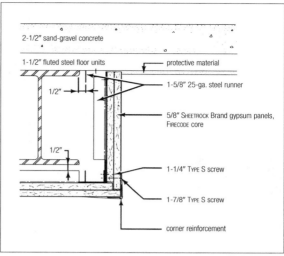

*UL Design N502
(beam only)*

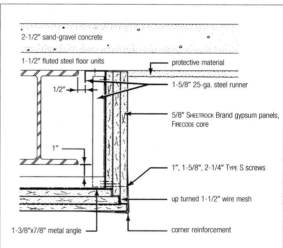

10

Column Fireproofing—
UL Design N514

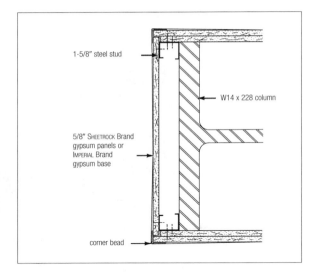

1-5/8" steel stud

W14 x 228 column

5/8" SHEETROCK Brand
gypsum panels or
IMPERIAL Brand
gypsum base

corner bead

Column Fire Protection

Steel column fire protection with lightweight and compact gypsum board enclosures offers fire ratings of 2, 3 or 4 hours depending upon construction. The board is held in place by a combination of wire, screws and steel studs. All attachments are mechanical; there's no waiting for adhesives to dry. See USG Technical Folders SA-920, *Plaster Systems*, and SA-923, *Drywall/Steel Framed Systems*, for more detailed information.

Curtain Walls & Penetration Fire-Stop Systems

Curtain Walls

Exterior curtain walls are nonaxial-load-bearing exterior walls. Steel studs used for curtain wall applications are modified channel types roll-formed from five thicknesses of steel. The same studs can provide wall framing for both drywall and veneer plaster systems. Exterior surfaces can be brick veneer, portland cement-lime stucco, decorative panels or siding materials. Also, USG Exterior Systems are available with stucco-look texture finishes over cement board, stucco or EIFS-type surfaces.

A wide selection of stud sizes and spacings has been identified to accommodate wind loads to 40 psf, wall heights to 32' at 15 psf, and a variety of building modules. For load and installation data on curtain walls, refer to USG Technical Folder SA923, *Drywall/Steel Framed Systems*. For curtain wall applications with DUROCK Brand Exterior Cement Board, see Technical Folder SA700, *Exterior Systems.*

INSULSCREEN 2100
Water-Managed EIFS

Masonry Exterior

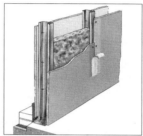

Gypsum Drywall Interior

Veneer Plaster Interior

Penetration Fire Stops

USG Fire Stop Systems for Floor and Wall Penetrations

Fire can pass from floor to floor or into adjacent spaces through over-sized floor or wall penetrations, including poke-through openings required for plumbing, telecommunication lines or other utility service.

USG Fire Stop Systems for Floor and Wall Penetrations employ FIRECODE Compound for a fire stop system to block smoke and flame from passing through openings in concrete floors and gypsum panel walls. Several different UL-classified through-penetration systems are available. Description of these systems may be found in Technical Folder SA727, *USG Fire Stop Systems*. These systems are classified in accordance with the standards ASTM E814 and UL 1479.

Installation When its use is called for, cut THERMAFIBER Safing insulation with a serrated knife slightly wider than the opening. Compress and tightly fit insulation with nominal density of 4.0 pcf completely around the penetrant. Note that the insulation thickness varies from system to system. Mix FIRECODE Compound according to the directions on the container. Using a trowel, putty knife or spatula, scoop the compound from its container and work it into the penetration opening. Apply compound to the thickness called for in fire-rated assembly on top of the safing insulation.

10

THERMAFIBER Fire/Smoke Stop System for Penetrations

Friction fit THERMAFIBER Safing Insulation to fill voids. Apply a layer of THERMAFIBER SMOKE SEAL Compound on top for floor penetration. Sandwich insulation between compound on both sides for wall penetrations. UL-Classified System Nos. CAJ-1020 and WL-1064. Insulation may be 2-1/2" or 3-1/2" thick and compound 1" or 2" thick, depending on test.

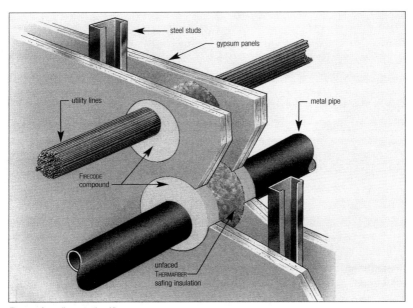

Fire stop for wall penetration, UL System No. W-L-1027 (metal pipe) and W-L-3023 (utility lines)

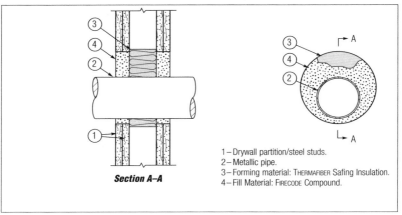

1 – Drywall partition/steel studs.
2 – Metallic pipe.
3 – Forming material: THERMAFIBER Safing Insulation.
4 – Fill Material: FIRECODE Compound.

Section A–A

Wall assembly—UL System No. W-L-1027 (metal pipe); F Rating—2 hr., T Rating—0 hr.

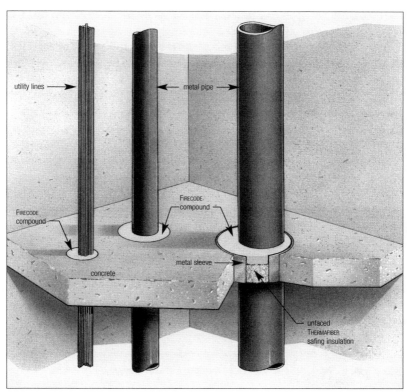

*Fire stop for floor
penetration, UL System Nos.
C-AJ-1081 and C-AJ-3045*

Head-of-Wall Construction Joints

10

Construction joints, where two fire-rated assemblies intersect, are evaluated under UL Standard 2079 for their ability to resist flame & temperature transmission as well as the hose stream, where required. Head-of-wall construction joints are intersections of wall to floor/ceiling or roof/ceiling. Other construction joints include wall to wall (expansion joint application), floor to floor (building joint application), or floor to wall.

Test parameters for head-of-wall assemblies are similar to those established for through-penetration fire stops, above. Systems may be tested and prescribed for either static (no floor or roof movement) or dynamic (to accommodate live load deflection) conditions.

Head-of-wall construction joints have common features, including: a) fire-rated assemblies for both the wall and floor/ceiling or roof/ceiling, b) a joint treatment system consisting of a forming material such as mineral fiber safing insulation to pack into openings, and a fill material such as FIRECODE Compound to seal all openings and passages.

Restraining angles also may be required to achieve the necessary flame and temperature barriers.

USG has had several head-of-wall assemblies tested under standard UL-2079. The illustration shows a head-of-wall assembly for a dynamic construction joint.

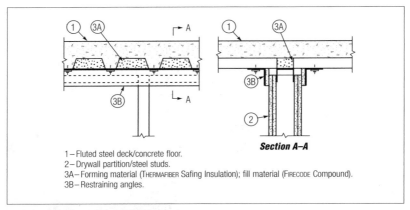

Section A–A

1 – Fluted steel deck/concrete floor.
2 – Drywall partition/steel studs.
3A – Forming material (THERMAFIBER Safing Insulation); fill material (FIRECODE Compound).
3B – Restraining angles.

*Head-of-wall joint treatment system for fluted steel
deck/concrete floor or roof/ ceiling and gypsum wallboard wall
assembly—UL System HW-D-0002.*

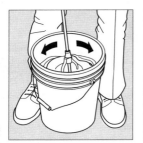

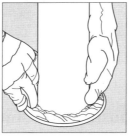

*FIRECODE Compound mixes easily
with water (or activator) at the
jobsite. There's less waste than with
caulking tube products.*

*When required by the specific
system, THERMAFIBER Safing Insulation,
the forming material, is fit snugly
into the penetration.*

*FIRECODE Compound is troweled into
the penetration to block particulate,
fire, sound, smoke and air movement
through the floor or wall.*

Air, Water and Vapor Control

**Air and Water
Infiltration**

Flashing and sealants as shown in construction documents and as selected by the architect and/or structural engineer should be provided to resist air and water infiltration. The flashing and sealants selected shall be installed in a workmanlike manner in appropriate locations to maintain continuity of air/water barriers, particularly at windows, doors and other penetrations of exterior wall.

All gypsum sheathing must be covered with No. 15 asphalt felt or an approved water and infiltration barrier to ensure water-tight construction. Asphalt felt should be applied horizontally with 2" overlap and attached to sheathing. Sheet barriers should be stapled to the sheathing according to manufacturer's directions. Accessories for stucco finishes should be made of zinc alloy with weep holes 12" o.c.

Vapor Retarders and Air Barriers

Proper use and placement of vapor retarders are important factors in modern, energy-efficient construction. Improper placement of a vapor retarder could produce condensation in exterior wall stud cavities and cause deterioration of the structure.

In cold climates, a vapor retarder is required on the warm interior side of the wall to restrict moisture from the warmer, humid air inside the building from penetrating through wall surfaces and causing condensation on colder surfaces within the cavity.

In climates where high temperature and humidity conditions are sustained, placement of a vapor retarder may be recommended on the exterior side. In any case, location and placement of vapor retarders should be determined by a qualified mechanical engineer.

Two vapor retarders in a single wall can trap water vapor between them and create moisture-related problems in core materials.

When a polyethylene vapor retarder film is installed on ceilings behind gypsum panels under cold conditions, it is recommended that ceiling insulation (batts or blankets) be installed before the board. If loose fill insulation is to be used above the ceiling, it must be installed immediately after the ceiling board is installed during periods of cold weather. Also the plenum or attic space should be properly vented. Failure to follow this procedure can result in moisture condensation behind the gypsum panels, causing board sag.

Note: Although nearly all vapor retarders are also air barriers, not all air barriers are vapor retarders. Standard SHEETROCK Brand Gypsum Panels, DUROCK Brand Cement Board, SHEETROCK Brand Gypsum Sheathing, No. 15 felt and industry building wrap and other common construction materials serve as air barriers, but not as vapor retarders.

10

Ceiling Sag Precautions

Water-based textures, interior finishing materials and high ambient humidity conditions can produce sag in gypsum ceiling panels if adequate vapor and moisture control is not provided. The following precautions must be observed to minimize sagging of ceiling panels:

1. Where vapor retarder is required in cold weather conditions, the temperature of the gypsum ceiling panels and vapor retarder must remain above the interior air dew-point temperature during and after the installation of panels and finishing materials.

2. The interior space must be adequately ventilated and air circulation must be provided to remove water vapor from the structure.

Most sag problems are caused by condensation of water within the gypsum panel. The placement of vapor retarders, climate, insulation levels and ventilation requirements will vary by location and climate, and should be reviewed by a qualified engineer if in question.

**Good Design
Practices**

A common error in buildings with suspended ceilings is to neglect treatment of drywall surfaces within the ceiling plenum on exterior walls. Since the plenum is not visible, care should be taken to make sure that this area is not overlooked. The drywall application and joint treatment should be carried all the way to the spandrel beam or floor structure above. Exterior ceilings and soffits are other areas that may be forgotten. Ceilings, soffits and cutouts for pipe, conduit, knee braces and vent penetrations should be carefully treated to avoid compromising the effectiveness of the vapor retarder and/or air barrier.

Penetrations in the exterior wall for windows, doors, outlets, HVAC and other fixtures or devices must be closed tight with sealant or tape.

Control joints should be carefully flashed and/or sealed to prevent water infiltration. Also, particular care should be taken to assure the integrity of the envelope for airtightness, vapor diffusion and thermal resistance, particularly at intersections and hidden penetrations. Details for floor/wall and roof/wall connections are the most difficult and important design challenges.

Planning, Execution & Inspection

Factors Affecting Results

Today's proven-quality products and high-performance systems permit installation of attractive, durable, trouble-free interiors that meet designers' specifications and owners needs. By using correct installation procedures and equipment, contractors can combine these products into systems with high quality results, thus reducing customer dissatisfaction, poor productivity, callbacks and decreased profitability.

This chapter identifies product, system, environmental, handling and storage, equipment, installation, workmanship and inspection factors that can affect the end results of a project.

Selection of Materials

In recent years, technological advances in building construction have resulted in new products and systems. Each requires systematic evaluation of performance and appearance characteristics in relation to cost, before selection and use. Evaluation may be done through benefit-cost analysis or life-cycle cost analysis, which considers the total cost of an assembly throughout its useful life. Building materials selection should always be based on total performance, including maintenance, not simply on initial construction cost or a budgeted cost figure. The following items merit consideration in systematically selecting products and systems for gypsum construction.

Satisfy User Needs

To satisfy the owner's functional requirements, it is basic to match products and systems to the end performance desired. For instance, such high-traffic areas as corridors may require hard-wearing, abuse-resistant surfaces available with specially designed products. Where quiet surroundings or isolation from noise is needed, systems with high resistance to sound transmission and surfaces that provide sound absorption are essential. Predecorated, low-maintenance surfaces may be justified in the form of vinyl-faced gypsum panels. In common walls between apartments, where greater cavity widths are needed to enclose plumbing lines, a system with adequate space in the cavity is called for. The objective is always to select products and systems that will improve the total performance of the building components.

Meet Regulatory Requirements

The performance of gypsum construction products and systems must comply with regulatory requirements established by local, state and federal agencies. Local and state building codes and insurance and lending agency requirements should be considered in material selection.

Identify Critical Performance

Any selection of appropriate materials should reflect product or system limitations. Such structural factors as limiting height and span, required number of screws, metal thickness, bracing spacing or maximum frame and fastener spacing should be carefully considered since they affect the flexural properties and strength of an assembly. Yield strength of all steel is not the same. Substitution by size alone is not recommended. System performance following any substitution of material or compromise in assembly design cannot be certified and may result in failure under critical conditions. It is important to note that extreme and continuous high humidity or temperatures may result in sag, joint deformation, poor appearance and possible deterioration of gypsum surface materials. Sealing and painting recommendations are important for proper performance of paints and other finishes.

Establish Performance Requirements

Fire Resistance Select ASTM E-119 fire-tested assemblies to comply with regulatory requirements, and construct the assembly according to specifications. If an assembly does not comply, work may be halted by the building inspector or installation may be rejected after completion.

Sound Control Owner's needs and regulatory requirements dictate the sound control needed. Many assemblies are available to meet requirements. Sound test data is obtained under ideal laboratory conditions per ASTM procedures, except as noted. For assemblies to approach testing performance, strict attention must be given to construction details, such as acoustical sealant, and installation. The isolation expected from an assembly can be negated by penetrations, perimeter leaks, accidental coupling of decoupled elements, incompatible surrounding structures and other faulty installation practices. The isolation may also be compromised by flanking sound, e.g., structure-borne sound carried via continuous concrete floors and other building elements, bypassing the sound rated assembly.

Structural Strength and Stability Select systems that provide adequate strength and acceptable deflection under live and dead loads as described in published USG performance tables. Shear or torque loads caused by shelving, sanitary basins, light fixtures and other accessories should also be considered. Shear forces from wind or earthquake may also require consideration. Cracking probably will occur in assemblies of sufficient strength or stiffness if adequate reinforcing is not provided.

Water and Moisture Choose products and systems that offer adequate resistance to water and high-moisture conditions. Gypsum wallboard products are not suitable under conditions of extreme and sustained moisture. Durock Cement Board is recommended as a substrate for ceramic tile under these conditions. Products manufactured from steel or other materials subject to corrosion must have a protective coating equal to the service conditions envisioned.

Humidity and Temperature Determine the environmental conditions to be expected during construction and use. Select products that offer high performance under these conditions or control the job environment. Plaster products should be installed at uniform temperatures above 55°F for 48 hours prior to and until 48 hours after the plaster application. These products may gradually deteriorate under sustained temperatures over 125°F. High humidity and temperatures may cause problems with veneer plaster finishes, gypsum plasters and gypsum board products.

11

Durability High-strength gypsum plaster, veneer plaster products and abuse-resistant drywall and gypsum fiber products offer high compressive strength and surface hardness to resist damage from impact and abrasion. For long-lasting, problem-free interiors, select products to meet functional needs.

Appearance Color, texture and surface gloss affect the final appearance of interior surfaces. Texture finishes offer a wide variety of effects for distinctive appearance. Glossy finishes highlight surface defects; textures hide minor imperfections.

Cleanability and Maintenance Select products according to functional requirements for washability and resistance to fading, staining and scuffing. Predecorated SHEETROCK Brand Vinyl-Faced Gypsum Panels offer a tough, stain-resistant vinyl surface easily cleaned with soap and water. Aggregated ceiling texture finishes cannot be washed but can be painted when redecoration is needed.

Light Reflection Select colors and finishes to meet appearance standards, illumination levels and other functional requirements. Strong side-lighting from windows or surface-mounted light fixtures may reveal even minor surface imperfections. The light strikes the surface obliquely, at a very slight angle, and greatly exaggerates surface irregularities. These conditions, which demand precise installation, increase chances for callbacks and should be avoided. If critical lighting cannot be changed, the effects can be minimized by skim coating the gypsum panels, applying SHEETROCK Brand First Coat primer, finishing the surface with texture finish or installing draperies and blinds, which soften shadows. As a preventive, use strong parallel-to-the-surface job lights to ensure a flat acceptable joint compound finish prior to priming, texturing and/or painting.

Interface and Compatibility Materials that come into contact with each other must be compatible. Differences in thermal or hygrometric expansion, strength of substrates or basecoats in relation to finish coats, thermal conductivity and galvanic action are common problem-causing situations. Tables of thermal and hygrometric coefficients for selected products are in the Appendix. The subject is too complex to be covered in detail here. Contact specific manufacturers for recommendations should questions arise. Following are some precautions of this kind associated with gypsum construction:

1. Gypsum surfaces should be isolated with control joints or other means where necessary to abut other materials, isolate structural movements, changes in shape and gross area limits.

2. Plaster may be applied directly to concrete block, however, with plaster over poured-in-place concrete, a bonding agent such as USG Plaster Bonder must be used.

3. Due to expansion differences, the application of high-pressure plastic laminates to gypsum panels or plaster generally is not satisfactory.

4. IMPERIAL Brand Gypsum Base and regular SHEETROCK Brand Gypsum Panels do not provide sufficient moisture resistance as a base for adhesive application of ceramic tile in wet areas. Use SHEETROCK Brand Gypsum Panels, Water-Resistant, FIBEROCK Brand Panels—Water-Resistant or DUROCK Cement Board.

5. Install resilient thermal gaskets around metal window frames to keep condensation from damaging wall surface materials. The gasket may also reduce galvanic action and resultant corrosion, which occurs when two dissimilar metals contact in the presence of moisture.

Vapor Control The use and proper placement of vapor retarders is extremely important in modern construction, with its increased use of thermal insulation brought about by the need for energy conservation.

Inattention to proper placement or omission of a vapor retarder may result in condensation in the exterior wall stud cavities. Cold climates typically call for a vapor retarder on the warm interior side of the wall. A vapor retarder may be required on the outside of the exterior wall for air conditioned buildings in climates having sustained high outside temperatures and humidity. A qualified mechanical engineer should determine location of the vapor retarder. Refer to local building codes for requirements or considerations in your project area.

Two vapor retarders on opposite sides of a single wall can trap water vapor between them and create moisture-related problems in the cavity materials.

When a polyethylene vapor retarder film is installed on ceilings behind gypsum panels under cold conditions, it is recommended that ceiling insulation be installed before the board or immediately after the board is installed (if the insulation is blown in). Also the plenum or attic space should be properly vented. Failure to follow this procedure can result in moisture condensation in the back side of the gypsum panels causing board sag.

Handling and Storage

Even quality products can contribute to problems during application and job failures if not protected from damage and improper handling. Generally, gypsum products should be stored inside at temperatures above freezing, protected from moisture and external damage and used promptly after delivery.

Inspect on Delivery

Products should be inspected for proper quantity and possible damage when delivered on the job. Incorrect quantities may result in job delays due to shortages or extra cost for overages that are wasted. Check products for such physical damage as broken corners or scuffed edges on gypsum board, wet board, bent or corroded steel studs and runners. Inspect containers for evidence of damage that may affect the contents. Look for damaged or torn bags, which could result in waste, lumpy joint compound, preset conventional plaster or veneer plaster finishes. Report any damaged material or shortages immediately.

11

Store in Enclosed Shelter

Enclosed protection from the weather is required for the storage of all gypsum products. Though not recommended, outdoor storage for up to one month is permissible if products are stored above ground and completely covered. Do not store gypsum products on gypsum risers. Use wood risers to prevent moisture from wicking up and wetting material. Various problems can result when these products get wet or are exposed to direct sunlight for extended periods.

Store gypsum boards flat on a clean, dry floor to prevent permanent sag, damaged or wavy edges or deformed board. Do not store board vertically. If board is stored on risers, the risers should be evenly spaced, no more than 28″ apart and within 2″ of the ends of the board.

The risers should also be placed directly under each other vertically.

Stack bagged goods and metal components off of damp floors and walls. Corrosion on corner bead, trim and fasteners may bleed through finishing materials. Ready-mixed joint compounds that have been frozen and thawed repeatedly lose strength, which may weaken the bond.

Protect From Damage

Locate stored stocks of gypsum products away from heavy-traffic areas to prevent damage from other trades. Keep materials in their packages or containers until ready for use, to protect them from dirt, corrosion and distortion. Damaged board edges are more susceptible to ridging after joint treatment. Boards with rough ends will require remedial action before installation, otherwise, deformation or blistering may occur at end joints.

Use Fresh Material

If possible, gypsum construction products should be ordered for delivery to the job just before application. Materials may become damaged by abuse if stored for long periods. To minimize performance problems caused by variable moisture conditions and aging, fresh plaster and veneer plaster finishes should be received on the job frequently.

Job Conditions

Many problems can be directly traced to unfavorable job conditions. These problems may occur during product application or they may not appear until long after job completion.

Recommendations for proper job conditions, given in the appropriate product application chapters here, should be closely followed. If job conditions are unfavorable, correct them before product installation. The following environmental factors can present problems in gypsum construction.

Temperature

Temperature can have a dramatic effect on the performance of gypsum products. Install gypsum products, joint compounds and textures at comfortable working temperatures above 50°F. In cold weather, provide controlled, well-distributed heat to keep the temperature above minimum levels. For example, if gypsum board is installed at a temperature of 28°F, it expands at the rate of 1/2″ for every 100 lin. ft. when the temperature rises to 72°F. At lower temperatures, the working properties and performance of plasters, veneer plaster finishes, joint compounds and textures are seriously affected. They suffer loss of strength and bond if frozen after application and may have to be replaced. Ready-mixed compounds deteriorate from repeated freeze-thaw cycles, lose their workability and may not be usable. Avoid sudden changes in temperature, which may cause cracking from thermal shock.

Humidity

High humidity resulting from atmospheric conditions or from on the job use of such wet materials as concrete, stucco, plaster and spray fireproofing often creates situations for possible problems. In certain kinds of gypsum board, water vapor is absorbed, which softens the gypsum core and expands the paper. As a result, the board may sag between ceiling supports. Sustained high humidity increases chances for galvanized steel components to rust, especially in marine areas where salt air is present. High humidity can cause insufficient drying between coats of joint compounds, which can lead to delayed shrinkage and/or bond failure. Jobs may be delayed because extra time for drying is required between coats of joint compound.

Low humidity speeds drying, especially when combined with high temperatures and air circulation. These conditions may cause dryouts in veneer plaster finishes and conventional plasters. They also reduce working time and may result in edge cracking of the joint treatment. Crusting and possible contamination of fresh compound, check and edge cracking are also caused by hot and dry conditions. Under hot, dry conditions, handle gypsum board carefully to prevent cracking or core damage during erection.

Moisture

Wind-blown rain and standing water on floors increases the humidity in a structure and may cause the problems previously described. Water-soaked gypsum board and plasters have less structural strength and may sag and deform. Their surfaces, when damp, are extremely vulnerable to scuffing, damage and mildew. Note that conventional drywall products should not be used in areas that have high humidity or the presence of moisture. SHEETROCK Brand Gypsum Panels, Water-Resistant, may be used in areas where occasional moisture or humidity are present. These panels are not intended for use in areas subject to constant moisture, such as interior swimming pools, gang showers and commercial food processing areas. DUROCK Brand Cement Board is recommended for these uses.

Ventilation

Ventilation should be provided to remove excess moisture, permit proper drying of conventional gypsum plasters and joint compounds and prevent problems associated with high-humidity conditions. For veneer plaster finishes, to prevent rapid drying and possible shrinkage, poor bond, chalky surfaces and cracking, air circulation should be kept at a minimum level until the finish is set. Rapid drying also creates problems with joint compounds, gypsum plasters and finishes when they dry out before setting fully and, as a result, don't develop full strength.

Sunlight

Strong sunlight for extended periods will discolor gypsum panel face paper and make decoration difficult. The blue face paper on veneer gypsum base will fade to gray or tan from excessive exposure to sunlight or ultraviolet radiation. Applying finishes containing alkali (lime) to this degraded base may result in bond failure unless the base is treated with an alum solution or bonding agent. Additional information on dealing with this problem is presented on page 392 and in PM4, *Sun-Faded IMPERIAL Brand Gypsum Base,* from USG.

11

Movement in Structures

Modern structural design uses lighter but stronger materials capable of spanning greater distances and extending buildings higher than ever before. While meeting current standards of building design, these frames are more flexible and offer less resistance to structural movement. This flexibility and resulting structural movement can produce stresses within the usually non load-bearing gypsum assemblies. Unless perimeter relief joints are provided to isolate these building movements, when accumulated stresses exceed the strength of the materials in the assembly, they will seek relief by cracking, buckling or crushing the finished surface.

Structural movement and most cracking problems are caused by deflection under load, physical change in materials due to temperature and humidity changes, seismic forces or a combination of these factors.

Concrete Floor Slab Deflection

Dead and live loads cause deflection in the floor slab. If this deflection is excessive, cracks can occur in partitions at the midpoint between supports. If partition installation is delayed for about two months after slabs are completed, perhaps two-thirds of the ultimate creep deflection will have taken place, reducing chances of partition cracking. This is usually a one-time non-cyclical movement.

Wind and Seismic Forces

Wind and seismic forces cause a cyclical shearing action on the building framework, which distorts the rectangular shape to an angled parallelogram. This distortion, called racking, can result in cracking and crushing of partitions adjacent to columns, floors and structural ceilings.

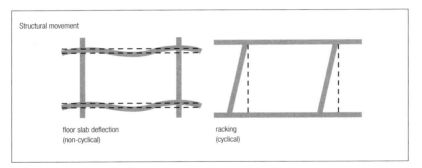

Structural movement

floor slab deflection
(non-cyclical)

racking
(cyclical)

To resist this racking, building frames must be stiffened with shear walls and/or crossbracing. Light steel-frame buildings are diagonally braced with steel strapping. Wood-frame structures are strengthened with let-in crossbracing and/or shear diaphragms of structural sheathing. On larger buildings, racking is resisted by shear walls and windbracing without considering the strength added by finishing materials. Moreover, the partitions must be isolated from the structure to prevent cracking caused by racking movement and distortion.

Thermal Expansion

All materials expand with an increase in temperature and contract with a decrease. In tall concrete or steel-frame buildings, thermal expansion and contraction may cause cracking problems resulting from racking when exterior columns and beams are exposed or partially exposed to exterior temperatures. Since interior columns remain at a uniform temperature, they do not change in length.

Exposed exterior columns can be subjected to temperatures ranging from over 100° to -30°F, and therefore will elongate or contract in length. The

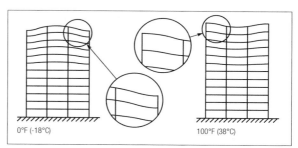

0°F (-18°C)   100°F (38°C)

amount of expansion or contraction of the exposed columns depends on the temperature difference and several other factors. (Structural movement caused by thermal differentials accumulates to the upper floors.) However, the stiffness of the structure resists the movement and usually full unrestrained expansion is not reached. A gypsum board wall 100′ long will expand 0.54″ when the temperature rises 50°F.

Racking, resulting from thermal movement, is greatest in the outside bays of upper floors in winter when temperature differentials are largest. To prevent major changes as described above, apply proper insulation to exterior structural members. The design should call for control joints to relieve stress and minimize cracking of surfaces.

Hygrometric Expansion

Many building materials absorb moisture from the surrounding air during periods of high humidity and expand; they contract during periods of low humidity. Gypsum, wood and paper products are more readily affected by hygrometric changes than are steel and reinforced concrete. Gypsum boards will expand about 1/2″ per 100′ with a relative humidity change from 13% RH to 90% RH (see Appendix for coefficients). Unless control joints are provided, hygrometric changes create stresses within the assembly, which result in bowed or wavy walls, sag between supports in ceilings, cracking and other problems.

Relief Joints

Select gypsum assemblies to provide the best structural characteristics to resist stresses imposed on them. As described previously, these systems must resist internal stresses created by expansion and contraction of the components and external stresses caused by movement of the structure. The alternative solution is to provide control and relief joints to eliminate stress buildup and still maintain structural integrity of the assembly.

11

To control external stresses, partitions and other gypsum construction must be relieved from the structural framework, particularly at columns, ceilings and intersections with dissimilar materials. In long partition runs and large ceiling areas, control joints are recommended to relieve internal stress buildup. Methods for providing relief and control joints are shown in Chapters 3, 4, 5, 6 and 8. These recommendations, for normal situations, provide for 1/4″ relief. Relief joints for individual structures should be checked for adequacy by the design engineer to prevent cracking and other deformations.

Cracking in High-Rise Structures

Contractors who install commercial partitions and ceilings should be aware of cracking problems caused by structural movement, deflection, expansion and contraction. These problems, described previously, usually are not due to faulty materials. Anticipated structural movement in the frame and floor system should be taken into account in the design of the building. It is better to solve potential problems with preventive measures before installation rather than attempting repairs afterward.

Some types of construction can be expected to cause cracking in gypsum assemblies if not handled properly. Following are clues to potential problems:

Flat Plate Design Particularly with column bay sizes exceeding 20′.

Exposed Exterior Columns and Shear Walls On buildings over 12 floors high and located in a cold climate.

Reinforced Concrete Structures Erected in cold weather, with partitions installed too soon thereafter. Creep deflection in the floor slab, a cause of partition cracking, is retarded in cold weather and accelerated in warm weather.

Structures Without Shear Walls or Proper Bracing Particularly if the plan is long and narrow, presenting a large wall area to withstand wind load.

Gypsum Systems Without Expansion Joints Long partition runs and large ceiling areas must have control joints to compensate for hygrometric and thermal expansion and contraction. Placement of control joints must be noted in the architectural or design plans.

When one or more of these conditions exists, it is wise to notify the owner, architect and general contractor, by letter, of the indicated possible problems and recommend corrective measures. If corrective measures are effective, all involved will be rewarded with a satisfactory performance, and costly complaints will be avoided.

Structurally Generated Noise

Loads of varying intensity can cause structural movement, which generates noise when two materials rub or work against each other. In high-rise buildings, variable wind pressure can cause a whole structure to drift or sway, causing structural deformation. Such deformation imparts racking stresses to the non-load bearing partition and can create noise.

As another annoyance, lumber shrinkage often results in subfloors and stair treads squeaking under foot traffic. This squeaking can be avoided by using adhesive to provide a tight bond between components and prevent adjacent surfaces from rubbing together.

Acoustical performance values (STC, NRC, CAC, IIC) are based on laboratory conditions. Such field conditions as lack of sealants, outlet boxes, back-to-back boxes, medicine cabinets, flanking paths, doors, windows and structure borne sound can diminish acoustical performance values. These individual conditions usually require the assessment of an acoustical engineer.

USG assumes no responsibility for the prevention, cause or repair of these job-related noises.

Lumber Shrinkage

In wood-frame construction, one of the most expensive problems encountered is fastener pops, often caused by lumber shrinkage, in drywall surfaces. Shrinkage occurs as lumber dries. Even kiln-dried lumber can shrink, warp, bow and twist, causing board to loosen and fasteners to fail. Gypsum surfaces can also crack, buckle or develop joint deformations when attached across the wide dimension of large wood framing members such as joists. Typically, this installation occurs in stairwells and high wall surfaces where the gypsum finish passes over mid-height floor framing, as in split-level houses.

Framing lumber, as commonly used, has a moisture content of 15% to 19%. After installation, the lumber develops about a 10% moisture content and consequently shrinks, particularly during the first heating season.

Wood shrinks most in the direction of the growth rings (flat grain), somewhat less across the growth rings (edge grain) and very little along the grain (longitudinally). Shrinkage tends to be most pronounced away from outside edges and toward the center of the member. When nails are driven toward the central axis, shrinkage leaves a space between the board and the nailing surface, as shown in the drawings on the next page.

Based on experiments conducted by the Forest Products Laboratory and Purdue University, the use of shorter nails results in less space left between the board and nailing surface after shrinkage (shown on next page) than with longer nails having more penetration. Using the shortest nail possible with adequate holding power will result in less popping due to shrinkage. Longer nails, however, usually are required for fire-rated construction, as specified by design requirements. Choose the proper nail length from the Selector Guide for Gypsum Board Nails on page 47.

The annular drywall nail, with an overall length of 1-1/4", has equivalent holding power to a 1-5/8" coated cooler-type nail, but the shorter length of the nail lessens the chances for nail popping due to lumber shrinkage, according to a study conducted at Purdue University.

Contractors can take several preventive measures to minimize fastener failures and cracking resulting from lumber shrinkage. Use the shortest recommended nails to reduce the likelihood of popping. Annular-thread (also called annular-ring) drywall nails are recommended because their design results in greater holding power than a smooth-shank nail of the same length and shank diameter (see pages 46-47). Type W screws are even better than the nails because they develop greater holding power and thus reduce possibilities for fastener pops.

The floating interior angle system effectively reduces angle cracking and nail pops resulting from stresses at intersections of walls and ceilings (see intersection detail). Gypsum boards should be floated over the side face of joists and headers and not attached. To minimize buckling and cracking in wall expanses exceeding one floor in height, either float the board over second-floor joists using resilient channels or install a horizontal control joint at this point.

11

Partition Corner

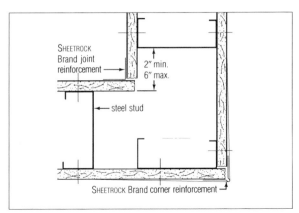

Using 2-1/2" nails.

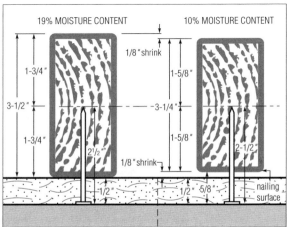

Using 1-1/2" nails.

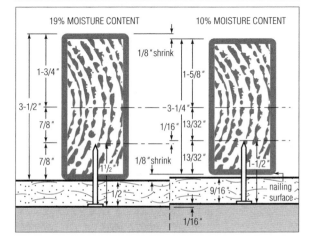

Workmanship

USG products are quality-tested and job-proven for fast, economical installation and problem-free results. Unfortunately, sometimes these products fail to achieve optimum performance after installation due to improper or unspecified application.

Follow Current Directions

The major cause of job problems and poor performance after application is failure to follow manufacturer's directions and architect's specifications. Application procedures should be checked regularly to conform with current manufacturer's recommendations. Product modifications to upgrade in-place performance may require slight changes in mixing or application methods. New products may require the adoption of entire new procedures and techniques.

Meet Specifications Fully

Building specifications are designed to provide a given result, but unless specified construction materials and methods are used and the proper details followed, the actual job performance will probably fall short of requirements. Excessive water usage, oversanding, improper surface preparation, substitution of materials, skimping and shortcuts should not be tolerated because they lead, inevitably, to problems.

Drywall and Plaster Tolerances

Standards of acceptability for installation of framing, drywall panels and joint treatment vary in different parts of the United States. Nevertheless, several organizations, including the Association of the Wall and Ceiling Industries International, Metal Lath/Steel Framing Association, Gypsum Association and American Society for Testing and Materials (ASTM), have published recommendations, standards and/or tolerances that may be required for a specific project. Similarly, references for tolerances and quality in plaster work have been published by AIA MasterSpec and Diehl's "Manual of Lathing and Plastering." Contractors and their customers should reach agreement before starting the project regarding which tolerance standards will be used to judge acceptability of the work. See the Appendix for further information on tolerances.

Equipment Selection

A large selection of equipment is available for gypsum construction and particularly for mechanical application of veneer plaster and texture finishes, conventional plasters and joint treatment (see Chapter 14, Tools & Equipment). The mechanical spray equipment chosen should be based on the type of material and the situations presented on each job. The size of the job, delivery volume required, portability and access through doorways also deserve consideration. Low maintenance and accessibility of parts for cleanup are important factors.

Using the wrong equipment for the job can cause serious problems. Improper equipment affects production as well as strength, workability, setting time and finished appearance.

Mixing

Equipment should provide the correct mixing action and mixing speed. Equally important are proportioning and mixing procedures required for

11

the particular material as shown in Chapters 5, 6 and 8. Poor mixing practices adversely affect material performance and can cause various problems.

Pumping

Equipment should have capacity sufficient for the job, hose size and pumping distance, and should be kept in good repair. To minimize abrasive wear in the pump mechanism, the pump type should be suitable for the aggregate and mixes being used. High plaster/sand ratios, small-diameter hoses and leakage increase the possibility of aggregate packing in the pump and hose. Use large-diameter hoses and no more hose length than needed. Small-diameter, long hoses cause pumps to wear faster and may lead to quick-set and low-strength problems in fluid materials.

Spraying

Nozzle or orifice size of the spray gun and air pressure used must be suitable for the material being applied. Improper nozzles and incorrect air pressures affect the spray pattern and may cause stoppage and aggregate fallout. With most veneer plaster finishing, a catalyst tank with metering device is required to adjust setting time.

Product Quality

Gypsum construction products from USG provide the essential requirements of economy, problem-free installation and high performance in fire and sound-rated systems. During manufacture, these products are carefully controlled to meet specific performance standards when applied according to directions and under proper job conditions.

Complaint Procedure

Should a probable product deficiency appear, stop using the suspected defective material immediately and ask your supplier to notify USG at once so that a representative can investigate the complaint and take remedial action. Do not continue to use improperly performing materials because the labor cost of replacement or reworking far exceeds the material cost.

Sampling

For analyzing suspected materials, obtain samples of the material that fully represent the complaint condition. Save bags, wrappers and packages (or write down the production codes) that will identify place and time of manufacture. For some complaints, samples of related materials such as aggregates, are also necessary. Weather conditions, mixing times and proportions of ingredients should be fully reported.

Substitution and Certification

USG will provide test certification for published fire, sound and structural data covering systems designed and constructed according to its specifications. Tests on USG products are conducted to meet the exact performance requirements of established test procedures specified by various building code agencies. Any substitution of materials or compromise in assembly design cannot be certified and may result in failure of a system in service, especially under critical conditions of load or fire exposure. Substitution of materials also usually will nullify acceptability of applicable fire tests.

How to Inspect a Job

Proper job inspection during installation many times reveals potential problem areas or procedures that produce unsatisfactory results. Corrective action taken immediately is usually less costly than callbacks to repair and perhaps rebuild walls and ceilings after the job is completed.

A complete understanding of job details, schedules and specifications is necessary to conduct proper inspection. If the assembly is to meet fire and sound-rating requirements, then construction details must also be known.

All walls and ceilings must be judged by these criteria and the contract conditions. Thus, it is important that drawings and specifications be complete, accurate and easily understood.

The job inspection phase of supervision is most important, and in many cases, will determine the success of the job. An accurate check should be made of the following major categories so that best results can be obtained.

Schedule of Inspection

Make job inspections at the following stages:

– When job is almost ready for materials delivery, in order to check environmental conditions and plan for delivery.

– When materials are delivered to the job.

– When framing is erected but before board or lath application.

– When gypsum board base layer and/or face layer are applied.

– When joints are treated; when veneer plaster finish or conventional plaster is applied.

– When job is substantially completed.

Delivery and Storage

When materials are delivered, check the following:

– First, check for shipping damage.

– See that materials meet specifications and are in good condition.

11

- Store gypsum boards flat, on the floor; store plasters and bagged goods flat, on a raised platform. Protect from moisture and damage by abuse.

- Protect framing materials from damage and moisture.

Framing Inspection

Framing members, either wood or metal, must meet architect's specifications and be free of defects. During and after framing construction, make the following inspections:

- See that wood and steel framing materials meet specifications as required by local building codes, regulations and standards. Also verify that sizes and gauges are appropriate based on limiting height tables.

- Check accuracy of alignment and position of framing, including bracing if required, according to plans and details. Make sure load-bearing steel studs are directly underneath the members they support.

- See that partitions are acceptably straight and true; ceilings are acceptably level.

- Measure spacing of studs and joists. Spacing should not exceed maximum allowable for the system.

- Look for protrusions of blocking, bridging or piping, and twisted studs and joists that would create an uneven surface. Correct situation before board attachment.

- Make sure there is appropriate blocking and support for fixtures and board.

- See that window and door frames, electrical and plumbing fixtures are set for the board thickness used.

- Check for proper position and attachment of resilient and furring channels.

- Review all wood and steel framing for compliance with minimum framing requirements outlined in Chapter 2.

- Examine steel studs at corners, intersections, terminals, shelf-walls, door and borrowed light frames for positive attachment to floor and ceiling runners. All load-bearing and curtain wall studs must be attached to runner each side, top and bottom. All load-bearing studs should sit tight against web of runner. Verify that appropriate gauge is used.

- See that steel stud flanges in field all face the same direction.

- See that preset door frames are independently fastened to floor slab and that borrowed light frames are securely attached to stud and runner rough framing at all jamb anchors.

Suspended Grillage

- Measure spacing of hangers, channels and studs to see that they are within allowable limits.

- Check ends of main runner and furring channels. They should not be let into, supported by, or in contact with abutting walls. Main runners should extend to within 6" of the wall to support a furring channel.

- Make sure furring channel clips are alternated and that furring channel splices are properly made.

- See that mechanical equipment is independently supported and does not depend upon the grillage for support.

- Inspect construction around light fixtures and openings to see that recommended reinforced channel support is provided.

Inspecting Drywall and Veneer Plaster Installations

Base Layer

- Verify that material being used complies with specifications and requirements of fire or sound rating.

- Make sure that proper perpendicular or parallel application of board is being used and that end joints are staggered.

- See that the recommended fasteners are being used, spaced and set properly.

- Check for proper use of acoustical sealant.

- Inspect installation to make sure thermal insulating or sound attenuation fire blankets are properly attached and fitted.

- Be certain vapor retarder is installed, if required, and sealed as required.

- Review appropriate system construction and application, and inspect for compliance with laminating recommendations and other construction procedures.

- See that required control joints are properly located and installed per architect's drawings.

Face Layer

- Verify material compliance.

- Look for high-quality workmanship. Cracked or damaged-edge boards should not be used. Board surfaces should be free of defects; joints correctly butted and staggered.

- Check for proper application method—perpendicular or parallel.

- Examine fasteners for compliance with specifications, proper spacing and application.

- Review adhesive application method and see that recommendations and specifications are being followed. Under adverse drying conditions resulting from high humidity, at either high or low temperature, drying of the laminating compound could be prolonged. Consult the setting time table on page 183 and the drying time table on page 186 for guidance.

- Inspect trim, corner beads and related components for alignment, grounds, secure attachment and proper installation.

- Make sure that acoustical sealant is applied around electrical outlets and other penetrations and that it completely seals the void.

Fasteners

- Make sure recommended or specified fasteners are used. Use of a specific fastener may be required by fire tests.

- See that fasteners are applied in such a manner that the board is flat against the framing.

- Observe whether board is held tightly against framing during application.

11

Test for loose board by pushing adjacent to the fastener. See that face paper is not broken when fastener is driven. If necessary, a second fastener should be driven within 1-1/2″ of the faulty one.

— Examine fastener positions. Fasteners should be at least 3/8″ in from edges and ends. Screws should not be set too deep; the screw head should be just below the surface of the wallboard.

— Make sure that fastener heads in veneer plaster assemblies are flush with the gypsum base surface, not dimpled.

Adhesives

— See that adhesive is applied to clean, dry surfaces only.

— So proper bond can be obtained, make sure that board is erected within allowable time limit after adhesive is applied.

— Measure size of bead and spacing, and see that a sufficient quantity is applied.

— Make sure temporary fastening and shoring holds panel tightly in place.

— Review appropriate adhesive application methods (see Chapter 3) and inspect for compliance.

Inspecting Drywall Joint Treatment

— Make sure panel surface is ready for joint treatment. Fastener heads should be properly seated below panel surface. Anything protruding above the plane of the drywall surface must be removed or sanded below the plane of the drywall surface. Gaps between adjacent panels should be prefilled with joint compound before taping begins. When a gap wider than 1/8″ is prefilled, the compound must be allowed to set or completely dry before taping.

— See that recommended mixing directions are followed (see Chapter 5). Only clean water and mixing equipment should be used. SHEETROCK Brand Setting-Type (DURABOND) and Lightweight Setting-Type (EASY SAND) Joint Compounds cannot be held over or retempered.

— Inspect joints and corners to see that tape is properly embedded and covered promptly with a thin coat of joint compound. Only compounds suitable for embedding should be used. Avoid heavy fills.

— Make sure compound is used at its heaviest workable consistency and not overthinned with water.

— Make sure joint compound is allowed to dry thoroughly between coats (see drying time guides on pages 183 and 186). Exception: SHEETROCK Brand Setting-Type (DURABOND) and Lightweight Setting-Type (EASY SAND) Joint Compounds need only be set prior to a subsequent application.

— Inspect second and third coats over joints for smoothness and proper edge feathering.

— See that fastener heads and metal trim are completely covered.

— See that the paper surface of the gypsum board has not been damaged by sanding.

— Make sure that all finished joints are smooth, dry, dust free and sealed before decoration.

**Inspecting
Veneer Plaster
Joint Treatment**

– See that corner bead is properly attached and aligned at all outside corners.

– See that control joints are properly installed where required.

– See that proper joint reinforcement is used—Under normal working conditions, joints of veneer plaster systems may be treated by applying IMPERIAL Brand Type P (pressure-sensitive) or Type S (staple) to the joints and then applying the veneer plaster basecoat or finish to preset the tape. However, there are a number of special situations that require the use of a setting-type joint treatment system:

· High building temperature, low humidity or excessive evaporation conditions fall in the "rapid drying" area of the graph (see page 214).

· Metal framing is specified.

· Wood-framing spacing of 24″ o.c. and a single-layer gypsum base veneer system is specified (5/8″ base with one-coat veneer finish and 1/2″ or 5/8″ base with two-coat veneer finish).

Under any of these conditions, use SHEETROCK Brand Joint Tape and SHEETROCK Brand Setting-Type (DURABOND) or Lightweight Setting-Type (EASY SAND) Joint Compound to treat all joints and internal angles. Allow joint treatment to set and dry thoroughly before plaster application.

– See that IMPERIAL Brand Tape is not overlapped at intersections.

– Be sure that all taped, preset IMPERIAL Brand Base joints are set before finish application begins.

– If gypsum base paper is faded, proper treatment is required (see page 392).

Inspecting Conventional Plaster Installations

Plaster Base

– See that material being used complies with specifications and fire or sound-tested construction.

– Review appropriate system construction and application, and inspect for proper installation practices.

– Check for proper application of base perpendicular to framing members, and see that end joints are staggered.

– Check for cracked and damaged edges of plaster base. These should not be used.

– Be sure recommended fasteners or clips are used and spaced properly.

– Check for proper use of acoustical sealant.

– Inspect installation to make sure that insulating blankets are properly attached and fitted.

– Be sure adequate supports are in place for fixture and cabinet applications.

11

**Grounds for
Plastering**

The thickness of basecoat plaster is one of the most important elements of a good plaster job. To ensure proper thickness of plaster, grounds should be properly set and followed. Check the following points:

- All openings should have specified plaster grounds applied as directed.

- If plaster screeds are used, the dots and continuous strips of plaster forming the screed must be applied to the ground thickness to permit proper plumbing and leveling.

- Grounds should be set for recommended minimum thickness for particular plaster base being used (see Chapter 8).

- Control joints should be installed as required for materials and construction with lath separated behind joint.

Job Conditions for Plastering

This phase of inspection is also important. Periodically make an accurate check of the following points:

- At no time should plastering be permitted without proper heating and ventilation.

- A minimum temperature of 55°F should be maintained for an adequate period before plastering, during plaster application and until the plaster is dry. Circulation of air is necessary to carry off excess moisture in the plaster, and a uniform temperature in a comfortable working range helps to avoid structural movement due to temperature differential.

- To prevent 'dryouts,' precautions must be taken against rapid drying before plaster set has occurred.

- Check temperature during damp, cold weather where artificial heat is provided.

- During hot, dry summer weather, cover window and door openings to prevent rapid drying due to uneven air circulation.

Plaster Application

After determining what materials are to be used on the job, refer to correct mixing and application procedures described in Chapter 8.

The visible success of the job is at stake with the finish plaster coat, and required measures should be taken to finish correctly:

- Check plaster type and mixing operation.

- See that proper plaster thickness is maintained.

- Inspect plaster surfaces during drying. Setting of basecoat plaster is indicated by hardening of plaster and darkening of surface as set takes place. Plaster that has set but not yet thoroughly dried will be darker in color than the unset portion. This accounts for the mottled effect as the plaster sets.

- Consult architect's specifications to see that proper surface finish is being used.

- Check temperature of building for proper finish plaster drying conditions.

Cleanup

For a complete job, cleanup is the final stage. All scaffolding, empty containers and excess materials should be removed from the job site. Floors should be swept and the building and site left in good condition for decoration and finishing.

Problems, Remedies
& Preventive Measures

Chapter 11 discussed problems associated with gypsum construction, many of which are beyond the control of contractors working from construction documents.

Other problems, resulting from improper job conditions and application practices, are the direct responsibility of the contractor and are controllable. In this chapter these problems as well as corrective remedies and preventive measures are discussed.

Drywall Construction

Almost invariably, unsatisfactory results show up first in the areas over joints or fastener heads. Improper application of either the board or joint treatment may be at fault, but other conditions existing on the job can be equally responsible for reducing the quality of the finished gypsum board surface.

To help determine the cause of a problem, what follows is a physical description of each defect along with a discussion of the factors causing unsatisfactory results. Also provided is a checklist that identifies possible causes for the irregularity as well as an index to the numerically listed problems, causes, remedies and preventions. By checking each numerical item listed for the defect, the exact problem cause can be determined and corrected.

Note that, because the proper installation procedures for FIBEROCK Brand products sometimes vary from the procedures used to install conventional drywall panels and gypsum base, the problems and remedies will vary as well. See the most current literature on FIBEROCK Brand Panels for recommendations to avoid installation problems.

| **Description of Defect** | **Fastener Imperfections** A common defect, which takes on many forms. May appear as darkening, localized cracking; a depression over fastener heads; pop or protrusion of the fastener or the surface area immediately surrounding the fastener. Usually caused by improper framing or fastener application. |

Joint Defects Generally occur in a straight-line pattern and appear as ridges, depressions or blisters at the joints, or darkening over the joints or in adjacent panel areas. Imperfections may result from incorrect framing or joint treatment application, or climatic conditions if remedial action has not been taken.

Loose Panels Board does not have tight contact with framing, rattles when impacted or moves when pressure is applied to the surface. Caused by improper application of panels, framing out of alignment or improper fastening.

Joint Cracking Appears either directly over the long edge or butt ends of boards, or may appear along the edge of taped joints. Often caused by structural movement and/or hygrometric and thermal expansion and contraction, or by excessively fast drying of joint compounds.

Field Cracking Usually appears as diagonal crack originating from a corner of a partition or intersection with structural elements. Also seen directly over a structural element in center of a partition. May originate from corners of doors, light fixtures and other weak areas in the surface created by penetration. Caused by movement described previously. Also, see Door and Window Openings on page 93 for use of control joints to minimize cracking.

Angle Cracking Appears directly in the apex of wall-ceiling or interior angles where partitions intersect. Also can appear as cracking at edge of paper reinforcing tape near surface intersections. Can be caused by structural movement, improper application of joint compound in corner angle or excessive build-up of paint.

Bead Cracking Shows up along edge of flange. Caused by improper bead attachment, faulty bead or joint compound application.

Wavy Surfaces Boards are not flat but have a bowed or undulating surface. Caused by improper board fit, misaligned framing, hygrometric or thermal expansion. Also see Handling and Storage on page 102 and Chapter 13 for proper procedure to keep boards flat before installation.

Board Sag Occurs in ceilings, usually under high-humidity conditions. Caused by insufficient framing support for board; board too thin for span; poor job conditions; improperly installed or mislocated vapor retarder; use of unsupported insulation directly on ceiling panels; or improperly fitted panels. Refer to appropriate chapters for proper job ventilation, storage and frame spacing, particularly with water-based texture finishes.

Surface Defects Fractured, damaged or crushed boards after application may be caused by abuse or lumber shrinkage. Also, see Discoloration below.

Discoloration Board surface has slight difference in color over joints, supports or fasteners. Caused by improper paint finishing, uneven soiling and darkening from aging or ultraviolet light.

Water Damage Stains, paper bond failure, softness in board core or mildew growth are caused by sustained high humidity, standing water and improper protection from water leakage during transit and storage. See page 102 and Chapter 13 for proper handling, storage and environmental conditions.

Checklist for Drywall Problems

To find the specific cause for a problem described above, check, on the following pages, all numerical references listed in the particular category.

Fastener imperfections	5, 8, 9, 10, 11, 12, 13, 14, 15, 16, 17, 18
Joint defects	1, 5, 6, 7, 11, 19, 20, 21, 22, 23, 24, 25, 26, 27, 28, 29, 30, 31
Loose panels	5, 8, 9, 10, 12, 13, 14, 15, 16, 17, 18
Joint cracking	5, 9, 20, 21, 22, 26
Field cracking	6
Angle cracking	20, 22
Bead cracking	20
Wavy surfaces	5, 8, 22
Board sag	5, 7, 14
Surface defects	2, 6, 28, 29, 30, 31
Discoloration	27, 28, 29, 30
Water damage	2, 4

12

Drywall Panel Problems

1. Panels— Damaged Edges

Fig. 1

Cause: Paper-bound edges have been damaged or abused; may result in ply separation along edge or in loosening of paper from gypsum core, or may fracture or powder the core itself. Damaged edges are more susceptible to ridging after joint treatment (Fig. 1).

Remedy: Cut back any severely damaged edges to sound board before application.

Prevention: Avoid using board with damaged edges that may easily be compressed or can swell upon contact with moisture. Handle gypsum panels with reasonable care.

2. Panels— Water-Damaged

Cause: During transit or storage, water has damaged panels from heavy rain, floods, broken pipes, etc. Water-damaged panels may be subject to scuffing and may develop paper bond failure or paper delamination from the gypsum core after application. They also may easily warp and deform. Dissolved glue from bundling tapes may damage board faces and cause them to stick together. If stored wet, may be subject to mildew. Prolonged soaking or exposure to water can soften gypsum core and destroy bond of the paper to the core.

Remedy: The amount of water exposure and the length of time exposed are both critical factors in preventing excessive losses. As soon as possible, dry wet board completely before using. Moisture damage delamination should not be present after thorough drying. Paper that is not totally bonded when the panel is moist often will reestablish its bond when panel is completely dry. If delamination exists after thorough drying, remove loose paper and patch area with SHEETROCK Brand Setting-Type (DURABOND or EASY SAND) Joint Compound. Replace board if there is extensive loose paper. Handle board cautiously and re-pile with bundles separated by spacer strips of gypsum board. Check incoming board for water stains or dampness. Protect carefully during shipment and storage. Do not erect damp panels; this may result in paper bond failure. Replace boards that have soft cores.

Prevention: Protect from high moisture conditions of any kind.

3. Panels— Paper Delamination

Cause: Manufacturing conditions, water damage.

Remedy: Manufacturing conditions or water damage causing delamination often can be treated as above. If board is received on job with paper delaminating, inspect delivery to determine extent of damage. Do not install or finish prior to contacting a USG representative. If delamination is minor, peel back paper to where it soundly bonds to board and treat with joint compound (ready-mix or setting-type).

Prevention: Protect from water damage.

4. Panels— Mildew

Cause: Mildew can occur on almost any surface depending on heat and humidity conditions. Gypsum panels that have become wet for any reason are susceptible to mildew growth.

Remedy: Ordinary soap and water may be used to clean moderately affected surfaces. Proper ventilation and/or heat should be used to thoroughly dry the affected area. Mildew growth may occur again if proper conditions are not maintained.

Prevention: Keep gypsum panels and the job site area as dry as possible to prevent mildew spores from blooming.

5. **Panels— Improperly Fitted**

Cause: Forcibly wedging an oversize panel into place bows the panel and builds in stresses preventing it from contacting the framing (Fig. 14, page 384). The result: following fastening, a high percentage of fasteners on the central studs probably will puncture the paper. May also cause joint deformation.

Remedy: Remove panel, cut to fit properly and replace. Fasten panels so that the board hangs flat against framing without binding against previously installed panels or framing. Apply pressure to hold panel tightly against framing while driving fasteners.

6. **Panels— Surface Fractured After Application**

a. **Cause:** Heavy blows or other abuse has fractured finished wall surface; too large a break for repair with joint compound.

Remedy 1: Cut a square-shaped section around damaged area with a utility knife or keyhole saw, (Fig. 2) then cut a plug of the same dimensions from a sound gypsum panel. Slip SHEETROCK Brand Drywall Repair Clips onto all four edges of the prepared hole and screw attach (Fig. 3). Mount replacement section and screw attach to clips (Fig. 4). Remove repair clip tabs (Fig. 5) and finish all four sides with SHEETROCK Brand Joint Tape and Compound. Apply and feather out second and third coats, sand and prime. Meets requirements of ASTM E-119 for repairing one-hour fire-rated wall. All patching components—except drywall—available in SHEETROCK Brand Drywall Repair Kit.

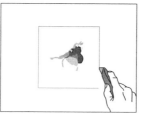

Fig. 2

Fig. 3

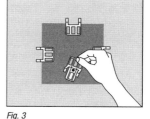

Fig. 4

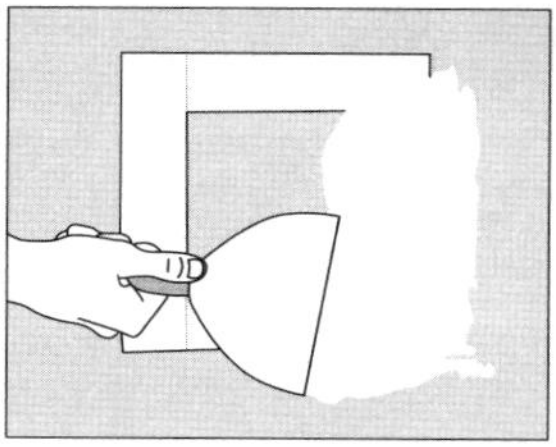

Fig. 5

12

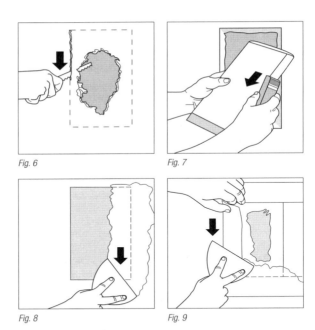

Fig. 6

Fig. 7

Fig. 8

Fig. 9

Remedy 2: Cut a square-shaped or triangular section around damaged area, with a utility knife or keyhole saw (Fig. 6); use a rasp or sanding block to slope edges inward at 45°. Cut corresponding plug from sound gypsum panel, sand edges to exact fit (Fig. 7). Butter edges (Fig. 8) and finish as a butt joint with joint compound (Fig. 9).

Remedy 3: An alternate repair technique (sometimes referred to as "California patch," "butterfly patch" or "hot patch") involves cutting a corresponding plug approximately 1-1/2" wider and longer that the cutout in the wall. Next, score through the back paper and core, snap the core and then peel the core away from the face paper so that an overlapping section remains around the perimeter of the plug. The plug is then edged with joint compound and inserted into the damaged area, and the overlapping face paper is used in lieu of tape for finishing with joint compound. Although this may be an acceptable method for certain applications, it provides a repair which is weaker and more difficult to finish than the methods noted above, because the patch will remain above the existing plane of the wall or ceiling. Also, this technique should not be used to repair fire-rated walls.

b. **Cause:** Attaching panel directly to flat grain of wide-dimensional wood framing members such as floor joists and headers. Shrinkage of wood causes fracture of board.

Remedy: As above, where appropriate, or repair as for joint ridging.

Prevention: To provide a flexible base to allow for movement of framing, attach RC-1 Resilient Channel to framing members and apply panels. Allow 1/2" space at bottom edges of board for movement. Or attach board directly to studs but allow 1/4″ separation between panels, and install Zinc Control Joint No. 093 (see single-layer application on page 113).

c. **Cause:** Knife scoring beyond corner of cutout for electrical boxes, light fixtures and door and window openings produces cracks in panel surface.

Remedy: Repair cuts with joint compound and tape before finishing.

Prevention: Stop score marks at corners, cut openings accurately.

d. **Cause:** Abnormal stress buildup resulting from structural deflection or racking discussed previously.

Remedy: Relieve stress, provide adequate isolation and retape, feathering joint compound over board area to disguise buildup.

Prevention: Provide proper isolation from structure to prevent stress buildup.

e. **Cause:** Excessive stresses resulting from hygrometric and/or thermal expansion and contraction discussed previously.

Remedy: Correct unsatisfactory environmental conditions, provide sufficient relief. Retape, feathering joint compound over board area.

Prevention: Correct improper job conditions and install control joints for relief in long partition runs and large ceiling areas (see pages 173-175).

7. **Panels—Ceiling Sag after Installation**

a. **Cause:** Too much weight from overlaid insulation; exposure to sustained high humidity; vapor retarder improperly installed or wetting causes ceiling panels to sag after installation. Also caused by installing board that is too thin for framing space.

Remedy: Remove sagged board or fur ceiling using RC-1 Resilient Channels; apply another layer of board. (Leveling of surface with joint compound, will not correct problems resulting from improper framing, unusual weight loads or recurring high moisture conditions.)

Prevention: Follow recommended frame spacing and attachment procedures and use recommended products only. Use SHEETROCK Brand Interior Gypsum Ceiling Board, where available. See "Ceiling Sag Precautions" on page 353.

b. **Cause:** Water-based textures wet face paper and weaken gypsum core, causing ceiling panels to sag after installation.

Remedy: Same as above.

Prevention: See Chapter 3 for proper frame spacing and application procedures. See "Ceiling Sag Precautions" on page 353.

12

Framing Problems

8. **Framing—Members Out of Alignment**

Cause: Due to misaligned top plate and stud, hammering at points "X" (Fig. 10) as panels are applied on both sides of partition will probably result in nailheads puncturing paper or cracking board. Framing members more than 1/4″ out of alignment with adjacent members make it difficult to bring panels into firm contact with all nailing surfaces.

Remedy: Remove or drive in problem fasteners and only drive new fasteners into members in solid contact with board.

Prevention: Check alignment of studs, joists, headers, blocking and plates before applying panels, and correct before proceeding. Straighten badly bowed or crowned members. Shim out flush with adjoining surfaces. Use adhesive attachment.

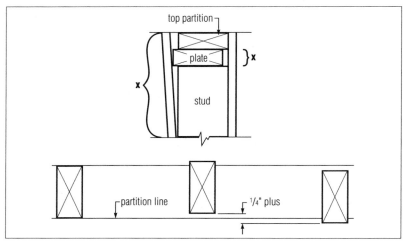

top partition
plate
stud
x
x
partition line
¹/₄" plus

Fig. 10

9. Framing— Members Twisted

Fig. 11

Cause: Framing members have not been properly squared with plates, presenting angular nailing surface (Fig. 11). When panels are applied, there is danger of puncturing paper with fastener heads or of reverse twisting of member as it dries out, with consequent loosening of board and probable fastener pops. Warped or wet dimension lumber may contribute to deformity.

Remedy: When moisture content in framing has stabilized after one heating season, remove problem fasteners and re-fasten with carefully driven Type W screws.

Prevention: Align all twisted framing members before board application. Also, see wood framing requirements on page 73.

10. Framing— Protrusions

Cause: Bridging, headers, fire stops or mechanical lines have been installed improperly so as to project beyond face of framing, preventing

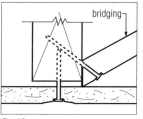

bridging

panels from contacting nail surface (Fig. 12). Result will be loose board, and fasteners driven in area of protrusion will probably puncture face paper.

Remedy and Prevention: Same as for Framing—Members Twisted, above.

Fig. 12

11. Framing (Steel)—Panel Edges Out of Alignment

Cause: Improper placement of steel studs or advancing in the wrong direction when installing panels can cause misalignment of panel edges and give the appearance of ridging when finished.

Remedy: Fill and feather out joint with joint treatment.

Prevention: Install steel studs with all flanges pointed in the same direction. Then install panels by advancing in the direction opposite the flange direction (Fig. 13).

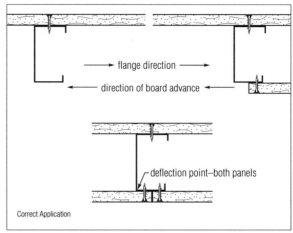

flange direction

direction of board advance

deflection point–both panels

Correct Application

Fig. 13

Fastener Problems

12. Fasteners— Puncturing of Face Paper

Cause: Poorly formed nailheads, careless nailing, excessively dry face paper or soft core, lack of pressure during fastening. Nailheads that puncture paper and shatter core of panel (Fig. 15) have very little grip on board.

Remedy: Remove improperly driven fastener, hold panel tightly and properly drive new fastener.

Prevention: Correction of faulty framing (see previous Framing Problems) and properly driven nails produce tight attachment with slight uniform dimple (Fig. 16). Nailhead bears on paper and holds panel securely against framing member. Use proper fastener or adhesive application. Screws with specially contoured head are best fastener known to eliminate cutting and fracturing. If face paper becomes dry and brittle, its low moisture content may aggravate nail cutting. Raise moisture content of board and humidity in work area.

12

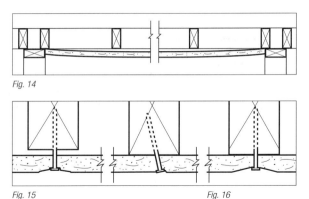

Fig. 14

Fig. 15   Fig. 16

13. Fasteners—Nails Loosened by Pounding

Cause: Applying panels to the second side of a partition can loosen nails on opposite side (lack of hand pressure during fastening). Particularly true when lightweight, soft lumber, undersized studs or furring are used.

Remedy: Check panels for tightness on the partition side where panels were first applied. If looseness is detected, strike each nailhead an additional hammer blow, being careful to not overdrive the nail.

Prevention: Use proper framing. Type W screws or adhesive application.

14 Fasteners—Unseated Nails

Cause: Flexible or extremely hard framing or furring does not permit nails to be properly driven. May result from undersized framing members, type of wood used, supports that exceed maximum allowable frame spacing or lack of hand pressure during fastening.

Remedy: Replace nails with 1-1/4″ Type W screws.

Prevention: Use proper framing (see Chapter 2), Type W screws or adhesive application. Apply pressure to hold panel tight against framing while driving fasteners.

15. Fasteners—Loose Screws

Cause: Using the wrong type screw for the application or an improperly adjusted screw gun results in a screw stripping or not seating properly.

Remedy: Remove faulty fastener and replace with a properly driven screw.

Prevention: Use screws with combination high/low threads for greater resistance to stripping and pullout; set screw gun clutch to proper depth.

16. Fasteners—Nail Pops From Lumber Shrinkage

Cause: Improper application, lumber shrinkage or a combination of both. With panels held reasonably tight against framing member and with proper-length nails, only severe shrinkage of the lumber normally will cause nail pops. But if nailed loosely, any inward pressure on panel will push nailhead through its thin covering pad of compound. Pops resulting from 'nail creep' (movement of nail resulting from lumber

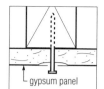

Fig. 17

shrinkage) occur when shrinkage of the wood framing exposes nail shank and consequently loosens panel (see Lumber Shrinkage on pages 365-366).

Remedy: Repairs usually are necessary only for pops which protrude 0.005″ or more from face of board (Fig. 17). Smaller protrusions may require repair if they occur in a smooth gloss surface or flat-painted surface under extreme lighting conditions. Those that appear before or during decoration should be repaired immediately. Pops that occur after one month's heating or more are usually caused wholly or partly by wood shrinkage and should not be repaired until near end of heating season. An often effective procedure for resetting a popped nail is to place a 4″ broad knife over the nail and hit with hammer to seat flush with surface. A more permanent method is to drive proper nail or Type W screw about 1-1/2″ from popped nail while applying sufficient pressure adjacent to nailhead to bring panel in firm contact with framing. Strike popped nail lightly to seat it below surface of board. Remove loose compound, apply finish coats of compound and paint.

Prevention: Proper nail application; use of lumber meeting framing requirements (see page 73); attachment with Type W screws or by adhesive application (see Chapter 3).

17. Fasteners— Panels Loosely Fastened

Cause: Framing members are uneven because of misalignment or warping; lack of hand pressure on panel during fastening. Head of fastener alone cannot pull panel into firm contact with uneven members. Also, see Panels—Improperly Fitted.

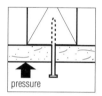

Fig. 18

Remedy: With nail attachment, during final blows of hammer, apply additional pressure with hand to panel adjacent to nail (Fig. 18) to bring panel into contact with framing.

Prevention: Correct framing imperfections before applying panels; for a more solid attachment, use 1-1/4″ Type W screws or use adhesive method (see Chapter 3). Apply pressure to hold panel tightly against framing while driving fasteners.

18. Fasteners— Bulge Around Fastener

Cause: Overdriving fasteners, driving them with the wrong tool or failing to hold board firmly against framing while driving fasteners can puncture and bulge face paper and damage core of board. Following application of joint compound or texture finish that wets the board paper can result in board bulging or swelling around fastener.

Remedy: Drive screw fastener close to damaged area, clean out damaged paper core, repair with SHEETROCK Brand Setting-Type (DURABOND) or SHEETROCK Brand Lightweight Setting-Type (EASY SAND) Joint Compound, and refinish.

Prevention: Use correct tool and drive fasteners properly. Also, see Fasteners—Panels Loosely Fastened.

12

Joint Problems

19. Joints— Blisters in Tape

Cause: Insufficient or overly thin compound was used under the tape; tape was not initially pressed into good contact with the compound;

overly thick (dry) compound was used; or too much compound was forced from under tape by application of excessive tool pressure when embedding.

Remedy: Open up blistered area by slitting tape. Fill cut with joint compound and press tape back in place with knife blade. When dry, smooth to level finish.

Prevention: Provide sufficient compound under entire tape.

20. Joints—
Edge Cracking

a. **Cause:** After joint treatment, straight narrow cracks along edges of tape result from: too rapid drying because of high temperature accompanied by low humidity or excessive drafts; improper application, such as overdilution of joint compound; use of wrong compound (topping instead of taping); excessive joint compound under tape; failure to follow embedding with a thin coat over tape; or cold, wet application conditions, which also may cause poor bond.

This problem, difficult to see when it first occurs, may not be discovered until decoration begins. However, the cause can be attributed to some aspect of the taping operation.

Remedy: Especially under hot, dry and/or drafty conditions, carefully examine all joints after taping applications have dried; repairs are more economical at this stage. Cut away any weakly bonded tape edges. Fill hairline cracks with cut shellac (2-to 3-lb.); groove out larger cracks with sharp tool; coat with shellac and allow to dry, then refill with joint compound; or cover cracks with complete joint treatment, including reinforcing tape; feather to surface level with plane of board.

Prevention: Use either SHEETROCK Brand Setting-Type (DURABOND) or SHEETROCK Brand Lightweight Setting-Type (EASY SAND) Joint Compound, which have the best built-in resistance to cracks. Place shielding devices over room openings to prevent drafts. Do not apply joint treatment over hot surfaces. Dampen floors if extra low room humidity condition is suspected. During cold weather, control heat at min. 55°F and supply good ventilation. Avoid practices listed under "Cause," above.

b. **Cause:** After joint treatment, cracks along edges of corner bead or trim can result from the same unsatisfactory conditions listed above for tape. Also can be caused by impact on the bead.

Remedy: Remove applied joint compound. Securely fasten corner bead or trim to framing beneath panels. Refinish bead with joint compound.

Prevention: Use SHEETROCK Brand Paper Faced Metal Tape On Bead and Trim, which eliminates edge cracking.

21. Joints—
Center
Cracking

a. **Cause:** Abnormal stress buildup resulting from structural deflection or racking discussed previously.

Remedy: Relieve stress. Provide adequate isolation and retape, feathering joint compound over broad area to disguise buildup.

Prevention: Provide proper isolation from structure to prevent stress buildup.

b. Cause: Excessive stresses resulting from hygrometric and/or thermal expansion and contraction discussed previously.

Remedy: Correct unsatisfactory environmental conditions. Provide sufficient relief; retape, feathering joint compound over broad area.

Prevention: Correct improper job conditions and install control joints for relief in long partition runs and large ceiling areas (see pages 173-175).

22. Joints— Angle Cracking

a. Cause: Too much compound applied over tape at apex of angle.

Remedy: After compound is completely dry, smooth out excess compound at apex. Fill only hairline cracks with compound. Do not apply additional compound, which will build up.

Prevention: Keep excess compound from corner, leaving only a small amount or no compound in apex.

b. Cause: Slitting or scoring reinforcing tape during application. May result from use of improper tool.

Remedy: If crack extends through the tape, retape and finish.

Prevention: Use proper tool for corner treatment.

c. Cause: Structural movement from two separate supports or framing members, which react independently to applied loads. Often occurs in wall-ceiling angles where wall is attached to top plate and ceiling is attached to floor or ceiling joists running parallel to top plate.

Remedy: Remove fasteners closer than 6″ from angle, retape and finish.

Prevention: Use "Floating Interior Angle" application described on page 138.

d. Cause: Structural or thermal movement resulting from two dissimilar materials or constructions.

Remedy: Remove tape, provide relief, finish with appropriate trim and caulk as required.

Prevention: Use channel-type or angle edge trim over gypsum board where two dissimilar surfaces interface.

e. Cause: Excessive paint thickness; application of paint under poor conditions.

Remedy: Correct unsatisfactory job conditions. Scrape away cracked paint. Fill and feather with joint compound. Prime and paint.

Prevention: Provide proper job conditions. Apply recommended thickness of prime and finish coats of paint.

12

23. Joints— High Crowns

Cause: Excessive build-up of compound over joint; compound not feathered out beyond shoulders, improper bedding of tape; framing out of alignment or panel edges not tight against framing; improper adjustment of tools; misuse of or worn tools.

Remedy: Sand joints to flush surface. Take care to avoid scuffing paper by oversanding.

Prevention: Embed tape properly, using only enough compound to cover tape and fill taper depression or tape itself at butt joints; feather compound wide enough to conceal.

24. Joints— Excessive and/or Delayed Shrinkage

Cause: (1) Atmospheric conditions—slow drying and high humidity; (2) Insufficient drying time between coats of compound; (3) Excessive water added in mixing compound; (4) Heavy fills. When a second coat of joint compound is applied over compound that has not yet dried, the first coat will dry more slowly and shrinkage will occur later than is typical. This slow shrinkage is termed "Delayed Shrinkage."

Remedy: See "Starved Joints," below.

Prevention: Allow each coat of joint compound to dry thoroughly before applying succeeding coat, or use a low-shrinkage SHEETROCK Brand Setting-Type (DURABOND) or SHEETROCK Brand Lightweight Setting-Type (EASY SAND) Joint Compound.

25. Joints— Starved Joints

Cause: This is a form of delayed shrinkage caused chiefly by insufficient drying time between coats of compound. May also be caused by insufficient compound applied over tape to fill taper, overthinning or oversmoothing of compound. Shrinkage usually progresses until drying is complete.

Remedy: Use fast-setting SHEETROCK Brand Setting-Type (DURABOND) or SHEETROCK Brand Lightweight Setting-Type (EASY SAND) Joint Compound or reapply a full cover coat of heavy-mixed compound over tape. Since this is heaviest application, most shrinkage will take place in this coat, making it easier to fill taper properly. Finish by standard procedure.

Prevention: Allow each coat of joint compound to dry thoroughly before applying succeeding coat, or use a low-shrinkage SHEETROCK Brand Setting-Type (DURABOND) or SHEETROCK Brand Lightweight Setting-Type (EASY SAND) Joint Compound.

26. Joints— Ridging

Cause: All building materials grow or shrink in response to changes in temperature and humidity. When they are confined to a specific space, such as gypsum panels in a partition or ceiling, they are put under stress, either compression or tension, depending on the temperature or humidity conditions. These stresses are relieved when the panel bends outward in the region of the joint. Once this bending takes place, the system takes a set and never returns to normal. It becomes progressively worse with each change of temperature or humidity. This progressive deformation appears as a continuous ridge along the length of joint, with a uniform fine, ridge-like pattern at the center.

Remedy: (1) Let ridge develop fully before undertaking repairs; usually six months is sufficient. Make repairs under average room conditions; (2) Smooth ridge down to reinforcing tape without cutting through tape. Fill concave areas on either side of ridge with light fill of compound. After this is dry, float very thin film of compound over entire area; (3) Examine area with strong sidelighting to make certain that ridge has been concealed. If not, use additional feathering coats of compound. Redecorate. Ridging can recur, but is usually less severe. Continuous wetting will aggravate condition.

Prevention: Where available, use SHEETROCK Brand Gypsum Panels, SW Edge, with the exclusive rounded edge designed to prevent ridging. Follow general recommendations for joint treatment (see Chapter 1) and approved application procedure, which includes back-blocking and laminated double-layer application to minimize potential ridging problems (see Chapter 3). Pay particular attention to temperature, ventilation, consistency of compound, prompt covering coat over tape, minimum width of fill, finish coats and required drying time between coats.

Finishing Problems

27. Finish— Discoloration

a. **Cause:** Differences in suction of panel paper and joint compound may lighten paint color or change gloss or sheen in higher-suction areas; most common when conventional oil-based paints are used. Also caused by texture differences between the face paper and finished joint compound or by overthinning of paint. May also occur over fasteners in ceilings subjected to severe artificial or natural side lighting. Suction differences may also cause greater amounts of texturing material to be deposited over high-suction areas, causing color differences when viewed from an angle. Before painting, face panel paper may be darkened from exposure to sunlight.

Remedy: Redecorate.

Prevention: Before painting or texturing, apply a prime coat of SHEETROCK Brand First Coat or undiluted interior flat latex paint with high solids content. Avoid roughening surface paper when sanding joint compound. Use strong job lights parallel to the surface to ensure a flat acceptable joint compound finish prior to priming, texturing and/or painting.

b. **Cause:** The use of preservatives in paint formulation. As the scientific community learns more about health hazards, additives to many products are changed or eliminated. Mercury, for example, was banned for use in paints in August, 1990. Some of these additives could cause a reaction resulting in an off-color appearance.

Remedy: A high-quality finish coat or coats will, generally, produce an acceptable finish.

Prevention: A good quality primer or SHEETROCK Brand First Coat and finish paint coat properly applied according to the paint manufacturer's recommendations will prevent most discoloration problems.

28. Finish— Gloss Variation With High Gloss Paints

Cause: Differences in suction of panel paper and joint compound, or texture differences between the face paper and finished joint compound (as stated in #27-a). Problem is accentuated by strong side lighting with slight angle of incidence to ceiling or wall surface.

Remedy: Redecorate.

Prevention: Before painting with a high gloss paint, apply a skim coat of joint compound over the entire wall surface or use a veneer plaster system. If skim coating is not done, the next best preventative measure is to apply a prime coat of SHEETROCK Brand First Coat.

12

29. Finish—
Joint Darkening

Cause: This condition occurs most commonly with color-tinted paint rather than white. Most severe when applied in humid weather when joints have not fully dried.

Remedy: Apply a prime coat of SHEETROCK Brand First Coat and repaint. Repaint only after all surfaces are thoroughly dry.

Prevention: Be sure joints are thoroughly dry before painting (see "Drying Time" on pages 185-186).

30. Finish—
Shadowing

Cause: Temperature differentials in outside walls or top-floor ceilings causes collection of airborne dust on colder spots of interior surface. Results in photographing or shadowing over fasteners, furring or framing. Most severe with great indoor-outdoor temperature variation.

Remedy: Wash painted surfaces, remove spots with wallpaper cleaner, or redecorate surfaces. Change air filters regularly.

Prevention: Use double-layer application with adhesively applied face layer. Use separately framed free-standing interior wall surface and insulate in void to reduce temperature difference between steel or wood components and panels.

31. Finish—
Decorating
Wallboard
Damaged by
Over-Sanding

Cause: Paper fibers of the exposed gypsum panel surface are scuffed and raised by over-sanding of the joints or use of sandpaper that is too coarse.

Remedy: Correct severe paper fiber raise with a light skim coat of a drying-type joint compound. Minor fiber raise may be treated by light sanding with very fine sandpaper or wiped down with a damp sponge or cloth.

Prevention: Good finish work with compound, feathered edges, etc. reduces the need for sanding, in general, limiting exposure to this kind of problem.

Veneer Plaster Construction

Many problems associated with veneer plaster construction have the same cause, remedy and prevention as with drywall systems. Similarity of problems appears in application of the base, framing irregularities, cracking due to structural movement, hygrometric and thermal expansion and fastener imperfections. The additional problems that follow are those specifically relating to veneer plaster finish construction. If solutions to your problems in veneer plaster construction are not described, check similar problems for drywall construction found earlier in this chapter.

Application Problems

1. Mixing—
Foaming Action
in Mixer

Cause: Use of USG Plaster Accelerator—Alum Catalyst as an accelerator when limestone aggregate is used.

Remedy: None. Dispose of batch.

Prevention: Use moulding plaster or quick-set gauging plaster as an accelerator when limestone aggregate is used. Or use sand aggregate.

Also, avoid entraining air from mixing with high-speed mixing paddle or wrong kind of paddle.

2. **Setting Time—Variable Set Time Within Batch**

   Cause: Insufficient or excessive mixing.

   Remedy: None. Dispose of batch.

   Prevention: Use proper drill speed; follow recommended mixing times (see pages 223-224).

3. **Slow Set— IMPERIAL and DIAMOND Interior Finish Plaster/ Basecoat**

   a. **Cause:** High air and mixing water temperature, in excess of 100°F.

   Remedy: Proper use of accelerator.

   Prevention: Avoid extremes of air and water temperatures.

   b. **Cause:** Contaminated mixing water or contaminated sand.

   Remedy: None.

   Prevention: Use drinkable water only.

   c. **Cause:** Excessive use of retarder.

   Remedy: None. Dispose of batch.

   Prevention: Follow recommendations for mix proportions and use of additives.

4. **Quick Set— IMPERIAL and DIAMOND Interior Finish Plaster/ Basecoat**

   a. **Cause:** Low air and water temperature below 40°F.

   Remedy: None. Dispose of batch.

   Prevention: Avoid extremes of air and water temperatures.

   b. **Cause:** Contaminated mixing water; dirty mixing equipment.

   Remedy: None. Dispose of batch.

   Prevention: Use drinkable water only. Clean set plaster residue from equipment after each batch. Always use clean mix equipment.

   c. **Cause:** Excessive use of accelerator.

   Remedy: None. Dispose of batch.

   Prevention: Follow recommendations for mix proportions and use of additives.

5. **Quick Set— IMPERIAL Finish Plaster and DIAMOND Interior Finish Plaster Only**

   Cause: Contamination; excessive use of aggregate and/or accelerator.

   Remedy: None. Dispose of batch.

   Prevention: Use drinkable water. Clean set plaster residue from equipment after each batch. Always use clean mix equipment. Follow recommendations for mix proportions and use of additives.

   12

6. **Workability— Stiff Working**

   Cause: Mixing action has improper or insufficient shear.

   Remedy: None. Use remainder of batch, if at all workable.

   Prevention: Follow recommendations for mixing time, drill speed and type of mixing paddle (see pages 223-224).

In-Place Problems

7. Bond Failure— Delamination of Finish Coat

Cause: Basecoat not left rough and open (rough for mechanical key and open as in porous); finish coat not properly scratched into basecoat to have necessary keying.

Remedy: Remove loose material, brush basecoat thoroughly, apply bonding agent and refinish.

Prevention: Follow application recommendations (see Chapter 6).

8. Bond Failure— DIAMOND Interior Finish Plaster

Cause: Application over faded (not normal blue color) gypsum base.

Remedy: Remove loose material, brush base clean, apply bonding agent and refinish.

Prevention: Do not store or apply base where it will be exposed to sunlight for an extended time. Where exposed, spray faded base with USG Accelerator–Alum Catalyst or USG Plaster Bonder before finish is applied (see No. 9 below).

9. Sun-Faded Gypsum Base

Cause: Exposure of gypsum base to sunlight for an extended period of time.

Remedy: When used with lime-containing plaster, such as DIAMOND Brand Interior Finish Plaster, sunfaded IMPERIAL Brand Gypsum Base face paper should be treated with USG Accelerator-Alum Catalyst or USG Plaster Bonder. This precaution is unnecessary when applying products that do not contain lime (IMPERIAL Brand finish Plaster, IMPERIAL Brand Basecoat Plaster and DIAMOND Brand Veneer Basecoat Plaster). For alum catalyst solution treatment, pour 3 pounds of USG Accelerator-Alum Catalyst slowly into one gallon of water and mix thoroughly. Allow the solution to stand until any undissolved material has settled, then strain solution into tank-type sprayer (such as garden sprayer). Spray solution onto faded IMPERIAL Brand Base face paper so that it is wet but not soaked. One gallon of solution should treat 750 sq. ft. of IMPERIAL Brand Gypsum Base. Begin finish plaster application before face paper treated with alum solution is completely dry. Caution: Alum treatment shortens setting time of DIAMOND Brand Interior Finish Plaster.

Prevention: See Problem No. 8.

10. Cracks— Joint Cracking

a. **Cause:** IMPERIAL Tape overlapped at joint intersections.

Remedy: Large cracks: apply SHEETROCK Brand Joint tape and SHEETROCK Brand Ready-Mixed Joint Compound (All Purpose or Taping) over the cracks. Minor cracks: flush out area with SHEETROCK Brand Ready-Mixed Joint Compound (All Purpose or Taping).

Prevention: Avoid overlapping tape at all joint intersections, including those at angles.

b. **Cause:** Improper steel stud placement. Gypsum base application advanced in wrong direction relative to flange direction.

Remedy: Repair with SHEETROCK Brand Joint Tape and SHEETROCK Brand Ready-Mixed Joint Compound (All Purpose or Taping).

Prevention: Install steel studs with all flanges pointing in same direction. Arrange gypsum base application so lead edge of base is attached to open edge of flange first (see Framing (Steel)—Panel Edges Out of Alignment on page 383).

c.   **Cause:** Overly rapid drying conditions.

Remedy: Repair with Sheetrock Brand Joint Tape and Sheetrock Brand Ready-Mixed Compound (All Purpose or Taping).

Prevention: Liberally sprinkle floor with water to raise humidity. Use Sheetrock Brand Joint Tape and Sheetrock Brand Setting-Type (Durabond or Easy Sand) Joint Compound on all joints. Allow compound to dry thoroughly before applying finish. Where steel stud framing is used, apply Sheetrock Brand Joint Tape and Sheetrock Brand Setting-Type (Durabond or Easy Sand) Joint Compound.

d.   **Cause:** Imperial Tape with steel framing.

Remedy: Repair with Sheetrock Brand Joint Tape and Sheetrock Brand Ready-Mixed Compound (All Purpose or Taping).

Prevention: Use only Sheetrock Brand Joint Tape and Sheetrock Brand Setting-Type Joint Compound (Durabond or Easy Sand).

---

11. Cracks— Field Cracking

Cause: Gypsum base installed with vertical joints extending from corners of door and window openings.

Remedy: Apply Sheetrock Brand Joint Tape and Sheetrock Brand Setting-Type (Durabond) Joint Compound; then finish with Sheetrock Brand Ready-Mixed Joint Compound (All Purpose or Taping). Prime and seal. This is a cosmetic treatment; there is no guarantee that cracks will not reopen.

Prevention: Install Zinc Control Joint No. 093 or cut base to fit around openings with joints centered above openings, not at corners.

---

12. Cracks— Craze and Map Cracking

Cause: Veneer plaster application too thin. Also can be caused by too rapid drying.

Remedy: Apply spackling putty. Prime and seal.

Prevention: Apply recommended thicknesses for both one- and two-coat work. Avoid excessive ventilation, which may cause rapid drying. When weather is hot and dry, sprinkle floor with water to raise humidity.

---

13. Blemishes— Blistering

a.   **Cause:** Loose paper on gypsum base as a result of improper cutting or from "peelers" caused by careless handling.

Remedy: Cut and remove unbonded paper, apply bonding agent if gypsum core is exposed, and refinish.

Prevention: Follow proper handling and cutting procedures.

b.   **Cause:** Troweling too early and lack of absorption; excessive material buildup.

Remedy: Minimize troweling and allow finish to become firm. Finish trowel over freshly set surface to eliminate blisters.

12

Prevention: Apply material in uniform thickness with minimum amount of troweling to produce smooth surface.

14. Blemishes— Joint Ridging and Beading	**Cause:** Joints not preset; excessive ventilation and poor heat control. Most likely to occur with one-coat applications. **Remedy:** Repair with Sheetrock Brand Ready-Mixed Compound (All Purpose or Taping). **Prevention:** Preset all joints before veneer plaster finish application; keep ventilation to minimum and control heat. In extremely hot, dry weather use Sheetrock Brand Joint Tape and Sheetrock Brand Setting-Type (Durabond or Easy Sand) Joint Compound as alternative joint reinforcement.
15. Blemishes— Spalling at Exterior Corners	**Cause:** Use of solid-flange drywall corner bead. **Remedy:** Remove all loose material and corner bead. Install expanded-flange corner bead and refinish. **Prevention:** Use expanded-flange corner bead.
16. Stains— Staining and Rusting	**Cause:** Use of improper fasteners, or exposed, improperly prepared metal trim. **Remedy:** Apply rust-locking primer over stains. **Prevention:** Use recommended coated fasteners (see Chapter 1). Apply rust-locking primer to all exposed metal.
17. Soft, Weak Surface— Dryouts	**Cause:** Too rapid drying conditions. **Remedy:** Fog-spray surface with water or alum solution to provide setting action. When set, apply Sheetrock Brand Ready-Mixed Joint Compound (All Purpose or Taping) for acceptably smooth surface. **Prevention:** Avoid extending set and/or temperature and humidity conditions, which cause rapid drying.
18. Soft, Weak Surface— Crumbly Areas	**Cause:** Use of excessive amount of sand aggregate and/or retarder. **Remedy:** Treat soft areas with penetrating sealer. **Prevention:** Allow minimum ventilation; use recommended amounts only of aggregate or retarder. Avoid prolonged set.

Cement Board Construction

Durock Brand Cement Board Systems require careful adherence to published installation procedures and high standards of workmanship.

1. Interior Tile System— Surface Fractured	**Cause:** Heavy impact punctures from moving equipment or vandalism. Holes resulting from previous fixture attachment. **Remedy:** Where tile can be removed without damaging the Durock Brand Cement Board—remove damaged tile by cutting and chipping tile. Scrape or grind bond coat down to skim coat. Tape any cracks with Durock Brand Tape. Reset tile and grout.

Where tile cannot be removed without causing excessive damage to the Durock Brand Cement Board, remove the damaged section by cutting through the tile and Durock Brand Cement Board. Install additional framing, screw attaching to existing framing at the same plane behind edge of existing surface, so that the perimeter of existing and new panels will be supported. Cut a patch of Durock Brand Cement Board that closely fits the opening. Apply a generous amount of organic adhesive to the edges of existing and new panel. Install panel and attach to framing with appropriate fasteners. Smooth and level adhesive at panel joints. Let adhesive cure for 24 hours before setting and grouting new tile.

2. **Delamination— Basecoat or Mortar**

Cause: Improper mixing procedures or improper basecoating techniques.

Remedy: Remove all material that is not properly bonded to the Durock Brand Panel surface. Apply a bonding agent such as Larsen's Weld-Crete; then reapply basecoat to the area.

Prevention: Always use the proper amount of clean potable water when mixing the material. Too much water will significantly reduce the bond strength of the material. Apply the material using a scratch and double back method. The tight scratch coat keys the material into the Durock Brand Panel surface.

3. **Delamination— Tile and Thin Brick**

Cause: Allowing the mortar to skin over before setting the tile or brick. Not back-buttering the tile.

Remedy: Scrape the mortar from the Durock Brand Panel surface. Apply a bonding agent to the Durock Brand Panel surface and allow to dry. Apply fresh mortar to the Durock Brand Panel and back-butter the tile and push into place.

Prevention: Do not allow the mortar to skin over. Back-butter the tile, slide into place, and beat in to ensure 100% coverage.

Texture Finishes

USG texturing materials offer a wide range of decorative yet practical finishes. Properly used, they can provide interest and variety in decoration while covering minor defects in the base surface. However, certain working conditions, application techniques or equipment problems can cause unsatisfactory results. The following list describes the problem, probable cause, remedy and prevention for particular situations.

Mixing Problems

1. **Mixing— Lumping of Wet Mix**

Cause: Too much water added to initial mix, making lumps difficult to break up.

Remedy and Prevention: Initial amount of water added to mix should be slightly less than recommended. After lumps are broken up, add remaining water.

12

2. Mixing—
Slow Solution
Time

Cause: Insufficient soaking and/or use of very cold water.

Remedy and Prevention: Allow materials to soak for up to two hours, as necessary, if using cold water.

3. Mixing—
Wet Mix Too
Thin

Cause: Addition of excessive water during initial mix. Also, insufficient soaking time in cold water.

Remedy and Prevention: Use recommended amount of water to ensure proper consistency. Allow materials to soak up to two hours, if necessary, when using cold water.

Application Problems

4. Application—
Excessive
Aggregate
Fallout in
Spraying

Cause: Excessive air pressure at nozzle; holding gun too close to surface being sprayed.

Remedy and Prevention: Use proper air pressure for type of material to be sprayed: low for SHEETROCK Brand Ceiling Spray Texture; high for SHEETROCK Brand Wall and Ceiling Spray Texture. (Consult appropriate USG Data Sheet for recommended air pressure.) Hold spray gun at proper distance from surface to prevent excessive bounce or fallout of aggregate.

5. Application—
Flotation of
Aggregate

Cause: Overdilution of job mix and/or lack of adequate mixing after water is added to control consistency.

Remedy and Prevention: Add correct amount of water as directed on bag to ensure proper suspension of materials in mix. Make certain that water is blended into mix.

6. Application—
Poor Coverage
with Spray
Finishes

Cause: Not enough water to bring texture material to proper spray viscosity and/or improper application, such as moving spray gun too slowly, overloading spray surface and using incorrect spray pressures.

Remedy and Prevention: Add proper amount of water as directed on bag. Use correct spray gun pressures and application technique to ensure uniform texture with maximum coverage.

7. Application—
Poor Hide

Cause: Overdilution of mix causing reduction in hiding power. Insufficient water in spray finishes causes poor material atomization, resulting in surface show-through. Also caused by overextending material or choosing incorrect spray pressures.

Remedy and Prevention: See above.

8. Application—
Poor Bond or
Hardness

Cause: Overdilution of jobmix results in thinning out of binder in texture. Contamination or intermixing with other than recommended materials can destroy bonding power.

Remedy and Prevention: Add proper amount of water as stated in bag directions. Always use clean mixing vessel and water. Never intermix with other products (except materials as recommended).

9. Application— Stoppage of Spray Equipment

Cause: Contamination of material or oversize particles can cause clogging of spray nozzle orifices. Also caused by using incorrect nozzle size for aggregate being sprayed.

Remedy and Prevention: Prevent contamination during mixing. Use correct nozzle for aggregate size of texture material.

10. Application— Unsatisfactory Texture Pattern

Cause: Improper spray pressure and/or worn spray equipment, either fluid or air nozzle. Also improper spraying consistency of mix and/or spraying technique.

Remedy and Prevention: Use recommended amount of water to ensure proper spraying consistency. Handle spray equipment correctly to achieve best results. Make certain that spray accessories are in good working condition; replace when necessary.

11. Application— Unsatisfactory Pumping Properties

Cause: Mix too heavy. Pump equipment worn or of insufficient size and power to handle particular type of texture.

Remedy and Prevention: Use recommended amount of water to ensure proper spraying consistency. Make sure that equipment is in good repair and capable of pumping heavy materials.

12. Application— Texture Build-Up

Cause: Texturing over a high-suction drywall joint (surface not properly primed) and/or allowing too much time between roller or brush application and texturing operation. Overdilution of texture material will produce texture build-up over joint.

Remedy and Prevention: Before texturing, apply a prime coat of SHEETROCK Brand First Coat or an undiluted, interior flat latex paint with high solids content. Use correct amount of water when mixing texture material. Allow safe time interval between application and final texturing.

Finish Surface Problems

13. Finish Surface— Poor Touchup

Cause: Touchup of a textured surface to completely blend with the surrounding texture is extremely difficult. A conspicuous touchup is caused either by texture or color variance.

Remedy: Perform touchup operation with extreme care; otherwise, re-texture entire wall or ceiling area.

14. Finish Surface—Joint Show-Through

Cause: Overthinned or overextended texturing material does not adequately hide the normal contrast between joint and gypsum panel paper. Also caused by improperly primed surface.

Remedy: Use correct amount of water when mixing texture material and apply at recommended rate of coverage until joint is concealed.

Prevention: Before texturing, apply a prime coat of SHEETROCK Brand First Coat or undiluted, interior flat latex paint with high solids content.

12

15. Finish Surface— White Band or Flashing Over Gypsum Panels

Cause: High-suction gypsum panel joint causes a texture variation, which often appears as a color contrast.

Remedy: Allow texture to dry, and paint entire surface.

Prevention: Before texturing, apply a prime coat of Sheetrock Brand First Coat or undiluted, interior flat latex paint with high solids content.

16. Finish Surface— White Band or Flashing Over Concrete

Cause: Damp concrete surface on which leveling compound has dried completely can produce results similar to those of high-suction joint.

Remedy: Allow texture to dry, and paint entire surface.

Prevention: Allow concrete to age for at least 60 days for complete dryout. Before texturing, apply a prime coat of Sheetrock Brand First Coat or undiluted, interior flat latex paint with high solids content.

17. Finish Surface— Joint Darkening

Cause: Application over damp joint compound, especially in cold and/or humid conditions.

Remedy: Allow texture to dry completely, and paint entire surface.

Prevention: Allow joint compound to dry completely before priming and texturing. Before texturing, apply a prime coat of Sheetrock Brand First Coat or an undiluted, interior flat latex paint with high solids content.

Conventional Plaster Construction

All USG basecoat and finish plasters are carefully manufactured and thoroughly tested before shipment. Along with the functional characteristics offered, USG plasters are carefully formulated for use under normal, prevailing weather conditions and with aggregates commonly used in the market.

Plasters are adversely affected by aging and abnormal storage conditions, use of the wrong aggregate and improper proportioning, all of which may affect the set, hardness and working properties of the material. Most plaster problems result from the following situations:

1. Adverse atmospheric and job conditions.
2. Set conditions too fast or slow.
3. Poor quality and incorrect proportioning of aggregate.
4. Improper mixing, application or thickness of basecoat or finish.
5. Incorrect lathing practices.
6. Dirty or worn mixing or pumping equipment.

Basecoat and finish coat plasters are so closely interrelated that problems pertaining to their use are treated together. No attempt is made here to discuss problems that might occur due to structural deficiencies. These were covered previously in this chapter. Plaster problems are classified under the specific existing condition. These are discussed in order, in the following groups:

1. Plaster cracks.

2. Blemishes.

3. Color variations and surface stains.

4. Weak, soft walls.

5. Bond failure.

6. Other porblems.

Cracking Problems	Connecting vertical, horizontal cracks at somewhat regular intervals, often in stepped pattern; also diagonal in appearance.

Material: Plaster over metal or gypsum lath.

a. **Cause:** Plaster too thin, insufficient plaster grounds.

   Remedy: Patch.

   Prevention: Apply plaster to proper thickness.

b. **Cause:** Weak plaster (through dryout or slow set).

   Remedy: Spray with alum solution to accelerate set.

   Prevention: Add accelerator to plaster mix to bring setting time to normal range.

c. **Cause:** Excessive use of aggregate.

   Remedy: Patch.

   Prevention: Use proper proportions of aggregate and plaster.

d. **Cause:** Failure to use Striplath reinforcement at potential weak points.

   Remedy: Cut out, reinforce and repair.

   Prevention: Install proper reinforcing.

e. **Cause:** Expansion of rough wood frames.

   Remedy: Remove plaster and lath as necessary. Seal frames and patch.

   Prevention: Seal frames. Cut basecoat along grounds prior to set. Install control joints over frames.

Material: Plaster over unit masonry.

a. **Cause:** Structural movement of masonry units.

   Remedy and Prevention: Correct masonry construction, provide movement relief, patch.

12

Material: Plaster over brick, clay tile or concrete block at door openings.

a. **Cause:** Poor lintel construction, improper frame construction.

   Remedy: Patch.

   Prevention: Use proper frame and lintel construction with self-furring metal lath reinforcement.

Fine cracks, random pattern, generally 1″ to 3″ apart. Includes shrinkage cracks, crazing, alligatoring, chip cracks.

Material: Gauged lime-putty finish over gypsum basecoat, used with any plaster base.

a. **Cause:** Insufficient gauging plaster-shrinkage of lime. Insufficient troweling during setting. Applied finish too thick. Basecoat too wet or too dry and too little or too much suction.

   Remedy: Apply spackling putty and primer-sealer.

   Prevention: Use sufficient gauging plaster, trowel sufficiently or properly condition basecoat before applying finish.

Fine cracks, irregular pattern, generally 6″ to 14″ apart; map cracking.

Material: Trowel finishes over gypsum basecoat—unit masonry plaster base.

a. **Cause:** Finish coat applied too thick.

   Remedy: Patch.

   Prevention: Apply finish coat to 1/16″ thickness but not more than 1/8″.

b. **Cause:** Improper timing of final troweling.

   Remedy: Patch.

   Prevention: Water-trowel as final set takes place (not before) to provide dense, smooth surface.

c. **Cause:** Retempering gauged lime putty.

   Remedy: Discard batch; make up new gauge.

   Prevention: Gauged lime putty should not be retempered once it has started final set.

Random pattern, usually less than 12″ apart, called map, shrinkage or fissure cracking.

Material: Basecoat over masonry.

a. **Cause:** High suction of masonry base.

   Remedy: If bond to base is sound and cracks are open 1/16″ or more, fill by troweling across cracks with properly aggregated plasters. If bond is sound, finish over fine cracks with highly gauged trowel finish or float finish. If curled at edges and bond is unsound, remove and reapply using proper plaster method.

   Prevention: Wet masonry with water to reduce suction before basecoat application.

b. **Cause:** Under-aggregating of basecoat; slow set.

   Remedy: Same as above.

   Prevention: Use 3 cu. ft. of aggregate per 100 lb. gypsum plaster (see Chapter 8 for proper proportion of aggregates). Discontinue use of job-added retarder and accelerator, if necessary, to obtain proper set.

c. **Cause:** Dryout condition.

   Remedy: Spray basecoat either with water or alum solution to thoroughly wet plaster. Proceed same as above.

   Prevention: In hot, dry weather, protect plaster from drying too rapidly before set. Spray plaster during set time if necessary.

Cracking at wall or ceiling angles.

....

Material: Plaster over gypsum lath.

a. **Cause:** Thin plaster.

   Remedy: Cut out and patch.

   Prevention: Follow correct application procedure.

b. **Cause:** Failure to use Cornerite reinforcement.

   Remedy and Prevention: Same as above.

Blemishes

Water-soluble, powdery crystals on surface, generally white but may be colored. Can be brushed off.

....

Material: Basecoat and finish plaster over concrete block or clay tile.

a. **Cause:** Efflorescence. As masonry units dry, water-soluble salts from units or mortar joints leach out and are deposited on the plaster surface.

   Remedy: After plaster surfaces are thoroughly dry, brush off efflorescence, apply oil-based sealer and paint.

   Prevention: On interior walls, eliminate source of moisture, remove efflorescence before plastering; decorate with oil-based sealer and paint. On exterior walls, eliminate moisture source, fur out, lath and plaster.

Pops or peak-like projections which fall out and create little craters or pits; often with final radial cracks.

....

Material: Gauged lime-putty finish.

a. **Cause:** Unslaked lime in mortar which slakes and swells after it is applied.

   Remedy: Remove core of "pops" and patch after popping has ceased.

   Prevention: Allow sufficient soaking time for normal hydrated lime or use double-hydrated lime or a prepared finish such as RED TOP Finish Plaster.

b. **Cause:** Contamination from foreign matter.

12

Remedy: Same as above.

Prevention: Eliminate source of impurity.

Material: Gypsum basecoat and finish.

a. **Cause:** Lumpy or undissolved retarder added on job. Retarder lumps swell or "pop" when wet.

Remedy: Cut out spots and patch.

Prevention: Completely disperse retarder before adding to mix water; mix well to distribute retarder throughout plaster.

Blisters in finish coat occur during or immediately after application.

Material: Gauged lime-putty finish.

a. **Cause:** Base too green (wet); insufficient suction; too much water used in troweling.

Remedy: After finish has set, trowel with very little water.

Prevention: Do not apply finish over green basecoat.

b. **Cause:** Finish too plastic.

Remedy: Same as above.

Prevention: Add small amount of very fine white sand to putty or increase amount of gauging plaster.

Excess material (slobbers) on finish surface.

Material: Gauged lime-putty finish.

a. **Cause:** Improper joining technique, excessive or improper troweling leaves excess material on finished surface.

Remedy: Scrape off excess material before decoration. Seal surface when plaster is dry.

Prevention: Previously applied finish should be cut square for completion of finish. Avoid excessive troweling at joining.

Peeling paint.

Material: Gauged lime-putty finish.

a. **Cause:** Paint applied over wet plaster.

Remedy: Scrape off peeled paint, allow plaster to dry, and redecorate.

Prevention: Be sure plaster is dry before decorating, and use a breather-type paint.

b. **Cause:** Weak finish. Plaster worked through set.

Remedy: Scrape off peeled paint, patch and decorate.

Prevention: Do not retemper or trowel finish after set.

Color Variations and Surface Stains

Streaks and discoloration.

Material: Lime finishes, gauged with gauging plaster or Keenes Cement.

a. **Cause:** Lime and gauging plaster not thoroughly mixed.
Remedy: Seal and decorate.

Prevention: Follow recommended mixing procedures.

b. **Cause:** Too much water used in troweling.

Remedy: Same as above.

Prevention: Apply as little water as possible in troweling.

c. **Cause:** Dirty tools or water.

Remedy: Same as above.

Prevention: Wash tools and use clean water.

Light and dark spots.

Material: Float finish.

a. **Cause:** Improper technique or too much water used in floating.

Remedy: Seal and paint to get uniform color.

Prevention: Follow recommended application procedures.

b. **Cause:** Spotty suction on basecoat which was dampened unevenly by throwing water on with a brush rather than by spraying with a fine nozzle.

Remedy: Same as above.

Prevention: Dampen basecoat uniformly using a fine spray.

Light or flat spots in light-color paint.

Material: Oil-based paint over gauged lime-putty finish.

a. **Cause:** Surface painted too soon after plastering (alkali in lime saponifies paint); paint pigments not limeproof.

Remedy and Prevention: Apply primer-sealer and repaint.

Material: Any colored paint over any plaster finish.

b. **Cause:** Non-uniform absorption results in uneven surface gloss and coloration.

Remedy and Prevention: Apply primer-sealer and repaint.

12

Yellow, brown or pink staining—yellowing.

Material: Any lime-putty finish over any basecoat and plaster base; generally occurs while surface is damp.

a. **Cause:** Contaminated aggregate.

Remedy: Apply primer-sealer and repaint.

Prevention: Use clean aggregate.

b. **Cause:** By-product of combustion from unvented fossil fuel space heaters.

Remedy: Same as above.

Prevention: Vent heaters to outside.

c. **Cause:** Tarpaper behind plaster base; creosote-treated framing lumber; tar or tar derivatives used around job; sulphur or chemical fumes.

Remedy: Same as above.

Prevention: Use asphalted paper. Remove source of air contamination.

Rust.

Material: Plaster over any plaster base.

a. **Cause:** Rusty accessories; or any protruding metal.

Remedy: Apply rust-locking primer-sealer and decorate.

Prevention: Use accessories made of zinc alloy or with hot-dip galvanizing. Do not use accessories that show rust prior to installation.

Soft, Weak Walls

Soft, white, chalky surfaces, occurring during hot, dry weather, usually near an opening.

Material: Gypsum basecoat over any plaster base.

a. **Cause:** Dryout. Too much water has been removed before plaster can set.

Remedy: Spray with alum solution or plain water to set up dryout areas.

Prevention: Screen openings in hot, dry weather; spray plaster during set; raise humidity by sprinkling floor with water.

Soft, dark, damp surfaces occurring during damp weather.

Material: Gypsum basecoat over any plaster base.

a. **Cause:** Sweat-out. Too little ventilation allows water to remain in wall for an extended period after plaster set. Some plaster has redissolved.

Remedy: Dry walls with heat and ventilation. If sweat-out condition continues, there is no remedy; remove and replaster.

Prevention: Properly heat and ventilate during plastering.

Soft, dark, damp surfaces, occurring in freezing weather.

Material: Gypsum basecoat over any plaster base.

a. **Cause:** Frozen plaster.

Remedy: If plaster freezes before set, no remedy except to remove and replaster.

Prevention: Close building, supply heat.

General condition; soft, weak walls; not spotty or due to slow set.

Material: Gypsum basecoat over any plaster base.

a. **Cause:** Too much aggregate or fine, poorly graded aggregate.

Remedy: No remedy; remove and replaster.

Prevention: Use properly graded aggregate and correct proportioning.

Weak plaster.

Material: Gypsum basecoat.

a. **Cause:** Extremely slow set.

Remedy: Spray with alum solution to accelerate set.

Prevention: Add accelerator to plaster mix to bring setting time within normal range.

Material: Gauged lime-putty finish over any basecoat.

a. **Cause:** Too little gauging with insufficient troweling; retempering; basecoat too wet.

Remedy: No remedy; remove and replaster.

Prevention: Use proper ratio of gauging to lime putty. Do not retemper plaster. Trowel adequately to ensure desired hardness.

Bond Failure

Basecoat separation.

Material: Gypsum basecoat over gypsum or metal lath.

a. **Cause:** Too much aggregate; plaster application over frost on lath; freezing of plaster before set; addition of lime or portland cement; excessive delay in plaster application after mixing; extremely slow set; retempering.

Remedy: No remedy except to replaster.

Prevention: Provide proper job conditions during plastering. Follow correct mixing and application procedures.

12

Brown coat separation from scratch coat.

Material: Gypsum basecoat plasters.

a. **Cause:** Weak scratch coat.

Remedy: None; remove and replaster.

Prevention: Use proper aggregate amount. Avoid retempering.

b. **Cause:** Failure to provide mechanical key in scratch coat.

Remedy: Roughen scratch coat and replaster.

Prevention: Cross-rake scratch coat to provide rough surface for brown coat.

c. **Cause:** Dryout of scratch coat.

Remedy: Water-spray scratch coat for thorough set before brown coat application.

Prevention: Provide proper job conditions during plastering; screen openings in hot, dry weather. Water-spray plaster during set. Raise humidity by sprinkling floor with water.

Finish coat separation.

Material: Gauged lime-putty finish applied over gypsum brown coat.

a. **Cause:** Brown coat too smooth, too dry, wet or weak; finish improperly applied.

Remedy and Prevention: Strip off finish, correct condition of brown coat and replaster.

b. **Cause:** Frozen finish coat.

Remedy and Prevention: Remove finish, provide sufficient heat during plastering, reapply finish.

c. **Cause:** Incomplete hydration of finish lime.

Remedy and Prevention: Remove finish; using properly proportioned double-hydrated lime or a prepared finish, reapply finish.

Other Problems

Slow Set—see Soft, Weak Walls.

Quick Set—plaster sets before it can be properly applied and worked.

Material: Gypsum basecoat over any plaster base.

a. **Cause:** Dirty water, tools or mixing equipment; excessive use of accelerator.

Remedy: Discard material as soon as it begins to stiffen; do not retemper.

Prevention: Use clean water, tools and equipment.

b. **Cause:** Mixing too long.

Remedy: See above.

Prevention: Reduce mixing time.

c. **Cause:** Poor aggregate.

Remedy: See above.

Prevention: Use clean, properly graded aggregate or add retarder.

d. **Cause:** Error in manufacture.

Remedy: See above. Send samples to manufacturer's representative.

Prevention: Add retarder.

e. **Cause:** Machine-pumping and application that exceed limits of time and distance pumped for plaster being used.

Remedy: See above.

Prevention: Add retarder. Use plaster designed for machine application.

Erratic Set—lack of uniformity in set.

Material: Gauged lime putty over gypsum basecoat.

a. **Cause:** Variable temperature.

Remedy and Prevention: Maintain uniform job temperature. In cold weather, heat building to min. 55°F.

Works hard or short, loses plasticity and spreadability. Does not carry proper amount of aggregate.

Material: Gypsum basecoat over any plaster base.

a. **Cause:** Aged or badly stored plaster.

Remedy: Obtain fresh plaster and mix equal parts with aged plaster or use less aggregate.

Prevention: Use fresh plaster.

b. **Cause:** Over-aggregating.

Remedy: None.

Prevention: Use proper proportioning.

Material: Gauged lime putty over gypsum basecoat.

a. **Cause:** Aged lime, partially carbonated; warehoused too long or improperly.

Remedy: None.

Prevention: Use fresh material.

b. **Cause:** Improper soaking, slaking. Low temperature during putty preparation.

Remedy: None.

Prevention: Use proper lime-putty preparation procedure. Do not soak at temperatures below 40°F.

12

Soupy Lime—too fluid for proper gauging and application.

Material: Lime putty.

a. **Cause:** Incorrect soaking.

Remedy: None.

Prevention: Follow directions for type of lime being used.

b. **Cause:** Cold weather, cold mixing water.

Remedy: None.

Prevention: The gelling action of lime is retarded when material is soaked in temperatures less than 40°F with cold water. Use warm water to quicken gelling.

Lime material too lumpy for proper blending with gauging plaster.

Material: Lime putty.

a. **Cause:** Old lime.

Remedy: None.

Prevention: Use fresh lime.

b. **Cause:** Damp lime.

Remedy: None.

Prevention: Protect lime from moisture on job and in storage.

c. **Cause:** Incorrect soaking.

Remedy: None.

Prevention: Follow soaking directions for type of lime used.

d. **Cause:** Excessive evaporation.

Remedy: Add proper quantity of water and allow to soak.

Prevention: Cover lime box with tarpaulin to reduce evaporation.

Safety Considerations, Material Handling

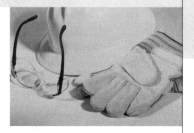

13

This chapter is an overview of the health and safety concerns that should be addressed when USG's products and systems are used at home in do-it-yourself projects or at professional construction sites. The chapter is not intended to be a comprehensive review but instead outlines some major issues, and refers to other sources for information and assistance. No attempt is made at completeness. We recommend that contractors seek the assistance of safety professionals, especially at the professional construction site, because there are many factors to be considered that are not included here.

Introduction

Construction can be a dangerous activity. This is intuitive to many people but it is also borne out by government statistics which show construction to be one of the occupations most likely to result in severe injury or death. The risks are present for "do-it-yourselfers" working around the home as well as for construction professionals.

The key to safety is training. Training leads to familiarity with the hazards and how to avoid them, and is the foundation of any safety program. For people involved in professional construction, guidance is provided by federal OSHA regulations and comparable state laws and regulations. As stated above, the assistance of a safety professional is invaluable. The construction industry, like most others, long ago passed the point where so-called common sense is sufficient by itself to avoid hazards. Instead, today's safety program requires knowledge of many technical issues that are not commonly understood.

For the "do-it-yourselfer" who works around the home, the best approach is to familiarize yourself with all the information available. Sources of information include Material Safety Data Sheets (MSDS) and product warnings. Also, literature produced by the Gypsum Association and guides issued by state and federal agencies can be helpful.

Safety risks can be caused by both physical dangers and health hazards. Physical hazards include, for example, heavy objects falling, panels breaking and electrical hazards. Health hazards are often less obvious and include, for example, the long term harm to the lungs and other organs caused by exposure to crystalline silica and mold, fungus and mildew that can grow on building materials after they get wet. Most people have little or no intuitive sense for what situations pose health hazards. Some of these hazards may be immediate and some may have a delayed effect. In addition, hazardous health effects can occur from a single exposure or as a result of long-term exposure. Thus, this part of safety awareness depends heavily on education. Warning labels and MSDSs are the primary initial sources of health hazard information.

Handling Wallboard and Other Panel Products

SHEETROCK Brand Gypsum Panels, IMPERIAL Brand Gypsum Base, DUROCK Brand Cement Board and FIBEROCK Brand Gypsum Panels are all heavy panels whose handling by machine or by hand poses the risk of serious injury.

A. Forklift Safety

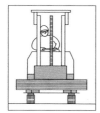

Board products and ceiling tile will first be moved by a forklift or similar device. It is absolutely essential that the equipment be rated capable of handling the loads. The forks should always be long enough to extend completely through the width of the load. Forks should also be extended far enough apart to support the load so that it will not break or fall. Gypsum panels are brittle compared to other building products, such as lumber. If not properly supported, individual panels or a whole lift can break.

SHEETROCK Brand Gypsum Panels and IMPERIAL Brand Gypsum Base:

— Fork spacing between supports should be one-half the length of the panels or base being handled so that a maximum of 4' extends beyond the supports on either end.

FIBEROCK Brand Gypsum Panels:

— Fork spacing should be similar to the above except that a maximum of only 3' should extend beyond the supports on either end.

Fork carriage spread in the range of 46" to 84" is suitable for handling most common lengths of board and panels.

Sometimes gypsum board manufacturers offer to band lifts of board at each end. This will aid in preventing deflection of the board when it is picked up with a forklift but it is not a substitute for proper fork spacing. Banding will not prevent board from breaking if the forks are not spaced far enough apart.

Other key items of forklift safety include:

— Always follow the forklift manufacturer's operating and maintenance instructions, especially concerning the load limits of the forklift.

— Always wear the safety belt when operating a forklift;

— Never move the forklift with the load elevated more than a few inches above the floor or ground surface;

— Never stand below or near a raised load;

— Observe all traffic rules in the loading or warehouse area;

— Never disable equipment back-up alarms or other safety devices;

— In heavy traffic areas, use a spotter to regulate forklift, pedestrian and other traffic.

13

412

For more information on forklift safety, see:

OSHA CFR, (800) 321-OSHA (6742)
National Safety Council, (800) 621-7619

B. Stacking Board

Generally, it is safer to stack board flat.

Gypsum Association literature states unequivocally that board should be stacked flat because stacking boards vertically against a wall poses a safety hazard. See "Handling Gypsum Board," Gypsum Association publication GA-801-93:

"Stacks of gypsum board are very heavy and can become unstable if proper stacking and handling procedures are not followed. Workers must always be extremely careful when stacking or working in an area where gypsum board is stacked. A 4' wide by 12' long by one-half-inch thick gypsum board can weigh over 80 pounds; this means a stack of only 25 boards weighs over a ton." (Page 2)

"Gypsum board should always be stored flat. Placing it vertically on edge for an extended period may damage the edges and can also cause the board to warp. Additionally, board stacked on edge can easily become unstable and accidentally fall over. Stacking gypsum board flat will lower the potential for a safety hazard." (Page 9)

However, there are some situations where stacking the board flat creates different safety hazards. For example, in residential construction where rooms are small and hallways narrow, contractors prefer that the board be stacked vertically against the wall so that tradespeople have room to move around. In these circumstances, board stacked flat could pose a tripping hazard.

Also in residential construction, floor load limits often are not sufficiently high to be able to accommodate a concentrated point load of gypsum panels, cement board or gypsum fiber panels in the center of the floor; instead, the safer procedure in this situation is to distribute the board in vertical stacks around the sides of the room. Sometimes, when different sizes or widths of board are required (for example, 5/8" for the ceiling and 1/2" for the walls) vertical stacking makes it easier for the wallboard hangers to find the board they need.

For all these reasons, in many if not most parts of the country, contractors prefer that the board be stacked vertically. When this is done, be sure to leave at least 4" to 6" of space between the bottom of the first board in the stack and the wall. Leaving less than 4" creates a risk that the stack could be pulled over; leaving more than 6" applies too much weight laterally against the wall.

C. Storage Conditions

Protecting wallboard and other products from rain, snow, sunlight and wind is important. Not only can the weather damage the board by soaking it, but exposure to weather can do other harm not immediately obvious. For example, moisture could affect the bond of the face paper to the gypsum core in a way that later creates problems in application and finishing. Also, ultraviolet (UV) exposure from sunlight will ruin the ability of plaster base panels (blue board) to act as a substrate for some veneer plasters.

More insidious, if wallboard is left unprotected and then installed, moisture in the wallboard can provide conditions favorable for mold, mildew and fungus growth which, as discussed below, poses not only esthetic problems, but also serious health consequences.

Although board products are very heavy, high winds across the flat surfaces of the board can provide "lift" just as with an airplane wing, and thus wind can send heavy pieces of gypsum wallboard flying through the air causing damage and serious injuries.

For more information see:

Handling Gypsum Board
Gypsum Association publication GA-801-93
Tel: (202) 289-5440

D. Lifting

SHEETROCK Brand Gypsum Panels, IMPERIAL Brand Gypsum Base, DUROCK Brand Cement Board, FIBEROCK Brand Gypsum Panels, joint compound packages (buckets or boxes), bags of plaster and ceiling tile packages are all very heavy, awkward loads posing the risk of severe back injury. Proper lifting techniques should always be observed: Keep the load close to your body and use your legs, not your arms, to lift. Use mechanical assistance such as pallet lifters or hand dollies wherever possible. Manual lifting and carrying should be confined to the shortest distance possible.

For more information see:

National Safety Council, (800) 621-7619

Other Physical Hazards

Pallets

Almost all pallets used to transport joint compound, plaster, plaster bags, ceiling tile, cement board and other construction materials are made of wood. Any pallets that are defective or incomplete (missing pieces) should be carefully unloaded and discarded from service. Not only will a broken pallet cause a spill and loss of the product, but it could also lead to serious injuries or death if heavy materials drop on people.

For more information see:

National Wooden Pallet and Container Association, (703) 527-7667

Eye Protection

Safety glasses or goggles protect eyes from a variety of hazards.

Eye protection should be worn at all times, not just when using power equipment. Some products, such as plasters containing lime, pose the risk of a chemical burn of the eye which could result in the loss of sight. However, even without a chemical burn, the mere physical impact of a trowel full of plaster dropped on the eye can cause severe injury or blindness. Eye protection (safety glasses or goggles) also protects the eyes from dust.

For more information, see:

National Safety Council, (800) 621-7619

13

Five-Gallon Bucket Child Drowning Warning

⚠ WARNING
⚠ ADVERTENCIA

Children can fall into bucket and drown.

Keep children away from bucket with even a small amount of liquid.

Los niños pueden caerse en el balde y ahogarse.

Mantenga a los niños alejados del balde, aunque éste contenga sólo una pequeña cantidad de líquido.

In the mid-1980's health officials noticed a pattern in some drowning deaths of very young children (less than three years of age). Several hundred deaths were reported of children drowning after falling into five-gallon buckets that were being used for household purposes (cleaning, storage, etc.). Some children drowned in as little as a few inches of liquid. Investigation showed that while children this age were developed enough to stand up and lean over into the bucket, their muscles were not strong enough to pull them out of the bucket. Also, because their heads were still large compared to the rest of the body, when they fell in, they could not get out. USG led the industry in putting a warning of this hazard on its five-gallon pails. It is a good example of a simple physical hazard that is not obvious. Many parents who would not dream of leaving their small children alone in a bathtub or by a pool might not recognize that a five-gallon bucket with a few inches of water also poses a drowning hazard.

Plaster Burn Warning

Occasionally people will use gypsum plaster in an art class or at home to make an imprint of a hand or other parts of the body. Sometimes, instead of an imprint, they will try to make a cast of the whole hand or other body part, completely enclosing it. This can lead to a serious injury because, as the plaster sets, it traps the hand or other body part, and enough heat is given off in the setting of the plaster to cause serious burns. For many years USG has placed the following warning on plaster products to alert users to this danger:

△ WARNING!

When mixed with water, this material hardens and becomes very hot—sometimes quickly. DO NOT attempt to make a cast enclosing any part of the body using this material. Failure to follow these instructions can cause severe burns that may require surgical removal of affected tissue or amputation of limb. Dust can cause eye, skin, nose, throat or respiratory irritation. Avoid eye contact and inhalation of dust. Wear eye protection. If eye contact occurs, flush thoroughly with water. If dusty, wear a NIOSH/MSHA-approved respirator. Prolonged and repeated exposure to respirable crystalline silica can cause lung disease and/or lung cancer. Use proper ventilation to reduce dust exposure. Do not ingest. If ingested call physician. Product safety information: (800) 507-8899.

KEEP OUT OF REACH OF CHILDREN.

Inappropriate Use of Plasters, Joint Compounds or Other Products

People sometimes use construction materials in situations for which they are not designed, which can cause serious risks of injury or death.

For example, a gypsum plaster should not be used to anchor porch, stadium or balcony railings where the plaster is exposed to the weather. This is an extremely dangerous misuse of gypsum plaster. Rain and snow weakens and dissolves exposed gypsum plaster. The resulting railing failure can cause death or at the very least, serious injury to people falling from the balcony, e.g., or to people on the ground below. In another example of misuse, a person using gypsum plaster as a substitute for the dietary calcium supplement prescribed by a physician can bring about serious medical problems. No gypsum-based construction product is designed for human consumption.

Health Hazards

Perhaps the greatest change in safety programs for the construction industry in the past several decades is the still-growing appreciation of the hazards posed by various chemicals or substances once used or still used in construction materials. These include, for example, asbestos, lead and silica. Note that *no* USG products currently contain any asbestos or lead.

Silica

Crystalline silica quartz which gets into the deep lung (i.e., is respirable) can pose a long-term health risk, including cancer and other severe and debilitating diseases. All dust should be avoided, not just silica-containing dust. Excessive dust strains the lungs and overcomes the body's defense systems. Every step should be taken to avoid the generation of dust. Any dust that is generated should be kept away from people on the job site. All of the following strategies should be pursued to minimize dust exposure:

– Avoid dust generation with power tools. Wherever a product can be scored and snapped as is the case with all of our gypsum panel products, this method should be used rather than power tools to trim the board.

– Where power tools are used, dust-control mechanisms should be employed. Even consumer power tools come with dust control kits, some of which hook up to shop vacs.

– Similarly, when mixing plaster or joint compound in powder form, care should be taken to create as little dust as possible when emptying the bags into the mixer. Ventilation should always be provided or, better yet, provide a local exhaust for the dust.

– Final finishing of joint compound may create excessive dust if the worker or "do-it-yourselfer" is not properly trained to apply joint compound. For years USG and other manufacturers in the industry have recommended wet sanding to reduce or eliminate dust levels. More recently, several equipment manufacturers have offered sanding equipment that uses a combination of wetting and/or local exhaust to remove the dust as it is being created.

13

Mold, Mildew, and Fungus

Mold, mildew, and fungus are all microorganisms which can, under the right conditions, find a suitable environment in which to grow and survive on building materials. Most often this growth is caused by moisture leaking into the building, although condensation, temperature, pH, lack of exposure to sunlight and several other factors also are involved.

In the past, mold and mildew were considered primarily as an esthetic problem which spoiled the appearance of the walls or ceilings and only secondarily as a mild health hazard affecting people with allergies or asthma. Today, the picture has dramatically changed and medical science recognizes that not only can these microorganisms cause potentially severe health problems in people with asthma or allergies, but they also can sometimes pose serious health threats even to people who do not have these conditions. A well-known example is the bacteria that causes the so-called "Legionnaires Disease." Others less well known, but receiving increasing attention in recent years, are organisms such as Stachybatris atra, a fungal pathogen which can grow on wallboard and many other materials in the presence of moisture.

The best way to address mold, mildew and fungus is to make sure that building materials do not get wet before installation and are not exposed to moisture inside the finished building. Traditional building practices, such as management of water away from the interior of the structure, not only constitutes the foundation of good construction practice, but also is the best way to avoid the growth of mold, mildew and fungus. Remove any building products suspected of becoming wet and having mold on them from the jobsite.

Fungicides and Mildewcides

Joint compounds are treated at the factory with fungicides to prevent mold growth in the bucket before the product is used, and to retard the growth of mold and mildew after the product is applied on walls and ceilings. The kinds and formulations of the fungicides and mildewcides have changed over the years. For example, decades ago joint compounds contained mercury-based biocides. These were discontinued by most manufacturers as the health hazards of mercury became better known. Today, USG generally uses tributyl tin benzoate as a mildewcide. However, the quantity of mildewcide or fungicide used in our joint compounds is minute and less than ever before. The amount used is less than 0.1 weight-percent, a quantity less than the reporting requirements of OSHA's Hazard Communication Standard.

Also, there are people who have special conditions (allergies, asthma, etc.) who will react differently and more strongly and adversely than the general population to these mildewcides and fungicides.

For further information, see the websites for EPA's Indoor Air Quality Home Page, American Lung Association Home Page and Canada's Indoor Environmental Program; they are listed at the end of this chapter.

Safety Tips for Installing Ceilings

Safety helmets, safety goggles/glasses and gloves are just three examples of safety equipment for use when installing acoustical ceilings.

When you arrive on the job, bring your safety helmet and cup-type eye goggles with you. Wear eye goggles whenever there is the possibility of eye injury, i.e., when using power-actuated tools, when doing over-head drilling, or when you hammer or drill into concrete.

Wear rubber soled shoes for good traction. Do not wear baggy or torn pants or shirts because these may catch on objects or moving equipment parts and cause injuries (e.g., falls).

Use a kit or tool belt to carry tools. Be very careful when using sharp tools or materials. If you are cut, obtain proper First Aid to avoid infection. If the injury is serious, seek professional help immediately.

Practice good housekeeping: keep work areas free of debris and neatly stack construction materials and panels. Secure these if necessary to prevent falling or sliding.

Personal protective equipment must be used to guard against the hazards of falling, flying or splashing objects, or exposure to harmful dusts, mists, fumes, vapors or gases. If respiratory protection is required, you must be medically certified that you are fit to wear a respirator and you must be properly fitted with the respirator.

Electrical Tools and Cables

Know how to properly use and maintain the power tools used for ceiling installations. Power-operated hand tools should be double insulated or grounded. Defective tools must be successfully repaired before use. Do not use electrical tools in wet conditions (e.g., wet floors). Do not hoist or lower a power tool by its electrical cord.

All cable in the work area must be covered or elevated to prevent damage. Frayed or worn electric cable must never be used. Extension cords must be protected against damage from traffic, sharp corners and projections. Flexible cord must be in continuous lengths without splices. When properly made, molded or vulcanized splices may be used.

When tools are equipped with guards, these must never be removed. The tools must be used with guards operating as they were designed to operate. Belts, gears, shafts or other moving parts must be guarded if there is any possibility that you can be exposed to the moving parts.

Power-Actuated Tools (e.g., Powder Fastening Tool)

These tools should be used only by persons who are properly trained and certified to use them. Powder-actuated tools must be oiled, cleaned and tested each day to make certain that safety devices are working properly. Other tips are as follows:

– Loaded tools must not be left unattended.

– Never point powder-actuated tools at anyone at any time.

– Always wear protective eyewear (goggles) when using these tools.

– Never use these tools in an explosive atmosphere.

– Use only cartridges and fasteners that are supplied by the manufacturer of these tools.

13

— Use these tools only in concrete, steel, mortar or masonry blocks. Use a small guard ("spall pad") when shooting directly into masonry materials to prevent a pin or material from flying free.

— Do not use these tools on wood, plaster, gypsum panels or similar materials unless such materials are backed by concrete, steel, mortar or masonry blocks. Consult with general contractor before using these tools. Some pre-stressed concrete joists have tension rods placed near the bottom of the concrete, and the architect may not permit the use of powder-actuated hangers.

— If the tool misfires, wait at least thirty (30) seconds before removing the tool from the work surface.

Saber and Band Saws

Get proper training on how to use these tools before operating them. Always wear safety goggles when operating saws. Do not wear loose clothing that could get caught in the moving blade.

Scaffolding

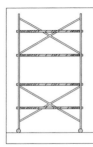

— The height of a scaffold must not exceed four times the minimum base dimension.

— Footings for a scaffold must be rigid and capable of supporting the maximum intended load without settling.

— Do not use barrels, boxes, bricks, concrete blocks or other unstable objects to support scaffolds.

— Casters on wheels must be locked to prevent movement.

— Use cross or diagonal bracing or both to properly brace scaffolds. Scaffolding must be upright, rigid and square. Make certain that poles, legs or uprights are plumb and securely braced to prevent displacement or swaying.

— Scaffolds with platforms 10′ or more above the ground must have guardrails and toeboards installed on all open sides and ends.

— Scaffolds 4′ to 10′ high ("Baker" scaffolds) and with a minimum horizontal dimension of less than 45″ must have guardrails installed on all open sides and ends of their platforms.

— When scaffolding is used as a passageway or work is to be performed under the scaffold, a screen (No. 18 gauge U.S. Standard wire 1/2″ mesh or equivalent) must be provided between the toeboard and guardrail and must extend the entire length of the opening.

— Scaffold planking must overlap a minimum of 12″ or be secured from movement.

— Planks must extend over end supports not less than 6″ and not more than 12″.

— An access ladder or equivalent safe access must be provided.

— Weak or damaged scaffolding parts or components (braces, brackets, ladders, etc.) must be immediately fixed or replaced.

Portable
Scaffolds

Portable scaffolds must be leveled and checked for safety each time they are moved. Do not adjust leg screws more than 12″. Move scaffolds only when the floor is level and free of obstructions. No one should ride on a scaffold that is being moved.

Ladders

Ladders with broken or missing rungs or steps, broken side rails or other defects must not be used at the jobsite.

– Do not use ladders as horizontal platforms, runways or scaffolds.

– Keep ladders out of doorways, driveways and passageways.

– Do not use metal ladders for electrical work or in areas where they may contact electrical conductors.

– Set a ladder such that its base stands 1′ of horizontal distance from the wall for every 4′ of ladder height. The base of the ladder must be level and stable.

– The top of the ladder side rails must extend at least 36″ above a landing.

– The area around the top and bottom of a ladder must be kept clear.

– When using a ladder hold the side rails with both hands when climbing up or down. Carry tools in a kit or on a tool belt when climbing a ladder.

– The feet of portable ladders must be placed on a substantial base (e.g., floor) before being used. Portable ladders must be secured at the top to prevent movement.

Additional Sources of Safety Information

Safety information is easier to find than ever before. OSHA and the comparable state agencies have done a tremendous amount of work in creating and making available materials that describe the hazards and how to prevent them in clear simple ways. Most of this material is also available on the Internet. Trade associations such as the Gypsum Association also make their materials available to the people who use Association members' products.

Organizations referenced throughout this chapter as sources for safety information are below. To contact any of these organizations, see "Agencies and Organizations" on pages 450-454 of the Appendix.

– Occupational Safety & Health Administration (see OSHA), U. S. Department of Labor

– National Safety Council (see NSC)

– National Wooden Pallet and Container Association (see NWPCA)

– American Society of Safety Engineers (see ASSE)

– American Industrial Hygiene Association (see AIHA)

– Gypsum Association (see GA)

13

– Ceiling and Interior Systems Construction Association (see CISCA); for further information about safety practices in installing ceilings, see the latest edition of (CISCA) Ceiling Systems Handbook.

Government agencies and non-profit organizations that may provide useful safety and health information are as follows:

EPA's Indoor Air Quality Home Page Contains information for the homeowner, schools, commercial buildings and environmental professionals on indoor air quality. It has extensive links to sites (http://www.epa.gov/iaq).

American Lung Association Home Page A national education program designed to help you make informed choices to improve your home's indoor environment (http://www.lungusa.org and http://www.healthhouse.org/iaq).

Canada's Indoor Environmental Program The Indoor Environmental Program integrates experimental, analytical and modeling competencies in the areas of lighting, acoustics, ventilation, indoor air quality, thermal comfort, energy efficiency and environmental psychology. The uniqueness of the Indoor Environmental Program lies in its integrated multi-disciplinary projects that combine the broad range of indoor environmental competencies with expertise from other IRC programs (http://www.nrc.ca/irc/ie).

Also listed below are several sources that you may want to consult further. Again, for professional construction, the advice and assistance of a safety professional is highly recommended.

– OSHA/National Association of Home Builders. Jobsite Safety Handbook. NAHB, 1201 15th St. N. W., Washington, DC 20005.

– Handling Gypsum Board, Gypsum Association Publication GA-801-93. Gypsum Association, 801 First Street, NE, #510, Washington, DC 20002; Tel: (202) 289-5440; Fax: (202) 289-3707; Western Office Tel: (602) 527-8466.

– Ceilings & Interior Systems Contractors Association (CISCA) 1500 Lincoln Highway, Suite 202, St. Charles, IL 60174; Tel: (630) 584-1919; Fax: (630) 584-2003:

Preventing the Fall: A Compliance Kit for OSHA's Fall Protection Standard. Includes a video, compliance manual, employee quiz, pocket checklist and employee training log. page manual. Member: $75.00; Non-member: $120.00.

Scaffold Safety Survival Kit. Includes a copy of the regulation, manuals for managers and employees, posters, and a videotape. Member: $70.00; Non-member: $110.00.

– Information available from the U.S. Department of Labor, OSHA/OICA Publications, P.O. Box 37535, Washington, DC 20013-7535:

Ground Fault Protection on Construction Sites—OSHA 3007.

Personal Protective Equipment—OSHA 3077

Fall Protection in Construction—OSHA 3146

Stairways and Ladders—OSHA 3124

- The following publications are available from the Superintendent of Documents, U.S. Government Printing Office, Washington, DC (202) 512-1800:

  Controlling Electrical Hazards—OSHA 3075 Order No. 029-016-00126-3; cost: $1.00.

  Hand and Power Tools-OSHA 3080—Order No. 029-016-00126-3; cost $1.00.

- Information available for purchase from the American National Standards Institute (ANSI), 11 West 42nd St., New York, NY 10036; Telephone: 212.642.4900 or 764.3274:

  ANSI A10.2-44 Safety Code for Building Construction

  ANSI A10.3-70 Safety Requirements for Explosive-Actuated Fastening Tools

  ANSI A12.1-67 Safety Requirements for Floor and Wall Openings, Railings, and Toe Boards

  ANSI A14.1 1-68 Safety Code for Portable Wood Ladders. Supplemented by ANSI A14.1a-77

  ANSI A14.2-56 Safety Code for Portable Metal Ladders, Supplemented by ANSI A14.2a-77

  ANSI A14.3-56 Safety Code for Fixed Ladders

  ANSI Z87.1-68 Practice of Occupational and Educational Eye and Face Protection

  ANSI Z89.2-69 Practices for Respiratory Protection

  ANSI Z89.1-69 Safety Requirements for Industrial Head Protection

Information available on the Internet
http//www.osha.gov:

A Guide to Scaffold Use in the Construction Industry. OSHA Pub. 3150 (1998), 77 pp. PDF file.

Selected Construction Regulations for the Home Building Industry. OSHA Regulation 29CFR 1926:
Subpart E - Personal Protective and Life Saving Equipment
Subpart I - Tools - Hand and Power
Subpart K - Electrical
Subpart L - Scaffolds
Subpart M - Fall Protection
Subpart X - Stairways and Ladders

13

Tools & Equipment

The Tools You Need

USG does not manufacture or distribute tools or equipment; however, suitably designed tools are essential for high-quality workmanship. Using the right tools for specific jobs can improve efficiency and reduce labor costs. This Chapter contains an extensive sampling of tools designed to meet the needs of acoustical, drywall, veneer plaster and plastering contractors. Some of the more commonly used hand tools can be found at building material dealers, hardware stores and home centers.

Framing and Acoustical Ceiling Installation Tools

Laser Alignment Tool
An extremely precise device that utilizes a visible laser beam for all construction alignment jobs. Provides maximum accuracy and speed for laying out partitions and leveling suspended ceiling grids.

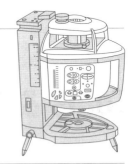

Power Fastener Driver
Used to drive fasteners into concrete or steel for attachment of framing members. Powder-driven model shown. Available in air-driven and powder-driven models.

End Cut Nippers
Lather's nippers for wire-tied attachments of metal lath, ceiling grid and framing components.

Metal Snips
Hand tool used to make straight cuts in steel framing components and trims. Several sizes and styles available. Models are available to make left and right curved cuts.

Channel Stud Shear
Cuts steel studs and runners quickly, cleanly without deforming. Has fixed guides for 1-5/8″, 2-1/2″ and 3-5/8″ sizes. For use with a maximum steel thickness of 20 ga.

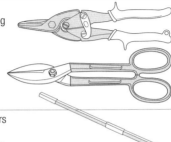

Circular Saw	Cuts steel studs, runners and joists of various gauges with appropriate abrasive metal-cutting blade. Hand-held and portable, it ensures easy on-site cutting and trimming. Use a carbide-tipped blade for cutting DUROCK Brand Cement Board. 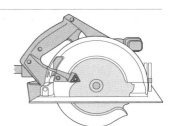
Chop Saw	The chop saw's abrasive metal cutting blade cuts all steel framing members. Its steel base can be placed on a bench, saw horse or floor for fast and efficient gang-cutting of members. 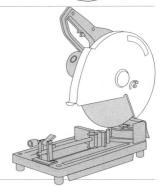
Band Saw	A variety of models are available for use in cutting steel framing members. (Not shown)
Cut-Off Saw	Gas powered for use where electricity is not available, this hand-held saw uses an abrasive blade and provides more power than a circular saw. 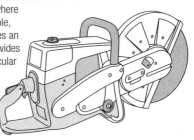
Stud Crimper	For setting and splicing metal studs, roughing-in door holders and window headers, setting electrical boxes and punching hanger-wire holes in ceiling grids. 

14

Combination Chalk Line Box and Plumb Bob

A plumb-bob shaped device that holds retractable chalk line and chalk. Single tool plumbs floor-ceiling alignments, snaps chalk line.

String Line

Strong nylon string that is stretched taught between two distant points, such as midpoints for ceiling grid wall angles, so that additional components can be aligned to the same level plane. (Not shown.)

Magnetic Spirit Level

Magnetized to attach to steel framing, this level assures member level and plumb. Typical length is 4'; available in 2'-7' lengths.

Water Level

Hose type level, filled with water. Especially useful for ceiling grid installation.

Locking Pliers/Clamps

Adjustable lock mechanism in the grip assures that the clamps hold securely. Excellent for holding steel framing and acoustical grid members in place during screw attachment.

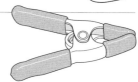

Spring Clamps

Faster and easier to use than locking clamps, and excellent for light-duty applications.

Lineman's Pliers

Square-nosed pliers with flat jaws and integral wire cutter. Flat jaws are used for joining wire such as suspension ceiling tie wire together by twisting; cutter is used for quickly removing excess.

Acoustical Punch Pliers   Plier type tool used for punching holes in acoustical ceiling grid tees for hanger wire attachment, or for wall angle corners or other joints that need to be secured by pop rivets.

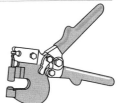

Pop Rivet Tool   Plier-type tool used to flare and secure pop rivets through prepared holes. Especially useful for securing wall angle corners or tee joints in suspended acoustical ceiling applications.

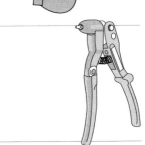

Serrated Knife   Knife with serrated edges makes cutting insulation easy.

Board and Lath Application Tools

Steel Rule   Retractable steel tape measure is essential for accurate measurements in preparation for cutting and attaching board.

T-Square   4' square is indispensable for making accurate cuts across the narrow dimension of board products. Also available in 54" length for wider panels.

Utility Knife   The standard knife for cutting board products. Has replaceable blade; extra blades store in handle.

14

Hook-Bill Knife

Useful for trimming gypsum boards and for odd-shaped cuts. (Also commonly known as linoleum knife.) Use a carbide-tipped version of this knife for scoring DUROCK Brand Cement Board.

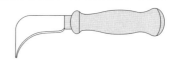

Drywall Saw

Short blade and coarse teeth (inset above) for cutting gypsum boards quickly and easily.

Keyhole-Type Utility Saw

Saw for cutting small openings and making odd-shaped cuts. Sharp point and stiff blade can be punched through board for starting cut.

Circle Cutter

Calibrated steel shaft allows accurate cuts up to 16″ diameter.

Electric Router

Used with specially designed bits for cutting openings in gypsum panels for electrical boxes, heating ducts and grilles, and other small passage ways. For cutting cement board or fiber-reinforced gypsum panels, other specialty bits are used.

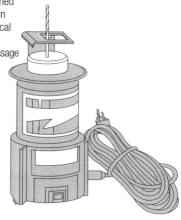

Tack Claw

A screw driver with claw attached. Gives user the opportunity to correct improper fastener attachment or remove fastener.

Rasp

Quickly and efficiently smooths rough-cut edges of gypsum boards. Manufactured model at left features replaceable blade and clean-cut slot to prevent clogging. Job-made model at right consists of metal lath stapled to a 2″ x 4″ wood block.

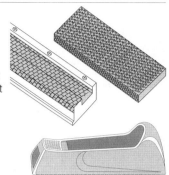

Lather's Hatchet

The standard nailing and cutting tool for gypsum lath.

Drywall Hammer

Has waffle-patterned convex face designed to compress gypsum panel face and leave desired dimple. Blade end is not for cutting but for wedging and prying panel. Not for veneer plaster bases, which require a tool with a flatter head.

Kick Lifter

Device is designed to move the panel forward as it lifts. Can be used for panels applied either perpendicular or parallel. Two types are shown.

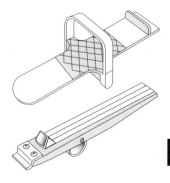

14

Panel Lift
Cradle-type lifter allows one-person application of drywall to sidewalls and sloped ceilings as well as level ceilings. Tripod base with rollers for easy movement.

Electric Screw Gun
Electric-power screw guns drive drywall screws in gypsum board attachment. Special chuck and tip control screw depth to assure that face paper is not broken. Also used for steel-stud framing and acoustical ceilings.

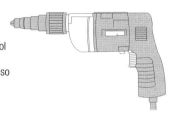

Cordless Screw Gun
Operates with power from battery pack which can be readily recharged. Drill body with special chuck and tip.

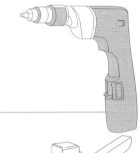

Pistol-Type Stapler
For attachment of insulation blankets to wood studs and to the inner face of gypsum boards in steel-framed assemblies. Also for attachment of corner beads, Striplath, Cornerite and fiberglass mesh tape.

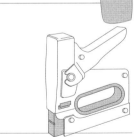

Electric or Pneumatic Stapler
Used for all staple attachment applications. Electric or pneumatic power assures greater staple leg penetration.

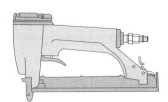

Caulking Equipment

Cartridge-Type Caulking Gun

Hand-operated apparatus uses 29-oz. cartridges. Bead size determined by cut of cartridge nozzle. Aids uniform application of adhesive. Smaller version uses 10-oz. cartridges.

Bulk-Type Caulking Gun

For high-volume applications. Cylinder is reloaded from bulk container of adhesive. Trigger mechanism withstands rough usage and offers minimum resistance to large bulk load of adhesive. Gun has 1-qt. capacity.

Loader Pump

Pump clamps on 5-gal. container to mechanically load bulk-type adhesive hand guns. Eliminates waste of hand and paddle loading.

Drum Extruder

Pumping machine designed for high-volume output of viscous material. Provides greater efficiency in the transfer, flow and spray of adhesives used to supplement or replace nail or screw attachment of panels and sheet material, especially flooring, partitions and ceilings. Large pumping equipment permits bulk material purchases, and contributes to job economy and waste reduction.

Most machine dispensing systems are available with a selection of pumps, flow valves, nozzles and accessories. Equipment manufacturers offer a wide choice of components to provide the exact system for the job.

Pail Extruder

For high-volume extrusion of adhesives from pails. Air power depends on viscosity (low, medium or high) of the material. Offered in portable or mobile units with pump, air regulators and gauge, pail ram, adapter and hose.

14

Mixing Equipment

Hand Mixer

For hand-mixing joint compounds. Available in several styles, all looking much like potato mashers. Model with rounded edge is especially effective for scraping material from sides of mixing bucket.

Heavy-Duty Drill

While hand mixing of joint compounds and textures is adequate, most applicators prefer electric mixers. Power mixing saves considerable time, particularly on large jobs where mixing in a central location is most convenient. Use a 1/2″ heavy-duty electric drill operating at a speed of 450-650 rpm. for joint compounds, 300-600 rpm for textures. Drills that operate at high speeds will whip air bubbles into the mix, rendering it unfit for finish coat purposes.

Use a 1/2″ electric drill with a no-load rating of 900 to 1,000 rpm for mixing veneer plasters.

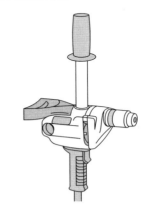

Joint Compound and Texture Mixing Paddle

Mixing paddles are available in various styles, such as the typical example shown. Paddles designed for joint compounds and textures, however, should not be used for mixing veneer plaster finishes. The latter require a special cage-type paddle (see below).

Veneer Plaster Mixer

The recommended mixer for USG veneer plaster finishes is a cage-type paddle. This paddle provides high shear action, necessary for proper dispersion of plaster ingredients in mixing water, and to develop high plasticity in

the mix. Operated at proper speed, the paddle mixes thoroughly, producing a virtually air-free plaster.

Plaster and Stucco Mixer	Standard paddle-type mixer for stucco and conventional plasters (not suitable for veneer plaster finishes). Available with capacities from 5 to 7 cu. ft. in either electric or gasoline-powered models.	
Lime Mixer	A vertical drum mixer that consists of an electric motor (which drives shaft-mounted paddles) mounted atop an open-end drum. Models are available for mixing double-hydrated lime. Lime mixers are typically made in 16- and 30-gal. sizes to accommodate one- and three-bag mixing assignments.	

Finishing Tools

Mud Pan	A pan, shaped like a bread pan, used as a joint compound carrier for the hand finisher. Edge of the pan is used for blade-cleaning. Available in a wide range of sizes and material composition, including stainless steel (preferred), plastic with removable knife-cleaning blade, galvanized steel and tinplate.	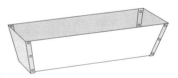
Hawk	Suitable for carrying any cementitious material by a hand applicator—joint compound, plaster, veneer finishes and stucco. Available in sizes from 8" x 8" to 14" x 14" and in aluminum and magnesium.	

14

Banjo

A box-type applicator that passes paper tape through a compartment filled with joint compound so that both materials are simultaneously applied to joints.

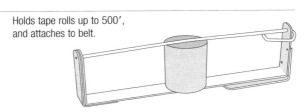

Tape Holder

Holds tape rolls up to 500', and attaches to belt.

Taping Knives

4", 5" and 6" knives are designed for taping, fastener spotting, angle taping and finishing; an 8" or wider knife for finish coating. The two narrower knives are available with either plain handle or with hammer-head handle. Other drywall finishing knives are available with blade widths from 1" up to 24". Long-handle models also available.

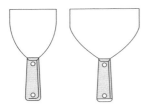

Convertible Hopper

Hopper holds and dispenses joint compound evenly onto paper-faced metal corner bead. Will accommodate both 90° and bullnose bead con-figurations.

Outside Roller Tool

Tool used to press paper faced metal corner beads into place for precise trim alignment.

Hand Sander

Sandpaper is attached with end clamps to the 3-1/4″ x 9-1/4″ base plate. Models include those with wood or aluminum handles.

Pole Sander

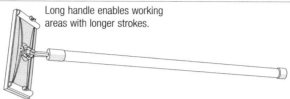

Long handle enables working areas with longer strokes.

Vacuum Power Sander

For fast and easy sanding of large areas. Vacuum dramatically reduces the amount of airborne particles.

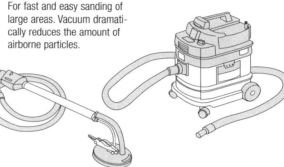

Angle Trowel

For interior corner finishing of veneer plaster and drywall jobs. Similar tool with narrower blades available for conventional plaster. May also be used to evenly apply joint compound.

Browning Rod

Also known as a straight edge. Available in various lengths from 4′ to 8′, browning rods or straight edges are stiff, rectangular rods used for leveling first or base coats of plaster, typically across grounds.

14

Feather Edge

Another broad tool, similar to a straight edge except precision tapered to enable feathering of plaster, generally from corners, intersections or terminations, out onto the plaster plane and into the field of already-applied plaster.

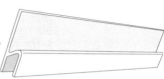

Slicker

A tool with a beveled edge often used in place of a darby, to level and smooth plaster coats.

Darby

For leveling, smoothing or floating plaster brown coat, where an especially true and even surface is desired. Made of wood, metal-edged wood or all metal. Notched darby (pictured) is for scratching basecoats.

Float

A device for leveling and straightening the finish coat or to correct surface irregularities. They are also used to produce a sand-finish effect on plaster surfaces. Floats typically are faced with hard rubber (shown), but may also be made of sponge rubber, cork, felt or carpet.

Angle Float

Angle floats are used for inside corner work with conventional plasters. Can be used for either brown or finish coat.

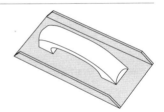

Blister Brush

Felt pad used to keep the plaster finish wet while finish troweling. This brush can also be used for wet-sanding joint compound.

Trowels

Available in several styles and in lengths from 10" to 16". Trowels are the standard tools for veneer plaster and conventional plaster work. Also used by drywall finishers.

Margin Trowel

A narrow trowel used to touch-up small areas, and for cleaning tools and equipment.

Pointer Trowel

Pointed trowel enabling finishing of sharp angles.

Scarifier

A wire-barbed tool for raking the wet surface of the scratch coat, so that the brown coat can key and bond correctly.

Scrub Brush

Needed for cleanup. Residue on tools or containers can affect performance of future material batches.

Mechanical Taping Tools

This line of specialized equipment is designed to speed and facilitate high-volume taping and joint finishing operations.

Hand Pump

Fills mechanical tools from 5-gal. pail.

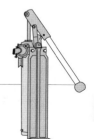

14

Automatic Taper　Tube-style device applies a metered amount of compound onto the tape, places the tape on the wall and cuts the tape to length. Works for flat joints or corners. The original taper is sold under the BAZOOKA® trade name.

Corner Roller　Used to embed tape in corner and force excess compound from under tape prior to using the corner finisher box.

Corner Applicator Head　Attaches to pole to wipe down and feather taping compound on both sides of a corner in one pass. This head is also used as an attachment with Corner Finishing Box (see below) for application of topping.

Corner Finishing Box　Application box used to apply joint compound to corners. It is used with an appropriate attachment, such as the Corner Applicator Head (above) or Paper-Faced Bead Applicator Head (below).

Paper-Faced Bead Applicator Head　Attaches to Corner Finishing Box for application of taping compound to corners prior to application of Paper-Faced Metal Bead.

Flat Finisher Box　Application box places a defined layer of compound 7"-12" wide on flat surfaces. Various handle lengths available to reach different height ceilings.

Hand Texture Equipment

Stucco Brush

For creating a variety of textures from stipple to swirl.

Texture Brush

Available in many sizes and styles, tandem-mounted brushes cover large area to speed texturing job. The texture brush may be attached to a pole for greater reach.

Wipedown Blade

Tool has hardened steel blade and long handle to speed cleaning of walls and floors after application of joint compound or texture materials. Straight wipedown blade is also used to knock down splatters to produce splatter-knockdown surface texture.

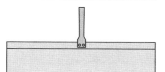

Roller

Standard paint roller is adapted to particular type of finish required. Roller sleeves available include short-nap, long-nap and carpet type in standard 9″ and 18″ widths.

Roller Pan

For use with roller. Some models can hold up to 25-lb. supply of mixed texture.

Glitter Gun

For spraying glitter on wet texture ceilings. Hand-crank model shown is most economical but is not as efficient as air-powered type (not shown).

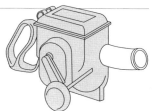

14

Spray Texture Equipment

Hopper Gun

This machine, with a spray gun and material hopper mounted together to form an integral unit, handles most types of drywall texture and fine-aggregate finish plaster materials. Material is gravity-fed through a hand-held hopper. Compressed air is introduced at the spray-nozzle orifice where texture material is atomized and applied to substrate.

Universal Spray Machines

When machine speed, air pressure and/or nozzle are adapted to material used, equipment in this group can handle drywall textures, veneer plaster finishes and conventional plasters, stucco and fireproofing materials.

Several factors must be considered in the selection of new equipment of this type, including: the type of material to be sprayed, type of finish desired, output volume required, the distance (horizontally and vertically) that the material is to be pumped, and portability of the machine through the halls and doorways in a building.

The following information is general in nature, offered to aid in the selection of new spray equipment. Equipment is discussed in terms of the commonly used types of pumping devices. Prospective equipment buyers should discuss their individual needs with manufacturers and users of the equipment.

Four pump types are available: Rotor-stator (Moyno), Peristaltic (squeeze-type), Piston (single and multi-piston), and Diaphragm. While the delivery of material is sufficient with each of these pump types, the mechanical differences may result in operational preferences of one type over the rest. Each operator must determine which will work best for his or her application. Depending on the size, much of this equipment can be trailer or truck mounted.

Rotor-Stator (Moyno) Pump

This pump uses a screw mechanism to pump material forward through a cylinder. The auger-type rotor is powered by an electrical or gas motor and rotates in place within a stationary metal sleeve that is lined with a pliable material such as rubber or neoprene (the stator) to assure rotor-to-stator contact and stop back flow. The auger (rotor) moves material from the hopper into the cylinder (stator) and drives it through the hose.

Rotor-stator pumps have a relatively high wear incidence with abrasive aggregates such as sand or perlite. However, they are particularly suited for pumping textures with polystyrene aggregates since these aggregates introduce "slip" into the mix and reduce pumping resistance. In addition, the smooth, constant delivery action makes rotor-stator pumps a good choice for very fine textures. The trailer-mounted rig shown is equipped with two separate self-contained mixing tanks and two rotor-stator pumps.

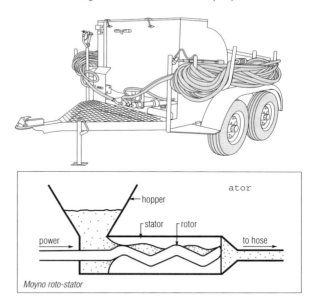

Moyno roto-stator

Peristaltic Pump

The action of this type of pump is like that of a wheel running lengthwise over a hose, squeezing material in the hose forward (the pump is sometimes called a "squeeze-type" pump). Multiple rollers pass over the pumping line and ensure smooth, constant material delivery. Offers the same benefits as the rotor-stator pump. Designed for long wear. Excellent for relatively low volume installations. The peristaltic pump set-up shown includes a hopper to hold material and is mounted on wheels for easy movement on the jobsite.

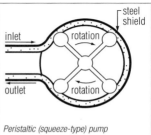

Peristaltic (squeeze-type) pump

14

Piston Pumps

Piston pumps operate on much the same principal as pistons in an automobile engine, drawing material into a cylinder through one port and out through another. In the case of a piston pump, the material is drawn from the hopper into a cylindrical chamber through a check valve as the piston is withdrawn. As the piston moves forward again, a check valve closes and the piston's ram action forces the material through the other check valve into the hose.

Single-Piston

In single-piston pumps, the material is drawn from the hopper into a large main cylinder and then into a smaller surge cylinder. The two-stage process assures continuous material flow and equalizes pressures within the chambers to keep pulsations at an acceptable level. Actual material flow into the hose is dictated by the action in the surge cylinder. The piston ram only displaces about half of the material in the cylinder and into the hose. As that action takes place at one end of the piston, a check valve opens at the other end, drawing more material into the main cylinder to renew the process.

Although single-piston pumps do deliver materials with some amount of surge, many operators who specialize in perlite texture work prefer them because of their low-wear, low-maintenance performance. These are high-volume pumps that can be metered for moderately fine textures.

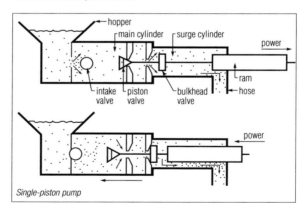

Single-piston pump

Multi-Piston

Pumps having two or more pistons share a common feature. All are designed to reduce surge to the lowest possible level. One piston is discharging material into a manifold (which in turns connects to the material hose), while another cylinder is recovering and drawing material from the hopper in preparation for a pump stroke.

In comparative terms, multi-piston pumps deliver the highest volume of material of all pump types. Like single-piston machines, these pumps can be metered down for a moderately fine texture.

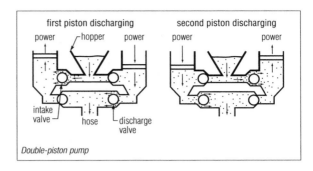

first piston discharging second piston discharging

Double-piston pump

Diaphragm Pump A diaphragm pump's operation is similar to a piston pump in that it draws material into a chamber with one action and discharges it with another. The difference is that the diaphragm itself enables the chamber size to expand and contract. As the diaphragm moves in one direction, material is drawn from the hopper into the chamber through a check valve. When the diaphragm moves in the other direction, that check valve closes and another opens, allowing material to move on into the hose.

The special advantage of a diaphragm pump is that the diaphragm separates the mechanical action of the pump from the material flow, making cleanup and maintenance easier. The set-up shown here has a material hopper placed above the pump, and the wheeled cart also has a self-contained compressor.

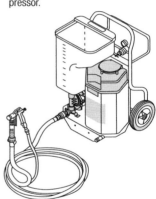

Hoses, Guns, Nozzles

Hoses Used to carry material from pump to nozzle. They vary in type and generally have a diameter of 3/4″ to 1″.

Pole Guns Used with any universal spray machines as well as largest of drywall texture machines described earlier in this section. Their length allows any operator to spray moderately high ceilings without scaffolding or stilts. Model shown has electric start-stop control. Also available with air start-stop control.

14

Texture Guns

Professional-type equipment for specific texture applications is manufactured by Binks, Graco and others. Each gun is designed for specific product applications, for instance the Binks Model 7E2 Type Texturing Gun is used for high volume or heavy texture designs, while the Binks Model 7D Type is for lighter textures. Follow the manufacturer's guidelines for selection to meet particular applications.

Nozzles

Provide for a variety of spray textures, and vary in orifice openings from 1/4″ to 5/8″.

Those used for conventional texturing are never larger than 1/2″.

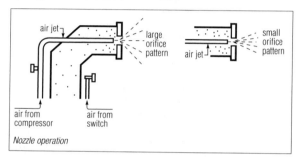

Nozzle operation

Spray Shield

Wide aluminum or plastic shield protects abutting wall or ceiling against overspray during spraying operation. Various widths available.

Miscellaneous Equipment

Joint Compound and Adhesive Spreaders

Made either commercially or by the applicator, these are used for applying joint compound in laminated gypsum panel assemblies.

A notched trowel is commercially available in either metal or disposable plastic. Depending on the notch configuration, these are often sufficient for job applications.

The spreader shown (below left) is easily made on the job. Stainless or galvanized sheet steel make the best spreaders. Other materials are *not*

satisfactory because compound tends to accumulate and dry in the notches. A good spreader blade has about the same stiffness as a plasterer's trowel.

Notches should be an inverted "V" shape, 1/2" deep, 3/8" wide at the base and spaced 1-1/2" to 2" o.c. A piece of wood dowel or window stop attached near top edge of blade provides a grip.

The tool shown (below right) is a laminating spreader that applies properly sized beads of adhesive at correct spacings.

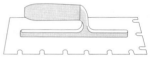

Gypsum Board Dolly

For efficient transport of gypsum boards around the floors of a building. The load, centered over large side wheels, is easily steered and moved by one worker.

Folding Trestle Horse

Top surface provides work surface or stand-on work platform. Legs adjust in increments.

14

446

Scaffold

Portable and easy to set up. Wheels lock for safety and security. Wide variety of sizes and types of scaffold are available to meet job requirements.

Stilts

Convenient way to reach high areas on drywall, veneer plaster and plaster jobs. Gives applicator full mobility plus height needed for ceiling work. Stilts have articulated joints to flex with ankle movement. Available in fixed-height and adjustable-height types (adjustable, articulated model shown).

Floor Scrapers

Scrapers have hardened steel blades and long handles to speed cleaning of floors after application of joint compound, plaster or texture materials. Blades are often replaceable.

Manufacturers

The following tool manufacturers provided illustrations or information for the creation of this chapter.

Ames Taping Tools and Systems, Duluth, GA

ITW (Binks) Industrial Finishing, Glendale Heights, IL

Bjorklund Manufacturing, Kirkland, WA

Dewalt Industrial Tool Company, Hampstead, MD

Empire Level Manufacturing Corporation, Waukesha, WI

Stanley Proto Industrial tools, Covington, GA

Graco Inc., Minneapolis, MN

Hilti, Inc., Tulsa, OK

Hyde Manufacturing Company, Southbridge, MA

Malco Products, Inc., Annandale, MN

Marshalltown Trowel Company, Marshalltown, IA

Milwaukee Electric Tool Company, Brookfield, WI

Pla-Cor Inc., Santee, CA

Porter-Cable Corporation, Jackson, TN

Quikspray, Inc., Port Clinton, OH

ITW Ramset/Red Head. Wood Dale, IL

Roto-Zip Corporation, Cross Plains, WI

S-B (Skil-Bosch) Power Tools, Chicago, IL

Spectra-Precision Inc., Dayton, OH

Spray Force Manufacturing, Fresno, CA

Wallboard Tool Company, Long Beach, CA

Wind-Lock Corp., Leesport, PA

14

Appendix

Agencies and Organizations

ACI	ACI International (American Concrete Institute) P.O. Box 9094 38800 Country Club Drive Farmington Hills, MI 48333	Phone: 248-848-3700 Fax: 248-848-3720 Website: http://www.aci-int.net/ E-mail: jtosca@aci-int.org
AGC	Associated General Contractors of America 333 John Carlyle Street Alexandria, VA 22314	Phone: 703-548-3118 Fax: 703-548-3119 Website: http://www.agc.org E-mail: info@agc.org
AFPA	American Forest & Paper Association 1111 19th Street NW, Suite 800 Washington, DC 20036	Phone: 202-463-2700 Fax: 202-463-2785 Website: http://www.afandpa.org E-mail: info@afandpa.org
AIA	American Institute of Architects 1735 New York Avenue, N.W. Washington, DC 20006	Phone: 202-626-7300 Fax: 202-626-7587 Website: http://www.aiaonline.com E-mail: aiaonline@aiamail.aia.org
A Ins. A	American Insurance Association 1130 Connecticut Ave., N.W. Washington, DC 20036	Phone: 202-828-7100 Fax: 202-293-1219 Website: http://www.aiadc.org E-mail: membership@aiadc.org
AIHA	American Industrial Hygiene Association 2700 Prosperity Avenue, Suite 250 Fairfax, VA 22031	Website: www.aiha.org
AISI	American Iron and Steel Institute 1101 17th Street, N.W. Washington, DC 20036	Phone: 202-452-7100 Fax: 202-463-6573 Website: http://www.steel.org E-mail: dwalson@steel.org
ANSI	American National Standards Institute 11 W. 42nd Street, 13th floor New York, NY 10036	Phone: 212-642-4900 Fax: 212-398-0023 Website: http://www.ansi.org E-mail: ansionline@ansi.org
APA	APA, The Engineered Wood Association (formerly: American Plywood Association) P.O. Box 11700 Tacoma, WA 98411	Phone: 253-565-6600 Fax: 253-565-7265 Website: http://www.apawood.org E-mail: help@apawood.org
ASA	Acoustical Society of America 2 Huntington Quadrangle Suite 1N01 Melville, NY 11747-4502	Phone: 516-576-2360 Fax: 516-576-2377 Website: http://asa.aip.org E-mail: asa@aip.org
ASC	Adhesive and Sealant Council, Inc. 7979 Old Georgetown Road Suite 500 Bethesda, MD 20814	Phone: 301-986-9700 Fax: 301-986-9795 Website: http://www.ascouncil.org E-mail: malinda.armstrong@ ascouncil.org

ASHRAE	American Society of Heating, Refrigerating and Air Conditioning Engineers, Inc. 1791 Tullie Circle, N.E. Atlanta, GA 30329	Phone: 800-527-4723 or 404-636-8500 Fax: 404-321-5478 Website: http://www.ashrae.org E-mail: ashrae@ashrae.org
ASSE	American Society of Safety Engineers 1800 E. Oakton Street Des Plaines, IL 60018	Phone: 800-380-7101 Website: www.asse.org
ASTM	American Society for Testing and Materials 100 Barr Harbor West Conshohocken, PA 19428-2959	Phone: 610-832-9585 Fax:: 610-832-9555 Website: http://www.astm.org E-mail: service@astm.org
AWCI	Association of the Wall & Ceiling Industries International 803 West Broad Street, Suite 600 Falls Church, VA 22046	Phone: 703-534-8300 Fax: 703-534-8307 Website: http://www.awci.org E-mail: info@awci.org
BIA	Brick Industry Association (formerly: Brick Institute of America) 11490 Commerce Park Drive Reston, VA 20191	Phone:703-620-0010 Fax: 703-620-3928 Website: http://www.brickinfo.org E-mail: cooney@bia.org
BOCA	BOCA International* (Building Officials and Code Administrators) 4051 West Flossmoor Road Country Club Hills, IL 60478	Phone: 708-789-2300 Fax: 708-799-4981 Website: http://www.bocai.org E-mail: info@bocai.org
CABO	Council of American Building Officials Now incorporated into International Code Council (see ICC)*	
CISCA	Ceiling and Interior Systems Construction Association 1500 Lincoln Highway, Suite 202 St. Charles, IL 60174	Phone: 630-584-1919 Fax: 630-584-2003 Website: http://www.cisca.org E-mail: cisca@cisca.org
CSI	Construction Specification Institute 99 Canal Center Plaza, Suite 300 Alexandria, VA 22314	Phone: 703-684-0300 or 800-689-2900 Fax: 703-684-0465
DRCI	Drywall Finishing Council 345 West Meats Avenue Orange, CA 92865	Phone: 714-637-2770 Fax: 714-921-8974 E-mail: none
EIMA	EIFS Industry Members Association 3000 Corporate Center Drive Suite 270 Morrow, GA 30260	Phone: 770-968-7945 Fax: 770-968-5818
GA	Gypsum Association 810 First Street, NE, Suite 510 Washington, DC 20002	Phone: 202-289-5440 Western Office: 602-527-8466 Fax: 202-289-3707 Website: http://www.gypsum.org E-mail: info@gypsum.org

* The International Code Council is an umbrella organization. It is composed of what was formerly CABO, and BOCA, ICBO and SBCCI which are all still operating separately and as part of ICC. Only CABO has changed its name to ICC at this point.

GSA	General Services Administration (U.S.) 1800 F Street, NW, Suite 6137 Washington, DC 20405	Phone: 202-501-0800 Fax: 202-219-1243 Website: http://www.gsa.gov E-mail: dave.barram@gsa.gov
HUD	Department of Housing & Urban Development (U.S.) 451 Seventh Street, SW Washington, DC 20410	Phone: 202-708-0417 (General phone number) Fax: 202-619-8129 (Administration Office) Website: http://www.hud.gov E-mail: no general e-mail
ICBO	International Conference of Building Officials* 5360 Workman Mill Road Whittier, CA 90601-2298	Phone: 800-284-4406 or 562-699-0541 Fax: 888-329-4226 Website: http://www.icbo.org E-mail: johnson@icbo.org
ICC	International Code Council* 5203 Leesburg Pike, Suite 708 Falls Church, VA 22041	Phone: 703-931-4533 Fax: 703-379-1546 Website: http://www.intlcode.org E-mail: staff@intlcode.org
ML/SFA	Metal Lath/Steel Framing Association; now a division of National Association of Architectural Metal Manufacturers (see NAAMM)	
NAAMM	National Association of Architectural Metal Manufacturers 8 South Michigan Avenue Suite 1000 Chicago, IL 60603	Phone: 312-332-0405 Fax: 312-332-0706 Website: http://www.naamm.org E-mail: naamm@naamm.org
NAHB	National Association of Home Builders 1201 15th Street NW Washington, DC 20005-2800	Phone: 800-368-5242 or 202-822-0200 Fax: 202-822-0559 Website: http://www.nahb.com E-mail: info@nahb.com
NCMA	National Concrete Masonry Association 2302 Horse Pen Road Herndon, VA 20171-3499	Phone: 703-713-1900 Fax: 703-713-1910 Website: http://www.ncma.org E-mail: ncma@ncma.org
NCSBCS	National Conference of States on Building Codes and Standards 505 Huntmar Park Drive, Suite 210 Herndon, VA 20170	Phone: 703-437-0100 Fax: 703-481-3596 Website: http://www.ncsbcs.org E-mail: rwible@ncsbcs.org Note: No general e-mail — above is for the Executive Director.
NEMA	National Electrical Manufacturers Association 1300 North 17th Street, Suite 1847 Rosslyn, VA 22209	Phone: 703-841-3200 Fax: 703-841-3300 Website: http://www.nema.org E-mail: mal_o'harpan@nema.org No general e-mail — above is for the President.

* The International Code Council is an umbrella organization. It is composed of what was formerly CABO, and BOCA, ICBO and SBCCI which are all still operating separately and as part of ICC. Only CABO has changed its name to ICC at this point.

NFPA	National Fire Protection Association 1 Batterymarch Park P.O. Box 9101 Quincy, MA 02269	Phone: 800-344-3555 or 617-770-3000 Fax: 800-593-6372 Website: http://www.nfpa.org E-mail: custserv@nfpa.org
NFoPA	National Forest Products Association This organization is now American Forest & Paper Association (see AFPA)	
NIBS	National Institute of Building Sciences 1090 Vermont Avenue, NW Suite 700 Washington, DC 20005-4905	Phone: 202-289-7800 Fax: 202-289-1092 Website: http://www.nibs.org E-mail: nibs@nibs.org
NLS	National Lime Association 200 North Glebe Road, Suite 800 Arlington, VA 22203	Phone: 703-243-5463 Fax: 703-243-5489 Website: http://www.lime.org E-mail: natlime@aol.com
NSC	National Safety Council 1121 Spring Drive Itasca, IL 60143-3201	Phone: 800-621-7619 Website: www.nsc.org
NTIS	National Technical Information Center U.S. Department of Commerce (Technology Admin.) 5295 Port Royal Road Springfield, VA 22161	Phone: 703-487-4650 Fax: 703-605-6900 Website: http://www.ntis.gov/ E-mail: info@ntis.fedworld.gov
NWPCA	National Wooden Pallet and Container Association 1800 North Kent Street, Suite 911 Arlington, VA 22209-2109	Phone: 703-527-7667 Eax: 703-527-7171 Website: http://www.nwpca.com
OSHA	U. S. Department of Labor Occupational Safety & Health Administration 200 Constitution Avenue Washington, DC 20210	Phone: 800-321-OSHA (6742) Website: www.osha.gov
PCA	Portland Cement Association 5420 Old Orchard Road Skokie, IL 60077	Phone: 847-966-6200 Fax: 847-966-6200 Website: http://www.portcement.org E-mail: bruce_mcintosh@port cement.org
PDCA	Painting and Decorating Contractors Of America 3913 Old Lee Highway, Suite 33B Fairfax, VA 22030	Phone: 800-332-7322 Fax: 703-359-2576 Website: http://pdca.org E-mail: gdomedion@pdca.org
RAL	Riverbank Acoustical Laboratories 1512 S. Batavia Avenue Geneva, IL 60134	Phone: 630-232-0104 Fax: 630-232-0138 Website: http://riverbank.iitri.org E-mail: jstangel@iitri.org
SBCCI	Southern Building Code Congress, Int'l.* 900 Montclair Road Birmingham, AL 35213	Phone: 205-591-1853 Fax: 205-591-9775 Website: http://www.sbcci.org E-mail: info@sbcci.org

* The International Code Council is an umbrella organization. It is composed of what was formerly CABO, and BOCA, ICBO and SBCCI which are all still operating separately and as part of ICC. Only CABO has changed its name to ICC at this point.

SIPA	Structural Insulated Panel Association 3413 56th Street NW, Suite A Gig Harbor, WA 98335	Phone: 253-858-7472 Fax: 253-858-0272 Website: http://www.sips.org E-mail: jimt@sips.org
TCA	Tile Council of America, Inc. 100 Clemson Research Blvd. Anderson, SC 29625	Phone: 864-646-8453 Fax: 864-646-2821 Website: http://www.tileusa.com E-mail: literature@carol.net
TPI	Truss Plate Institute 583 D'Onofrio Drive, Suite 200 Madison, WI 53719	Phone: 608-833-5900 Fax: 608-833-4360 Website: none E-mail: flow@tpinst.org
UL	Underwriters Laboratories, Inc. 333 Pfingsten Road Northbrook, IL 60062-2096	Phone: 847-272-8800 Fax: 847-272-8129 Website: http://www.ul.com E-mail: northbrook@ul.com
ULC	Underwriters Laboratories of Canada 7 Crouse Road Scarborough, Ontario M1R 3A9 Canada	Phone: 416-757-3611 Fax: 416-757-1781 Website: http://www.ulc.ca E-mail: ulcinfo@ulc.ca
WHI	Warnock Hersey International Inc. Intertek Testing Services 530 Garcia Avenue Pittsburg, CA 94565	Phone: 925-432-7344 Fax: 925-432-3576 Website: http://www.warnock hersey.com E-mail: hstacy@itsqs.com

* The International Code Council is an umbrella organization. It is composed of what was formerly CABO, and BOCA, ICBO and SBCCI which are all still operating separately and as part of ICC. Only CABO has changed its name to ICC at this point.

Rating Fire Endurance

(ASTM E119, UL 263 and NFPA 251) This is the standard test for rating the fire resistance of columns, girders, beams, and wall-partition, floor-ceiling and roof-ceiling assemblies. It is published by three organizations, designated above, and is essentially the same for all three.

The test procedure consists of the fire endurance test for all assemblies (not individual products) and, in addition, a hose stream test for partition and wall assemblies. The test specimen assembly must meet the following requirements:

1. Structural elements subjected to the test must support the maximum design loads applied throughout the test period. Columns, beams, girders and structural decks must carry the load without failure.

   This test does not imply that the test specimen will be suitable for use after the exposure. Some specimens are so damaged after one hour of exposure that they would require replacement, even though they meet all of the requirements for a 4-hr. rating.

2. No openings may develop in an assembly that will permit flames or hot gases to penetrate and ignite combustibles on the other side.

3. An assembly must resist heat transmission so that temperatures on the side opposite the fire are maintained below designated values. The temperature of the unexposed surface is measured by thermocouples covered with dry refractory filter pads attached directly to the surface. In the case of walls and partitions, one thermocouple is located at the center of the assembly, one in center of each quarter-section, and the other four at the discretion of the testing authority.

The integrity of walls and partitions is evaluated in the hose stream test that examines the construction's ability to resist disintegration under adverse conditions. The hose stream test subjects a duplicate sample to one-half of the indicated fire exposure (but not more than one hour), then immediately to a stream of water from a fire nozzle at a prescribed pressure and distance. This test evaluates the impact, erosion and cooling effects of a hose stream directed at the exposed surface. If there is a breakthrough on the unexposed side, sufficient to pass a stream of water, the result is test failure.

The time-temperature curve used for the fire endurance test is shown on page 458. The temperature of the furnace is obtained from the average readings of nine thermocouples, symmetrically located, and placed 6" from the exposed surface of walls and partitions, or 12" from the exposed surface of floors, ceilings and columns.

Conditions for Hose Stream Test

Resistance Period	Water Pressure At Base of Nozzle		Duration of Application, Min. per 100 ft.²(9.29²) Exposed Area
	lbf/in.²	kPa	
8 hr. and over	45	310	6
4 hr. and over if less than 8 hrs.	45	310	5
2 hr. and over if less than 4 hrs.	30	207	2-1/2
1-1/2 hr. and over if less than 2 hr.	30	207	1-1/2
1 hr. and over if less than 1-1/2 hr.	30	207	1
Less than 1 hr., if desired	30	207	1

Surface Burning Characteristics

(ASTM E84, ANSI 2.5, NFPA 225 and UL 723) The characteristics of interior finish materials that are related to fire protection are:

- ability to spread fire, and

- quantity of smoke developed when burning

Materials that have high flame spread and produce large quantities of smoke are considered undesirable, especially when used in areas where people assemble or are confined.

The flame spread test (Surface Burning Characteristics of Building Materials) is often referred to as the Steiner Tunnel Test, after its originator.

In the test, a 20" x 25' sample, forming the roof of a rectangular furnace, is subjected to a fire of controlled severity, placed 12" from one end of the sample. Where the flame contacts the sample is considered to be 4-1/2' from the fire, so the test is actually conducted over 19-1/2' of the sample.

The time required for the flame to travel the 19' to the end of the sample, along with the smoke and heat produced, is compared with similar figures for red oak which is arbitrarily given the value of 100 for these two characteristics, and inorganic reinforced board which is given the value of 0.

Smoke developed is measured by means of a photoelectric cell connected to an ammeter which indicates changes in smoke density.

Obviously, the indices developed in the tunnel test are relative, but enough is known about the burning characteristics of materials to make these indices reliable for building code specifications.

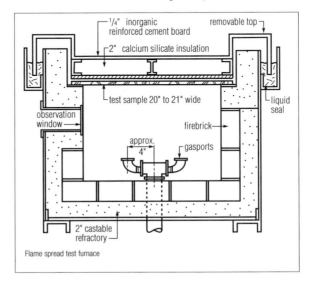

Flame spread test furnace

Most building codes divide materials into four classes, based on the Flame Spread Indices. The numbering and range of each class varies with the different codes, but they generally follow this pattern:

Class I (Class A)—0-25   Class III (Class C)—76-200

Class II (Class B)—26-75   Class IV (Class D)—over 200

Surface Burning Characteristics (per ASTM E84)

Product	Flame Spread	Smoke Developed
SHEETROCK Brand Gypsum Panels	15	0
SHEETROCK Brand Interior Gypsum Ceiling Board	15	0
SHEETROCK Brand Lay-In Ceiling Tile	15	0
SHEETROCK Brand Exterior Gypsum Ceiling Board	20	0
SHEETROCK Brand Gypsum Panels, Water-Resistant	20	0
SHEETROCK Brand Vinyl-Faced Gypsum Panels		
Pumice	20	25
Suede	15	25
Presidio	15	25
Granite	15	25
Linen	15	25
Country Weave	20	35
Textile (Type I, Fabric-Backed)*	25	70
Brittany (Type I, Fabric-Backed)*	25	55
THERMAFIBER Sound Attenuation Fire Blankets	15	0
DUROCK Cement Board, Underlayment and Exterior Cement Board	5	0

*Comply with Federal Specification CCC-2-408C, Type 1.

Through-Penetration Fire Stops

(ASTM E814)

ASTM E119 is the guide for assessing fire performance of most construction products and assemblies. However, ASTM E814 Fire Tests of Through-Penetration Fire Stops has been developed in recognition of the special role these constructions play in fire protection.

This standard test is applicable to through-penetration fire stops of various materials and construction. Fire stops are intended for use in openings in fire-resistive walls and floors. They consist of materials that fill the opening around penetrating items such as cables, cable trays, conduits, ducts and pipes and their means of support. See Chapter 10 for more information on through-penetration fire stops.

The test method considers the resistance of fire stops to an external force simulated by a hose stream. Two ratings are established for each fire stop. An F Rating is based upon flame occurrence on the unexposed surface, while the T Rating is based upon the temperature rise as well as flame occurrence on the unexposed side of the fire stop.

A fire stop shall be considered as meeting the requirements for an F Rating when it remains in the opening during the fire test and hose stream test within the following limitations:

1. The fire stops shall have withstood the fire test for the rating period without permitting the passage of flame through openings, or the occurrence of flaming on any element of the unexposed side of the fire stops.

Time Temperature Curve for Fire-Endurance Testing (ASTM E119)

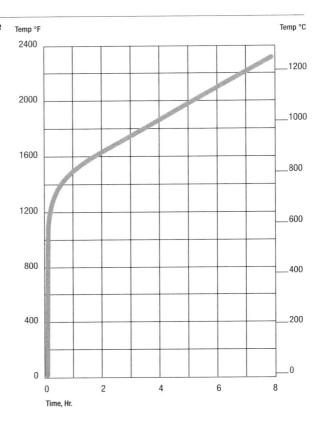

2. During the hose stream test, the fire stop shall not develop any opening that would permit a projection of water from the stream beyond the unexposed side.

A fire stop shall be considered as meeting the requirements for a T Rating when it remains in the opening during the fire test and hose stream test within the above limitations for F Rating; and: The transmission of heat through the fire stops during the rating period shall not have been such as to raise the temperature of any thermocouple on the unexposed surface of the fire stop or on any penetrating item more than 325°F above its initial temperature.

Head-of-Wall Construction Joints

Construction joints, where two fire-rated assemblies intersect, are evaluated under UL Standard 2079 for their ability to resist flame and temperature transmission as well as the hose stream, where required. Head-of-wall construction joints are intersections of wall to floor/ceiling or roof/ceiling. Other construction joints include wall to wall (expansion joint application), floor to floor (building joint application, or floor to wall. See Chapter 10 for more information on head-of-wall construction joints.

Test parameters for head-of-wall assemblies are similar to those established for through-penetration fire stops, above. Systems may be tested and prescribed for either static (no floor or roof movement) or dynamic (to accommodate live load deflection) conditions.

Head-of-wall construction joints have common features, including a) fire-rated assemblies for both the wall and floor/ceiling or roof/ceiling, b) a joint treatment system consisting of a forming material such as mineral fiber safing insulation to pack into openings, and a fill material such as FIRECODE Compound to seal all openings and passages. Restraining angles also may be required to achieve the necessary flame and temperature barriers.

USG has had several head-of-wall assemblies tested under standard UL-2079. These assemblies are recognized by ICBO (ER-2331).

Determination of Sound Transmission Class (STC)

Testing for airborne sound transmission is performed under rigidly established procedures set up by the American Society for Testing and Materials (ASTM procedure E90-90). Several independent acoustical laboratories across the nation are qualified to perform the tests. Although all are presumably reliable and follow the ASTM procedure, the results tend to vary slightly. For this reason, test results from more than one laboratory should never be compared on an exact basis.

Tests are conducted on a sample assembly, at least 2.4 m x 2.4 m in size. The assembly is installed between two rooms constructed in such a way that sound transmitted between the rooms by paths other than through the assembly is insignificant. Background noise in the rooms is monitored to ensure it does not affect test results.

The sound source consists of an electronic device and loudspeaker which produce a continuous random noise covering a minimum frequency range of 125 to 4,000 Hz (Hertz—cycles per second). Note for comparison that human speech is approximately 125 to 8,000 Hz. Panel diffusers and/or rotating vanes are set up so noise is diffused and the sound level is measured at several microphone positions in each room. Readings are taken at sixteen 1/3-octave frequency-band intervals. Average sound levels in the receiving room are subtracted from the corresponding sound levels in the source room. The differences (sound levels of the actual transmission) are recorded as transmission-loss values (adjustments are made for test room absorption and test assembly size).

Sound Test Sample Assembly

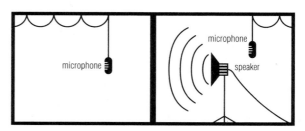

These transmission-loss values are then plotted on a frequency band–sound pressure level graph and the resulting curve is compared to a standard reference contour. The Sound Transmission Class (STC), as defined by the rating procedure set forth in ASTM E413-87, is determined by adjusting the reference contour vertically until the decibel (dB) total of all frequency bands on the test curve that are below the reference contour does not exceed 32, and no point on the test curve is more than 8 dB below the reference contour. Then, with the reference contour adjusted to meet these standards, its transmission loss at 500 Hz (500 cycles per second) is taken as the STC (dropping dB unit).

An alternative procedure, frequently used for the measurement of sound transmission loss under field conditions, is given in ASTM Standard Test Method E336-90. This may be used to obtain a Field Sound Transmission Class (FSTC).

Determination of Sound Transmission Class

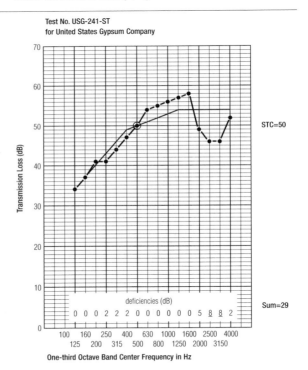

Test No. USG-241-ST
for United States Gypsum Company

Reproduced above is the graph of an actual sound transmission-loss test of a drywall partition, Test No. USG-241-ST. The partition is rated at STC 50 with the reference contour adjusted to meet the standards outlined above. The deficiencies at 2,500 Hz and 3,150 Hz are 8, the allowable maximum.

The total of all points below the criterion curve is 29, three points less than the 32 allowed.

The reference contour itself is plotted to allow for subjective human response to sound pressure at the 16 frequency bands measured. Because the human ear is less sensitive to low-frequency sound pressure than to high frequencies, the reference contour has been adjusted to allow some additional noise at low frequencies. This avoids down-rating test results because of noise levels that are least objectionable to people. The ASTM test procedure explains the use of STC in the following excerpt from E413.

"These single-number ratings correlate in a general way with subjective impressions of sound transmission for speech, radio, television and similar sources of noise in offices and buildings. This classification method is not appropriate for sound sources with spectra significantly different from those sources listed above. Such sources include machinery, industrial processes, bowling alleys, power transformers, musical instruments, many music systems and transportation noises such as motor vehicles, aircraft and trains. For these sources, accurate assessment of sound transmission requires a detailed analysis in frequency bands."

Noise Reduction Coefficient (NRC)

Noise Reduction Coefficient (NRC) is a measure of the sound absorption characteristics of an acoustical product. In accordance with the reverberation room test method, ASTM C423, panels are tested for sound absorption in the frequency range of 100 to 5000 hz. The actual NRC value is determined by averaging the sound absorption values in the four main frequency bands of 250, 500, 1000, and 2000 hz. These values represent the majority of the range of the human voice. The greater the NRC, the better the overall sound absorption of the acoustical material, providing a room that will have less reverberation and echo.

Ceiling Attenuation Class (CAC)

Ceiling Attenuation Class (CAC) is a numerical rating used to characterize sound traveling between two horizontally adjacent spaces sharing a common ceiling plenum. CAC is measured using test standard ASTM E1414. Sound is introduced into a room and measured in that room. Then the same sound is measured in the adjacent room (other side of the partition from where sound was introduced). The CAC value is calculated using sound measurements in both rooms. Any sound that could pass directly through the partition is already calculated and factored out. Higher CAC values indicate greater attenuation of sound into and through the plenum.

Articulation Class (AC)

Articulation Class (AC) is a single numerical rating used to identify the degree of transmitted speech intelligibility between office spaces. This rating is particularly useful for open plan offices. AC provides an indication of the degree to which occupants will be able to understand and/or be disturbed by conversation occurring elsewhere in the office space. AC is determined by following the test procedure outlined in standard ASTM E1111, which measures sound levels in a source space and then at varying distances beyond a barrier screen. The derived value is a combination of the sound reflection characteristics and sound absorption characteristics of the acoustical product being tested in a prescribed assembly.

Determination of Impact Insulation Class (IIC)

Impact sound originates when one body strikes another, such as in the case of footsteps, hammering and objects falling. Even though some of the sound energy is eventually conducted to the air, the sound is still classified as impact.

Impact sound travels through the structure with little loss of energy if the structure is continuous and rigid. Thus, tenants without enough heat can pound on a radiator and notify the superintendent (and all other tenants as well) of the situation.

Transmission of impact sound can be controlled by isolation, absorption and elimination of flanking paths, and offset by the introduction of masking sound. Limpness in the construction affects transmission of impact sound, but is difficult to introduce because of the structural requirements of the assembly.

Mass plays a secondary role in the isolation of impact sound. The benefit of mass in a sound-control construction is its resistance to being set into vibration. In retarding airborne sound, this is very effective because the sound energy is small. With impact sound, the energy is greater and is applied directly to the construction by the sound source with little energy loss. Thus, the mass of that surface is immediately set into motion. For this reason, concrete slab construction at $100lb/ft.^2$ is only slightly more effective in retarding impact sound than simple wood frame construction at $10 \ lb/ft.^2$.

Although leaks in a floor-ceiling assembly must be sealed to stop transmission of the airborne sound associated with impact, they play little part in retarding the transmission of structure-borne sound.

Absorbing Impact Sound

The use of sound attenuation blankets is as effective in controlling impact sound as for airborne sound. Of course, unless the opposite surfaces of the assembly (floor and ceiling) are isolated or decoupled, sound travels through the connecting structure.

Structural Flanking Paths

One of the most frequent causes of sound performance failure in a floor-ceiling assembly is flanking paths. Impact sound produces high energy at the source. This energy follows any rigid connection between construction elements with little loss. For example, in a child's tin-can telephone, sound travels better through the tight string stretched between the cans than through the surrounding air.

Some of the most common flanking paths are supplied by plumbing pipes, air ducts and electrical conduit rigidly connected between floor and ceiling. Continuous walls between floors, columns or any other continuous structural elements will act as flanking paths for impact sound. In fact, any rigid connection between the two diaphragms transmits impact sound.

Determination of Impact Insulation Class

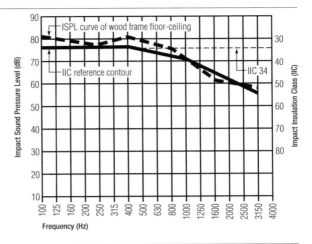

Methods of Impact Rating

Assemblies designed to retard transmission of impact sound are tested for performance as prescribed by ASTM Standard Method E492-90. The floor-ceiling assembly is constructed between two isolated rooms, and microphones are positioned in the receiving room to record the pressure of transmitted sound.

The impact sound source is a standard tapping machine. It rests on the floor of the test assembly and drops hammers at a uniform rate and impact energy. The sound produced depends to a large extent on the floor surface material. Carpet and pad, for example, greatly improve IIC ratings. The transmitted sound is measured and recorded at several microphone locations and four locations of the tapping machine. Results are corrected to a standard absorption so that results from different laboratories may be compared.

These results, recorded at sixteen 1/3-octave bands, are plotted and compared with a standard reference contour in much the same manner as Sound Transmission Class determinations, except that deficiencies lie above the contour.

Impact sound rating methods were established by the Federal Housing Administration (now HUD). The earliest was a single-number rating system called Impact Noise Rating (INR) and published in FHA 750.

The current rating system is described in E989-89. To determine this Impact Insulation Class (IIC), the ISPL curve is plotted on a graph as shown above. The reference contour is then shifted to the lowest point where no point on the ISPL (Impact Sound Pressure Level) curve is more than 8 dB above it, and the sum of all ISPL deviations above it is no more than 32 dB. The location of the reference contour at 500 Hz is projected to the IIC scale, right of graph, to read IIC rating.

The IIC relates to STC ratings with respect to acceptability, and is a positive number. IIC values will usually be 51 points above the corresponding former INR values, but some deviations can occur. Tests must be analyzed individually against IIC criteria.

Abuse-Resistant Systems

Abuse resistance has grown in importance as designers have realized that it is often less expensive from a life-cycle cost perspective to address abuse resistance in critical areas in the initial project stage than to pay the high on-going costs of maintaining and repairing regular drywall partitions.

Defining Abuse Resistance Abuse resistance may be defined as the ability of a system to resist three levels of damage: (1) Surface damage (from abrasion and/or indentation); (2) Penetration (through to the wall cavity from sharp or blunt impact); (3) Security breach (through the entire assembly from ballistics or forced entry). For more detailed information on abuse resistance, please see publication SA929, *United States Gypsum Company Abuse Resistant Systems.*

Categories of Abuse Resistance

Assemblies designed to have appropriate strength will lessen maintenance and repair costs. Five usage categories have been created by USG to help you determine the appropriate level of abuse resistance needed. Each category is described below with *minimum* performance values that apply. All categories represent an improvement over standard interior partition construction.

USG-Defined

Level	Description	Performance Types			
		Abrasion	Indentation	Hard-Body Impact	Soft-Body Impact
Category 1 Light duty	A basic upgrade to standard drywall. Provides improved resistance to incidental surface and impact damage.	15 cycles	0.15 in.	30 ft.-lbs.	120 ft.-lbs.
Category 2 Moderate duty	Provides moderate resistance to incidental surface and impact damage from people and objects.	30 cycles	0.13 in.	40 ft.-lbs.	180 ft.-lbs.
Category 3 Heavy duty	Provides resistance to heavy surface and impact abuse from people and objects.	100 cycles	0.10 in.	80 ft.-lbs.	210 ft.-lbs.
Category 4 Extreme duty	Provides resistance to extreme levels of surface and impact damage from hard objects.	500 cycles	0.08 in.	110 ft.-lbs.	300 ft.-lbs.
Category 5 Security	For areas requiring forced entry and ballistic resistance.	1000 cycles	N/A	N/A	N/A

Abuse-Resistant Systems By Category

The following table illustrates abuse-resistant systems for all categories or levels of abuse-resistance that apply to walls. Systems based on drywall, veneer plaster, conventional plaster, gypsum fiber and concrete masonry units (CMU) are described.

System	Assembly Substrate	Finish	Surface Damage Abrasion (Cycles)	Indentation Depth (in.)	Penetration Hard-Body[4] (ft.-lbs.)	Soft-Body[4] ft.-lbs.	Fire Rating[1] (hours)	Sound[4] (STC Rating)	Partition Width[2] (in.)	System Weight[2] (psf)	Cost Index[3]	Applications
Category 1	Basic Upgrade to standard drywall. Provides some resistance to surface abuse and impact.											
Light Duty	1/2" Fiberock VHI	Joint Treatment Only	30	0.14	69.5	240	N/A	40 (est.)	4-5/8	2.3	1.11	Stairways, family rooms, primary grade classrooms, public spaces in health-care facilities.
	5/8" Fiberock AR	Joint Treatment Only	30	0.14	35	150	1	41	4-7/8	2.9	1.18	
	1/2" Sheetrock AR	Joint Treatment Only	20	0.15	35	120	1	45 (est.)	4-5/8	2.2	1.05	
	1/2" Imperial Base	1-Coat Diamond Veneer	30	0.12 (est.)	21	60	N/A	45	4-3/4	3.1	1.2	
	5/8" Imperial Base Base	1-Coat Diamond Veneer	30	0.12	30	120	1	47	5	3.3	1.35	
Category 2	Provides moderate resistance to incidental impact and abrasion from bodies and objects.											
Moderate Duty	5/8" Fiberock VHI	Joint Treatment Only	30	0.14	99	>300	1	41	4-7/8	2.9	1.27	Multifamily stairways, entries and common areas, middle/high school classrooms, college lecture halls, mailrooms, retail corridors/public areas.
	5/8" Fiberock AR	2-Coat Veneer[6]	1000	0.09	62.5	180	1	42 (est.)	4-3/4	4.9	1.84	
	5/8" Imperial AR	1-Coat Diamond Veneer	30	0.09	54.6	180	1	45 (est.)	5	3.3	1.35	
	5/8" Sheetrock AR	Joint Treatment Only	20	0.13	45	150	1	45 (est.)	4-7/8	2.7	1.15	
	5/8" Sheetrock AR	2-Coat Diamond Veneer[5]	30	0.12	62.5	180	1	46 (est.)	4-7/8	3.6	1.78	
	3/4" Ultracode	2-Coat Veneer[6]	1000	0.09	50	180	1	48 (est.)	5-1/4	3.9	2.01	
Category 3	Provides resistance to intentional and heavy surface and impact abuse from people and objects.											
Heavy Duty	5/8" Fiberock VHI	2-Coat Veneer[6]	1000	0.09	115 (est.)	>300	1	42 (est.)	5	4.9	1.92	High-risk multifamily entries, stairways, common areas, school corridors and gyms, college dorms, healthcare corridors, payroll rooms and loading areas.
	5/8" Imperial AR (2 layers)	2-Coat Imperial Veneer[7]	1000	0.09	84	210	2	51	6-1/8	6.3	—	
	3.4# Lath	1-Coat Imperial Veneer	1000	0.08	90	N/A	1	45 (est.)	—	7.5	2.26	
	8" Hollow CMU	Joint Treatment Only	>700	0.018 (est.)	70	N/A	1	44	8	38.00	—	

Note: "est." indicates estimated value.

(1) See publication SA923 for specific fire rating information. (2) Weights and widths are based on completed systems (panels on both flanges of studs). (3) Cost index base of 1.00 corresponds to single-layer Type X paper-faced gypsum panel each side of 3-5/8", 20-ga. steel framing, 16" o.c., joint treatment only. (4) Minimum 3-5/8", 20-ga. steel framing at 16" o.c. is recommended for abuse-resistant assemblies, and was used for the hard-body, soft-body and acoustical testing shown in this publication. Framing spacing of 24" o.c. will likely reduce the impact resistance of an assembly, while framing of 12" o.c. will likely improve the impact resistance. (5) Two-coat system consists of Diamond Brand Veneer Basecoat Plaster and Diamond Brand Interior Finish Plaster. (6) Two-coat system consists of Diamond Brand Veneer Basecoat Plaster and Imperial Brand Finish Plaster. (7) Two-coat system consists of Imperial Brand Basecoat Plaster and Imperial Brand Finish Plaster.

System / Substrate	Assembly	Finish	Surface Damage — Abrasion (Cycles)	Surface Damage — Indentation Depth (in.)	Penetration — Hard-Body[4] (ft.-lbs.)	Penetration — Soft-Body[4] (ft.-lbs.)	Fire Rating[1] (hours)	Sound[4] (STC Rating)	Partition Width[2] (in.)	System Weight[2] (psf)	Cost Index[3]	Applications
Category 4	Provides resistance to intentional and heavy surface and impact abuse from people and objects.											
Extreme Duty	5/8" FIBEROCK VHI (2 layers)	2-Coat Veneer[6]		0.09		>360 (6 impacts)		51 (est.)		7.8		Low-risk and youth detention, psychiatric wards, payroll rooms and loading areas
	STRUCTO-BASE #9 Lath	1-Coat IMPERIAL Veneer		0.08		N/A		45 (est.)		7.5		
	8" Core-Filled CMU	Parge or prime and paint		0.018 (est.)		N/A		45 (est.)		95.0		
Category 5	For areas requiring forced-entry and ballistic resistance											
Secure	12-Gauge STRUCTOCORE	1-Coat IMPERIAL Veneer		0.023		N/A		45		35.0		Government, military, embassies and consulates, high-detention, bank vaults.
	18-Gauge STRUCTOCORE	1-Coat IMPERIAL Veneer		0.023		N/A		45		35.0		
	8" Core-Filled CMU	Parge or prime and paint		0.018 (est.)		N/A		56		95.0		

Note: "est." indicates estimated value.

(1) See publication SA923 for specific fire rating information. (2) Weights and widths are based on completed systems (panels on both flanges of studs). (3) Cost index base of 1.00 corresponds to single-layer Type X paper-faced gypsum panel each side of 3-5/8", 20-ga. steel framing, 16" o.c., joint treatment only. (4) Minimum 3-5/8", 20-ga. steel framing at 16" o.c. is recommended for abuse-resistant assemblies, and was used for the hard-body, soft-body and acoustical testing shown in this publication. Framing spacing of 24" o.c. will likely reduce the impact resistance of an assembly, while framing of 12" o.c. will likely improve the impact resistance. (5) Two-coat system consists of DIAMOND Brand Veneer Basecoat Plaster and DIAMOND Brand Interior Finish Plaster. (6) Two-coat system consists of DIAMOND Brand Veneer Basecoat Plaster and IMPERIAL Brand Finish Plaster. (7) Two-coat system consists of IMPERIAL Brand Basecoat Plaster and IMPERIAL Brand Finish Plaster.

Fixture Attachment-Drywall and Plaster Systems

Fixture Attachment Load Table

Fastener Type	Size in.	Size mm	Base Assembly	Allowable Withdrawal Resistance lb.	Allowable Withdrawal Resistance N[1]	Allowable Shear Resistance lb.	Allowable Shear Resistance N[1]
toggle bolt or hollow wall fastener	1/8	3.2	1/2" gypsum base or panels	20	89	40	178
	3/16	4.8		30	134	50	223
	1/4	6.4		40	178	60	267
	1/8	3.2	1/2" gypsum base or panels	70	312	100	445
	3/16	4.8	& 25 ga. steel studs	80	356	125	556
	1/4	6.4		155	690	175	779
No. 8 sheet metal screw	—	—	1/2" gypsum base or panels	50	223	80	356
TYPE S bugle head screw			& 25 ga. steel base	60	267	100	445
TYPE S-12 bugle head screw	—	—	1/2" gypsum base or panels	85	378	135	601
			& 20 ga. steel insert				
TYPE S pan head screw	—	—	25 ga. steel to 25 ga. steel	70	312	120	534
two bolts welded to steel insert	3/16	4.8	grab bar attachment	175	779	200	890
	1/4	6.4		200	890	250	1113
bolt welded to 1-1/2" channel	1/4	6.4	plumber's bracket	200	890	250	1113
	5/16	7.9	see drawing on page 140	200	890	300	1334
plug and screw	#6	—	metal or gypsum	10	45	40	178
	#8	—	lath and plaster[2]	20	89	50	222
	#12	—		30	133	60	267
Toggle bolt or hollow wall fastener	1/8	3.2	Metal or gypsum	75	334	50	222
	3/16	4.8	lath and plaster[2]	125	556	140	623
	1/4	6.4		175	778	150	667

(1) Newton. (2) Plaster having compressive strength of at least 900 psi was used to develop this data.

Drywall, Plaster and Acoustical Ceiling Installation Tolerances

Standards of acceptability for installation of framing, drywall panels and joint treatment vary in different parts of the United States. Nevertheless, several organizations, including the Metal Lath/Steel Framing Association, Gypsum Association and American Society for Testing and Materials (ASTM), have published recommendations, standards and/or tolerances that may be required for a specific project.

Similarly, references for tolerances and quality in plasterwork and acoustical ceilings are available. References for tolerances and quality in plasterwork have been published by AIA MasterSpec and Diehl's "Manual of Lathing and Plastering." For acoustical ceilings construction, see the appropriate ASTM standards (page 474) or "Code of Practices for Acoustical Ceiling System Installation" in the Ceilings and Interior Systems Construction Association (CISCA) *Ceiling Systems Handbook.*

Contractors and their customers should reach agreement before starting the project regarding which tolerance standards will be used to judge acceptability of the work.

Gypsum Board Screw Usage

The number of fasteners used to install gypsum board varies with framing spacing, screw spacing, panel orientation and panel size. The charts below show estimated screw usage per thousand square feet of gypsum board for both horizontal and vertical board attachment. Allowance should be made for loss.

Horizontal Board Attachment (Screws/1000 ft.²)

Framing Spacing

4' x 8' Board	Screw Spacing (Inches)			
	8	12	16	24
8"	2844	2031	1625	1219
12"	1969	1406	1125	844
16"	1531	1094	875	656
24"	1094	781	625	469
4' x 10' Board				
8"	2800	2000	1600	1200
12"	1925	1375	1100	825
16"	1488	1063	850	638
24"	1050	750	600	450
4' x 12' Board				
8"	2780	1980	1590	1190
12"	1900	1360	1090	820
16"	1460	1050	840	630
24"	1030	730	590	440

Vertical Board Attachment (Screws/1000 ft.²)

Framing Spacing

4′ x 8′ Board	Screw Spacing (Inches)			
	8	12	16	24
8″	2844	1969	1531	1094
12″	2031	1406	1094	781
16″	1625	1125	875	625
24″	1219	844	656	469
4′ x 10′ Board				
8″	2800	1925	1488	1050
12″	2000	1375	1063	750
16″	1600	1100	850	600
24″	1200	825	638	450
4′ x 12′ Board				
8″	2771	1896	1458	1021
12″	1979	1354	1042	729
16″	1583	1083	833	583
24″	1188	813	625	438

Comparing Plaster Systems

The chart below compares conventional plaster and veneer plaster systems to help in selection for specific job applications.

Characteristics	Comments			
1. Conventional Plaster Best system to attain a uniform, monolithic, blemish-free, smooth surface with excellent wear resistance.				
2. IMPERIAL Brand Basecoat with selected finish shown below, "A" through "E"	**Finish Plaster Rating** **(No. 1 Best—No. 4 Acceptable)**			
	Productivity	Hardness	Workability	Ease to Achieve Smooth Surface
A. IMPERIAL Brand Finish Ultimate in surface hardness and abrasion resistance. Easily textured. Low productivity and hard to achieve a completely smooth finish.	4	1	4	4
B. DIAMOND Brand Interior Finish Plaster Single-bag, ready-to-use finish. Moderate high strength. Acceptable workability. Extremely adaptable to textured finishes. Satisfactory smooth finish.	2	2	2	3
C. Regular Gauging Lime Putty Highest productivity. Best workability. Joinable, easiest to achieve a monolithic finish. Only moderate surface hardness.	1	4	1	1
D. STRUCTO-GAUGE Gauging Lime Putty (1:1) Hardest dense putty finish. Moderate workability and ease of application. Excellent finish appearance.	2	3	2	2
E. RED TOP Keenes Cement, Lime Putty and Sand Unique, only truly retemperable material. Best choice for coloring or tinting large plaster wall areas. Ultimate choice for texturing. Can be floated for extended time period.	Due to its unique nature, Keenes is not rated with above finishes.			
3. IMPERIAL Brand Finish (one-coat) Monolithic, smooth or textured appearance Ultimate in surface hardness. Primarily intended for direct application to plaster base. Achieves high productivity due to compatibility with absorbent surface of plaster base. Ready for finishing in 48 hours with favorable drying conditions.	Fast completion shortens construction time, brings in paying tenants faster, thus reducing interest paid on project construction loan.			
4. DIAMOND Brand Interior Finish Plaster Monolithic appearing. Hard, wear-resistant surface. Provides texture desired. Ready for final finish in as little as 48 hours under favorable drying conditions. Greatest coverage for single coat application over special absorbent surface of plaster base. Lowest cost veneer system.	See comment on IMPERIAL Brand Finish.			

Metric Terms and Metric Equivalents

Basic Units

Quantity	Metric (SI) Unit	Symbol	U.S.A. equivalent (nom.)[1]
Length	millimeter	mm	0.039 in.
	meter	m	3.281 ft.
			1.094 yd.
Area	meter	m^2	10.763 ft.^{2}
			1.195 yd.^{2}
Volume	meter	m^3	35.314 ft.^{3}
			1.307 yd.^{3}
Volume (Fluid)	liter	L	33.815 oz.
			0.264 gal.
Mass (Weight)	gram	g	0.035 oz.
	kilogram	kg	2.205 lb.
	ton	t	2,204.600 lb.
			1.102 tons
Force	newton	N	0.225 lbf.
Temperature (Interval)	kelvin	K	1.8°F
	degree celsius	°C	1.8°F
Temperature	celsius	°C	(°F-32)5/9
Thermal Resistance		$K \bullet m^2$	5.679 ft.$^2 \bullet hr \bullet$°F
		W	Btu
Heat Transfer	watt	W	3.412 Btu/hr.
Pressure	kilopascal	kPa	0.145 lb./in.^{2} (psi)
	pascal	Pa	20.890 lb./ft.^{2} (psf)

(1) To convert U.S.A. units to SI units, divide by U.S.A. equivalent

Prefixes (Order of Magnitude)

Prefix	Symbol	Factor
mega	M	$1000000 = 10^{+6}$
kilo	k	$1000 = 10^{+3}$
centi[1]	c	$0.01 = 10^{-2}$
milli	m	$0.001 = 10^{-3}$
micro	μ(mu)	$0.000001 = 10^{-6}$

(1) Limited use only.

Metric Conversion

The table below provides metric equivalents for the dimensions of USG products. "Soft" conversions merely apply a conversion factor that translates feet and inches (according to which the products were manufactured) into metric units; "hard" metric measurements are given for products actually manufactured in metric sizes.

Metric Equivalents

Dimension	Conversion Type[1]	Ft./In.	mm[2]
SHEETROCK Brand Gypsum Panels			
Thickness	Soft	1/4″	6
		3/8″	10
		1/2″	13
		5/8″	16
		3/4″	19
		1″	25
Width	Hard	24″	600
		48″	1200
Length	Hard	8′	2400
		10′	3000
		12′	3600
Steel Stud Framing			
Thickness (gauge)	Soft	0.0179 (25)	0.45
		0.0270 (22)	0.69
		0.0329 (20)	0.84
Depth	Soft	1-5/8″	41
		2-1/2″	64
		3-1/2″	89
		3-5/8″	92
		4″	102
Length	Hard	8′	2400
		10′	3000
		12′	3600
THERMAFIBER Insulation			
Thickness	Soft	1″	25
		1-1/2″	38
		2″	51
		3″	76
		4″	102
		6″	152
Width	Hard	16″	400
		24″	600
Length	Hard	48″	1200

(1) Conversion Type: "Soft" is metric relabeling with no physical change of dimension; "hard" is a physical change to the metric dimension shown. (2) Conversion factors: Inches X 25.4 = mm; Feet X 304.8 = mm.
Notes: Availability: Items above are not stocked in metric lengths or widths. Minimum quantity orders may be required. Lead time should be determined; upcharges may apply. Geographic availability may vary and should be verified for the project location.
Lengths: Shown on SHEETROCK Brand Gypsum Panels and steel stud framing for illustration purposes only.
Framing Spacing: 16″ o.c. converts to 400 mm o.c.; 24″ converts to 600 mm o.c.

Specification Standards

The listings following contain existing standard specifications that apply to USG materials described in this handbook. Where ASTM, local codes, etc., require product variance, consult your USG representative.

Specification Standards

Product	ASTM Designation
Plaster	
RED TOP gypsum plaster	C28
RED TOP two-purpose plaster	C28
RED TOP wood fiber plaster	C28
STRUCTO-LITE plaster	C28
RED TOP gauging plaster	C28
RED TOP keenes cement	
regular	C61
quick trowel	C61
STRUCTO-GAUGE plaster	C28
STRUCTO-BASE plaster	C28
IMPERIAL plaster	C587
DIAMOND plaster	C587
Gypsum Lathing	
ROCKLATH plaster base 3/8" & 1/2"	C37
IMPERIAL gypsum base 1/2" & 5/8"	C588
Lime	
RED TOP and GRAND PRIZE finish limes	C206 type N
IVORY finish lime	C206 type S
Gypsum Panels	
SHEETROCK Brand (plain) (foil-back)	C36
SHEETROCK Brand sq. edge	C36
SHEETROCK Brand tap. edge	C36
SHEETROCK Brand bev. edge	C36
5/8" SHEETROCK Brand FIRECODE Core	C36
SHEETROCK Brand FIRECODE C core	C36
SHEETROCK vinyl-covered	C960
SHEETROCK Brand water-resistant	C630
SHEETROCK Brand gypsum coreboard panels	C442
SHEETROCK Brand shaft wall liner panels	C442
SHEETROCK Brand exterior gypsum ceiling board	C931
SHEETROCK Brand interior gypsum ceiling board	C1395
FIBEROCK Brand panels—abuse-resistant	C1278
FIBEROCK Brand panels—VHI abuse-resistant	C1278
Cement Panels	
DUROCK Brand cement board	C1325 (ANSI A 118.9)
DUROCK Brand exterior cement board	C1186 (ANSI A 118.9)
Sheathing	
SHEETROCK Brand gypsum sheathing	C79
Joint Treatment	
SHEETROCK Brand joint compounds	C475

Specification Standards (continued)

Product	ASTM Designation
Accessories	
Structural steel joists, runners	C645, C955, A568, A653,
	A792 (alum.-zinc coating),
	A591 (galv. coating)
25, 22 ga. studs,	C645, A568 (steel), A653,
25, 22 ga. runners	A463 (alum. coating),
	A792 (alum.-zinc coating)
	A591 (galv. coating)
20 ga. studs, 20 ga. runners	C645, A568 (steel),
	A653 (galv. coating),
	A792 (alum.-zinc coating)
	A591 (galv. coating)
RC-1 resilient channels	A568 (steel),
	A525 (galv. coating),
	A792 (alum.-zinc coating)
Zinc Control Joints	C841
Dur-A-Bead corner bead	C1047
Sheetrock Brand metal trims	C1047
Shaft wall/area separation wall studs	A653
	A792 (alum.-zinc coating)
	A591 (galv. coating)
Drywall screws	C1002, C954
Sheetrock Brand acoustical sealant	C834
Acoustical Units—Prefabricated	
Cast ceiling panels	C423, C523, C635, C636,
Water-felted ceiling panels	C117, E84, E119, E1264
Ceiling Suspension System	
Donn Grid	C635, C363, C645,
	C841, E119, E1264
Mineral Fiber Insulation	
Thermafiber sound atten. fire blanket	C665

ASTM Application Standards

There are also standards for application of many of the products in this Handbook. See the specification standards listed below for more information.

Application Standards

Product	Application Standard
Standard Practice for Installation of Metal Ceiling Suspension Systems for Acoustical Tile and Lay-In Panels	C636
Specification for Installation of Steel Framing Members to Receive Screw-Attached Gypsum Panel Products	C754
Specification for Application and Finishing of Gypsum Board	C840
Specification for Installation of Interior Lathing and Furring	C841
Specification for Application of Interior Gypsum Plaster	C842
Specification for Application of Gypsum Veneer Plaster	C843
Specification for Application of Gypsum Base to Receive Gypsum Veneer Plaster	C844
Specification for Installation of Load-Bearing Steel Studs and Related Accessories	C1007
Specification for Application of Gypsum Sheathing	C1280
Standard Practice for Application of Ceiling Suspension Systems for Acoustical Tile and Lay-In Panels in Areas Requiring Moderate Seismic Restraint	E580

ASTM Standards for Performance Specifications and Test Methods

Performance Specifications and Test Methods

ASTM E-84, Standard Test Method for Surface Burning Characteristics of Building Materials, describes the method of establishing Flame Spread and Smoke Developed values.

ASTM E-119, Standard Test Methods for Fire Tests of Building Construction and Materials, describes the method of establishing fire-resistant hourly ratings for floor/ceiling and/or roof/ceiling construction assemblies. Underwriters Laboratories, Inc. Fire Resistance Designs are established under this test method.

ASTM E-136, Standard Test Method for Behavior of Materials in a Vertical Tube Furnace at 750 °C, describes the method for determining the acceptability of a material for use in noncombustible construction.

Fed. Spec. 209, Clean Room and Work Station Requirements for Controlled Environments, describes the method of establishing Clean Room Classification values.

ASTM C-367, Standard Test Methods for Strength Properties of Prefabricated Architectural Acoustical Tile or Lay-in Ceiling Panels, describes the method of establishing strength properties of acoustical ceiling tiles and panels.

ASTM E-413, Standard Classification for Rating Sound Insulation, provides criteria to establish Ceiling Attenuation Class (CAC) of an acoustical ceiling, similar to STC ratings for walls.

ASTM C-423, Standard Test Method for Sound Absorption and Sound Absorption Coefficients by the Reverberation Room Method, describes the method of establishing Noise Reduction Coefficient (NRC) values.

ASTM C-635, Standard Specification for the Manufacture, Performance and Testing of Metal Suspension Systems for Acoustical Tile and Lay-in Panel Ceilings, provides classification criteria by load capacity, along with manufacturing tolerance, coating, and inspection criteria for suspension systems.

ASTM E-1110, Standard Classification for Determination of Articulation Class, provides criteria to establish ceiling Articulation Class (AC) of an acoustical ceiling, generally applies to open plan ceilings in lieu of a NRC rating.

ASTM E-1111, Standard Test Method for Measuring the Interzone Attenuation of Ceiling Systems, describes the method of establishing Articulation Class (AC) values.

ASTM E-1264, Standard Classification for Acoustical Ceiling Products, (Correlates with Federal Spec. SS-S-118 "Sound Controlling Acoustical Tiles and Panel"), provides general classification by type and form, acoustical rating qualification, light reflectance coefficient qualification, and surface burning fire classification of acoustical ceiling tiles and panels.

ASTM E-1414, Standard Test Method for Airborne Sound Attenuation Between Rooms Sharing a Common Ceiling Plenum (Adaptation of the AMA-I-II-1967 "Test Method for Ceiling Sound Transmission Test by Two-Room Method"), describes the method of establishing Ceiling Attenuation Class (CAC) values.

ASTM E-1433, Standard Guide for Selection of Standards on Environmental Acoustics, is intended to assist acoustical consultants, architects, specifiers and others in understanding ASTM standards in environmental acoustics, as referenced in E-413, E-1110,E-1264, etc.

ASTM E-1477, Standard Test Method for Luminous Reflection Factor of Acoustical Materials by Use of Integrating-Sphere Reflectometers, describes the method of establishing Light Reflectance (LR) values.

Products/UL Designations

The USG products listed below are identified in the UL Fire Resistance Directory by the designations shown.

Products/UL Designations

UL Type Designation	Drywall, Cement Board and Plaster Board Products
R	SHEETROCK Brand Gypsum Panels
SCX	SHEETROCK Brand Gypsum Panels, FIRECODE Core
C	SHEETROCK Brand Gypsum Panels, FIRECODE C Core
WRX	SHEETROCK Brand Gypsum Panels, FIRECODE Core, Water-Resistant
WRC	SHEETROCK Brand Gypsum Panels, FIRECODE C Core, Water-Resistant
AR	SHEETROCK Brand Abuse-Resistant Gypsum Panels
SLX	SHEETROCK Brand Gypsum Liner Panels
ULTRACODE	SHEETROCK Brand Gypsum Panels, ULTRACODE Core
SHX	SHEETROCK Brand Gypsum Sheathing, FIRECODE Core
FCV	SHEETROCK Brand Gypsum Panels, FIRECODE Core, Vinyl-Covered
FB	SHEETROCK Brand Formboard
IPR	IMPERIAL Brand Plaster Base
IP-X1	IMPERIAL Brand Plaster Base (Type X)
IP-X2	IMPERIAL Brand Plaster Base (Type C)
IP-X3	IMPERIAL Brand Plaster Base, ULTRACODE Core
DUROCK	DUROCK Brand Cement Board
DUROCK Exterior	DUROCK Brand Exterior Cement Board
UC	ULTRAWALL Panel (Type C)
UL Type Designation	**Acoustical Tile and Panel Products**
FC-CB	Gypsum Lay-In Ceiling Tile
AP or AP-1	ACOUSTONE Ceiling Product (LINEAR EXPRESSIONS, SANDRIFT, FROST, GLACIER, "F" FISSURED Ceiling Panels)
GR	AURATONE FIRECODE Ceiling Product (Omni, Fine Fissured II, Omni CLIMAPLUS, Fissured Ceiling Tile)
FR-83 or GR-1	AURATONE FIRECODE Ceiling Product (Illusion, Aspen, Omni, Natural Fissured II, Fine Fissured II, Omni CLIMAPLUS, Fissured, Pin Perforated II, Pebbled, IMPACTION, Radar CLIMAPLUS, Ceiling Panels)
FR-81 or FR-83	AURATONE FIRECODE Ceiling Product (Rock Face CLIMAPLUS, Clean Room CLIMAPLUS Ceiling Panels)
FR-4	CERAMIC HERITAGE Ceiling Product (CERAMIC HERITAGE CLIMAPLUS Ceiling Panels)
M	AURATONE METAL FACE Ceiling Product (METAL FACE CLIMAPLUS Ceiling Panels)
FR-X1	X Technology FIRECODE Ceiling Product (ORION CLIMAPLUS, ECLIPSE CLIMAPLUS, MILLENIA CLIMAPLUS [clay back] Ceiling Panels)

Permeance—USG Products

Permeance—USG Products

Moisture Vapor Permeance

Product[1]	Finish	Perms[2,3]
Gypsum Panels		
3/8" SHEETROCK Brand Regular		35.3
1/2" SHEETROCK Brand Regular		34.2
1/2" SHEETROCK Brand Regular	1-coat flat latex paint	28.3
1/2" SHEETROCK Brand Regular	2-coats flat latex paint	28.4
1/2" SHEETROCK Brand Regular	2-coats gloss enamel (oil)	1.0
5/8" SHEETROCK Brand Regular		26.6
5/8" SHEETROCK Brand FIRECODE Core		28.6
1/2" SHEETROCK Brand FIRECODE C Core		31.8
5/8" SHEETROCK Brand FIRECODE C Core		25.9
1/2" SHEETROCK Brand Water-Resistant		30.2
5/8" SHEETROCK Brand Water-Resistant FIRECODE C Core		30.2
5/8" SHEETROCK Brand Water-Resistant FIRECODE Core		26.7
1/2" SHEETROCK Vinyl-Faced		
Pumice Pattern		0.8
Suede		0.6
Presidio		0.6
Granite		0.6
Linen		0.5
Country Weave Pattern		0.8
Textile (Type I, Fabric-Backed) [4]		1.0
Brittany (Type I, Fabric-Backed) [4]		2.1
1" SHEETROCK Brand Gypsum Liner Panel		24.0
Gypsum Base		
1/2" IMPERIAL Brand		28.8
1/2" IMPERIAL Brand	DIAMOND Brand Interior Finish Plaster	24.4
1/2" IMPERIAL Brand	1 coat IMPERIAL Finish Plaster	5.3
1/2" IMPERIAL Brand	IMPERIAL Brand Basecoat/ IMPERIAL Brand Finish Plaster	8.0
5/8" IMPERIAL Brand		26.9
1/2" IMPERIAL Brand FIRECODE C		30.0
5/8" IMPERIAL Brand FIRECODE C		26.2
3/8" gypsum base and 1/2" gypsum plaster, metal lath and 3/4" gypsum plaster		20.0
Gypsum Sheathing		
1/2" SHEETROCK Brand Gypsum Sheathing, Regular		23.3

(1) All foil-back products, less than 0.06 perms.
(2) All tests comply with ASTM E96 (desiccant method).
(3) Grain per sq. ft. per in. of water vapor pressure difference (grain/ft.^{2}-h.-in.-Hg) (grams/m^2/24 hours).
(4) Comply with Federal Specification CCC-2-408C, Type I

Thermal Coefficients of Linear Expansion of Common Building Materials

Unrestrained 40°—100°F. (4°—38C.)

Material	Coefficient x10-6in./ (in.°F)	x10-6 mm/ (mm.°C)
Gypsum Panels and Bases	9.0	16.2
Gypsum Plaster (sanded 100:2, 100:3)	7.0	12.6
Wood Fiber Plaster (sanded 100:1)	8.0	14.4
STRUCTO-LITE Plaster	7.3	13.1
Aluminum, Wrought	12.8	23.0
Steel, Medium	6.7	12.1
Brick, Masonry	3.1	5.6
Cement, Portland	5.9	10.6
Concrete	7.9	14.2
Fir (parallel to fiber)	2.1	3.8
Fir (perpendicular to fiber)	3.2	5.8

Hygrometric Coefficients of Expansion (unrestrained)

	Inches/Inch/% R.H. (5%—90% R.H.)
Gypsum Panels and Bases	7.2×10^{-6}
Gypsum Plaster (sanded 100:2, 100:3)	1.5×10^{-6}
Wood Fiber Plaster (sanded 100:1)	2.8×10^{-6}
STRUCTO-LITE Plaster	4.8×10^{-6}
Vermiculite Gypsum Plaster (sanded 100:2)	3.8×10^{-6}

Thermal Resistance Coefficients of Building and Insulating Materials[1]

Thickness			Density		Resistance (R-Value)	
in	mm	Product	lb/ft³	kg/m³	hr.ft.² °F/Btu	K.m²/W
2-2-1/2	50.8-63.5	THERMAFIBER Mineral Fiber Insulation (SAFB)	2.5	48.1	7.7-9.3	1.23
3-3-1/2	76.2-88.9	THERMAFIBER Mineral Fiber Insulation (SAFB)	2.5	48.1	11.1-13.0	1.94
5 1/4-6	133.4-152.4	THERMAFIBER Mineral Fiber Insulation (SAFB)	2.5	48.1	19.4-22.2	3.35
1	25.4	Extruded Polystyrene Insulation	2.2	35.2	5.00	0.88
1/2	12.7	SHEETROCK Brand Gypsum Panels	43	690.2	0.45	0.08
5/8	15.9	SHEETROCK Brand Gypsum Panels	43	690.2	0.56	0.10
1/2	12.7	SHEETROCK Brand Gypsum Panels, FIRECODE C Core	50	800.9	0.45	0.08
5/8	15.9	SHEETROCK Brand Gypsum Panels, FIRECODE and FIRECODE C Core	50	800.9	0.56	0.10
1/2	12.7	IMPERIAL Brand Gypsum Base	43	690.2	0.45	0.08
5/8	15.9	IMPERIAL Brand Gypsum Base	43	690.2	0.56	0.10
1/2	12.7	IMPERIAL Brand Gypsum Base, FIRECODE C Core	50	800.9	0.45	0.08
5/8	15.9	IMPERIAL Brand Gypsum Base, FIRECODE and FIRECODE C Core	50	800.9	0.56	0.10
3/8	9.5	ROCKLATH Plaster Base	50	800.9	0.32	0.06
1/2	12.7	SHEETROCK Brand Gypsum Sheathing	50	800.9	0.45	0.08
1/2	12.7	Sanded Plaster	105	1681.9	0.09	0.02
1/2	12.7	Plaster with Lightweight Aggregate	45	720.8	0.32	0.06
4	101.6	Common Brick	120	1922.2	0.80	0.14
1/2	12.7	DUROCK Brand Cement Board	72	1153.3	0.26	0.05
1/2	12.7	DUROCK Brand Exterior Cement Board	72	1153.3	0.26	0.05
4	101.6	Face Brick	130	2082.4	0.44	0.08
1	25.4	Portland Cement Stucco with Sand Aggregate	116	1858.1	0.20	0.04
4	101.6	Concrete Block, 3-oval Core, Cinder Aggregate			1.11	0.20
8	203.2	Concrete Block, 3-oval Core, Cinder Aggregate			1.72	0.30
12	304.8	Concrete Block, 3-oval Core, Cinder Aggregate			1.89	0.33
—	—	Vapor-Permeable Felt			0.06	0.01
—	—	Vapor-Retarder Plastic Film		Negl.	—	
1	25.4	Stone			0.08	0.01
1 x 8	25.4-203.2	Wood Drop Siding			0.79	0.14
3/4 x 10	19.1-254.0	Beveled Wood Siding			1.05	0.18
3/4-3-1/2	19.1-88.9	Plain Air Space, non-reflective[2]			0.92	0.17

(1) All factors based on data from 1981 ASHRAE Handbook of Fundamentals, Factors at 75°, mean temperature. (2) Conditions: heat, flow horizontal; mean temperature 50°F; temperature differential 30°F; E (emissivity) 0 82.

USG Plant Locations

USG Plant Locations

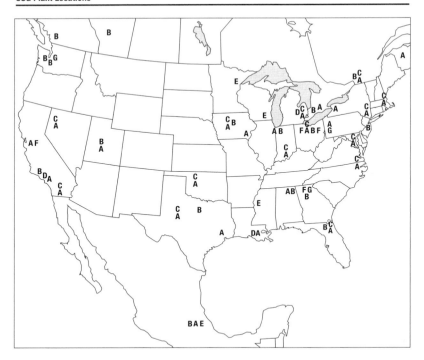

Legend	
A	Gypsum Board
B	Joint Treatment and Textures
C	Gypsum Plasters
D	Cement Board Products
E	Acoustical Ceilings
F	Acoustical Suspension Systems and Specialty Products
G	Trim

A	**Gypsum Board**	Aliquippa, PA Baltimore, MD Boston, MA Bridgeport, AL Detroit, MI East Chicago, IN Empire, NV Fort Dodge, IA Fremont, CA Galena Park, TX Gypsum, OH Hagersville, Ontario, Canada Jacksonville, FL Montreal, Quebec, Canada	New Orleans. LA Norfolk, VA Oakfield, NY Plaster City, CA Port Hawkesbury, Nova Scotia, Canada Puebla, Mexico Santa Fe Springs, CA Shoals, IN Sigurd, UT Southard, OK Sperry, IA Stony Point, NY Sweetwater, TX
B	**Joint Treatment and Textures**	Auburn, WA Bridgeport, AL Chamblee, GA Dallas, TX East Chicago, IN Edmonton, Alberta, Canada Fort Dodge, IA Gypsum, OH Hagerville, Ontario, Canada	Jacksonville, FL Montreal, Quebec, Canada Port Reading, NJ Puebla, Mexico Sigurd, UT Surrey, British Columbia, Canada Tacoma, WA Torrance, CA
C	**Gypsum Plasters**	Baltimore, MD Boston, MA Detroit, MI Empire, NV Fort Dodge, IA Gypsum, OH Jacksonville, FL	Montreal, Quebec, Canada Norfolk, VA Plaster City, CA Shoals, IN Southard, OK Stony Point, NY Sweetwater, TX
D	**Cement Board**	Detroit, MI New Orleans, LA	Santa Fe Springs, CA
E	**Acoustical Ceilings**	Cloquet, MN Greenville, MS	San Juan, Mexico Walworth, WI
F	**Acoustical Suspension Systems and Specialty Products**	Oakville, Ontario, Canada Stockton, CA Westlake, OH	Cartersville, GA Medina, OH
G	**Trim**	Auburn, WA Cartersville, GA	Wierton, WV

USG Literature

Complete technical data on USG products and systems can be found in the USG Architectural Technical Literature series. Those folders applying to drywall, cement board, acoustical ceilings, insulation and plaster construction are listed below with their appropriate CSI numbers. Copies of literature are available through USG sales offices.

Folder No. & Description		CSI No.
General		
SA100	Construction Selector	
Thermal and Moisture Protection		
SA700	Exterior Systems	07240
SA727	USG Fire Stop Systems	07840
Suspension Systems		
SC2000	Ceiling Systems	09120
Lath, Plaster		
SA920	Plaster Systems	09210
Gypsum Drywall		
SA923	Drywall/Steel-Framed Systems	09250
SA924	Drywall/Wood-Framed Systems	09250
SA925	USG Area Separation Fire Wall/Party Wall Systems	09250
SA926	USG Cavity Shaft Wall Systems	09250
SA927	Gypsum Panels & Accessories	09250
Prefinished Panels		
SA928	Sheetrock Brand Vinyl-Faced Gypsum Panels	09720
Abuse-Resistant Systems		
SA929	Abuse-Resistant Systems	09250
Tile Accessories		
SA932	Durock Brand Cement Board Systems	09305
Finishing Materials		
SA933	Sheetrock Brand Textures and Finish Products	09940
Ceiling Systems		
SC2000	Acoustical and Specialty Ceilings	09500
Security Walls		
SA1119	Structocore Security Wall Systems	11190

Glossary

Absorption The taking up and holding or dissipating of matter or energy, as a sponge takes up water. Absorption is the opposite of reflection. Porosity is a term that describes the absorption qualities of certain materials, such as wallboard paper.

Accelerator An additive that shortens the time for gypsum plasters or setting-type joint compounds to set.

Acoustical Panels Normally a 24″ x 24″ or larger piece of prefinished material with various surface finishes installed in a suspension system to provide improved sound absorption qualities.

Acoustic Privacy Sound-control design with assemblies provided between two spaces for the purpose of preventing passage of airborne sound and dampening impact sound.

Acoustical Ceiling Sound-absorbing and/or sound attenuating modules held in a suspended grid. A system having highly effective sound-absorbing and/or sound attenuating qualities.

Acoustical Ceiling Board (Lay-In Panel) Acoustical material used in conjunction with a lay-in grid system, usually in 24″ x 24″ or larger panels.

Acoustical Consultant Trained professional in recommending solutions to sound problems and design facilities to meet specific sound criteria. Also acoustical engineer or acoustician.

Acoustical Sealant Special caulking material designed to seal gaps and cracks to reduce sound flanking in an assembly. For example, SHEETROCK Acoustical Sealant, from USG.

Acoustical Tile Normally a 12″ x 12″ or 12″ x 24″ piece of prefinished material with various surface finishes installed in a concealed suspension system or cemented to a ceiling or upper wall surface to provide sound absorption qualities.

Acoustics Science dealing with the production, control, transmission, reception and effects of sound, and the process of hearing. The acoustics of a room are those qualities that, together, determine its character with respect to distinct hearing.

Admixture Any substance added to a plaster component or plaster for the purpose of modifying its properties.

Aggregate Sand, gravel, crushed stone or other material that is a main constituent of portland cement concrete and aggregated gypsum plaster. Also, polystyrene, perlite and vermiculite particles used in texture finishes.

AIA American Insurance Assn., successor to the National Board of Fire Underwriters and Nonprofit Organization of Insurance Companies. Also, American Institute of Architects.

Airborne Sound Sound traveling through the medium of air.

All Purpose Joint Compound A compound formulated and manufactured to serve as a taping or finishing compound, or both.

Ambient Light The generally available, surrounding or pervading light in the area, coming from all sides, including outside light coming in through windows.

ANSI American National Standards Institute, a nonprofit, national technical association that publishes standards covering definitions, test methods, recommended practices and specifications of materials. Formerly American Standards Assn. (ASA) and United States of America Standards Institute (USASI).

Anchor Metal securing device embedded or driven into masonry, concrete, steel or wood.

Anchor Bolt Heavy, threaded bolt embedded in the foundation to secure sill to foundation wall or bottom plate of exterior wall to concrete floor slab.

Annular Ring Nail A deformed shank nail with improved holding qualities specially designed for use with gypsum board.

Area Separation Wall Residential fire walls, usually with a 2- to 4-hour rating, designed to prevent spread of fire from an adjoining occupancy; extends from foundation to or through the roof. Identified by codes as either "fire wall," "party wall" or "townhouse separation wall."

Articulation Class A classification to rate the degree of speech recognition allowed to transmit through ceilings or partitions.

ASA Formerly American Standards Assn., now American National Standards Institute (ANSI).

ASTM Formerly American Society for Testing and Materials, now ASTM, a nonprofit, national technical society that publishes definitions, standards, test methods, recommended installation practices and specifications for materials.

Attenuate The act of resisting the passage of sound energy.

Attenuation In acoustics, the diluting or holding back of the energy of sound waves as they pass through a material. Materials are rated for their ability to prevent sounds from traveling through them (see Ceiling Attenuation Class, CAC).

Back Blocking A short piece of gypsum board adhesively laminated behind the joints between each framing member to reinforce the joint. Also, may be a method of attaching additional framing to support gypsum board where no framing is present.

Backup Strips Pieces of wood nailed at the ceiling-sidewall corner to provide fastening for ends of plaster base or gypsum panels.

Balloon Frame Method of framing outside walls in which studs extend the full length or height of the wall.

Bar Joist Open-web, flat truss structural member used to support floor or roof structure. Web section is made from bar or rod stock, and chords are usually fabricated from "T" or angle sections.

Basecoat The first layer or layers of plaster applied over a lath or other substrate. The first application is normally called a scratch coat and the second application is referred to as a brown coat.

Basecoat Floating The finishing act of spreading, compacting and smoothing of the basecoat plaster to a reasonably true plane.

Batten Narrow strip of wood, plastic, metal or gypsum board used to conceal an open joint.

BCMC Board for the Coordination of Model Codes; part of the Council of American Building Officials Association (CABO).

Beam Loadbearing member spanning a distance between supports.

Bearing Support area upon which something rests, such as the point on bearing walls where the weight of the floor joist or roof rafter bears.

Bed To set firmly and permanently in place.

Bending Bowing of a member that results when a load or loads are applied laterally between supports.

Board Foot (Bd. Ft.) Volume of a piece of wood, nominal 1″ x 12″ x 1′. All lumber is sold by the board-foot measure.

BOCA Building Officials Conference of America, a nonprofit organization that publishes the National Building Code.

Bonding Agent A material applied to a surface to improve the quality of the bond between it and the succeeding plaster application. For instance, monolithic concrete and cement board require the addition of a bonding agent before applying plaster.

Brick Veneer Non-loadbearing brick facing applied to a wall to give appearance of solid-brick construction; bricks are fastened to backup structure with metal ties embedded in mortar joints.

Bridging Members attached between floor joists to distribute concentrated loads over more than one joist and to prevent rotation of the joist. Solid bridging consists of joist-depth lumber installed perpendicular to and between the joists. Cross-bridging consists of pairs of braces set in an "X" form between joists.

Brown Coat The second coat in three-coat gypsum plaster application.

Building Construction Joint A designed division of a building that allows movement of all component parts of the building, in any plane, which may be caused by thermal, seismic, wind loading or any other force. The construction of the separation is accomplished by one of the following methods: (1) manufactured devices suitable for this application, or (2) by field fabrication of suitable materials.

CABO Council of American Building Officials Association, made up of representatives from three model codes. Issues National Research Board (NRB) research reports.

CAC See Ceiling Attenuation Class.

Calcine The process of heating a mineral to produce a change in the chemical composition of the mineral, ranging from the removal of chemically combined water through the reduction of the mineral to its oxide state.

Calcined Gypsum A dry powder; primarily calcium sulfate hemihydrate, resulting from calcination of gypsum; cementitious base for production of most gypsum plasters; also called plaster of paris; sometimes called stucco.

Calcium Sulfate The chemical compound $CaSO_4$.

Camber Curvature built into a beam or truss to compensate for loads that will be encountered when in place and load is applied. The crown is placed upward. Insufficient camber results in unwanted deflection when the member is loaded.

Cant Beam Beam with edges chamfered or beveled.

Cant Strip Triangular section laid at the intersection of two surfaces to ease or eliminate effect of a sharp angle or projection.

Carrying Channel Main supporting member of a suspended ceiling system to which furring members or channels attach.

Casement Glazed sash or frame hung to open like a door.

Casing The trim around windows, doors, columns or piers.

Ceiling Attenuation Class (CAC) A sound rating developed especially for acoustical ceilings. The sound ratings are determined by AMA1-II ceiling sound transmission tests. Results were previously called CSTC value.

Ceiling STC (CSTC) Obsolete. See Ceiling Attenuation Class.

Cement Board A factory-manufactured panel, 5/16″ to 5/8″ thick, 32″ to 48″ wide, and 3′ to 10′ long, made from aggregated and reinforced portland cement.

Chalk Line Straight working line made by snapping a chalked cord stretched between two points, transferring chalk to work surface.

Class A A fire classification for a product with a flame spread rating of no more than 25 and a smoke developed rating not exceeding 50, when tested in accordance with ASTM E84.

Cladding Gypsum panels, gypsum bases, gypsum sheathing, cement board, etc. applied to framing.

Coefficient of Thermal Conductance (C) Amount of heat (in Btu) that passes through a specific thickness of a material (either homogeneous or heterogeneous) per hr., per sq. ft., per °F. Measured as temperature difference between surfaces.

The "C" value of a homogeneous material equals the "k" value divided by the material thickness:

$$C = k/t \text{ where } t = \text{thickness of material in inches}$$

It is impractical to determine a "k" value for some materials such as building paper or those only used or formed as a thin membrane, so only "C" values are given for them.

Coefficient of Thermal Conductivity (k) Convenient factor represents the amount of heat (in Btu) that passes by conduction through a 1″ thickness of homogeneous material, per hr., per sq. ft. per °F. Measured as temperature difference between the two surfaces of the material.

Coefficient of Heat Transmission (U) Total amount of heat that passes through an assembly of materials, including air spaces and surface air films. Expressed in Btu per hr., per sq. ft., per °F temperature difference between inside and outside air (beyond the surface air films). "U" values are often used to represent wall and ceiling assemblies, floors and windows.

Note: "k" and "C" values cannot simply be added to obtain "U" values. "U" can only be obtained by adding the thermal resistance (reciprocal of "C") of individual items and dividing the total into 1.

Coefficient of Hygrometric Expansion See Hygrometric Expansion.

Coefficient of Thermal Expansion See Thermal Expansion.

Column Vertical loadbearing member.

Compression Force that presses particles of a body closer together.

Compression Strength Measures maximum unit resistance of a material to crushing load. Expressed as force per unit cross-sectional area, e.g., pounds per square inch (psi).

Concrete Footing Generally, the wide, lower part of a foundation wall that spreads the weight of the building over a larger area. Its width and thickness vary according to weight of building and type of soil on which building is erected.

Conduction, Thermal Transfer of heat from one part of a body to another part of that body, or to another in contact, without any movement of bodies involved. The hot handle of a skillet is an example. The heat travels from the bottom of the skillet to the handle by conduction.

Construction Joint A designed division of a building that allows movement of all component parts of the building in any plane, which may be caused by thermal, seismic, wind loading or any other force. Construction joints are sometimes confused with control joints.

Convection Process of heat carried from one point to another by movement of a liquid or a gas (i.e. air). Natural convection is caused by expansion of the liquid or gas when heated. Expansion reduces the density of the medium, causing it to rise above the cooler, more dense portions of the medium.

Gravity heating systems are examples of the profitable use of natural convection. The air, heated by the furnace, becomes less dense (consequently lighter) and rises, distributing heat to the various areas of the house without any type of blower. When a blower is used, the heat transfer method is called "forced convection."

Core (of gypsum board) The hardened material filling the space between the face and back papers consisting substantially of rehydrated gypsum with additives.

Corner Brace Structural framing member used to resist diagonal loads that cause racking of walls and panels due to wind and seismic forces. May consist of a panel or diaphragm, or diagonal flat strap or rod. Bracing must function in both tension and compression. If brace only performs in tension, two diagonal tension members must be employed in opposing directions as "X" bracing.

Corner Post Timber or other member forming the corner of a frame. May be solid or built-up as a multi-piece member.

Creep Plastic flow or deformation of a material or a composite resulting from the sustained application of a force or load. Creep is typically greater at higher temperatures.

Creep Deflection Permanent deflection in a building system caused by deformation under a sustained force or load. An example of creep deflection is the sag in concrete floor slabs of a new building caused by sustained dead and live loads on the floor. This deformation or sag often causes partition cracking when the center of a partition span occurs near the area of greatest creep deflection. Creep deflection is a structural problem that decreases after a building stabilizes, one or two years after construction. Another cause of partition cracking, sometimes confused with that from creep deflection, is racking of structural components. Partition cracking caused by racking as a result of thermal expansion and contraction or wind loads on the building must be treated in some way, such as by the use of control or expansion joints.

Cripple Short stud such as that used between a door or window header and the top plate.

Critical Light Strong, angular or harsh light that can show imperfections in reflecting surfaces. Most common sources are skylights, wall sconces and directed track lights such as those used in art galleries.

Curtain Wall Exterior wall of a building that is supported by the structure and carries no part of the vertical load except its own. Curtain walls must be designed to withstand wind loads and transfer them to the structure.

Cycle (Acoustic) One full repetition of a motion sequence during periodic vibration. Movement from zero to +1 back to zero to -1 back to zero. Frequency of vibration is expressed in Hertz (cycles per second see Frequency).

Dead Load Load on a building element contributed by the weight of the building materials.

Decibel (dB) Adopted for convenience in representing vastly different sound pressures. The sound pressure level (SPL) in decibels is 10 times the logarithm to the base 10 of the squared ratio of the sound pressure to a reference pressure of 20 micropascals. This reference pressure is considered the lowest value at 100 Hz that the ear can detect. For every 10 dB increase or decrease in SPL, a sound is generally judged to be about twice or half as loud as before the change.

Decoupling Separation of elements to reduce or eliminate the transfer of sound, heat or physical loads from one element to the other.

Deflection Displacement that occurs when a load is applied to a member or assembly. The dead load of the member or assembly itself causes some deflection as may occur in roofs or floors at mid-span. Under applied wind loads maximum deflection occurs at mid-height in partitions and walls.

Deflection Limitation Maximum allowable deflection is dictated by the bending limit of the finish material under the required design load (e.g.,usually 5 psf for interior partitions). Often expressed as ratio of span (L) divided by criterion factor (120, 180, 240, 360). For example, in a 10' or 120" high wall, allowable deflection under L/240 criterion equals 120"/240 or 1/2" maximum.

Selection of limiting heights and spans are frequently based on minimum code requirements and accepted industry practice as follows: (a) L/120 for gypsum panel surfaces and veneer plaster finish surfaces, (b) L/240 for conventional lath and plaster surfaces, (c) L/360 for mechanically attached marble or heavy stone to walls; however, support for its own weight should be from the floor or separate supports. Although some building codes permit these deflections, more conservative criteria are frequently advised so that applied loads are not visible or esthetically unacceptable.

Deformation Change in shape of a body brought about by the application of a force internal or external. Internal forces may result from temperature, humidity or chemical changes. External forces from applied loads can also cause deformation.

Density The quantity per unit volume of a material; the mass of a substance per unit volume.

Design Load Combination of weight (dead load) and other applied forces (live loads) for which a building or part of a building is designed. Based on the worst possible combination of loads.

Desulfo Gypsum Calcium sulfate dehydrate (gypsum) produced as a byproduct of scrubbing industrial smoke stacks to meet environmental clean air standards. Also known as synthetic gypsum.

Dew Point The temperature at which air becomes saturated with moisture and below which condensation occurs.

Direct Lighting Lighting aimed at objects or surfaces. Direct lighting mounted in ceilings de-emphasizes the ceiling surface and highlights horizontal surfaces, such as work surfaces and the floor. A combination of both direct and indirect illumination can produce a positive effect on the space and save money.

Door Buck Structural element of a door opening. May be the same element as the frame, if frame is structural, as in the case of heavy steel frames.

Dot A small lump of plaster placed on a surface (usually scarified basecoat) between grounds to assist the plasterer in obtaining the proper plaster thickness and aid in aligning the surface.

Double-Hung Window Window sash that slides vertically and is offset in a double track.

Double-Up Successive plaster coat application with no setting or drying time allowed between coats; usually associated with veneer plastering. The double-up coat is applied (from the same mix) to a scratch coat over gypsum base.

Drip Interruption or offset in an exterior horizontal surface, such as a soffit, immediately adjacent to the fascia. Designed to prevent the migration of water back along the surface.

Drywall Generic term for interior surfacing material, such as gypsum panels, applied to framing using dry construction methods, e.g., mechanical fasteners or adhesive. See Sheetrock Brand Gypsum Panels.

Edge (of gypsum board) The paper-bound edge as manufactured.

End (of gypsum board) The end perpendicular to the paper-bound edge as manufactured. The gypsum core is always exposed.

Expansion Joint See Building Construction Joint and Construction Joint.

Efflorescence A deposit of white, powdery, water-soluble salts on the surface of masonry or plaster. It is caused by the migration of the dissolved salts to the surface; also called "whiskering" or "saltpetering."

Exterior Insulation and Finish Systems (EIFS) Exterior cladding assembly consisting of a polymer finish over a reinforcement adhered to foam plastic insulation that is fastened to masonry, concrete, building sheathing or directly to the structural framing. The sheathing may be cement board, gypsum sheathing or other acceptable substrate.

Extrapolate To project tested values, assuming a continuity of an established pattern, to obtain values beyond the limit of the test results. Not necessarily reliable.

F & T Ratings Flame-resistance and temperature ratings usually associated with "Through-Penetration" Testing. "F rating" or flame-resistance rating is the time period a firestop system remains in place during an ASTM E814 fire test, but "T rating" is the time period it takes for the temperature on the unexposed surface, the firestop and the penetrating item to rise 325 °F above the initial temperature.

Factor of Safety Ratio of the ultimate unit stress to the working or allowable stress.

Fascia Board Board fastened to the ends of the rafters or joists forming part of a cornice.

Fast Track Method that telescopes or overlaps traditional design-construction process. Overlapping phases as opposed to sequential phases is keynote of the concept.

Fatigue Condition of material under stress that has lost, to some degree, its power of resistance as a result of repeated application of stress, particularly if stress reversals occur as with positive and negative cyclical loading.

Feather The gradual thinning of joint compound from the thickness over the joint to the outer edge of a coat.

Finish Coat The final layer of plaster applied over a basecoat or other substrate.

Finish Coat Floating The finishing act of spreading, compacting and smoothing the finish coat plaster or stucco to a specified surface texture.

Finishing Compound (See Topping Compound).

Fire Endurance Measure of elapsed time during which an assembly continues to exhibit fire resistance under specified conditions of test and performance. As applied to elements of buildings, it shall be measured by the methods and to the criteria defined in ASTM Methods E119, Fire Tests of Building Construction and Materials; ASTM Methods E152, Fire Tests of Door Assemblies; ASTM Methods E814, Fire Test of Through-Penetration Fire Stops; or ASTM Methods E163, Fire Tests of Window Assemblies.

Fireproof Use of this term in reference to buildings is discouraged because few, if any, building materials can withstand extreme heat for an extended time without some effect. The term "fire-resistive" or "resistant" is more descriptive.

Fire Resistance Relative term, used with a numerical rating or modifying adjective to indicate the extent to which a material or structure resists the effect of fire.

Fire-Resistive Refers to properties or designs to resist effects of any fire to which a material or structure may be expected to be subjected.

Fire-Retardant Denotes substantially lower degree of fire resistance than "fire-resistive." Often used to describe materials that are combustible but have been treated to retard ignition or spread of fire under conditions for which they were designed.

Firestop Obstruction in a cavity designed to resist the passage of flame, sometimes referred to as "fire blocking."

Firestop System A system for protecting against the spread of fire through a penetration in a wall or floor where a pipe or other penetrant passes through a fire-rated system. A firestop is the specific construction using materials designed to fill the annular space around the penetrant for the purpose of preventing the passage of fire through the fire-resistive partition or floor/ceiling assembly.

Fire Wall Fire-resistant partition extending to or through the roof of a building to retard spread of fire. See Area Separation Wall.

Flame Spread Index of the capacity of a material to spread fire under test conditions, as defined by ASTM Standard E84. Materials are rated by comparison with the flame-spread index of red oak flooring assigned a value of 100 and inorganic reinforced cement board assigned a value of 0.

Flammable Capability of a combustible material to ignite easily, burn intensely or have rapid rate of flame spread.

Flanking Paths Paths by which sound travels around an element intended to impede it, usually some structural component that is continuous between rooms and rigid enough to transmit the sound. For example, a partition separating two rooms can be "flanked" by the floor, ceiling or walls surrounding the partition if they run uninterrupted from one room to the other. Ducts, conduits, openings, structural elements, rigid ties, etc., can be sound flanking paths. The acoustic effect of sound flanking paths is dependent on many factors.

Flashing Strips of metal or waterproof material used to make joints waterproof, as in the joining of curtain wall panels.

Flexural Strength The maximum load sustained by a standard specimen of a sheet material when subjected to a bending force.

Footcandle the measurement of light emitted over distance. One foot candle is the amount of direct light thrown by one international candle onto a surface one foot away and equal to one lumen per square foot.

Footing Lower extremity of a foundation or loadbearing member that transmits load to load-bearing substrate.

Force Amount of applied energy to cause motion, deformation or displacement and stress in a body.

Foundation Component that transfers weight of building and occupants to the earth.

Framing Member Stud, plate, track, joist, furring and other support to which a gypsum panel product, or metal plaster base is attached.

Frequency (Sound) Number of complete vibrations or cycles or periodic motion per unit of time.

Furring Member or means of supporting a finished surfacing material away from the structural wall or framing. Used to level uneven or damaged surfaces or to provide space between substrates. Also an element for mechanical or adhesive attachment of paneling.

Gable Uppermost portion of the end wall of a building that comes to a triangular point under a sloping roof.

Gauging Plaster Combine with lime putty to provide setting properties, to increase dimensional stability during drying, and to provide initial surface hardness in lime finish coats.

Girder Beam, especially a long, heavy one; the main beam supporting floor joists or other smaller beams.

Green A term to describe freshly applied plaster that has set, but has not dried.

Ground A piece of wood or metal attached to the framing or plaster base so that its exposed surface acts as a gauge to define the thickness of plaster to be applied. Also a term to denote plaster thickness. Also see Screed.

Grout Gypsum or portland cement plaster used to fill crevices or to fill hollow metal frames.

Gusset Wood or metal plate riveted, bolted, glued or pressed (wood trusses) over joints to transfer stresses between connected members.

Gypsum The mineral consisting primarily of fully hydrated calcium sulfate, $CaSO_4 \bullet 2H_2O$ or calcium sulfate dihydrate.

Gypsum Fiber Panels Gypsum panels with fiber reinforcement concentrated on each face of the panel. They are part of a new-technology series of panel products, called FIBEROCK® Brand Panels, which produce stronger, more abuse-resistant, water-resistant walls and ceilings than those produced with conventional drywall. There are variations for interior drywall applications in dry and wet areas, sheathing applications and flooring applications. Also, a very-high impact (VHI) product is further reinforced on the backside by a fiberglass mesh.

Gypsum Lath A gypsum board used as the base for application of gypsum plaster.

Gypsum Molding Plaster A calcined gypsum plaster used primarily for plaster casts or molds, sometimes used as a gauging plaster.

Gypsum Neat Plaster A calcined gypsum plaster without aggregate; common usage is for gypsum plaster used for basecoats.

Gypsum Plaster The generic name for a family of powdered cementitious products consisting primarily of calcined gypsum with additives to modify physical characteristics, and having the ability, when mixed with water, to produce a plastic mortar or slurry which can be formed to the desired shape by various methods and will subsequently set to a hard, rigid mass.

Gypsum Sheathing A gypsum board used as a backing for exterior surface materials, manufactured with water-repellent paper and may be manufactured with a water-resistant core.

HUD Housing and Urban Development, federal agency.

HUD Manufactured Home Standards Officially, the Manufactured Home Construction and Safety Standards, a national, pre-emptive building code covering manufactured homes. Includes the following agencies: DAPIA—Design Approval Primary Inspection Agency, and IPIA—Production Inspection Primary Inspection Agency.

HVAC Heating, ventilating and air conditioning. (American Society of Heating, Refrigerating & Air Conditioning Engineers, Inc. "ASHRAE" Guide is the technical reference source.)

Header Horizontal framing member across the ends of the joists. Also the member over a door or window opening in a wall.

Head of Wall A type of construction joint where two fire-rated assemblies intersect. Head-of-wall assemblies occur where a wall intersects a floor/ceiling or roof/ceiling. In these construction details, a fire-protective assembly is needed to protect against the spread of fire. An example is where a partition intersects a fluted steel deck. Head-of-wall and other construction joints are evaluated under UL Standard 2079 for their ability to resist flame and temperature transmission as well as hose stream.

Heat Form of energy thought to be characterized by the rate of vibration of the molecules of a substance. The hotter the substance, the faster the molecules vibrate. On the other hand, when there is no heat present it is thought the molecules will be at rest, which theoretically occurs at absolute zero, -459.7 °F (-273.2 °C or 0.0 K).

Heat Quantity (Btu) Common unit of measure of the quantity of heat is the British Thermal Unit (Btu). One Btu is the amount of heat required to raise one pound of water from 63 ° to 64 °F (1 Btu = 1055.06 J). This is about the amount of heat given off by one wooden match. A pound of coal can produce 13,000 Btu.

Heat Transfer Heat always flows toward a substance of lower temperature until the temperatures of the two substances equalize. It travels by one or more of three methods: conduction, convection or radiation.

Heel of Rafter Seat cut in a rafter that rests on the wall plate.

Hemihydrate The dry powder, calcium sulfate hemihydrate, resulting from calcination of $CaSO_4•2H_2O$, calcium sulfate dihydrate. See calcined gypsum.

Hertz The units of measure of sound frequency, named for Heinrich H. Hertz. One Hertz equals one cycle per second.

Honeycomb Any substance having cells suggesting a mass of cells such as those built by the honeybee. Some hollow-core doors use the honeycomb principle in their construction.

Hydrate To chemically combine with water as in the hydration of calcined gypsum or slaking of quicklime. Also the product resulting from this combination.

Hygrometric Expansion All materials, particularly those of organic origin, expand and contract in relation to their moisture content, which varies with environment. The Hygrometric Coefficient of Expansion is expressed in "Inches Per Inch Per Percent Of Relative Humidity." Example: gypsum board has a coefficient of 7.2 x 10-6 in. per in per % R.H. This means that with an increase in relative humidity of from 10% to 50%, a gypsum board wall 300 ft. long will have an unrestrained linear expansion of 1.0368" or 1-1/32".

ICBO International Conference of Building Officials, a nonprofit organization that publishes the Uniform Building Code.

ISO International Standards Organization, an organization similar in nature to ASTM.

Impact Insulation Class (IIC) Single-number rating used to compare and evaluate the performance of floor-ceiling constructions in isolating impact noise. The advantages of this rating system are positive values and the correlation with Sound Transmission Class (STC) values-both providing approximately equal isolation at a particular value. The IIC rating is used by building agencies for specifying minimum sound-control performance of assemblies in residential construction.

Impact Noise Rating (INR) Obsolete rating system for floor-ceiling construction in isolating impact noise. INR ratings can be converted to approximate IIC ratings by adding 51 points; however, a variation of 1 or 2 points may occur.

Incombustible See Noncombustible.

Indirect lighting Reflected light. For ceilings, this is typically light from luminaires distributed upward. A combination of both direct and indirect illumination can produce a positive effect on the space and save money.

Industrial Construction Construction of residential or commercial structures in a factory environment. Includes HUD-Code manufactured homes as well as residential and commercial modular construction.

Insulation (Thermal) Any material that measurably retards heat transfer. There is wide variation in the insulating value of different materials. A material having a low density (weight/volume) will usually be a good thermal insulator.

Interpolate To estimate untested values that fall between tested values.

Jamb One of the finished upright sides of a door or window frame.

Jamb Stud Wood or metal stud adjacent to the door jamb.

Joint Tape A type of paper, fabric or glass mesh commonly used with joint compounds to reinforce the joints between adjacent gypsum boards.

Joist Small beam that supports part of the floor, ceiling or roof of a building.

Joist Hanger Metal shape formed for hanging on the main beam to provide support for the end of a joist.

Keene's Cement An anhydrous gypsum plaster characterized by a low mixing water requirement and special setting properties, primarily used with lime to produce hard, dense finish coats. Complete name is Red Top Keenes Cement.

Key The grip or mechanical bond of one coat of plaster to another coat, or to a plaster base. It may be accomplished physically by the penetration of wet mortar or crystals into paper fibers, perforations, scoring irregularities, or by the embedment of the lath.

Kiln-Dried Lumber Lumber that has been dried and seasoned with carefully controlled heat in a kiln.

Label Service (UL) Program allowing a manufacturer to place Underwriters Laboratories Inc. labels on its products that have met UL requirements. A UL representative visits the manufacturing location to obtain samples of the products for testing by UL. In some cases, samples are also purchased on the open market for testing. The public is thereby assured that products bearing the UL label continually meet UL specifications.

Lamination Placing a layer of gypsum board over another gypsum board or over another substrate using an adhesive product for attachment.

Laser Level A mechanical device whose primary function is to establish level or plumb lines on a construction site with an extreme degree of precision. In acoustical ceiling installations it uses a high-intensity light beam that rotates in a level plane. See Tool Chapter for more information.

Lath A metal or gypsum (or wood in the past) material applied separately to a structure to serve as a base for plaster.

Lay-In Panel Any panel designed to be supported by an accessible suspension system.

Leaks (Sound) Small openings at electrical boxes and plumbing, cracks around doors, loose-fitting trim and closures all create leaks that allow sound to pass through, reducing the acoustical isolation of a wall, floor or ceiling system.

Ledger Strip Strip fastened to the bottom edge of a flush girder to help support the floor joists.

Life-Cycle Costing Selection of the most economical material and systems based on initial costs, maintenance costs and operating costs for the life of the building.

Limiting Height Maximum height for design and construction of a partition or wall without exceeding the structural capacity or allowable deflection under given design loads.

Lintel Horizontal member spanning an opening such as a window or door. Also referred to as a Header.

Live Load Part of the total load on structural members that is not a permanent part of the structure. May be variable, as in the case of loads contributed by the occupancy, and wind and snow loads.

Load Force provided by weight, external or environmental sources such as wind, water and temperature, or other sources of energy.

Load-Bearing Partition A partition designed to support a portion of the building structure.

Loudness Subjective response to sound pressure, but not linearly related thereto. A sound with twice the pressure is not twice as loud. See Decibel.

Louver Opening with slanted fins (to keep out rain and snow) used to ventilate attics, crawl spaces and wall openings.

Lumen A standard unit of light emission measurement. Generally speaking, one lumen is the amount of light emitted by one candle. More strictly defined, a lumen is the unit of measure for the flow of light through a unit solid angle from a uniform point source of one international candle.

Luminaire A complete lighting unit, consisting of a lamp or lamps together with parts designed to distribute the light, to position and protect the lamps and to connect to the power source.

Mass Property of a body that resists acceleration and produces the effect of inertia. The weight of a body is the result of the pull of gravity on the body's mass.

Mechanical Bonds The attachment created when plaster penetrates, into or through, the substrate, or envelops irregularities in the surface of the substrate.

Metric Terms Metric units shown as equivalents in this handbook are from the International System of Units in use throughout the world, as established by the General Conference of Weights and Measures in 1960. Their use here complies with the Metric Conversion Act of 1975, which committed the United States to a coordinated voluntary conversion to the metric system of measurement.

Refer to the pages 470-471 in Appendix for metric units and conversion factors applicable to subjects covered in this handbook. For additional information, refer to ASTM E380-76, Standard for Metric Practice.

Miter Joint formed by two pieces of material cut to meet at an angle.

Model Code Building code, written and published by a building-official association, available to states, counties and municipalities for adoption (for a fee) in lieu of their own, e.g. Uniform Building Code, Standard Building Code, National Building Code.

Modular Building A structure intended for residential or commercial use that is at least partially completed in a factory complying with state or local code requirements.

Module (1) In architecture, a selected unit of measure used as a basis for building layout; (2) In industrialized housing, a three-dimensional section of a building, factory-built, shipped as a unit and interconnected with other modules to form the complete building. Single-family units factory-built in two halves are usually referred to as "sectionals."

Modulus of Elasticity (E) Ratio between stress and unit deformation, a measure of the stiffness of a material.

Moment of Inertia (I) Calculated numerical relationship (expressed in in.^{4}) of the resistance to bending of a member, a function of the cross-sectional shape and size. A measure of the stiffness of a member based on its shape. Larger moments of inertia indicate greater resistance to bending for a given material.

Mortar A mixture of gypsum plaster or portland cement with aggregate or hydrate lime, or both, and water to produce a trowelable fluidity.

Moulding (also Molding) Narrow decorative strip applied to a surface.

Mud Slang term for joint compound.

Mud Pan Rectangular, angle-sided pan, shaped like bread pan, used by joint finisher to handle portions of joint compound. Straight-cut lip of pan assures that taping knife can be regularly cleaned.

Mullion Vertical bar or division in a window frame separating two or more panes.

Muntin Horizontal bar or division in a window frame separating multiple panes or lights.

Music/Machinery Transmission Class (MTC) Rating developed by U.S. Gypsum Company to isolate music and machinery/mechanical equipment noise or any sound with a substantial portion of low frequency energy. This rating system is not currently in common use.

NBFU National Board of Fire Underwriters, now merged into the American Insurance Assn.

NBS National Bureau of Standards, a federal agency.

NCSBCS National Conference of States on Building Codes and Standards, a nonprofit organization formed to increase interstate cooperation and coordinate intergovernmental reforms of building codes.

NFPA National Fire Protection Association. An international technical society that disseminates fire prevention, fire fighting and fire protection information. NFPA technical standards include the National Electrical Code which is widely adopted.

NFoPA National Forest Products Association.

Nail Pop The protrusion of the nail usually attributed to the shrinkage of or use of improperly cured wood framing.

Neutral Axis The plane through a member (at the geometric center of the section in symmetrical members) where the fibers are neither under tensile nor compressive stress.

Noise Reduction Coefficient (NRC) Arithmetic average of sound absorption coefficients at 250, 500, 1000 and 2000 Hz.

Nominal Term indicating that the full measurement is not used; usually slightly less than the full net measurement, as with 2″ x 4″ studs that have an actual size when dry of 1-1/2″ x 3-1/2″.

Noncombustible Definition excerpted from the ICBO Uniform Building Code:

1. Material of which no part will ignite and burn when subjected to fire.

2. Material having a structural base of noncombustible materials as defined, with a surface not over 1/8″ thick that has a flame spread rating of 50 or less.

The term does not apply to surface finish materials.

Octave Interval between two sounds having a basic frequency ratio of two. The formula is 2n times the frequency, where n is the desired octave interval. The octave band frequency given in sound test results is usually the band center frequency, thus the 1000 Hz octave band encompasses frequencies from 707 Hz to 1414 Hz (n=± 1/2). The 1000 Hz one-third octave band encompasses frequencies from 891 Hz to 1122 Hz (n = ± 1/6).

OSU Ohio State University, an independent fire-testing laboratory which is currently inactive.

Parapet Wall Extension of an exterior wall above and/or through the roof surface.

Penny (d) Suffix designating the size of nails, such as 6d (penny) nail, originally indicating the price, in English pence, per 100 nails. Does not designate a constant length or size, and will vary by type (e.g., common and box nails).

Performance Specification States how a building element must perform as opposed to describing equipment, products or systems by name.

Perimeter Relief A gap left around the perimeter of a wall, floor or ceiling membrane, such that it will not be in direct contact with the membrane of adjoining assemblies. This gap is normally caulked with acoustical sealant.

Perm A unit of measurement of Water Vapor Permenance (ASTN E96). Also, see Permeance.

Permeance (water vapor) The ratio of the rate of water vapor transmission (WVT) through a material or assembly between its two parallel surfaces to the vapor pressure differential between the surfaces. Metric unit of measuring is the metric perm, 1 g/24 h. x m² x mm Hg; U.S. unit, 1 grain/h x ft.² x in. Hg.

Permeability The property of a porous material that permits a fluid (or gas) to pass through it; in construction, commonly refers to water vapor permeability of a sheet material or assembly and is defined as water vapor permeance per unit thickness. Metric unit of measurement, metric perms per centimeter of thickness. Also, see Permeance.

Photographing See Shadowing.

Pilaster Projecting, square column or stiffener forming part of a wall.

Pillar Column supporting a structure.

Pitch of Roof Slope of the surface, generally expressed in inches of vertical rise per 12″ horizontal distance, such as "4-in-12 pitch."

Plaster Base Gypsum panel with specially treated face paper to serve as a stable backing for plaster applications. Two types of plaster base are available; one type is usually 3/8-in. thick, 16 in. wide and 4 feet long and is used for conventional (thick) coat plastering. The other is typically 1/2-in. or 5/8-in. thick and 4 feet wide (lengths vary) and is used for veneer plaster system applications.

Plaster Bonder See Bonding Agent.

Plate "Top" plate is the horizontal member fastened to the top of the studs or wall on which the rafters, joists or trusses rest; "sole" plate is positioned at bottom of studs or wall.

Platform Floor surface raised above the ground or floor level.

Platform Framing Technique of framing where walls can be built and tilted-up on a platform floor, and in multi-story construction are erected sequentially from one platform to another. Also known as "Western" framing.

Plenum Chamber in which the pressure of the air is higher (as in a forced-air furnace system) than that of the surrounding air. Frequently a description of the space above a suspended ceiling.

Plenum Barrier Vertical surface framed from the structure above to the finished ceiling and sealed to prevent the passage of air.

Porosity The propensity of certain materials, such as wallboard paper, to absorb water.

Portland Cement Hydraulic cement produced by pulverizing clinker consisting essentially of hydraulic calcium silicates, usually containing one or more forms of calcium sulfate as an interground addition.

Prescription Specification Traditional procedure used on building projects to describe by name products, equipment or systems to be used.

Purlin Horizontal member in a roof supporting common rafters, such as at the break in a gambrel roof. Also, horizontal structural member perpendicular to main beams in a flat roof.

Racking Forcing out of plumb of structural components, usually by wind, seismic stress or thermal expansion or contraction.

Radiation Transfer of heat energy through space by wave motion. Although the radiant energy of heat is transmitted through space, no heat is present until this energy strikes and is absorbed by an object. Not all of the radiant heat energy is absorbed; some is reflected to travel in a new direction until it strikes another object. The amount reflected depends on the nature of the surface that the energy strikes. This fact explains the principle of insulating foil and other similar products that depend on reflection of radiant heat for their insulating value.

Radiant heat travels in straight lines in all directions at about the speed of light. In radiant heating systems, heat is often radiated down from the ceiling. As it strikes objects in the room, some is absorbed and some reflected to other objects. The heat that is absorbed warms the object, which, in turn, warms the surrounding air by conduction. This warmed air sets up gentle convection currents that circulate throughout the room.

Rafter That member forming the slanting frame of a roof or top chord of a truss. Also known as hip, jack or valley rafter depending on its location and use.

Rafter Tail That part of a rafter that extends beyond the wall plate—the overhang.

Ready-Mixed Plaster A calcined gypsum plaster with aggregate added during manufacture. Ready-mixed plaster is a powder product that requires the addition of water.

Reflected Heat See Radiation.

Reflected Sound Sound that has struck a surface and "bounced off." Sound reflects at the same angle as light reflects in a mirror; the angle of incidence equals the angle of reflection.

Large curved surfaces tend to focus (concave) or diffuse (convex) the sound when reflected. However, when the radius of the reflecting surface is less than the wavelength of the sound, this does not hold true. Thus, a rough textured surface has little effect on diffusion of sound.

Reflective Insulation Material that reflects and thus retards the flow of radiant heat. The most common type of reflective insulation is aluminum foil. The effectiveness of reflective barriers is diminished by the accumulation of dirt and by surface oxidation.

Relative Humidity The ratio of actual water vapor pressure to the saturation water vapor pressure at the same temperature, expressed as a percentage.

Retarder An admixture used to delay the setting action of plasters or other cementitious materials.

Reverberation Persistence of sound after the source stops. When one hears the 10th, 20th, 50th, 100th, etc., reflection of a sound, one hears reverberation.

Reverberation Time Essentially the number of seconds it takes a loud sound to decay to inaudibility after the source stops. Strictly, the time required for a sound to decay 60 dB in level.

Ridge Peak of a roof where the roof surfaces meet at an angle. Also may refer to the framing member that runs along the ridge and supports the rafters.

Rise Measurement in height of an object; the amount it rises. The converse is "fall."

Riser Vertical face of a step supporting the tread in a staircase.

Rough Framing Structural elements of a building or the process of assembling elements to form a supporting structure where finish appearance is not critical.

SBCCI Southern Building Code Congress International, nonprofit organization that publishes the Standard Building Code.

Sabin Measure of sound absorption of a surface, equivalent to 1 sq. ft. of a perfectly absorptive surface.

Safing Firestop material in the space between floor slab and curtain wall in multi-story construction.

Safing Off Installation of fire safety insulation around floor perimeters, between floor slab and spandrel panels. Insulation helps retain integrity of fire resistance ratings.

Scab Small piece or block of wood that bridges several members or provides a connection or fastening between them.

Screed To level or straighten a plaster coat application with a rod, darby or other similar tool. Also, as a noun, see Ground. Screeds are made from basecoat plaster; they are created between plaster dots or grounds.

Section Modulus (S) Numerical relationship, expressed in in.^{3}, of the resistance to stress of a member. It is equal to the moment of inertia divided by the perpendicular distance from the neutral axis to the extremity of the member.

Set The hardening and hydration of a gypsum plaster or setting-type joint compound. See Setting Time.

Setting Time The elapsed time required for a gypsum plaster or setting-type joint compound to attain a specified hardness and strength after mixing with water.

Shaft Wall Fire-resistant wall that isolates the elevator, stairwell and vertical mechanical chase in high-rise construction. This wall must withstand the fluctuating (positive and negative) air-pressure loads created by elevators or air distribution systems.

Shadowing An undesirable condition where the joint finish shows through the surface decoration.

Shear Force that tends to slide or rupture one part of a body from another part of the body or from attached objects.

Sheathing Plywood, gypsum, wood fiber, expanded plastic or composition boards encasing walls, ceilings, floors and roofs of framed buildings. May be structural or non-structural, thermal-insulating or non-insulating, fire-resistant or combustible.

SHEETROCK Leading brand of gypsum panel for interior wall and ceiling surfaces, developed and improved by United States Gypsum Company. There is only one SHEETROCK Brand Gypsum Panel.

Shoring Temporary member placed to support part of a building during construction, repair or alteration; also may support the walls of an excavation.

Sill Horizontal member at the bottom of door or window frames to provide support and closure.

Sill Plate Horizontal member laid directly on a foundation on which the framework of a building is erected.

Slab Flat (although sometimes ribbed on the underside) reinforced concrete element of a building that provides the base for the floor or roofing materials.

Soffit Undersurface of a projection or opening; bottom of a cornice between the fascia board and the outside of the building; underside of a stair, floor or lintel.

Sole Plate See Plate.

Sound Absorption Conversion of acoustic or sound energy to another form of energy, usually heat.

Sound Attenuation The reduction of sound energy as it passes through a conductor, resulting from the conductor's resistance to the transmission.

Sound Barrier A material installed in a plenum or partition to prevent the passage of sound from one area to another. Sound-deadening board and lead sheet or special insulations make good sound barriers.

Sound Insulation, Isolation Use of building materials or constructions that will reduce or resist the transmission of sound.

Sound Intensity Amount of sound power per unit area.

Sound Pressure Level (SPL) Expressed in decibels, the SPL is 20 times the logarithm to the base 10 of the ratio of the sound pressure to a reference pressure of 20 micropascals. See Decibel.

Sound Transmission The transfer of sound energy from one place to another, through air, structure or other conductor. Unwanted sound in a room may be the result of sound transmission from sources outside the room. The degree to which this sound transmission is acceptable depends on the quantity and source of the sound and the use of the adjacent space. Sound transmitted at a level below the receiving room ambient level would be acceptable.

Sound Transmission Class (STC) Single-number rating for evaluating the effectiveness of a construction in isolating audible airborne sound transmission across 16 frequencies. Higher numbers indicate more effectiveness. Tested per ASTM E90.

Span Distance between supports, usually a beam or joist.

Spandrel Beam Horizontal member, spanning between exterior columns, that supports the floor or roof.

Spandrel Wall Exterior wall panel, usually between columns, that extends from the window opening on one floor to one on the next floor.

Speed of Sound Speed of sound in air varies with atmospheric pressure and temperature, but is the same at all frequencies. For most architectural work, the speed of sound should be taken as 1,130 ft./second.

Splayed Hangers Hangers installed at an angle rather than perpendicular to the support grid or channel.

Square Edge An acoustical tile is considered square-edge material when the edge of the tile is not beveled; it creates a hairline joint when installed. Drywall panels also may have square edges; however, drywall edges are typically tapered.

Stile Vertical outside member in a piece of mill work, as a door or sash.

Stirrup Hanger to support the end of the joist at the beam.

Stop Strip of wood fastened to the jambs and head of a door or window frame against which the door or window closes.

Strain Unit deformation in a body that results from stress.

Stress Unit resistance of a body to an outside force that tends to deform the body by tension, compression or shear.

Stringer Heavy horizontal timber supporting other members of the frame in a wood or brick structure; a support also for steps.

Structure-Borne Sound Sound energy imparted directly to and transmitted by solid materials; such as building structures.

Strut Slender structural element that resists compressive forces acting lengthwise.

Stucco

1. A mixture of portland cement and aggregate designed for use on exterior surfaces or interior surfaces exposed to high levels of moisture. May also contain hydrated lime to improve working characteristics.

2. A gypsum plaster mix including aggregate for use on interior surfaces.

3. Calcined gypsum used to produce plaster, gypsum wallboard and related products. This terminology is specific to the gypsum processing industry.

Stud Vertical load-bearing or non-load bearing framing member.

Subfloor Rough or structural floor placed directly on the floor joists or beams to which the finished floor is applied. As with resilient flooring, an underlayment may be required between subfloor and finished floor.

Substrate Underlying material to which a finish is applied or by which it is supported.

Surface Burning Characteristic Rating of interior and surface finish material providing indexes for flame spread and smoke developed, based on testing conducted according to ASTM Standard E84.

Suspended Ceiling A ceiling that is hung from the structure with wire hangers.

Synthetic Gypsum A chemical product, consisting primarily of calcium sulfate dehydrate ($CaSO_4 \bullet 2H_2O$) resulting primarily from an industrial process. Also, see Desulfo Gypsum.

Take-Up The loss of water of a plaster into the absorptive substrate during application, as evidenced by a moderate stiffening of the plaster coat.

Tapered Edge An edge formation of gypsum board which provides a shallow depression at the paper-bound edge to receive joint reinforcement. Typical edge on drywall panels; edges may also be square.

Taping Compound (Sometimes called embedding compound.) A compound specifically formulated and manufactured for use in embedding of joint reinforcing tape at gypsum board joints.

Task Lighting Lighting directed to a specific work surface or area to provide illumination for tasks.

Temperature Measurement of the intensity (not quantity) of heat. The Fahrenheit (°F) scale places the freezing point of water at 32° and the boiling point at 212°. The Centigrade or Celsius (°C) scale, used by most countries and in scientific work, places the freezing point of water at 0° and the boiling point at 100°. On the Kelvin (K) scale, the unit of measurement equals the Celsius degree and measurement begins at absolute zero 0° (-273°C).

Tensile Strength Maximum tensile stress that can be developed in a given material under axial tensile loading. Also the measure of a material's ability to withstand stretching.

Tension Force that tends to pull the particles of a body apart.

Thermal Expansion All materials expand and contract to some extent with changes in temperature. The Thermal Coefficient of Linear Expansion is expressed [Inches Per Inch Per Degree Fahrenheit]. Example: gypsum board has a coefficient of 9.0×10^{-6} in. per in. per °F. This means that with an increase in temperature of 50°, a gypsum board wall 100 ft. in length will have a linear expansion of 0.54″ or an excess of 1/2″. The expansion characteristics of some other building materials are more pronounced; a 50° temperature increase would produce expansion in a 100′ length of approx. 3/4″ in aluminum, 3/8″ in steel and 1/2″ in concrete.

Thermal Resistance (R) Resistance of a material or assembly to the flow of heat. It is the reciprocal of the heat transfer coefficient: (1/C, or 1/U)

For insulating purposes, low "C" and "U" values and high "R" values are the most desirable.

Threshold Raised member at the floor within the door jamb. Its purpose is to provide a divider between dissimilar flooring materials or serve as a thermal, sound or water barrier.

Through Penetrations An opening through a fire-resistive partition or floor/ceiling assembly caused by the need to have a penetrating item pass through it. Through penetrations usually require the use of a firestop system to protect against the spread of fire through the opening.

Through Penetration Firestop A system for sealing through-penetrations in fire-resistant floors, walls and ceilings.

Time-Temperature Curve Rate of rise of temperature in a fire-testing furnace.

Toenail Method of fastening two boards or studs together as in a "T" by driving nails into the board that forms the stem of the "T" at an angle so they enter the other board and cross each other.

Tongue-and-Groove Joint Joint where the projection or "tongue" of one member engages the mating groove of the adjacent member to minimize relative deflection and air infiltration; widely used in sheathing, flooring and paneling. Tongues may be in "V," round or square shapes.

Topping Compound A compound specifically formulated and manufactured for use over taping or all purpose compounds to provide a smooth and level surface for the application of decoration.

Transmission Loss (TL) Essentially the amount, in decibels, by which sound power is attenuated (decreased) by passing from one side of a structure to the other. TL is independent of the rooms on each side of the structure and theoretically independent of the area and edge conditions of the structure.

Tread Horizontal plane or surface of a stair step.

Trimmer Double joists or rafters framing the opening of a stairway well, dormer opening, etc.

Truss Open, lightweight framework of members, usually designed to replace a large beam where spans are great.

UBC Uniform Building Code document promulgated by the International Conference of Building Officials.

U of C University of California, an independent fire-testing laboratory.

"U" Factor Coefficient of heat transfer, "U" equals 1 divided by (hence, the reciprocal of) the total of the resistances of the various materials, air spaces and surface air films in an assembly. See Thermal Resistance.

UL Underwriters Laboratories Inc.—not-for-profit laboratory operated for the purpose of testing devices, systems and materials as to their relation to life, fire and casualty hazards in the interest of public safety.

USASI United States of America Standards Institute, now American National Standards Institute.

Vapor Retarder Material used to retard the flow of water vapor through walls and other spaces where this vapor may condense at a lower temperature.

Veneer Plaster Calcined gypsum plaster specially formulated to provide specific workability, strength, hardness and abrasion resistance characteristics when applied in thin coats (1/16″ to 3/32″ nom.) over veneer gypsum base or other approved base. The term thin-coat plaster is sometimes used in reference to veneer plaster.

Water-Absorption The amount of water absorbed by a material under specified test conditions commonly expressed as weight percent of the test specimen.

Water-Repellent Paper Gypsum board paper surfacing which has been formulated or treated to resist water penetration.

Water Vapor Transmission The rate of water vapor flow, under steady specified conditions, through a unit area of a material, between its two parallel surfaces and normal to the surfaces. Metric unit of measurement is 1 g/24 h. x m^2 x mm Hg. Also, see Permeance.

Wavelength (Sound) Wave is one complete cycle of sound vibration passing through a medium (such as air) from compression through rarefaction and back to compression again. The physical length of this cycle is termed the wavelength. Wavelength in air vary from about 11/16″ for a 20,000-cycle per sec. (See Frequency) sound, to approximately 56-1/2′ for a 20-cycle per sec. sound (the two approximate extremes of human hearing sensitivity). There are waves outside of this range, but generally, they cannot be heard by humans.

Weep Hole Small aperture at the base of an exterior wall cavity intended to drain out trapped moisture.

Wet Sand To smooth a finished joint with a small-celled wet sponge. A preferred method to reduce dust created in the dry sanding method.

WHI Warnock Hershey International, an independent fire-testing laboratory.

Wood-Fibered Plaster A calcined gypsum plaster containing shredded or ground wood fiber added during manufacture.

Key Word Index

C

510

E

516

W

Alphabetical Index to Tables

USG Corporation

To contact your local USG sales office or representative,
call toll-free: 877-874-6655

To reach the USG product information and literature line,
call toll-free: 800-874-4968
or see the USG website (http://www.usg.com).

Industrial Division

Information about products from the Industrial Division
of USG Corporation can be obtained by
calling: 800-487-4431
or see the Industrial Gypsum Division website (http://igd.com).

Additional Copies

The *Gypsum Construction Handbook* can be purchased at many
technical and specialty bookstores across the U.S.
To inquire about where to obtain copies of any of these versions,
call: 1-800-874-8624 or see the USG website (http://www.usg.com).